PRODUCTIVITY CHANGE, PUBLIC GOODS AND TRANSACTION COSTS

ECONOMISTS OF THE TWENTIETH CENTURY

General Editors: Mark Perlman, *University Professor of Economics, Emeritus, University of Pittsburgh* and Mark Blaug, *Professor Emeritus, University of London; Professor Emeritus, University of Buckingham and Visiting Professor, University of Exeter*

This innovative series comprises specially invited collections of articles and papers by economists whose work has made an important contribution to economics in the late twentieth century.

The proliferation of new journals and the ever-increasing number of new articles make it difficult for even the most assiduous economist to keep track of all the important recent advances. By focusing on those economists whose work is generally recognized to be at the forefront of the discipline, the series will be an essential reference point for the different specialisms included.

A list of published and future titles in this series is printed at the end of this volume.

Productivity Change, Public Goods and Transaction Costs

Essays at the Boundaries of Microeconomics

Yoram Barzel

Professor of Economics
University of Washington, US

ECONOMISTS OF THE TWENTIETH CENTURY

Edward Elgar

Published by
Edward Elgar Publishing Limited
Gower House
Croft Road
Aldershot
Hants GU11 3HR
England

Edward Elgar Publishing Company
Old Post Road
Brookfield
Vermont 05036
USA

British Library Cataloguing in Publication Data
Barzel, Yoram
Productivity Change, Public Goods and Transaction Costs: Essays at the Boundaries of Microeconomics. – (Economists of the Twentieth Century Series)
I. Title II. Series
338.5

Library of Congress Cataloguing in Publication Data
Barzel, Yoram.
Productivity change, public goods and transaction costs : essays at the boundaries of microeconomics / Yoram Barzel. — 1st ed.
p. cm. — (Economists of the twentieth century)
1. Microeconomics. 2. Industrial productivity. 3. Public goods. 4. Transaction costs. I. Title. II. Series.
HB172.B34 1995
338.5—dc20 94–28682
CIP

Printed and bound in Great Britain by
Hartnolls Limited, Bodmin, Cornwall

ISBN 1 85898 076 3

Contents

Acknowledgements

The publishers wish to thank the following who have kindly given permission for the use of copyright material.

Academic Press Inc. for article: 'The Rate of Technical Progress: The "Indianapolis 500"', *Journal of Economic Theory*, **4**(1) (February 1972), pp. 72–81.

American Economic Association for articles: 'The Market for a Semipublic Good: The Case of the *American Economic Review*', *American Economic Review*, **LXI**(4) (September 1971), pp. 665–74; 'Assets, Subsistence, and The Supply Curve of Labor' with Richard J. McDonald, *American Economic Review*, **LXIII**(4) (September 1973), pp. 621–33.

Basil Blackwell Ltd for articles: 'The Demand Curves for Giffen Goods are Downward Sloping' with Wing Suen, *Economic Journal*, **102**(413) (July 1992), pp. 896–905; 'Ronald Coase on the Nature of Social Cost as a Key to the Problem of the Firm' with Levis A. Kochin, *Scandinavian Journal of Economics*, **94**(1) (1992), pp. 19–31, 33–6.

The Econometric Society for article: 'Some Observations on the Index Number Problem', *Econometrica*, **31**(3) (July 1963), pp. 391–9.

Elsevier Science Publishers for articles: 'Productivity in the Electric Power Industry, 1929–1955', *Review of Economics and Statistics*, **XLV**(4) (November 1963), pp. 395–408; 'Optimal Timing of Innovations', *Review of Economics and Statistics*, **L**(3) (August 1968), pp. 348–55.

J.C.B. Mohr Verlag for article: 'Transaction Costs: Are They Just Costs?', *Journal of Institutional and Theoretical Economics*, **141**(1) (March 1985), pp. 4–16.

Journal of Law and Economics and University of Chicago for articles: 'A Theory of Rationing by Waiting', *Journal of Law and Economics*, **XVII**(1) (April 1974), pp. 73–95; 'An Economic Analysis of Slavery', *Journal of Law and Economics*, **XX**(1) (April 1977), pp. 87–110; 'Some Fallacies in the Interpretation of Information Costs', *Journal of Law and Economics*, **XX**(2) (October 1977), pp. 291–307; 'Measurement Cost and the Organization of Markets', *Journal of Law and Economics*, **XXV** (April 1982), pp. 27–48; 'Confiscation by the Ruler: The Rise and Fall of Jewish Lending in the Middle Ages', *Journal of Law and Economics*, **XXXV** (April 1992), pp. 1–13.

Kluwer Academic Publishers for articles: 'Two Propositions on the Optimum Level of Producing Collective Goods', *Public Choice*, Spring (1969), pp. 31–7; 'Is the Act of Voting Rational?' with Eugene Silberberg, *Public Choice*, **XVI** (Fall 1973), pp. 51–8; 'Voting Behavior, Efficiency, and Equity' with Robert T. Deacon, *Public Choice*, **XXI** (Spring 1975), pp. 1–14.

The MIT Press for articles: 'The Determination of Daily Hours and Wages', *The Quarterly Journal of Economics*, **LXXXVII** (May 1973), pp. 220–38; 'The Allocation of Resources by Voting' with Tim R. Sass, *The Quarterly Journal of Economics*, **94** (August 1990), pp. 745–71.

Prentice-Hall Inc. for article: 'The Testability of the Law of Demand' in William F. Sharpe and Cathryn M. Cootner (eds), *Financial Economics: Essays in Honor of Paul Cootner*, 1982, pp. 233–45.

Sage Publications Inc. for article: 'The Origins of Democracy in England', with Edgar Kiser, *Rationality and Society*, **3**(4) (October 1991), pp. 396–422.

The University of Chicago Press for articles: 'The Production Function and Technical Change in the Steam-Power Industry', *Journal of Political Economy*, **LXXII**(2) (April 1964), pp. 133–50; 'Productivity and the Price of Medical Services', *Journal of Political Economy*, **77**(6) (November/December 1969), pp. 1014–27; 'Excess Capacity in Monopolistic Competition', *Journal of Political Economy*, **78**(5) (September/October 1970), pp. 1142–9; 'Investment, Scale, and Growth', *Journal of Political Economy*, **79**(2) (March/April 1971), pp. 214–31; 'Private Schools and Public School Finance', *Journal of Political Economy*, **81**(1) (January/February 1973), pp. 174–86; 'An Alternative Approach to the Analysis of Taxation', *Journal of Political Economy*, **84**(6), (December 1976), pp. 1177–97.

Western Economic Association for articles: 'The Effect of the Utilization Rate on the Division of Labor' with Ben T. Yu, *Economic Inquiry*, **XXII**(1) (January 1984), pp. 18–27; 'Competitive Tying Arrangements: The Case of Medical Insurance', *Economic Inquiry*, **XIX**(4) (October 1981), pp. 598–612; 'The Entrepreneur's Reward for Self-Policing', *Economic Inquiry*, **XXV** (January 1987), pp. 103–16; 'Knight's "Moral Hazard" Theory of Organization', *Economic Inquiry*, **XXV** (January 1987), pp. 117–20.

Every effort has been made to trace all the copyright holders but if any have been inadvertently overlooked the publishers will be pleased to make the necessary arrangements at the first opportunity.

Introduction*

Israel

I was born in Jerusalem in 1931 and reached my teens during the Second World War. Political issues occupied much of my own and my friends' thinking through the waning years of the British Mandate over Palestine. I avidly read the economic section of the newspaper and was excited by the left-wing political discourse of the youth movement. After a brief and painless army service and a stay of a few months on a kibbutz, I started to think about college. With parental financial support, this sounded like more fun than going to work. There were then just two institutions of higher learning in Israel: the Technion (now the Israeli Institute of Technology) in Haifa, and the Hebrew University in Jerusalem. Attending the Technion was out of the question as that would have meant staying in my home town, so in 1950 I enrolled in the Hebrew University.

A friend told me that his sister was studying 'political economy' at the Sorbonne. The idea appealed to me and I decided to follow suit. But 'political economy' was not offered at the Hebrew University, so I reluctantly settled on majoring in plain economics.

My most important freshman course was a year-long Introduction to Economics taught by Don Patinkin. I very quickly discovered that I loved the subject even though it bore no relation to economic issues as they appeared in the daily newspapers, which is what I thought 'political economy' was about. I devoted most of the little time I spent on studying to this course. However, since my English was rudimentary, for the first few months I spent more time with the dictionary than with the required text.

I can't say that the course gave me a solid grasp of either the principles or the foundations of economics. I found it hard to see the whole for the parts, a problem that continued to plague me for a long time. In spite of this, I managed to make some sense of bits and pieces of what I encountered in my studies. I still operate in this fashion, and not only when it comes to economics.

Patinkin was a wonderful teacher, a gifted expositor who instilled great enthusiasm for the subjects he was teaching. On him rested practically the whole analytical program in economics. He did not teach intermediate price theory but, by the time I had completed my MA, I had taken his courses in advanced price theory, macro, business cycles and international trade.

During that period Patinkin was completing his *magnum opus*, *Money, Interest and Prices*. He exposed his students to the material he was developing, thus creating an atmosphere of intense excitement in the macro course. He also wrote articles, participated in a number of government commissions and ran the Economics Department. He placed his most advanced students in graduate programs abroad

* Thanks to my wife, Dina, and to my daughters, Osnat and Tamar, for their helpful suggestions.

and later recruited some of these and others to the economics faculty at the Hebrew University. How he managed to do all this is hard to fathom, but he accomplished it without sacrificing personal contact with his students.

I took the course in intermediate price theory in my sophomore year. The instructor had studied with George Stigler at Colombia University. He was neither a very good teacher nor a great economist, but in this year-long course the substantial readings provided the opportunity for a thorough study of the subject. These consisted of four books: Alfred Marshall's *Principles*, George Stigler's *Price Theory*, and intermediate texts by Boulding and Bain. I was alternately excited and exasperated by Marshall, I suppose it depended on my mood. Stigler's conciseness made his book difficult to comprehend; a great deal of discipline, which I did not have, was required to study it, but what I did understand filled me with satisfaction. It took longest to understand his jokes. My fellow students and I quickly dismissed the other two texts as shallow; there was no sense of a great mind behind either of them.

I had made only a halfhearted effort in most of my courses thus far, but towards the end of the year I found myself engrossed in price theory material. For a week's time, preparing for the final exam, I worked harder than I ever had in my life. At the end of that week I started to get a feel for economics – the capacity to address systematically real-world problems – that has stayed with me to this day.

I took another course in price theory, this one taught by Abba Lerner. Lerner had come from the US to Israel as a consultant to the government. He was thought to have accepted the job because it gave him a golden opportunity to implement his socialist ideas, since the government was then dominated by socialists (the Mappai party). He was keen on equating marginal costs to marginal valuations everywhere. Not surprisingly, however, the 'socialist' government had little use for Pareto efficiency and preferred to subsidize its supporters and penalize the rest. Lerner displayed 'disloyalty' when he publicly denounced these policies. Apparently he was greatly disheartened by that experience. It seems, however, that he enjoyed living in Israel. He knew Hebrew very well and nobody minded his nonconformity – in fact, with his sandals and long hair, this is how a biblical prophet might have looked. He chose to stay in Israel for a couple of years which gave him plenty of time to teach.

In terms of preparation, Lerner was probably the laziest teacher I ever had, perhaps equating his marginal cost to his marginal revenue. ... There was a single text for the course: his *Economics of Control*. He assigned one chapter for each class meeting and one student to discuss it. Each chapter seemed simply to reiterate the principle of equating on the margins. I was invariably bored by the hapless student who had been given the responsibility of describing it. Before long, however, Lerner would start to ask questions, prodding us to discuss the material critically. He was most effective in getting us thoroughly involved in the discussion. He would gently make us realize the power and applicability of the principle of equating on the margin to conventional and unconventional problems of allocation. Lerner was at his best when he summarized the period's discourse. His exposition was crystal clear and the economic reasoning brilliant. The central issues were separated from the subsidiary ones, and every one of our numerous mistakes was weeded out in the process. Lerner's brilliance more than compensated for his slipshod preparation.

Of everything I read while studying for the MA, two articles made an especially strong impression on me: 'Factor Price Equalization' by Paul Samuelson and 'The Case for Flexible Exchange Rates' by Milton Friedman. I was not surprised by the wonderful piece by Samuelson since he had written the elementary text I was raised on (at the time I failed to realize that not all elementary texts were written by the best economists). The flexible exchange rate paper, however, was my first encounter with Friedman and I was flabbergasted. Not only was I greatly impressed by the substance of the argument and by its incisive presentation but, having already developed a 'bias' for the market, I was gratified to see such a convincing additional case for it.

Towards the end of my sophomore year I began to work part time at the Energy Department of the Israeli government, mostly as a compiler of statistical data. When it was time to write my master's thesis, I chose a topic I could pursue there: the efficiency of the gasoline tax. My training equipped me with a solid base for the economic aspect of such a study, but left me totally unprepared when it came to empirical methods. Although I had taken several courses in statistics, the only worthwhile one in the program was that on probability. Taught by Dvoretsky, who was often dazzling, its material was not useful for empirical work. The instructors in economics were not much help in empirical method either, so I had to improvise as well as I could.

My main focus in the thesis was on the substitution between gasoline and diesel. Gasoline was then taxed at a much higher rate than diesel. I collected some data on the cost of operating gasoline and diesel trucks of different sizes and then estimated their costs under equal tax rates. I concluded that the differential tax rate did not induce much substitution, and that on that score the tax distortion was modest. Though I had never heard of Harberger, my thesis seemed to presage that he would become my mentor.

In spite of my rudimentary methods, this project gave me a taste for empirical research that would shape my work for years to come. When I decided to continue studying towards a PhD, I was thinking primarily in terms of a program that dealt with real data. Here, too, the guidance by the economics faculty in Jerusalem proved inadequate; nor was my own search terribly effective. For a while I wanted to specialize in location theory or industrial economics because I thought that only in these fields did one do empirical work, but I did not know where to find such programs. I relaxed my criteria and decided to try my luck in the US.

During this period I made and lost one of the closest friends of my life, a fellow student named Yehuda Grunfeld. Yehuda had a profound influence on me. He was smart, very imaginative and charismatic without being conceited. Sadly, this friendship lasted only a short time. He died in a drowning accident when just 31 years old.

I first got to know Yehuda well in an army reserve unit to which we both belonged. He was ahead of me in his studies, so we did not share many courses, but we spent a great deal of time together, discussing economic problems and his pet idea of a world government. A short time later I joined him in the Energy Department where he was writing his master's thesis on the economics of blending oil-refinery output. I was in fact witnessing the independent invention of linear programming. His version was apparently fairly primitive, but quite effective. Soon after getting his MA he went to the University of Chicago to study for a PhD; when I arrived at Chicago, he had just been appointed assistant professor. During the next two summers he ran two projects at the Transportation Center of Northwestern University where I acted as one of his assistants. I had great fun with the empirical research and was paid handsomely. I thoroughly enjoyed Yehuda's company, but it was to be for the last time. He passed away the following summer. He had a rich personal life, magically touching his numerous close friends, and was at the beginning of a brilliant career. He remains the only person of my acquaintance to whom I feel the title of 'leader' truly applied.

Chicago

When concluding my search for a graduate program, Chicago was not at the top of my list. This was due partly to financial considerations and partly to lack of information, for Chicago was in fact foremost in empirical work in economics. However, after I arrived in the States I visited Yehuda and realized that the empirical emphasis for which I was searching was then almost unique to Chicago. When Chicago offered to 'sweeten the pot', my decision was made.

The intellectual atmosphere at Chicago was electrifying; the economics faculty was free of deadwood and did virtually no consulting. Small talk occurred, of course, but it occupied only a small fraction of our time, the rest of which was relentlessly overtaken by economics. Already then, in Chicago, 'economics' meant nearly everything. Although Gary Becker was no doubt a major contributor to that view, he was not in Chicago then. Indeed, during my first year, neither were Friedman or Stigler. The atmosphere of total involvement was contagious. You couldn't spend two minutes in the company of most graduate students without hearing about the marginal cost of something. I became avidly involved in these discussions in and out of the classroom. In Israel, I had seldom taken part in course discussions, but I became quite aggressive in the classroom immediately after arriving at Chicago, an unplanned, but quick, adjustment to the Chicago style.

At Chicago, of course, the market was king. On my second day there I had lunch with several advanced graduate students. One of them asked what I thought of the US. Since I had never seen freeways before, I said that I was amazed at the sight of the West Side Highway in New York. I added that I was surprised no tolls were charged during rush-hour to reduce the traffic jams. Two members of the group looked at each other and burst out laughing. I was not sure what was funny. One of them explained: 'If you know that already, what more is there for you to learn at Chicago?'. I didn't fully grasp the significance of that remark then. I thought that everybody knew that tolls reduce congestion. Only after I left did I discover that Chicago differs slightly from the rest of the world.

During the early 1950s the Cowles Commission resided at the University of Chicago, with Chicago at the forefront of econometrics and, to a lesser degree, mathematical economics. However, by 1957 when I arrived, the Cowles Commission had transferred to Yale. The search for replacements went slowly. During my entire stay at Chicago there were neither theoretical econometricians nor high-powered mathematical economists on the staff. The sole exception was Trygve Haavelmo who visited Chicago during my first year. I took his course in econometrics and found it very stimulating, but most of the material, unfortunately, was over my head. None of the courses in my program was 'formal', not even Haavelmo's. Indeed, the graduate sequence in statistics, taught in the business school by Harry Roberts, was one of the most informal courses I took. It was partly based on Allen Wallis's notes, which provided a peculiar but powerful feel for statistics. Although little time was spent on theorems, heavy emphasis was placed on rigor in the application phase.

In my first quarter I took a course in price theory from Harberger who was quite a casual instructor. The age difference between us is not large and, since I already had my MA, I initially assumed that I was as good an economist as he was. A few weeks later I was willing to acknowledge that he did perhaps have an edge since I had yet to demonstrate my superiority. ... Eventually, I also realized that Harberger had (and probably still has) the knack of winning an argument without making the loser feel like a fool. By the end of the quarter I decided that I wanted both to become a member of his workshop and for him to be my dissertation adviser. I was delighted to have both wishes granted.

I spent four years at Chicago. By my reckoning, Harberger was there a total of 21 months during that period! Yet he provided all the help I needed, which was quite a bit. Having him as an adviser also gave me a sense of how to get involved in others' research, which I continue to enjoy.

The workshop system was a great innovation for writing dissertations, its main advantage being the 'socializing' of the writing process. One could see how others were going about it and take part in their progress; one also had a forum for presenting one's own ideas and the benefit of hearing the unadorned reactions of others. Moreover, the discussions often spilled over into hallways and offices. We all took part in each other's work. Writing a dissertation under these conditions was not all that desolate a process.

Chicago was full of impressive individuals. The most prominent among them were Friedman and Stigler. Neither was at Chicago during my first year when I was engaged in all the required course work, so I only audited Friedman's course on price theory and Stigler's on industrial organization. I also attended Friedman's workshop for one term. I did not, however, attend Stigler's industrial organization workshop, a fact which is quite amazing. The significance of both Aaron Director and Ronald Coase, who attended that workshop, completely eluded me. Perhaps this was because the workshop was held in the Law School; Director and Coase were both on the Law School faculty and not in economics, and I was not (and still am not) interested in law. Not many economics departments, not to speak of law schools, can boast that they had at any one time a pair of economists who could match Director and Coase. Twenty years later my work was to belong within the scope of that workshop and Director was to become one of my best friends.

Towards the end of my second year I started to look for a dissertation topic. Several of the doctoral students who preceded me had worked on the estimation of demand functions, concentrating mainly on durable goods. I decided instead to study something related to supply and narrowed my choice to factors that might shift the curve. It took me several months to find an industry that was subject to significant shifts and for which adequate data were available. I settled on the electric power industry which, according to John Kendrick, had experienced a huge increase in productivity during the previous three decades. Moreover, this being a regulated industry, a great deal of data on it were available. Chicago hated regulations but loved the data they generated.

My objective was to determine what accounted for the change in output per unit of input – Kendrick's measure of productivity. I considered this productivity measure a 'residual' and tried to shrink it as much as I could. I hypothesized that, even under constant technology, output per unit of input could increase by a shift to larger plants and by a more intense use of existing plant. I estimated the coefficients for these variables from a cross-section and applied the results to the period covered by Kendrick. I concluded that the bulk of the productivity increase was the result of exploiting existing scale economies and of the more intensive use of available plants, induced by demand increase and by a change in its pattern. Not much remained for 'technical advance'. My work was received well by all except Stigler, who was one of my committee members. He said it was 'fine' but added, without elaborating, that he was not interested in this kind of work. It took me several years to realize that he was looking for the testing of hypotheses rather than 'estimation', by which time I had adopted that view as well.

Seattle

In the autumn of 1961 my job search brought me to Seattle, where I still am today. Few people were neutral to Chicago and its graduates then. Some schools would not consider Chicago graduates, while others were eager to have them. The University of Washington belonged in the latter category. Indeed, I found the Economics Department most congenial. Don Gordon was its dominant intellectual figure and I greatly enjoyed, and benefited from, his company. As sometimes happens, much of his creativity got embedded in the writing of others, including my own.

My arrival in Seattle came at a time of phenomenal expansion in the Economics Department which grew from about 20 the year before I arrived to about 30 the year after. This growth was accompanied by substantial turnover. Among this large and fluid crowd it was not hard to find plenty of both professionally and personally compatible individuals. For some reason, however, the Department was always quite contentious and seldom ran peacefully. Within a decade, with the exception of Doug North, those to whom I was closest had left. Don Gordon and Walter Oi went to the University of Rochester, while Al Hynes and John Floyd chose the University of Toronto. However, Doug North, who became chairman after the first two had gone, hired Steve Cheung which proved momentous to the whole Department, and especially to me, in the 1970s and 1980s.

My main research interest during the 1960s was in the supply side of micro-economics. I first extended my empirical work on electricity production and had fun switching from a mechanical calculator to a (main-frame) computer. One problem I dealt with in my dissertation was the construction of a quantity series, which required a quantity index. In the process of publishing the main dissertation results (Chapter 2), I also managed to have accepted 'Some Observations on the Index Number Problem' in *Econometrica* (1963), probably one of the least technical papers ever published in that journal (Chapter 1). This study empirically exploits the revealed preference principle to bracket the true change in quantity; it is the only time, I believe, that revealed preference has been applied in this way.

My research branched off into two areas: the measurement of productivity change, and innovations. The former led to one paper – 'Productivity and the Price of Medical Services' – in which I used medical insurance coverage as a proxy for a constant quality service (Chapter 4). After completing this, I decided to move into other research areas. Regarding innovations, I first attempted to do empirical work on patents, using data from Israel. Given the uniqueness of patents, simply counting them seemed unsatisfactory. I decided to give more weight to important than to unimportant patents, and concluded that 'importance' should be measured as the net value of each. That led me to the startling conclusion that all patents should be weighed at zero. The reason was quite simple: under competition among potential inventors, the net expected profit from every invention should be zero, hence the weights. One logical implication of this result was to abandon the project. ... I felt impelled, however, to ponder the returns from innovation, which ultimately led to my best-known paper – 'Optimal Timing of Innovations' – published in 1968 by the *Review of Economics and Statistics* (Chapter 6).

In my attempt to deal with this issue, I confronted the notion of the 'public domain' for the first time in my own research and only then began to think seriously about it. Given that the knowledge underlying innovations lies in the public domain, I concluded that the zero-profit condition was the result of competition (but was not a condition for efficiency), and that it produced the non-optimal result of premature innovations. When I attempted to publish the paper containing this result, the *JPE* rejected it specifically on the grounds that this argument was wrong. In 1971, however, the *JPE* published my paper 'Investment, Scale, and Growth' that relied on the same idea (Chapter 8). Subsequently, Dasgupta and Stiglitz published a series of articles based on the timing of innovation results.

During the late 1960s and early 1970s I continued to work on the timing of innovations and other activities subject to decreasing cost, on problems of public goods and on a host of diverse issues. My most eccentric paper, which is also shortest on economic content, is on the Indianapolis 500 (Chapter 5). Only its concern with speed may explain why it is in the *JET* set. Another isolated paper is on monopolistic competition.

My dissatisfaction with conventional textbook treatment triggered two studies on labor. In one I argue that the assumption of a linear budget constraint – which implies that the (per-hour) productivity of a worker is invariant whether he works one, eight or 24 hours a day – is unreasonable. Relaxing that assumption led to the conclusion, among others, that what we usually call 'the wage rate' is actually the average wage in a take-it-or-leave-it wage-hours package, and is not the appropriate rate for marginal decisions (Chapter 9). The other textbook problem is in drawing the individual labor supply as sloping downward only after initially sloping upward. When the wage rate is very low, however, a person whose entire income comes from work must spend the maximum possible amount of time working just to survive. As the wage rate rises, such a person obviously cannot work more, and may work less. Dick McDonald helped me to formalize the results; in the process we expanded the model to account for non-labor income, determining the conditions under which the textbook result may hold. This paper was published in the *AER* in 1973 (Chapter 10).

Late in 1971, towards the end of a year-long visit to England, I read an article on 'Discrimination by Waiting Time in Merit Goods' by Nichols, Smolinsky and Tideman (*AER*, 1971). I was greatly intrigued by the subject, but found some of their results unsatisfactory and thus worth reworking. I started to look into this problem after returning to Seattle. This research marks the beginning of a remarkable relationship with Steve Cheung.

Steve came to Seattle in 1969 and it took us much of the first year to size each other up. By the time I had returned from the next year's sabbatical in England, Al Hynes and John Floyd, two of my closest colleagues, had left the University. Steve had a keen interest in the rationing-by-waiting problem which I had started to work on, and it was natural for us to try to collaborate. Steve had come from Chicago, where he had spent the previous three years as an assistant professor, much of the time with Coase. At UCLA he had taken some graduate price theory from Armen Alchian and had written his dissertation on sharecropping under him. On arrival in Seattle he was, in my current view, the top transaction-cost property-rights economist in the profession. I perceived right away that his was a protean force and also that his line of thinking provided the organizing framework I was lacking.

I was not the only one to appreciate Steve's talents. John McGee was probably the first to recognize his extraordinary abilities, and Doug North, who was then chairman, did not take long to see his potential. Doug provided Steve, and the kind of program he advocated, full support, which included hiring Levis Kochin, a move Steve strongly recommended. Kochin's knowledge of fact, organized by economic reasoning, is probably unequalled in the profession, and for years now he has been my closest colleague. He is not renowned, however, for his orderliness or for timekeeping. Thus Doug took it on himself to support (in addition to Steve) one more unconventional character.

Until the late 1960s, the Department was considered good in applied economics and very good in economic history. By the end of the 1970s economic history was strengthened further, to a substantial degree because of its interaction with the transaction cost group, the latter coming very close to the top of the profession in its specialty. Unfortunately, by the early 1980s, the whole edifice had disintegrated. North and Cheung were allowed to slip away, with an almost audible sigh of relief from those seeking a conventional, or perhaps a staid, Department. The price was paid in mediocrity. The Nobel Prize was eventually awarded to a 'former' University of Washington faculty member, Doug North, in 1993.

During the 1970s Steve and I spent something like half our time at work together and numerous hours at home talking to each other on the telephone. In this intense interaction, I provided a set of tools and problem-solving skills which was almost ideally suited to analyze the kinds of issues that interested us. While I was concerned with the rationing-by-waiting problem, Steve was working on the closely related topic of price controls, part of his project on rent control in Hong Kong. We encountered numerous common puzzles and attacked them from all angles with great zest. On my part, at least, the gain in understanding was exhilarating.

The main ingredient common to rationing-by-waiting and to price control is that allocation is not random; on the contrary, people will compete for any commodity that the government either provides free of charge or sells at a below-market price under a price control. The outcome of this competition depends on the criterion by which the good is allocated among demanders. Those with a comparative advantage in meeting the criterion will be the ones to acquire it, making the outcome determinate. The net gain to a marginal person would be zero; the aggregate net gain to participants is necessarily less than the total value of what is given away or placed under a price control.

It took me a long time to realize that the same analysis was fully applicable to private markets where, because of the prohibitive cost of delineating all attributes, some of them are provided at no marginal charge. The other side of the coin is that various apparent 'inefficiencies', such as queues, are present in private, competitive markets. One cannot infer that inefficiency exists simply as a result of observing phenomena such as queues that result from government action.

The rationing-by-waiting paper marked the beginning of my almost exclusive research interest in transaction cost issues during the last two decades. There was one exception, however – my obsession with the law of demand, which began around 1968. Two colleagues, Lowell Bassett and Tom Borcherding, were at that time trying to determine whether factors of production can become Giffen goods. I participated in demonstrating that no Giffen good could emerge in a competitive industry. Even if the production function does accommodate such a good, the Giffen good may emerge only if produced in the inefficient part of its domain. This is inconsistent with cost minimization and can be avoided by altering the scale of operations of the firm (and the number of firms).

Reflecting on this result, I became convinced that an analogous relationship must apply to individuals. I reasoned that the 'scale' (or income) of individuals is determined endogenously, by gambling for instance, and, consequently, that individuals too are able to avoid the Giffen good trap. Intermittently for many years I tried to figure out whether I was right. I was successful in demonstrating for a special case that an individual who is prone to the Giffen good problem will increase his utility by holding an asset portfolio containing more than the commensurate amount of the inferior good. For such a person the income and the substitution effects are in the same direction, so the demand curve must be negatively sloped.

For years, I posed to technically better-skilled colleagues the challenge of proving the proposition for the general case. Only in the early 1990s was this challenge met. Wing Suen, a former student of mine, was able to prove that individuals will gain by taking steps ahead of time to avoid the trap, and that no Giffen good can then emerge. The result was published in the *EJ* in 1991 – after a 'gestation' period of almost a quarter of a century (Chapter 18)!

While wrestling with the Giffen good problem, I arrived at a related demand analysis result. I realized that, under a wide set of conditions, individuals are expected to arrange their endowments so as to reach their consumption point before any price change. This is the case regarding a change in rent when one lives in one's own house, and also regarding the change in any price when one's wage is tied to the cost-of-living index. The income effect is simply absent under such price changes. For this reason, using the conventional method of adjusting income in the estimation of demand is plainly wrong. These ideas were published under the title 'The Testability of the Law of Demand' in the memorial volume for Paul Cootner (reprinted here as Chapter 17).

My rationing-by-waiting paper was followed by one on taxation. The idea for the paper came to me almost unconsciously. I sensed that there was an argument regarding taxation that was analogous to that on rationing-by-waiting: first, it should be possible partially to avoid the tax and, second, competition for the avoided tax would be of the same nature as competition for the free good. It took me a long time to articulate the idea, not only to others, but also to myself. I remember spending an airplane trip, returning from an annual AEA meeting, trying to explain the idea to Gene Silberberg. All I got in response was a look in his eyes which said, 'What does this crazed man want from me?'. When finally able to make sense of the idea, I found it extremely valuable because it underlies the notion that free attributes are everywhere, and that their allocation is a dominant transaction cost problem.

In the per-unit tax case, what corresponds to the free attribute is the ability to pack more 'substance' into each taxed unit, thereby reducing the tax burden. I hypothesized that, as measured, the price of a taxed commodity could rise by more than the tax. Applying the notion to cigarettes, the hypothesis was not rejected. The results were published as 'An Alternative Approach to the Analysis of Taxation' (Chapter 20). An amusing example can be cited from the 1920s when the tax on cigarettes was first imposed. The tax was set on a per-cigarette basis. A cigarette producer then introduced very long cigarettes. After paying the 'unit' tax, the user divided each cigarette into several shorter ones. To ease this job, the producer perforated the cigarettes at convenient division points. Eventually, the Treasury added a maximum length specification to the definition of cigarettes.

In 1977, I published a book jointly with Chris Hall who was then a graduate student. In *The Political Economy of the Oil Import Quota* (Stanford University Press), we pursued the idea that, because the quota was valuable, people spent resources to effect it and to qualify for it. Since, for instance, small refiners earned higher proportional quotas, we predicted that refiners would take steps to become 'small'. I had received a grant to work on the quota problem and hired Chris as an assistant, but he very quickly and decisively earned promotion to co-author. One of the best economists I have met, from the beginning of his graduate studies Chris demonstrated a profound understanding of economics. I am constantly impressed by his beautiful empirical work which, unfortunately, transcribes awkwardly to the printed page. Our friendship continues to this day and (though we are half a globe apart) I enjoy talking economics with him more than with anybody else.

I next set out to write the paper 'An Economic Analysis of Slavery' (Chapter 21) which had its origin in the teaching of price theory. Friedman's brief analysis in his price theory text about the effect of the prohibition of slavery, such as on the return to investment in human capital, intrigued me. Every time I taught price theory I spent a little more time on the subject. Around 1970, Bob Fogel came to Seattle to give a seminar. I was away that day, but on returning I was told about his remarkable finding that slaves got more calories per day than poor whites did. To my way of thinking, it would have been remarkable had they *not* received more calories. After all, owners could not extract a high level of output on a continuing basis unless they supplied the commensurate amount of calories. In any case, I decided right then that I would like to work on slavery.

I started doing so in earnest after *Time on the Cross* by Fogel and Engerman (Little, Brown, 1974) was published. I did more reading on slavery than on any other problem I have encountered. In this regard, it is my most empirical work. It was also a bit frustrating. I would form new hypotheses on why this or that practice was observed, usually while reading a monograph or an article on slavery, then seek new data to test the new hypothesis. But with each new data source, typically from another society and era, there existed other differences that required a reformulation of the problem and still newer data for a valid test. Even though I think well of the paper that emerged, I was never able to overcome this sense of inability to resolve satisfactorily the problem.

I worked on the slavery problem mostly in 1974–75, during a year-long visit to the Hoover Institute at Stanford. The best thing that happened to me during that visit was meeting Aaron Director. In spite of a full generation gap, he became one of my closest friends. We had endless conversations on the slavery problem. Indirection was his method. He would bring up an observation, such as some debate on a slavery issue in the British parliament, and try to deduce the motive for the action taken. As a rule, I could not explain the action, and Aaron seldom offered reasons of his own. Nevertheless, after several conversations I realized I was gaining a better understanding of issues that I thought I had already fully grasped.

Aaron was very critical of the use of unnecessary or overly complex terminology, often stating that 'property rights' was one of these superfluous terms. When I asked what was wrong with it, he said that in the cases he had come across, demand-supply analysis would have been entirely adequate. He was persuaded neither by my claim that what he saw was a biased sample, nor by my attempt to provide better examples. Convinced of my case, I decided to set my idea down in writing. The paper that emerged was titled, somewhat whimsically, 'Transaction Costs: Are They Just Costs?' (Chapter 25). I was greatly relieved when Aaron accepted my argument that the existing framework was inadequate and also that competition does not necessarily bring about Pareto conditions. I was elated when he referred to the paper as written 'for me'.

I never wrote a joint paper with Steve Cheung, but we came close to it once. Around 1975 Zvi Griliches visited us to give a seminar. During lunch, in the course of a conversation on radicals in the Economics Department at Harvard, Zvi described some of the early 'market signaling' results by Michael Spence. I was immediately convinced they were wrong, but needed some time to demonstrate to myself why. The next day I told Steve about Spence's results, and he elucidated the problem so quickly as to make me a bit envious. We decided then that we would collaborate on exploring that issue. To get the ball rolling, I wrote a few pages and gave them to Steve, and subsequently handed him longer and longer manuscripts. Steve never responded. I do not know why. So I completed the paper on my own.

The title of the paper, 'Some Fallacies…' (Chapter 22) alluded to Frank Knight's celebrated article on social cost. It was my first methodological paper in the transaction cost area. Its main point is that, under the assumptions of Spence's model, people can always find profitable arrangements that shun information whose net social value is negative. Another result is that when transaction costs are positive, people may suppress potentially wasteful activities. I suggested that this result may explain the restrictions De Beers places on its approved traders in inspecting the diamonds it proffers, and the 'block booking' of films offered to movie theaters.

The paper 'Measurement Cost and the Organization of Markets' (Chapter 24) is the most crucial to my understanding of the methodological problems associated with the costs of transacting. For a long time I was trying to get a toehold on these issues by studying insurance practices. My thinking proved to be very messy and my advancement slow until I hit on the magic word 'measurement'. Once pronounced, the thing started to fall into place. What may explain the transformation is that, with measurement, one's attention is immediately focused on marginal costs and benefits, and one no longer has to operate on an all-or-nothing basis, which is natural in the context of insurance.

To exchange, the buyer must know what he receives from the seller. The cost of measurement of a commodity or service increases as it is made more complete, more accurate and more widely available. Transactors wish to economize on this cost but, when they do, one or both can be exploited by the other. This problem does not disappear even where numbers are large. In the paper I analyze these problems and form hypotheses regarding the methods and institutions employed to resolve them. Among other things, this paper may be the first to argue that the violation of marginal principles is not inconsistent with competition. It also reiterates Cheung's claim in his rent control paper that such discrepancies do not imply waste.

In 1981, the Department at the University of Washington decided to add a course on property rights to the undergraduate curriculum. Cheung taught it first, and then promptly moved away. North taught it next, and likewise moved away. In the process of preparing for the course when my turn came, I realized that I had developed a great deal of new material. I decided then to write a book on the subject. This was published in 1989 by The Cambridge University Press entitled *Economic Analysis of Property Rights*.

The unifying theme of the book is that, in every exchange, some attributes of the transaction are not constant and are too costly to price. Failure to price these attributes amounts to placing them in the public domain. Transactors attempt to maximize the value of their exchange in the face of that difficulty. The free attributes that remain unpriced and unconstrained will be consumed to the point where their marginal value is zero. In other cases, transactors will restrict their own actions in various ways. These include, among others, quantity constraints, operating on a wage rather than piece-rate contract, making commitments not to change prices, making guarantees and consenting not to exercise rights (which may appear as the attenuation of rights). Although the book is not empirical, it contains numerous refutable implications that can test the model.

In the 1980s, I, like many other economists, started to dabble in 'political economy' problems. Although this was what I had thought of studying when first at college, I quickly lost sight of it, coming back only with the general awakening to the subject by economists. I made a minor foray into the topic of voting (with Gene Silberberg, Chapter 14) in the early 1970s, but that was an isolated effort. My interest in voting was renewed in the mid-1980s. The problems that I thought were worth studying seemed at first intractable. It occurred to me that since voting is also practised in the business world, the study of business voting could be a good introduction to the study of voting in general. The next big leap was the realization that voting and other procedures within firms are introduced into their constitution by entrepreneurs. All of a sudden I had the seed of a profit-maximizing theory of the constitution.

These ideas led to a paper (with Tim Sass) on voting. In it we construct and test a model of voting as applied to condominiums. The main hypothesis, supported by the data, is that the developers of condominium projects formulate voting and other procedures to minimize the opportunities for wealth-transfer among owners (Chapter 28).

With these results in hand, I began to wonder whether the rationale for voting in the political sphere was the same. One candidate for the role of entrepreneur is a dictator. He is able to implement voting and related procedures, and can reap the benefits of associated gains. The model I started with, however, was seriously deficient as it could not cope with the fact that most dictators are in no hurry to take advantage of the opportunities apparently available to them. Eventually I concluded that the personal security of the dictator could be the main restraining factor, and with that I decided to try to apply the idea.

I am doing much of this work by myself, but some of it jointly with Edgar Kiser, a sociologist here with similar interests. This body of work, however, is difficult to 'sell', and thus far only one paper (jointly with Kiser) has been published – 'The Origins of Democracy in England' (Chapter 29).

The dictator faces a fundamental trade-off between security and material wealth. He is safer keeping subjects under his yoke, and supervising their inputs allows tight control. The tighter the control, however, the smaller their output and the smaller the amount the dictator can extract. The more freedom he allows, the more they become residual claimants of their actions and the larger the amount he can extract. But subjects granted freedom and the opportunity to accumulate wealth are also better able to depose their ruler. The granting of freedoms, then, is expected to be accompanied by safeguards for the ruler as well as his subjects. As a final point here, subjects that accumulate wealth and power are attractive partners for various projects, especially for war. Large-scale projects with many partners require decisions to be made by voting. My hypothesis is that voting institutions and other constitutional provisions do not necessarily reflect a striving towards democracy, but rather the attempt by the ruler and his most prominent subjects to bolster further their wealth, while at the same time protecting it from confiscation.

This model is being applied in several projects that are at different stages of completion. In one of the joint studies with Kiser we determine that, in broad terms, the model is supported by the steady constitutional progress that occurred in medieval England, and by its initial progress and subsequent decline in medieval France. Other studies include a comparison between medieval England and France regarding the relationship of voting rights to tax payment; the emergence of the state from 'primitive' conditions; the cause of a certain type of revolt; the city-state, and the evolution of the English parliament.

For the time being this subject is, and probably will continue to be, my main research interest.

PART I

PRODUCTION FUNCTIONS AND PRODUCTIVITY

Econometrica, Vol. 31, No. 3 (July, 1963)

SOME OBSERVATIONS ON THE INDEX NUMBER PROBLEM

BY YORAM BARZEL[1]

A Laspeyres index of total input in the electric power industry was constructed. The nature of the bias imbedded in such an index, and its relation to the Paasche index and its bias, are investigated. Means to evaluate the actual size of the bias and means to reduce it are devised.

IT IS well known that the Laspeyres quantity index, which is derived by weighting each of the individual quantities by its base year price, gives a biased estimate of the true change. In a study of productivity change in the electric power industry [**1**], the author used such an index to measure changes in aggregate input. This index increased from 100 in 1929 to 169.6 in 1955.[2] Since this is a biased estimate, it became desirable to determine the direction and size of bias, and to devise means of minimizing it. The conclusions drawn from the investigation of the index number problem in that context are relevant to many other studies which make use of index number estimation.

The estimate of the change in inputs required to move from the original position to a new position obtained by means of the Laspeyres index has an upward bias. It overstates the quantity of input required to produce the change in output. On the other hand, measuring the required change in input by means of the Paasche index leads to a downward bias.[3] The biases of the two indexes are demonstrated in Figure 1. A and B are the observed quantities of labor (measured along the horizontal axis) and capital (measured along the vertical axis) in the first and second periods respectively. P_A and P_B are the respective price lines, and I_A and I_B are isoquants tangent to P_A and to P_B at A and B respectively. Finally, V_A and V_B are radius vectors through A and B, V_A intersects P_B at b and I_B at b', and V_B intersects P_A at a and I_A at a'. In the Laspeyres case, P_A, the price line of the first period is used as an approximation for the isoquant I_A. The movement along P_A from A to a is supposedly a movement along an isoquant, and the distance aB is the Laspeyres measure of the increase in inputs necessary to move from A to B (or more accurately, from I_A to I_B). It is obvious that this quantity is too big and should rather be $a'B$. The distance aa' measures the Laspeyres bias. If, however, the price line P_B is used as an approximation for an isoquant, in this case for I_B, the movement from B to b is supposedly along the isoquant, and representing the substitution effect, and the distance bA is the measure of change in inputs necessary to move from A to B. This

[1] An earlier version of this paper is a part of my Ph.D. dissertation described in [**1**]. I am indebted to my colleague, Judy G. Thornton, for valuable comments.

[2] For the source of this and all subsequent estimates see Barzel [**1**].

[3] An extensive analysis of the index number problem is presented in [**4**].

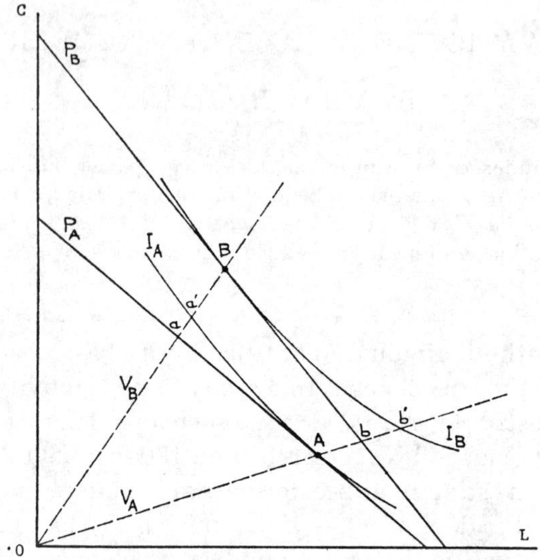

FIGURE 1.—Reference graph for the index number problem.

is the Paasche measure. It is an underestimate of the true quantity $b'A$ and the size of the bias is bb'.

These conclusions, however, are reversed if the curves considered are concave rather than convex. This would be the case when one is concerned with the movement from one transformation curve to another.[4] Since transformation curves are concave they lie below the corresponding price lines. In this situation the Laspeyres has a downward bias, and the Paasche has an upward bias. The confusion becomes complete when one is simultaneously concerned with transformation curves and the corresponding tangential indifference curves. Under these circumstances, the Laspeyres is biased upwards when compared to the true change of indifference curves, and downwards when compared to the true change of transformation curves, and conversely for the Paasche.

The magnitude of both biases is a function of two factors: the curvature of the isoquants and the relative price change. The larger each of these is (holding the other constant) the larger the bias. A common procedure for reducing the bias due to relative price changes is to change weights frequently. By frequently changing the weights, comparisons with wide price changes are avoided, hence the bias reduced.[5] Also, by reducing the span of time

[4] See Bergson [**2**, pp. 32–34].

[5] This statement should be qualified. It is clear that a large price change would lead to a larger bias than a small price change (other things held constant). However, the comparison is between the bias due to one large change in prices and the sum of biases due to a series of small price changes (summing up to the large one). It can be

TABLE I

COMPARISON OF SOME INPUT INDEXES FOR 1955 (1929=100)

	Laspeyres	Paasche	Laspeyres / Paasche
1. Chained annually	169.6	165.7	1.024
2. Fixed weights	182.5	153.1	1.192

between the periods compared, the danger of a substantial change in the form of the production function is reduced. Consequently, the index of total input in the electric power industry was calculated as a chain-linked index. For each of the twenty-six pairs of consecutive years from 1929 to 1955 an index of input was calculated and the index for the period as a whole was calculated as the product of the twenty-six individual indexes. The first row in Table I presents the Laspeyres and the Paasche chain-linked indexes and the ratio of the two. It should be noted that the two are within three per cent from each other.

In comparison with the annually linked indexes, input indexes with fixed weights were also computed. The Laspeyres index uses only first year prices for the whole period and the Paasche only last year prices. These indexes are presented in the second row of Table I. Using one set of weights for the whole period instead of changing the weights every year, the spread between the Paasche and the Laspeyres indexes increases from less than three per cent to more than nineteen per cent.

Kendrick [3] measured productivity over a long period of time for a large number of industries. In each case, he combined different inputs to an index of aggregate input also using the Laspeyres measure. His indexes, however, are chain-linked every few years. The years selected as links are those statistical benchmark years[6] which were also at the peaks of the business cycles. It is interesting to compare the results of linking annually the input indexes in the power industry to those obtained from linking the indexes of the benchmark years—1929, 1937, 1948, and 1953. The results of this comparison are presented in Table II.

The two sets of results correspond closely. There are, however, two important (and partially related) differences between them. First, in 1948 the Paasche input index is larger than the Laspeyres in the benchmark linked indexes. Second, the spread between the Laspeyres and the Paasche is reduced for the benchmark linked indexes compared to the annually linked ones.

shown that if the function considered is homogeneous the statement in the text is correct. It seems correct for all "normal" circumstances, but it is not necessarily true in the general case.

[6] When certain censuses were conducted.

TABLE II

COMPARISON OF INPUT INDEXES CHAIN-LINKED ANNUALLY AND CHAIN-LINKED ONLY IN BENCHMARK YEARS (1929 = 100)

	Chained Annually		Chained in Benchmark Years	
	Laspeyres	Paasche	Laspeyres	Paasche
1937	101.7	99.7	100.4	98.7
1948	123.6	120.9	120.5	121.3
1953	156.0	153.6	153.9	152.4

The Laspeyres and the Paasche indexes were compared as an attempt to bracket the true index. The previous results indicate that bracketing is not automatically guaranteed. On the surface it seems that the Laspeyres index overstates the shift from A to B (in terms of Figure 1) and the Paasche understates it, and consequently bracketing is necessary. The actual comparison, however, is not between A and B but between isoquants I_A and I_B. Isoquants do not always bear constant proportional relation along any radius vector, and consequently the relative change in (total) input required to move from one isoquant to another is not necessarily constant and depends on the points of comparison. This means that generally there is no unique way of measuring the change unless a single radius vector is considered. In terms of Figure 1, the Laspeyres index overstates the required increase in inputs from I_A to I_B along V_B, and the Paasche understates the required increase along V_A. Since the required increase along the two isoquants is not always the same, bracketing is not a necessary result.[7]

One should take care not to interpret this conclusion as an argument against any attempt to construct an aggregative index. Although there is no uniquely correct index, the range of potential indexes may be narrow enough to justify using one. The remainder of this paper is devoted to the examination of this range.

What are the conditions under which the Paasche measure would be bigger than the Laspeyres? In terms of Figure 1, the question is when does the relation $aB/aO < Ab/AO$[8] hold? The conditions turn out to be very

[7] The two indexes were conceived as a combination of two steps. The first step is a movement along a price line (representing an isoquant), and the second is along a radius vector. If the order of the steps is reversed, that is, the first movement is along a radius vector and the second along a price line (not drawn in Figure 1), the numerical values of the indexes would not be affected. However, the Laspeyres comparison is meaningful only along V_B. The Laspeyres measure bears no necessary relation to Ab' the change along V_A; it could overstate it, be equal to it, or understate it. It bears a necessary relation only to the change along V_B where it is always an over-estimate. Similarly, the Paasche comparison is meaningful only along V_B.

[8] Recall that aB/aO is the Laspeyres measure and Ab/AO is the Paasche measure.

simple. This inequality holds when the slope of I_B at B is less than the slope of I_A at A (that is, the relative quantity moves in the same direction as relative price). More generally, the two observed points lie on two radius vectors V_A and V_B. The condition $aB/aO < Ab/AO$ will be satisfied when the observed point lying on the higher radius vector (i.e., with a greater angle with respect to the horizontal axis) is on the price line with the lesser slope.

Proof. Suppose the slopes of the two price lines are equal, then $aB/aO = bA/AO$ (OBb is a triangle, and aA is parallel to bB). If the slope of the line through B is greater than that through A (as is the case in Figure 1), $aB/aO > Ab/AO$ since aB, aO, and AO are unchanged while Ab is smaller. If the slope of the line through B is smaller, $aB/aO < Ab/AO$ and only then the the Paasche is bigger than the Laspeyres.

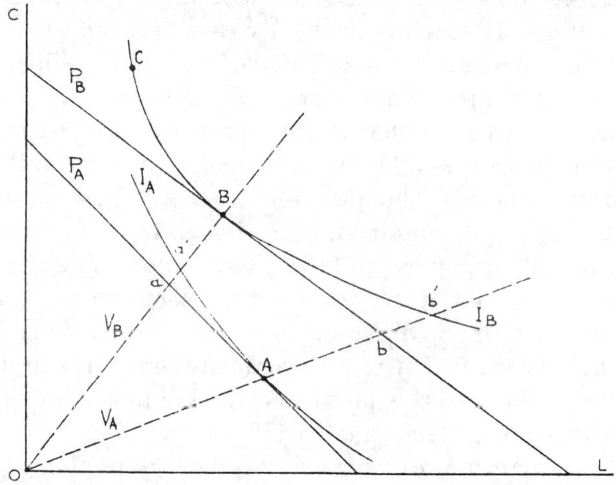

FIGURE 2.—Reference graph for the index number problem.

The case of non-bracketing is demonstrated in Figure 2. The notation used in Figure 2 is the same as that used in Figure 1. Notice that the price of capital and its quantity increased from A to B. It is clear that Ab, the Paasche measure, is bigger than aB, the Laspeyres measure, even though the Paasche understates the true quantity Ab' (along V_A) and the Laspeyres overstates the true quantity $a'B$ (along V_B). This can be written as:

$a'B$	$<$	aB	$<$	Ab	$<$	Ab'.
(True measure along V_B)		(Laspeyres)		(Paasche)		(True measure along V_A)

Notice that if the second period quantities would be at C rather than at B

(but still on isoquant I_B) the Laspeyres again would become bigger than the Paasche. This is so not because the indexes are now more accurate but rather because the bias became larger.

The foregoing analysis indicates why in case of homogeneity the Laspeyres index will be always bigger than the Paasche. In a homogeneous production function, isoquants bear constant proportional relations along any radius vector. The slopes of all the isoquants are the same along any given radius vector, hence any point which is to the left of any other must have also a bigger slope, and then the Laspeyres is always bigger than the Paasche. Even though in general an observation where the Laspeyres is bigger than the Paasche does not guarantee bracketing, in the case of homogeneity there is no ambiguity, and the bracketing rule always works.

The production function of the electric power industry seems to be non-homogeneous,[9] and in this case even when the Laspeyres index is bigger than the Paasche, bracketing does not always hold. Sometimes it will and sometimes it will not. It depends on the distance between the two isoquants at the points of comparison and on the size of the biases. When the twenty-six annual Laspeyres input indexes are compared with the corresponding Paasche indexes, it turns out that in thirteen cases the Laspeyres is bigger than the Paasche, in six cases the two are equal, and in seven the Laspeyres is smaller than the Paasche. The question arises as to how much confidence one can have in the results obtained, even though for the period as a whole the results using the Laspeyres are bigger than those using the Paasche. It should be noted, first, that in the seven comparisons where the Laspeyres is smaller than the Paasche the difference between the two is very small. This is reassuring, but not sufficient to give complete confidence in the results. A more satisfactory answer to this problem can be obtained along the lines of Samuelson's revealed preference analysis.[10]

In Figure 3 the quantities of labor and capital[11] were plotted as a scatter diagram, each point representing one year. Through each point the price line of the respective year was drawn (also one radius vector for orientation). Compare now the years 1934 and 1935 (lower left part of the figure). The quantities of 1935 could be purchased with 1934 "budget"; 1935 quantities are below the price line that goes through the 1934 quantities. Hence, 1934 lies on a higher isoquant than 1935. The isoquant of 1935 is below that of 1934 and also above 1935's price line (except at the point of tangency), which

[9] See Figure 2; also [**1**, pp. 49–57].

[10] Samuelson [**5**, Chapter VI]. The index number problem is also discussed in this chapter.

[11] Fuel is omitted from this discussion since its introduction will complicate the analysis substantially while adding very little to the results because of its relative unimportance.

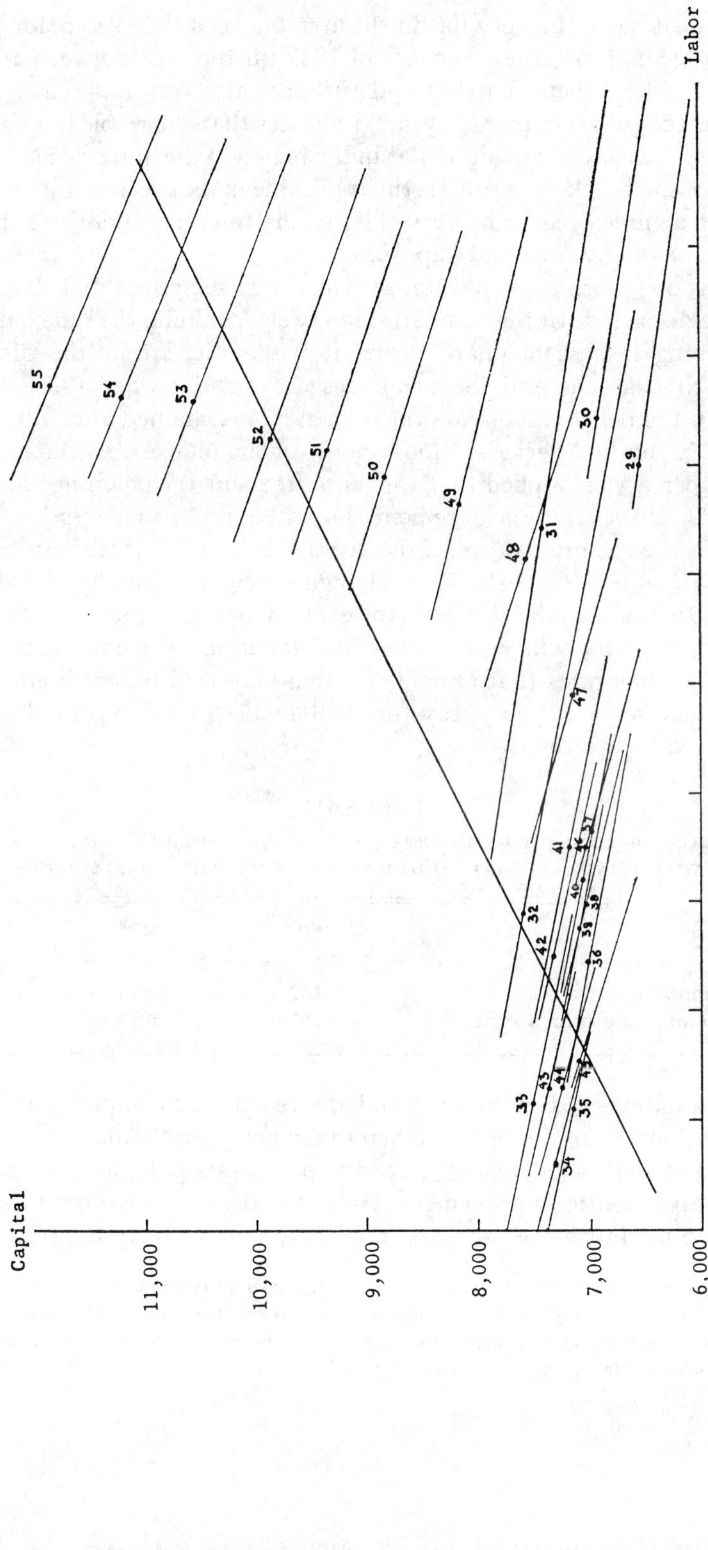

FIGURE 3.—Scatter diagram of the quantities of labor and capital and the corresponding price lines.

means that it has to be very flat in the area between the 1935 point and the 1934 point. Similarly, the isoquants of 1932 (in the area between 1931 and 1932) and of 1942 (between 1941 and 1942) are also very flat. This evidence (as well as that of other pairs of years) indicates that the whole isoquant map has to be well behaved and quite flat in the region of the observations. If such is the case, the bracketing rule is still applicable in most cases, and when it is not, the true index has to be very close to the computed one, and the error could not be of any practical importance.

There is one more point of interest which was suggested in Table II that should be discussed. In the comparison between chaining the index annually and chaining it in benchmark years, it was noticed that the dispersion between the Paasche and the Laspeyres was smaller when the index was chained in the benchmark years than when it was chained annually. This is not entirely due to "perverse" movements of the indexes. In the beginning of this paper it was implied that the more frequent the chaining, the better the results. However, this statement should be qualified. Suppose that P_1, P_2, and P_3 are the price ratios of the years 1, 2, and 3 respectively. Suppose also that $P_1 \neq P_2$, $P_1 = P_3$. Then, changing weights annually and chaining will lead to the familiar biases. However, if only P_1 (or P_3) is used for weighting, no error will be involved in comparing year 1 to year 3. This example demonstrates that annual chaining may lead to larger errors than chaining less frequently in a way that will avoid "jumping points" such as P_2 in the relative prices.

TABLE III

COMPARISON OF 1955 INPUT INDEXES (1929 = 100) WHEN CHAINED ANNUALLY WITH CHAINING THAT MINIMIZES RELATIVE PRICE VARIATIONS

	Laspeyres	Paasche	Laspeyres / Paasche
Chained annually	169.6	165.7	1.024
Chained to minimize price variation	167.4	166.4	1.006

Such an index was computed,[12] and the results are compared with those of annual chaining in Table III. When the indexes are chained annually, the Paasche and the Laspeyres are already very close, and there is very little room for an absolute improvement. However, the relative improvement by chaining to minimize the "jumps" in relative prices is very impressive. The

[12] The price ratio between labor and capital was plotted against time. Then a smooth curve connecting 1929 with 1955 was drawn by free hand. The points lying on or close to the curve were selected for computing the index. No formal procedure to minimize price variation was devised.

main drawback of this procedure is that comparisons are made between years that may be far apart, and if the production function is not stable, the comparisons might turn out to be meaningless. The choice of the unit of time which is short enough depends on the problem at hand. In the study that originated this discussion, where change was the main problem, it did not seem appropriate to stretch the periods of comparison, especially since the absolute pay-off was very low. The fact that the spread of the indexes is reduced when they are chained in benchmark years compared to annual chaining is a reflection of the relative price stability between peaks of the business cycles, an indication of the soundness of Kendrick's choice of points of comparison.[13]

As mentioned in the beginning of this paper, the index which was used in the productivity study was a Laspeyres index, chain-linked annually. The choice of a Laspeyres index rather than Paasche is arbitrary. Bergson[14] argues that since the Laspeyres is measured along V_B (V_2 in his notation), it better represents the second period quantities. This is correct, but not relevant to the problem. The comparison is between quantities of two periods, and the index number problem arises because different quantities change by different proportions. There is no meaning to the proposition that one set of quantities is more representative than the other, and, consequently, the Laspeyres is as appropriate (or as inappropriate) as the Paasche.

The University of Washington

REFERENCES

[1] BARZEL, YORAM: "Productivity in the Electric Power Industry, 1929–1955," unpublished Ph.D. dissertation, Department of Economics, University of Chicago, 1961.

[2] BERGSON, ABRAHAM: *The Real National Income of Soviet Russia Since 1928*, Cambridge: Harvard University Press, 1961.

[3] KENDRICK, JOHN W.: *Productivity Trends in the United States*, Princeton University Press, 1961.

[4] RUTTAN, VERNON W.: "Technological Progress in the Meat Packing Industry, 1919–47," unpublished Ph.D. dissertation, Department of Economics, University of Chicago, 1952.

[5] SAMUELSON, PAUL A.: *Foundations of Economic Analysis*, Cambridge: Harvard University Press, 1948.

[13] When an aggregative index is constructed on a monthly (or quarterly) basis, even if there is sufficient information for changing weights every month, the above discussion suggests that annual changes in weights would be more appropriate than monthly or quarterly changes. This way the bias introduced by seasonal fluctuations in weights would be avoided.

[14] [2, pp. 32–34].

Reprinted from
THE REVIEW OF ECONOMICS AND STATISTICS
Published by Harvard University

Vol. XLV, No. 4, November 1963

PRODUCTIVITY IN THE ELECTRIC POWER INDUSTRY, 1929–1955*

Yoram Barzel

THIS study investigates the output per unit of input technique as a measure of productivity. This technique has become quite common in recent years (namely, in the works of Fabricant, Abramovitz, Solow, Schultz, and most recently and on the largest scale, Kendrick). It obtained its prominence mainly because it requires very little prior knowledge of the production process.

In fact, the entire problem of measurement of changes in productivity is a consequence of our inadequate knowledge of the production process. The ideal way of obtaining an answer to this problem is by means of studying the shifts in the production function, which is fully specified in form (implicitly taking into account economies of scale) and in conventional inputs (labor, capital, and raw materials). The availability of this function for different points of time would reduce the problem of measuring productivity changes to the study of the shift pattern in the function over time. In this Utopian world of perfect knowledge, we would possess an exact and unambiguous tool for measuring productivity. Unfortunately, we do not know the functional form relating inputs to output. The problem is further complicated because we do not know whether the shifts in the production function are neutral.

These considerations indicate that caution is important in trying to measure productivity with the aid of the production function, particularly when the latter has to be derived from the same set of data used for measuring productivity. Despite these difficulties, progress is possible. The output-per-unit-of-input technique provides us with a means of measuring productivity change while avoiding the problem of simultaneously deriving the production function.

The next few paragraphs examine the assumptions which underlie the output-per-unit-of-input technique.

In this discussion these symbols will be used:
O = output quantity,
I_i = input quantities,
P_i = input prices,
MP_i = input marginal productivities, and
Q_{12} = Productivity Index defined as productivity in year 2 relative to productivity in year 1.

(Subscripts 1 and 2 refer to years 1 and 2, respectively.)

If the industry studied has a production function which is homogeneous to the first degree (that is, if there are no economies or diseconomies of scale), the relation

$$O = \Sigma I_i \, MP_i \qquad (1)$$

holds.

If the industry studied is also operating competitively, the factors of production are paid the value of their marginal product, and (1) may be replaced with

$$O \sim \Sigma I_i \, P_i. \qquad (2)$$

(The symbol $\sim$ denotes proportionality. The relation is that of proportionality and not of equality because the left side is measured in physical units while the right side is measured in money units.)

When relation (2) is considered specifically for year 1 it is written as

$$O_1 \sim \Sigma I_{i1} \, P_{i1}. \qquad (2')$$

Now suppose that inputs in year 2 are assigned marginal productivities proportional to their prices in period 1, then

$$O_2^* \sim \Sigma I_{i2} \, P_{i1}. \qquad (3)$$

O_2^* is the output that would have been produced in year 2 had the production function and factor marginal productivities stayed constant. O_2 is the output actually produced in period 2 under technical conditions different from those of year 1. We can now write

* This study is based on an unpublished Ph.D. dissertation (same title), University of Chicago, 1961. I am greatly indebted to A. C. Harberger and Z. Griliches for helpful advice and comments. M. J. Bailey, J. C. Hause, A. A. Rees, J. Rothenberg, and G. J. Stigler made valuable suggestions. The study was supported financially by the Public Finance Workshop and by a Ford Foundation Fellowship.

$$Q_{12} = \frac{O_2}{O_2^*}. \qquad (4)$$

O_2^* is the production one would expect in year 2 if input quantities are those actually used in year 2, but under technical conditions of year 1, while O_2 is produced with the same inputs but under technical conditions of year 2. Hence, the ratio of the two is a measure of the change in production technique from year 1 to year 2.

When (3) is divided by (2′) we obtain an equality (instead of proportionality) relation

$$\frac{O_2^*}{O_1} = \frac{\Sigma I_{i2}\ P_{i1}}{\Sigma I_{i1}\ P_{i1}}. \qquad (5)$$

Multiplying through by O_1 we obtain

$$O_2^* = O_1 \frac{\Sigma I_{i2}\ P_{i1}}{\Sigma I_{i1}\ P_{i1}}. \qquad (5')$$

(4) can be rewritten by substituting (5′) into it,

$$Q_{12} = \frac{O_2\ \Sigma I_{i1}\ P_{i1}}{O_1\ \Sigma I_{i2}\ P_{i1}}. \qquad (6)$$

All the quantities in the right side of (6) are observable, and so the productivity index can be measured.

The application of this technique to any particular industry should be handled with great care. Relation (6) is derived under very restrictive conditions, and violation of any of them might bias the results. Thus, when productivity changes in any particular industry are studied by using the technique suggested above, the effect of violating any of the conditions — of no economies of scale, of competition, and of no changes in the marginal productivity of the inputs between the two years compared — should be determined.

The restrictions under which the suggested method operates are quite serious. However, the restrictions imposed by the main alternative — the production function approach — are much more serious. The output-per-unit-of-input method avoids the specification of a production function. If input weights (prices) are changed frequently, the only assumption underlying the production function is that of no economies of scale. The production function approach, on the other hand, requires the specification of the production function and of the pattern of shifts in the function over time. This is clearly much more restrictive and much more difficult to handle than the output-per-unit-of-input approach.

The present study deals with one industry — the privately owned electric power industry.[1] First, the variables that enter into the measurement formula and the series of observations that represent these variables are evaluated. Then, annual productivity changes from 1929 to 1955 are measured using the method presented above. These results are then subjected to tests of the effects of violating any of the underlying assumptions. Finally, the results are compared with those obtained through the production function approach.

I. — Output, Inputs, and the Productivity Index

The electric power industry produces electricity and distributes it to the final consumer. The measurement unit of electricity output is a kilowatt hour (kwh). Even though it seems that all kwh are identical, careful examination reveals that economically (and physically) kwh have many dimensions, which affect their cost differently for different customers. Major sources of divergence are the differences between different classes of customers and the varying quantities consumed by individuals within each class. The relative importance of the different classes and the proportion of large and small customers within classes change over time. Consequently, each kwh has to be weighted according to its particular cost of production.[2]

There is a great deal of information on the relation between the amounts demanded per customer and the rates for these amounts in *Typical Electric Bills*, an annual official publication of the Federal Power Commission. Using data from this publication, four scatter diagrams relating number of kwh per month to the rate per kwh for four classes of customers [3] were plotted. Two phenomena are immediately

[1] The public sector and the commercially-operated-for-own-use sector of the electric power industry are excluded.

[2] The cost difference between peak and off-peak consumption is treated through the load factor. See section VI below.

[3] *Typical Electric Bills* gives information about four groups of customers: (1) residential, (2) commercial light service, (3) commercial power service, (4) industrial service.

apparent. First, there are two distinct relations between price and quantity, one for residential customers, and the other for all commercial customers. Second, both relations are negative,[4] and linear on a semi-log scale. As price falls linearly, quantity increases exponentially. These cross-sectional relations show a great deal of stability in their general shape and in their relation to each other throughout the period of the study. The rates for 1940, a year at the center of the study period (1929–1955), were chosen to derive the estimates for the price quantity relations.[5] With this information and the price quantity relation, corrected output for every year was obtained in the following way. The average quantity consumed by residential customers in 1929 was 42 kwh per month. We read the price per kwh for this particular quantity (after converting it to logarithms) from the residential regression. This price is the weight of each residential kwh for 1929. The prices (weights) of electricity for small and large commercial customers are derived in the same fashion from the commercial regression. The quantities consumed by the three groups are weighted by their respectively derived prices; and the sum of the three weighted quantities is the 1929 corrected output. Similar computations are carried out for the other years of the study to obtain the annual series of corrected output.[6]

Kendrick's[7] estimate of output is a weighted average of the number of kwh produced, where the weights are the prices of one kwh for the different classes of customers. The quantitative differences between unweighted output, corrected output, and Kendrick's weighted output, are very substantial, as can be seen from Table 1.

TABLE 1. — OUTPUT INDEXES (1929 = 100)

	1953	1955
Corrected output	293.9	326.2
Unweighted output	404.9	481.0
Kendrick's weighted output	491.0	n.a.

The difference between the corrected and unweighted output reflects the increase in the amount of electricity consumed per customer, which resulted in a reduction in the cost per kwh. The average quantity of electricity consumed by each residential customer increased more than five-fold from 1929 to 1955; that by each small commercial customer more than three-fold; and that by each large commercial customer more than seven-fold. At the same time, consumption of residential electricity (which is more costly at the observed range) increased from 15 per cent to 27 per cent of total electricity consumed. This last factor explains the difference between Kendrick's weighted output and the unweighted output. The comparison is for 1929–1953 and not for 1929–1955 because Kendrick's study terminates in 1953.

The three major inputs of the electric power industry are: labor, capital services, and fuel. Reliable annual series of the quantities and prices of these inputs are available.[8]

In conventional studies of the production function and of productivity, generally, only

[4] The average rates are constructed in a way that guarantees that this relation is actually the rate structure and not just points on the demand curve.

[5] Two regressions, one for residential and one for commercial customers, were run. They are of the form $p = a + b \log q$, where p is the rate in cents per kwh and q is the corresponding (monthly) quantity in kwh. The regression equation for residential customers is $p = 9.055 - 2.590 \log q$, the r^2 is .99986 which, for four observations (two degrees of freedom), is significant at 1 per cent. The regression equation for commercial customers is $p = 7.263 - 1.148 \log q$, the r^2 is .981 which is also significant at 1 per cent (nine observations). Information on total amount of electricity consumed by the three major groups of customers (residential, small commercial, and large commercial) as well as the average amount consumed by each customer at each group is available.

[6] Section III discusses the applicability of these rates as measures of cost.

[7] J. W. Kendrick, *Productivity Trends in the United States*, National Bureau of Economic Research (Princeton University Press, 1961), Appendix H.

[8] The series of labor input, in man-hour per year, and of the returns per man-hour, were constructed by Kendrick, *ibid.* The series of the quantity of capital were constructed by M. J. Ulmer in *Capital in Transportation, Communications, and Public Utilities: Its Formation and Financing*, National Bureau of Economic Research (Princeton University Press, 1960). These series were extended to 1955 using statistics of the Bureau of Labor Statistics, Department of Commerce, and Edison Electric Institute. The series of return on capital (defined as the sum of net profits, taxes on income, interest payments, and depreciation) were obtained from Edison Electric Institute statistics. The series of the rate of return on capital is the ratio between total returns on capital and the stock of capital for the respective year. The series of quantities and prices of fuel were also obtained from Edison Electric Institute except prices for a few early years, which were obtained from Survey of Current Business statistics.

labor and capital are considered. The third major input — raw materials (which do not contribute to the value added) — is excluded. Hence, the question arises whether raw materials should be incorporated in the productivity measure in this study; [9] and the answer is in the affirmative. The procedure of excluding materials is wrong. It probably stems from studies of the economy as a whole where raw materials are just outputs of some intermediary production stages and inputs of others, and cancel out for the economy as a whole. But they do not cancel out for individual industries. For these, they are one of the factors of production which may be substitutable for other factors. Furthermore, entrepreneurs who try to increase productivity do not restrict themselves to labor and capital alone; they would attempt to save raw materials as well. In short, there is no reason for treating raw materials on the industry level asymmetrically with the other factors.

It is well known that fuel, the main raw material in the electric power industry, is substitutable for capital. If fuel is excluded from the productivity measure, the shift from steam to hydro power, as a result of relative price change, would appear as a fall in productivity.[10] Moreover, if fuel is saved as a consequence of productivity increases, it would not at all be captured by the productivity measure which would be biased downwards. Consequently, fuel is included explicitly in computing the productivity index in this study.

The productivity index for the period 1929–1955 was computed as a chained index, chaining the 26 indexes of the 26 pairs of consecutive years. Each index for a pair of years uses the first year prices of factors as weights, that is, a Laspeyres quantity index. In Chart 1, the individual year-to-year productivity changes are plotted against time. Table 2 presents the productivity index for the period as a whole and the (geometric) means of the annual productivity index. It also presents, for comparison, the productivity index with unweighted kwh, and its mean. This productivity measure is a point estimate. The degree of confidence one can have in it is a function of the error to which it is subject. In the following three sections, the most important sources of potential error are considered in some detail.[11]

CHART 1. — YEAR-TO-YEAR CHANGES IN PRODUCTIVITY 1929–1955

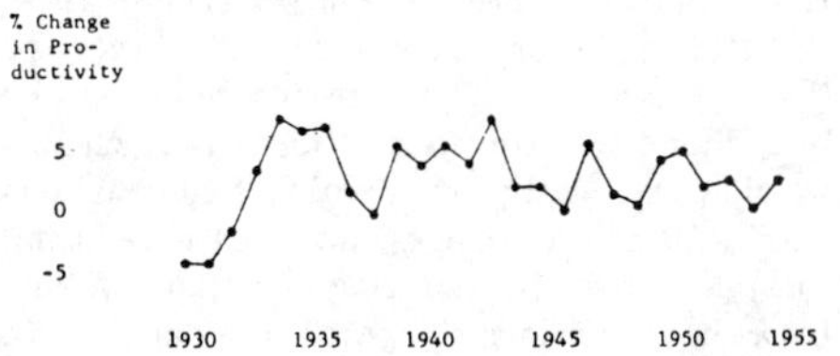

TABLE 2. — THE PRODUCTIVITY INDEXES AND THEIR MEANS

	1955 index (1929 = 100)	Geometric mean of annual indexes
Productivity with corrected output	192.0	102.54
Productivity with unweighted output	283.4	104.09

II. — The Productivity Measures and the Index Number Problem

The estimation technique used above introduces an error in the productivity measure in assuming a linear production function while in fact the production function is not linear. These errors are identical with the common index number bias. The use of first year prices as weights yields results equivalent to the Laspeyres quantity index. Under stationary conditions, the estimate of the change in inputs required to move from the original to the new position obtained by the Laspeyres index has an upward bias; the Paasche index (also under stationary conditions) has a downward bias.[12]

[9] Paradoxically, in some studies productivity is identified with fuel efficiency.

[10] If raw materials are netted from output also, productivity would not be affected by the shift to hydro power, but this is not always done. Kendrick, for example, does not net input of materials from his electricity output.

[11] For a discussion of the effect of random errors in the observations and for further detail on problems of output and inputs see my dissertation.

[12] An extensive analysis of the index number problem is presented in my dissertation, pp. 25–35. See also Vernon W. Ruttan, "Technological Progress in the Meat Packing Industry, 1919–47" (unpublished Ph.D. dissertation, Department of Economics, University of Chicago, 1952).

The size of both biases is a function of two factors: the curvature of the isoquants, and the relative price change. The larger each of these is (holding the other constant), the larger the bias. A common procedure for reducing the bias due to relative price changes is to change weights frequently, thus avoiding comparisons with wide price changes, and hence reducing the bias. Also, by reducing the span of time between the periods compared, the danger of a substantial change in the form of the production function is reduced.

Table 3 presents a few variants of the productivity index. In the top line the indexes are linked annually, that is, the weights are changed every year. It should be noted that the correspondence between the Laspeyres and the Paasche measures is very good.[13] For comparison with the annually linked indexes, productivity indexes with fixed weights were also computed. The Laspeyres index uses only first year prices for the whole period and the Paasche only last year prices. These indexes are presented in the bottom line of the table. Using one set of weights for the whole period instead of changing the weights every year, the spread between the Paasche and the Laspeyres indexes increases from less than 3 per cent to more than 19 per cent.

TABLE 3. — COMPARISON OF SOME 1955 PRODUCTIVITY INDEXES (1929 = 100)

	Paasche	Laspeyres	Paasche / Laspeyres
Productivity, annually chained	197.2	192.0	1.027
Productivity, fixed weights	213.0	178.7	1.192

It is also interesting to compare the results of linking the indexes annually with those of linking them only in (statistical) benchmark years — the procedure followed by Kendrick. These results are presented in Table 4, and show a close similarity. However, there are two important (and partially related) differences. First, in 1958 the Paasche productivity index is smaller than the Laspeyres in the benchmark linked indexes. This is a reflection of the fact that the two indexes are not estimates of the same quantities, and consequently, bracketing is not guaranteed.[14] However, careful examination of the relation between the quantities of the factors and their relative prices indicates, nevertheless, that both indexes are good approximations of the true quantity. Second, the spread between the Paasche and the Laspeyres is reduced for the benchmark linked indexes compared with the annually linked ones. This is due to the relative price stability between peaks of the business cycle — the benchmark years. This choice of base years is an indication of the soundness of Kendrick's choice of points of comparison.

TABLE 4. — COMPARISON OF PRODUCTIVITY INDEX CHAIN LINKED ANNUALLY AND CHAIN LINKED ONLY FOR BENCHMARK YEARS, 1929 = 100

	Chained Annually		Chained in Benchmark Years	
	Laspeyres	Paasche	Laspeyres	Paasche
1937	114.0	116.5	115.8	117.7
1948	163.9	168.1	168.5	167.4
1953	187.9	191.6	191.2	193.0

III. — Monopoly and the Productivity Measure

One of the assumptions underlying the productivity formula is that of competition in the industry considered. It is conceivable that some monopoly power is exercised by the electric power industry,[15] and that some monopoly profit is earned. Thus, using the observed rate of return on capital as equal (or proportional) to the value of its marginal productivity may lead to a bias in the estimation of productivity. The output measure is also vulnerable if considerable monopoly power is exercised. If electric rate differentials among customers do not reflect genuine cost differentials, but instead reflect discriminatory practices, then the proper output measure is not the one which weights output by customer class [16] and by the average quantity consumed by customers within classes, but merely the total number of kwh consumed.

[13] Recall that the productivity indexes are the inverse of the input indexes, hence the Paasche index is an overestimate, and the Laspeyres an underestimate.

[14] See P. A. Samuelson, *Foundations of Economic Analysis* (Harvard University Press, 1948), Ch. VI.

[15] Or rather by the individual firms in the industry, each in its own market area.

[16] Kendrick's procedure of weighting output.

In order to determine whether the electric power industry is actually exercising monopoly power to a significant extent, several tests are performed: first, the observed rate of return on capital in the power industry is compared with that of alternative investments; second, the effect of an (arbitrarily) lower rate of return on productivity is studied; third, a single competitive output price is "imposed," and total revenue reduced accordingly, to see how far the rate of return would fall, and whether this rate is consistent with competitive rates of return on capital.

Stigler's study on capital and return in manufacturing [17] provides us with a rate of return which can be used as a standard of comparison. The rate of return in all manufacturing, constructed by Stigler, is the ratio of the sum of interest payments and net profit to all assets. For the years 1938–1955, Stigler's rate of return in manufacturing is 7.2 per cent [18] while the rate of return in the power industry is 6.4 per cent.[19] These comparisons are far from being conclusive, because of the lack of an ideal yardstick with which the observed rate of return in the power industry can be compared. Still, it is clear that whatever monopoly power this industry has, it is not overwhelmingly strong.

Although monopoly profits are not large, one has to determine what effect they might have on the productivity measure. When the gross rate of return is halved — certainly a very extreme reduction — the measure of productivity for the entire period increases by 6 per cent using the Paasche method, and by 2 per cent using the Laspeyres. Since monopoly profits, if at all present, account for much less than half of the gross rate of return, their effect on the productivity measure is negligible.

The power industry is accused of being a discriminatory monopolist because different customers are charged different rates for an identical product. Under these circumstances the observed rate of return on capital overstates the marginal productivity of capital because it does not exclude the discriminatory returns. If the lowest available rate is considered as the competitive rate, the differences between that rate and other available rates are discriminatory profits. The sum of these differences, each multiplied by the respective quantity, is an estimate of discriminatory return. When this estimate is subtracted from the total return, the remainder is an estimate of the competitive return on capital.

When this analysis is applied in the power industry, two possible levels of discrimination should be considered: (1) discrimination among different classes of customers (such as residential, small commercial, and large commercial); (2) discrimination within each class according to the quantity demanded by the individual customer.

In 1940 the observed gross rate of return on capital [20] was 19.5 per cent. Assume first that discrimination was exercised within classes but not among classes. If the implied monopolistic returns are removed, the rate of return falls to 9.8 per cent before depreciation (and to 4.6 per cent after depreciation, but before taxes). Similarly, assuming discrimination among classes (but not within them), the implied competitive rate of return falls to 6.2 per cent (after depreciation but before taxes).[21] Finally, assuming discrimination among and within classes, a negative net rate of return on capital would be implied.

The low rates of return on capital implied in these calculations do not support the contention that differential electricity pricing is an indication of discrimination rather than a reflection of cost differentials.[22] Coupled with the previous results, we may conclude that the

[17] George J. Stigler, *Capital and Rates of Return in Manufacturing Industries*, National Bureau of Economic Research (Princeton University Press, 1963).

[18] This figure is based on book value of assets; however, he shows that at least for 1938–57, there is very little difference between book value and constant dollar value. Stigler's figures are more accurate for these years than for the earlier years.

[19] For the entire period, Stigler's rate is 5.8 per cent, and that for the power industry 7.8 per cent.

[20] The rate of return in this case includes all profits before taxes, interest payments, and depreciation. Capital itself is essentially the market value of the assets (and not of the firms). We selected 1940 since it is not an atypical year (the average rate of return for the period as a whole is 17.7 per cent). Estimates for this year were also used for deriving the rate structure.

[21] Stigler's rates are after taxes.

[22] Some additional evidence is furnished in Table 6 showing that residential electricity required different proportions of inputs than commercial electricity. More spe-

monopoly power of the electric power industry is not substantial. Hence the observed rate of return can be used in the productivity formula without undue damage, and weighting output by the observed prices gives a better approximation to the desired concept of output than does unweighted output.[23]

IV. — Returns to Scale and the Load Factor

The productivity formula implies the assumption that there are no economies or diseconomies of scale in the industry studied. This is probably the most vulnerable assumption contained in this formula, at least for the power industry. The formula implies that, except for productivity changes, output changes in the same proportion as inputs. Any deviation from this proportionality is considered productivity change. However, if between two time periods the industry experiences some (dis)economies of scale, the productivity measure will be biased. The measure is still valid as a measure of output per unit of input. But it no longer can be considered as an estimate of shifts in the production function.

This section is an attempt to evaluate the importance of economies of scale in the power industry and of the effect of changes in the level of the use of capacity, which lead to consequences similar to those of the scale effect. Estimates of the two effects will be used as a correction factor of the productivity measure.

One important aspect of economies of scale — that of supplying electricity to the individual customer — is discussed in detail in Section I above on the output of the industry. It is claimed there that economies of scale in supplying large quantities of electricity to the individual customer are very important. The average quantity consumed by the individual customer increased very substantially from 1929 to 1955 (Section I above), and if the claim is correct, this increase in average consumption per customer accounts for some 48 per cent of the productivity change during the period.[24] Evidence presented in Sections III and V below corroborate the claim of economies of scale at the size of customer level.

Other, and more familiar, aspects of economies of scale are those of the industry size and of the plant size, that is, external and internal economies, respectively. External economies do not seem to be of great importance in this industry, and even if they are, they cannot be determined within the context of this study. This is because the two basic measures of industry size, the output and the input — are components of the productivity measure. Thus, we are prevented from relating the productivity measure to size, which should determine the effect of the latter on the former, by the spurious relation between the two.

The sum of the factor powers in a Cobb-Douglas production function is a measure of external economies. An unrestricted Cobb-Douglas production function was fitted to the data (with time as an additional variable to account for shifts in the function), and the results found to be entirely unreliable (Section VII below). The divergence of the sum of the powers from unity cannot seriously be considered as reflecting the returns to scale rather than just a statistical twist. Hence, this approach also fails to estimate the effect (if any) of external economies on the productivity measure.[25]

---

cific evidence on this point is provided in W. Iulo, *Electric Utilities: Costs and Performance* (Pullman: Washington State University Press, 1961). He shows (Table 43, p. 103) that the cost of producing electricity (per kwh) is increasing with the proportion of residential consumption and falling with the average size of residential and commercial customers.

[23] The electric power industry, as a "public utility," is subject to government regulations in some of its activities. In particular, there is a certain "fair" rate of return on capital which should not be surpassed. It is conceivable (though with unknown likelihood) that prices are discriminatory, and also that the industry over-invests in order to reduce its over-all rate of return on capital down to the "fair" level. Because the likelihood of such behavior (and certainly its importance, if present) is unknown, this has to be left as an open question.

[24] If the Kendrick measure of output is used (which is more appropriate for this purpose) the increase in average consumption per customer accounts for even more than 48 per cent of the productivity change.

[25] See R. Solow, "Technical Change and the Aggregate Production Function," this REVIEW, XXXIX (August 1957), 312–20, in which he estimated productivity using a method similar to that used here. In a reply (this REVIEW, XL [November 1958], 413), he then fitted a Cobb-Douglas production function to the inputs, and outputs corrected for productivity change, in order to learn about the returns to scale. However, the method used imposes constant returns to scale on the corrected data, hence, one can learn nothing more from these data about the returns to scale.

We turn now to internal economies — economies which are due to plant size. Here, as in the case of economies of scale in consumption, a cross sectional relation is used to determine the effect of the variable. The cross section results are then applied to the time series. The cross section basic set of data [26] relates to certain characteristics of steam plants operating in 1959. The sample is confined to plants that were initially operated in the years 1953–1955. From these observations all plants that added to capacity (or made other major changes) during 1959 were excluded. Three variables were constructed from these data: (1) productivity, defined as output per unit of cost, where output is number of kwh produced during 1959 and cost is the sum of capital service cost (13.5 per cent [27] of the original cost of equipment), production expenses (exclusive of fuel), and fuel expenses (computed at $25 [28] per BTU); (2) a size variable, measured as the installed generating capacity of each of the plants in kw; and (3) load factor,[29] measured as the number of kwh produced during 1959 per installed kw. Productivity is the dependent variable in the cross sectional regression, and size and load factor are the independent variables. Scatter diagrams of the dependent variable on each of the independent variables indicate that the relations are logarithmic. The scatters also indicate that four observations are entirely out of the range of the rest of the sample in all the variables. The inclusion of these observations probably would have increased the correlation, but would have also dominated the whole relation; hence, they are dropped from the sample. The final size of the sample is fifty.

A regression of the logarithms of the observations was run, and the results presented in Table 5. The coefficient of plant size is positive and highly significant, which indicates that there are economies of scale to size of plant in this industry. The numerical size of the coefficient, .109, means that when plant size is increased by 10 per cent, productivity will increase by 1.09 per cent (or conversely, the cost of producing one kwh will fall by 1.09 per cent).

TABLE 5. — CROSS SECTION REGRESSION RESULTS OF THE EFFECT ON PRODUCTIVITY OF PLANT SIZE AND OF LOAD (LOGARITHMS)

	R^2	Plant size	Load factor
Coefficient	.835	.109	.373
Standard error		.013	.053

Strictly speaking, these results are not applicable to the time series. The time series contain not only steam plants (the cross section's domain) but also hydroelectric plants. However, steam plants comprise about 80 per cent of capacity and production of the power industry. Also, the cross section is on the plant level, while the rest of the study includes distribution as well as production, and economies of scale might not be the same for the two sets of operations. Still, if we are willing to assume that the cross sectional size coefficient can be applied to the entire operations of the plants in the industry, it turns out that 23 per cent of the productivity change in the period 1929–1955 should be attributed to increase in average plant size over the period.[30]

Time series regressions with variables corresponding to those of the cross section give results that point in the same direction as those of the cross section, but the coefficients vary considerably among regressions (which differ from each other in the productivity measure used and also in the form of the observations, whether in their original form or in first differences). This is mainly a consequence of a strong common trend present in the time series, that affects substantially the regression results.

We turn now to the load factor. It seems clear that the load factor should have a strong effect on the productivity measure. The load

The divergence of the sum of coefficients from unity is probably a consequence of imposing constant shares while shares were not exactly constant.

[26] U.S. Federal Power Commission, *Steam-Electric Plant Construction Cost and Annual Production Expenses, 12th Annual Supplement* (Washington, 1959).

[27] The average gross rate of return in 1953–55.

[28] Median fuel price for these plants in 1959.

[29] The load factor is discussed in more detail subsequently.

[30] Here also only steam plants are considered. The data were obtained from *Historical Statistics of the United States, Colonial Times to 1957*, U.S. Bureau of the Census (Washington, 1960) Series S46. The average size of steam plant increased from about 13,000 kw in 1929 to 86,000 kw in 1955. The cross section sample range is 28,000–1,400,000 kw, which does not cover the whole time series range. However, there is no sign of non-linearity in the cross sectional relation, and the results can be safely extrapolated to the non-overlapping area.

factor increased substantially over the period of the study. The average number of hours that each installed kw was used during the year increased from 3,125 in 1929 to 4,843 in 1955 — an increase of over 50 per cent. The effect of the load factor, along with the effect of the size variable, was estimated in the cross sectional regression, and the results presented in Table 5. The coefficient of the load factor obtained the right sign, is highly significant, and implies that when the load factor is increased by 10 per cent, productivity will rise by 3.73 per cent. Applying this result to the time series, the load factor accounts for 18 per cent of the productivity increase from 1929 to 1955. The qualifications regarding the limited scope of the cross section apply here also.[31] Again the time series regressions produced results which point in the right direction, but which are not too stable.

What is the effect of the factors discussed above on the productivity measure? Output (in unweighted kwh) per unit of total input increased from 100 in 1929 to 283.4 in 1955 (Table 2). Economies of scale in distributing electricity to the individual customer account for 48 per cent of this productivity measure, and when subtracted, it falls to 192.0 $\left(=\frac{283.4}{1.48}\right)$ (Table 2). Economies of scale due to increase in plant size account for 23 per cent of the productivity change, and reduce the previous measure to 156.1. Changes in the load factor account for an additional 18 per cent, which reduces the productivity measure further to 132.3.

In summary, total productivity increase from 100 to 283.4 is composed of four (multiplicative) components — 48 per cent of the increase is due to increased customer size, 23 per cent to increased plant size, 18 per cent to increased load factor, and 32 per cent to "pure" (or rather unexplained) productivity.

V. — The Structure of the Industry

During the course of discussion in previous sections, some supposedly existing relations in the industry were treated as known facts. These asserted relations, which were obtained through casual observations, played an important part in the analysis of some of the problems discussed. These assertions are: (1) factor prices affect the demand for factors; (2) residential electricity is different from commercial electricity; (3) hydroelectric plants differ from steam plants; and (4) using the existing (generating) capacity at different levels substantially affects the production costs.

In this section the validity of these assertions is tested, and a set of multiple regressions was run. These regressions are an attempt to explain the changes in the ratios of the factors of production through time. The explanatory variables are the quantitative counterparts of those previously mentioned. The test consists of finding out whether each of the independent variables contributes significantly to the explanation of the dependent variables.

Labor, capital, and fuel are the main factors of production in the power industry. Three ratios of these factors were constructed and (the logarithms of) these ratios were the dependent variables:[32] (1) log $\left(\frac{P_L}{P_c}\right)$, (2) log $\left(\frac{P_c}{P_F}\right)$, (3) log $\left(\frac{P_L}{P_F}\right)$, (4) kwh per installed kw (the load factor), (5) residential use of kwh as percentage of total kwh, (6) installed hydroelectric kw as percentage of total installed kw, and (7) kwh generated by hydroelectric plants as percentage of total.

The role of relative prices in these factor demand functions is obvious.[33] The role of the other independent variables needs clarification. The power industry produces electricity and distributes it to the final consumers. Production is carried on partially in steam plants, and partially in hydroelectric plants.[34] Some of this electricity is distributed to residential customers, and the rest to commercial customers. If the production function of electricity in steam plants differs from that in hydroelec-

[31] However, the range of the load factor in the cross section is 2700–8200, so there is no problem of extrapolation.

[32] However, each of the three regressions contains only a subset of five independent variables.

[33] There is no serious problem of identification in this case. It can be safely assumed that at each point of time, the factor supply curves facing the industry are infinitely elastic. The prices are then given to the industry, which in turn determines the quantities purchased at those prices.

[34] Electricity is also produced in internal combustion plants, but in negligible magnitude.

TABLE 6. — TIME SERIES REGRESSION RESULTS EXPLAINING THE RATIOS OF FACTORS OF PRODUCTION

	Dependent Variable (in logarithms)	Independent Variables							
		R^2	$\log \frac{P_L}{P_c}$	$\log \frac{P_c}{P_F}$	$\log \frac{P_L}{P_F}$	kwh per installed kw	Residential kwh / total kwh in per cent	Installed hydro kw / total kw in per cent	Hydro generated kwh / total kwh in per cent
Coefficient	L/C		− .482		− .547	.053	.490	− .788	
t ratio		.901	−4.38		−5.52	5.30	2.18	−3.05	
partial r			.69		.77	.76	.43	.55	
Coefficient	C/F		.245	.308		− .192	− .140	.962	
t ratio		.992	3.22	.043		−21.33	− .70	4.15	
partial r			.58	.09		.98	.15	.67	
Coefficient	L/F		− .333		− .466	− .118	.480		.322
t ratio		.997	−4.63		−7.28	−13.11	3.36		3.19
partial r			.71		.85	.94	.59		.57

tric plants, and if the "distribution" functions for commercial and residential customers are not the same, then the aggregate production function could be completely specified by factor prices alone only if the proportions of the components remained constant through time. The latter condition is not met for the time period of this study, and therefore, some correction for changing factor proportions must be made.

To illustrate this point, suppose that the price of fuel increases, and at the same time the hydroelectric section of the industry contracts. Under these conditions, the quantity of fuel may increase, and it might seem that the quantity of fuel demanded goes up as its price goes up. However, if the ratio of hydroelectric production of electricity to total production is considered explicitly as a separate variable, prices can play their proper role once more.[35] Similar, though less obvious, effects might appear as a consequence of change in the consumption pattern. Here the variable which accounts for changes in pattern is the ratio of residential consumption to total consumption. The load factor may also be viewed as a "disaggregative" variable. The same quantity of output can be produced with little machinery used intensively, or with more machinery used less intensively.

Table 6 summarizes the regression results.

[35] It may be argued that the contraction of the hydroelectric section is also a consequence of price changes, such as an increase in the prices of hydroelectric sites. This may well be the case. However, in the present context such prices are not accounted for explicitly, and some other variables have to account for these changes.

The first impression conveyed by these regressions, that of the high value of the multiple coefficients of determination, should not be accepted at face value. The observations are over time, and a strong common trend is present in virtually all of the variables. A more meaningful statistic is the partial coefficient of correlation which shows the effect of the respective variable on the dependent variable, after the effect of others (and hence of the common trend) is accounted for. Most of these coefficients are not only highly significant, but also have high absolute values which indicate high explanatory power.

The first set of regression coefficients, that of the price ratios, is difficult to interpret. Barring statistical difficulties in the estimation of these coefficients, in each regression one of the coefficients should be the familiar elasticity of substitution, and the other comparable to a "cross" elasticity of substitution. However, ominous statistical difficulties are present,[36] and

[36] Note first that $\log \frac{P_L}{P_C} + \log \frac{P_C}{P_F} = \log \frac{P_L}{P_F}$. This linear dependence bars the estimation of the three elasticities simultaneously. One of the price ratios has to be eliminated, and the choice is arbitrary. However, the results depend on this choice. Suppose that $\log \frac{P_L}{P_F}$ is eliminated and a regression of the form $\log \frac{L}{C} = b_0 + b_1 \log \frac{P_L}{P_C} + b_2 \log \frac{P_C}{P_F} + U$ is run, and b_1 and b_2 are the estimates obtained for the "elasticities." If, instead, $\log \frac{P_C}{P_F}$ is eliminated and the regression $\log \frac{L}{C} = d_0 + d_1 \log \frac{P_L}{P_C} + d_2$

the estimates cannot be viewed in this naive manner. In spite of these difficulties, two conclusions can be drawn from the regression results. (1) The elasticities of substitution are certainly not zero. The quantities demanded respond to price changes. The factors of production are not used in fixed proportions (even when the other variables are held constant). (2) The production function is not of the Cobb-Douglas form. In the Cobb-Douglas production function, the "cross" elasticities are zero. A change in the price of fuel does not affect the ratio of labor to capital. All three coefficients estimated in the regression are significantly different from zero.[37]

The remaining results are easier to interpret. The regression coefficients of the load factor $\left(\frac{kwh}{kw}\right)$ indicate what happens to the demand for factors when capacity is held constant while output is allowed to change. If capacity is held constant, in essence capital is also held constant. One would then expect a positive relation between load and log $\frac{L}{C}$ and a negative relation between load and log $\frac{C}{F}$ (that is, positive with log $\frac{F}{C}$). The two regression coefficients have the expected signs, and are highly significant. The third coefficient, between load and log $\frac{L}{F}$, is negative, which is plausible and also statistically significant.

The regression coefficients of the residential versus the commercial electricity consumption indicate that, as the relative importance of residential consumption increases, the demand for labor relative to capital and also labor relative to fuel, rises. These are reasonable results. It seems that the distribution of electricity to residential customers is more labor intensive than the distribution to commercial customers. The third coefficient, the effect of residential consumption on the ratio between capital and fuel, is negative, but insignificant.

The next two variables are similar to each other. Both measure the relative importance of hydroelectricity and can be discussed together. One would expect that as the importance of hydroelectricity increases, the demand for labor and for capital relative to the demand for fuel will increase. Also, although with somewhat less confidence, it can be stated that when the importance of hydroelectricity goes up, so would the demand for capital relative to labor. The three coefficients have the expected sign and are significant.

The results of these regressions strongly confirm some of the more important casual observations in previous sections. In particular, these results establish the assertion that residential electricity uses different factor combinations than commercial electricity, and hence, unweighted kwh are not the correct unit of output; also that the load factor has a strong effect on the use of the factors, and hence, might have a significant effect on productivity in the industry.

The next question of interest is: "What is the effect, if any, of productivity change per se on the relative demand for the factors?" When the cumulative productivity index is introduced in the previous regressions as an additional variable, it has a clear-cut effect only on one pair of factors — the ratio between labor and fuel. Adding the productivity variable to the first regression, where the dependent variable is log L/C, does not affect the multiple coefficient of determination; the regression coefficient of the additional variable is insignificant, and the other coefficients lose their sharpness. In short, this is a severe case of multicollinearity.

The effect of the productivity variable on the second regression, with log C/F as the dependent variable, is almost as bad. The coefficient of productivity change is $-.210$ and its standard error is .131, which makes the coefficient significant at 90 per cent, but not at 95 per cent. Again, the other coefficients lose their sharpness, and the R^2 is not increased substantially.

However, the productivity variable has a clear-cut effect on the third regression where

log $\frac{P_L}{P_F} + V$ is run, it can be shown that $b_1 \neq d_1 = b_1 - b_2$, and also $d_3 = b_2$. It seems that the true elasticity of substitution is neither b_1 nor $d_1 (= b_1 - b_2)$ What is the true elasticity? I do not know.

[37] The previous remark would not apply here, because if the true "cross" elasticities are zero, the difficulties disappear.

TABLE 7. — TIME SERIES REGRESSION RESULTS OF THE EFFECT OF PRODUCTIVITY ON THE RATIO OF LABOR TO FUEL

	Dependent Variable (in logarithms)	R^2	Independent Variables: $\log \frac{P_L}{P_c}$	$\log \frac{P_L}{P_F}$	kwh per installed kw	Residential kwh / total kwh in per cent	Hydro generated kwh / total kwh in per cent	Cumulative productivity (1929=100)
Coefficient			−.333	−.466	−.118	.480	.322	
t ratio	*L/F*	.997	−4.63	−7.28	−13.11	3.36	3.19	
partial *r*			.71	.85	.94	.59	.57	
Coefficient			−.403	−.601	−.134	.456	.664	.086
t ratio	*L/F*	.998	−5.84	−8.12	−13.40	3.65	4.41	2.77
partial *r*			.79	.88	.95	.63	.71	.53

the dependent variable is the ratio between labor and fuel. The regression results are presented in Table 7 along with the last regression from the previous table for comparison. Here the R^2 is improved substantially,[38] all the partial regression coefficients become more significant, and the coefficient of the productivity variable itself is significant. Its positive sign indicates that when productivity is increasing, the demand for fuel is falling faster than that for labor. This means that productivity changes favor labor relative to fuel; the production function is shifted in a fashion so that at the previous input ratio between the two, the marginal productivity of labor increases more than that of fuel.

It can be said now that productivity affects labor favorably relative to fuel. It can also be said that productivity probably affects fuel favorably relative to capital. If these two results are combined, it can be said that productivity probably affects labor favorably relative to capital.[39]

VI. — An Alternative Measure of Productivity

Whenever the problem of measuring productivity arises, an immediate method comes to mind. This is to fit a production function to the observed data and to add time as an independent variable in order to account for the shifts in the function through time. These shifts, if they capture what they are supposed to, are a measure of the (average) changes in productivity. This method differs from the one used in this study in several respects. It assumes that productivity changes are basically constant through time and that the deviations are randomly distributed around the constant. It also assumes that aside from these shifts in the function, the function itself is stable through time, that is, the shifts are neutral. The specific form of the function imposes a further limitation. In particular, the Cobb-Douglas production function assumes that the elasticity of substitution between factors is −1 (that is, constant factor shares). The Cobb-Douglas production function approach has one advantage over the method used in this study; it requires considerably less data on the factors of production, their quantities, but not their prices. Because of the widespread use of this method, and because it requires less data, it is worth while to compare its results with those obtained by the method used in this study.

Four regressions of the form $\log y = \log a + \Sigma b_i \log x_i + t \log c$ where y is output, x_i the inputs, and t time, were run; two where output is corrected, and two where output is unweighted. In each pair, one incorporates fuel as an input, and the other excludes it. The results of these regressions are presented in Table 8. The very high values of the coefficients of determination are, to a substantial extent, a reflection of the common trend present in the dependent and in the independent variables; hence this parameter is not very informative. All the other results are extremely unsatisfactory. In those regressions where fuel is included, its coefficients are much higher than the fuel's share of total factor receipts

[38] When the R^2 is increased from .997 to .998 the unexplained variance falls from .003 to .002, i.e., by one-third.

[39] Note that the three regression equations are not independent. In fact the sum or the difference of each two is approximately equal to that of the third (approximately and not exactly, because the independent variables are not identical, and also because the minimization process is not the same).

TABLE 8. — REGRESSION RESULTS OF FITTING COBB-DOUGLAS PRODUCTION FUNCTION WITH TIME AS AN ADDITIONAL VARIABLE, AND THE TRANSFORMS OF THE TIME COEFFICIENT

Dependent Variable	R^2	Labor coefficient (and s.e.)	Capital coefficient (and s.e.)	Fuel coefficient (and s.e.)	Sum of labor, capital, and fuel coefficients	Time coefficient (and s.e.)	Derived 1955 productivity index (1929 = 100)	Annual average of productivity index
Corrected output	.998	.218 (.043)	.375 (.041)	.337 (.036)	.930	8.711 (1.082)	168.5	102.0
Unweighted output	.997	− .108 (.048)	.341 (.046)	.717 (.040)	.950	6.048 (1.211)	143.6	101.4
Corrected output	.991	.498 (.067)	.266 (.035)		.764	18.382 (.667)	300.5	104.3
Unweighted output	.981	.498 (.132)	.108 (.168)		.597	26.656 (1.312)	493.2	106.3

(the fuel share ranged between 7 and 15 per cent). When fuel is excluded, the importance of capital is diminished. The share of capital in value added ranged between 55 and 70 per cent — much more than indicated in the last two regressions. Not only are the estimates of the individual factor coefficients unreliable and unstable, the same is true also for their sums, which supposedly should measure the returns to scale.

The estimates of productivity change are also very unstable, and bear no correspondence to the previous estimates. In particular, in the first pair of regressions, the productivity estimate, where output is weighted, turns out to be higher than that were output is unweighted. This is a very weird result because the unweighted output increased much faster than the weighted output.

The year-to-year changes in productivity may be obtained from the production function approach if it is assumed that the residual terms in the regressions are due solely to productivity changes; [40] hence they measure the deviations of the individual productivity changes from their trend line. The first differences of these deviations correspond to the annual productivity index used in this study. When the two are correlated, the coefficient of determination obtained is .47, which is significant, but not too high.

[40] In fact, the method followed in this study also lumps together the residual of an observed from an expected quantity as productivity change. But deviations from a regression line are restricted in their pattern, while this study's method does not impose any such restriction.

These results indicate that the production function approach should not be used for studying productivity. It is not only a poor method for estimating changes in productivity, but also for estimating the parameters of the production function. The failure of the production approach is a consequence of two factors. One is the multicollinearity present in time series. The other is the restrictions that this approach imposes on the data, such as a given form of the production function, constant parameters of the function, and smooth shifts in the function through time.

VII. — Summary

The central problem of this study is the examination of the appropriateness of the output-per-unit-of-input technique as a measure of productivity change. If this technique of measuring productivity change is used, three potential sources of bias should be examined: first, the conventional index number bias; second, the presence of monopoly which may bias the results by invalidating the equality between prices and marginal product (and marginal cost); and third, the presence of economies or diseconomies of scale, which may introduce a bias because the output-per-unit-of-input formula as a measure of productivity implicitly assumes constant returns to scale.

A measure of change in output per unit of input was obtained for the private sector of the electric power industry for the years 1929–1955. This measure was subjected to several tests to determine how much it is affected by the considerations mentioned in the preceding paragraph, and how it should be corrected in order to represent productivity change.

It is found that if the weights (prices) used in the measurement formula are changed annually, the index number bias introduced is very small — approximately 1 per cent of the productivity measure. However, if a single set of weights is used for the entire period, the bias becomes substantial — approximately 10 per cent of the productivity measure. Hence, if the weights are changed frequently, most of the index number bias can be avoided.

The effect of monopoly on the productivity measure in the power industry turns out to be unimportant. Although the extent of monopoly power of the industry is not determined accurately, it is clear that this power is not strong enough to affect the results substantially.

The effects of economies of scale prove to be of extreme importance for this industry. Three types of economies of scale are taken explicitly into account: first, economies due to the scale of the individual customer in order to take account of the decreasing relative importance of overhead costs in providing electricity to larger customers; second, economies of scale of plant in the production of electricity; and third, economies associated with the operation of plants at a higher load factor. The 1940 rate structure was used for estimating the effect of the first type of economies of scale, while the other two were estimated on the basis of a cross section of fifty plants built between 1953 and 1955. Whereas the output-per-unit-of-total-input approach states that total factor productivity in the electric power industry in 1955 was 2.83 times that in 1929, the study shows that this can be represented as a product of four distinct factors:

(1) 1.48, due to the increase of the average amount of electricity purchased by customers in both the residential and commercial classes;
(2) 1.23, due to the increased average size of plant;
(3) 1.18, due to higher average load factor; and
(4) 1.32, the residual, which is the best estimate of pure technical advance in this industry over the period 1929–1955.

In addition to these sources of bias, many studies of productivity are subject to bias also because only labor and capital are regarded as inputs, while raw materials are disregarded. In such a case, improved techniques that save raw materials will not be counted as productivity increases. In this study, raw materials are accounted for explicitly.

Finally, a test of the appropriateness of measuring technical advance by fitting a (Cobb-Douglas) production function with a time trend is undertaken. The test proves to be quite unfavorable to this technique because of the restrictions it imposes on the data and the common trend in the time series involved.

We conclude that the technique of measuring productivity change as the change in output per unit of input, at least for the power industry, is not appropriate. It leads to very sizable bias in estimating productivity change. However, the sources of the bias are known, and in this particular case its size is estimated, and the productivity measure corrected accordingly. When these corrections are made, this technique becomes quite accurate, and is superior to the most common alternative — a production function with time trend approach.

Reprinted from The Journal of Political Economy
Vol. LXXII, No. 2, April 1964
Copyright 1964 by the University of Chicago
Printed in U.S.A.

THE PRODUCTION FUNCTION AND TECHNICAL CHANGE IN THE STEAM-POWER INDUSTRY[1]

YORAM BARZEL
University of Washington

I. INTRODUCTION

Most production-function studies impose highly simplified production-function forms on their data as the basis for empirical as well as for theoretical work. Such a choice is dictated by paucity of data, and also by the simplicity and elegance of the simpler forms. The repetitious use of the simple forms (and in particular of the Cobb-Douglas production function) has almost created the belief that the world actually behaves according to these stylized models.

This study sets out to examine whether such simple forms are appropriate, or whether their use is likely to be misleading. The abundance of high-quality data for the electric-power industry (produced by the regulatory agency) provides an opportunity to determine, at least for this industry, whether a more complex and a more sophisticated form of the production function will contribute to the understanding of the production process. An important by-product of this study is that of providing better understanding of the operations of this particular industry. Although a substantial number of studies of this industry are already in existence,[2] the data are far from being exhausted, and there is much room for additional work.

The problems specifically considered are as follows: How does the scale of the plant affect the quantities used of each of the three major inputs in the steam-power industry—labor, fuel, and capital? How do variations in the intensity of the use of the plant affect the quantities of the inputs? How do changes in relative factor prices affect these quantities? What is the effect of the aging process of the plant on the use of fuel and labor? What has been the pattern of technical advance and how have the individual inputs been affected by this advance? And finally, how can an appropriate price index for capital inputs be constructed?

II. GENERAL FRAMEWORK

The common approach to production function studies is to write the general production function $y = f_1 (x_1, \ldots , x_n)$ where y is output and the x_i are inputs of the conventional factors of production. For concrete applications, it is necessary to specify the form of this function. If the form is assumed to be of the Cobb-Douglas type, we can write $y = a\pi x_i^{b_i}$ and then proceed to use this form

[1] I am indebted to D. F. Gordon for many valuable comments.

[2] See, e.g., M. Nerlove, "Returns to Scale in Electricity Supply" in *Measurement in Economics* (Stanford: Stanford University Press, 1963); J. Johnston, *Statistical Cost Analyses* (New York: McGraw Hill Book Co., 1960) pp. 44–73; R. Komiya, "Technological Progress and the Production Function in the United States Steam Power Industry," *Review of Economics and Statistics*, XLIV (May, 1962), 156–66; W. Iulo, *Electrical Utilities—Costs and Performance* (Pullman: Washington State University Press, 1961); Y. Barzel, "Productivity in the Electric Power Industry, 1929–1955," *Review of Economics and Statistics*, Vol. XLV (November, 1963).

to estimate the parameters of the function. This procedure, however, not only severely limits the parameters to be estimated, but also is subject to a very serious statistical drawback, when applied to the steam-power industry, because the conventional inputs are not sufficient for describing the production function of this industry.

The distribution of output over time in the steam-power industry is not entirely up to the firm. Consequently, output is a function not only of the size (capacity) of the plant but also of the extent to which this plant is utilized. This consideration is usually taken into account by introducing an additional variable, the "load factor," which is defined as the percentage of the annual number of hours in which the plant is utilized.[3] In addition, the electric-power industry is supposed to enjoy substantial economies of scale. In order to account for this factor, the size of the unit, usually measured by number of installed kilowatts (kw.), is also introduced into the production function.

We have now

$$y = f_2(x_1, \ldots, x_n, \text{utilization factor, size})\,.$$

If we again specifically consider the Cobb-Douglas form, defining output as number of kilowatt hours (kwh.) produced, we have

$$\text{total kwh.} = a\pi x_i^{b_i}\,\text{load}^{d_1}\,\text{size}^{d_2}$$

but

$$\text{load} \equiv K\,\frac{\text{total kwh.}}{\text{installed kw.}}$$

(where K is a proportionality constant),

and

$$\text{size} \equiv \text{installed kw.},$$

so that

$$\text{output} \equiv \text{total kwh.} \equiv K\,(\text{total kwh.}) \times \frac{\text{installed kw.}}{\text{installed kw.}} \equiv K\,(\text{load} \times \text{size})\,.$$

Thus the introduction of considerations of scale and of level of plant utilization to the production function leads to an identity relation between the dependent and independent variables in the production function ($d_1 = d_2 = 1$).[4]

An alternative approach for studying the production function is through the demand for the factors of production.[5] The demand for a factor of production is a function of three sets of forces: (1) the demand for the final product produced by the factor; (2) relative factor prices; and (3) the state of the arts. Thus we can write $x_i = g\ (y, p_i, \ldots, p_n)$, where y and the p_i's represent the demand for the product and relative factor prices respectively, while g represents the state of the arts.[6]

The detailed form of such a function is different for labor and fuel than for capital. Once a plant is installed, it is likely to remain in its original form for quite a few years, and no further major investment in it is expected to be undertaken. On the other hand, the rigid commitment of capital is not accompanied by a similar commitment of fuel and labor, the quan-

[3] Load factor = total annual kwh./installed kw. × total annual hours × 100 = percentage of time in utilization, where kw. stands for kilowatt, the standard unity of capacity in this industry, and kwh. stands for kilowatt hour, the standard unit of output.

[4] I am indebted to L. Telser for this point. This argument applies to any form of the production function, except that in general the relation would only approximate an identity.

[5] For his own reasons Komiya (*op. cit.*, p. 158) also rejects the explicit production function approach in favor of the demand for factors approach.

[6] M. Nerlove (*op. cit.*) points out that due to economic and institutional considerations, output is a predetermined variable in this industry. This is another reason for treating output as an independent rather than a dependent variable.

tities of which can be adjusted to new conditions as they arise. So while for the study of the quantity of capital we are mostly concerned with future conditions as anticipated when the investment decision is undertaken, for the study of the quantities of labor and fuel we are concerned also with the realized values of the relevant variables while the plant is actually in operation. Consequently, in the formulation of the demand function for capital, only expectational variables are taken into account, while for labor and fuel realized variables are considered as well. The demand functions for labor and fuel will be discussed first.

III. DEMAND FOR FUEL AND LABOR

Using total output as the sole measure of the demand for the product is not entirely satisfactory. Two plants, one twice as big as the other, can produce the same quantity of output if the bigger plant operates at half the level of the smaller. Since it is unlikely that the two would require the same amounts of labor or fuel, it becomes desirable to distinguish between the effects of size and of utilization level on the demands for labor and fuel. Size and utilization factors can be introduced directly into the demand functions by using the relation, output = total kwh. = $K \times$ load $\times$ size (where K is a factor of proportionality), and substituting the latter for the former.

The use of the load-factor variable is subject to an objection similar to that advanced against the unqualified use of output as a measure of demand. If the anticipated average load factor for a certain plant is 80 per cent, it is likely that the plant will be designed for such a level of operation. If that plant happens to operate in a certain year at 60 per cent of capacity, one would expect it to use amounts of labor and fuel different from those used in a plant (of equal capacity) that was designed in the first place to operate at 60 per cent of capacity and actually operated at this level. A way to account for such differences is to decompose the output variable further to

$$\text{output} = K \times \text{size} \times (\text{antipated average load}) \times \frac{\text{actual load}}{\text{anticipated average load}},$$

and to consider each of the three elements in the product separately. This is the highest level of "decomposition" considered in this study.[7]

Only one price ratio is considered for the demand for labor and fuel, and this is the ratio of the price of fuel to that of labor (p). The price of capital, the other other major production factor, is not considered explicitly, due to difficulties in defining and measuring this variable.

The argument advanced for the decomposition of the load factor applies to the price variable as well. One would expect the anticipated average price level (which influences fuel and labor demanded through the design of the equipment) to have a different effect on the demand for a factor than do deviations from this average. This is again taken into account by decomposing the price variable into

$$p = (\text{anticipated average } p) \times \frac{(\text{actual } p)}{(\text{anticipated average } p)}$$

and by considering separately the two components of the product.

[7] G. J. Stigler, "Production and Distribution in the Short Run," *Journal of Political Economy*, XLVII (June, 1939), 305–27, drew a distinction between plants that are designed to operate at a certain constant level and plants designed to operate at the same average level, but with some variation over time. Here it is assumed that all plants are designed for variable outputs, but that the average output differs for different plants.

Since some of the plants are observed not only when they are new but also subsequently, an age-of-plant variable is introduced to differentiate among such plants. Finally the observations cover plants that started operations over a fairly substantial span of time—between 1941 and 1959. A set of variables to account for differences between plants of different vintages is therefore introduced. We can now write the demand function for fuel as

$Q_f = g_f$ (size, anticipated average load, load index, anticipated average price, price index, age, date of installation)

and similarly for labor. The form selected for statistical estimation is the log linear form,

$$\log y_f = \sum_i b_i \log x_i \quad i = 0, \ldots, 19,$$

where y_f is input of fuel, in B.T.U. (British Thermal Units), during the year that

x_0 = a constant

x_1 = plant size measured by the number of installed kilowatts

x_2 = anticipated average load of plant, measured by the observed load factor in first full year of operation

x_3 = a within-plant index of x_2, over time

x_4 = anticipated average input price ratio measured as the ratio of the average price of fuel per B.T.U. to the average labor cost per man-year in the first year of operation of plant

x_5 = a within-plant index of x_4, over time

x_6 = age of plant defined as accumulated number of hours of operation

x_7–x_{19} define a set of dummy variables, where x_7 has a value of 10 for plants that started operation in 1943 and 1 for other years. x_8–x_{19} are similarly defined for 1948–59 plants.[8] (The transformation of the above values into logarithms converts them to 1 and 0, respectively.)

[8] Note that there is no dummy variable for 1941, which is used as a base year.

The above list of variables contains a description of how the variables were actually measured. The two variables, x_2 and x_4, require further explanation. The selection of observations on the first year of operations to represent the anticipated average values of the variables is based on two considerations. First, past experience is usually used as a basis for forming expectations about the future, and the first year of operations is the closest to the past and is most likely to conform to it. Second, because in the sample some plants are observed over several years while others are observed only for one year, it is impossible to form a consistent estimate from observations on any year other than the first.[9]

The log-linear functional form selected for estimation assumes constant elasticities of substitution, and constant elasticities of factor quantities with respect to size, but leaves the magnitudes of these parameters to be determined by estimation. Similarly, the form allows each factor to follow its own path of technical advance so that factor proportions may change over time in the absence of changes in scale or in relative prices, due to the effects of differential rates of technical advance. This form is very flexible and imposes fewer restrictions on the production function than those commonly used. In contrast, the Cobb-Douglas production function implies a unitary elasticity of substitution between factors and identical returns to scale for all factors, and, when a time

[9] Such a procedure inevitably leads to errors in the observations. It can be shown that, while the coefficients of x_3 and x_5 will be unbiased, those of x_2 and x_4 will be biased toward the coefficients of x_3 and x_5, respectively.

trend is introduced, it also implies neutral technical change.[10]

IV. THE FUEL REGRESSION

The results of the fuel regression are presented in Table 1. Since the variables are all in logarithms, the regression coefficients are partial elasticities.

Returns to scale.—The partial elasticity of the quantity of fuel used with respect to size is .896. This coefficient is significantly different from 1. A 99 per cent confidence interval for this coefficient covers the range from .884 to .908. Although economies of scale of size indicated by the coefficient are far from being trivial, it is easy to overestimate their importance. The average plant size is continuously growing over time. The (geometric) mean plant size in the sample increased from 26,600 kilowatts for plants that started to operate in 1941 to 98,400 for plants that started to operate in 1959, a 3.70-fold increase. A given output from a typical 98,400-kilowatt plant (holding load and other variables constant) would require, however, only 14.6 per cent less fuel than from a typical 26,600-kilowatt plant.[11]

The load factor.—The coefficient of the average (or rather, the first year) load factor was .85 with a standard error of .013, which indicates that this variable is significantly different not only from zero but also from unity. Since increase in the load factor is in a sense an increase in the scale of operations it is interesting to compare the coefficient of the load factor with that of size. The coefficient of the latter is .048 larger than the coefficient of the former. The standard error of the difference is .015 and the t-ratio for testing the difference from zero is 3.20 which is highly significant. Thus the decomposition of output into its scale and load components seems justified.

TABLE 1

RESULTS FROM FUEL REGRESSION

Variable	Regression Coefficient	t-Ratio
Size	.896	196.623
Load	.848	67.532
Load index	.893	67.721
Relative price	−.040	− 4.314
Relative-price index	−.074	− 3.374
Depreciation	−.013	− 1.913
Dummy for 1943	.026	2.311
Dummy for 1948	.007	.671
Dummy for 1949	.002	.231
Dummy for 1950	.009	.898
Dummy for 1951	−.008	− .876
Dummy for 1952	−.014	− 1.451
Dummy for 1953	.012	1.200
Dummy for 1954	−.008	− .932
Dummy for 1955	−.040	− 4.118
Dummy for 1956	.020	2.076
Dummy for 1957	.044	3.494
Dummy for 1958	−.039	− 3.187
Dummy for 1959	−.040	− 2.812

$R^2 = .9904$.

The index of the load factor.—The coefficient of the within-plant load factor is .89, and is significantly different from unity. It is also significantly larger than the coefficient of the between plants load factor (the difference is .045, and the t-ratio of the difference is 2.87). We may conclude that this further decomposition of output is also justified, since the two components lead to different demand coefficients for fuel.

These three variables, the product of which is a measure of total output, ex-

[10] A neutral technical change or a neutral change in scale, unaccompanied by a change in relative prices, will leave the relative factor quantities constant.

[11] This number reflects a change in productivity for the entire output. A 1 per cent increase in size will require a 0.9 per cent increase in fuel input, and so the productivity increase for the additional output is 10 per cent, while the productivity increase for the entire output is only 0.1 per cent.

plain between them the bulk of the variance in the use of fuel by different plants, and within plants over time. The other variables, from this viewpoint, play minor roles. Some of them, however, are significant and are interesting in their own right.

The relative price of fuel.—The coefficient of the price of fuel relative to labor was $-.040$; this is a low coefficient, but it is significantly different from zero ($t = 4.314$). This coefficient is not equivalent to the elasticity of substitution between fuel and labor, since it measures not the effect of relative factor prices on *relative* quantities, but the effect of relative factor prices on the quantity of one factor only. The problem of obtaining the magnitude of the elasticity of substitution is discussed below, in connection with the results of the labor regression.

The regression coefficient of the within-plant price index is $-.079$ and its t-ratio is 3.374. This coefficient is larger than that of the expected price; however, the t-ratio of the difference between the two coefficients (which is .0384/.0216 = 1.778) is not significant at the 5 per cent level.

Depreciation.—The attempt to estimate the effect of the age of plant on the use of fuel did not lead to significant results. The sample, however, covers a span of only twenty years, and the useful life of an electric generator is considerably longer. Moreover, there are only ten plants in the sample for which observations for ten years or more are available (the longest series of observations covers seventeen years). Most of the plants were observed for only three to five years. The coefficient obtained for the depreciation variable is $-.013$ which, after the appropriate transformations, indicates that with every year added to the life of the plant, the amount of fuel used falls by about 2 per cent.[12] This result, which is contrary to expectations, was not, however, substantiated when separate coefficients were estimated from two subsamples of plants (one contains "young" plants aged four years or less, and the other contains "old" plants aged five years or more).[13] The coefficient for the "young" plants was .00307 (with a t-ratio of 1.099) and of the "old" plants $-.00249$ (with a t-ratio of 1.725). When an alternative definition of age, the calendar age rather than the accumulated use of the plant, was examined, the results did not change much. I conclude that for the first ten years of the life of the plant, and possibly also the next ten years, the efficiency of the use of fuel is affected very little by the age of the plant.

Technical change.—This is represented by the shifts in the fuel function between plants of different vintage years. If the fuel regression contains all the factors affecting the demand for fuel, a shift in the function is a result of technical change or, more accurately, of a change in the quality of the equipment. Before running the regression described above, separate regressions, one for each vintage year,[14] were run. While no formal test was conducted, it appeared quite clear that except for changes in the constant term, the function remained stable between years. Consequently, dummy variables for changes in the constant term only were introduced.

[12] The antilog of the regression coefficient, -1.03, indicates the factor by which the amount of fuel changes with one additional year of full time operation. Since on the average plants operated at about 60 per cent of capacity, the annual change in the quantity of fuel is about -2 per cent.

[13] The sample was subdivided in an attempt to determine whether plants start to deteriorate only after several years of operation.

[14] Except for 1959, for which the number of degrees of freedom is too small.

The most striking feature of the set of coefficients of the dummy variables is their small size. The base year is 1941 and the regression coefficients obtained are comparisons of the year under consideration with that year. The coefficient for 1959, −.040, indicates that the amount of fuel required to produce one kilowatt hour was 9.6 per cent[15] lower in 1959 than in 1941. The annual rate of improvement in productivity over the period is quite unstable. In fact the coefficient of the dummy variable for 1957 is +.044, which indicates a 10.6 per cent *fall* in fuel efficiency between 1941 and 1957. When the entire pattern of shifts in the function is examined, however, it seems that 1959, rather than 1957, is on the trend line of the change in fuel efficiency (see Fig. 1). The shifts in the fuel function over time will be discussed further below, along with the shifts in the labor and capital functions.

V. THE LABOR REGRESSION

The effects of measurement errors in the quantity of labor variable (and its price) are probably much more serious than for any of the other variables in this study. Labor quantity is measured as "average number of employees" in each plant in a given year. This average might contain errors (or rather elements of non-homogeneity) due to differences in the total number of hours a worker worked during the year as between years,[16] between plants at a point of time, and possibly even within plants due to improper weighting of part-time work, and due to differences in the quality of labor both cross-sectionally and over time. The same considerations carry over to the estimate of the wage rate. While the multiple coefficient of determination for the fuel regression is .99, that for the labor regression with an identical set of independent variables is only .81.[17] Still some of the estimates are very interesting. The regression results are presented in Table 2.

It should be emphasized from the outset that it is not at all clear in this case that pooling the data on individual vin-

TABLE 2

RESULTS FROM LABOR REGRESSION

Variable	Regression Coefficient	*t*-Ratio
Size	.626	47.237
Load	.169	4.624
Load index	.054	1.402
Price	−.267	−9.803
Price index	−.259	−3.816
Depreciation	.010	.527
Dummy for 1943	.156	4.718
Dummy for 1948	.046	1.413
Dummy for 1949	.093	3.412
Dummy for 1950	−.023	−.760
Dummy for 1951	−.013	−.477
Dummy for 1952	−.089	−3.219
Dummy for 1953	.009	.305
Dummy for 1954	−.028	−1.041
Dummy for 1955	−.157	−5.543
Dummy for 1956	−.002	−.066
Dummy for 1957	−.026	−.709
Dummy for 1958	−.130	−3.697
Dummy for 1959	−.208	−5.017

$R^2 = .8079$.

tage years into a single regression, using only dummy variables for the differences in the constant terms, is appropriate, since the results of the regression for the individual vintage years were not very stable between years. Consequently, the discussion of the results of the pooled regression includes references to results from the regressions for the individual years.

Economies of scale.—The size coeffi-

[15] Antilog of .04011 = 1.096.

[16] An attempt to correct for this factor by converting man-years to total number of hours worked over the year did not improve the results.

[17] The original variance in the labor variable, however, is less than one-half of the variance in the fuel variable.

cient, −.626, does not differ much from those of most of the individual years studied and is probably a reliable point estimate. The economies of scale with respect to labor are considerably more pronounced than those with respect to fuel. The increased efficiency in the use of labor due to the 3.70-fold increase in plant size between 1941 and 1959 is about 63 per cent, since the amount of labor required in a typical 1959 plant compared to a typical 1941 plant increased by a factor of 2.27 only. The differential response of the demand for labor as compared to that for fuel implies that as plant size is changing the relative amounts of the two factors also have to change. When plant size is increased, the amounts of both fuel and labor increase more slowly than output; but labor increases even more slowly than fuel, and consequently its share has to fall. This leads to the seemingly paradoxical conclusion that while economies of scale are more pronounced for labor than for fuel, as plants grow bigger the importance of the differential in terms of total factor productivity is falling, since the relative share of labor is falling and there is less room for saving in this factor.

The load factors.—The load coefficient is .169 and its *t*-ratio 4.624. This regression coefficient is lower than most of the individual year coefficients, which center around .350. In either case the coefficient is far below unity which means that plants of equal size, designed to operate at different levels of capacity, will not vary substantially in the amount of labor used.

This phenomenon is even more pronounced in the case of variations in the use of capacity within plants. The coefficient for this variable is .054, and it is not significantly different from zero. It is slightly higher in the individual years but not significant in most cases. It may be concluded that if this variable has any effect, it is extremely small. It is interesting to note the lack of symmetry between labor and fuel in their response to changes in the load factor. When the load factor varies within plants, the response of fuel is quite close to a proportional change, while there is practically no response at all in the use of labor.[18] Within plants fuel is practically the only factor of production reacting to changes in load.

Relative prices.—The coefficients of the relative price of labor and of the within-plant changes in this variable are −.267 and −.259, respectively. Both are significant but both are subject to negative spurious correlation due to common (though inverse) errors in the measurement of the quantity of labor and its price, which pull both coefficients toward unity.

One can attempt to approximate the elasticity of substitution between labor and fuel by summing the price coefficients emerging from the two regressions. This procedure is equivalent to taking the ratio of the two quantities as the dependent variable and the price ratio as the independent variable. The sum of these coefficients would be the elasticity of substitution between labor and fuel, except for one important reservation arising from the presence of the third input, capital.[19]

[18] Harry G. Johnson has pointed out that this may be partly due to the fact that labor is measured in man-years rather than in man-hours.

[19] When the price of fuel increases, the quantity of fuel demanded falls not only because the price of fuel relative to the price of labor increases but also because the price of fuel relative to the price of capital increases. When the price of labor falls, the amount of fuel demanded falls—this time, however, only because fuel is more expensive relative to labor, but not to capital. Even though the price of capital is not included explicitly in the model, it affects the price coefficients of labor and fuel. There is no way to disentangle the effect of the price of capital from

The sum of the labor and fuel price elasticities is −.307 for expected price and −.338 for changes around this price. The standard errors are less than .1,[20] so that the two coefficients are significantly different from zero and one. This again indicates that at least for this industry the Cobb-Douglas production function, which implicitly assumes an elasticity of substitution of −1, is unacceptable.[21] However, the fact that these coefficients are significantly different from zero indicates that factor quantities are responsive to price changes (rather than that these numerical results are unbiased estimates of the corresponding elasticities).

Depreciation.—The coefficient of the depreciation variable was .010, indicating that as a plant grows a year older, the demand for labor goes up by about 1.5 per cent. This coefficient, however, is not significantly different from zero. The coefficients of the individual years displayed a similar pattern, being on the whole insignificant. When the accumulated use measure of depreciation was replaced by the calendar age as a measure of depreciation for two subsamples of the study, the results were practically the same. But when the two variables were introduced simultaneously, both became highly significant. The coefficient of the accumulated use variable (with a t-ratio of about 4) indicated a substantial depreciation (or rather increase in maintenance), in one case of about 8 per cent per year and in the other 26 per cent per year. The coefficient of the calendar age variable was also highly significant, and indicated a *reduction* in the use of labor as the plant gets older; in the one case by 4 per cent per year and in the other by 42 per cent. My conjecture is that the two coefficients reflect two distinct forces that operate in opposite directions. One is the deterioration of equipment over time, which requires more labor for maintenance purposes. The other is a combination of improvements in the quality of labor and improvements in methods of using labor inside the plant. The first is basically a function of the extent to which a plant is used, and the second is highly correlated with the flow of time. In the two subsample years selected, calendar age is correlated with accumulated use, but not perfectly so; consequently the introduction of the two variables into the same regression leads to partial separation of the two forces.

Technical change.—The shifts in the labor function over time show a pattern similar to that of the fuel function, but the magnitude of the shifts is larger. The coefficient of the dummy variable for 1959 is −.208, indicating that for a given level of output the amount of labor required for plants installed in 1941 was 1.61 larger than that required for plants installed in 1959. While the shift over time was not smooth, the downward trend is even more pronounced than in the fuel function. Part of the explanation for the difference between the rates of change in the two functions lies, prob-

the relation between labor and fuel, since there are three elasticities of substitution between three factors, but there are only two independent price ratios. I conclude that the sum of the two price coefficients is an upward-biased estimate of the elasticity of substitution between labor and fuel.

[20] The standard errors of the components of each sum are available, and even though estimates of the covariances between them are not available, they cannot exceed $\sqrt{[V(a)\ V(b)]}$, where $V(a)$ and $V(b)$ are the variances of the components. Using this inequality relation, it turns out that the two standard errors cannot exceed .037 and .091, respectively.

[21] Komiya (*op. cit.*) experimented with fitting a Cobb-Douglas production function to the data. The results were not satisfactory, and he proceeds to reject the possibility of factor substitution without taking account of the possibility that the poor results might stem from an inappropriate functional form rather than from the absence of substitutability.

ably, in the improvement in labor quality (though presumably this should be captured by the relative price variable). The shift in the function is explored further below.

VI. CAPITAL IN THE POWER INDUSTRY

Dependent and independent variables.—The concept of the quantity of capital employed in the industry is very elusive and must be handled with great care. The number of generators obviously is not a correct measure since there are generators of many sizes and qualities. The number of installed kilowatts, which is frequently used as a measure for generator size, is superior but is not entirely satisfactory either. Generators of equal capacity can differ substantially in the amount of collaborating factors required to produce a given output. Such quality differences have to be accounted for in a measure of the quantity of capital. Consequently, the number of installed kilowatts as the sole measure of the quantity of capital has to be rejected. Finally, the value of capital can be deflated by the price index of capital. This would be the right measure if the price index were the appropriate one. But what is the appropriate price index of capital? It cannot be obtained unless the quantity units are appropriately defined, which leads us back to the point where we started. In order to overcome these difficulties the variable that was selected for explanation was the total undeflated value of the plant. The total value can be conceived as the "quantity" of the plant times the price per unit of quantity. In the regression equation there is an attempt to account for both elements in the value of the plant. In attempting to explain the variance in the value of the plant, it is implicitly assumed that at any point in time, all customers are confronted by the same price for a given generator. While for fuel and for labor cross-sectional price differentials were allowed for, they are not allowed for in the case of the price of capital. It is also assumed that discrimination among buyers of electrical equipment, if present, is not correlated with the independent variables included in the regression. Over time, however, prices of plants are allowed to vary.

Four variables are introduced to account for the quantity (and quality) of capital. These are the number of installed kilowatts, the load factor, the price of fuel, and the price of labor. The number of kilowatts variable is an obvious measure of size. The use of the load factor deserves explanation. The higher the load factor at which a plant is expected to operate, the more desirable it becomes to obtain equipment that can cope with the heavier strain, and consequently the higher the cost of the equipment. The first-year load factor is again used as a proxy for the anticipated (average) load factor. A similar rationale applies to the introduction of the anticipated prices of labor and fuel. The higher they are the stronger is the incentive to invest more in equipment that is more efficient in the use of these factors. Here also the observed first year prices of labor and of fuel are used as proxies for the corresponding anticipated prices. These prices are basically price ratios since cross-sectionally the price of capital is (assumed) constant, and since changes in the level of prices over time are accounted for by dummy variables. Finally, dummy variables are introduced to estimate the shift in the constant term over time. These shifts are partly due to inflationary trends over the period, and partly due to technical improvements in equipment that made the production of a given amount of electricity with less capital possible. An attempt to separate the two trend factors is described below.

The regression results, based on 178 observations (one per plant) are presented in Table 3. Results from preliminary regressions for the individual year indicated that only the constant terms differed from year to year, while the regression coefficients remained quite stable between years.

Economies of scale.—The coefficient of the size variable is .815. This coefficient is significantly smaller than unity, indicating that there are economies of scale in the capital cost of the plant. The magnitude of these economies of scale is different from those of both labor and fuel. They are less than in labor, but more than in fuel. The 3.70-fold increase in average plant size from 1941 to 1959 requires only a 2.90-fold increase in expenditures for plant (compared to 3.25-fold for fuel and 2.27-fold for labor).[22]

The price of quality.—The elasticities of the cost of equipment with respect to the prices of labor and of fuel and with respect to the load factor are all positive, as expected, and all significantly different from zero.[23] They all indicate that the quality of equipment is an important factor in the determination of its price. The regression coefficient of labor price indicates that a one per cent increase in anticipated labor cost leads to a .271 per cent increase in the original investment in the plant, presumably in labor-saving devices. Similarly a one per cent anticipated increase in fuel cost leads to a .186 per cent increase in investment in plant, presumably to improve the thermal efficiency of the plant and to reduce the burden of the higher fuel cost. Finally, the coefficient of the load factor is .117—the percentage increase in investment in plant in response to a one per cent increase in anticipated load factor. Even though the absolute magnitudes of these coefficients are not large,[24] being quite far from unity, they are all highly significant and indicate that the production of electricity does not require fixed proportions of inputs and that a given output can be obtained with different factor combinations.[25] The particular combina-

TABLE 3

RESULTS FROM CAPITAL REGRESSION*

Variable	Regression Coefficient	*t*-Ratio
Size	.815	39.410
Labor price	.271	4.077
Fuel price	.186	3.921
Load factor	.116	3.739
Dummy for 1943	.091	1.412
Dummy for 1948	.134	2.142
Dummy for 1949	.267	4.897
Dummy for 1950	.232	3.827
Dummy for 1951	.309	5.743
Dummy for 1952	.244	4.428
Dummy for 1953	.213	3.831
Dummy for 1954	.246	4.609
Dummy for 1955	.253	4.504
Dummy for 1956	.260	4.875
Dummy for 1957	.162	2.428
Dummy for 1958	.281	5.215
Dummy for 1959	.183	3.042

*The coefficients of the dummy variables are obtained from a different regression than the rest of the coefficients. For explanation see text below.

$R^2 = .9437$.

[22] In my "Productivity in the Electric Power Industry, 1929–1955," *op. cit.*, I estimated the returns to scale as a single parameter. The results presented here indicate that this oversimplified approach is erroneous. A similar and more obvious error was to consider the effects of changes in the load factor as uniform with respect to all inputs.

[23] Since the errors in measuring the price of labor due to non-homogeneity in labor quantity are not likely to be correlated with the cost of equipment, the significance of the coefficient of the labor price variable indicates that variability in this variable is not entirely due to quality differences, but also to some genuine differences in wages.

[24] Here errors in the variables lead to the conventional downward bias in the regression coefficients.

[25] Recall that the definition of the industry is quite narrow; only steam power plants are considered.

tion which is eventually selected is quite sensitive to economic incentives.

Shifts in the function.—The shifts over time in the capital function are obtained from the set of coefficients of the dummy variables. These coefficients, as presented in Table 3, are obtained from a regression which excluded the price of labor and the price of fuel. The presence of these price variables, which are measured in current prices, would lead to a downward-biased estimate of the coefficients of the dummy variables.[26] It is worth mentioning that the coefficients of all the dummy variables in the regression that excludes the price variables are larger than the corresponding coefficients from the regression where no variables are excluded.

The pattern of the shifts in the function over time is of a rapid increase up to 1951—a rise from 100 in 1941, to 185 in 1949, to a peak of 204 in 1951. After 1951, the pattern is one of fluctuations with no clear-cut trend. This pattern corresponds well with the general trend in prices over these two decades. A striking feature of this pattern is its negative correlation with the shifts in the fuel and labor functions. This relation is explored further below.

Total capital versus equipment only.—The cost of capital variable considered here is inclusive of all capital expenditures; it includes not only equipment, but also structure and improvements and land. The equipment constitutes about 75 per cent of the total, structure and improvements about 24 per cent, and land 1 per cent. The last two items are sometimes excluded from the analysis on the ground that "the construction component . . . varies considerably, depending upon the site conditions . . . weather conditions . . . and number of generating units."[27] It seems to me undesirable to exclude any individual element of the capital expenditures on such arbitrary grounds. While it may be true that these are "non-equalizing" differentials, it is more appropriate to let the data determine which formulation is more advantageous. An additional regression was run with the same set of independent variables as before, but with cost of equipment only as the dependent variable. The fit, as measured by the multiple coefficient of determination, favors by a small margin the exclusion of expenditures other than on equipment; the R^2 goes up from .9437 to .9511 and the regression explains an additional 12 per cent of the remaining variance.[28] The regression coefficients indicating the scale factor are quite close in the two cases, and the difference between them indicates that economies of scale are a bit more pronounced for total capital than for equipment only.

The regression coefficients of the three other non-dummy variables are substantially different in the two formulations, as can be seen in Table 4. Total capital is much more sensitive than its equipment component to changes in each of these three variables. These results show that not only is the equipment purchased designed to economize on the use of la-

[26] Viewed geometrically, changes of a given magnitude in the price of capital would appear as vertical shifts in the function when only the price of capital is considered, thus the entire price change would be reflected in the shift of the constant term; the shifts become diagonal when some of the independent variables are prices, and then only part of the change is reflected in the shift of the constant term. The slope of the regression in the price dimensions, however, is not biased by the inclusion of these current prices variables.

[27] Komiya, *op. cit.*, p. 159.

[28] The original variance of the two capital variables is almost identical. In fact, the more inclusive variable has a smaller variance, but the difference is not sufficient to upset the conclusion in the text.

bor where wages are high, but that even more labor saving devices are incorporated in the plant through the design of series regressions in which the dependent variable was the series of the coefficients of the dummy variables of the capital

TABLE 4

COMPARISON OF SOME REGRESSION RESULTS FOR TWO FORMULATIONS OF CAPITAL

Variable	Equipment Only		Total Capital	
	Regression Coefficient	*t*-Ratio	Regression Coefficient	*t*-Ratio
Price of labor	.223	3.570	.271	4.077
Price of fuel	.127	2.847	.186	3.921
Load factor	.088	3.001	.117	3.739

structure and improvements. A similar argument applies to fuel and to the load factor. This discussion indicates that the exclusion of structures from total capital leads to the loss of valuable information about the production process in this industry. The time pattern of the dummy variables from the two capital regressions is presented in Figure 1, as are also the time patterns of the dummy variables from the fuel and the labor regressions.

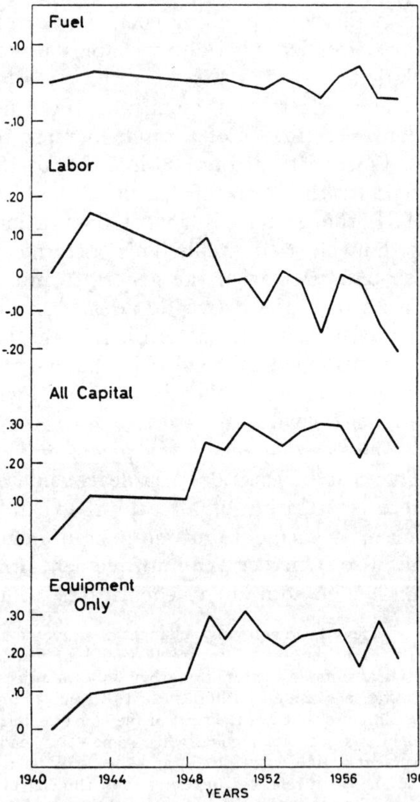

FIG. 1.—The time pattern of the the dummy variables.

VII. PRICE INDEX OF ELECTRICAL PLANT AND EQUIPMENT

We now are in a position to discuss together the shifts over time of the fuel, labor, and capital functions. The shifts in the value of equipment function are a combination of shifts in the quantity of equipment and in its price. The shifts in the price component reflect inflationary trends in the economy as well as special factors affecting the price of electrical equipment. The shift in the quantity component is comparable to the shift in the fuel and labor functions, reflecting the increased ability to produce a given amount of output with less inputs. An attempt to separate the two components was undertaken by running a few time-function. The independent variables were some measures of price changes to account for the price component and the dummy variables from the fuel and labor regressions to account for the quality component, the reasoning being that improvements in fuel and labor efficiency will be correlated with the price of equipment.

Three alternative price-level variables were considered. The first was the GNP price deflator, reflecting the general price trends in the economy. The second was the price index of electrical machinery and equipment.[29] The third is a combined index of wages in the electrical machinery industry[30] and steel prices.[31] All price indexes were transformed into logarithms. The regression results are presented in Table 5.

In all cases the coefficients of the price variables are less than unity (although not significantly so), indicating that the price of capital increases more slowly than do the prices of labor and steel, the major inputs in the production of capital; more slowly than the price index of machinery as calculated by the Department of Commerce; and more slowly than the general price level as reflected by the GNP price deflator. The GNP price deflator itself reflects, to some degree, the increase in productivity in the economy as a whole. Since capital in the steam-power industry rises in price more slowly than the general price level, the increase in productivity in the production of this capital is more pronounced than the increase in productivity in the economy as a whole, at least as reflected by the GNP price deflator.

The interpretation of the coefficients of the dummy variables is quite complex and not entirely satisfactory. The causal relationship between the two sets of dummy variables can work both ways. If the manufacturers of electrical plant

TABLE 5

RESULTS FROM ALTERNATIVE REGRESSIONS FOR SHIFTS IN CAPITAL FUNCTION OVER TIME*

INDEPENDENT VARIABLES	DEPENDENT VARIABLE†					
	1	2	1	2	1	2
GNP price deflator	......	......	.927	.960	......	......
			(.183)	(.194)		
Price index of electrical machinery	.900	.939	......	......	......	......
	(.191)	(.196)				
Hourly earnings in electrical machinery industry	......	......	......	......	.373	.794
					(.663)	(.612)
Steel price	......	......	......	......	.394	.062
					(.625)	(.578)
Dummy coefficients from labor regression	.933	.702	.617	.368	.876	.603
	(.313)	(.323)	(.255)	(.267)	(.376)	(.347)
Dummy coefficients from fuel regression	−2.525	−1.997	−1.953	−1.393	−2.428	−1.856
	(.914)	(.942)	(.831)	(.869)	(1.040)	(.961)
R^2	.730	.759	.755	.775	.693	.780

* Entries in this table are regression coefficients and their standard errors.

† Dependent variable 1 is the series of regression coefficients of the dummy variables from the regression on all capital. Dependent variable 2 is the series of regression coefficients of the dummy variables from the regression on equipment only. Sample size is 14.

[29] U.S. Department of Commerce, *Business Statistics* (Supplement to the *Survey of Current Business*), 1961, p. 39.

[30] *Ibid.*, p. 72.

[31] *Ibid.*, p. 158.

and equipment are able to improve their product in terms of labor and fuel efficiency, they can increase the price of equipment. On these grounds we would expect negative regression coefficients for the two (independent) dummy variables. On the other hand, if the price of equipment is rising independently, labor and fuel would be substituted for capital and this would appear as a reduction in efficiency of equipment, leading to positive coefficients for the two variables. Since the price of capital was not incorporated in the fuel and labor regressions, the coefficients of the two dummy variables reflect these two opposing forces. It seems that the former is stronger in the case of fuel, while the latter dominates in the case of labor.[32] Although it is impossible to separate the two effects, the results are not meaningless. They indicate that both forces are in operation—that labor (and fuel) are substituted for capital when its price goes up, and that improvements in fuel (and labor) efficiency lead to higher price of equipment.[33] Price increases due to higher efficiency should be netted out, at least in principle, from the price index of equipment since they reflect quality improvements rather than mere price increases.

One more comment on the price index of electrical equipment is in order at this juncture. Due to economies of scale, and due to the increase in average plant size over time, consumers today pay lower prices for electricity than they would have paid in the absence of economies of scale. These economies are partly due to the higher labor and fuel efficiency of bigger plants. They are also due to the lower capital cost of bigger plants. Should such reductions in cost be incorporated in the price index of electrical equipment? The allocation of such economies of scale is arbitrary. One may argue that these economies are a consequence of the increase in size and in geographical concentration of consumer units that enables utilities to install larger plants. Alternatively, one may argue that the manufacturer of the equipment should be credited with such economies since he is the one responsible for the construction of equipment that becomes more efficient at larger size. It seems convenient to adopt the latter attitude and to construct the price index of plant and equipment accordingly. Table 6 presents the price indexes per installed kilowatt of electrical equipment only and of electrical plant and equipment. These indexes take explicit account of two factors. The first is that the price of electrical plant and equipment of a given size increased more slowly than the GNP deflator (Table 5). The second is that the price per unit of capacity declines when size increases (Table 3).[34] Due to the ambiguity of the results regarding the quality of the equipment, this factor is not included in the con-

[32] When the two variables are introduced separately into the regressions their signs are not affected, but they become entirely insignificant. Only when both appear in the same regression are they significant, even though the correlation between the two is quite high (.756).

[33] Komiya, *op. cit.*, also investigates the shift in the function over time. However, his observations on capital are deflated by a price index. Since the deflator series would in general already incorporate any shifts in the function, it is not surprising that Komiya does not observe any significant shifts in his capital regressions.

[34] For a 1 per cent increase in the GNP deflator the "all capital" price index is increased by .927 per cent (obtained as the coefficient of the GNP deflator in Table 6), and for a 1 per cent increase in (geometric mean plant size, the price index is reduced by 0.185 per cent (0.185 = 1 − 0.815/0.815 is the size coefficient in the capital regression).

struction of the index.[35, 36] The gaps in the indexes (1942 and 1944–47) are not serious since very few plants were constructed in those years, and consequently there is no clear meaning to an index for such years.

The two indexes reflect the upward trend in general prices on the one hand, and the reduction in cost of plant (per kilowatt) due to the increase in average plant size over the period. The index for all capital goes up more slowly than that of equipment only since economies of scale are a bit more pronounced for all capital. Also, all capital has a slightly lower coefficient with respect to the GNP deflator. The increase in both indexes is considerably more moderate than that in the Department of Commerce price index for electrical machinery and equipment, which increased from 70.1 in 1941 to 154.4 in 1959, a 2.2 fold increase. Finally, the two indexes do not have a very smooth time pattern. This is mainly due to the fact that the average plant size has substantial fluctuations aside from its upward trend.

TABLE 6

PRICE INDEX PER INSTALLED KILOWATT OF ELECTRICAL PLANT AND OF ALL CAPITAL (1941 = 100)

Year*	Equipment Only	All Capital
1941	100.0	100.0
1943	104.5	103.3
1948	176.4	173.9
1949	146.3	143.4
1950	140.3	137.3
1951	171.7	168.3
1952	157.6	153.9
1953	148.4	144.4
1954	167.8	163.9
1955	151.4	147.3
1956	175.0	170.6
1957	169.6	164.9
1958	168.4	163.4
1959	163.3	158.1

* The index for any year is for plants that had their first complete (calendar) year of operation at that year. They were installed earlier and started to operate the year before. If we want to "date" a plant according to when it started operation, the entire index should be moved backward—1940 would be 100, 1942 would be 104.5, etc.

VIII. SUMMARY

The result which emerges most prominently from this study (as in most other steam-power-industry studies) is that there are substantial economies of scale in this industry. The economies of scale are not uniform over all factors of production. They are most pronounced for labor, less so for capital and even less for fuel. This feature indicates that the Cobb-Douglas production function is inappropriate for studies of this industry.

In addition to economies of scale, there are substantial economies in the more intensive use of the available plants. Such economies are obvious in the case of capital. They are very important in the case of labor, which is almost a fixed factor after a plant is installed. Even fuel can be saved by operating the plant more intensively; the use of fuel increases less than proportionately with output. If plants are designed in advance to operate at a higher level of capacity, this increases the fuel efficiency further, but at the cost of increasing somewhat the labor and capital costs.

Factor substitution, contrary to prevalent notions, is not absent. It operates not only in the long run, when it is possible to incorporate price information in the design of equipment, but also for existing plants. The elasticity of substitution between labor and fuel however, is far below unity (which is another in-

[35] However, the capital regressions take explicit account of contemporaneous differences in quality, and the dummy variables are free from these quality differences.

[36] For a comprehensive discussions of such corrections see I. Adelman and Z. Griliches, "On an Index of Quality Change," *Journal of American Statistical Association*, Vol. LVI (September, 1961).

dication of the inappropriateness of using the Cobb-Douglas form for this industry). Depreciation, at least for the first ten years of operations, does not seem to be of great importance. This, however, may be due to the incorporation of some new techniques in plants already in existence.

Since fuel is the only input whose quality was actually held constant over the period, it is the only one for which the effects of technical advance would be detected at all clearly. As it turns out, while technical advance should be credited with an increase in fuel efficiency, such improvements are far from being overwhelming and fall short of the increase in fuel efficiency due to economies of scale.[37] The increase in labor efficiency is much more pronounced than that of fuel, however, and so presumably is the increase in the quality of labor. There are indications that capital requirements (holding size constant) are falling over time, but it is impossible, within the present framework, to evaluate the magnitude of these changes.

Finally, the price index of capital for the electrical industry (and the price index of equipment only), when appropriately constructed, shows a much more moderate increase between 1941 and 1959 than either the GNP price deflator or the price index for electrical equipment as constructed by the Department of Commerce.

[37] Similar conclusions were reached in my previous study covering production and distribution of electricity by the entire power industry. See Barzel, *op. cit.*

APPENDIX

A. THE DATA

The entire data for the core of the study, where a power plant is the basic unit of observation, are obtained from a single source—the Federal Power Commission's Annual Supplements to "Steam-Electric Plant Construction Cost and Annual Production Expenses." The plants incorporated in the sample were all installed between 1941 and 1959. The time pattern of the sample is shown in Table A1. A plant is observed annually from its first year of full time operation, until any major change is undertaken in it (or until 1960, the last year for which data were available at the time of the study). All these plants are privately owned, and the sample covers practically all such plants except those for which information is insufficient.

B. STATISTICAL PROCEDURES

Estimates of the parameters of the demand for factors functions, with all observations transformed into logarithms, are obtained by multiple regression. Two types of variables are considered in the functions of the demand for fuel and of the demand for labor. One varies between plants, and the other within plants. However, both types are incorporated within the framework of a single regression. Consequently, the total sample size of 801 does not appropriately represent the number of degrees of

TABLE A1

TIME PATTERN OF THE SAMPLE

Year of Installation	No. of Plants*	Average No. of Years Observed per Plant
1941	8 (7)	63:8 = 7.9
1943	8 (7)	38:8 = 4.8
1948	9 (8)	42:9 = 4.7
1949	17 (16)	75:17 = 4.4
1950	12 (9)	56:12 = 4.7
1951	19 (17)	78:19 = 3.7
1952	19 (15)	70:19 = 3.7
1952	18 (15)	60:18 = 3.3
1954	22 (18)	86:22 = 3.9
1955	24 (14)	81:24 = 3.4
1956	24 (18)	74:24 = 3.1
1957	9 (6)	26:9 = 2.9
1958	18 (18)	32:18 = 1.8
1959	13 (10)	20:13 = 1.5
Total	220 (178)	801:220 = 3.6

* Numbers in brackets are for observations used in capital regressions; in a few cases the data on this variable were incomplete and so some observations had to be dropped from the sample.

freedom for the between-plants variables. The number of the within-plants observations is 581 (=801 − 220) which should be used as the basis for calculating degrees of freedom for the within-plant variables. Furthermore, many plants are observed for more than one year, and the observations on the between-plants variables are duplicated for such plants. Some plants are observed over more years than other plants, and consequently such plants obtain unduly large weight in the regression. This is particularly so for the older plants in the sample. But, since the total number of plants is so large (and since the number of older plants is rather small), the loss in efficiency can be disregarded for practical purposes.

[4]

Productivity and the Price of Medical Services

Yoram Barzel

University of Washington

I

The increase in the price of medical services over the last few decades measured in the Consumer Price Index (CPI) has exceeded the total for all other items. The clear implication is that not only have medical services become relatively more expensive but also that the production of these services is subject to a smaller productivity advance than are products and services in the rest of the economy. Table 1 summarizes the relevant figures. It is the argument of this paper that these figures are a poor reflection of productivity change and that in fact the rate of increase of productivity in the medical services has exceeded somewhat the overall productivity increase in the rest of the economy.

The CPI (U.S. Department of Labor, relevant issues) attempts to provide a measure of the income compensation required to maintain the consumer at a given utility level. It seems clear that the commodities and services constituting the base for the index should be arguments in the consumer's utility function.

TABLE 1
THE CPI AND SOME OF ITS MEDICAL COMPONENTS

Time Period	All Items	All Medical Care	Physicians' Fees	Hospital Daily Service Charges
1935–64 (1935=110)	226.2	241.17	217.6	608.8
1945–64 (1945=100)	172.4	207.7	185.3	445.8

SOURCE.—U.S. Department of Labor, Bureau of Labor Statistics (relevant issues).

I wish to thank W. Y. Oi for valuable comments, W. H. Nam for assistance in organizing the data, my wife for the computer program, and the National Science Foundation for financial support.

Medical commodities and services which are arguments in this function can be discussed most conveniently using the framework recently introduced by Lancaster (1966). Following Lancaster, the individual's utility function $U(Z)$ is a function of characteristics (Z_i's) of commodities and services. Each characteristic, in Lancaster's formulation, may be "produced" by more than one commodity (Y_k), so that

$$Z_i = \sum_k b_{ik} Y_k,$$

where b_{ik} is the amount of Z_i per unit of the kth commodity. Commodities purchased by the individual, then, are inputs in the production function of utility. When we concentrate on the health component of the utility function, the more important Z_i's are the level of health of the individual and the psychic cost of illness. If the function relating the medical commodities and services purchased on the market (Y_k's) to the health characteristics in the utility function (Z_i's) is homogeneous of the first degree, then the price index of these inputs would also be the price index of the health output. But one of the major inputs on the part of the household is the time lost due to illness. Since conventional price indices totally ignore this input, the price index will be biased to the extent that this input varies disproportionately to other inputs. Moreover, for the price index of medical inputs to be a valid measure of the price of output, the inputs must be of constant quality over time.[1] Hospital daily room charges and fees for physicians' visits are two major medical components of the CPI. It is hard to argue on a priori grounds that the quality of these two components is constant over time.[2]

An additional problem arises when, instead of a single individual, we consider an average over many individuals. For this average to be meaningful, the health level of the population has to remain constant over time. Changes in factors such as nutritional standards on the one hand and changes in the age distribution toward a higher proportion of younger and older individuals on the other cast some doubt on the constancy of medical "needs" of the population over the last few decades.

Horton's study on medical care in the U.S. Navy (1966) provides many of the elements required to evaluate the order of magnitude of the discrepancy between the medical component of the CPI and the ideal measure of such a price index. By concentrating on the Navy and Marine Corps, Horton was able to study a group which experienced very little age variation over time; for example, between 1932 and 1959, over 90 percent of the force was less than forty years old (Horton 1966, p. 116). He found that

[1] Or, alternatively, the production function transforming inputs into outputs should be constant over time and not be subject to technical change.

[2] It should be pointed out that daily room charges are also a poor measure of the cost of inputs, since the amount of capital, labor, and materials per patient per day may (and does) vary widely.

for the period 1932–62, the number of "M.D.'s equivalents"[3] per 100,000 force fell from 2,670 in 1932 to 1,864 in 1962. The number of hospital beds per 100,000 force fell from 8,315 in 1932 to 1,621 in 1962 (Horton 1966, table 8 and appendix table 1).[4] During the same period, all indices of health in the Navy and Marines point upward. For example, the number of days per man lost due to disease and injury fell from 28.3 (24.5 for disease alone) in 1932 to 9.5 (7.5 for disease alone) in 1962. Similarly, the death rate per 1,000 fell from 3.35 in 1932 (1.68 for disease alone) to 1.56 (0.29 for disease alone) in 1962 (Horton 1966, appendix table 2). In short, these results indicate a dramatic improvement in productivity. The Medical branches of the Navy and Marines offer medical services that correspond to both hospital and nonhospital medical care in the civilian sector. It is unlikely that the productivity advance in the Navy was restricted to the nonhospital element. When output of the medical industry is measured as the dollar value of reduced sick time. Horton obtains a productivity increase of 5.3–7.3 percent per year for 1932–62. These rates, while subject to certain qualification,[5] are considerably above those obtained by Kendrick (1961) for the entire economy. If the rate of increase of medical factor prices did not exceed that for the whole economy, the faster rate of productivity advance in the medical industry should result in a slower rate of price increase than that for the entire economy. The change in the cost of capital equipment to the medical industry is unknown, but there seems to be no a priori reason to believe that it changed differently from that of other industries. The cost of labor input to the medical industry increased more slowly than that for the entire economy.[6] Given the above considerations, we may conclude that the true price index of medical care increased more slowly than the overall CPI and that the price index for hospital services very likely followed that same pattern.

II

The previous remarks indicate that, to obtain a meaningful price index for medical care, attention should be focussed on the population's health level. The ideal way to approach this problem is to determine how much it would

[3] Medical personnel were aggregated according to their wages, using doctors as the basic unit.

[4] The correct variable here is the amount of capital equipment per navy man. These series are not available. The series of the number of beds probably did not rise as fast as the capital series. Such a bias, however, seems insufficient to reverse the main conclusions.

[5] One qualification is indicated in a previous footnote; another is that it is implicitly assumed that the level of health of navy recruits was constant over the period. Still another qualification is due to the inherent difficulty of evaluating human life.

[6] For the period studied by Horton (1966), average annual earnings per full-time employee tripled for the entire economy and only doubled for medical services (U.S. Department of Commerce, relevant issues).

cost to maintain the consumer's health at a constant level at different points in time (after appropriate correction for normal change in health due to age). Such cost series would constitute the base for the health component of the CPI, since the consumer would receive, if compensated according to the index, the precise amount that would keep him at a constant level of utility. At the moment, this method would require a major large-scale research project. I believe that eventually such an effort should be undertaken.[7]

The technique adopted here, while far from ideal, gets us a substantial part of the way toward that goal; its point of departure is the health insurance plan. Consider a particular health insurance contract providing a certain coverage. A subscriber attempting to allocate his resources among all activities will demand medical service consistent with equilibrium. When that equilibrium is displaced due to curable medical problems, the subscriber will take advantage of the insurance until the problems are resolved, at which time his health is restored to its previous equilibrium level. In generalizing this statement, we may conclude that the medical insurance will be used in such a way as to maintain the health level of the subscriber constant.[8]

If this is what the individual subscriber attempts to do, the insurance company's expenses in each period will be such as to maintain the health of that subscriber at a constant level. Two major components contribute to these costs: the particular medical experience of the subscriber and the change over time of treating any given medical problem. If we succeed in separating and removing the random element of the individual experiences, the systematic element remaining will provide us with the actual cost of maintaining health at a constant level, and we can then construct a conceptually valid price index of medical services.

Several conditions have to be satisfied in order to identify and separate that cost element. The most obvious, and the one most easily satisfied, is that the number of individuals covered by the insurance be large, so that the random element in the medical experience of each subscriber will wash out. Since data are available for millions of insured individuals, this is not a serious problem.[9]

[7] Scitovsky (1967) provides an attempt in that direction. She does not, however, take into account changes in the quality of treatment; more particularly, she ignores the effect of changes in the incidence of illnesses. For a more detailed evaluation of this article, see my "Comment" (Barzel 1968).

[8] This constancy is a "comparative statics" type; equilibriun is upset, and we compare the new equilibrium with the old. Obviously, the "dynamics" of the problem are also relevant: the speed of recovery is an argument in the utility function. The data used below, however, are not suitable to take this factor into account. We also abstract here from the problem that the equilibrium level of health may change with age.

[9] In the case of epidemics, when large groups are struck at the same time, the random elements may not be sufficiently independent to wash out. This does not seem to be a serious problem for the period covered by the present study—1945–64.

The other conditions are less satisfactorily met and can be discussed more profitably after the data used in this study are described. Some eighty nonprofit insurance organizations provide nonhospital medical care, covering mainly physician's fees, in forty-five states and the District of Columbia to over 50 million individuals (subscribers and their family members). The plans offered are intended primarily, but not entirely, for low-income groups. Subscribers' benefits are in the form either of direct services or of cash indemnity. These insurance organizations, approved by the local medical societies, usually report to the American Medical Association, which in turn, annually or biennially, publishes a summary of the basic features of each of the plans. These publications provide the main source of data for this study. The number of insurance organizations that provided usable data for this study and their total numbers of subscribers are presented in table 2.

Each insurance organization establishes for its main policies a rate structure affected not only by medical costs but also by insurance costs; the latter, however, are not very large. The insurance organizations pay out most of their income as benefits (and services) to their subscribers—89.4 percent of their total revenues in 1964 (National Association of Blue Shield Plans 1965, p. 246). Since this proportion has been reasonably constant for the last few years, we may conclude that the insurance component in the medical insurance rates has only a minor effect on the results.

The rates compiled for the price index are based on the experience of each insurance organization with its own subscribers. The question arises

TABLE 2

Year	Number of Insurance Organizations	Number of Subscribers (in Thousands)
1945	32	2,047
1946	47	3,740
1947	63	6,524
1948	67	9,386
1949	74	13,022
1950	77	20,008
1951	78	25,506
1952	77	31,066
1953	77	35,438
1954	77	39,398
1956	77	50,799
1957	77	55,403
1958	75	56,999
1960	63	50,418
1962	54	44,472
1964	49	42,962

of whether the subscriber population remains stable over time with respect to medical needs. Several factors may affect these needs. The individual subscriber probably makes more use of his insurance as he grows older. Membership in virtually all the insurance plans included in the study grew steadily over the period; whether this increase altered the age structure of participants is a moot question. I see no reason to presume, however, that the age structure did change significantly over the period.

Regarding the family size of the subscriber, again there is no presumption of a significant shift. Here, however, something more can be said. Most insurance organizations provide a number of optional plans, each with its own rates: one for the individual subscriber, one for subscriber and wife, and one for the family. The first two avoid the problem of the size of the subscribing unit; to the extent that their price indices diverge from that of the index for the family rate, it could be explained in part as due to changes in family size.

The most difficult problem pertains to possible changes in health level of the population as a whole, which may be due to two related factors. First is that increases in per capita income probably lead to improvements in nutrition and other factors affecting health. Consequently, it seems plausible that the amount of medical care needed to keep the level of health constant is declining over time. On the other hand, if medical care is a superior good—and casual observations indicate that it is—then the demand for medical services will increase with income. In the present context, this may be reflected in demand for a larger range of services to be covered by the insurance plans and in demand for improvements in the quality of services already provided. To the extent that the insurance organization responds to such demands, this may appear explicitly on the descriptions of coverage by the various plans as well as in the maximum payment allowed for a given treatment. To the extent that such coverage changes occur, they are explicitly taken into account in a way to be described below. It is interesting to note that not a single case was found where coverage was reduced; all changes were expansions. It is highly probable that changes in the quality of coverage frequently go unreported and that the majority of such changes are improvements not captured by our price indices. We may therefore conclude that income changes lead to two biases that tend to offset each other, although their relative sizes remain unknown.

III

If we were to attempt to restrict the study to plans that were in operation throughout the period and that did not change their coverage, we would be left with few, if any, observations. Some insurance organizations went in and out of operation during the period; many added and dropped specific insurance schemes; and, most importantly, many changes were instituted in

TABLE 3
MONTHLY RATES CHARGED (IN DOLLARS)

Year	Plan 1	Plan 2	Plan 3
t_1	5	2	8
t_2	7	3	8
t_3	7	3.5*	9

the coverage of individual insurance plans over the period. Consequently, a major problem is that of combining series that overlap only part of the time.

This problem is resolved by making consecutive comparisons between pairs of adjacent years by using *all* available information for each pair of years and then linking together consecutive pairs. When this approach is used, the coverage of consecutive pairs is not uniform, since the plans used in different pairs of years usually do not completely overlap. Different plans differ widely in the rates they are charging; consequently, the series of the average rates are not meaningful.[10] The linked price index, however, is meaningful—since each price relative for a pair of years is based on a comparison of exactly the same set of plans.

A simple numerical example illustrates the problem. Suppose we have data on three insurance plans for three years, as shown in table 3. The simple arithmetic average of the monthly rates of the three plans for t_1 is five dollars. The average for t_2 is six dollars. If we set the price index for t_1 as 100, the index for t_2 is $6/5 \times 100 = 120$. For t_3 the rate for plan 2 is starred to indicate a change in the coverage of the plan. The rates for years t_2 and t_3 for plan 2 refer to basically different commodities and consequently should not be used in computing the pure price change.

The arithmetic average of the remaining two plans is eight dollars per month, but it is quite clear that the price index did not rise to $8/5 \times 100 = 160$. If, however, we compare the two plans that did not change in coverage between t_2 and t_3, we get a change from an average price of \$7.50 in t_2 to \$8.00 in t_3. The price index in t_3 with t_2 set at 100 is $8/7.5 \times 100 = 106.7$. We obtain the price index of t_3 in terms of t_1 by linking the two indices: $120 \times 106.7/100 = 128.0$. This index utilizes the maximum amount of information. Although plan 2 contributes nothing to the price index from t_2 to t_3, if it were to be disregarded altogether, some relevant information would be wasted regarding the change in rates from t_1 to t_2,

In the computations of the actual indices, the size of the insurance organization is also taken into account. The averages computed are not

[10] In fact, we have two average rates for each year: one for comparing it with the previous year and one for comparing it with the subsequent year.

simple averages, but weighted—the weights being the total number of subscribers (including all family members covered) of the insurance organization in the earlier of the pair of years being compared.

IV

Insurance plans studied here are classified according to whether they are offered to groups or to individuals, whether they cover only medical or medical and surgical expenses, and whether they are for subscriber alone, for subscriber and wife, or for subscriber and family. Altogether these comprise twelve plans. A few more plans are offered (such as coverage for subscribers over sixty-five years of age), but information is too scanty to permit their being included in this study.

First, results regarding one of the plans are presented and discussed in detail. The rest of the results are discussed subsequently. The plan first discussed covers medical and surgical costs for a family insured through a group. This plan is chosen because it is more comprehensive and because most insurance organizations offer such coverage. The results, along with some related series, are presented in table 4. Two striking results come out of table 4. The first, and more obvious, is that the price index of medical services as constructed here not only increased less than the CPI "Physicians' Fees" component (the main item covered by the insurance studied here) but even less than the general CPI. The second result is more easily recognized in figure 1, where the three indices are delineated, letting 1947–49 = 100. The Physicians' Fees component of the CPI is hardly distinguishable from a pure trend. On the other hand, the index calculated from insurance data not only portrays a great deal of variability

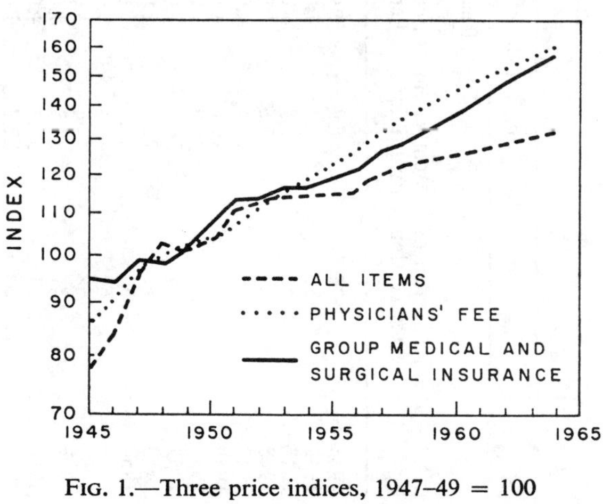

FIG. 1.—Three price indices, 1947–49 = 100

TABLE 4

Year	Group Medical and Surgical Insurance for Family								From Consumer Price Index (Setting 1945 = 1.00)	
	No Change in Coverage				Including Change in Coverage					
	Number of Observations	Membership (in Millions)	Relative Change during Period	Change Relative to 1945	Number of Observations	Membership (in Millions)	Relative Change during Period	Change Relative to 1945	Physicians' Fees	All Items
1945–46 . .	25	1.8	1.001	1.001	25	1.8	1.001	1.001	1.049	1.085
1946–47 . .	36	3.2	1.040	1.041	36	3.2	1.040	1.041	1.117	1.241
1947–48 . .	46	5.3	1.002	1.042	46	5.3	1.002	1.042	1.161	1.337
1948–49 . .	48	7.6	1.038	1.082	49	7.7	1.037	1.081	1.182	1.324
1949–50 . .	51	10.4	1.046	1.132	52	10.4	1.046	1.131	1.201	1.337
1950–51 . .	54	16.2	1.056	1.196	54	16.2	1.056	1.195	1.245	1.444
1951–52 . .	53	21.0	1.006	1.203	57	21.4	1.007	1.203	1.300	1.475
1952–53 . .	61	26.7	1.024	1.231	62	27.2	1.023	1.231	1.335	1.486
1953–54 . .	61	29.4	1.001	1.232	63	31.3	1.001	1.232	1.374	1.493
1954–56 . .	56	33.4	1.036	1.277	62	34.9	1.049	1.292	1.464	1.510
1956–57 . .	64	44.5	1.047	1.336	64	44.5	1.047	1.352	1.528	1.563
1957–58 . .	58	44.4	1.018	1.360	62	47.3	1.022	1.381	1.580	1.606
1958–60 . .	47	37.3	1.057	1.438	50	38.1	1.063	1.468	1.675	1.644
1960–62 . .	41	36.4	1.087	1.563	42	36.5	1.087	1.595	1.768	1.681
1962–64 . .	38	32.7	1.066	1.665	38	32.7	1.066	1.700	1.853	1.724

over the period but, with the exception of the first few years, shows that variability to be correlated with the overall CPI. In fact, if we restrict the comparison to the period 1949–64, the correlation is quite good. For the period as a whole, physicians' fees increased faster than the index compiled from insurance rates by about 0.6 percent per year. This indicates that physicians' productivity is increasing at the rate of 0.6 percent per year—that a visit accomplishes 0.6 percent more than a similar visit a year earlier. Productivity change, measured as a difference between input and output prices, is the cause of the difference.

Most of the increase in productivity occurred in the earlier part of the period. When 1947–49 is set equal to 100 in figure 1, it becomes clear that relative to the CPI, the insurance data index rose more slowly until the late forties and at about the same rate until the late fifties; only toward the end of the period did it rise faster than the CPI. Compared with the Physicians' Fees component, the insurance data increased more slowly until 1956, and from then on the two increased at about the same rate.

We turn now to a comparison between the two series constructed here—the one just discussed, which holds insurance coverage constant, with the series which relates to all plans whether coverage remained constant or not. As mentioned above, all observed changes in the insurance plans were expansions, rather than contractions, of coverage. There are four distinct types of expansion: an increase in the variety of medical conditions covered; an increase in the number of days of treatment allowed under the insurance; an increase in the maximum expense allowed for a given type of medical condition; and an increase in the minimum income that qualifies the subscriber to receive medical services without extra charges.[11] The nature of the first type of expansion is obvious. In the case of the second, it should be noted that, even when the number of days allowed is constant, medical advances that shorten the duration of an illness increase the effective coverage of the insurance.

The nature of the other two is quite complex and calls for some elaboration. The allowance for a given medical treatment serves a dual purpose. In cases where the insurance is a service type and physicians are compensated by insurance alone, the level of such allowance is designed to attract physicians to participate. In cases where the insurance is of the indemnity type, the physicians' allowance may be supplemented by extra charges to the patient. According to a large-scale study[12] of these plans in 1964, 77 percent of total costs to members were paid by insurance. There are no figures as to the level of these payments in other years. Such charges, according to letters from a number of the insurance organizations, are, however, fairly constant over time. In any case, there is little room for

[11] Many insurance organizations specifically allow the physician to charge rates higher than the prescribed minimum if the patient's income exceeds a certain amount.

[12] National Association of Blue Shield Plans (1965).

these charges to rise over time if 77 percent of all costs were covered at the end of the period. Adjustments in the amounts allowed can be viewed, then, as designed to maintain the real value of the insurance plan constant.[13] When the price index is constructed, they are not treated as changes in the quality of the insurance coverage.[14]

The last change is in the definition of "minimum income." About two-thirds of the subscribers considered here participate in plans combining service and indemnity elements. As long as the subscriber's income is below the prescribed minimum, he has a service contract. But if his income exceeds the minimum, he may be charged additional fees above those paid by the insurance; he then has an indemnity contract. Since per capita money income is rising at about 4 percent per year (the period considered is 1950–64), the "minimum income" has to be adjusted at a similar rate to maintain coverage constant. The actual rate of adjustment is about 1 percent per year, which implies a constant drift of subscribers from service contract to the more costly indemnity contract. It is not possible to evaluate accurately either the extent of the drift or the extra cost involved. The 77 percent cited in the previous paragraph, however, is due to this factor also, so the bias cannot be too large. Still, this downward bias in the results has to be kept in mind.

Two additional factors tend to improve the effective value of the insurance plans. One is simply the increase in availability of such insurance over the period considered. Not only did the number of insurance organizations increase, but most of them now offer many more options than at their inception. And with the growth of the plans, it is likely that subscribers have become more knowledgeable in the advantageous use of their insurance and are now able to obtain superior service.

The differences between the constant- and nonconstant-coverage series are basically those between a constant- and nonconstant-quality series. While the constant quality index increased from 100 in 1945 to 166.5 in 1964, the index uncontrolled for quality change rose to 170.0. The improvement in coverage for this particular plan, as reflected by the difference between the two indices, is quite small.

The price indices for the remaining eleven constant-coverage insurance plans are presented in figure 2.[15] Nongroup insurance is a relatively novel phenomenon; data are available only since 1949, and even for subsequent years, figures are still less abundant than those for group insurance. So we

[13] It should nevertheless be pointed out that, in the event of some downward trend in the percentage paid out by insurance, the indicated productivity figures would be lower: for a 1 percent fall in coverage, productivity would also fall by 1 percent.

[14] If the amount allowed is changed to cover a better service rather than increased cost, this will constitute a change in quality. Such changes, however, cannot be distinguished from each other; consequently, the "constant quality" price index may be biased upward.

[15] Tables containing information on all twelve insurance plans may be obtained from the author.

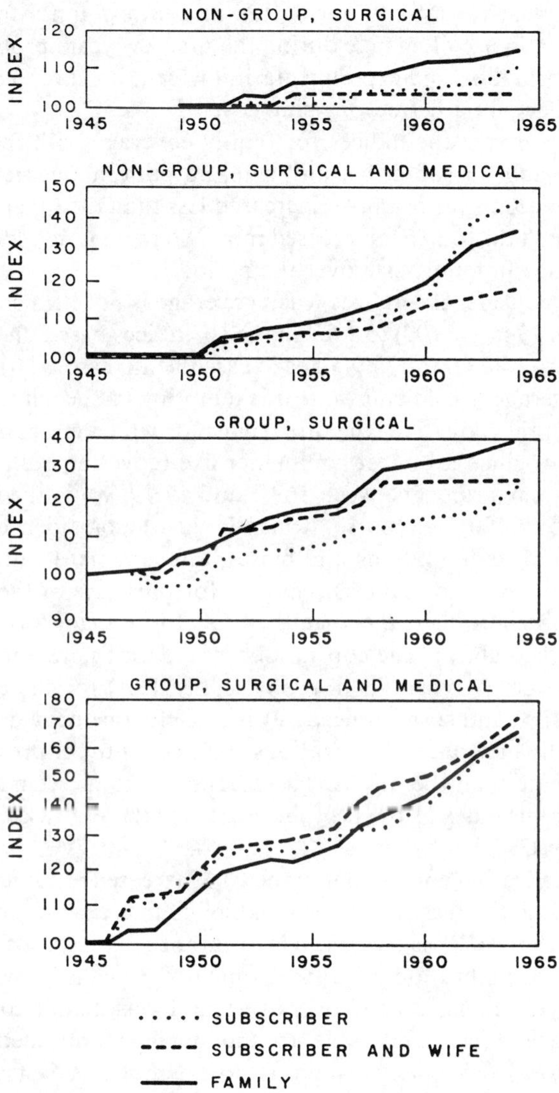

FIG. 2.—Medical insurance price indices (no change in coverage)

have to rely mainly on results garnered from group-insurance experience. The six price indices obtained from group insurance did not increase uniformly, but ranged from 124.0 to 172.6 in 1964 (1945 = 100). This divergence probably reflects changes in relative costs of different plans and adjustments of insurance rates to reflect costs better. Still, the entire range is below the Physicians' Fees component of the CPI that increased from 100 in 1945 to 185.3 in 1964.

The time pattern of the six indices is quite similar—slight change during the first few years followed by changes correlated with the CPI: a fast rise for 1950–51, relative stability during the mid-fifties, and a fast rise from 1960 on. The absence of change during the first few years probably reflects a period of formation and experimentation which, however, could not last long, particularly in a period of rising costs.[16]

When we compare the indices for family coverage with those for subscriber alone and for subscriber and wife, no pattern emerges. The index for subscriber alone, for example, increased less than the other two in three instances, but in the fourth it increased most. So there is no indication of an effect of change in family size over the period.

Let is now consider the indices when coverage is not held constant. The increase from 1945 (= 100) to 1964 in the six indices based on group insurance ranges from 133.0 to 173.9. In each case the increase is larger than that when the coverage is held constant. It is tempting to speculate on the phenomenon that the indices for the three plans for which information is most abundant and which are most comprehensive (covering both medical and surgical problems) range between 169.1 and 173.9, while the CPI is 172.4 in 1964 (1945 = 100). Of course, it may be just a coincidence.

If, in spite of its limitations and biases, one accepts the notion that an index based on insurance data is preferable for purposes of the CPI to one based on physicians' fees, a choice then has to be made from the twelve indices described above. The constant-coverage index presented in table 3 represents coverage (basically for physicians' fees) for the entire family for both medical and surgical needs. It is also the one provided most consistently by the insurance organizations; consequently, it provides a more reliable estimate than the others. These considerations seem sufficient for the choice of this index as the best substitute for the Physicians' Fees component in the CPI.

The hospitalization component in the CPI increased at a much faster rate than the Physicians' Fees component and, of course, rose still more sharply compared with the CPI as a whole. The insurance plans discussed above do not provide hospitalization insurance, which is typically provided to their members by additional Blue Cross coverage. I was unable to obtain hospital insurance data comparable to the medical and medical-surgical insurance data. Consequently, there is no attempt to construct the price index for hospital care.

The results obtained by Horton (1966) leave little doubt that productivity increased in the medical industry as a whole at least as fast as in the rest of the economy; consequently, the price of medical services could not have increased to the extent indicated by the medical component of the CPI.[17]

[16] The indices for the nongroup rates show very little change for 1949–53, their initial period of operation.

[17] The hospital room charges in the CPI fail to account for the possible substitution of more intensive treatment, induced in part by the increasing time cost of staying in the hospital. They also fail to correct for the change in the age structure of the population toward a higher proportion of younger and older people.

References

American Medical Association. *Voluntary Prepayment Medical Benefit Plans.* Chicago: American Medical Assoc., relevant years.

Barzel, Yoram. "Comment." *A.E.R.* (September 1968).

Horton, Melvin E. "An Economic Analysis of Progress in the Medical Care of the U.S. Navy and Marine Corps Personnel." Ph.D. dissertation, Univ. Wash., 1966.

Kendrick, John W. *Productivity Trends in the U.S.* Princeton, N.J.: Princeton Univ. Press (for Nat. Bur. Econ. Res.), 1961.

Lancaster, Kelvin J. "A New Approach to Consumer Theory." *J.P.E.* (April 1966).

National Association of Blue Shield Plans. *The Blue Shield.* Chicago: Nat. Assoc. Blue Shield Plans, December 1965.

Scitovsky, Anne A. "Changes in the Costs of Treatment of Selected Illnesses, 1951–1965." *A.E.R.* (December 1967).

U.S. Department of Commerce. *Survey of Current Business.* Washington: Government Printing Office, relevant issues.

U.S. Department of Labor, Bureau of Labor Statistics. *Consumer Price Index.* Washington: Government Printing Office, relevant issues.

Reprinted from JOURNAL OF ECONOMIC THEORY
Vol. 4, No. 1, February 1972

Printed in Belgium

The Rate of Technical Progress: The "Indianapolis 500"

YORAM BARZEL

Department of Economics, University of Washington, Seattle, Washington 98105

Received July 9, 1970

Automobile racing has been an annual occurrence in Indianapolis (except during the two World Wars) since 1911. The race course differs little today from its condition for the first competition,[1] and the distance to be covered remains 500 miles.[2] Many aspects of the race, however, were frequently tinkered with, particularly in the earlier years: for example, the requirements for qualifying, the number of competitors, and the maximum engine size. But these changes do not seem to have been systematic and did not appreciably affect the outcomes of the races, as will be indicated below. The steady progress in racing performance appears to have been largely due to improvements in driving skills, in the racing cars, in car maintenance, and in ancillary equipment.

In what follows, technical advance is equated with progress in winning speed, and time is used as a proxy for the "cause" of that progress. Technical advance surely depends upon such factors as research and accumulated experience, and not merely upon the passing of time. But if time is correlated with the factors contributing to progress, it can be used as a proxy for all such factors. The appropriateness of equating speed with progress will be touched upon below.

The manifestation of technical progress by the speed of the winning car is measured with great accuracy, much more so than in most other studies of technical progress. We have, then, the opportunity to test hypotheses for which the usual data are too crude. When interpreting the results we should bear in mind that while improvements in the racing cars, in driving skills, etc., proceeded constantly, the cars themselves had to be retained to the exclusion of other types of vehicles, a constraint not normally imposed on technical progress. For that reason, the measured

[1] The surface was first cobblestone, and during the late thirties the course was gradually paved in asphalt. All factual data for years 1911–1967 were obtained from the handsome volume by Fox [3] and those for 1968 and 1969 from almanacs.

[2] This was reduced to 300 miles in 1916 and the race was stopped at 400 miles in 1926 and at 345 miles in 1950 because of rain.

rate of progress probably understates the rate that would be achieved in the absence of such a constraint.

This paper is concerned with the pattern of the average speed (or of its inverse, average time) of each winning car from 1911 to 1969. The upward trend in speed is unmistakable: the winning average speed in 1911 was 75 mph and this has increased quite steadily to 156 mph in 1969, as shown in Fig. 1. We seek answers to two basic questions. First, was the rate of progress stable? Second, did the interruption of the race during the World Wars adversely affect the racing performance? Of several simple functional forms with respect to which the rate of progress could be constant, four are considered here: (1) a semilogarithmic relation for

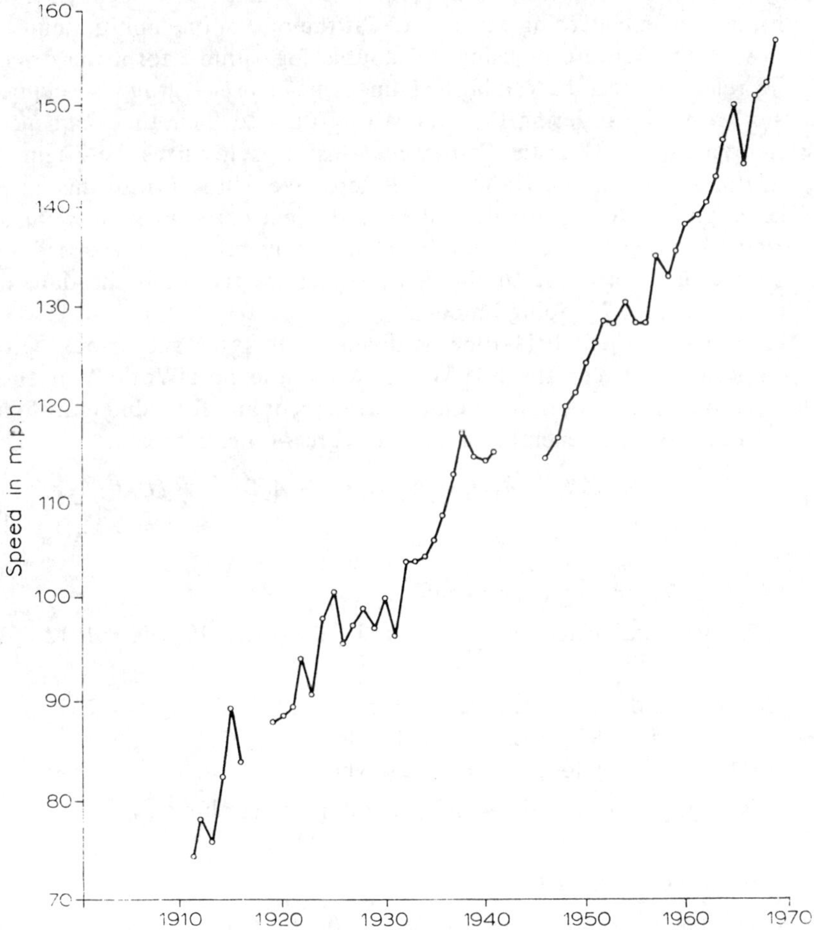

FIGURE 1

which the proportionate increase in speed is constant over time; (2) a linear relation for which the progression of winning speed is arithmetic; (3) an inverse relation for which the winning time declines at an arithmetic rate (i.e., at an accelerating percentage rate); and (4) a double logarithmic relation.

The two World Wars may have affected racing through war-related technical advance on the one hand and through the interruption of the activity on the other. To the extent that progress is due to "learning by doing," the war years were lost to racing. This possibility, combined with the notion that a double logarithmic relation exists between the winning speed and time, conforms to a major version of a learning-by-doing model recently advanced by Fellner [2]. His model is ideally suited to processes where learning accumulates at the rate of one unit per unit of time. As a prerequisite of using the double logarithmic form the origin of the relation must be established on some *a priori* grounds. Fellner measures time by ordering the events according to their time sequence, assigning a value of 1 to the first event. This implicitly fixes the origin of the relation, since the logarithm of 1 is zero. We will return to this later.

The empirical work is divided into two distinct parts. First we want to determine whether time can "best" explain the average winning speed, its logarithm, or its inverse. In the second part we try to fit the data to Fellner's "learning by doing" model.

The period studied, 1911-1969, is divided into three subperiods—pre-World War I, between the two World Wars, and post-World War II—allowing in each case both for a different intercept and for a different slope for each group. The general form of the regression equations is

$$f_i(S) = A_0 + B_0T + A_1D_1 + B_1(D_1T) + A_2D_2 + B_2(D_2T) + e, \qquad i = 1, 2, 3, \quad (1)$$

where

A's and B's are regression coefficients,

T is the actual year of a race minus 1910 (so that 1911 is 1, 1912 is 2, etc.)

D_1, D_2 are dummy variables such that
$D_1 = 1$ for 1911–1916 and 0 elsewhere,
$D_2 = 1$ for 1946–1969 and 0 elsewhere,

S is average speed of the winning car in miles per hour with $f_1(S) = S$, $f_2(S) = \log s$ and $f_3(S) = 500/S$, and

e is a random error term.[3]

[3] For the three years in which the race was cut short $f_3(S)$ is not the actual winning time, but rather the winning time proportionately adjusted for 500 miles.

A_0 and B_0 are, respectively, the constant and the slope for the interwar period; A_1 and B_1 are, respectively, the differential constant and the slope for the pre-World War I years (as compared with interwar years); and A_2 and B_2 are, respectively, the differential constant and the slope for the post-World War II years. A single slope for the entire regression (i.e., failing to reject the hypothesis $B_1 = B_2 = 0$) would indicate a common rate of progress for the whole period. A single intercept for the entire period would indicate that the trend of progress in the two pre-World War periods continued through the two wars, and that the war years in which the race was suspended were not lost to racing.

The regression results for the three forms are presented in Table I. For none of these can we accept either the hypothesis that $A_1 = A_2 = 0$, or the hypothesis that $B_1 = B_2 = 0$. The resumption of racing after the wars, then, did not proceed on the previous path, and the rate of advance did not remain uniform for the whole period.

Consider now the logarithm of speed regression—the easiest one to interpret. The regression as a whole is obviously highly significant and serial correlation as measured by the Durbin–Watson (DW) statistic is absent. From 1911 to 1916—the first subperiod—speed is predicted to increase at the rate of 3.1% per year.[4] The speed predicted for 1919, the first year of racing after the World War I interruption, is 88.5 mph, or just 1.6% above that of 1916 (87.1 mph).

The improvement in the entire three-year span in which the race was interrupted was, then, smaller than a one-year improvement in previous years. From 1919 to 1941 predicted speed increased at the rate of 1.3% per year to reach 116.1 mph in 1941, a very substantial drop from the 3.1% per year achieved in the pre-World War I years. Racing resumed in 1946, and a speed of 116.7 mph is predicted for that year—a mere half of 1% above that of 1941. The interwar rate of improvement in speed of 1.3% applies also to the post-World War II years, since the regression coefficient for the differential growth rate for that period is extremely small and totally insignificant. The rate of advance, then, after a short burst before World War I settled at a steady 1.3% per year for the remaining of the period, halting, however, with the interruptions of the two world wars.

A similar interpretation may be applied to the other two functional forms; the results are summarised in Table II in terms of growth rates.

[4] The regression coefficient of the slope "common" to the entire period is 0.0054, to which the pre-World War I slope coefficient of 0.0079 has to be added. The anti-logarithm of the sum of the two is 1.031, i.e., an annual growth rate of 3.1% for those years.

TABLE I

Regression Results, with "t" Ratios in Brackets

Dep. Variable	A_0 (common constant)	B_0 (common slope)	A_1 (pre-WWI constant)	A_2 (post-WWII constant)	B_1 (pre-WWI slope)	B_2 (post-WWII slope)	R^2	DW
Speed	76.46	1.27	−4.23	−19.80	1.22	.38	.987	1.753
	(43.77)	(15.28)	(−1.40)	(−4.80)	(1.91)	(3.34)		
Log speed	1.8982	.0054	−.0376	−.0221	.0079	−.0001	.986	1.956
	(256.50)	(16.02)	(−3.07)	(−1.32)	(3.07)	(−.18)		
$\frac{500}{\text{speed}}$	6.172	−.061	.695	−2.720	−.128	.016	.983	2.115
	(74.52)	(−15.57)	(4.86)	(−1.39)	(−4.26)	(2.89)		

TABLE II

Predicted Rates of Growth

Period	First subperiod		*WWI* Interruptions	Second Subperiod		*WWII* Interruptions	Third Subperiod	
Dep. Variable	1911–12	1915–16	1916–19	1919–20	1940–41	1941–46	1946–47	1968–69
Speed	3.3	2.9	.8	1.4	1.0	.2	1.4	1.0
Log speed	3.1	3.1	1.6	1.3	1.3	.5	1.3	1.3
$\frac{500}{\text{speed}}$	2.9	3.3	1.9	1.0	1.4	.4	1.0	1.4

The basic features of the logarithmic regression are reproduced in the other two, i.e., the interwar annual rate of improvement was virtually identical with the post-World War II rate, both rates being less than half that for the pre-World War I years, and the two world wars were totally lost in terms of racing performance. The improvement in the three-year span 1916–1919 was approximately the single-year rate of subsequent years, while for the entire five-year span 1941–1946 the gain was less than for a single year in any of the racing periods.

How can we determine which of the three regressions is "best?" The R^2 is not an appropriate measure, since the dependent variable differs among the three versions. A method to compare members of a family of functional forms that includes all those introduced above is provided by Box and Cox.[5]

They proceed by showing that by transforming the dependent variable y into

$$y^{\lambda} = \begin{cases} [(y^{\lambda} - 1)/\lambda] & (\lambda \neq 0) \\ \log y & (\lambda = 0) \end{cases}$$

it is possible to obtain directly a maximum log likelihood estimate of $\lambda - L \max(\lambda)$. Given a value of λ, a regression is run using the transformed dependent variable. The log likelihood of λ, except for a constant term, is calculated as

$$L \max(\lambda) = \frac{N}{2} \log \left(\frac{RSS}{N} \right) + (\lambda - 1) \sum_{i=1}^{N} \log y_i ,$$

where RSS is the directly obtained residual sum of squares, N is the number of observations, and y_i is the dependent variable in the original units.

In our problem the three forms of the dependent variable are: the linear, where $\lambda = 1$; the logarithmic, where $\lambda = 0$; and the inverse, where $\lambda = -1$. The log likelihood of λ in each of the three regressions is as follows:

$$\begin{aligned} L \max(\lambda &= 1) = -\ 20.94 \text{ —— linear,} \\ L \max(\lambda &= 0) = -\ 2.87 \text{ —— logarithmic,} \\ L \max(\lambda &= -1) = -\ 9.45 \text{ —— inverse.} \end{aligned}$$

Thus the logarithmic form gives the highest log likelihood. To construct a confidence interval around $\hat{\lambda}$ (the maximum log likelihood over the entire range) the approximate relation

$$L \max(\hat{\lambda}) - L \max(\lambda) < \tfrac{1}{2}\chi^2{}_1(\alpha)$$

[5] Box and Cox [1] consider a somewhat more general functional form, and the application of their method is more general than implied in the text. See also [4].

can be used to give a $100(1-\alpha)$ % confidence interval. Since $\chi_1^2(.05) = 3.84$, the 95% confiderence interval around L max$(\hat{\lambda})$ is 1.92. In our case, the differences among the three log likelihood values all substantially exceed 1.92; so we can be confident that the logarithmic form is significantly better than the other two.

The choice of the best form may appear of little importance since within the observed range the three predicted lines almost coincide. The results, however, become quite sensitive to the choice of λ for prediction purposes. If we try to predict the results for the year 2000, say, assuming no interruption of the race, we find that the average speed would increase to 201.5 mph according to the linear regression, to 222.7 mph according to the semilogarithmic regression, and to 262.8 mph according to the inverse of speed regression. The differences are obviously substantial, and our results clearly indicate that the best prediction is that based on the semilogarithmic form.

On the surface, the basic regression results appear to be consistent with Fellner's "learning-by-doing" model in two major respects. First, the war years during which experience was not accumulated were lost to racing as implied by Fellner's model. Second, the double-logarithmic functional form he derives implies a positive rate of progress that first declines rapidly and after a relatively short period, continues to decline but only at a very slow pace. This corresponds to the slowdown in the rate of advance after World War I as obtained in the above regression results. It is, then, of some interest to try to find how the "Indianapolis 500" data fit the double logarithmic form. If Fellner's actual procedure is followed closely, the time origin is placed at the date of the first race. But the notion is hard to accept that no automobile racing experience was accumulated prior to 1911. Consequently, an attempt was made to find what starting date would give the best possible results in terms of the R^2 and in terms of the serial correlation.[6]

[6] Fellner [2] in his empirical work regressed the logarithm of the winning performance in each of 22 Olympic events either on the sequence number of the Games in which the event took place or on the logarithm of the sequence number. The logarithm of the sequence is extremely sensitive to the placing of the origin of the sequence. It seems, however, that Fellner did not fully recognize the importance of this point. He viewed as an anomaly the fact that, in his regressions of performance in different events in the Olympic Games, the 200-meter dash had a better fit by use of the semilogarithmic than of the double logarithmic form. That dash, however, did not take place in 1896, the first modern Olympics, but was begun in 1900. If the experience gained, say in the 100- and 400-meter dashes in 1896 was relevant to the 200-meter dash, then perhaps the correct origin for that event is 1896 and not 1900 as set by Fellner. Altogether, of the 22 events examined by Fellner, 9 fit better in the double-logarithmic form, and 13 in the semi-logarithmic form. Of the first nine, 7 started with the first Olympic Games in 1896 and only two were added later. On the other hand, of the 13 events that fit the

When the origin is set at 1911 the R^2 for the double logarithmic relation is .868 and the Durbin–Watson statistic is .372, which is highly significant.[7] The R^2 increases steadily as the origin is pushed back and reaches a maximum value of .982 around the year 1830. The serial correlation becomes less pronounced as the origin is moved back, as shown by the fact that the Durbin–Watson statistic increases steadily towards 2 for at least 100 years. Even if we rely on the R^2 as our sole criterion, the date of the origin precedes by several decades the invention of the automobile. We have to conclude, then, that while our results in their broad outline are in agreement with Fellner's model, the data do not fit that model at all tightly.

Since Fellner's model calls for only a single independent variable, its comparison with a regression employing five independent variables may seem unfair. But a semilogarithmic relation, using only a single independent variable, fits the data better than a double logarithmic form with 1911 as origin. This is true whether time is directly used or is measured as the sequence number of the race, as with Fellner's model. Only when the origin of the double logarithmic form is moved back some thirty years, i.e., to around 1880, does the fit (and serial correlation) of the double logarithmic form become as good as those of the single variable semilogarithmic form.

Returning to the Indianapolis 500 itself, after World War II the race became highly stylized. In 1948 the number of cars in the race had been finally fixed at 33. For over a decade, most cars were of a single make, having a four cylinder engine with a displacement of about 250 cubic inches. Many of these features of the race were unique to that period. Previously the number of cars in the race varied all the way from 21 (1913) to 42 (1933). Similarly, the maximum engine displacement had spanned

---

semilogarithmic form better, only 5 started in 1896, the other 8 started at later dates. These 13 events may, in fact, have been generated by a double-logarithmic process; but if their *true* origin occurred earlier than the first Olympic Games in which they took place, one might expect the semilogarithmic form to fit the data better than the double logarithmic form.

[7] Since time is the basic independent variable here, an ordering of observations according to their time sequence for purposes of calculating serial correlation becomes identical with ordering the observations according to the value of the independent variable. Indeed, if one is to order observations according to the values of an independent variable and then perform a serial correlation test (such as the Durbin–Watson test), one would in fact parametrically test for the linearity of the relation with respect to that independent variable. Such a test may be used as a preliminary procedure to decide whether to use the Box–Cox [1] method. In our particular problem, the presence of a significant serial correlation indicates some combination of serial correlation and nonlinearity, since time is the basic independent variable. The presence of a significant serial correlation when simple regressions were run is one of the reasons for inserting dummies in the previous set of regressions.

the range from 91 cubic inches (1926–1929) to almost 600 cubic inches (1911–1912). Lacking any thorough mechanical and racing expertise, I would have expected engine size and the number of cars in the race to exert a strong effect on the racing performance. To my surprise, it turned out that neither of these factors is capable of explaining virtually any of the remaining variability in the regression residuals.[8]

Speculating *ex post*, these results may indicate that extra power is largely offset by a loss in manoeuvrability and perhaps by increased requirements for fuel and pit stops. A similar argument applies to the effect of the number of cars in the race. Fewer cars in the race result in less congestion, but the number of potential winners is also reduced. It seems that here, also, the two forces may more or less cancel each other within the observed range.

Of other changes which took place some are not easy to quantify and for some data are not readily available. Qualification rules changed frequently, as did rules regarding the technical specifications of the cars. Until 1922, and then from 1930 to 1937, a mechanic was normally added (and in some years required), and, for some races, relief drivers were allowed. The only systematic effect detected in all the regressions is the declining variance over time, particularly pronounced in the regression for elapsed time where the average absolute residual for the pre-World War I years is more than three times that of post-World War II. The pattern of a falling variance is consistent with the fact that the tinkering with the rules occurred most frequently in the earlier years of the race.

Technical advance, as manifested in racing and statistically analyzed here, certainly does not give full information on economic advance, since racing as a good has many dimensions of which winning speed is only one. For example, it is widely claimed that manufacturers of automotive equipment learn a great deal from racing. No systematic information is available to me regarding the cost of achieving the improvement in performance; this cost, however, is not negligible and in all likelihood is not constant through time. We may speculate that with the increase in the absolute size of the automotive industry, with the observed increase in the size of the crowd watching the "Indianapolis 500"[9] and with the substantial increase in prize money,[10] it is likely that the amount of resources devoted to racing is increasing. In spite of this probable increase, the rate of improvement in technology failed to accelerate. So it would seem that,

[8] Similarly, for years within which engine size varied considerably, the engine size of the winning car could be found anywhere within the range.

[9] The "Indianapolis 500" authorities do not release attendance figures.

[10] Placement prizes varied little before World War II and were close to $60,000 in most of those years. After World War II, these prizes increased spectacularly to exceed $500,000 in recent years.

within the constraining conditions of the "Indianapolis 500," returns to investment in technical advance are diminishing.

Finally, while the two World Wars led to a vast military expenditure to improve automotive products, the impact on subsequent automobile racing performance was nil. This is not consistent with the frequent assertion that specific research in one area may lead through "spillover" to improvements in a much wider sphere. On the other hand, the same result is consistent with the "learning-by-doing" hypothesis. The drastic fall in the rate of advance after the first few years of racing is also consistent with Fellner's notions, although we have seen that Fellner's specific functional form does not fit the data well.[11]

Acknowledgments

I am indebted to Robert D. Lamson, Roger L. Miller, and Potluri Rao for their comments, and to Richard McDonald for most competent assistance. The paper was revised while I was visiting University College, London on a Ford Foundation Fellowship.

References

1. G. E. P. Box and D. R. Cox, An analysis of transformations, *J. Royal Statist. Soc. Ser. B.* **26** (1964), 211–243.
2. William Fellner, Specific interpretation of learning by doing, *J. Econ. Theory* **1** (1969), 119–140.
3. Jack C. Fox, "The Indianapolis 500," World Publishing, Cleveland, 1967.
4. Paul Zarembka, Functional form in the demand for money, *Amer. Statist. Assoc. J.* **63** (1968), 502–511.

[11] A postscript: Two additional races were held in Indianapolis between the initial submission and the final typing of this paper. In the first race (1970), the winning speed was 155.7 mph compared with a speed of 156.5 mph predicted by the semilog regression. In the second the winning speed was 157.7 mph, a shade above the predicted speed of 157.4 mph. These two years, then, clearly conform to the past trend.

Printed in Belgium by the St. Catherine Press Ltd., Tempelhof 37, Bruges

PART II

OPTIMAL TIMING

[6]

OPTIMAL TIMING OF INNOVATIONS

Yoram Barzel *

IT is widely recognized that when innovators are unable to realize the full benefits generated by their innovations the profit motive may not provide an incentive strong enough for them to innovate at the socially optimal rate. On the other hand, it has not been recognized that competition between potential innovators to obtain priority rights (and profits) from innovations can result in premature applications of discoveries.

The basic knowledge used by innovators is a free public good. Were this knowledge owned, its proprietor would introduce an innovation at the time when its present value would be maximized. However, since the basic knowledge is costless to the innovator, he introduces a discovery when it first becomes profitable instead of waiting until profits are maximized. Basic knowledge is thus overexploited comparably to public roads, fisheries, and oil and water pools,[1] although in this case the excessive use of resources takes the form of their premature application.

A simple numerical example illustrates this proposition. Suppose that an outlay of $2000 is required to activate a given innovation which saves $1 per unit of output of a certain product. The innovator, referred to here as the individual (or group) that develops the innovation for commercial use, will set the royalty rate at $1. Suppose that the interest rate is 10 per cent and that output is 200 in year t and increases by 10 units every year. Table 1 indicates three alternative earning streams for the potential innovator with a capital stock of $2000. Line 1 is the earning stream obtained from innovating immediately. Since output in year $t-4$ is 160, at a royalty rate of $1 per unit total earnings that year are $160 and will increase with output at the rate of $10 per year. Line 2 is the earning stream obtained from keeping the $2000 invested elsewhere in the economy at 10 per cent. Line 3 is the earning stream if the sum is invested as in Line 2 until year t and then diverted to the innovation.

Obviously, the innovator will be best off by selecting the earning stream indicated by Line 3. So will society as a whole, since Line 3 represents a dominant earning stream. However, as long as any competitor by innovating at $t-1$ (or even earlier) could earn more than 10 per cent he has an incentive to push back the date of the innovation. If entry is not restricted we would expect the discovery to be introduced when it would earn just 10 per cent ($t-10$ in this example). This will result in an earning stream as indicated by Line 1 (with present value equal to that indicated by Line 2), which is clearly inferior to the earning stream represented by Line 3.

TABLE 1. — EARNING STREAMS FROM THREE ALTERNATIVE INVESTMENT POLICIES (IN DOLLARS)

Year	$t-4$	$t-3$	$t-2$	$t-1$	t	$t+1$	$t+2$	$t+3$	$t+4$
1. Innovating immediately	160	170	180	190	200	210	220	230	240
2. Investing elsewhere	200	200	200	200	200	200	200	200	200
3. Best combination	200	200	200	200	200	210	220	230	240

The current controversy regarding the development of supersonic transport (SST) is a dramatic case in point. This technically feasible

* The author thanks John E. Floyd, Donald F. Gordon, J. Allan Hynes, Edwin Mansfield, Walter Y. Oi, and Henry Wan, Jr. for many valuable comments. This study was supported by a grant from the Center of Comparative Studies in History and Growth of the University of Washington.

[1] See, for example, F. H. Knight, "Some Fallacies in the Interpretation of Social Cost," *The Quarterly Journal of Economics* (1924), reprinted in *Readings in Price Theory*, Stigler and Boulding (eds.) (Chicago: Richard D. Irwin, 1952); and H. S. Gordon, "The Economic Theory of a Common Property Resource: the Fishery," *Journal of Political Economy*, LXII (Apr. 1954), 124–142.

innovation is of doubtful profitability. Stephen Enke, for example, states that ". . . perhaps a best guess is an overall program rate of return of 0 to 5 per cent." Since he recommends ". . . continuation only so long as the program is expected to earn a rate of return comparable to that expected by United States industry," [2] he seems to reject the SST project. But even a sufficient rate of return would not assure that its introduction would be optimal. The SST investment should be postponed until the *marginal* rate of return — not the average — is sufficient. The competition between the American SST, the British-French "Concord," and possibly the Russian SST, leads to further misallocating of resources since, while collectively the best introduction date is probably in the 1980's, a considerable advantage will accrue to the competitor who arrives on the scene first.

Many of the main features of the model presented in this paper are indicated by the above illustrations. Innovations are assumed to be currently possible: we have the necessary blueprints and these are free. To make the innovation commercially feasible, however, a once-and-for-all investment is required. Once developed, the innovation can be used indefinitely at no cost.[3] Innovations in our model are endogenous to the system. They are introduced when they become profitable. If the economy is stationary, an innovation that proves profitable would have been profitable all along, since no relevant parameters change through time. Similarly, a presently unprofitable innovation will remain unprofitable indefinitely and no innovation, as defined here, will be introduced.

If the output of a commodity affected by an innovation is expanding over time, as in the examples, the innovation will become progressively more profitable, since the cost of introducing the innovation is independent of the output affected while the revenues are proportional to the output.[4] This characteristic of innovations provides an explanation of their role in economic growth. When population is growing, the output of most commodities will also grow, endowing previously unprofitable innovations with profitability. If innovations are introduced at their optimal dates, their contribution to wealth will *always* be larger than could have been supplied by the same resources employed elsewhere in the economy. However, competition among potential innovators may deprive innovations of all their special economic value. The rest of the paper presents a more formal and more detailed discussion of these issues.

Timing of Innovations

The model is set to determine the date for which an innovation is socially optimal, the date for which it maximizes profit for its owner, and its net contribution under either situation to the income (or wealth) of society. The date of introducing an innovation so as to maximize the innovator's profits will diverge from the socially optimal introduction date depending on several market conditions. To keep the number of possible comparisons manageable, the basic model is first based on a number of highly simplified assumptions, as follows:

1) The capital cost of developing an innovation is constant and equal to I dollars.[5]

2) The innovation, adopted without delay by the entire industry, reduces the cost of each unit of output by k dollars without affecting its quality.[6]

3) The demand for the competitively produced output is X_o in the initial period ($t = o$) and is presumed to grow at a continuous rate p. Hence, demand at time t will be $X_t = X_o e^{pt}$.

4) The royalty rate is set at $h = k$ dollars per unit of output. If the innovation is being applied at the initial period, total royalty earnings for the period are $hX_o = S_o$.

[2] Stephen Enke, "Government-Industry Development of a Commercial Supersonic Transport," *American Economic Review*, LVII (May 1967), 71–79.

[3] We are mainly concerned with the basic knowledge used in the innovating process and not with the appropriate pricing of services generated by innovations.

[4] This idea, of course, is not new. Its first systematic presentation that the author is aware of is in Jacob Schmookler's "The Level of Inventive Activity," this REVIEW, XXXVI (May 1954), 183–190.

[5] The investment, I, should include accrued interest for the gestation period.

[6] To the extent that implementation of the innovation entails constant costs per unit of output, k should be taken as net of such costs. Similarly, fixed implementation costs should be included in I.

5) Only one innovator is associated with a given innovation.

6) The instantaneous and constant rate of discount is r.

7) The parameters of the system are widely and accurately known.

Assumptions 6) and 7) are maintained throughout this paper. The effects of changes in all other assumptions will be examined in subsequent sections, in most cases, individually, however the combining of such changes is straightforward. Assumption 4) is quite strong and calls for a short comment. The royalty rate is set to equal the saving due to the innovation. Since no benefits are "passed" to the consumer, the only beneficiary is the innovator himself. Consequently, the overall supply conditions of the commodity and the equilibrium price (and quantity) both remain constant; there are no externalities, and if we determine the innovator's profits, we also have the social saving.

We will examine now the exact point in time at which an innovation investment should be undertaken.[7] Since benefits generated by an innovation are spread over time, and since the innovation investment may be undertaken in the future, the profitability of the innovation is measured by its net present value, R_o. The present value of an innovation is the difference between the discounted stream of benefits that grow at the rate p per period and the discounted value of the investment in the innovation. If the stream of benefits begins when the innovation investment is completed, at time t, the present value of the innovation is

$$R_o = \int_t^{\infty} S_o e^{-(r-p)\tau} d\tau - Ie^{-rt}. \tag{1}$$

When we examine expression (1), it becomes clear that if $p \geqq r$, R_o goes to infinity, and so this has to be ruled out as an economic impossibility. For $r > p$, when we evaluate (1) we obtain

$$R_o = \frac{S_o e^{-(r-p)t}}{r-p} - Ie^{-rt}. \tag{2}$$

The value of t, $t(m)$, which will maximize the present value of the innovation, is

$$t(m) = \frac{\ln r + \ln I - \ln S_o}{p}. \tag{3}$$

Expression (3) is indeterminate for $p = 0$ (that is, for the stationary state).[8] For $p < 0$, when output is declining, $t(m)$ is negative, indicating that the innovation should have been introduced in the past. We may concentrate, then, on the relevant values of p which lie in the interval $0 < p < r$. The higher the initial benefits (S_o) and the faster the rate at which they grow, (p), the smaller is $t(m)$ and the earlier the introduction date for maximum present value. Conversely, the larger the investment required (I) and the higher the discount rate (r), the later the maximizing introduction date.

When the solution for $t(m)$ is examined, it turns out that at the point $t(m)$

$$S_o e^{-(r-p)t(m)} = rIe^{-rt(m)}. \tag{4}$$

Dividing through by $e^{-rt(m)}$ we obtain

$$S_o e^{pt(m)} = rI, \tag{4'}$$

which gives us (4) in current values. Expressions (4) or (4′) imply that the innovation should be introduced at the point when the present value of the savings per unit of time due to the innovation is equal to the present value of the alternative earnings of the innovation investment per unit of time, i.e., when the marginal revenues (of royalty earnings) become large enough to cover the marginal cost (of foregone interest).

Using the equality in (4) we can substitute for S_o in (2). We obtain for the maximized present value, $R_o(m)$,

$$R_o(m) = \frac{rIe^{-rt(m)}}{r-p} - Ie^{-rt(m)}$$
$$= \left(\frac{r}{r-p} - 1\right) Ie^{-rt(m)}$$
$$= \frac{p}{r-p} Ie^{-rt(m)}, \tag{5}$$

which gives the present value of the innovation at time o in terms of the original investment. The present value, it should be emphasized, is net of the capital cost Ie^{-rt}. The present value

[7] Stephen E. Marglin in *Approaches to Dynamic Investment Planning* (Amsterdam: North-Holland Publishing Co., 1963) investigates the optimal timing of "lumpy" investment and arrives at conditions equivalent to ours (his "myopic rules"). He then, however, investigates a different range of problems.

[8] The economic interpretation of this result is that if $S_o > rI$ the innovation is always profitable, and the earlier it is undertaken, the more profitable it becomes. If $S_o < rI$, it is never profitable.

of the innovation at time $t(m)$, $R_m(m)$, is

$$R_m(m) = \frac{R_o(m)}{e^{-rt(m)}} = I\frac{p}{r-p} \qquad (6)$$

or, stated slightly differently,

$$\frac{R_m(m)}{I} = \frac{p}{r-p}. \qquad (6')$$

Expressions (6) and (6′) indicate the value of the innovation at the time of its introduction — $t(m)$; (6) indicates its absolute net value and (6′) indicates the net value per dollar of investment. If, for example, $p = 0.5r$, then $R(m) = I$, and the net contribution of the innovation to the stock of wealth over and above the normal return is equal to the innovation investment itself. Although innovations relevant to a given industry may differ in scale, the ratio $p/r - p$ remains constant and these innovations will contribute to the stock of wealth equally per dollar of innovation investment. However, since each may differ with respect to the time at which its present value is maximized, we may expect subsequent innovations to afford a continuing contribution to the stock of wealth.

The contribution of an innovation to wealth depends critically on the presence of a positive growth rate of output, the magnitude of the contribution depending on the ratio of the growth rate of output to the discount rate. Since $Ip/(r - p)$ is net of the cost of capital, this is a measure of the net contribution of investment in the given innovation in terms of the capital stock. The corresponding income flow is $rIp/(r - p)$, which is the annuity equivalent of the net contribution of the innovation to the income flow.

From expression (2) we can obtain the point in time $t(z)$ for which the net present value of the innovation will be zero. By equating R_o to zero we obtain

$$t(z) = \frac{\ln(r-p) + \ln I - \ln S_o}{p}. \qquad (7)$$

Comparing (7) with (3) we see that $t(z) < t(m)$ since $p > 0$, and the point of zero present value will be reached earlier than the point of maximum present value.

A simple diagram may be useful in illustrating some of the points presented above. In figure 1, $S_oe^{-(r-p)t}$ represents the flow of discounted benefits, and rIe^{-rt} represents the flow of discounted costs. Note that the innovation investment is converted here to its equivalent flow, which appropriately represents the alternative cost of capital.

FIGURE 1

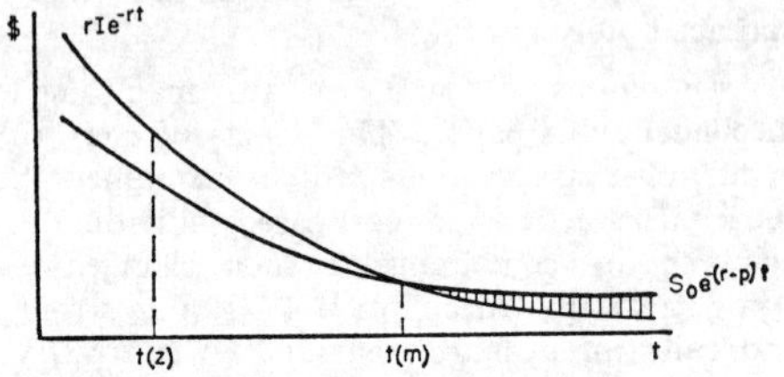

If the investment is delayed from t to $t + 1$, the cost saving will be the interest that the capital earns elsewhere in the economy. The present value of this interest saving is rIe^{-rt}. Both curves are declining exponentially; the benefits, however, decline more slowly due to the positive rate of growth in output. At any date earlier than $t(m)$ — in which the two curves intersect — the innovator's costs per unit of time will be larger than his benefits. He will be better off not to undertake his investment activity so early. Conversely, at any date later than $t(m)$ the benefits per unit of time will be larger than the costs, and he could have increased his total profits by advancing the date of his investment activity. At $t(m)$, benefits are equal to costs, and this is the profit maximizing date. The shaded area between the two curves to the right of $t(m)$ represents the net present value of the innovation. If the innovation investment is undertaken at $t(z)$, the net present value will be zero, since the present value of losses between $t(z)$ and $t(m)$ is equal to the present value of profits beyond $t(m)$. It should be noticed that if the innovation is introduced between $t(z)$ and $t(m)$, even though the present value is not maximized, it is larger than zero.

Relaxation of Assumptions

In the preceding discussion, the timing of an innovation has been considered optimal if its present value is maximized. Under the stated conditions, maximum private value is identical with maximum social present value.[9] It was

[9] In determining the optimal timing, the royalty rate was

also shown that the present value of an innovation will become positive before the maximum will be reached. Whereas a sole innovator in maximizing his profits will introduce the innovation at $t(m)$, any competitive innovator must take into account the effect of the action of others on his profit position. In particular, the first to complete the innovation will rob subsequent introductions of all economic value, since for him the marginal cost of the completed innovation is zero while for others the continuing costs of development are positive.[10] Any competitive innovator will realize that prior to $t(m)$ some other will have profited by an earlier introduction. Since the present value of the innovation is larger than zero at any date later than $t(z)$, the date of introduction may be pushed all the way back to $t(z)$. Threat of entry thus will drive profits to zero; in this case, however, the nullified profits would have represented the net value of the innovation to society. As considered here, the basic wasteful effect of competition lies not in duplicating the use of resources but in using these resources prematurely, when they would have earned a higher return elsewhere in the economy.[11]

The innovator's profits may diverge from the social benefits if the royalty rate h' charged by the innovator is less than k — the amount saved per unit of output. This is illustrated in figure 2, where $S_o e^{-(r-p)t}$ now represents the discounted private benefits (where $S_o = h'X_o$), and $S^*_o e^{-(r-p)t}$ represents the discounted social

FIGURE 2

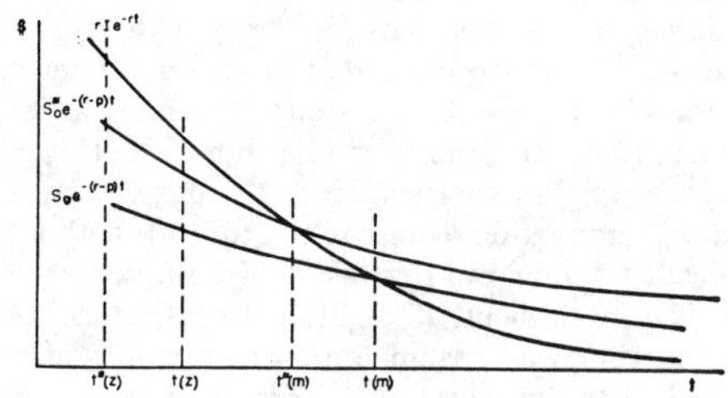

benefits ($S^*_o = hX_o = kX_o$). At $t(m)$ the innovation will be of maximum present value to the innovator but no longer so to society. The maximum present value to society will have occurred at $t^*(m)$, which is necessarily earlier than $t(m)$ since $S^*_o > S_o$. Similarly, if the innovation is introduced at $t(z)$, the present value of the innovation to the innovator will be zero, but it will be positive for society as a whole.

The royalty rate, however, is not determined arbitrarily: the controlling innovator will select that which maximizes his profits. If the adoption of the innovation is immediate and complete (as implicitly assumed through previous discussion) then under a wide range of commodity-demand conditions the maximizing royalty rate will exhaust the entire saving due to the innovation. If the adoption rate is gradual and is a function of the royalty rate, then the profit-maximizing royalty rate will be less than the entire saving and private profits will again diverge from social benefits.

While the assumption of a constant rate of growth of output, p, is very convenient, nothing of substance is changed if p varies by industry. Not even this degree of constancy is essential to the qualitative results. It is however essential that p be positive at least part of the time, since if p is negative all the time, any potential innovation will become less profitable with the decline of the volume of output to which it would have been applied. This restriction is necessary but not sufficient; it is required also that there be a t for which the present value will be positive. At $t(m)$, the value of t for which R_o is maximized, we obtain an equality similar to that in (4), which, in terms of figure 1, is the point where the two curves intersect.

set equal to the innovation's cost saving, even though the marginal cost of applying the innovation after its introduction is zero. If perfect price discrimination is allowed, the level of the benefit curve in figure 1 will shift upward and both $t(m)$ and $t(z)$ will be reached somewhat earlier. However, in this case as in the case of a single royalty rate of size h, all benefits from the innovation accrue to the innovator. The difference in the level of benefits is only of minor importance to the argument of this paper.

[10] One of the effects of a patent system is to legally deprive late innovations of their economic value. In the absence of a legal monopoly to the first innovator, potential innovators may eventually be attracted by the existing royalty rate, although they cannot expect the rate to remain at that level once the duplicated innovation competes for the same market.

[11] A conceptual way to overcome this kind of misallocation is by granting (or by auctioning) monopoly rights on potential innovations before resources are committed to the innovating activity. If the decision is left to the grantee of these rights, in order to maximize his present value he will undertake (or contract for) the innovation investment at that point in time which is also socially optimal.

The form of the revenue curve will depend, of course, on the time path of the growth rate in output. It is also clear that $t(z)$, the value of t for which $R_o = 0$, will occur at a date earlier than $t(m)$. It is not possible, however, to obtain a simple expression for the present value of an innovation comparable to (5) without specification of the time path of output.

The investment, I, required to introduce an innovation was assumed in the previous discussion to be constant. This assumption is justified if factor prices and the state of knowledge are held constant. Let us maintain the assumption of constant factor prices, but not that of a constant state of knowledge.[12] A breakthrough in basic knowledge may be viewed as reducing the investment required to introduce a given innovation. If this investment is now $I^* < I$, the profitability and the timing of the innovation will be affected. Figure 3 contains the same two curves presented in figure 1 and, in addition, a curve reflecting the new and lower investment cost. Before the breakthrough, the points of maximum and of zero profits are $t(m)$ and $t(z)$ respectively. The corresponding points after the breakthrough are $t^*(m)$ and $t^*(z)$. If the increase in knowledge takes place before $t^*(z)$, competition between innovators may lead to an introduction date, $t^*(z)$, where the innovation has a zero net present value,[13] and the advancement in basic knowledge is economically wasted due to its premature application. On the other hand, if the basic knowledge is applied after $t^*(z)$, the present value of the innovation is bound to be positive. Disregarding the intrinsic value of basic knowledge, the economy will be better off if such knowledge becomes available rather later than earlier, with $t^*(z)$ as the reference point. If the innovator is unable to capture all the benefits generated by the innovation, the social benefits are greater than his own, and the results are modified correspondingly.

FIGURE 3

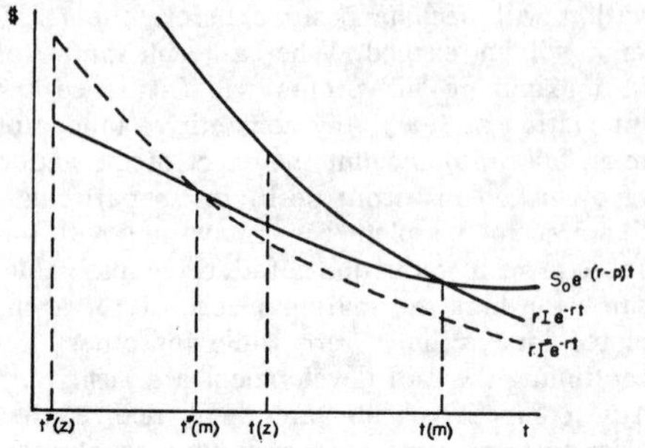

What effect might the subsidization of innovating activity exert on growth? Under competitive conditions, the cost of the innovation to the innovator is the cost to society. Subsidies typically reduce the cost to the innovator but not to society. In the absence of subsidy, the introduction date for potential innovators competing with each other is $t(z)$, in terms of figure 2; but with subsidies (which would lower the curve rIe^{-rt} in figure 2) the introduction date will shift to a date earlier than $t(z)$ or even, if the subsidy is large enough, earlier than $t^*(z)$. The social present value will then be negative and the innovation subsidy will actually retard the growth of the economy.

The above discussion has been restricted to cost-saving rather than to product-creating innovations. To consider the effects of removing this restriction, let us classify commodities as intermediate or final. For the first class, the distinction is immaterial, since either sort of innovation would lead to cost reduction in the final product.

In the case of final consumer goods, a profit-maximizing innovator who contemplates the introduction of a totally new final commodity will here, as elsewhere, compare the costs, which are constant, with the return, which will be proportional to output. But what is the relevant output? We can conceive of the demand for an entirely new commodity (or for a modified existing commodity) as existing prior to its introduction but without explicit market manifestations. When the economy expands, the demand for all commodities — including that for the not-yet-introduced commodity — also expands. The potential profitability of innovation in the new commodity

[12] While it is conceivable that the level of knowledge is itself affected by economic forces, there is no attempt to explore these forces here. What may be explored, using the model presented in this paper, is the effect of such changes on economic growth.

[13] It is assumed here again that benefits for the innovator and for society as a whole are identical.

increases until eventually its present value becomes positive. So the same forces that make cost-saving innovations profitable will also make innovations in new commodities profitable.

The contribution of such innovations to growth is more difficult to assess. The consumer's surplus caused by a new commodity that sells for one dollar is not the same as that caused by adding one dollar's worth of output for an existing commodity. It is greater but how much greater is impossible to say. The ratio $p/r - p$, a measure of the extra profitability of a dollar invested in the innovation, is computed by valuing all the units produced in terms of the marginal unit. This may be appropriate for a commodity already in the market; but for a new commodity, the average value is more than the marginal value, and so the ratio $p/r - p$ understates that contribution. The profitability of the innovation will be larger if (perfect) price discrimination is practiced; but in the usual case where the commodity is sold at a single competitive price, profits will reflect only part of its contribution. Since under a single-royalty rate the innovator will not capture all the generated benefits, his optimal time of introducing the innovation will be later than would be desirable from the social viewpoint. Figure 3 also illustrates the above conclusions. It is assumed that in period o, S_o represents the benefits captured by the innovator, while $S^*_o > S_o$ represents all benefits. The results, then, become the same as those reached above where the royalty rate is less than the cost savings. If the innovator is in the position of a perfectly discriminating monopolist, the curve $S^*_o e^{-(r-p)t}$ will represent the present value of his benefit, and the optimal introduction date for him will become $t^*(m)$ rather than $t(m)$. It is not easy to conceive, however, of conditions under which such discrimination could be exercised.

Concluding Remarks

Technical change is now almost universally considered the major cause of growth in per capita income experienced in the Western world over the last few centuries. Yet, with few exceptions such as Arrow's "learning by doing" argument,[14] technical change is treated as exogenous to the economic system,[15] a trend imposed on the production function making it shift outward systematically over time. Technical change, however, does not descend on us like manna. Resources have to be employed to generate such change, and it is not obvious that these invariably are better occupied by innovation than by other activities.

In this paper it is shown that innovations are induced, since they become more profitable with the expansion of output. The amount of resources devoted to innovating activity, however, is in general not the optimal one because of the pressure of two opposing forces. On the one hand, competition between potential innovators tends to make this amount too large; on the other, the inability of innovators to capture all the benefits tends to make the amount too small. The results are summarized in table 2. In the first row, when all benefits are captured by the innovator either there is no economic growth due to innovations or else innovators are the sole beneficiaries from that growth. When benefits are diffused the innovation will always lead to economic growth, but only by sheer coincidence will it lead to *maximum* growth, which may be missed because the innovation is introduced either too early or too late. The rate of growth is always positive if the innovation is introduced too late. It may fall to zero with too-early introduction or even become negative if innovational activity is subsidized.[16, 17]

[14] Kenneth J. Arrow, "The Economic Implications of Learning by Doing," *Review of Economic Studies*, XXIX (June 1962), 155–173.

[15] C. Kennedy, in "Induced Bias in Innovation and the Theory of Distribution," *Economic Journal*, LXXIV (Sept. 1964), 541–547, and more recently, Paul A. Samuelson in "A Theory of Induced Innovation Along Kennedy Weisacker Lines," this REVIEW, LXVII (Nov. 1965), 343–356, do not treat changes in technology as entirely exogenous. However, they are concerned mainly with the "bias" of technical advance and its relation with economic forces within the economy. They do not try to make advance per se internally determined.

[16] An additional case of some interest is that of monopoly at the commodity level. Here the profit-maximizing introduction date, due to a lower level of output, will be later than that reached under competitive conditions. But under monopoly, innovations are likely to be introduced within the firm, resulting in output expansion and lower price as well as avoiding the resource waste involved in competition among innovators.

[17] The analysis in this paper is basically a partial equilib-

rium analysis and is inadequate in two instances. First, the presence of investment opportunities in developing new innovations will lead to an increase in the rate of return on capital, as contrasted with a situation where such opportunities are absent, and this will itself contribute to growth in the economy. Second, innovations having a positive present value generate an increase in income, releasing resources to produce additional commodities to satisfy the added demand induced by the increased income. The resultant increased scale of output reinforces the economies of scale to innovations.

TABLE 2

		State of Competition in Innovational Activity [a]	
		Monopoly	Competition
Portion of Benefits Accruing to the Innovator	All	Optimal social timing Maximum private PV Maximum social PV	Introduction date too early Zero private PV Zero social PV
	Part	Introduction date too late Maximum private PV Positive social PV	Introduction date indeterminate Zero private PV Positive social PV

[a] PV stands for (net) present value.

[7]

The Market for a Semipublic Good: The Case of the *American Economic Review*

By YORAM BARZEL*

Operationally, the theory of public goods is now at a serious impasse.[1] The two optimum conditions—the total condition and the marginal condition—cannot be simultaneously applied in actual policy. The total condition, requiring that total benefits are not less than total costs, cannot be applied unless benefits can be evaluated. To appraise these, we have to know something about individual utilities or, in operational terms, we have to know something about demand for the public good. But if the marginal condition, equating price to marginal cost, is actually used, no market data is generated. This is because the marginal cost of producing an extra unit of service from an already produced public good is zero, and, in fact, we normally fail even to keep track of the quantity demanded at this price. So here we find ourselves in a position where the total condition cannot be evaluated. Alternatively we may forgo pricing at marginal cost and in this way obtain data on the demand for the public good at some positive price; but then the marginal condition is necessarily violated, and there is no a priori information to suggest that this is less wasteful than violating the total condition.[2] Buchanan's suggestion (see p. 194) to use the model of a perfectly discriminating monopolist to resolve the dilemma does not, as Samuelson has pointed out (see 1967, p. 199), bring any new operational elements into the picture.

I

In this paper an attempt is made to get around the dilemma by studying, not a purely collective good, but a semipublic good—*The American Economic Review* (*Review*). The commodity considered here, unlike a TV signal, is not strictly a public good. The ideas contained in a publication such as the *Review* constitute the core of its public-good component, since their availability to some does not reduce their availability to others. However, ideas are not directly "consumed." For the consumer to obtain access to ideas, they must be published and disseminated at costs which increase with the number of consumers. Casual empiricism suggests that the costs of printing and distributing such a publication are roughly proportional to circulation volume. On the other hand, the costs of editing and setting the publication in print may be an extension of the public-good aspect of this commodity where costs are independent of the volume of output. It thus seems proper to consider the *Review* as a semipublic good—a mixture of a purely public and purely private good. It is important to note at the outset that, while the above considerations are common to other kinds of publications, in this case the cost of the original research is borne not by the consumer but by scholars, universities, and foundations, etc. In this respect the learned journals differ from books and magazines priced so as to pay the authors' fees or royalties. Rather, ironically enough,

* Visiting research fellow, University College, London, on leave from University of Washington. I wish to thank John E. Floyd and George Borts for their comments. Richard McDonald provided most able assistance.

[1] See in particular the exchanges (1964) between Jora Minasian and Paul Samuelson and between James Buchanan, Minasian, and Samuelson in 1967.

[2] The situation is analogous to the "uncertainty principle" in physics where, of two related variables, one can be measured only at the cost of foregoing measurement of the other.

they resemble commercial TV where the cost is not covered by the viewer but by the program benefactor, the advertiser.

It should also be noted that the *Review* is at least in part a producer rather than a consumer good. Consequently, the demand for it is a derived demand and the utility generated by it is "derived utility."[3] With this reservation in mind, it is appropriate to apply the analysis for collective consumption goods to this good as well.

In the literature on public goods, the discussion usually focuses on the public good itself, comparing the utility derived to cost. Here we will focus instead on the flow of services generated by the public, or the semipublic, good. The two approaches should, of course, produce identical results, and the choice between them is simply a matter of convenience. The service flow approach is more convenient for the present purpose.

In exploring the relation between pure public goods and semipublic goods, concentration upon the semipublic good might at first appear to be an undesirable compromise. However, in reality the conceptual difference between the two is minor. We can write a simplified version of the total cost function for the flow of services from the good under consideration (a single issue of the *Review*) as $TC=aX+C$, where TC is total cost, X is the level of output, and a and C are constants. In the case of a purely public good, $C>0$ and $a=0$, while in the case of a semipublic good, $C>0$ and $a>0$ (for a purely private good $C=0$, $a>0$).[4] Notice, then, that for both the pure public good and the semipublic good, the average cost function declines throughout with the marginal cost necessarily below the average cost. Thus, once we take into account the presence of a positive marginal cost (the a term) in the semipublic good,[5] most of the propositions for a purely public good will hold for a semipublic good as well.

In terms of the information potentially available, however, the difference between the two is of considerable importance. Since the marginal cost is zero, if the purely public good is priced to equate price with marginal cost, no market information is generated. If, on the other hand, a semipublic good is priced at marginal cost, it may provide us with information that purely public goods cannot—market information on utility generated. In other words, due to its purely private component, a semipublic good affords information on quantities and prices, and if this information is sufficiently varied, we may be able to obtain an approximation of its demand function.

Furthermore, if one tries to give examples of purely public goods, the list is almost exhausted after national defense, TV signals, and lighthouses. On the other hand, it is easy to compose a long list of semipublic commodities, to include books, magazines, newspapers (in fact everything printed), records, tapes, electricity where the power plant is not used to capacity, and so on. Since the policy problems raised by semipublic goods are of the same nature as those for purely public goods, obtaining information on the subject is important on its own.

II

The main objectives of the empirical work are to obtain estimates of the cost of producing the *Review* and of the benefits derived from it, to determine whether the optimum conditions of producing such a good are met and, if not, what may be done to meet them.

In the empirical work, data problems often

[3] Richard Schmalensee has recently shown that under monopoly conditions, the observed increase in consumers' surplus due to a fall in price of a factor of production may be an underestimate of the true change in welfare.

[4] If "all enjoy in common" a collective good, the case where $a=0$ characterizes a pure collective good, since no additional cost is necessary for an additional consumer to enjoy it. If $C=0$ we are at the other extreme where there is no element of communality. We occupy the in-between situation of a semipublic good if $C>0$, constituting the common component of the good, and $a>0$, constituting its private component. (A broader definition of a semipublic good is where the marginal cost is positive but less than average cost.)

[5] This may be done by netting the demand curve from these costs. The resulting relationship between quantity and price may be thought of as a demand curve for a purely public good.

prevent correct measurement of some of the desired quantities. On the demand side, observed price is not the subscription rate for the *Review* but membership dues to the American Economic Association. For some but not all years the inside cover of the *Review* states what portion of the dues applies to subscription. It is not possible, however, to buy the subscription at that price, so this information is neither complete nor operational. We have to view the demand, then, as comprising both the *Review* itself and other services provided to members by the association, such as organizing of meetings, supplying of directories and special supplements, and vesting of prestige in its members. To the extent that the level of such extra services did not vary much over the period studied, the misspecification of the demand function on this account may be ignored. It will be shown below that the actual level of these services did in fact remain quite stable. An additional service provided by the Association since 1963 is in publishing a second journal, the *Journal of Economic Abstracts* succeeded later by the *Journal of Economic Literature*. To avoid the effects on price and cost of these additional publications, the empirical work is terminated at 1965, the last year before the price of the *Review* was increased to meet the additional cost of the new publication. We will see later what can be said regarding these additional publications.[6]

On the cost side we encounter a different problem that is probably much more significant; this is that two major cost elements associated with the *Review* are not borne by it: the cost of doing the original research (i.e., writing the "editorial copy") and the cost of refereeing. Who is bearing these costs? The latter seem to be borne entirely by the referees. However, they presumably get adequate psychic compensation from performing this function, since they are doing it voluntarily, and there is no need to view this aspect of publication as involving any net social cost.

The problem of the cost of research going into the *Review* cannot be dismissed so easily. True, part of it may be a consumption good to those engaged in it; for this part, as for refereeing, there is no problem. But, quite clearly, a substantial portion of the research would not have been forthcoming had it not been paid for either by universities, directly in support or indirectly in salary increases, or by other institutions with the objective of promoting knowledge. The institutions providing the funds almost never benefit directly from the research. Rather, their support for research is a recognition of the public good aspect of research and of the need for nonmarket sources of funds to sustain it.

The direct users and beneficiaries of the research results are the readers of the *Review*. It is thus appropriate to ask, What are the total consumers' benefits to readers of the *Review* and are these large enough to justify the use of resources devoted to research and to its publication? To the extent that the publication component of costs is met by subscription fees the above question is reduced to a comparison between the consumers' surplus derived from the *Review* and the cost of research. While data on the cost of research going into the *Review* are not available, an estimate of the benefits may be used to determine what research costs can be justified by demand considerations.

In the empirical work, then, we will on the one hand, attempt to establish the demand curve for the *Review*. On the other, we will try to obtain an estimate of the cost function of publishing the *Review* (but not of conducting the original research). First, we want to establish whether the casual notion of economies of scale (or its counterpart, declining average cost) is valid in regard to editing the *Review*; then we will try to de-

[6] It is sometimes claimed that since a single copy of the *Review* can be, and frequently is, read by many, this is another dimension of the public good aspect of the *Review* and the observed demand thereby understates the total demand. It should be recognized, however, that the owner of a copy of the *Review* has the option of excluding others from using it. If he does not do so, the demand of these other users is reflected in the utility and demand function of the owner of the copy. This is parallel to the utility from and market manifestation of the demand for guest-room furniture by the host rather than by the guest.

termine the interactions of such economies with the change in demand patterns over time.

The American Economic Association publishes annually, in the *Papers and Proceedings* (*Proceedings*), a financial report as well as data on circulation and on the size of the journal in terms of the number of pages. The period covered in the regression analysis is 1930–65; consistent time-series are available only from 1930, and 1965 is the last year before fees were increased to cover the *Journal of Economic Abstracts*. Since the format of the journal changed little over that period there is no need to worry about this aspect of quality. On the other hand, the number of pages per issue shows a rising trend over time. This variable, then, should be controlled in the estimation process.

To account for economies of scale in production we consider the following:

total real cost = f (number of pages, circulation).

The basic unit of output is the printed page, and output can be expanded either by an increase in circulation while holding the size of the *Review* constant, or alternatively by increasing the number of pages while maintaining the level of circulation. The estimation form used is:[7]

$$TC = a_0 + a_1P + a_2P^2 + a_3C + a_4C^2 + a_5PC + U$$

where TC is total real annual cost of publishing and printing, P is the annual number of pages,[8] C is average annual circulation,[9] and U is the random term. In the absence of economies or diseconomies of scale, only a_5 will differ from zero. If any of the other a's differs from zero, average cost will in general, differ from marginal cost.

The regression results (with t-ratios in brackets), using an alogarithm that maximizes R^2 ,are:

$$\underset{(16.18)}{TC = 27{,}171} - \underset{(5.09)}{5.067C} + \underset{(3.33)}{.000104C^2} + \underset{(3.71)}{.0041CP} \qquad R^2 = .976 \quad D\text{-}W = 2.18$$

The goodness of fit, the absence of serial correlation, and the sharpness of the coefficients are all gratifying. A closer examination of the results reveals some peculiarities at the lower range of the variables, probably reflecting the fact that during the early 1930's, a period during which circulation and the number of pages in the *Review* declined, total nominal costs remained fairly constant and total real costs increased.

Abstracting from these first few years, the results largely conform to the casual notions of an absence of economies of scale with respect to the size of the *Review*, and the presence of such economies to its circulation.[10] The latter, however, persisted only until circulation reached some 16,000 (around 1962), at which point the marginal cost of an extra copy became equal to the average cost. This finding is consistent with the actual experience of the AEA. Given the tendency of the Association for average cost pricing and the lag in price adjustments, as circulation grew prior to 1962, while average cost was falling, the Association found itself quite regularly in the "black." In more recent years, as circulation has continued to grow along with a rising average cost, deficits have become more common, eventually resulting in an increase in real price.

It is important to repeat that the cost of the original research is entirely independent of circulation and of the size of the *Review*.

[7] I am indebted to Sanford Berg for drawing to my attention that the logarithmic form I used in an earlier draft is inconsistent with the theoretic formulation.

[8] TC and P are defined for the *Review* alone, to exclude the *Proceedings*, since the latter is not edited by the editorial staff of the *Review*. The deflator used for TC is the wholesale price index exclusive of food and farm products.

[9] Circulation is taken as the number of copies of the *Proceedings* issue printed during the given year; it is almost identical with the average number of copies of the *Review*. Circulation at 3,700 was lowest in 1934 and at 20,000 was highest in 1965. The annual number of pages ranges from 792 in 1932 to 1,327 in 1965.

[10] Regressions for the *Proceedings* issue where recorded costs are almost entirely for printing and circulation, are even clearer in showing no scale economies with respect to these activities.

TABLE 1—REGRESSION RESULTS FOR THE DEMAND FUNCTION*
(t ratios in brackets)

	Price	No. of *BA*'s	No. of Pages in *Review* Alone	No. of Pages in *Review* & *Proceedings*	R^2	*D-W*
1.	−.50	1.01		−.15	.96	.25
	(3.02)	(10.20)		(.69)		
2.	−.53	.73	.78		.96	.24
	(3.23)	(4.49)	(1.42)			

* All variables in logarithms.

Had this cost item been included in the total cost, its only effect would have been to correspondingly increase the constant term. This in turn would mean an increase in average cost with no effect on the marginal cost.

III

So much for the cost side; we will now turn to demand considerations. How should close substitutes to the *Review*, particularly other economic journals, be handled in this context? Since prices of close substitutes tend to move together over time, it is difficult statistically to separate the own elasticity from the cross-elasticity. If we allow only the own price to enter, we tend to get the industry demand elasticity—that facing the individual producer when all producers in the industry change prices together. But this is precisely what we would like to obtain, since the basic choice is between doing and not doing the research at all, rather than between doing the research for the *Review* versus doing it for some other journal. The problem is complicated, however, by the fact that during the period considered the range of substitutes has broadened, with the inception of such journals as *Econometrica*, *The Review of Economic Studies*, and *The International Economic Review*. This, of course, has lowered the effective price of substitutes but in a way extremely difficult to take into account empirically. The trend in the real price of the *Review* over the period of study is basically downwards, the same direction of change as in the newly introduced substitutes; but, of course, the latter fell in price more than the *Review*. Subscribers, then, have had a greater incentive to switch to these substitutes than would have been the case if all the prices had changed by the same proportion. Consequently, not explicitly accounting for the new journals introduces a downward bias to the estimate of elasticity of the industry demand obtained by observing the *Review* alone. It is interesting to observe that these new journals themselves probably represent a response to the increase in market size and to the resultant sufficiently expanded demand for such highly specialized products.

With the above caveats, the general form of the demand function is:

$$q = f(\text{real price, real per capita income, population, number of pages})$$

For estimation, the form used is:

$$\log C = b_0 + b_1 \log Pr + b_2 \log Y + b_3 \log Pop + b_4 \log P + V$$

where C is circulation, P is the number of pages, and V is the random term. Pr is price, defined as the annual subscription rate deflated by the consumer price index, and Pop is population, alternatively defined as total labor force or as total number of individuals possessing bachelors' degrees.[11] It is not at all clear that per capita income is the relevant variable here, since the *Review* as mentioned above may be considered a producer rather than a consumer good. In the actual regressions this variable was never significant and, in fact, had a negative sign. Consequently, the results with this variable present are omitted from the findings presented in Table 1. As to the choice between the labor force or the number of *BA*'s, the latter per-

[11] Ideally, we would like to measure the size of the industry consuming the commodity under consideration. The best measure of the size of the relevant industry is membership in the American Economic Association. This however, may lead to somewhat spurious results. The number of *BA*'s was considered as a reasonable alternative. This was measured as a 25-year moving sum of *BA*'s granted up to the given year; for 1917–1957, where the number of new *BA*'s is not available for odd years, it was interpolated from the two adjacent even years.

forms slightly better. It is also, on a priori grounds, a better proxy for industry size, the results are reported only for the number of *BA*'s.

The most impressive result is that of the price coefficient. It is quite stable from one regression to another (including those not reported here) and has a consistently small standard error. The size of the coefficient, indicating a demand elasticity of about 0.5, may appear low. But one should bear in mind another aspect of this commodity as a public good—that for the individual a second copy has very little, if any, use. Thus a fall in price may induce additional demand by new readers but virtually no additional demand by current readers.[12] The number of *BA*'s (as well as the labor force) is highly correlated with the number of pages, and it is hard to sort out their individual effects. In any case it seems that the combined number of pages in the *Review* and *Proceedings* is not a relevant variable. Therefore, regression 2 may be considered the better. In subsequent sections, I use the results of demand regression 2 dealing with the *Review* alone.

IV

Let us now turn to see how these results can be interpreted in reference to the public-good problem. Again, we seek answers to two basic problems. One is whether to engage in producing the good at all—the total condition. The other is what quantity of resources should be devoted to that good—the marginal condition. To answer the first we have to determine whether the area below the demand curve is at least as large as the total resource cost of producing the journal, where the alternative cost of the resources engaged in research for the *Review* is included in the cost. Here, however, we do not attempt to measure the resource cost of doing research. Instead we attempt to measure the benefits from such research, thereby obtaining a measure of the maximum amount of resources that should be devoted to that activity.

The area under the demand curve, taking the form of the demand equation and using the numerical results of regression 2, is given by

$$\int_{Pr}^{\infty} (\text{antilog} - 4{,}147) \qquad (Pop)^{.729}(P)^{.781}(Pr)^{-.529}dPr$$

The area, of course, depends on the values taken by the three variables. However, before inserting such values, it should be recognized that it does not make much sense to pretend that we can safely extrapolate the demand curve to an infinite price.[13] On the other hand, if we restrict ourselves to the observed range of prices, we obtain a highly conservative estimate of the area under the demand curve. The highest real price observed is that for 1941, when the annual subscription rate was $5.00 and the consumer price index stood at 51.3 (1957–59 = 100). The lowest real price observed is for 1961, ($6.00 deflated by 104.2). The 1941 real price is then higher than that of 1961 by some 80 percent. Using this range of prices and the 1961 levels of the number of *BA*'s (6,371,000) and number of pages (1168), the value of the above integral, in regression units, is 24.55 − 19.16 = 5.39. Since the price index is 100 for 1957–1959 and the quantity is measured in units of a hundred, when adjusted the area becomes $53,900 (in 1957–59 prices).[14] This represents the extent by which 1961 subscribers to the *Review* benefited by not having to pay the 1941 price.

In diagrammatic terms, this is shown in Figure 1, where D_{61} reflects demand in 1961 and the intersection point of this curve with

[12] On the other hand, consumers are limited in terms of buying less than one whole unit. So a fall in price normally will lead to shifts from buying zero units to buying one unit.

[13] In this case the area is infinite, so we can disregard this as an economic impossibility. (Or are we experiencing Nirvana by merely having the *Review*?)

[14] The value of $53,700 is a point estimate and subject to a sampling error. It should be viewed, then, only as pointing to orders of magnitudes involved. The same applies to all subsequent estimates. Also, it contains an element of upward bias due to the above mentioned bias in estimating the demand elasticity.

AC reflects that fact that the *Review* normally covers its costs through subscription fees. The portion under the curve bounded by P_{41} and Q_{61} is a measure of total benefits from the *Review* under the assumption that the demand curve has an elasticity of .53 up to the 1941 price and then becomes perfectly elastic. The area P_{61}xQ_{61} represents actual *Review* office and publication costs, and the area bounded by P_{41}, P_{61}, and D_{61} is the "consumers' surplus" evaluated above at \$53,900.

The value of \$53,900 should not be entirely attributed to the fall in price from 1941 to 1961. The values of the other independent variables also changed, and it is of interest to try to allocate the \$53,900 among these factors. In 1941 the *Review* had some 20 percent fewer pages than in 1961, and the estimated number of *BA*'s was less than half of the 1961 level. Thus, the shift in quantity demanded is due not only to a move along the demand curve but to a shift of the curve itself. Again, when we now compare the area below the curve in 1941 and in 1961, we ignore the "upper tail" of the demand curve and the change in the upper tail between the two periods. When the area under the curve due to shifts in demand is calculated we obtain $\$10{,}000\times\{(25.55-19.16)-(10.90-8.51)\}=\$30{,}000$. So, out of the \$53,900 area below the 1961 demand curve bounded by the 1961 and 1941 prices, \$30,000 may be attributed to a shift in demand and the remainder, \$23,900 to a shift along the demand curve.[15] In terms of Figure 1, the \$30,000 is the area bounded by the two prices and lying between the two demand curves, and the area to the left of D_{41} is measured as \$23,900. The former is a measure of the added consumer benefits due to the increase in number of consumers and of the improvement in the quality of the product (in terms of number of pages). The latter is a measure of the realization of economies of scale, resulting in a fall in real price of the *Review*.

The \$30,000 might be further broken down into two components: the number of *BA*'s and the number of pages. They are, respectively, \$21,900 and \$8,100. The shift in demand producing the \$21,900 figure is basically due to an increase in the size of the economy (in terms of population and in terms of per capita income, both reflected here by the number of *BA*'s). As the economy expands, demand curves tend to shift outward, and the value of a public good grows correspondingly. Since the cost of the public good is independent of the intensity of its use, the difference between its value and its cost grows with the economy's size, thereby increasing "productivity" in the economy. In fact we may want to consider the entire \$30,000—or even the \$53,900—figure as the appropriate one, since both the increase in number of pages and the fall in price can be viewed as a response to the increase in circulation.

If we assume that the *Review* itself typically breaks even in its financial operations, and if we further assume (without much conviction) that the total condition was just met in 1941, the annual amount of resources devoted to research for the *Review* could have increased from the 1941 level by as much as \$53,900 (in 1957–1959 prices) without violating the total condition. This, of course, still fails to account for the change in the upper tail of the curve.

A mild attempt to account for this upper tail is to assume that the demand function retains its form for a certain price range but above that point becomes perfectly elastic. If we assume that the price at the upper end of the range is twice that of the 1941 real price, the consumers' surplus increases from \$53,900 to \$149,100. If we allow the price at the upper end to be three times the 1941 level, the area increases further to \$220,400 (see Figure 1).

When for purposes of comparison with 1941 we use 1965 (the last year included in the study) rather than 1961, we find the number of *BA*'s and the number of pages have increased but the price of the *Review* has also gone up. The 1965 consumers' surplus arising from not having to pay the 1941 price is \$39,000. Now if the price at the upper

[15] Such allocation necessarily contains an arbitrary element.

end of the range is twice the 1941 price we get $158,600, and it if is three times the 1941 price we get $248,500. All these figures represent an attempt to approximate the total condition. They reflect, of course, only the benefit side of the picture, against which we may match total cost.

Let us now consider the marginal condition. For a commodity such as the *Review* or, for that matter, many other public goods, the units in which it is desirable to count output are far from obvious. Output can be expanded by printing more copies of the *Review* without changing its contents, or output can be expanded by devoting more resources to improve the quality of the papers going into the *Review*. Also the size of the *Review* can be increased by either adding more issues per year or by increasing the number of pages per issue.

The last alternative seems to be most reasonable to investigate further. This is one of the ways in which the *Review* has expanded in the past, and it is relatively easy to control. Thus, let us investigate the effect which a 1 percent increase in the size of the *Review* may have on total cost and on total benefits. Given the 1965 conditions, this is equivalent to about thirteen extra pages, the length of a typical article. Without a change in price, this would imply a shift in the demand curve to the right by .776 of 1 percent (the regression coefficient above for number of pages). This means an increase of $300 in consumers' surplus when the demand curve is bound by the 1941 price,[16] $1,200 if bound by twice that price, and $1,900 if bound by three times that price. In addition, the number of copies demanded increases by .78 of 1 percent and at the given price of the *Review*, revenues increase by the same proportion. Circulation in 1965 was 20,000 and the subscription rate $8.00. The increase in revenue, then, will be about $1,100 (in 1957–1969 prices). This addition to revenues, however, will be more than matched by the added expenses of $1,400

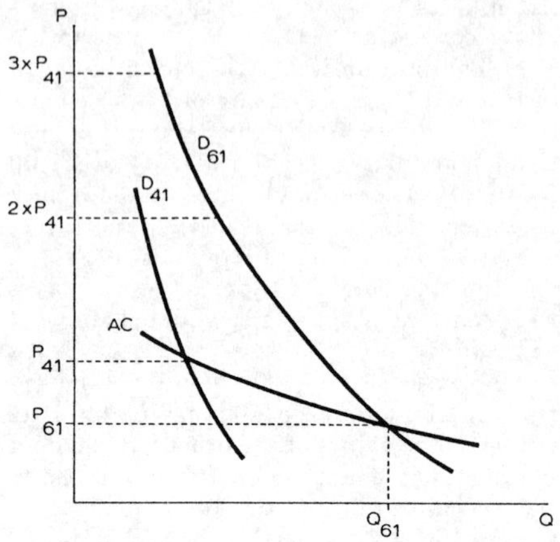

FIGURE 1

due to increased circulation cost and additional editing and publishing of the extra pages. Apart from this $300 excess of cost over revenue, the question boils down to determining whether the total research cost required to generate one more article[17] of the same average quality as the other *Review* articles is less than $300, between $300 and $1,900, or more than $1,900. The first figure provides a lower bound as to the value of the article; the middle range still probably does not overestimate its value; but if total cost of an article exceeds $1,900, there may be serious doubts as to whether the benefits generated by the article are sufficient to cover the added cost.

An important qualification should now be made here to the way in which the marginal condition was implicitly applied above, with regard to the timing of research and publication. The decision rule which should be applied is the maximization of the present value of the research investment. The research for a given journal article may be undertaken at different points in time. Since publishing research at a given date excludes it from being published at any other date,

[16] The 1965 real price, however, is only about 35 percent higher than the 1941 real price. With the 1941 price constituting an upper bound on demand, consumers' surplus is necessarily low.

[17] Only a fraction of the articles written are published, and the cost of the unpublished ones (the "dry holes") should be counted as part of the total cost.

the article may be considered as mutually exclusive with itself over time. If demand is growing steadily over time, as is the case for the *Review*, maximizing the present value of an article necessarily leads to a positive present value. Consequently the break-even point in terms of the total condition—i.e., when net present value is equal to zero—is not an optimal point: the activity has to be postponed until the appropriate marginal condition is satisfied, when the time rate of change in benefits is equal to that in costs.[18] In fact, under the stated conditions the marginal condition is the necessary and sufficient condition for optimum.

V

In discussing the demand for the *Review*, it was mentioned that subscribers receive benefits from the Association in addition to the *Review* itself. We propose to measure the value of these services to subscribers as the difference between 1) the real subscription fees and 2) the costs associated with the *Review*, defined as predicted (real) costs from the above cost equation. For all but one year, the difference, in 1957–59 values, varied between \$2.50 and \$4.30 with no apparent trend. The changes from year to year mostly reflect the drift in costs and in real fees on the one hand and in the discrete changes in fees on the other. We may thus conclude that while demand by subscribers is for both the *Review* and the other services provided by the Association, disregarding the latter in the demand equation does not lead to a serious distortion of the results.

Since 1963, the AEA has been publishing a second journal: the *Journal of Economic Abstracts* in the years 1963–68 and the *Journal of Economic Literature* (*JEL*) since 1968. How does this fact relate to the rest of the study? From 1963 to 1965, the *Journal of Economic Abstracts* was priced separately from the *Review* and did not affect either the subscription fees or the cost of the *Review*. Since 1969 the format of the latter has been drastically changed, and at the same time, the *Journal of Economic Abstracts* was superseded by the *JEL*. It is not possible to separate the simultaneous effects of the two changes.

Over the 1966–68 period, however, the format of the *Review* was the same as in the previous years. Given the subscription rate and the number of *BA*'s for these years, it is possible to predict what would have been the quantity demanded (i.e., circulation of the *Review*) in the absence of the new journal. The difference between the actual number of subscribers and that predicted can be attributed to the introduction of the *Journal of Economic Abstracts*. However, given the positive serial correlation in the demand regression, we should expect the residuals for 1966–68 to be at the same level as for the immediately preceding years. The residuals for 1963–65 averaged approximately .07, indicating a positive deviation of about 17.5 percent. The average difference between (the logarithms of) the observed and predicted subscription for 1966–68 is about .125, or a positive deviation of about 33 percent. We thus conclude that subscription to the *Review* increased by about 13.5 percent (antilog of $.125-.07=.055$) in response to the introduction of the *Journal of Economic Abstracts*.

VI

The main purpose of this paper has been to obtain some empirical evidence on the demand for a semipublic good, the *Review*, and thereby to demonstrate that at least for semipublic goods there exists a partial solution to the operational dilemma in which the theory of public goods is mired. It is true that the empirical analysis is incomplete, due to lack of data on the cost side on the part of contributors to the *Review*.

This, however, should not be a serious shortcoming in terms of assessing the degree to which the optimum conditions are met for other collective goods, since for many of these the required cost data are relatively easy to obtain. It should be pointed out in closing that even for a commodity such as a TV signal, some usable market data are available to estimate demand. Expenditures

[18] For a detailed discussion of this point, see Stephen Marglin and my article.

on TV sets reflect demand for programs. Expenditures on individual and centralized antennas also reflect demand and sometimes can be used to determine the demand for a specific extra channel. Such information obviously cannot provide accurate estimates of the demand for TV signals, even less of that for specific programs. Nevertheless, given the current state of knowledge as to the demand for TV signals, analysis of the available data may be valuable in making the theory of public goods operational.

REFERENCES

Y. Barzel, "The Optimal Timing of Innovations," *Rev. Econ. Statist.*, Aug. 1968, *50*, 548–55.

J. M. Buchanan, "Public Goods in Theory and Practice: A Note on the Minasian-Samuelson Discussion," *J. Law Econ.*, Oct. 1967, *10*, 193–97.

S. A. Marglin, *Approaches to Dynamic Investment,* Amsterdam 1963.

J. R. Minasian, "Television Pricing and the Theory of Public Goods," *J. Law Econ.*, Oct. 1964, *7*, 71–80.

———, "Public Goods in Theory and Practice Revisited," *J. Law Econ.*, Oct. 1967, *10*, 205–07.

P. A. Samuelson, "Public Goods and Subscription TV: Correction of the Record," *J. Law Econ.*, Oct. 1964, *7*, 81–83.

———, "Pitfalls in the Analysis of Public Goods," *J. Law Econ.*, Oct. 1967, *10*, 199–204.

R. Schmalensee, "Consumer's Surplus and Producer's Goods," *Amer. Econ. Rev.*, Sept. 1971, *61*, 682–87.

[8]

Investment, Scale, and Growth

Yoram Barzel

University of Washington

There are many economic activities where the cost function can be approximated by a fixed initial cost and a constant (sometimes zero) marginal cost as with book publishing, public utilities, and innovations. In the absence of technical advance, an economy that grows in scale could nevertheless exhibit growth in per capita income by taking advantage of the economies of scale afforded. To the extent, however, that these production processes are in the public domain, overinvestment, manifested either in premature entry or in duplication of resources, will occur, and the growth potential, to a large extent, will be lost.

Almost without exception, the theoretical research on economic growth identifies technological change as the sole cause of steady-state expansion of an economic system. This body of literature has completely overlooked a source of development potentially present in an environment of unchanging technology—the existence of activities subject to economies of scale. When the scale of the economy expands due to population growth the economy is able to take advantage of projects that are profitable at large scales only. It is shown in this paper that such projects typically will add to the *net* stock of wealth of the economy and increase per capita income; also that innovations are an important subset of the set of projects contributing to growth. A number of complications arising from the noncompetitive nature of projects subject to economies of scale are investigated, and we see that neither an uncontrolled economy nor an economy controlled by current institutional arrangements is likely to reach the full potential afforded by the scale economies. Numerous examples of investment projects subject to scale economies are brought up in the course of the discussion; they serve not only to illustrate the theory but also to convey the wide range of such projects and their importance.

I am indebted to J. Allan Hynes and to an anonymous referee for valuable comments.

Consider first an economy in competitive equilibrium. In the absence of limiting factors on the one hand and of technical advance on the other, when population is growing the steady-state-equilibrium capital stock of such an economy will grow proportionately. Total output, then, will also grow proportionately, and income and wealth per capita will remain constant. One of the properties of such an economy is that the rate of return on investment is equal to the discount rate. Consequently, the net present value of investment projects undertaken in the process of expansion is zero, and the present value of potential investment projects is zero or less. In other words, the stock of wealth cannot be increased by diverting capital from one project to another. Investment can be increased by reducing current consumption but, given the discount rate in the economy, the present value of the resulting consumption stream will be less than that of the currently selected stream. In the absence of technical change, then, such an economy cannot achieve growth in its stock of wealth per capita and in its income per capita.

An implicit assumption underlying the above model is that the production function of each of the commodities produced is homogeneous to the first degree and the production process is perfectly divisible. Maximum efficiency, or minimum average cost, then is achieved at low levels of output. These are necessary assumptions if the economy is to be in competitive equilibrium. In this paper we examine in detail the consequences of dropping the assumption of divisibility, so that for the relevant range commodities may be produced under conditions of declining average cost.

It is generally agreed that many commodities are produced under such conditions. Taking this into account does not merely add "noise" to the competitive model—it fundamentally affects the results. For illustration, consider a commodity that can be produced by two distinct but already existing technologies. Suppose that one is a "small-scale" technology so that a plant of optimal size can supply only a small fraction of total demand, whereas the other is a "large-scale" technology by which the optimal-size plant can supply several times the total quantity currently consumed, but at a lower cost per unit. Let us postpone the discussion of the optimal date of introducing the large-scale plant. Suppose it is constructed when, due to population growth, demand has increased sufficiently to use its entire capacity. It will then have a net positive present value, since that same output can be produced by small-scale technology only when using a larger amount of resources. The economy has expanded sufficiently to take advantage of the large-scale technology and can undertake a project with a positive net present value, while the net present value of the next best alternative is zero.

Economies of scale are commonly associated with public utilities, but they are prevalent in other fields as well. In many artistic endeavors production is subject to such economies. In the motion picture industry, for example, the final output is the viewing of the film by the public. The marginal cost of the film services, of showing the film to an additional viewer,[1] is probably constant; but since the marginal cost of showing the movie to the first viewer requires the production of the film itself, the average cost of all output units beyond the first is falling. In this case there is no serious capacity limit on the volume of services that can be generated from a single film. Consequently, in a growing economy, if the production of the movies is sufficiently postponed it will eventually obtain a positive present value regardless of its cost of production.

The same type of argument applies to the production of books, where the writing process composes the initial fixed cost and the printing and distribution the constant marginal cost; of paintings and their reproduction; of music and its recordings, etc. This argument also applies to innovations which require certain developmental costs, but which when available can generate services indefinitely at no cost (see Barzel 1968).

A source of confusion in grasping the distinction between investment in a competitive industry and investment in a decreasing-cost industry arises from the fact that one optimum condition for a competitive industry is that the rate of return on investment equal the economy's discount rate. This condition results in a zero net value for such an investment. One should avoid the notion that the criterion of investing when the present value is zero should be applied under noncompetitive conditions.[2] Even though Marglin (1963), Arrow (1964), and Barzel (1968) have already shown that the optimizing rule to be applied is that of the *maximization* of the present value of investment, it is worthwhile to present the argument briefly once more.

I. The General Framework

Consider an economy on a balanced growth path where, due to population growth, the demand for all commodities expands at a constant exponential rate and relative prices of existing commodities remain constant. We will concentrate on a single commodity, not yet in production.

[1] Or to a group of viewers in a single showing.

[2] In personal conversations I have frequently been told that the argument against equating the present value to zero belabors the obvious; but this error is constantly made, and often by eminent economists. Robert Fogel, for example (1966), states that investments in the space projects should be undertaken when benefits cover costs, that is, when present value is zero. And Hirshleifer, DeHaven, and Milliman (1960, p. 152) prescribe: "Adopt any project for which the present value . . . is greater than zero." But if a project is mutually exclusive with itself over time, and its present value increases with time, should the project be undertaken when its present value just exceeds zero? It should be postponed and undertaken when present value is maximized.

The demand for it, although latent, also grows at the economy's growth rate. The price elasticity of demand, not necessarily constant along a given demand schedule at a point in time, depends on the usual forces. At a given price, the price elasticity is constant through time due to the nature of shift in demand. While the question of price setting is deferred to later sections, it is important to note that if marginal cost is constant (as assumed below), whether price is equated to marginal cost, as would be socially optimal, or is set at the point where marginal cost equals marginal revenue, it will not change through time. Since in this case the price, whether optimally chosen or not, will remain constant through time, the path of the quantity demanded will exhibit a rate of growth equal that of the economy. Total revenue, then, will also grow at the same rate.[3] In the remainder of this section revenues are assumed equal to the area below the demand curve, as would be the case for a perfectly discriminating monopolist who equates marginal revenues with marginal price. This assumption will be critically evaluated below.

Suppose that total cost of supplying the commodity has two components: a once-and-for-all "fixed" investment and an additional cost which is constant per time period.[4] After the decision is made to undertake the project, costs under the above assumptions are independent of the level of output; in other words, the marginal cost is zero. If all costs are capitalized, it becomes clear that average cost is basically inversely proportional to output. An example of such a commodity is electricity generated in a large-scale hydroelectric project whose annual maintenance cost is largely independent of the volume of output.

As time goes on, the profitability of introducing and commencing to supply the commodity increases, since revenues increase over time while costs do not. The crucial questions, then, are when to undertake the once-and-for-all investment and what implications arise from different investment policies. We will concentrate on two alternative policies: equating the present value of the investment to zero, or maximizing its present value. We will show that the second is socially optimal, whereas the first may prevail under current circumstances. The net present value of the investment project R_o, is used since we wish to compare different time flows. We want to find what happens to R_o when the starting point

[3] Marglin (1963) concentrates on the case where quantity is fixed and price (rather than quantity) grows steadily. Nevertheless many of the results of this paper apply under the conditions specified by him.

[4] The initial investment is considered as constant throughout the paper; similarly, the time pattern of revenues is considered as given. The case where variable costs are proportional to output rather than constant per unit of time is considered below (particularly in n. 15).

of the project is allowed to change. Given our assumption, the starting point of the project is the only variable subject to decision.[5]

If we denote by $t(z)$ the point in time for which the present value is equal to zero ($R_o = 0$), it is found that at the point in time the investment is made, the rate of change in (discounted) benefits is less than the rate of change in (discounted) costs.[6] In other words, if investment is

[5] This is the first of a series of footnotes providing a more formal and more complete presentation of the verbal model in the text and its results. Total revenue is

$$S = g(t) \,, \tag{1}$$

so that

$$\frac{\partial S}{\partial t} > 0 \,, \tag{2}$$

where t is time and S is total revenue per unit of time. If we assume a constant (positive) rate of growth in revenues we get

$$S = g(t) = S_o e^{pt} \,, \tag{1'}$$

where S_o is revenues in time t_o, and p is the growth rate. Total cost of supplying the commodity is

$$C = I + f(t) \,, \tag{3}$$

and we assume that after the initial investment I is made,

$$\frac{\partial C}{\partial t} = f'(t) = a \,. \tag{4}$$

The net present value, R_o, is

$$R_o = \int_T^\infty g(t)e^{-rt}dt - Ie^{-rt} - \int_T^\infty f'(t)e^{-rt}dt \,, \tag{5}$$

where r is the discount rate. Substituting (1′) and (4) into (5) we obtain an explicit expression for R_o,

$$R_o = \int_T^\infty S_o e^{-(r-p)t}dt - \int_T^\infty ae^{-rt}dt - Ie^{-rt} \,. \tag{6}$$

Note that for $p \geq r$, $R_o \to \infty$, and this can be ruled out as an economic impossibility. (The importance of this result to the balanced-growth literature is obvious.) When the integrals in (6) are evaluated for $p < r$ we obtain

$$R_o = \frac{S_o e^{-(r-p)t}}{r-p} - \frac{ae^{-rt}}{r} - Ie^{-rt} \,. \tag{7}$$

[6] Solving for t for which $R_o = 0$, we obtain

$$t(z) = \frac{1}{p}\left[\ln\left(I + \frac{a}{r}\right) - \ln S_o + \ln (r-p)\right] \,. \tag{8}$$

The implications of (8) can be evaluated by considering the rate of change in costs and benefits at time $t(z)$. The time derivative of (7) is postponed, the resources released would earn more when employed elsewhere than they earn in this particular project.

In this case, then, use of the rule of equating the present value to zero (the "myopic" investment rule) leads to a nonoptimal solution. The more general optimizing rule that applies to both competitive and noncompetitive situations is that the present value of the *marginal* unit of investment is zero. In competition, the marginal and the average are the same, but not so for decreasing-cost industries. It will now be shown that, in fact, the socially optimal solution in this case is maximization of present value.

That such maximization is a superior investment criterion is well known.[7] Its superiority is particularly relevant in cases where the investment projects considered are mutually exclusive. In this paper, the projects considered are all mutually exclusive over time. Building a hydroelectric project preempts the site not only from other contemporaneous projects but also from similar projects at different points in time. Similarly, a given innovation at a point in time excludes, as an economic activity, the duplication of that innovation at any subsequent point in time. The justification for applying the principle of maximization of present value over space holds equally well over time.

It is clear from previous discussion that to maximize present value the time to invest is when the rate of change in revenues is equal to the rate of change in cost.[8] It should be noted from comparing expressions (8) and

---

$$\frac{\partial R_o}{\partial t} = -S_o e^{-(r-p)t} + ae^{-rt} + rIe^{-rt} . \tag{9}$$

When we insert into (9) the solution for $t(z)$, it is found (for $p > 0$) that at the time the investment is made, the first term on the right of (9), the discounted benefit, is less than the sum of the second and third terms, representing the variable costs and the interest cost on the fixed investment (both discounted to the present).

[7] See Hirshleifer (1958). Note that we assume perfect capital markets, so that problems of credit rationing do not arise.

[8] Present value has an extreme value when (9), the time derivative of the net present value—(6) or (7)—is equated to zero. We obtain

$$S_o e^{-(r-p)t} = ae^{-rt} + rIe^{-rt} . \tag{10}$$

The second derivative of (9) is

$$\frac{\partial^2 R_o}{\partial t^2} = e^{-rt}[(r - p)S_o e^{pt} - ra - r^2 I] . \tag{11}$$

Upon examination it turns out that for the relevant values of p, $0 < p < r$, (11) is negative, so the solution for t in (10) is a maximum. If we denote $t(m)$ as the solution for the maximizing value for t, the explicit expression for $t(m)$ is

$$t(m) = \frac{\ln (rI + a) - \ln S_o}{p} = \frac{\ln \left(I + \frac{a}{r}\right) - \ln S_o + \ln r}{p} . \tag{12}$$

(12) in footnotes 6 and 8, respectively, that $t(m)$, the starting date for the maximization of present value, is always later than $t(z)$, the starting date for equating the present value to zero.

At this point, a figure will be useful in permitting a better understanding of the problem. In figure 1*A*, points on the revenues-flow curve represent potential revenues at each point in time. Revenues rise exponentially at a constant rate. The costs-flow curve is constant over time after the initial investment is converted to its equivalent flow. Figure 1*B* is identical with 1*A* except that all the points on the curves for costs flow and revenues flow are discounted to present terms. We are able to convert the initial fixed investment to its equivalent flow, since the timing is a free variable and the alternative cost per period of these resources is what they can earn elsewhere during that period. The point $t(m)$ at which the two curves intersect is the optimal investment date. If investment takes place earlier, at a time such as $t(z)$, at each point between time $t(z)$ and time $t(m)$ costs are higher than revenues, and resources could earn more elsewhere. Beyond that date resources earn less elsewhere. At the point $t(m)$ marginal cost is equal to marginal revenue.[9] The net present value of the investment is the (discounted) area between the two curves to the right of $t(m)$.[10] Since at $t(z)$ the net present value is zero, the area between the two curves in figure 1*B* in the range $t(z)$ to $t(m)$ is identical in size, but with opposite sign, with the area between the curves to the right of $t(m)$.

When we compare the timing of the investment under the rule of equating the present value to zero with that of maximizing the present value, we can see that since $t(z) < t(m)$ the latter leads to a later date of

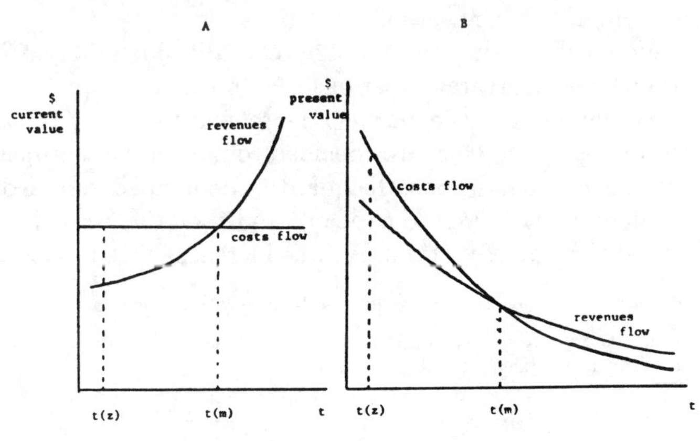

FIG. 1

[9] Marginal with respect to time, and not with respect to output volume at a point in time.

[10] Since the rate of growth in S is p, and the discount rate is $r > p$, the discounted net benefits are finite.

investment.[11] Then the decision rule to invest when present value is equal to zero calls for a premature diversion of resources into the investment project under consideration. We can now evaluate the maximum net present value. This is always positive and can be expressed as a simple function of the value of the fixed investment and the capitalized value of the running cost. This function increases with the initial level of revenues and with the rate of growth in revenues, and falls with the rate of discount.[12]

If projects of the kind described above are available, an economy that would otherwise experience growth of income proportional to the growth of population would be able, by taking advantage of its increasing scale, to increase its per capita stock of wealth and concurrently its per capita income. It should be emphasized again that this growth in per capita income is entirely independent of technical change. The economic advance will be achieved even when technology is entirely constant.

II. The Relevance of the Formal Model

Two important questions arise regarding the relevance of the above model. First, since the conditions specified are unlikely to be met in full in the "real world," we have to investigate the effects of divergences from these conditions on the results obtained. Second, can we expect the economy to take full advantage of the economies of scale, or will the inherently noncompetitive nature of the projects considered prevent any positive results? The first problem is now discussed; the second will be considered in the following section.

It was assumed above that the average cost falls indefinitely. Consider now the case where the average cost has the "normal" shape but, due to the temporary small size of the market, the relevant range of the average cost is downward-sloping. Once it is decided to undertake a project characterized by such cost conditions, the quantity demanded, due to demand expansion, will eventually exceed capacity and then the limited quantity will be rationed through a continuous price increase. This is basically the

[11] The difference between the two is $[\ln r - \ln(r - p)]/p$ periods.

[12] By inserting the value of t from (12) into (7) and using the equality in (10), we obtain the maximum net present value, $R(m)$:

$$R_o(m) = e^{-rt(m)}\left(I + \frac{a}{r}\right)\frac{p}{r - p}. \tag{13}$$

The first component of (13), $e^{-rt(m)}$, is simply a discount factor for the rest of the expression to bring it to present terms. The second term, $I + (a/r)$, is the capitalized value of all costs. The product, $[I + (a/r)]e^{-rt(m)}$, is the present value of all costs discounted to time zero. The net present value, $R_o(m)$, then, is a product of the present value of total cost by the factor $p/(r - p)$. It is necessarily positive, since for $0 < p < r$, $p/(r - p) > 0$.

case considered by Marglin (1963). With the exception of limitations on natural resources, this situation cannot proceed indefinitely. Sooner or later it will be worthwhile to construct additional plants, and then conditions of "natural monopoly" no longer prevail. In terms of figure 1*A*, the revenue curve as viewed by the individual firm does not continue to rise indefinitely; it will eventually fall to the level of minimum average cost—the competitive level. It is obvious that the optimal time to invest is still when the rate of change in benefits is equal to the rate of change in cost, as in $t(m)$; but the present value of the investment is less than when the average cost falls indefinitely. The contribution of such projects to wealth depends on the difference between the average cost at current levels of output and the minimum average cost and on the speed of reaching the minimum point.

It was assumed above that "variable" costs are constant per unit of time. In the communication field the total cost of producing a book, say, has as a fixed component the writer's and editorial costs, while the costs of printing and distribution are probably proportional to the number of books printed. For such cases, the cost conditions specified above have to be modified, since the "variable" component is now proportional to output rather than constant per unit of time. The solutions for $t(z)$ and for $t(m)$ are somewhat different from those obtained above, but the differences are of only secondary importance.[13]

A special case of some interest arises where the demand for a commodity or a service is short lasting, as in the case of news and of fashion items.

[13] If we denote the variable cost corresponding to S_o by a_o, for $R_o = 0$, the solution for $t(z)$ is

$$t(z) = \frac{\ln I - \ln (S_o - a_o) + \ln (r - p)}{p}, \tag{8'}$$

and for R_o = maximum we obtain

$$t(m) = \frac{\ln I - \ln (S_o + a_o) + \ln r}{p}. \tag{12'}$$

In the case of innovative services where the cost of the first service unit is equal to the total cost of the innovation while the cost of all subsequent units is 0, that is $a_o = 0$ in (8′), this represents a pure public good (if $a_o > 0$, it is a semipublic good). Here the solutions for the two values of t are

$$t(z) = \frac{\ln I - \ln S_o + \ln (r - p)}{p}, \tag{8''}$$

$$t(m) = \frac{\ln I - \ln S_o + \ln r}{p}. \tag{12''}$$

Notice that if we define $S_o' = S_o - a_o$, which is net revenue after deducting costs proportional to output, (8′) and (11′) become essentially the same as (8″) and (11″), which allows us to treat semipublic goods basically in the same way as pure public goods.

Consider a fashion designer with sketches for "minishoes" for teenage girls, whose number grows at an exponential rate. Let us assume that within a month after they are introduced, no matter which month is selected, a constant fraction (depending on the price elasticity) of all teenage girls will purchase one pair, and after the month is over, not a single pair will be sold. When should the designer make the initial investment to introduce his minishoes if he wants to maximize his profits? Maximizing the present value is again the proper criterion, since the project is mutually exclusive over time. As before, maximization of present value leads to an investment date later than that for equating the present value to zero.[14] In terms of figure 1*B*, since all sales are completed within one month, different points (or one-month segments) on each of the curves should be viewed as alternatives to each other and $t(m)$ will occur when the positive vertical distance between the (discounted) revenue curve and the (discounted) cost curve is maximized, whereas zero present value occurs at the intersection of the curves. This case illustrates the fact that while most of the discussion in this paper is concerned with multiperiod production, the model is also applicable to commodities for which the entire output is consumed in one period, as long as production of the commodity in one period precludes its production in other periods.

Another assumption has been that revenues increase at a constant rate, equaling the population's rate of growth. Population, however, does not grow at a constant rate. Nor is per capita income constant, in part due to the positive present value generated by projects such as those discussed above. If the income elasticities for different commodities are not the same, the rate of growth in demand will not be constant over time and will differ among commodities. For inferior commodities, if population growth is not sufficient to compensate for negative income effects,

[14] The present value of this venture is

$$R_o = S'_o e^{-(r-p)t} - Ie^{-rt}, \tag{14}$$

where S_o is defined in n. 5 above and p is the growth rate of the population of teenage girls. Maximum present value is obtained by differentiating R_o with respect to t and equating to zero,

$$\frac{\partial R_o}{\partial t} = -(r-p)S'_o e^{-(r-p)t} + rIe^{-rt} = 0. \tag{15}$$

Solving (15) for t we obtain

$$t(m) = \frac{\ln r + \ln I - \ln (r-p) - \ln S'_o}{p}. \tag{16}$$

When the present value is equated to zero we obtain

$$t(z) = \frac{\ln I - \ln S'_o}{p}. \tag{17}$$

demand may even fall. In other words, while the rate of growth in demand is positive for most commodities and services, it cannot be considered as constant over time or as uniform among commodities. The results obtained for the net present value of projects of the type discussed above can be conceived now only on an average for the economy. We can no longer explicitly derive $t(m)$ and evaluate the maximum present value. However, we can state the conditions for a maximum. The marginal condition, as before, is that the rate of change in (discounted) net revenue should equal the (discounted) interest cost on capital. In addition, to obtain a maximum rather than a minimum, the revenue curve must intersect the cost curve from below. Finally, the net present value has to be positive.[15] These conditions require that at least some of the time the rate of growth in revenues has to be positive. Figure 2, where the two flow curves are drawn in present-value terms, illustrates the above conclusions. The cost curve declines exponentially; the revenue curve first falls slowly, then "catches" the cost curve at $t(m)$, and finally slips behind again. The two intersections m and n give two solutions for extreme values; m, where the cost curve is intersected from below, is a maximum, and n is a minimum. Finally, for $R_o > 0$, the area contained by the revenue curve to the right of $t(m)$ has to exceed the area below the cost curve to the right of $t(m)$—that is, the difference between the horizontally lined area and the vertically lined area has to exceed zero.[16] As long as $R_o > 0$, the construction of such a project will add to the stock of wealth. The crosshatched area between $t(z)$ and $t(m)$ is equal in size and opposite in sign to the net present value at $t(m)$, indicating that the net present value is zero at $t(z)$, but positive between $t(z)$ and $t(m)$.

All the cases discussed in this section differ from the case of the previous section. But the differences are all secondary in terms of the main thesis of this paper: Projects manifesting economies of scale will have,

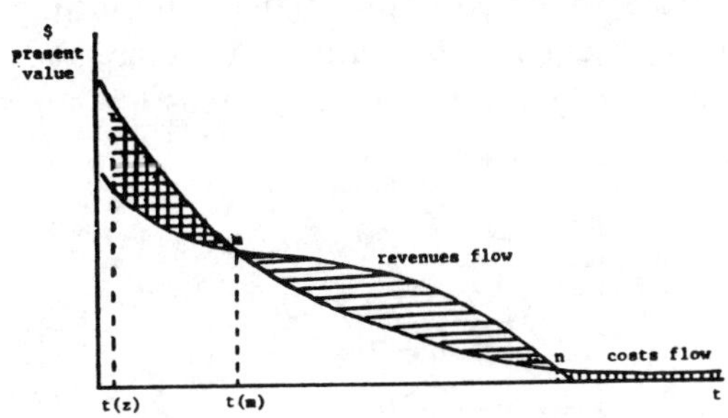

FIG. 2

[15] This condition always holds if revenues grow indefinitely at an exponential rate.

[16] If there are avoidable costs, the project should be abandoned at the point in time when total avoidable costs exceed the benefits; results in the text are to be modified accordingly.

when undertaken at the optimal time, a positive net present value. In all cases, the investment rule requiring that the internal rate of return be equal to the market discount rate will lead to a premature application of resources that will rob these projects of their potential contribution to net wealth.

III. The Divergence between Private and Social Returns and the Determination of $t(m)$

The major point of the previous discussion is that under a wide range of conditions an expanding economy should be able to increase its per capita income by exploiting projects offering scale economies. The question then arises whether, given the current institutional setting, the economy possesses the mechanism to take advantage of the opportunities afforded. The projects that could increase the stock of wealth are invariably natural monopolies, and we can no longer assume that the efficiency associated with competition will prevail. Divergences between private and social costs and returns may be initiated by two distinct sets of forces: the first to be discussed is well recognized; the second is not.

The Natural Monopoly Problem

The projects considered here operate under conditions where marginal costs are less than average costs. If the services generated are sold at a single profit-maximizing price, two sources of misallocation arise. One is that total consumers' benefits are greater than their costs. A socially desirable project is not necessarily privately profitable and may fail to be undertaken. Even if the project is undertaken, the level of output is too small, since price is higher than marginal cost. In figure 3, *VTR* is a static demand curve, from which costs proportional to output are netted out. At *OQ*, marginal cost is equal to marginal revenue, and *OP* is the (net) profit-maximizing single price. Total revenues are represented by the

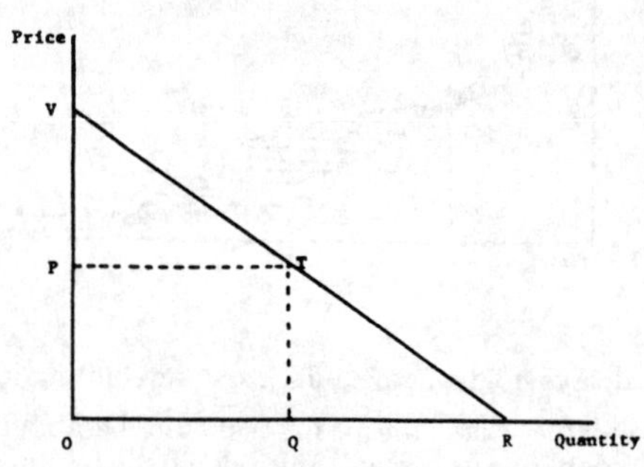

FIG. 3

rectangle *OPTQ*. The triangle *PTV* represents consumers' surplus,[17] the extra amount that consumers are willing to pay for the amount sold. The producer, however, charges the single price *OP* for the entire output, so the consumers' surplus does not enter his decision function. Similarly, output expansion from *OQ* to *OR* will increase the difference between consumers' benefits and producer costs by the area of the triangle *QRT*[18] which also does not enter the producer's decision function. In other words, the triangle *VRO* corresponds to a point on the revenue curves in figure 1 that includes all benefits. The revenues to the monopolist are only *PTQO* and will result in a lowering of the revenue curves. From the social standpoint the investment will take place too late, and the subsequent quantity produced will be too small. Both of these sources of resource misallocation could be eliminated if the producer would practice perfect price discrimination, since his revenues then would be identical with total consumers' benefits as assumed in Sections I and II. Such discrimination, however, is seldom accomplished. Thus, misallocation will persist and investment will take place too late.

The "Public Domain" Problem[19]

Not recognized in the current context is that aspect of divergence between the private and social viewpoint which stems from the absence of property rights on certain factors of production. The productive agent in the public domain is the production technology where the output enjoys decreasing cost. It was shown above that if a project is undertaken at its optimal time it will generate a positive net present value. If a single entrepreneur had control over the technology involved he could appropriate that present value. But if the technology is in the public domain, as frequently occurs, the opportunity for earning a rate of return above the market rate will attract into the activity additional resources in two forms—one involving duplication of effort, the other premature investment. In either case resources will continue flowing into the activity until the private rate of return will be reduced to that in the rest of the economy, and the potential latent in the large-scale technology will be wasted.[20]

[17] Assuming that the demand curve is income-compensated.

[18] For a linear demand curve, the producer's net revenues (*OQTP*) are exactly one-half of total consumers' benefits for the output level *OR*.

[19] The source of misallocation discussed in the previous section is first abstracted from; later the two are considered together.

[20] Joint maximization by producers and consumers could prevent the waste of resources. The number of potential entrants may be too large to make joint maximization on the part of producers practicable; similarly, it is hard to see consumers organizing to maximize jointly.

For illustration, suppose that the score of one of Bach's cantatas is newly discovered. Consider the sale of records of this cantata as the only source of revenue and utility from that cantata. To produce records, the cantata has to be performed, recorded, etc., and we assume that the marginal cost beyond the first record is constant. If net revenues from the record sales will increase with time, we can find $t(m)$, the point in time for the initial production and sales that will maximize the present value of this artistic investment project. Suppose that $t(m)$ happens to be twenty years hence. The copyright on the score, however, expired long ago and is now in the public domain. The question then arises which of the many recording firms will be the lucky one to produce the records and to increase its own net present value. The answer is that in a profit-world none of them will. Time $t(m)$ is not the profit-maximizing date for any of the firms. For them any value of $R_o > 0$ is preferable to $R_o = 0$—the latter reflecting their profits if they do nothing. As long as $R_o > 0$, all firms have an incentive to produce this particular record. By virtue of the public-domain aspect of the score, entry is free, and competition as to who will be the first to come out with the record is bound to bring R_o to zero. If the date of entry were determined by the above competitive forces but entry were to be limited to the first firm producing the record, the discussion would be complete. In terms of figure 1 or 2, the record will be introduced at time $t(z)$. If, however, additional firms are also permitted to record that piece (and it is not clear that they would do so) the initial producer cannot count on obtaining all the revenues but must take into account potential sales of records of the same cantata by other recording firms. More resources will enter the industry until the present value is reduced to zero. So, regardless of the entry pattern that may emerge, the present value of this endeavor will be driven to zero either through the premature application of resources or through duplication of effort, at which point the newly discovered score is deprived of all its potential net economic value. Had Bach's heirs maintained the copyright on the cantata and charged the profit-maximizing royalties, it is obvious that the net present value of the cantata would be positive rather than zero.[21]

Misallocation, then, may arise as a result of two distinct forces. Since some production agents are in the public domain, investment is too large

[21] This problem is common to many projects in the communications field, broadly defined. If many economists are equally able to write an elementary text, even if they are profit maximizers the text cannot be expected to be introduced at its optimal time. If the copyright of the ideas originally contained in journal articles and monographs could be exercised, the original authors could enforce an optimal publication date for the textbook simply by demanding the appropriate royalties. But since the ideas in the original papers have in fact entered the public domain, textbook writers can use them at no cost and will compete among themselves until their profits are eliminated either by introducing the text too early or by introducing too many texts.

or too early. Due to monopolistic elements in selling the output generated by an investment project, investment is too little or too late. Even though the two forces pull in opposite directions, since their magnitude depends on entirely different sets of factors we cannot expect that the final result will be optimal,[22] except by chance. Moreover, in many cases one of the forces may be absent, and in such a case misallocation is certain to occur. In many "public utility" type projects, no problems arise from factors of production which are in the public domain. If the utilities are not publicly controlled, their timing of investment will be optimal when they discriminate perfectly. In practice, it is unlikely that this condition is fully satisfied; consequently the timing of investment is too late for optimality.

In the case of patentable inventions, the production agent which is in the public domain is the basic knowledge needed to invent. Assuming that patent protection is effective, two possibilities should be considered. The first arises where a patent is easily obtained and there is no need to invest heavily to demonstrate its applicability. In this case the inventor is actually able to appropriate the relevant knowledge and the patent owner can time his major developmental investment without fear of competition;[23] but even in such a situation, due to the finite elasticity of demand for the patent services, royalty revenues are usually less than the social benefits, and the timing of the main investment will be too late. If, on the other hand, the major innovating investment has to be made as a condition of obtaining the patent, competition among inventors to obtain priority rights will lead to a too-early investment. If the two forces operate together, timing will be indeterminate relative to the socially optimal.[24]

IV. Some Current Government Policies

We will consider here only two of the major government policies—direct investment and ceilings on private rates of return—in their effect on the production of the class of goods discussed in this paper. Direct government investment in roads, dams, etc., has two major relevant characteris-

[22] Even if we neglect here the desirable output expansion from *OQ* to *OR* (fig. 3).

[23] The time limitation on patent rights (abstracted from in the text) will lead to a *delay* in patenting activities, since the present value of the royalties must exceed the cost of patenting during the seventeen years in which the patent is protected. The patent owner stands to profit most from seventeen "good" years, and in a growing economy the future contains the better years.

[24] The production of knowledge, of nonpatentable innovations, and of other factors that fall fully or in part in the public domain will be too low and too late, since the private return is less than the social return. This is a problem additional to those discussed in the text. I am indebted to the referee for this point.

tics. One is that an investment is considered worthy when the sum of all benefits, private and social, just exceeds cost. The other is that services generated by such projects are seldom priced so as to recover the original investment. This pricing policy may be conceived as an attempt to produce the socially optimal quantity where price is equal to marginal cost.[25] If a project is constructed when its benefit-cost ratio equals 1, its present value will be zero. Since demand typically grows over time, delaying the project will yield a positive present value, whereas if it is constructed when the present value is zero, its potential contribution to wealth will be entirely wasted.

Ceilings on private rates of return are common in the public utilities sector. If set at the competitive level they will have an effect similar to that of using a benefit-cost ratio equal to 1. Here, however, we have to distinguish whether all the benefits accrue to the utilities. If the utilities' revenues equal the social benefits generated by their services, private and social net present value is zero. But if social benefits exceed the utilities' revenues, the rate-of-return ceiling may induce them to invest earlier than when they maximize present value; while the private present values are zero, the social ones consequently are positive.[26] Government policy toward patents was touched upon in the previous section. Other government policies (such as investment subsidies, research grants, etc.) can be easily analyzed using the above framework, and there is no need to discuss them here.

In all the cases discussed above, whether with or without government intervention, the present value of the projects considered will never be negative.[27] Even though the present value would not, in general, equal the maximum obtainable (from the social standpoint), it will still be positive in many instances. Consequently, assuming that limiting factors are unimportant, when the economy expands the net wealth per capita will increase and, with it, so will per capita income.

V. Concluding Remarks

In the last few sections, the difference in utility between the marginal unit consumed and submarginal units played an important role in the analysis. When we consider the contribution of any firm to income, we should take into account not only its revenues but also the consumers' surplus enjoyed by the consumers of its output. In a competitive indus-

[25] Problems of crowding are ignored here.

[26] The utilities, of course, have other means to reduce their rate of return.

[27] An exception to this may arise if the government subsidizes investment to the extent where the social rate of return from a project is less than the market rate of discount.

try, however, the demand curve facing an individual firm is perfectly elastic, and consumers' surplus generated by the marginal firm is zero; so in considering the effect of an additional firm on output this is not an issue. Even in the case of an existing monopoly, consumers' surplus is not a crucial problem since the most intensive demand is already satisfied and the expansion of output will involve relatively small welfare triangles.[28]

This problem is then of importance mainly in the case of new commodities (or for "old" commodities whose prices may be drastically reduced). The investment projects considered in this paper would not be restricted to production of new commodities. *All* new commodities, however, are produced under conditions of falling average costs due to the initial investment required to produce the first unit. If average costs were not falling, these commodities would have been introduced in the past. We may conclude that under conditions considered in this paper, consumers' surplus is of great operational importance.

The above model was developed under the assumption that individuals attempt to maximize their present value. The range of activities contains many—such as inventing and artistic creation—where individuals may be motivated by factors other than personal profit. We still may claim that they maximize, but we then have to add psychic benefits to the pecuniary benefits (or else recognize that the alternative costs are less than their pecuniary market choices).

Let us instead assume that these activities are not rationally motivated; can we still make positive statements regarding the effects of such activities on growth? Suppose that the amount of resources devoted to these activities grows proportionately with income. At what rate would the benefits increase? For activities undertaken at period t_o, designate by S_o', the present value of the benefits from which costs proportional to output are netted out. If in t_1 the amount of resources devoted to such activities is the same as in t_o, we may expect that they will have the same economic characteristics.[29] Since, however, the economy expands at the rate p, the value of the benefits at t_1 from the new projects will be $(1 + p)S_o'$. And since the amount of resources devoted to such activities also expands at that rate S_1', the net present value of the benefits at t_1, will be $S_1' = (1 + p)^2 S_o'$. Whatever the level of the initial benefits relative to the amount of resources devoted to these activities, the benefits grow at twice the rate of cost and eventually will exceed cost. So, even if resources are allocated among such activities in a random fashion, sooner or later they will necessarily provide for a net increase in the stock of wealth.

[28] This statement should be qualified if the demand curve is elastic at low price levels, particularly for pure public goods (where $MC = 0$).

[29] If there is an infinite set of outcomes to choose from and the choice in each period is random, the expected value of the economic characteristics will be constant.

References

Arrow, Kenneth J. "Optimal Capacity Policy, the Cost of Capital, and Myopic Decision Rules." *Ann. Inst. Statis. Math.*, vol. 16, nos. 1, 2 (1964).

Barzel, Yoram. "The Optimal Timing of Innovations." *Rev. Econ. Statis.* 50 (August 1968): 348–55.

Fogel, Robert W. "Railroads as an Analogy to the Space Effort: Some Economic Aspects." *Econ. J.* 76 (March 1966): 16–43.

Hirshleifer, Jack. "On the Theory of Optimal Investment Decision." *J.P.E.* 66 (August 1958): 329–52.

Hirshleifer, Jack; DeHaven, James C.; and Milliman, Jerome W. *Water Supply.* Chicago: Univ. Chicago Press, 1960.

Marglin, Stephen E. *Approaches to Dynamic Investment Planning.* Amsterdam: North Holland, 1963.

PART III

LABOR

[9]

THE DETERMINATION OF DAILY HOURS AND WAGES *

Yoram Barzel

In *The Theory of Wages* [1] the daily wage rate concept is contrasted with that of the hourly rate. In discussing the daily wage, Hicks clearly recognizes the dependence of productivity per hour on the number of hours worked in determining the length of the working day. Although not pushing this relationship very far, he does go substantially farther than subsequent economists who, as a matter of course, consider the constraint facing the individual as an externally determined hourly wage rate independent of the number of hours worked.[2] Analysis based on the assumption that daily hours of work have no effect on productivity per hour will be designated in the rest of this paper as the "standard approach." [3] The purpose of this paper is explicitly to inquire into and to take account of the interdependence between hours and productivity.

I. The General Framework

We will concentrate on a single individual assumed to possess skills best suited to a given industry.[4] What can plausibly be said

* I acknowledge deep gratitude to H. Gregg Lewis, who generously extended himself to provide me with his unpublished work in the area, from which I benefited greatly. My basic approach is similar to Lewis's, but the difference in emphasis and detail is such that full responsibility is mine for any errors in this paper. I am indebted to John E. Floyd, to Roger L. Miller, and to Jacob Mincer for their comments. Finally, the paper is greatly improved in presentation and in substance due to Sherwin Rosen's painstaking suggestions. I did some of the work on this paper while visiting at University College London, supported by a Ford Foundation Fellowship.

1. J. R. Hicks, *The Theory of Wages* (New York: Macmillan, 1932).

2. A notable exception is found in Sherwin Rosen, "On the Interindustry Wage and Hours Structure," *Journal of Political Economy*, LXXVII (March/April 1969), 249–73. Rosen's departure point is the effect of specific investment in labor on hours worked.

3. It is not easy to find detailed discussion of these issues. However, a relatively comprehensive one is presented by Tibor Scitovsky, *Welfare and Competition* (Chicago: Irwin, 1951), ch. V.

4. "Best" should mean "of highest value." An individual may find, however, that the industry in which his earnings are highest for an eight-hour day is not the same as for a four-hour day. We will assume here that one industry

about the relation between his productivity and the number of hours he works in a typical day? Productivity is zero between the time a worker "punches his card" and the time he reaches his actual work spot; as he gets organized, productivity will rise slowly. It is generally accepted that eventually, as the length of the working day approaches a critical value (maybe twelve or fourteen hours), total product will reach a maximum.[5] I will assume that between these two extremes productivity changes smoothly. In terms of the hourly (marginal) product, the sequence begins at zero, rises for a while, reaches a maximum, and then declines until toward the end of the day it again becomes zero. The hourly product curve $E'(H)$ with respect to the hours of the day will then appear as in Figure I. Any point on the daily product curve $E(H)$ in Figure I is the area to that point under the $E'(H)$ curve, the former reaching its maximum when the latter falls to zero. This may be contrasted with the standard assumption that the hourly product is constant and that total daily product (and hence the budget constraint) is a straight line through the origin.[6] The $E'(H)$ and $E(H)$ functions are conceived as long-run relations — each point is obtained after full adjustment in capital equipment, number of shifts, etc., has taken place.[7]

Even though much of the subsequent analysis is on the individual level, it should be tied up with that of the industry; thus we will better understand the conditions under which the individual operates while also guarding against the pitfalls of aggregation. The discussion is restricted to competitive conditions, free of institutional constraints. As long as the product per hour is constant, it is a relatively simple matter to obtain aggregate demand and supply for labor in an industry even if working hours are not uniform, since all hours are of equal weight. Where product per hour is not con-

---

is best for all hours. The assumption is relaxed in my "The Firm's Offer and the Individual Choice of Daily Hours and Wages" (mimeographed).

5. The word "total" in this context is used as the net contribution of the individual for the *total* number of hours worked. It is not the total product of all factors but rather the extra product due to labor.

6. We encounter a nonlinear budget constraint in a variety of other circumstances, as when quantity discounts are available or when the interest rate changes with the amount borrowed.

7. In a recent monograph, when addressing the question of daily hours, M. R. Fisher discusses in detail the individual's allocation of time among activities and the intensity of effort applied for each unit of time. The factors affecting these decisions, according to Fisher, are numerous and intricate. Our approach, although consistent with Fisher's, is simpler by virtue of being more mechanistic, and it carries stronger (and more easily refutable) implications. Fisher, *The Economic Analysis of Labor* (London: Widenfeld and Nicolson, 1971).

stant, we make the following assumptions: (1) hours per man may vary among, but not within, firms; (2) workers are all equally productive, but their taste for leisure may differ; (3) the demand is for effective labor only — i.e., the firm is indifferent between different combinations of hours per man and number of men for any given level of effective labor.

Given these assumptions, the demand for labor in terms of effective units is straightforward. The supply, however, is more complicated. A change in the effective wage rate will lead to a change not only in the number of men but also in the number of hours for each man; these hours have to be transformed into effective units to obtain the quantity supplied. The intersection of the supply and demand schedules will determine the wage rate and the quantity of effective labor. While it should be recognized at this point that the slope of the supply curve is not necessarily positive, we assume a unique and stable equilibrium.

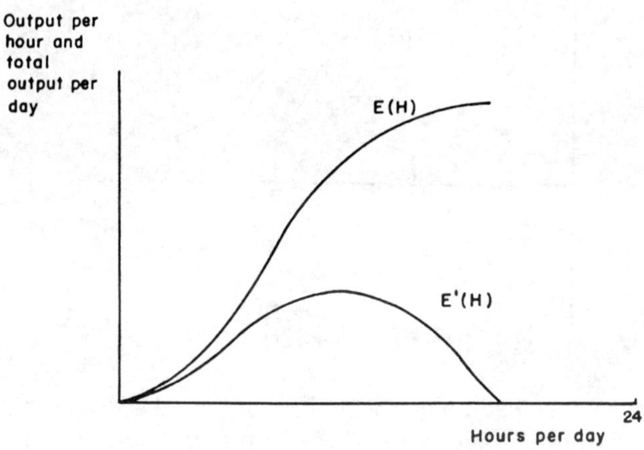

FIGURE I

Given the wage rate (and using the relation $W = \frac{\partial Q}{\partial L} P_Q$ where W is the wage rate, P_Q is product price, and $\frac{\partial Q}{\partial L}$ is the marginal product of labor), we can transform Figure I into value terms by first accounting for the overall marginal product of labor and then multiplying the $E(H)$ curve by the price of the product to obtain the value of daily product (see Appendix). Following the convention of measuring working hours from right to left[8] with respect to the choice between labor and leisure, we obtain in Figure II the *VDP* (value of daily product) curve. The *VDP* curve then is arrived at by turning $E(H)$ around and multiplying it by a constant.

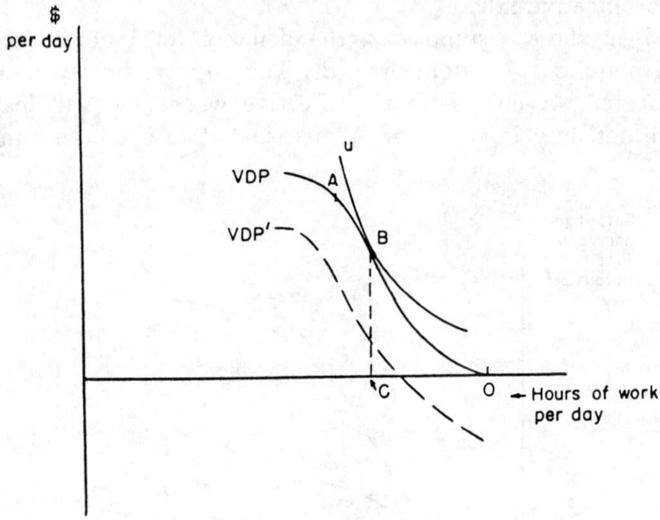

FIGURE II

At point B, for example, the individual works $0C$ hours, and his contribution to the net value of the firm is BC dollars. The counterpart to the *VDP* curve in the standard analysis is the budget constraint (wage line). Since all individuals are assumed equal in terms of their productive ability, their *VDP* curves are the same. But because their tastes are diverse, the tangency point between an indifference curve and the *VDP* curve will differ among individuals. Consider an individual with indifference curve U reflecting his taste for goods as compared with leisure.[9] Point B, where he is working $0C$ hours and being paid BC dollars per day, is his best position, since U is the highest indifference curve consistent with his productive ability.[1]

8. Hebrew being this writer's native language, moving from right to left seems rather natural.

9. The indifference curves reflect not only the choice between leisure and work but also the direct cost of work (such as extra food). An alternative procedure is to work with a *VDP* concept from which this "productive" consumption is netted out. Presumably a slave owner will operate at the maximum point of such a curve.

1. The possibility of multiple tangencies is ignored. The possibility that the indifference curve tangent to the *VDP* curve at B will intersect it to the right of B is important in determining labor-force participation.

How will labor be allocated among firms in the industry? An equilibrium condition here is that the level of hours chosen by every firm will be such that, given the effective wage rate, there is no excess demand or supply at any level of hours. To see this, consider a group of individuals who are currently employed for daily pay and hours as indicated by point *A* but who recently have acquired a taste for leisure so that their indifference curve is tangent to *VDP* at *B*. Since they would be better off at *B*, there will be excess supply of workers at *C* hours (and shortage at the longer hours). Wages for *C* hours will fall, and firms operating at *C* will earn more than normal profits. This will induce additional firms to offer *C* hours rather than the previous level. This process will continue until daily wages for any number of hours are proportionate to the amount of effective labor.[2]

Three major implications stem from the above analysis:

1. As long as tastes are diverse, profit maximization dictates a nonuniformity of hours across firms.

2. *VDP* is the (nonlinear) budget constraint facing the individual who, by selecting the firm to work for, can attain his desired package of daily hours and wages.[3]

3. The observed average hourly wage will differ among those working different numbers of hours and, except by accident (as at point *A*), will not equal the wage for a marginal hour, simply because productivity for the marginal hour is different from that for the average hour.

Employment contracts, we argue, will simultaneously specify daily wages and daily hours. Average hourly wages can, of course, be calculated but have little operational significance. If average wage is less (more) than the value of the marginal hour at equilibrium, employers will not permit employees to work less (more) than the agreed-upon hours at the average rate, and employees will refuse to work additional (fewer) hours at that rate. So when a newspaper reports a labor contract at $3.00 per hour, this should be interpreted at $3.00 per hour for (say) an eight-hour day. In the "small print" of the contract it becomes obvious that the rate does not apply at the margin: overtime rates are usually higher, and no provision is made for fewer hours. More on this later.

It should be emphasized that as long as a worker is on his *VDP*

2. For a more formal demonstration, see Appendix.

3. The nonlinearity of the *VDP* curve is due to the heterogeneity of different hours in terms of effective labor. The similarity of the curve to that obtained when considering the law of variable proportions is accidental.

curve, he is paid according to his marginal product — in the sense of the value of the marginal product along the industry demand curve. The curvature of the budget constraint does not reflect imperfections in the labor market but rather the change in his productive capacity with respect to the hours of the day.

An additional consideration relevant to the total daily product curve is that some costs associated with each worker are not related to the intensity of his work.[4] Such costs shift the daily product curve from *VDP* to *VDP′*, a parallel shift downward by the daily amount of the costs. As a result, the right-hand segment of the *VDP* curve becomes negative and uneconomic. Once such costs are accounted for, the assumption that the demand is for effective labor only is far less restrictive than might have appeared at first sight.

Costs independent of the intensity of work may be incurred by the employer, as frequently happens with on-the-job training, or by the individual worker, as with formal education. In the former case, observed points for hours and wages will fall on the *VDP′* curve; in the latter they will fall on the *VDP* curve. In the final analysis, the *VDP′* is the appropriate curve, since it contains all the relevant costs and represents the net wealth position of the individual.

II. Productivity Changes and Nonlabor Income

The shape of the *VDP* curve is determined by characteristics of the individual worker in relation to his working environment. The height of the curve is determined by the wage per effective unit of labor, and this may change due to changes in the industry demand for labor or supply of labor to it. To analyze the effect of such a change, we make the following assumption: The *relative* shape of the *DP* (or *HP*) curve in Figure I is independent of the scale of output, of factor proportions, and of improvements in labor quality over time. For example, if labor productivity goes up due to an increase in the amount of capital, it is assumed that the change is proportionate for all hours of the day. Consequently a change in the effective wage rate will lead to a proportional vertical shift in

4. A major component of this is the cost of training. Given the expected length of employment, the cost per day (abstracting from the discount factor) is the ratio of total training cost to the expected number of days on the job. This is the factor emphasized by Rosen, "Interindustry Wage and Hours Structure." See also Ronald C. Ehrenberg, "Absenteeism and Overtime Decisions," *American Economic Review*, LX (June 1970), 352–57.

the entire gross *VDP* curve. One such proportional shift is portrayed in Figure III, where, for any given number of hours, the ratio of gross productivity in VDP_1 to that in VDP_0 is constant. Notice that each point on the demand curve of labor is associated with a different *VDP* curve.

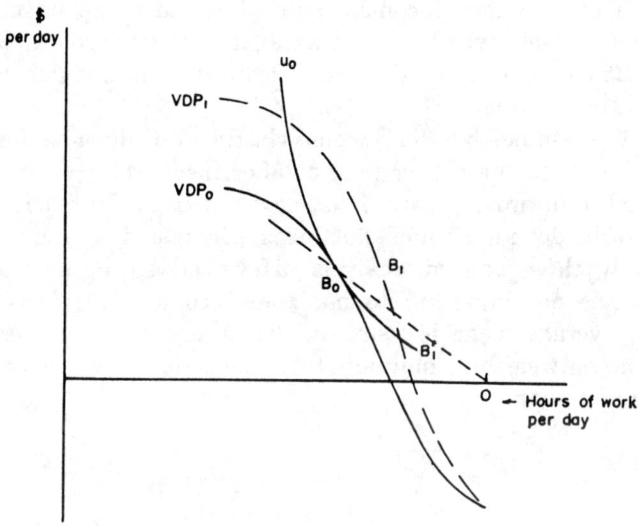

FIGURE III

We want now to explore, at the individual level, the change in the equilibrium daily wages and hours associated with such a productivity change. In Figure III, U_0 is the indifference curve tangent to VDP_0 at B_0. What can be said about B_1, the equilibrium point on VDP_1? Theoretical considerations alone tell us very little; B_1 can be either to the right or to the left of B_0, and hours may either increase or fall, as with the standard analysis. Furthermore, the average wage at B_1 may be *less* than at B_0. This last result is ruled out by assumption when the wage rate is considered as independent of the number of hours worked, since an increase in productivity then necessarily implies an increase in average wage. Here, however, a change in productivity is a change in the entire schedule; while for any given number of hours the average product on the higher curve is above that on the lower one, the new higher schedule contains some points with lower average product than those appearing in the lower schedule. If the income effect of the demand for leisure is strong enough (making all other goods inferior), working hours may be sufficiently reduced to cause a decline in the average product.[5] As can be seen in Figure III, the average hourly wage at B'_1 is less than B_0, and B'_1 cannot a priori be ruled out as a potential point of tangency with an indifference curve higher than U_0.

Labor is not the only income source of an individual. The presence of nonlabor income, assumed to be independent of the *VDP* curve itself, will lead to a parallel shift upwards in the *VDP* curve. The extent of the shift is basically the income per day from the nonwork source.

If we assume that the income elasticity of demand for leisure is positive, then the higher the nonlabor income, the farther to the right is the optimal point. This means that the number of hours worked will decline as nonlabor income increases, a result also obtained by the standard analysis. However, since the wage rate per hour is not invariant to nonlabor income, and if, as will be argued, average wage is rising in the observed range, the shorter hours of the wealthier individual will lead to a lower hourly wage rate for his labor.

III. Overtime

Whereas theoretical considerations alone are not sufficient to determine at which side of A (Figure II) the equilibrium point will lie, knowledge of some overtime practices may help in narrowing the range in which the tangency point actually falls. The employer usually determines the amount and the timing of overtime work. The employee accepts such an arrangement provided that he is paid at a previously agreed-upon rate. Under normal conditions we would expect no overtime work. No point other than B (Figure II) is preferable to the employer and to the employee simultaneously. The latter will insist on achieving an indifference curve no lower than U; the former will demand to stay on *VDP* or below. To justify overtime, either demand for labor or taste for leisure must change. The fact that discretion as to overtime is left with the employer at predetermined terms indicates that the deciding factor is value of the product rather than utility, the change being a (temporary) increase in such value. Since $0C$ hours are already con-

5. Average product may fall also if hours are increased in response to productivity increase. This is even less likely to happen in reality because, if the productivity increase is large, there may be no point on VDP_1 between B_0 and the maximum of VDP_1 with average productivity less than at B_0.

tracted for, the shift in the *VDP* curve will originate at point *B* where overtime starts.

The overtime rate reflects the terms under which the worker is willing to substitute leisure for other commodities, given that the normal length of the working day is 0*C* hours. That overtime rates are substantially above the average hourly pay suggests that at *B* the marginal product is higher than the average product. To see this, suppose that the tangency point is to the left of *A* where the average product exceeds the marginal product. An upward shift in the *VDP* curve will increase the value of the marginal hour, and the employer will be willing to pay a higher *marginal* wage rate. Still, this does not guarantee an overtime rate higher than the previous average rate. Moreover, since overtime work calls for a discrete change in hours, and since, in the range considered, the marginal product is declining, to justify an overtime rate 50 percent above the average rate, the *VDP* curve would have to increase substantially more than 50 percent. On the other hand, if *B* lies to the right of *A* (as drawn in Figure II), marginal product to begin with is higher than average product and is increasing, so even a moderate increase in the *VDP* curve may justify a substantial premium for overtime as compared with average hourly pay. Since we observe that small changes in demand lead to overtime, we may conclude that in all likelihood *B* lies to the right of *A*.[6]

IV. The Effect of Training

The effect of training on the *VDP* curve can be broken into two main components: (1) It will raise the level of the curve, since training makes the individual more productive; as with other changes in productivity, we assume that the entire gross *VDP* curve will shift proportionately upwards. (2) It will reduce the level of the *VDP* curve by a constant amount reflecting training costs as allocated per working day. To the extent that the employee bears the training cost, the question whether training is achieved through formal education or on the job is immaterial for our discussion. An individual will engage in training if thereby he can reach a higher indifference curve.

Suppose for a moment that the optimal training investment

6. Martin S. Feldstein shows that for a cross-section of British industries the elasticity of output with respect to hours is about 1.5–2.0 times larger than that of output with respect to men. Feldstein, "Specification of the Labor Input in the Aggregate Production Function," *Review of Economic Studies,* XXXIV (Oct. 1967), 375–86.

leads to a net shift from VDP_0 to VDP_1 and that VDP intersects VDP_0 at the old optimum point B (see Figure IV). VDP_2 is the new (gross) productivity level, and the training cost is BD. Under the new conditions the individual is still able to purchase the old "basket" of leisure and goods. Given the assumed nature of the shift from VDP_0 to VDP_1, the slope of VDP_2 at D is larger (in absolute value) than that of VDP_0 at B. Since VDP_1 is parallel to VDP_2, VDP_1

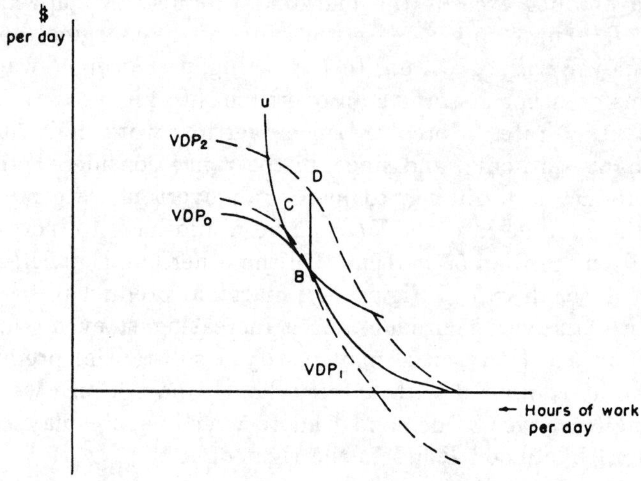

FIGURE IV

is steeper than VDP_0 at B, and the new equilibrium point C is to the left of the old one.[7] Consequently, the new marginal wage rate (at C) is higher than the old one (at B). And if, as suggested above, the average wage is below the marginal wage at B, the move from B to C will also be associated with an increase in the average wage (net of training cost).

The assumption that VDP_0 and VDP_1 intersect at B is equivalent to restricting the effect of training to a substitution effect, since at B the cost and return from training are the same and so the (apparent) income effect is zero. If the cost of training is more than BD, as long as training is worthwhile, the above qualitative result is unchanged. Thus we arrive at the unambiguous result that training that is only marginally profitable will necessarily

7. Lindsay reaches a similar conclusion while using a budget constraint that is linear but does not go through the zero point. C. M. Lindsay, "Measuring Human Capital Returns," *Journal of Political Economy*, LXXIX (Nov./Dec. 1971), 1195–1215.

lead to longer working hours. We now want to allow for training that does generate a positive income effect, as when training costs fall short of *BD*. If leisure is not inferior, the income effect will tend to reduce hours, and the final outcome is ambiguous, as with changes in productivity. It should be borne in mind, however, that training costs dampen the change in income, increasing the likelihood that the substitution effect will dominate. In fact, reasoning in reverse, we may say that a fall in the number of hours worked is consistent with a substantial income effect. The fall in hours during the earlier decades of this century may be the result of such divergence between returns and costs.[8]

V. Minimum Wage and Wage Ceiling

Consider now a legally enforced minimum hourly wage. If the minimum wage is set below the actual hourly wage, it will have no effect. If it is set above the highest possible average wage, no wage is mutually acceptable to both worker and employer, and the worker will be laid off. Since, however, the actual equilibrium point *B* does not represent the highest achievable average wage, a minimum wage above the current wage but below the maximum will not lead to unemployment. This can be seen in Figure V, where the minimum wage, W_{min}, cuts the *VDP* curve at *D* — between *B*, the equilibrium point, and *A*, the highest average point. The area above W_{min} but below the *VDP* curve represents points all acceptable to the employer. The highest indifference curve in this area is the one passing through *D* — the point with the smallest number of hours. Within the employers' acceptable region, competition will then force the number of hours to *D*, the level most preferred by employees. Given the minimum wage constraint, *D* is therefore the equilibrium point, and the minimum wage will result in a larger number of hours. Still, *D* lies on a lower indifference curve than *B*. Note that the minimum wage will lead to fewer hours if *B* lies to the left of *A*. Note also that in both cases zero hours may be the *chosen* point.

The possibility that a minimum wage law will increase the

8. Carroll and Ihnen show that the private rate of return to some technical schooling was 25.9 percent and that graduates of the technical school worked 2.7 hours per week less than graduates of secondary school. This indicates to us that with such a high rate of return, the income effect was dominant; hourly wages, however, are not given. A. B. Carroll and L. A. Ihnen, "Costs and Returns of Postsecondary Technical Schooling," *Journal of Political Economy*, LXXV (Dec. 1967), 862–73.

number of hours of some workers changes another result of the standard analysis.[9] Figure VI draws the demand and supply curves

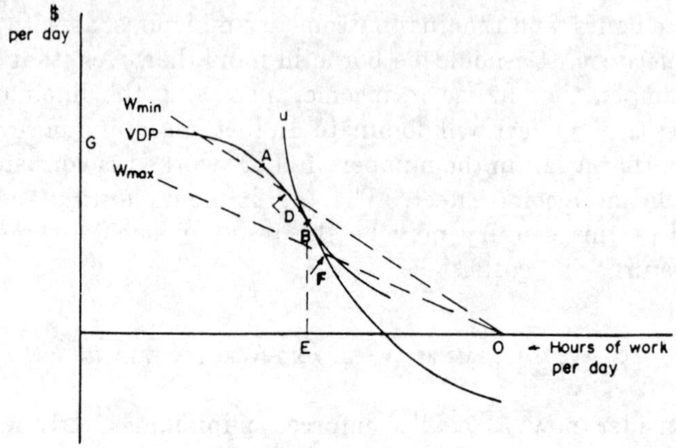

FIGURE V

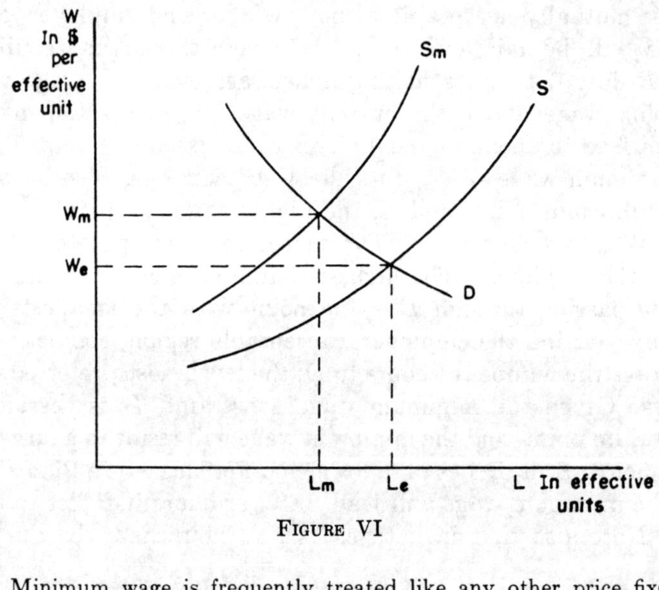

FIGURE VI

9. Minimum wage is frequently treated like any other price fixed at a level above the market price and resulting in excess supply or unemployment. This analysis is not entirely satisfactory where the productivity and wages of different workers vary greatly. If we do not account for quality differences, it would appear that the unemployed workers are as productive as those that remain employed. But when quality differences are acknowledged, it becomes clear that the minimum wage most probably acts to the detriment of those with low productivity. As previously noted, the analysis in the text is labeled "standard" in the sense of considering wage for an individual as independent of his hours.

of labor with labor measured in efficiency units rather than in actual man-hours. For every wage level in efficiency units, the actual wage per hour has to be calculated for each worker. By standard analysis those whose actual hourly wage is below the minimum are excluded from S. A minimum wage law, then, will shift the supply curve from S to S_m to exclude those who do not meet the minimum wage criterion. With a shift in supply to S_m, employment will decline from L_e to L_m, and the wage rate of the remaining workers will rise from W_e to W_m.

But once it is recognized that (average) hourly wage is itself a function of the number of hours and that, as indicated above, for some workers a minimum wage will lead to an increase in the number of work hours, the shift in supply is not fully accounted for by S_m. The net shift depends on the relative importance of two opposing influences: some workers are totally excluded from the market while others offer a larger number of hours at the minimum wage. In the absence of empirical evidence as to the relative strength of the two influences, the conclusion is unwarranted that wages will rise for those workers whose initial wages are above the minimum.[1]

We now analyze a wage rate ceiling such as may be imposed in an attempt to counter inflation. Again, theoretical considerations alone are insufficient to determine the direction of the change. An effective wage ceiling has to pass below B and, as shown in Figure V, will cut the *VDP* curve at three points: at zero hours of work; at F, which lies between 0 and B; and at G, to the left of B. To the employer, the zero point and any point on the line segment *DF* will be acceptable. Which will be preferred by the worker is impossible to say on a priori grounds.[2] In general, it will be advantageous to both employer and employee to report and pay wages for more hours than the actual ones. One way of achieving this is by upgrading workers. But if the wage ceiling is literally adhered to, the attempt to fight inflation or to reduce the pecuniary cost of war pro-

1. Support for minimum wage legislation by highly productive workers suggests that the shift in the conventional supply curve is the dominant influence. Since minimum wages usually apply to broad categories of workers, it is not entirely appropriate to assume that the *VDP* curve will not shift along with the shift in the general wage level.

2. If the preferred point lies between F and G, the value of the labor is higher than its pay, and producers have an incentive to expand output. If they are able to expand, output will increase, resulting in a fall in product prices and in the value of the marginal productivity of labor, thereby shifting down the entire *VDP* curve. This process will continue until the *VDP* curve cuts the ceiling wage line at its point of tangency with an indifference curve. The analysis is further complicated by the fact that at the ceiling wage rate a labor "shortage" may arise, and the desired output expansion may not materialize.

duction may result in a reduction in output from that achieved at *B*.

VI. Some Aspects of Market Demand and Supply

As we move down along the demand curve for efficient units of labor, the increase in quantity will be met by some combination of changes in number of man-days and in hours and efficiency per man-day. As we have already seen, it is not possible to say a priori what will happen to the equilibrium number of hours as the *VDP* curve shifts down. One possibility is that the number of hours will increase sufficiently so that fewer man-days will be demanded. In the United States, where the eight-hour day (and forty-hour week) have been the rule for the last three decades, a move along the demand curve of labor will probably be accompanied with a change in the number of man-days, with hours per day remaining constant.[3] For the earlier part of the century in the United States, and in many other countries today, an upward move along the demand curve may be accompanied by shorter hours, in which case it is not possible to determine the direction of change in the number of man-days demanded.

When considering supply conditions, the units employed should be the same as those used for demand. Consequently, any consideration of man-hours and man-days must take into account the efficiency of different hours. That this determination of hours per day combines considerations of demand (productivity) and of supply (utility) needs no further discussion. A couple of labor force participation considerations are, however, needed here. For the unattached individual, an upward shift in the *VDP* curve (i.e., in the objective conditions facing him) unambiguously implies a larger likelihood of labor force participation. But a change in market opportunities for one member in a family may affect the labor-leisure choice of others. In particular we cannot rule out such possibilities as that an upward shift in the *VDP* curve for both husband and wife may cause the wife to quit her job in spite of the improved terms of work. This sort of analysis, however, cannot be applied to the economy as a whole, since the supply curve reflects conditions at a point in time and under a given total productive capacity in the economy, whereas an increase in *all VDP* curves must reflect an increase in this capacity.[4]

3. The income effect is probably stronger than implied above, since it may account for the reduction in the number of days worked per year.

4. By the same token, there is scant theoretical basis for the backward

The upshot of this discussion on market demand and supply is that labor's unique characteristics preclude any such straightforward qualitative statements as can be made regarding, say, the effect of taxing a commodity on its equilibrium quantity and price. Work itself is an argument in the individual's utility function, and productivity per hour and value of labor change with the hours offered by the individual.

VII. Concluding Remarks

If, as asserted in this paper, labor productivity changes with the number of daily hours, the use of the average hourly wage as a measure of labor's marginal productivity is inappropriate. It should be replaced with a whole function relating total daily wages to total daily hours, where the average hourly wage does not, in general, equal the wage for the marginal hour.

This inequality invalidates a number of major implications of the standard analysis that assume that the two are identical. For instance, by standard analysis a minimum wage law would unambiguously result in an increase in the wage level of those remaining employed; it is here indicated that this is not a necessary result. Again, since the model suggests that productivity of the last hour of a "normal" day exceeds average productivity, the shorter the hours individuals choose to work, the lower the average hourly rate. Thus, part-time workers such as women, students, and wealthier persons will be paid a low rate rather than the full-time workers' rate as implied by standard analysis. We also cannot rule out, a priori, the possibility of a fall in the average wage resulting from an increase in labor productivity. These results are testable, as are other implications of the analysis in this paper that differ from those of the standard analysis; consequently the relative merits of the two are subject to empirical determination.

Appendix [5]

The Individual's Supply

The individual has a utility function

$$U = U(C, L),$$

bending portion of the supply curve of labor for the labor market as a whole. The historical evidence actually portraying the shape of the curve as a negative slope with no bend was obtained when the productivity of the economy was not held constant but was rising substantially.

5. I am greatly indebted to R. J. McDonald for his help with the Appendix.

where C is commodities and L is leisure. He possesses time (twenty-four hours a day) and some initial assets providing a daily flow of income, A.

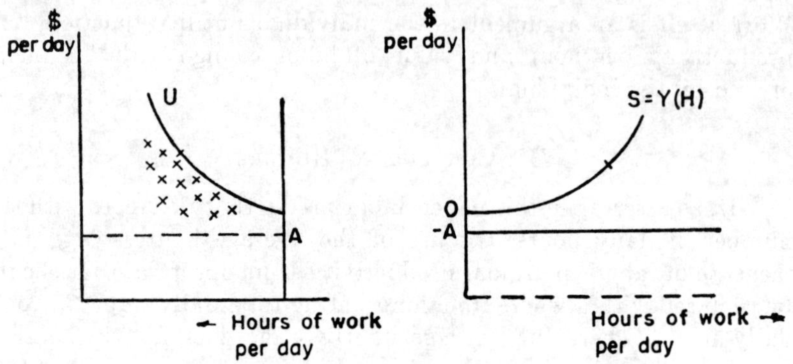

FIGURE VII(a) and VII(b)

The opportunities open to the individual in the labor market are composed of points, one to a firm, where the coordinates of a point indicate the daily number of dollars a firm is willing to pay the individual in exchange for a given number of hours of work per day. This is illustrated in Figure VII(a). U is the highest indifference curve passing through any of the points, and this point will be the chosen employment.[6]

$S=Y(H)$ in Figure VII(b) is the number of hours the individual is willing to supply to the chosen employer at different levels of total daily pay. This curve is a mirror image of the indifference curve in Figure VII(a) (after deducting asset income). Given that the indifference curve has a negative slope throughout, the curve $Y(H)$ slopes up monotonically; its slope $\frac{dY}{dH}$ is (minus) the marginal rate of substitution between money income (commodities) and leisure. When converted to dollars per hour, it provides a constant real income supply curve, which has a positive slope throughout due to the convexity of the indifference curve.

The Firm

The firm that buys factors and sells its product in perfectly competitive markets is a profit maximizer. Its production function is given by $Q=F(\sum_{i=1}^{M} Ei(Hi), K)$, where K is the capital stock (or any other factor), Hi is the number of hours of the ith employee,

6. Note that a change in conditions leading to a change in employment will normally involve a finite change in hours of work per day.

$Ei(Hi)$ is the effectiveness or productivity of the employee for the given number of hours, and M is the number of employees. We define total labor input, L (and implicitly the notion of effectiveness or productivity), as

$$L = \sum_{i=1}^{M} Ei(Hi),$$

so that the production function is now the traditional $Q = F(L, K)$. The profit function is

$$\pi = P_q F(L, K) - \sum_{i=1}^{M} Yi(Hi) - P_k K,$$

where P_q is the price of output and P_k is the price of capital.

We now assume that within the labor supply facing a single firm all workers are identical both in productivity (so that $Ei(Hi) = E(H)$) and in their supply functions (so that $Yi(Hi) = Y(H)$). We can then write

$$\pi = \pi(H, M, K) = P_q F(M \cdot E(H), K) - MY(H) - P_k K.$$

Necessary conditions for maximum are

$$\text{(A)} \quad \frac{\partial \pi}{\partial H} = P_q \cdot F_L(L, K) \cdot M \cdot E'(H) - M \cdot Y'(H) = 0$$

$$\text{(B)} \quad \frac{\partial \pi}{\partial M} = P_q \cdot F_L(L, K) \cdot E(H) - Y(H) = 0$$

$$\text{(C)} \quad \frac{\partial \pi}{\partial K} = P_q F_k(L, K) - P_k = 0.$$

For $M \neq 0$ we can rewrite (A) as

$$P_q \cdot F_L(L, K) E'(H) = Y'(H).$$

The value of the marginal hour to each worker (in terms of commodities) has to equal the contribution of the marginal hour to the value of output. We can write condition (B) as

$$P_q F_L(L, K) \cdot E(H) = Y(H),$$

indicating that the pay to a marginal (full-time) worker is equal to his contribution to output.[7]

Considerations of second-order conditions indicate that we cannot rule out the possibility of multiple tangencies between $E(H)$ and $Y(H)$ and that we have to watch for tangencies that are at the minimum rather than the maximum point; this could happen in the region of increasing returns to the $E(H)$ function. Specifically, in addition to the standard concavity assumptions on the production function $F(L, K)$, we must have $P_Q E''(H) F_L(L, K) < Y''(H)$.

Finally, it is possible to show that a change in product price will result in a change in M but not in H. This is because M can be augmented at a constant cost, but increasing H requires a move along the individual's upward sloping curve $Y(H)$, which increases (at equilibrium) at a higher rate than $E(H)$.

7. We abstract here from the fact that M has to take integral values.

The Industry

We wish to determine the relative rate of pay for workers working different numbers of hours. We assume that while both tastes and productivity vary among workers, the industry considered contains so many firms that each is able to secure a work force of identical workers,[8] and that each firm operates as a price taker in the labor market. All firms also have the same production function and obtain their capital from a single capital market.

Suppose now that firm j earns a positive (net) profit while all other firms earn zero profits. Given that in its segment of the labor market the supply point is $Y_j(H_j)$, the firm will employ labor to satisfy its marginal condition

$$P_q F_L(L_j, K_j) E_j(H_j) = Y_j(H_j).$$

Now, if conditions in the labor market are such that pay of each type of labor is proportionate to its productivity, i.e.,

$$\frac{Y_j(H_j)}{Y_k(H_k)} = \frac{E_j(H_j)}{E_k(H_k)},$$

where k is some other firm in the industry, then F_L has to be the same for both firms, since firm k will operate where

$$P_q F_L(L_k, K_k) E_k(H_k) = Y_k(H_k)$$

and since P_c, P_q, and F are common to both firms. Similarly, it is easy to show that F_K is the same to both, and the two combined imply that the relation $L_j = L_k$ has to hold.[9] But then both revenues and factor payments are the same to the two firms, and firm j cannot earn a positive profit. So positive profits imply that the equality

$$\frac{Y_j(H_j)}{Y_k(H_k)} = \frac{E_j(H_j)}{E_k(H_k)},$$

cannot hold. Conversely, when the equality does not hold and positive profits are present, new firms will enter the "cheap labor" segment of the market and bid up the wage payment until the ratio of pay to productivity in this segment of the market is the same as in all others.

Notice that the above process will generate for all workers with the same $E(H)$ an opportunity set composed of points on $E(H)$, a point to each firm catering to that segment of the labor force. These points constitute a subset of that presented in Figure VII(a). The rest of the points in that diagram represent opportunities in other industries.

The above is a condition relating a whole day's pay to a whole

8. Or a narrow enough range of workers so that the differences within its work force can be ignored.

9. If the production function is homogeneous of degree one in L and K, then $\frac{L_j}{K_j} = \frac{L_k}{K_k}$ rather than $L_j = L_k$ has to hold, but the final conclusions are not changed.

day of work. A similar condition has to hold for a marginal change in hours. For a single individual we have

$$\frac{E'_j(H_j)}{E_j(H_j)} = \frac{Y'_j(H_j)}{Y_j(H_j)},$$

and, given the above market equality for whole days, we have to have

$$\frac{Y'_j(H_j)}{E'_j(H_j)} = \frac{Y'_k(H_k)}{E'_k(H_k)}$$

or equivalently

$$\frac{Y'_j(H_j)}{Y'_k(H_k)} = \frac{E'_j(H_j)}{E'_k(H_k)}.$$

The ratio of pay to productivity for the marginal hour, then, has to be equal across individuals in the industry.

UNIVERSITY OF WASHINGTON

[10]

Assets, Subsistence, and The Supply Curve of Labor

By YORAM BARZEL AND RICHARD J. McDONALD*

The "backward bending" supply curve of labor is now accepted as a matter of course by most economists. It has no doubt been perplexing to observe that the most commonly employed types of utility functions do not yield such curves under the usual textbook analysis of the problem.[1] Particular preference maps have been found that generate backward bending curves;[2] however, they are nonparametric, leading to difficulties of estimation, and upon closer examination seem to imply counter-intuitive results. We will show that taking into account the wealth position of an individual on the one hand and survival consideration on the other greatly expands the variety of shapes that can be derived for the supply curve from some simple utility functions. The use of a specific simple utility function also implies some severe restrictions on the form the supply curve can take, rendering it testable. Empirical evidence is shown to support the conclusion that the supply curve is monotonic. We will also show that the notion that the aggregate supply curve of labor slopes down rests, in part, on an error of aggregation, and that the empirical evidence usually cited in support of the negative slope, when correctly interpreted, cannot be so construed.

I. The Supply Curve of the Individual

A curious method is commonly employed to derive the accepted shape of the supply curve of labor. The typical text first points out (following Lionel Robbins) that a wage change results in an income as well as a substitution effect and, noting the importance of leisure in the individual budget, concludes reasonably enough that the supply curve may, in some of its range, have a negative slope. But then the discussion proceeds without further analysis to suggest something about a turning point in the curve—that the curve will turn back only after an initial positive slope. In Milton Friedman's words, ". . . *beyond* some point the income effect dominates the substitution effect" (1966, p. 204, italics added) and the change in sign is explained by the statement that ". . . in a primitive society, the initial low wage rate at which the income effect becomes dominant reflects a lack of familiarity with market goods and a limited range of tastes. As tastes develop and knowledge spreads, the point at which the income effect dominates tends to rise." The sign change seems to apply only to a primitive society, the value at which this occurs seems to shift around, and its explanation is rather lame. Although Friedman is only one of many economists to accept uncritically the backward bending shape of the supply curve,[3] his argument is singled out precisely because of his usual astuteness and the advanced nature of the text.[4]

* University of Washington. Some of the work on this paper was done while Barzel was visiting University College, London, supported by a Ford Foundation Fellowship.

[1] For example, a Cobb-Douglas utility function yields a perfectly inelastic supply curve.

[2] See, for example, Giora Hanoch.

[3] J. R. Hicks apparently was the first to introduce the backward bend, but he failed to offer any satisfactory explanation.

[4] To cite one more example, Paul Samuelson in his elementary text also subscribes to the backward bending shape of the supply curve.

Consider now a point on the supply curve of labor and observe what happens to the income change due to *successive* wage increases. The effect of the first wage increase is independent of whether the supply curve at that point has a positive or a negative slope, not those of the second and subsequent wage changes. If the supply curve has a positive slope, the number of hours affected by subsequent wage changes is larger and, other things equal, the income effect tends to grow stronger and stronger.[5] The converse will occur if the income effect dominates in the first place, rendering the slope of the supply curve negative. These "self-correcting" tendencies give some basis for expecting the supply curve to eventually become vertical.

The asset holdings of the individual play an important (and thus far largely neglected) role in determining the shape of the supply curve of labor.[6] If we consider an extremely wealthy individual, it seems intuitively clear that as long as work itself is not a commodity, no labor will be offered at the lowest range of wages; assuming continuity of preferences and the absence of indivisibilities, an infinitesimal amount will be supplied at the point of entry into the labor market. From there, at least for awhile, the curve *has* to slope upwards.

On the other hand, for an individual with no wealth whatsoever and no income source other than his own work, the very lowest wage will be insufficient for survival. As wages increase, a point will be reached where survival becomes possible if he supplies the highest physically possible amount of labor. For such an individual, as the wage rate continues to rise, the amount of labor supplied *cannot* increase; given that leisure is a commodity, the supply curve has to have a negative slope right from its *very beginning*. It will be suggested in the following analysis that we predominantly observe just such an initially negatively sloped curve eventually tending to become perfectly inelastic.

To proceed with the formal analysis, we consider an individual who derives satisfaction from the consumption of two goods: market purchased commodities, denoted by C, and leisure, denoted by R. Assume that the preferences of the individual can be characterized by a function $f(C', R')$, which at a point (C', R') in the commodity space indicates the individual's marginal rate of substitution between the two commodities at that point.

That is,

$$\frac{dC'}{dR'} = -f(C', R')$$

for small movements leaving the consumer as well off as he was before. The accepted range of this function is for $C', R' \geq 0$. But it should be recognized that unless some positive level of consumption of C is reached, survival is not possible, and so for some positive values of C a preference map cannot be said to exist. Similarly, survival considerations may dictate a certain minimal level of leisure (or rest) time. Notice that the roles played by the two survival requirements are not symmetric since all individuals are endowed with more time than is needed for survival but not all have sufficient assets for survival. Denote by S the minimal required consumption of goods per day, and by T the minimal required leisure time and define C and R as $C=C'-S$ and $R=R'-T$. We now assume that the arguments in the marginal rate of substitution are C and R so that

[5] Of course, it is possible that as wages rise the rate of change of labor supply, with respect to a change in income, may change sufficiently to negate this tendency.

[6] Kenneth Boulding notes the role of assets but does not proceed to examine it fully (pp. 800–01). He, too, draws a backward bending supply curve of labor even though his illustrations (pp. 210–11) demonstrate only a negative slope and not a turning point.

$$\frac{dC}{dR} = -f(C, R) \tag{1}$$

along an indifference curve, for C, $R>0$. This transformation, while innocuous as long as f is not further specified, is a substantive one once specific properties are assumed for the preference map, as we shall do below. We also assume that $f(C, R)$ is positive, differentiable, and that preferences are characterized by a diminishing marginal rate of substitution. Thus

$$\frac{d^2C}{dR^2} = f(C, R)f_1(C, R) - f_2(C, R) > 0 \tag{2}$$

for movements along an indifference curve, and for all C, $R>0$, where f_1 and f_2 are, respectively, the partial derivatives of f with respect to C and R.

The individual is subject to constraints on time and expenditures. The time constraint is $R+T+L=D=24$, where D is the length of the day and L is labor hours.[7] Given the notion of required rest time, it is more convenient to write the constraint as

$$R + L = D - T = D' \tag{3}$$

where D' is the fixed number of hours whose composition can be allocated to leisure or labor.

The expenditure constraint is $Y=WL+PA=PC'$, where Y is money income, W is the money wage rate (or the shadow wage if the individual is self-employed), P is the price of market commodities, and A is per day nonwage income in units of consumption goods. By rearranging and substituting from (3) for L, we get

$$C + wR = wD' + A - S \tag{4}$$

where $w=W/P$. Equation (4) has as its variables C and R, the two arguments in the marginal rate of substitution. Notice that if $wD'<S-A$, then even if the individual works the physically maximum number of hours, he will not earn enough to survive. In other words, unless the condition

$$w > \frac{S - A}{D'} \tag{5}$$

is satisfied, C and R cannot both be positive, and the function f is not defined.

We assume that the individual chooses the most preferred combination that he can attain, given that he is able to survive.[8] Necessary and sufficient conditions for this to be the bundle (C_0, R_0), given (5), are that C_0 and R_0 satisfy the equations (2) and (4), together with

$$f(C_0, R_0) = w \tag{6}$$

This last condition is independent of the transformation previously imposed on the origin of the function f.

Comparative statics results can be obtained by differentiating conditions (4) and (6) partially, first with respect to A and then with respect to w. The resulting slopes of the demands for consumption and leisure with respect to the wage rate are

$$\frac{\partial C}{\partial w} = f/(ff_1 - f_2) + (D' - R)\frac{\partial C}{\partial A} \tag{7}$$

$$\frac{\partial R}{\partial w} = -1/(ff_1 - f_2) + (D' - R)\frac{\partial R}{\partial A} \tag{8}$$

Now we want to concentrate on the effects of wage changes on the quantity of labor supplied. Because of equation (3) we can write

$$\frac{\partial L}{\partial w} = 1/(ff_1 - f_2) - (D' - R)\frac{\partial R}{\partial A} \tag{9}$$

The first term of the right-hand side of

[7] No substantive change is involved if we carry the analysis in terms of some other time unit, such as a week or a year. More importantly, our analysis is equally relevant to market-employed as to self-employed individuals.

[8] If $wD'=(S-A)$, the consumer will thus choose $C=0$, $L=D'$ rather than to work less and starve.

(9) is the pure substitution effect and is necessarily positive, due to the convexity of the preference map. The second term, assuming that leisure is not an inferior commodity, is also positive but is preceded by a minus sign. It is clear from this formulation that without further specification of the consumer's preferences, it is impossible to say which of the two effects will dominate.[9] Notice, however, that if we are in a region where the income effect dominates, as w increases the term $(D'-R')$ is declining, tending to diminish the strength of the entire income term. The converse is true if the substitution effect dominates.

We now introduce a more specific form of the consumer's preference. This will allow more definite and more readily refutable empirical implications. The more detailed specifications will be introduced in two steps. First, the function $f(C, R)$ will be restricted to be homothetic. In this case the marginal rate of substitution between (net) consumption and leisure is a function only of the ratio in which the two goods are consumed. Equation (9) can now be rewritten as

$$\frac{\partial L}{\partial w}=\frac{1}{w}\,\frac{R}{(C+wR)}\,[C(\sigma-1)+(A-S)] \tag{10}$$

where σ is the elasticity of substitution between net consumption and net leisure.[10] So the slope of the supply curve depends on the signs of $(\sigma-1)$ and of $(A-S)$.[11] In the special case $\sigma=1$, where the preferences imply a Cobb-Douglas type of utility function, the sign of the slope of the supply curve hinges entirely on the sign of $(A-S)$. In general σ need not be constant but will vary with the ratio C/R. Letting $x=C/R$, it can be shown that

$$\frac{\partial\sigma}{\partial w}=\frac{1}{x}\,(1-\sigma-\sigma\epsilon)$$

where ϵ (itself a function of x) is defined by

$$\epsilon=\frac{h''(x)\cdot x}{h'(x)}$$

and $h(x)$ is the marginal rate of substitution as defined in the Appendix. Then, using the definition of σ, we have

$$\frac{\partial\sigma}{\partial w}=\frac{\sigma}{w}\,(1-\sigma-\sigma\epsilon)$$

and since our assumptions about the preference map impose no restrictions on the sign or magnitude of ϵ, nothing a priori can be said about the direction of change of σ as wages vary. Thus, if we do not restrict σ to a constant value, the supply curve can assume virtually any shape and therefore will have no testable implications.

The second step in specifying preferences, then, is to constrain σ to a constant value. This will also further simplify matters and allow for easy graphical interpretation. The marginal rate of substitution takes the particular form

$$f(C, R)=\left(\frac{1-\alpha}{\alpha}\right)\left(\frac{C}{R}\right)^{1/\sigma} \tag{11}$$

where $0<\alpha<1$.[12] The above assumptions

[9] If consumption C is assumed to be a normal good, then the demand for it (with respect to w) must be positively sloped, due to the restriction that the individual can consume no more than D' hours of leisure.

[10] See the Appendix.

[11] The terms in the square brackets in (10) are grouped differently than is conventional. Since $A-S-C=-wL$, these terms represent the income effect, while $C\sigma$ represents the substitution effect.

[12] Equation (11) would follow from any monotonically increasing function of the *CES* utility function.

$$V(C, R)=[\alpha C^{-\beta}+(1-\alpha)R^{-\beta}]^{-1/\beta}\qquad \text{for } \beta\neq 0$$

$$V(C, R)=C^{\alpha}R^{1-\alpha}\qquad \text{for } \beta=0$$

defined for $0<\alpha<1$ and $-1<\beta<\infty$. The elasticity of substitution is then equal to $1/(1+\beta)$. This specification is a generalization of the class of utility functions generating the so-called linear expenditure system of demand equations introduced by Laurence Klein and Herman Rubin, and more recently adopted by Richard Stone.

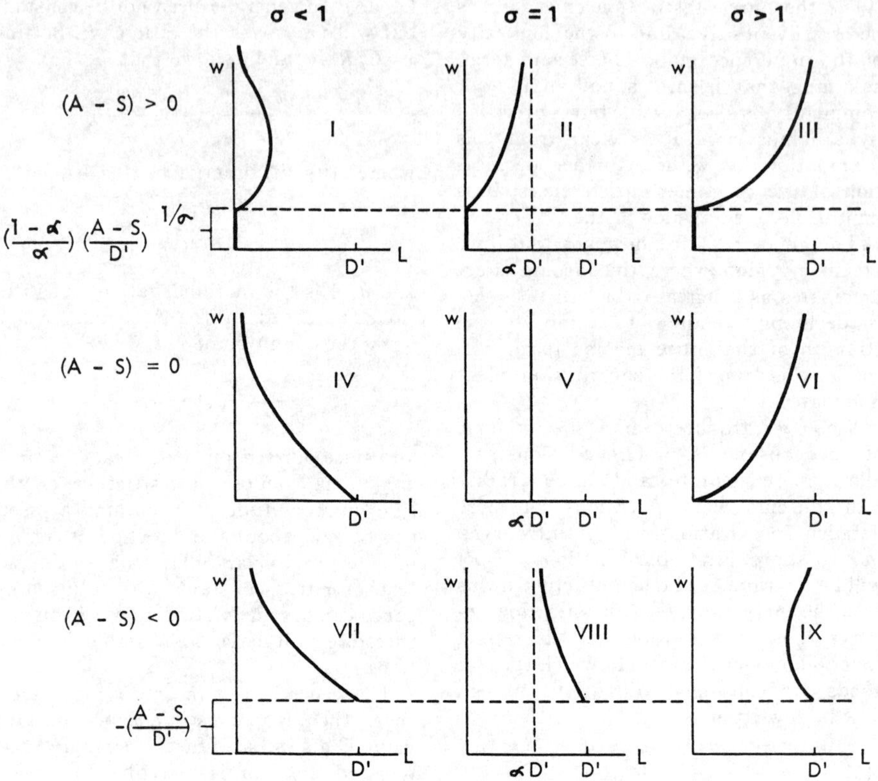

FIGURE 1

may appear to be highly restrictive; nevertheless, depending on the signs of $(\sigma-1)$ and $(A-S)$, we get the textbook characterizations of the supply curve as well as some novel ones.

The nine panels in Figure 1 are drawn for cases where $\sigma \gtreqless 1$ in combination with $(A-S) \gtreqless 0$. This set of diagrams gives us a whole gamut of possible results—monotonically rising and falling, perfectly inelastic, and both backward and forward bending. So the assumptions made regarding the form of the preference map do not turn out to be as restrictive as might first appear.[13] Notice that in the three figures with $(A-S)<0$ the supply curve is not defined for wage rates below $(S-A)/D'$.

The second row of panels (IV–VI) where $A-S=0$ corresponds to the conventional treatment of the supply of labor where both A and S are implicitly assumed equal to zero. It is easy to see, by comparing the second row with the first and with the third, the crucial importance of these two

[13] One important restriction is the linearity of the Engel curves. See Samuelson (1948). Given our subsistence requirements, the Engel curves do not necessarily go through the origin.

factors.[14] If assets are large enough, the supply curve will always have an initial region with a positive slope (and will be monotonic for $\sigma \geq 1$). If assets alone are insufficient to provide for survival, the supply curve will always slope negatively initially (and will be monotonic for $\sigma \leq 1$).[15] Consider an individual possessing no income source other than his own labor. If we do not explicitly take into account survival considerations, then the second row will appear pertinent. An individual with a utility function leading to $\sigma > 1$ would, at the lower wage range, then prefer to die from starvation rather than to earn enough for survival. This absurd result points to the reasonableness of transforming the preference function as we did.

There is no a priori reason to accept any one of these cases. It is important to note, however, that since few individuals, even in Western countries, start their working career with asset holdings sufficient for survival, the third row of diagrams represents the wealth conditions of most individuals. For some individuals, however, $A > S$; for those, we should observe, at least in part of the range, a positive relation between wages and hours, and in such cases the vertical intercept itself will rise with the level of asset holdings. It will be shown that empirical evidence conforms closely to the *C-D* case illustrated in Panel VIII.

II. The Negative Income Tax and the Supply of Labor

The preceding analysis can easily be adapted to determine the effects on the supply of labor of a variety of tax and transfer schemes. Of current interest are those tagged as "guaranteed annual income" or "negative income tax." Under most of these the individual whose income exceeds some "break-even" level, denoted here by Y_b, is being taxed and the individual whose income falls short of that level is being subsidized. For simplicity let us assume that the marginal rate of tax does not vary with income, that is, the rate of tax (which is also the rate of subsidy) is constant. If we denote this rate by t, the floor on income is tY_b.

The disposable income available to the individual, denoted by Y_d, is given then by

$$Y_d = Y + t(Y_b - Y) \tag{12}$$

where $Y = wL + A$. The budget constraint now becomes, after manipulations similar to those used to derive (4),

$$C + (1-t)wR = (1-t)(wD' + A) + tY_b - S \tag{13}$$

$$= (1-t)wD' + (A - S) + t(Y_b - A) \tag{13'}$$

The condition for an interior maximum is now

$$f(C, R) = (1-t)w \tag{14}$$

Again, assume the preference map to be homothetic, then the same comparative static techniques used to derive (10) give us

$$\frac{\partial L}{\partial w} = \frac{1}{w}\,\frac{R}{[C + (1-t)wR]}\{C(\sigma - 1) + [(1-t)A - (S - tY_b)]\} \tag{15}$$

This result is essentially the same as (10), with the wage rate deflated by the tax (and subsidy) rate, and with the term in the square brackets corresponding to $[A - S]$ in (10). The term $(1-t)A$ is net-of-tax nonwage income, and $(S - tY_B)$ is the portion of subsistence not covered by

[14] In analyzing the labor-leisure problem many authors implicitly assume that labor is the only source of income. As can be seen by comparing the second with the first (and third) row of diagrams, this may result in a serious error.

[15] An important omission in our analysis is the possibility that an individual may be able to forestall starvation by consuming part of his stock of wealth in addition to the flow of income resulting from it. This is, of course, only a short-run solution. A fuller treatment of this problem would require bringing time considerations explicitly into the analysis.

the guaranteed minimum income. As before, the sign of the term in the outer brackets determines the sign of $\partial L/\partial w$. For the case where $\sigma = 1$, the supply curve is positively sloped if net nonlabor income exceeds the "net" subsistence term. It is not possible to determine a priori the effect of the tax plan on this final term, since the tax lowers net nonlabor income while the existence of the income floor weakens the force of the survival requirements.

Given, however, the notion of a minimum survival requirement, it would seem that if a guaranteed income has any meaning at all, it has to at least suffice for survival. We want, then, to examine the case where $tY_b \geq S$. The terms in square brackets in equation (15) must then be positive. The possible cases then reduce to those in the first row of Figure 1 (with trivial modifications in interpretation of the terms). The supply curve will always slope upwards initially, and may slope upwards throughout. Only when σ is sufficiently less than one is it possible for the labor supply to turn into a negatively sloping curve.

To understand the effects of the plan more completely, it is helpful to find the effect of a change in the tax rate on the supply of labor. This can be done by differentiating equations (13) and (14) partially with respect to the tax rate t. The result of these operations is shown in equation (16).

$$\frac{\partial L}{\partial t} = \frac{R[C(1-\sigma) + (S - Y_b)]}{(1-t)[C + (1-t)wR]} \tag{16}$$

Again the effect on the labor supply cannot be determined a priori, and it would take another series of nine figures to depict all of the possibilities. Notice that it is the break-even level of income, and not the floor (tY_b) on income, that is opposed to survival consumption S. Since the break-even level Y_b must be greater than the floor tY_b, and the floor in turn must exceed subsistence (see preceding paragraph), it is plausible that the break-even level will exceed subsistence. If this is the case, the effect of an increase in the tax (and subsidy) rate will be to decrease the labor supply (unless σ is sufficiently smaller than unity). Note also that at $Y = Y_b$ the tax is zero; consequently, for $Y = Y_b$ a change in the tax rate leads to a substitution effect but not to an income effect. As a final result, the partial effect of changes in the level of break-even income on labor supply can be found to be

$$\frac{\partial L}{\partial Y_b} = \frac{-tR}{[C + (1-t)wR]} \tag{17}$$

which is negative, given that $0 < t < 1$.

III. The Aggregate Supply Curve

The individual's demand for leisure is derived under the assumption that (in competition) the wage rate is an exogenously determined parameter; a change in the wage rate will lead to an income or wealth effect, in addition to the substitution effect. The central interest in this paper is with the uncompensated demand curve. So the demand for leisure in (8) and subsequently contains both a substitution and an income effect. It is well known that when considering the aggregate demand for a commodity, price is an endogenously determined parameter and, more importantly, that the net wealth effect will tend to zero. This recognition is one of the major contributions of general equilibrium analysis. Milton Friedman (1949) and subsequently Martin Bailey, in identically titled articles, "The Marshallian Demand Curve," both stress that in the aggregate, at a point in time, wealth effects tend to wash out due to the constraint imposed by the resource endowment of the economy. And in the absence of wealth effects, no Giffen goods are possible, and the aggregate demand curve for leisure, as for any other good, has to slope down throughout.[16] But elsewhere in their writings, when drawing the supply curve of labor, both Friedman and Bailey allow for a negatively sloped portion of the curve. Friedman (1966) does not specify the level of aggregation, but Bailey (1962) clearly discusses the economy-wide supply curve of labor.

A possible explanation for such inconsistency is that empirical evidence strongly indicates a negative relation between the wage rate and the supply of labor. To the extent that this relation is observed in cross-sections, it is usually obtained for subgroups in truly partial equilibrium settings, and the evidence is not pertinent in determining the shape of the aggregate relation. As for time-series, the *ceteris paribus* is clearly violated. Comparisons are made between points in time for which the total productive capacity of the economy is not held constant. In other words, over time we observe not only the substitution due to an increase in real wages but also the effects of a net increase in real wealth. The wealth increase is not the result of the change in wage; if anything, it is the cause of the change in wage. Under these conditions, a negative relation between the quantity of labor supplied and the wage rate is easily understood, but this does not reflect on the slope of the supply curve at a point in time where wealth is constant.

This is not to imply that the aggregate supply curve of labor can never slope downwards or that (in the aggregate) Giffen goods can never be observed. These phenomena are not ruled out on a priori grounds, but may occur only under much more stringent conditions than usually specified. Suppose that the proceeds of a tax imposed on capital are used to subsidize labor. The relative price of labor will increase, and individuals supplying labor will experience positive wealth effects. On this account, the slope of the supply curve may become negative. On the other hand, individuals, in their capacity as owners of capital, will experience negative wealth effects and will demand less leisure and offer more labor services. For an individual whose capital holdings are exactly proportionate to the quantity of labor he supplies, the two income effects will cancel out. The other extreme is where all but one individual have no capital whatsoever while a single individual owns the entire capital stock of the economy. The wealthy owner will increase his labor supply as a result of the decline in his wealth by at most twenty-four hours a day. Since his contribution will be a minute fraction of the total, the aggregate supply curve can easily be negatively sloped. The actual situation is somewhere in between these two extremes and while the notion that the aggregate supply curve may slope down at a point in time is greatly weakened, it cannot be entirely rejected on a priori grounds.

IV. The Empirical Evidence

In *The Price of Leisure*, John Owen compiled *U.S.* time-series spanning the years 1901–61 for (among other things) the number of weekly hours of work and the corresponding real hourly wage. A number of important adjustments to the raw data make these series particularly useful for our purposes, especially in adjusting weekly hours for vacations and holidays and in excluding working students from the series from 1940 on.

The data, however, should be interpreted with great care. The coverage is for "private, non-agricultural wage and salary workers." If we assume, as seems reasonable, that the larger the asset holdings of an individual, the larger the chance that he will become self-employed, then the

[16] By the same token, it is not surprising that Stigler's search for Giffen goods is in vain. See George Stigler.

above classification of workers is biased towards individuals with low asset holdings. This has strong implications in interpreting the time-series. First, we saw that when the wage is parametric, the supply curve of individuals will vary substantially according to whether their level of assets is such that $A-S>0$ or $A-S<0$; this is evident in a comparison of the first and third rows of panels in Figure 1. In particular, as asset holdings increase, the relation $A-S<0$ will change to $A-S>0$, and at the same time, individuals will tend to drop out of the class of workers covered by the series. The individuals covered by the time-series, then, have particular asset holdings that will tend to bias the observed relation towards a negative slope.

Second, as noted above in the section on aggregation, to the extent that the change in wages is not accompanied by a shift in the transformation curve, the income effect on wage earners will be more or less matched by an income effect in the opposite direction on asset owners. But since the latter tend to be excluded from the sample, the effect on them is missed, and again the aggregative curve is biased towards a negative slope.[17]

In addition, during the period covered a dramatic shift occurred in productivity, and the observed increase in wage earners' incomes was not at the expense of asset holders. Consequently, the evidence afforded by the aggregative time-series corresponds more closely to that of the individual where wages are parametric and where increased wages mean a higher level of income than to the aggregative supply curve at a point in time where total income is constant.

The above discussion leads us to view the time-series as being obtained from a population for which asset holdings are not

[17] These two biases, however, are fortunate from the viewpoint of identifying the parameters of the underlying utility function.

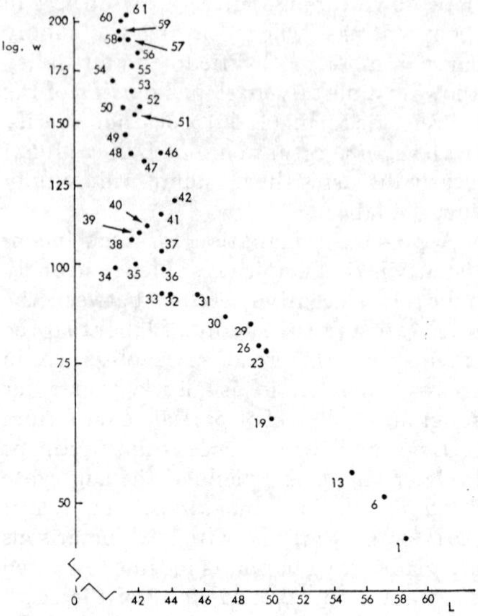

FIGURE 2

high (though perhaps rising) and to view the wage changes as parametric. So the data may narrow down the range of utility functions consistent with the evidence by shedding some light on the constanty of σ and on its value.

The data are plotted in Figure 2, where the horizontal axis measures hours worked per week and the vertical axis measures (on a logarithmic scale) the index of real wages. Individual points are identified according to their year. From 1901 to 1929 only selected points are available; from 1929 to 1961 the data are annual except for the omission of the war years, 1943–45.

The pattern that emerges conforms closely to Panel VIII of Figure 1, where $A-S<0$ and where $\sigma=1$.[18] During the first half of the period, from 1901 to the

[18] We should bear in mind that each of the diagrams in Figure 1 is drawn for a constant level of nonwage income. Since nonwage income is not held constant in the actual data, and since such income may be correlated with the level of wages, a possibility of a bias is present.

mid-1930's, real wages doubled, and weekly hours fell from 58 to about 42. During the second period, from the mid-1930's to 1961, real wages doubled again but hours remained virtually constant, particularly so if the war-related years are ignored. From 1948 to 1961, the range of variation of weekly hours is in the narrow band between 40.4 (1954) and 42 (1952) with no apparent trend.[19] This corresponds to the Cobb-Douglas utility function where the supply curve approaches asymptotically a positive number of hours.[20] Given that American wages in 1901 were substantially above those required for subsistence, the above evidence is insufficient to determine the minimum levels of consumption and rest.

Owen's data go only to 1961 and cover a very broad class of workers. During the 1960's real wages continued to increase, but weekly hours showed very little, if any, decline. Weekly hours for all production workers fell from 38.6 in 1961 to 37.0[21] (the coverage does not differ much from Owen's but the hours are unadjusted). This decline, however, is entirely due to a decline in hours in wholesale and retail trade (from 38.3 to 35.1); none of the other four subclasses, which include mining, construction, manufacturing and finance, showed any decline. Note that both 1961 and 1971 had high unemployment rates. The last decade, then, conforms to the pattern of the earlier period.

An interesting empirical implication (also useful for testing the conclusion that the utility function is Cobb-Douglas) is that as wages go up the divergence with respect to hours of work tends to disappear as between the capitalist and noncapitalist classes, i.e., between those with $A-S>0$ and those with $A-S<0$. Casual notions suggest that working habits of wealthier individuals in the United States do not differ much from those of less well-off individuals. Casual notions also suggest that the "leisure" class is quite prominent in poor countries where the real wages are low. These notions, if correct, tend to support the hypothesis that $\sigma=1$. Of course, a more careful and systematic analysis of the evidence is necessary to determine whether these casual notions are correct.

V. Some Further Comments

The attainable (survival) consumption set used in the preceding analysis was of a simple, "fixed coefficient" nature. A more complicated (and perhaps more realistic) formulation, allowing some substitution between the two commodities in meeting the requisites of survival, would in principle cause few difficulties in the formal theory.[22] However, the notion of net consumption (above survival) would then have little intuitive appeal, and it thus might be impossible to find a formulation of preferences yielding simple expressions like equations (8) and (9) for the slopes of the demand curves. The assumptions used do, however, seem to strike a reasonable balance between complicating the analysis severely and ignoring subsistence needs completely, since they allow simple types of preferences to generate a wide variety of types of demand (supply) curves.

Thus Hanoch verges on an error when he asserts (p. 639) that *CES* utility functions cannot produce backward bending

[19] The range will be further narrowed if we take account of cyclical fluctuations in unemployment, which are negatively correlated with the number of hours.

[20] It is interesting to note that since the end of the Second World War, weekly hours in Great Britain are also almost constant. There, however, the number is around 48 hours per week, The difference of about 7 hours per week between the two countries is an interesting puzzle.

[21] See the *Monthly Labor Review*.

[22] Provided that the new attainable set is convex. Otherwise, it may be impossible to even define convex preferences over the entire set of attainable consumption bundles. See Arrow and Gerard Debreu (1954) and Debreu.

supply curves and that a *C-D* utility function produces a vertical supply curve. His failure to take into account the wealth position and subsistence requirements of the individual has led him to use an unnecessarily complicated utility function to get his desired qualitative results. His illustration of a "conventional" supply curve, with $(A-S)$ implicitly set at zero, shows how unreasonable one can get if minimum consumption is not specified. Since his supply of labor becomes zero at all wage rates below $w=1$,[23] his consumer then would apparently prefer to starve to death rather than work and live at a wage less than 1.

In empirical studies of the supply of labor, the asset position of the individual is seldom taken into account. But a comparison of the first and third rows of Figure 1 clearly shows that even when assets are present we cannot simply add nonwage income as another variable in, say, a regression equation. Clearly, the coefficient for the wage rate depends on the level of nonwage income, and it even changes sign as assets pass through the level $A=S$. A simple relation allowing for no interaction effects, even if statistically "significant," gives average results for diverse groups of individuals, which in this case are entirely meaningless. More specifically, in a sample with assets distributed on both sides of the subsistence level, the estimated effect of the wage rate on the supply of labor will be biased toward zero. Given the model formulated above, however, the correct specification for the labor supply is shown by equations (A 10) and (A 11) of the Appendix. Equation (A 11), where it is assumed that $\sigma=1$, can be readily estimated by standard techniques; (A 10) poses more of a problem but could also be estimated if the hypothesis that $\sigma=1$ is not tenable.

[23] The units of w are not specified; thus, the entry point into the labor market is *not* invariant to the choice of units for the consumption good. His specific utility function in our notation is:

$$V(R, C) = R \exp\left[-\exp\left(-\frac{C}{R}\right)\right]$$

Appendix

To derive equation (10) it will be convenient to solve explicitly for the effects of asset changes on the demands for C and R. We can differentiate equations (4) and (6) totally to get

$$dC + w dR = dA + (D' - R)dw$$

$$f_1 dC + f_2 dR = dw$$

Letting dw be zero and recalling that at equilibrium $w=f$, we see that the partial effect of income on leisure is

$$\text{(A 1)} \qquad \frac{\partial R}{\partial A} = f_1/(ff_1 - f_2)$$

Substituting this into (9) and rearranging, we have

$$\text{(A 2)} \qquad \frac{\partial L}{\partial w} = f_1/(ff_1 - f_2)\left[\frac{1}{f_1} - (D' - R)\right]$$

$$= \frac{1}{w} f_1/(ff_1 - f_2) \cdot \left[\frac{f}{f_1} - (C + S - A)\right]$$

where the budget constraint (4) has been used to substitute for $(D'-R)$ and we have again used $w=f$.

Assume now that the individual's preferences are homothetic in C and R, so the marginal rate of substitution is a function only of the ratio of consumption to leisure—that is, $f(C, R)$ is homogeneous of degree zero—so we may write

$$f(C, R) = h\left(\frac{C}{R}\right)$$

Then f_1 and f_2 can be written as

$$\text{(A 3)} \qquad f_1 = \frac{h'}{R'}; \qquad f_2 = -\frac{C}{R}\frac{h'}{R}$$

and we have

$$(A\ 4)\quad ff_1 - f_2 = \frac{h'}{R}\,\frac{(C + hR)}{R} > 0$$

by convexity. So it must be true that $h' > 0$. The income effects then become

$$(A\ 5)\quad \frac{\partial R}{\partial A} = \frac{R}{(C+wR)} \text{ and } \frac{\partial C}{\partial A} = \frac{C}{(C+wR)}$$

where the derivation of the latter parallels that for leisure.

The elasticity of substitution between the net quantities of consumption and leisure is defined as

$$\sigma = \frac{d\left(\frac{C}{R}\right) \Big/ \left(\frac{C}{R}\right)}{df/f}$$

where the differentials are for movements along an indifference curve. When preferences are homothetic this is simply

$$(A\ 6)\quad \sigma = \frac{Rh}{Ch'}$$

and then we have

$$(A\ 7)\quad \frac{f}{f_1} = \frac{Rh}{h'} = C\sigma$$

Equations (A5) and (A7) may then be substituted into (A2) to yield (A8).

$$(A\ 8)\quad \frac{\partial L}{\partial w} = \frac{1}{w}\,\frac{R}{(C + wR)} \cdot [C(\sigma - 1) + (A - S)]$$

Working in a parallel manner, equation (7) can be rewritten as

$$(A\ 9)\quad \frac{\partial C}{\partial w} = \frac{C}{(C + wR)}\,[R(\sigma - 1) + D']$$

It can also be shown that no weaker specifications on the individual's preferences will give these results.

The further assumption that the elasticity of substitution is a constant yields the explicit supply function

$$(A\ 10)\quad L = \frac{\left(\frac{\alpha}{1 - \alpha}\right)^{\sigma} w^{\sigma} D' - (A - S)}{\left(\frac{\alpha}{1 - \alpha}\right)^{\sigma} w^{\sigma} + w}$$

which reduces to

$$(A\ 11)\quad L = \alpha D' - (1 - \alpha)\left(\frac{A - S}{w}\right)$$

when $\sigma = 1$. This is the supply function that would be generated by a Cobb-Douglas type of utility function.

REFERENCES

K. J. Arrow and G. Debreu, "Existence of an Equilibrium for a Competitive Economy," *Econometrica*, July 1954, *22*, 265–90.

M. J. Bailey, "The Marshallian Demand Curve," *J. Polit. Econ.*, June 1954, *62*, 255–61.

———, *National Income and the Price Level*, New York 1962, p. 34.

K. E. Boulding, *Economic Analysis*, 3d ed., New York 1955.

G. Debreu, *Theory of Values: An Axiomatic Analysis of Economic Equilibrium*, New York 1959.

M. Friedman, *Price Theory*, rev., Chicago 1966, p. 204.

———, "The Marshallian Demand Curve," *J. Polit. Econ.*, Dec. 1949, *57*, 463–94; reprinted in *Essays in Positive Economics*, Chicago 1953.

G. Hanoch, "The 'Backward-Bending' Supply of Labor," *J. Polit. Econ.*, Dec. 1965, *73*, 636–42.

J. R. Hicks, *Value and Capital*, 2d ed., Oxford 1946, p. 37.

L. R. Klein and H. Rubin, "A Constant Utility Index of the Cost of Living," *Rev. Econ. Stud.*, 1948–49, *15*, 84–87.

J. D. Owen, *The Price of Leisure*, Rotterdam 1969.

L. Robbins, "On the Elasticity of Demand for Income in Terms of Effort," *Economica*, June 1930, *29*, 123–29.

P. A. Samuelson, "Some Implications of

'Linearity'," *Rev. Econ. Stud.*, 1948–49, *15*, 88–90.

———, *Economics*, 8th ed., New York 1970.

G. J. Stigler, "Notes on the History of the Giffen Paradox," *J. Polit. Econ.*, Apr. 1947, *55*, 152–56.

R. D. Stone, "Linear Expenditure Systems and Demand Analysis: An Application to the Pattern of British Demand," *Econ. J.*, Sept. 1954, *64*, 511–27.

Monthly Labor Review, U.S. Department of Labor, July 1972, p. 82.

THE EFFECT OF THE UTILIZATION RATE ON THE DIVISION OF LABOR

YORAM BARZEL and BEN T. YU*

The recognition that investment in human capital depends on its utilization (*i.e.*, the number of hours it is used) is offered as an explanation of diverse phenomena such as of tourists' behavior, women's participation rate in the labor force, and the decline of investment in human capital with age.[1] In this paper we examine the way the utilization rate of human capital affects specialization. We demonstrate that even if training in each specialty is subject to diminishing returns or rising cost, the utilization effects of human capital would prompt two identical individuals to specialize their training, and therefore hours of work, in different occupations.

In section I the main argument is presented with the aid of a numerical example. In section II the proposition is demonstrated more formally and its relation to the conventional intertemporal labor-leisure model is shown. Countering forces that might deter complete specialization are discussed, and the shortcoming of the Harrod neutral assumption is shown in section III.

I. UTILIZATION RATE AND SPECIALIZING: A NUMERICAL EXAMPLE

A numerical example serves to illustrate our main idea. Suppose that when a worker faces identical wage rates, say $1.00, in activities A and B, which are identical to him, he spends four hours a day at each activity so that his total daily earnings are $8.00 (first row of table 1). Suppose further that exogenous conditions have changed (*e.g.*, his initial wealth has declined) and that he wants to work two more hours. The higher number of working hours means the return to education is higher and, as a result, investment in education increases. How would the person allocate the two extra hours and the increase in educational investment between the two activities?

TABLE 1

Educ. in A	Working Hours in A	Wage in A	Earning in A	Educ. in B	Working Hours in B	Wage in B	Earning in B	Total Earning
0	4	$1.00	$ 4.00	0	4	$1.00	$4.00	$ 8.00
$10,000	5	1.20	6.00	$10,000	5	1.20	6.00	12.00
$20,000	5	1.30	6.50	0	5	1.00	5.00	11.50
$20,000	10	1.30	13.00	0	0	1.00	0	13.00

One might expect that the person would allocate equal hours and investments to each activity since they are identical by assumption. This conclusion, however, is incorrect. Consider first the equal time allocation to the two activities. If the person

*University of Washington and University of California, Los Angeles.

1. See Becker (1975), Polachek and Mincer (1974).

intends to devote one extra hour to each activity, education in both activities would increase by the same amount. As a result of the higher education and investment, the wage rate in both activities rises. The magnitude of the wage increase depends on the wage-education relationship as determined in a competitive labor market. For example, suppose that the wage-education relationship, $w(E)$, is as in table 2. If (given the expected working hours) the wealth maximizing level of education is \$10,000 for each activity, the hourly wage increases to \$1.20 in both activities, and total earnings are \$12.00 (row two in table 1).

TABLE 2

Educational Expense	Wage
0	\$1.00
\$10,000	1.20
\$20,000	1.30
\$30,000	1.35

But the individual has a better alternative. Suppose he allocates all his educational expenditures of \$20,000 to A. The wage rate in A increases even more, though at a diminished rate — to \$1.30 in the example, but the wage rate in B decreases to \$1.00. If one extra hour is allocated again to each activity, total earnings are only \$11.50 (row three in table 1). If, however, he allocates all hours to the higher wage activity, total earnings are \$13.00 (row four in table 1), which exceeds those of the equal time allocation scheme.[2]

The economics of table 1 may be summarized in a simple proposition: the expectation of a higher utilization rate in a particular activity results in a larger accumulation of human capital specific to that activity. The greater accumulation, in turn, results in a higher wage rate in the activity, which feeds back to substituting working hours into that activity. Once the substitution commences, it continues until it is complete. Thus, the effect of utilization on human capital implies that specializing in market time and in education simultaneously is preferred to diversifying the two activities.

Consider a second individual, identical to the person above in every respect including his wage rates and training opportunities. By the same reasoning, we expect his utilization rate and his incentive to specialize to be the same as the first person's. However, the activity in which he chooses to specialize may be different. In fact, in a general equilibrium context, one should expect that some individuals specialize in A while others specialize in B.

2. Another way to look at the problem is to translate the set of numbers in the text into cost of education terms. Diminishing returns in the wage-education function would then be a rising marginal cost of education. Maximization implies that an individual will equate the marginal return to education with the marginal cost. Under competition, however, an individual would have to choose the least costly way of obtaining the education (analogous to the point of minimum average cost). We thank an anonymous referee for suggesting the analogy.

The numerical example illustrates the underlying force that generates an apparent difference in "natural talents." It began with two identical individuals confronted with two economically equal activities. It concludes with two distinct activities with each individual having a "comparative advantage" (as measured by the higher wage) in only one of the two activities. This conclusion can be found in the writings of Adam Smith:

> The difference of natural talents in different men is, in reality, much less than we are aware of; and the very genius which appears to distinguish men of different professions, when grown up to maturity, is not upon many occasions so much the *cause*, as the *effect* of the division of labour. The difference between the most dissimilar characters, between a philosopher and a common street porter, for example, seems to arise not so much from nature, as from *habits*, *custom*, and *education*. (*The Wealth of Nations*, p. 15, emphases added.)

Smith's incentive to specialize, however, primarily arises from trade, whereas our result arises from the utilization rate. The difference is most obvious in a Robinson Crusoe world. In such a world, there is no trade and Smith's proposition is not applicable. The utilization effect, however, is applicable to Crusoe, who can spend resources in training himself to fish or to hunt, but he may choose to specialize in only one activity.[3]

II. SPECIALIZING WITHIN THE FRAMEWORK OF LABOR-LEISURE CHOICE

How would the effect demonstrated in the last section relate to the conventional labor-leisure choice model? Consider an individual who can allocate his working hours, H, between two productive activities, A and B. Output, interpreted either as the market earning of the individual or the physical goods and services produced by him, can be specified more generally as $f(h_A, h_B)$ where h_A, h_B are the hours spent on the two activities respectively.[4] A conventional labor-leisure choice model would specify the following objective function:

$$\max_{h_A,\, h_B,\, x,\, \lambda} U(x, 24 - h_A - h_B) + \lambda(f(h_A, h_B) - x), \tag{1}$$

where $U(x, \ell)$ is the utility of the individual which is a function of real goods and services (purchased or produced), x, and leisure, ℓ.

Alternatively, consider that the individual maximizes his earning (or output) subject to the number of hours he wants to work. *I.e.*,

$$\max_{h_A,\, h_B,\, \mu} f(h_A, h_B) - \mu(H^* - h_A - h_B), \tag{2}$$

where H^* is the solution to the following utility maximization problem:

3. Two implicit assumptions in our numerical example are the absence of job-specific fatigue and activity complementarity in terms of working hours or of training. These assumptions are relaxed below.

4. The "extent of the market," then, is assumed to be so large that the individual has no effect on the market wage.

$$\max_{x,\,H,\,\lambda} U(x, 24 - H) + \lambda(f^*(H) - x), \tag{3}$$

where $f^*(H)$ is the optimal solution value of (2).[5]

Straightforward differentiations show that the first order conditions of (1) are identical to those in (2) *and* (3). Furthermore, since the choice variables in (3) do not involve h_A and h_B, the problem in (1) can be analyzed recursively by first obtaining the solution values in (2) independently of the subsequent solution values in (3). In other words, if we can demonstrate a tendency to specialize in (2) for all values of H, it certainly should be valid for the particular optimal value of H in (3).

The solution values to (2) rely critically on the mathematical properties of the function $f(\cdot)$. To establish the proposition that a difference in comparative advantage would evolve even for identical individuals, we assume that the individual's earning function is of the following linear form:

$$f(h_A, h_B) = W_A \cdot h_A + W_B \cdot h_B, \tag{4}$$

where W_A and W_B are the wage rates (or the marginal products) in the two activities respectively.

Given the functional form in (4), the solution to (2) may be easily seen by the aid of a diagram. In figure 1 an "iso-earning line," *ST*, and a "budget line," *BT*, are drawn with h_A and h_B on the two axes. The slope of the iso-earning line is constant, $-W_A/W_B$, its linearity follows from the assumption of linear earning function and implying the absence of fatigue and job complementarity. The slope of the budget line is -1. If the individual has no endowed comparative advantage between the two activities, $W_A/W_B = -1$, the iso-earning curve will coincide with the constraint leading to multiple solutions. On the other hand, if he has an endowed natural talent, $W_A/W_B \neq -1$. The slope of the iso-earning curve will differ then from the slope of the constraint, leading to a corner solution as drawn.

FIGURE 1

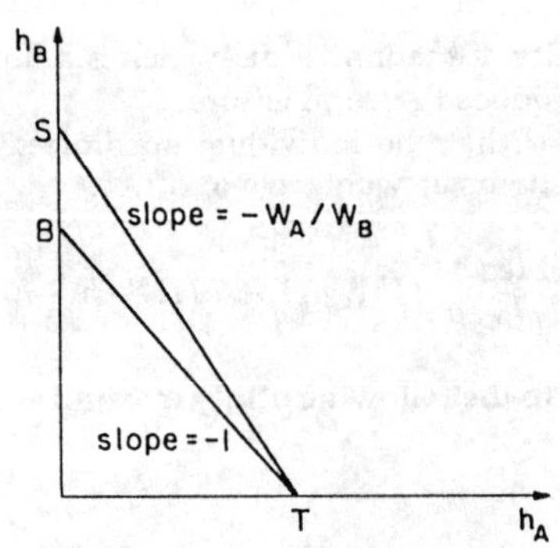

5. H^* is determined by maximizing the utility of the individual subject to a labor-leisure constraint with the wage rate equal to max (W_A, W_B).

The procedure of analyzing specialization as described by (2) and (3) does not change with the introduction of training. So long as the training decision is guided by wealth maximization, the training possibility alters only the shape of the earning function $f(\cdot)$, and the recursive procedure described is still consistent with utility maximization. Since the training decision in the context of intertemporal labor-leisure choice model has been analyzed extensively in the literature, we note here only the first order condition regarding human capital accumulation. In a two period model, it may be shown that the maximizing level of education is a function of (i) the increase in wage rate (or marginal product) due to a unit increase in education, (ii) the post-training working hours, *i.e.*, the utilization rate of human capital, (iii) the interest rate, and (iv) the opportunity cost of education. Thus, if T_2 is the total hours available in the second, post-training period, t_2 is the post-training leisure hours, $W_2(E)$ is the post-training wage rate as a function of education, W_1 is the opportunity cost of training (*i.e.*, the wage rate) in the first period, and $t(E)$ is the amount of training time, the first order condition becomes

$$\text{(5)} \qquad \frac{1}{(1+r)}(T_2 - t_2)\frac{\partial W_2}{\partial E} - (W_1 \frac{\partial t}{\partial E} + 1) = 0.$$

The significance of equation 5 has not been emphasized sufficiently in the literature,[6] perhaps because it is only one of the many first order conditions that can be derived from a global utility maximization model; and methodologically, it is incorrect to derive comparative dynamics results from one equation amidst a set of first order conditions. However, in our working paper (1981), we reduced the set of first order conditions into a single first order condition as described in (5) by a two-period indirect utility maximization procedure. The approach clarifies some ambiguities in the rate of return calculations in human capital accumulation; it also illustrates how working hours can affect human capital accumulation. More precisely, we argued that the exogenous variables (*e.g.*, initial wealth) analyzed in many of the global utility maximization models affect human capital accumulation only *because* these variables affect the utilization rate. This clarification, of course, has no bearings on the main results in the existing utility maximizing models since the latter are primarily concerned with the overall effects of various exogenous variables — it does not matter how these exogenous variables work through the system. However, for other sets of problems such as the one contemplated here, re-emphasizing the mechanism inside the "black box" demonstrates how the $f(\cdot)$ function (and thus the issue of specialization) would be affected by training possibilities.

Formally, the linear function in (4) can be re-specified and the objective function of (2) becomes

$$\text{(6)} \qquad W_A(E_A(h_A)) \cdot h_A + W_B(E_B(h_B)) \cdot h_B + \mu(H^* - h_A - h_B),$$

6. Thus, even though equation (2) is implicit in the pioneering model of Ghez and Becker (1975), it is given no explicit interpretation. In fact, that approach hs been subsequently criticized by Blinder and Weiss (1976, p.451), as "merely stating the first order conditions." In Heckman (1976) and Rosen (1977), similar first-order conditions were derived, but the breakdown of a separation theorem in human capital was alleged. For instance, Rosen (1977, p. 31), argues that "... once leisure is considered, life utility rather than present values of net earnings must be equalized across occupations in full market equilibrium."

where $E_i(h_i)$, $i = A, B$, summarizes the adjustment implicit in equation (5), and $W_i(E_i)$ is the market reward to education, $E_i' > 0$ and $W_i' > 0$. Comparing (6) and (2), the effects of the utilization rate on specialization become immediately obvious. The constraints in both expressions are identical, but the iso-earning curve in (6) is concave whereas that curve is linear in (2) (see Appendix I). Thus, complete specialization is necessarily implied even if the two activities, A and B, are *ex-ante* identical.

III. THE EFFECTS OF DIMINISHING RETURN AND COMPLEMENTARITY ON SPECIALIZING

It is easy to imagine conditions reducing the individual's tendency to specialize completely, so that he may choose to be trained in several activities. In conventional textbook trade models,[7] specialization is viewed as the outcome of several opposing factors: (i) diminishing return in producing a particular product; (ii) complementarity in producing several products, and (iii) trading possibilities. The first refers to the signs of the second partial derivatives of the production possibility frontier, and the second refers to the sign of the cross partials of the production possibility frontier. Both factors may lead to the concavity of the frontier which,[8] together with the convexity of indifference curves, determine the nonspecialization solution in autarky. The third factor refers to the existence of a market price line, reflecting differences in wages or in endowments across individuals and encouraging specialization. Considering the three factors jointly, the degree of specialization is usually viewed as the outcome of a three-way tug of war.

Transaction cost considerations may also deter complete specialization. For example, when a substantial cost is involved in enforcing contracts having multiple characteristics or when a small exchange value is involved, a person may work at several activities even though there is an apparent gain from specializing.

Our analysis in the previous two sections does not deny the existence of these detering effects; it merely highlights the utilization effect which is absent from conventional considerations. The key to understanding the economic force at work is the substitutability in the utilization rate between the two activities. If the first hour of activity B has the same productivity as the Hth hour of activity A after $(H - 1)$ hours have been spent on A, complete specialization will necessarily result. It is a small extension to incorporate countering forces as cases of less than perfect substitutes. For example, job-specific fatigue is comparable to job-specific diminishing return. In the presence of such diminishing return, the marginal wage rate of a particular activity should fall as the number of hours applied to it increases. Incorporating this force into (5), we indeed can have an interior solution. (See Appendix II for details.)

It is a common assumption that education is Harrod neutral; supposedly it augments market and nonmarket time *equally.*[9] The analysis in previous sections cautions that such formulation may be inconsistent with a more general maximization framework. Even if countering forces are present, the effect of the utilization rate on specialization would still be partially at work, in the sense that the larger the fraction of a person's time spent on an activity, the more that person invests in education

7. For example, see Hirshleifer, chapters 7 and 8.

8. This is commonly stated in terms of the second order conditions.

9. See Michael (1973) and Heckman (1976). The assumption was apparently made to attain tractability.

for that activity. Furthermore, the wage-education relationship in different activities may differ. Therefore, it seems highly improbable that the opposing effects are so coincidental that the educational mix acquired is precisely the one rendering it Harrod neutral.

IV. CONCLUSIONS

We argue that the positive relationship between utilization rate and human capital accumulation results in specialization. Although specialization is usually thought to arise from trade, the utilization effect is present even in a Robinson Crusoe world. In fact, one can argue that it is specialization that results in trade, rather than the other way around.

The distinction has just begun to find its way into the literature. Both Becker (1981) and Rosen (1983) have noted increasing returns due to utilization, and have recognized the potential of using this concept in other areas of analysis. Rosen (1983), for example, has linked the utilization effects with the work by Krugman (1982) on international trade. We see possibilities for extension of the argument to other areas as distinct and as unrelated as biological evolution theories and research and development strategies.

APPENDIX I
THE CONCAVITY OF THE ISO-EARNING CURVE

The first order conditions of (6) are:

(AI.1) $$\frac{\partial w_A}{\partial E_A} \cdot \frac{\partial E_A}{\partial h_A} \cdot h_A + w_A(E_A(h_A)) - \mu = 0.$$

(AI.2) $$\frac{\partial w_B}{\partial E_B} \cdot \frac{\partial E_B}{\partial h_B} \cdot h_B + w_B(E_B(h_B)) - \mu = 0.$$

(AI.3) $$H^* - h_A - h_B = 0.$$

The second order matrix D is

$$D = \begin{vmatrix} F_{h_A h_A} & 0 & -1 \\ 0 & F_{h_B h_B} & -1 \\ -1 & -1 & 0 \end{vmatrix}$$

F denotes the objective function in equation (6) and $F_{h_i h_i}$ denotes the second order derivative of F with respect to h_i, $i = A, B$.

The curvature of the iso-earning curve is determined by the sign of

$$|D| = -F_{h_A h_A} - F_{h_B h_B}, \qquad \text{and}$$

(AI.4)

$$F_{h_i h_i} = \left[\frac{\partial^2 w_i}{\partial^2 E_i} \cdot \left(\frac{\partial E_i}{\partial h_i} \right)^2 + \frac{\partial w_i}{\partial E_i} \cdot \frac{\partial^2 E_i}{\partial^2 h_i} \right] \cdot h_i + 2 \frac{\partial w_i}{\partial E_i} \cdot \frac{\partial E_i}{\partial h_i} .$$

However, the maximizing level of E_i is determined by:

$$\text{(AI.5)} \qquad \frac{h_i \cdot \dfrac{\partial w_i}{\partial E_i}}{(1+r)} = 1 + \frac{\partial t}{\partial E_i} \cdot W_1 .$$

where W_1 denotes the foregone wage during training.

Totally differentiating (AI.5) with respect to h_i yields:

$$\text{(AI.6)} \qquad \frac{\partial w_i}{\partial E_i} + h_i \cdot \frac{\partial^2 w_i}{\partial^2 E_i} \cdot \frac{\partial E_i}{\partial h_i} = 0.$$

Multiplying both sides of equation (AI.6) by $\partial E_i/\partial h_i$ and substituting it into (AI.4), we have:

$$F_{h_i h_i} = \frac{\partial w_i}{\partial E_i}\left(h_i \frac{\partial^2 E_i}{\partial^2 h_i} + \frac{\partial E_i}{\partial h_i}\right),$$

with $\dfrac{\partial w_i}{\partial E_i} > 0, \ \dfrac{\partial E_i}{\partial h_i} > 0$, and $\dfrac{\partial^2 E_i}{\partial^2 h_i} \gtreqless 0.$

But so long as we assume that the effect of utilization on accumulation is not dampened, $\partial^2 E_i/\partial^2 h_i > 0$, and $F_{h_i h_i} > 0$.

Thus, $|D| < 0$, and the iso-earning curve must be concave.

APPENDIX II
THE CONCAVITY OF THE ISO-EARNING CURVE WITH FATIGUE

In the presence of an activity specific fatigue, earning can no longer be specified as the product of a constant wage rate and working hours. Let $L_A(h_A, E_A(h_A))$ be the earning function in A, and $L_B(h_B, E_B(h_B))$ be that in B. $\partial L_i/\partial h_i$ is the marginal wage rate in activity i, $i = A, B$. Fatigue implies that $\partial^2 L_i/\partial^2 h_i < 0$.

An increase in education in an activity will raise the marginal wage rate, *i.e.*, $\partial^2 L_i/\partial E_i \partial h_i > 0$. Education also increases earning directly, *i.e*, $\partial L_i/\partial E_i > 0$, but subject to diminishing return, $\partial^2 L_i/\partial^2 E_i < 0$ because of fatigue. The individual maximizes total earning subject to the predetermined number of hours he wants to work, H^*. He maximizes

$$\text{(AII.1)} \qquad L_A(h_A, E_A(h_A)) + L_B(h_B, E_B(h_B)) + \mu(H^* - h_A - h_B),$$

with respect to h_A, h_B and μ.

First order conditions imply:

$$\text{(AII.2)} \qquad \frac{\partial L_A}{\partial h_A} + \frac{\partial L_A}{\partial E_A} \cdot \frac{\partial E_A}{\partial h_A} - \mu = 0.$$

$$\text{(AII.3)} \qquad \frac{\partial L_B}{\partial h_B} + \frac{\partial L_B}{\partial E_B} \cdot \frac{\partial E_B}{\partial h_B} - \mu = 0.$$

$$\text{(AII.4)} \qquad H^* - h_A - h_B = 0.$$

$\partial L_i/\partial h_i$ is equivalent to $w_i(E(h_i))$ in (AI.1) and (AI.2) and $\partial L_i/\partial E_i \cdot \partial E_i/\partial h_i$ is equivalent to $\partial w_i/\partial E_i \cdot \partial E_i/\partial h_i \cdot h_i$ in (AI.1) and (AI.2).

The second order matrix D is

$$\begin{vmatrix} L^{AA} & 0 & -1 \\ 0 & L^{BB} & -1 \\ -1 & -1 & 0 \end{vmatrix}$$

The curvature of the iso-earning curve is determined by the sign of $|D| = -L^{AA} - L^{BB}$.

Whether the iso-earning curve is concave or convex, therefore, depends on the signs of L^{AA} and L^{BB} and on the relative magnitude of the two terms. L'' can be written as,

$$L'' = \frac{d^2L_i}{d^2h_i} = \frac{\partial^2 L_i}{\partial^2 h_i} + \left(\frac{\partial^2 L_i}{\partial E_i \partial h_i}\right) \cdot \frac{\partial E_i}{\partial h_i}$$

$$+ \frac{\partial E_i}{\partial h_i}\left[\frac{\partial^2 L_i}{\partial h_i \partial E_i} + \frac{\partial^2 L_i}{\partial^2 E_i} \cdot \frac{\partial E_i}{\partial h_i}\right] + \frac{\partial L_i}{\partial E_i} \cdot \frac{\partial^2 E_i}{\partial^2 h_i} .$$

Although there are forces of increasing returns, *i.e.*, $\partial^2 L_i/\partial E_i \partial h_i > 0$, $\partial E_i/\partial h_i > 0$, $\partial L_i/\partial E_i > 0$, fatigue implies $\partial^2 L_i/\partial^2 h_i < 0$; diminishing return in education implies $\partial^2 L_i/\partial^2 E_i < 0$; and diminishing effect of utilization on education implies $\partial^2 E_i/\partial^2 h_i < 0$. Thus, the sign of L'' depends on the relative magnitude of increasing returns *vs.* diminishing return, and the sign of D depends on the relative magnitude of L^{AA} *vs.* L^{BB}. With job complementarity, we assume $L_i(h_i, E_i(h_i), h_j)$, $i, j = A, B$. The second order matrix then would involve extra terms of L''. This provides additional forces resulting in non-specialization.

REFERENCES

Barzel, Yoram, and Yu, Ben T., "The Interdependence Between the Accumulation of Human Capital and Its Utilization," University of Washington, 1978, revised 1980.

Becker, Gary S., *Human Capital*, 2nd ed., New York, New York, Columbia University Press, 1975.

__________, *A Treatise on the Family*, Cambridge, Massachusetts, Harvard University Press, 1981.

Blinder, Alan S., and Weiss, Yoram, "Human Capital and Labor Supply: A Synthesis," *Journal of Political Economy, 84*, No. 3, June 1976.

Ghez, Gibert R., and Becker, Gary S., *The Allocation of Time and Goods Over the Life Cycle*, New York, New York, Columbia University Press, 1975.

Heckman, James J., "A Life Cycle Model of Earnings, Learning, and Consumption," *Journal of Political Economy, 84*, No. 4, Part 2, August 1976, 511-544.

Hirshleifer, Jack, *Price Theory and Applications*, 2nd ed., Prentice-Hall.

Krugman, P. R., "Intraindustry Specialization and the Gains from Trade," *Journal of Political Economy, 89*, No. 5, October 1981.

Michael, Robert T., "Education in Non-market Production," *Journal of Political Economy, 81*, No. 2, March/April 1973, 306-327.

Mincer, Jacob, and Polachek, Solomon, "Family Investments in Human Capital: Earnings of Women," *Journal of Political Economy*, 82, No. 2, March/April 1974.

Rosen, Sherwin, "Human Capital: A Survey of Empirical Research," *Research in Labor Economics*, ed., Ronald G. Ehrenberg, Greenwich, Connecticut, Jai Press, Volume I, 1977.

__________, "Specialization and Human Capital," *Journal of Labor Economics*, Vol. 1, No. 1, January 1983, *43*.

Smith, Adam, *The Wealth of Nations*, New York, The Modern Library, 1937.

PART IV

PUBLIC CHOICE

[12]

TWO PROPOSITIONS ON THE OPTIMUM LEVEL OF PRODUCING COLLECTIVE GOODS*

Yoram Barzel
University of Washington

What is the optimal level of government for the production of collectively produced goods? Consider the question of mosquito control. The good demanded is "dead mosquitoes." In Figure 1 D_A, D_B, and D_C reflect demand curves of three individuals, each representing one third of the population in the political unit--say,

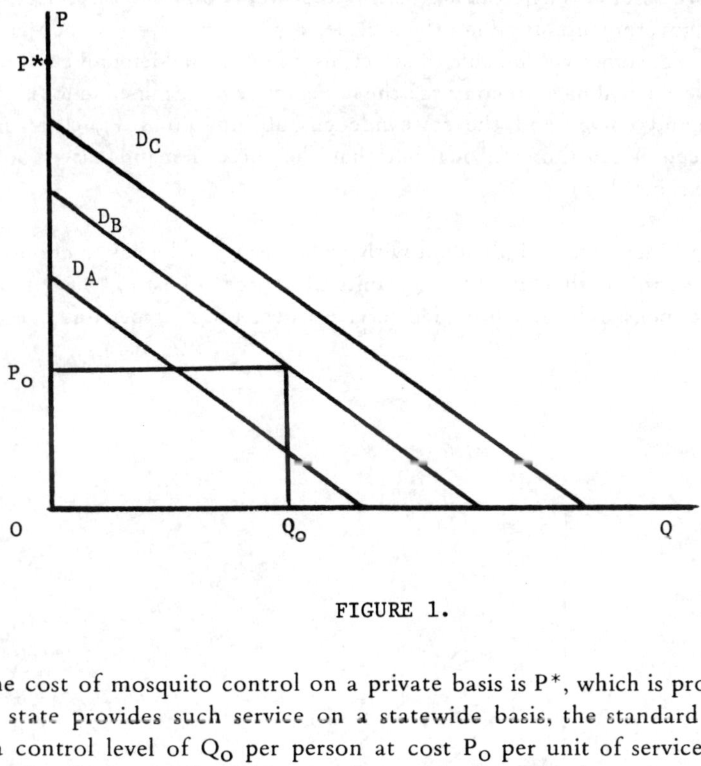

FIGURE 1.

a state. The cost of mosquito control on a private basis is P*, which is prohibitive; but if the state provides such service on a statewide basis, the standard solution indicates a control level of Q_o per person at cost P_o per unit of service.[1] If the economies of scale in providing this service are already realized at a lower level of activity, and if the three groups of consumers can be easily segregated, it is obvious that a superior solution can be achieved by providing individuals in each group not the common quantity Q_o but the respective quantities demanded by them at price P_o. This, of course, is well-known. Tiebout[2] further suggested that if the three levels of service are offered in three localities, consumers will gravitate towards the locality that best agrees with their desires.

This paper is concerned with situations where economies of scale are not exhausted and where it is thus more costly to supply the service on a smaller scale, and with situations where segregation of consumers into homogeneous groups is not easy. The discussion of the first problem is basically at the individual level, and no interpersonal comparisons are necessary. The discussion of the second does involve such comparisons.

Under what conditions would an individual opt to go with the local group rather than with the entire state? Obviously, he will compare the returns and costs in the two situations and choose the one where the difference in favor of returns is larger. We assume that costs are distributed evenly among consumers, at whatever level of government supplying the service. For returns, we assume that at the local level the consumer will be able to select his point on the demand curve, while at the state level he will have to consume the collectively determined amount. In Figure 2, the demand curves and the statewide equilibrium point P_oQ_o of Figure 1 are reproduced. We assume throughout that the three demand curves are linear and have the same slope.

Consider first an individual with demand D_C. If he has to choose between a state government that provides Q_o units of service at cost P_o per unit and between a more expensive locally provided service where the cost per unit is P_x but where

Figure 2.

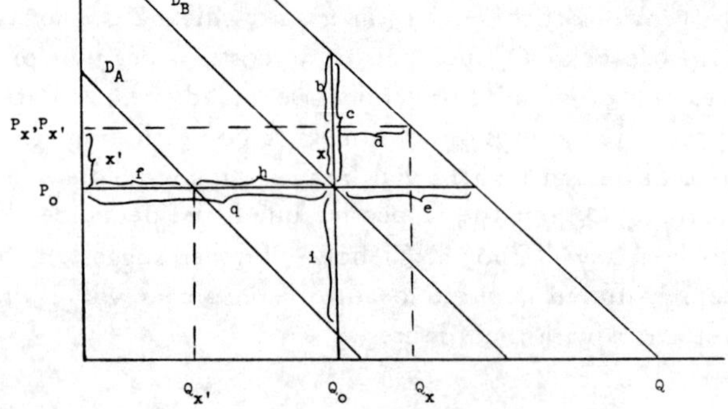

the amount supplied is Q_x, he will compare the rectangle of size xq (see Figure 2) -- which is the added cost to him of not being able to pay P_o for Q_o units-- with the extra return $\frac{bd}{2}$ which is his added benefit of being allowed to consume Q_x, the quantity demanded by him at price P_x. If $xq > \frac{bd}{2}$ he will choose the state, and if $xq < \frac{bd}{2}$ he will opt for the local supply of the service.

It can be shown[3] that the value of x (the increase in price) for which the two will be equal is:

$$x = \beta\,(q + e - \sqrt{(q+e)^2 - e^2}\,)\ ,$$

where β is the absolute value of the slope of the demand curve.[4] In addition to depending on the slope of the demand curve, the change in price entirely depends on q, the quantity actually supplied at price P_o, as compared with e, the excess demand at that price. The larger the latter is, the more price increase the consumer can afford without being worse off.

A similar computation can be performed for an individual whose demand curve is D_A and who at P_o would like to consume the quantity f--an amount smaller than the quantity (q_o) he actually consumes and pays for.[5] If (as assumed above) D_B is at half the distance between D_A and D_C the two triangles with vertexes at P_oQ_o, representing the loss of consumer's surplus to the two groups, are of equal size. But when we try to determine the price at which an individual with demand D_A will be indifferent between local and state service, the symmetry, as shown below, disappears.

We want to find for an individual with demand D_A the increase in price, x',[6] that will equate the extra cost of local supply with the extra benefit. Consider the area of the trapezoid bounded by P_x', and P_o, and by D_A (see Figure 2). This trapezoid represents the extra cost due to the increase in price. The area of the triangle $\frac{hi}{2}$ reflects the "deadweight" of the excessive quantity consumed at price P_o.[7] When we solve for the value of x' that equates the two we get

$$x' = \beta\ (\sqrt{f^2 + h^2} - f\ ),$$

which is a function of the slope of demand, and of the quantity actually consumed at the higher price --f-- and of the excess quantity consumed at price P_o--h. Again, the larger this excess is, the higher the price that would be tolerated under local supply.[8] Notice that for a given change in price the benefit here is always larger than with D_C, since $\frac{hi}{2} > \frac{bd}{2}$, and that the trapezoid described above is always smaller than the rectangle xq. Consequently, an individual with demand D_A will always be willing to accept a higher unit cost than an individual with demand D_C. This asymmetry is clearly seen in Figure 3 below.

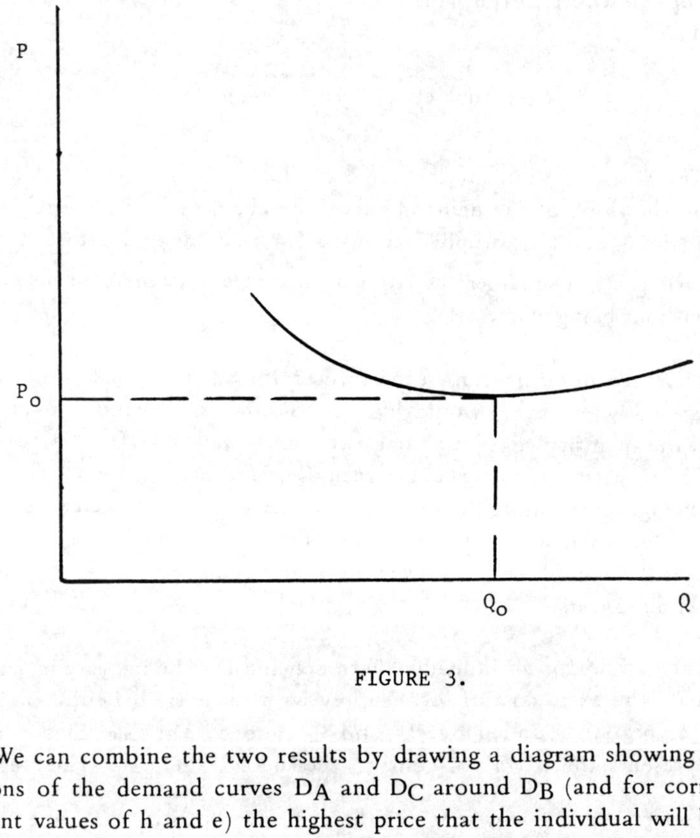

FIGURE 3.

We can combine the two results by drawing a diagram showing for different positions of the demand curves D_A and D_C around D_B (and for correspondingly different values of h and e) the highest price that the individual will be willing to pay (given β and P_o) for a local rather than a state supply. This is represented in Figure 3. It is important to realize that the bottom point of the curve is at height P_o, reflecting the fact that individuals with demand D_B are perfectly happy with state supply. It should be emphasized that if individuals with demand D_A and D_C find it advantageous to operate on a local basis, the cost per unit will also increase to the middle group, who will thus lose from such a change. If they are able to bribe individuals in the two other groups, the curve drawn in Figure 3 will flatten somewhat.[9]

35 TWO PROPOSITIONS

The analysis leading to Figure 3, basically answering the question of the degree to which individuals are willing to sacrifice economies of scale in favor of diversity of taste, involved the utility calculus of the individual. In analyzing the problem of grouping individuals into subgroups, we assume that economies of scale attainable by the entire state can also be realized by any of the subgroups. In pursuing the problem of subgrouping, it is necessary to make interpersonal comparisons. We assume that the value of an extra dollar is the same for all individuals in the group.[10] We also assume, as before, that all demand curves have a slope of $-\beta$ and that the quantity supplied to all individuals within a group is the same. We may begin by asking what is the optimal quantity if supply is at the state government level. The answer is that arithmetic mean of all quantities demanded (at the given price per unit) is the optimal amount. This can be proved by noting that the deadweight loss to an individual with demand D_C (see Figure 2) is the area of the triangle $\frac{ce}{2}$. Since the demand slope of the demand curve is $-\beta$, we have $c = e\beta$ and we can rewrite the area of the triangle as $\frac{\beta}{2}e^2$, which is a quadratic function of e--the excess demand at price P_o. We denote by e_i the excess demand for the ith individual, where i goes over all individuals in the group. We want to find the quatity, Q*, for which the expression $\Sigma \frac{\beta}{2}e_i^2 = \frac{\beta}{2}\Sigma e_i^2$ will be minimized, since this is the sum of the deadweight losses to all individuals. The arithmetic mean of the individual Q's, being a least square estimate, has this property and consequently is the optimal common quantity to be supplied to all individuals in the group.

We now maintain that *any* kind of subgrouping is preferable to a single group. This can be easily demonstrated by using the "sum of squares" identity so common in analysis of variance. This identity states that $\Sigma\Sigma(x_{ij} - \bar{x}_{i.})^2 + \Sigma\Sigma(\bar{x}_{i.} - \bar{x}_{..})^2 \equiv \Sigma\Sigma(x_{ij} - \bar{x}_{..})^2$ where x_{ij} are the individual observations, $\bar{x}_{i.}$ is the mean of x_{ij} over the group i, and $\bar{x}_{..}$ is the overall mean of all the observations. Stated in words, this expression says that the sum of square deviations of the individual observations around the overall mean is identical with the sum of squares of the observations around their own group means plus the sum of squares of the group means around the overall mean. Let us recognize that $\bar{x}_{..}$ can be identified with the mean quantity demanded by all individuals in the state at price P_o, $\bar{x}_{i.}$ the mean quantities for the subgroups, and x_{ij} the individual quantities demanded (by individual j in group i) at the common price. Individuals are allocated to subgroups by some arbitrary procedure. The total surplus loss due to a single price is $\frac{\beta}{2}\Sigma\Sigma(x_{ij} - \bar{x}_{..})^2$,[11] and the surplus loss due to subgrouping is $\frac{\beta}{2}\Sigma\Sigma(x_{ij} - \bar{x}_i)^2$. It is obvious that the former has to be larger than the latter, the difference being $\frac{\beta}{2}\Sigma\Sigma(x_{i.} - \bar{x}_{..})^2$, which is necessarily a positive quantity. So no matter how we slice the state into local groups, under the stated assumptions the deadweight welfare losses have to fall. Of course, the more homogeneous the individual groups are, the smaller the expression $\Sigma\Sigma(x_{ij} - \bar{x}_{i.})^2$ and the better off we are. But even a *purely random* allocation of individuals into groups is preferable to supplying the service at the state level.

It would be desirable now to combine the analysis of subgrouping and of economies of scale. Unfortunately, this is beyond the resources of this writer.

APPENDIX

We want to obtain the value of x for which, in terms of Figure 2,

$$(1) \quad \frac{b.d}{2} = x \cdot q.$$

Since the slope of D_C is $-\beta$,

$$(2) \quad \beta = \frac{b}{d} \quad \frac{b+x}{e} \quad \text{or } d = \frac{b}{\beta} \text{ and } \beta e - x = b.$$

Using (2) we can write the left side of (1) in terms of e and x

$$(3) \quad \frac{bd}{2} = \frac{b^2}{2\beta} = \frac{(\beta e - x)^2}{2\beta}.$$

Using (3) we can rewrite (1) as

$$(4) \quad \frac{(\beta e - x)^2}{2\beta} = xq,$$

which after some manipulations can be written as

$$(5) \quad x^2 - 2\beta(e+q)x + \beta^2 e^2 = 0.$$

Solving this quadratic equation for x we then get

$$(6) \quad x = \beta(e+q) \pm \sqrt{(e+q)^2 - e^2}.$$

The positive root of the solution does not make any economic sense, so the solution to x becomes

$$(7) \quad x = \beta(e+q) - \sqrt{(e+q)^2 - e^2}.$$

A similar procedure is used to obtain x'.

FOOTNOTES

*The example used in this paper was presented in a lecture by Gordon Tullock at the University of Washington in the Spring of 1968. In addition to this lecture, which aroused my interest in the problem, there are a number of papers in this general field which were, at that time, circulating in mimeographed form but which are beginning to come into publication. The paper read by Tullock, published in this issue, is different from the one read at the University of Washington but was in existence at that time. The paper he read at the University of Washington is to be published in the May issue of The American Economic Review. Further, Jerry Rothenberg read a paper "Decentralization Externalities, Equity and Inter-Governmental Relations" at a National Bureau of Economics conference organized by Julius Margolis at Princeton in 1968. This paper, together with a comment by Tullock, was published in the proceedings of this conference. Mancur Olson who has been working in this area using an essentially similar approach, will also have a paper on the subject in the proceedings issue of The American Economic Review this year.

[1] A justification of this solution is presented below.

[2] Charles M. Tiebout, "A Pure Theory of Local Expenditures," JOURNAL OF POLITICAL ECONOMY, LXIV (October, 1956), 416-24.

[3] See appendix.

[4] q and e have the dimensions of quantity; by multiplying them by B, which is the ratio of price to quantity, we obtain a result having the dimensions of price.

[5] Notice that an individual with demand $D_A < D_B$ may be worse off with the public good than without it. This is never the case for an individual with demand $D_C > D_B$.

[6] To avoid clutter in Figure 2, x' and $P_{x'}$ are drawn as identical with x and P_x.

[7] The possibility that D_A will cut the horizontal axis at a quantity less than Q_o is ignored here.

[8] Noting that q = f+h and that h is the excess supply, so that -h is the excess demand, we can write $x' = \beta\ (\sqrt{(q-h)^2 + h^2} - (q-h)\ )$. Recalling that e is the excess demand in the expression for x, the similarity between the solutions for x and for x' is clear.

[9] I find it too complicated to calculate the change in the form of the curve presented in Figure 3 if compensation takes place. It is particularly difficult since, given the configuration of D_A and D_C around D_B, individuals with demand D_A will opt for a local supply at a different price per unit than individuals with demand D_C. Furthermore, the cost per unit to the two groups would not in general be equal. It should be noted that at a given per unit increase in cost, the loss to the individuals with demand D_B is about half way between the losses to individuals with D_A and with D_C.

[10] If compensation payments are actually made, the assumption in the text is the appropriate one. It is also important to note that once it is decided to produce the service collectively, decisions as to the appropriate amount always contain interpersonal comparisons. It is desirable to make the rule for such comparisons explicit.

[11] Or $\frac{\beta}{2} \sum e_i^2$, using the notation of the previous section.

Private Schools and Public School Finance

Yoram Barzel
University of Washington

In his article "Efficiency Aspects of Local School Finance," Barlow (1970) attempts to compare empirically an actual level of schooling with the optimal one. His basic premise is that individuals (or households) are private maximizers in their voting behavior. A household will vote in favor of a higher tax if its valuation of the extra return exceeds the tax increase on it. Barlow concludes that for Michigan, in 1956, the actual level of schooling provided fell short of the optimal.

Barlow's work, in my view, is an important contribution to positive political economy, particularly in providing actual measurements in an area where measurement is scarce and difficult. Necessarily, one has to make simplifying assumptions to obtain empirical results. The objective of this paper is to examine critically and then to modify, within the framework and data employed by Barlow, one of the crucial assumptions; this leads to a reversal of most of his major results.

Schooling as a Public Good

The assumption involved is an implicit one—that schooling is provided by the public sector only. This will occur either because households do not choose to use private schools, even though they may, or because public schooling is compulsory. Although in fact public schooling is not compulsory, Barlow implicitly so treats it; and in overlooking the existence of private schools he also treats schooling as if it were a purely public good.

Barlow defines the optimum level of education as that level for which the vertical summation of individual demands equals the marginal cost of supplying education to that number of individuals. If education is a purely public good, the amount available to one is available to all. Thus everybody obtains the same quantity, and with the uniformity in quan-

I benefited greatly from James M. Buchanan's comments, particularly in discussing the public-good aspect of education, as well as from the valuable suggestions of Thomas E. Borcherding. This paper was written while I was visiting at University College, London. A summer grant from the Earhart Foundation is gratefully acknowledged.

tity, the vertical summation of individual demand curves can be carried out. But the fact that a commodity is publicly supplied at a uniform rate to all does not make such a commodity a public good, that is, fully divisible in consumption. We want, then, to see whether the notion that education is a public good is consistent with observed behavior; a question totally ignored by Barlow.

That schooling is not a purely public good on the production side is obvious. To accommodate more students, more teachers and larger schools are necessary, and this is more expensive. In fact, beyond a relatively small unit size it seems that schooling is a constant-cost industry. On the consumption side, however, schooling may be conceived of as a public good in that the returns from education are widely diffused and not restricted to the person being educated. The more nearly schooling approaches the nature of a purely public good, the smaller will be the return to the student relative to the return to society as a whole.

Considering the notion of the demand for education, we have to distinguish clearly between that demand manifested by voters' behavior toward schooling expenditures in the public sector and that manifested through the private sector. In the former, an increase in the level of schooling applies to all. Because an individual's demand for an extra unit of schooling in public schools is satisfied only when all obtain an extra unit of schooling, his demand will reflect the direct benefits from that unit as well as indirect benefits from the fact that everybody else obtains an extra unit. The externality then is basically internalized, and observed demand reflects all the returns. On the other hand, no such internalization takes place in the case of private education; the external benefits are not an argument in the individual's demand function, since the increase is restricted to the individual demander (or to a small group of demanders).

Consider a community of, say, 1,000. If education is a purely public good, private education will not take place unless the individual's valuation of a unit of education is in the order of 1,000 times greater than for those obtaining education through the public sector. We would, then, expect to observe extremely little private education. We should further ask what is the area over which education may be a public good. If it is the country as a whole, education would hardly be worthwhile on a state level, not to speak about the local or private level, since most of the benefits would dissipate out of the local unit. We would not observe state (or local) education, just as we do not observe states undertaking measures for defense.

The federal government, however, is not the main supporter of education, and most states leave education to local units.[1] We may conclude,

[1] In attempting to determine the optimal level of schooling Barlow treats (most of) Michigan as a single unit; he ignores the fact that there are several dozen school dis-

then, that at best the benefits from education are very narrowly diffused and that the motivation for public supply derives from considerations other than that education is a "public good." The fact that private education is widely observed side by side with public education implies not only that education is not a purely public good but also that if it does indeed contain any public-good component, it must be quite small. Furthermore, common observation indicates that many childless voters vote against educational expenditures favored by the majority.[2] Such behavior is inconsistent with the notion that education is largely a public good.[3] We conclude, then, that the evidence favors the notion that, by and large, education is a private good. In the rest of this paper it is maintained that the uniformity of public education (and the vertical summation of demand allowed by it) is imposed by institutions rather than by the technology of the good itself.

The Calculus of Private School Users

The actual quantity supplied publicly[4] is the quantity desired by the crucial voter—the median voter when majority rule applies (as assumed here)—and this quantity will differ in general from the optimal one. Whether the actual quantity is optimal or not, it is the same to all households.[5] But the quantity demanded, which depends on the price facing the household and on its income, varies greatly among them.[6] Private schools provide an opportunity to obtain the desired quantity.

Given that public schools are financed by taxes, as long as a household remains within the school district it is not exempted from paying the (school) taxes merely by its refusal to make use of the public school's services. A household will nevertheless choose a private school if the net

tricts in the state, even though he is using observations on school districts in his empirical work.

[2] In a school levy voters' survey in the State of Washington in 1970, it was found that 43 percent of those who voted for the levy had no school-age children, while 66 percent of those who voted against it had no children of school age (Washington State Temporary Special Levy Study Commission 1971, p. 343).

[3] An alternative explanation in terms of transfers from the minority to the majority of voters is offered below. The lowest income households, as shown below, do not benefit much, if at all, from these transfers. So the state supply of education cannot be viewed as means of helping those currently poor, and the subsidies to the next generation's poor are achieved, in part, by taxing the poor of the present generation.

[4] It is an unfortunate source of confusion that the term "public good" sometimes means a good supplied by the government and sometimes a good which is not partitionable. It is hoped that the context will clarify the appropriate meaning.

[5] This is an oversimplification (recognized by Barlow), particularly in that the number of children per household is not constant. This simplifying assumption will be retained in the numerical analysis. The effect of dropping it is discussed briefly toward the end of the paper.

[6] Again, as Barlow recognizes, other factors may also affect demand. This assumption is also retained in the numerical analysis, and later examined critically.

benefits from obtaining the desired (instead of the uniform) quantity exceed the extra cost. For households demanding a quantity smaller than that supplied by the public schools, the cost of private schooling will always exceed the net benefits, since benefits are negative and the cost positive. But the net benefits may outweigh the extra costs for those demanding a quantity larger than that supplied by public schools. We wish to determine whether any of the Michigan households considered by Barlow will be better off with private schooling.[7]

A number of working assumptions (essentially Barlow's) should be spelled out before such analysis. Schooling is considered a constant-cost industry, so the total quantity of education is proportionate to expenditures on schooling. Note that quantity can be increased either by increasing the number of students or by increasing the expenses per student, that is, the quality of schooling. We will assume that the cost per unit in private schools is the same as in public schools. Public schools, it is assumed, are entirely financed by residential property taxes. Given that property assessments vary across households, the "price" of schooling facing each household varies accordingly. More or less public schooling is achieved by raising or lowering the property tax millage. Finally, it is assumed that the median voter always obtains the quantity of education he desires.[8]

We will now show that the median or crucial voter has, in general, less than the median income. As income rises, the quantity of education demanded goes up, and so do property taxes. Barlow's findings for Michigan indicate that as income rises, the value of the benefits from an increased level of schooling rises faster than the extra tax cost. The marginal benefit-burden ration, then, rises with income, and the level of public education desired will also increase with income. Consider now a vote on the proposition to increase the level of education above that desired by the median-income individual. The half below him whose marginal benefit-burden ratio is lower will vote against an increase, and the quantity voted for cannot exceed that desired by the median voter. However, when considering the proposition of reducing the level of education below that desired by the median-income individual, the situation is quite different. Those with income just above the median will vote against reduction. But we cannot be sure that those substantially above will vote in the

[7] Barzel (1969) shows what premium an individual would pay to get the amount desired by him rather than the uniform amount collectively supplied. Buchanan (1970) generalizes to the case where private arrangements can supplement collective ones. But because of the constraint on students' time, private schooling is not a satisfactory supplement to regular schooling, and normally private schooling is substituted entirely for public schooling. This is why Buchanan's approach is not applied here; I rather consider public and private schools as mutually exclusive for the individual household.

[8] This implies that voters are in control of the educational bureaucracy rather than being controlled by it as frequently suggested.

same way. As income rises, the discrepancy between the level of education desired and the uniform amount supplied publicly rises, which makes private education progressively more attractive. When the discrepancy is large enough, private schooling may be preferred. The availability of private schools changes the marginal benefit-burden ratio for the highest-income individuals from more than one to zero. The individuals who opt for private education will vote for a reduction in the level of public education, since thereby their taxes will be reduced.[9] Since all those with less than median income will also vote for reduction, the level of education voted for will fall short of that desired by the median-income voter. Barlow's model is then adequate only if the incentive to use private schools is weak. Then, even though private schools may be permitted, no one will take advantage of that option, and the level of public schooling voted for is that desired by the median-income individual.

When the higher-income households move out of the public school system, they themselves now obtain whatever amount of education they desire.[10] Their tax contribution then is basically a transfer payment—entirely from the rich to the rest of the community. The clear-cut regressive nature of financing public schools through property taxes present in Barlow's model no longer holds.

The decision of high-income households to switch to private schools will affect the vote on actual level of public schools in two major ways. First, as the level of public schooling considered for voting declines, high-income households will experience a fall in their marginal benefit-burden ratio from more than one to zero. So, whereas in the absence of private schools they would have supported an increase in the level of public schooling, they will favor as little of it as possible when private schools are permitted. As the high-income household's voting allegiance changes, the position of the median (crucial) voter will move to a lower income level, and the support level for public schooling will decline.

Second, as this reduction in the level of public schooling leads more high-income households to switch over, those that remain within the public school system are presented with a continually increasing gift, in that fewer and fewer households make claim on the schooling resources. In other words, as the level of schooling declines, the (average) tax price to those remaining also goes down. While in the subsequent empirical work the average rather than the marginal price is taken into account, it is important to recognize that the marginal price is the appropriate decision

[9] Households with no school-age children (or with no prospective school-age children if the educational expenses are durable) will always vote for a zero level of education.

[10] If a school of some minimum size is required before costs become constant, as is probably the case, considerations of the optimal uniform quantity of schooling provided within each private school become relevant. In that case the framework provided by Barzel (1969) has to be superimposed on the one discussed here.

TABLE 1

SOME DATA ON MICHIGAN HOUSEHOLDS, 1956

Households	Residential Property Tax ($)	Household Income ($)	Marginal Benefit-Burden Ratio	Distribution of Households (%)	Cumulative Distribution of Households (%)
A	54	1,249	0.04	11.3	11.3
B	68	2,851	0.14	9.5	20.8
C	73	4,028	0.26	11.6	32.4
D	77	5,291	0.41	13.5	45.9
E	86	6,530	0.56	23.8	69.7
F	103	9,390	0.94	19.1	88.8
G	162	20,321	2.56	11.2	100.0

SOURCE.—Barlow (1970, table 1).

variable. To estimate the effect on the margin, however, requires more information than we have (and possibly more than the crucial voter may have).[11] Since the average price rises with the level of schooling, the marginal price is higher than the average price; thus use of the average price results in upward bias in stating the actual level of public schooling. Consequently, the results are biased against our main thesis: that some households will prefer private schooling.

The Numerical Results

When Barlow's data are examined, it is found that indeed his highest income group is better off by switching from public to private education. In Barlow's study, the population is divided into seven groups ordered in terms of property tax (and in terms of income) per household, group A being at the bottom and G highest on the list. The data are presented in table 1, adopted from Barlow's table 1. We assume, for simplicity, that within groups all households are identical. The median-income household is in group E, and according to Barlow's model the crucial voter resides in this group. Consequently the tax rate will be such that this group will be in equilibrium. But if group G prefers private schooling, it will vote for the lowest possible taxes. When households are ordered according to the amount of education they desire, group G will thus be at the bottom, followed by A, B, etc. The median voter in that case will be in group D

[11] A convenient feature of Barlow's model is that the quantity of education received by a household is proportional to its tax payment, so that the information needed for the household's decision is straightforward and fairly easy to obtain. It is unlikely that a household could estimate with any degree of confidence the effect of the change in price facing it, since it depends on the fraction of households switching to private schooling induced by the (marginal) decline in the quantity of public schooling.

rather than in E, and the level of public schooling will be such as to satisfy group D. I will now show that G is better off with private education.

In using private education, group G will improve its position by getting the amount of education it desires (rather than the quantity of public education that satisfies group E), but, of course, it has to pay the cost of the private education. To obtain numerical estimates of these two magnitudes we use the log-linear demand curve adopted by Barlow along with the numerical values of the coefficients he obtained. Barlow, it seems, abstracted from private education when deriving his estimates. Correcting for this error, however, does not seem to substantially affect the results, as will be suggested below.

Barlow's demand function is

$$Q_i = kY_i^{\alpha} P_i^{\beta} \quad \text{with} \quad \alpha = 0.67,\ \beta = -0.34,$$

where Q_i is the quantity demanded by group i, Y_i is its income, and P_i is the price facing it.[12] We can specify the units of Q to make $k = 1$, and k can be dropped. The median voter, by hypothesis, is in equilibrium, obtaining the quantity of education he demands given the tax price facing him. If the median voter is in group D, then that group is in equilibrium; since the tax bill of group D is \$77, $P_D \cdot Q_D = 77$, and we can write

$$P_D \cdot Q_D = 77 = Y_D^{0.67} P_D^{1-0.34} = 5{,}291^{0.67} P_D^{0.66},$$

where \$5,291 is the income of group D. Solving for P_D, we obtain $P_D = 0.1198$. The corresponding quantity Q_D is 642.8.

The price facing group E when the median voter is in this group rather than in D differs from P_D because of two factors. The first, a basic feature in Barlow's model, is that while the quantity of schooling is the same for both groups, the tax burden on group E is \$86 compared with \$77 for group D. The second is that for the median voter to be in group E, group G must have remained within the public school system, whereas when the median voter is in group D, group G has abstained from public education. When group G uses private schooling, the tax revenues are spent on a smaller group. Since 88.8 percent of the households are in groups A–F, compared with 11.2 percent in group G, the subsidy from the abstaining group to those using public education amounts to (100 − 88.8)/88.8, or almost one-eighth. The price to group E therefore increases by that factor when the median voter shifts from group D to group E. The price facing group E then is

[12] Barlow used observations from the public school sector. If schooling contains a nontrivial public-good component, then his estimated demand function substantially overstates demand for private education, as pointed out above. This distinction allows one, in principle, to test whether schooling is a public good, since, if it is, our estimate of the extent of actual private schooling is too high.

$$P_E = 0.1198 \times \frac{86}{77} \times \frac{100}{88.8} = 0.1507.$$

The quantity of schooling desired by group E, given the price, is

$$Q_E = 6530^{0.67} \times 0.1507^{-0.34} = 684.7$$

(where $Y_E = 6{,}530$). Group G has the choice of receiving the uniform 684.7 units of public schooling while paying a tax commensurate with that quantity, or else buying its schooling privately, thereby obtaining the amount it desires while simultaneously paying a tax commensurate with 642.8 units of public schooling (the amount desired by group D). To make the comparison we have to calculate the price of private schooling, the consumer's surplus from obtaining the desired rather than the common level of schooling, and the change in tax.

To obtain the price of private schooling, we assume, as stated above, that the cost of schooling is constant per unit and is the same for private as for public schools. The (weighted) average tax burden per household is \$89.59, or 4.2 percent more than the burden on group E. Since the price faced by group E is 0.1507, the average cost of schooling is 0.1569, and this is the per-unit price facing group G when using private education. The quantity they demand at this price is

$$Q_G = 20{,}321^{0.67} \times 0.1569^{-0.34} = 1{,}445$$

(where $Y_G = \$20{,}321$). We can also determine the marginal valuation of the 685th unit of education for group G, denoted by $P_G{}^*$, from the relation

$$684.7 = 20{,}321^{0.67} P_G{}^{*-0.34}$$

to obtain $P_G{}^* = 1.410$.

Now consider figure 1. If group G opts for private education, it will purchase 1,445 units at a price of 0.1569 per unit: a total outlay of \$226.7. If households in group G prefer public schooling and vote for it, since now the median voter will be in E, they will get 684.7 units of schooling. The shaded area reflects the gross benefits due to obtaining the desired rather than the uniform quantity. This area is

$$\int_{P=0.1569}^{P=1.410} 20{,}321^{0.67} P^{-0.34} dP - 684.7(1.410 - 0.1569) + (1445 - 684.7) \times 0.1569 = 1{,}119.5 - 857.8 + 119.3 = 381.0.$$

An additional benefit to group G is the reduction in taxes. Since group D demands only 642.8 units of schooling compared with 684.7 for group E, by voting for less schooling it will reduce its tax burden from \$162 to \$152.1—a saving of \$9.9. So we obtain the net benefit from private schooling as:

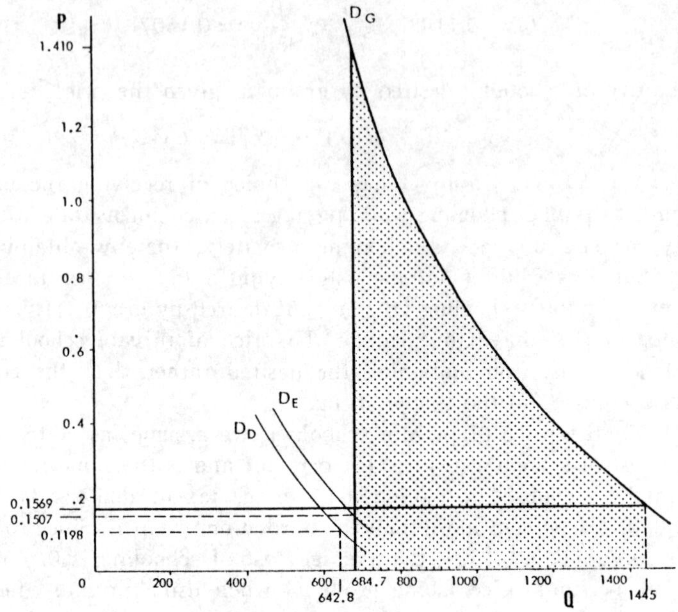

FIG. 1

$$\text{change in consumer surplus} + \text{reduction in tax} - \text{cost of private schooling} = \text{net benefit:}$$

$$\$381.0 + \$9.9 - \$226.7 = \$174.2.$$

Consequently, households in group G are better off with private schooling and will vote for the lowest possible level of school taxes. The same procedure can be used to determine whether households in group F are also better off with private education. It turns out, however, that they would lose almost $100 by opting for private schools.

Some Further Issues

The above results, when turned around a bit, may provide a clue as to why education, which we argue is a private good, is provided to a large extent publicly. It was just indicated that group F will lose some $100 if opting for private schools. But if all education were private, they would not have to pay school taxes, which also amount to about $100. For the lower half of this group, public schooling is preferable, since the value of the subsidy from group G exceeds the loss in not obtaining the optimal quantity. Groups D and E are clearly better off with public schooling, and probably so is group C. These groups comprise close to 60 percent of all households. So even if schooling is a purely private good, we can expect a majority of the voters to support public schooling, which results in an income transfer favorable to them.[13] This transfer is at the expense of the highest income group, but in the process the lowest income group is also made worse off by receiving, and partly paying for, more of the good than they desire.

Imagine a system where public education is compulsory and private education is banned. How would this compare with the present combination of public and private schools? We have demonstrated that group G is better off when private schools are available than when public schooling is compulsory. With the availability of private education, group D is in equilibrium and is obviously better off compared with the schooling level that satisfies group E. Groups A–C are also better off, since the discrepancy between their actual positions and their desired positions is now smaller. But what can we say about groups E and F? They are now further away from their desired positions, but on the other hand they benefit, as do Groups A–D, from the subsidy provided by group G and from the reduction in their tax. We can determine numerically which of the two forces dominates. It is enough to make the determination for group F, since if that group is now better off, group E is even more so, being closer to equilibrium. As it turns out, group F is in fact better off, since the benefit of the "subsidy" is larger than the loss occasioned by the move away from the desired quantity.[14] We encounter here a remarkable phenomenon. Had public education in Michigan been compulsory, then removal of that restriction would have made *every* household group better off—a most uncommon feature in public policies. This discovery of a genuinely Pareto-optimal policy move suggests that there may be similar wholly beneficial instances elsewhere in the economy. This seems an attractive area for search by economists.

When taken at face value, our results suggest that 11.2 percent of the Michigan households in 1956 would have used private rather than public schools.[15] In the next few paragraphs we will discuss briefly some estimation problems abstracted from above and point out the effects of additional factors that may affect the fraction of students attending private schools.

The price and income elasticities used above were derived by Barlow

[13] This still leaves unexplained why only *some* private goods are singled out for public supply.

[14] The value of the "subsidy" to group F is about $10, the tax reduction is about $6, and the loss in consumer surplus is about $5: a net gain of some $11. The net gain to group E is about $15.

[15] Actually, in 1955–56, 15.7 percent of all Michigan kindergarten and elementary school children attended nonpublic schools. Some nine-tenths of those, however, attended Catholic schools (U.S., Department of Health, Education, and Welfare 1960, chap. 2, pp. 114–17). The figure of 11.2 percent pertains to household rather than children. It should be noted that the number of children per household is not constant, and that many families in the highest income groups do not have school-age children.

apparently under the assumption that (within each school district) all schooling is public. To the extent that private schooling is utilized, the income of the crucial voter is below the median. By the same token, because of the indirect subsidy from users of private schools, the school tax paid by the median voter overstates the per-unit price facing him. The wider the dispersion of income within a school district, the more pronounced is the effect of these errors of specification. It does not seem, however, that these errors are correlated with the dependent variable, so they can be treated as random measurement errors. Such errors would bias both coefficients downward (in absolute terms). A higher value of income elasticity would strengthen the conclusions reached above; a higher value of price elasticity would weaken them. The two tend to cancel each other, but the net effect cannot be determined in the absence of additional data.

Given that households are grouped into a small number of income (and tax) classes, some of them quite diverse, the group means used above provide only a rough approximation to the true values. The errors are both in being unable to pinpoint the income and the tax of the median voter and in not having access to the entire income distribution of groups F and G to determine the break-even point for using private rather than public schools. It does not seem, however, that correcting for these factors would make much difference. Groups D and E are fairly homogeneous, so the error in using the group means as an estimate of the median cannot be large. As to the distribution of income within groups F and G, we saw that the gain from private schooling to group G is substantial, while group F has a strong incentive to use public schools. The break-even point therefore appears to be in the neighborhood of the actual division line between the two groups.[16]

A more serious problem arises from the fact that (most of) Michigan is treated as a single unit in comparing the actual with the optimal quantity of public schooling. Since Michigan actually contains many individual school districts, the analysis is correct only if the distribution of income (as well as of other relevant characteristics) is the same in all districts.[17] Similar individuals do have an incentive to belong to the same school district; therefore, within such districts private schooling may be unimportant. While we may expect a fair amount of private schooling in Detroit, probably little of it will be found in the city's middle-class suburbs.[18]

[16] It is possible, but not checked for, that some households with income higher than the average of group F ($9,390) but less than that for group G ($20,321) are net losers when the median voter moves from group E to group D.

[17] Recent court decisions in California and Texas require uniform education within states. If the decisions are upheld and applied to other states, the uniformity of population within school districts would not matter any more.

[18] I was unable to obtain data at less than the state level to test the proposition. There is some evidence, however, to the effect that the larger the community size, the less satisfaction there is with children's education (*Gallup Opinion Index* 1969).

By far the least satisfactory assumption is that the demand for education by a household is a function only of its income and of the price facing it. Obviously, the demand for public education by families with more than the average number of children is underestimated. The quality of education is not uniform even within a single school district, and this quality is probably positively correlated with income. Finally, and most important, education is a multidimensional commodity, and even households homogeneous in income and price may exhibit a taste for different kinds of education. Parochial schools are the most prominent manifestation of such diversity, but the existence of many other types of private schools indicates the pervasiveness of this phenomenon.[19]

The above-mentioned factors (along with still others such as sources of finance to the public school system other than the residential property tax) render the 11.2 percent more a reference point than an actual estimate of the proportion of households using private schools.

To what extent does the actual level of schooling differ from the socially optimal one? Barlow arrives at the conclusion that the quantity of schooling is less than optimal by showing that for the crucial voter (with public schooling only), the marginal benefit-burden ratio at efficiency is about 0.5. In that case, the optimal quantity exceeds the quantity desired by the crucial voter. But by demonstrating that group G will not remain in the public school system, that result is drastically modified.[20] The relative contribution of the different groups to the school tax is unaffected by the behavior of group G, but the shares in the benefits are tripled for all groups other than G, since group G's share in the benefits when using public schools is about two-thirds. Consequently, whereas the marginal benefit-burden ratio for group D in Barlow's model is 0.41, the exclusion of group G changes this to about 1.2; this means that for groups A–F combined, the quantity of public schooling exceeds the optimal one. Given, however, the low price elasticity, the actual quantity exceeds the optimal quantity by less than 10 percent. Group G, of course, gets its optimal quantity.

The concept of the "efficient quantity" is itself meaningful only when uniformity is imposed. If schooling is in fact a private good, allocation

[19] Proponents of the notion that education is a "public good" have to face the question of whether all education, or only public education, is a public good. If all education is a public good, then private schools should not be discriminated against in terms of tax support. If, on the other hand, only public education is a public good, the social output falls when students transfer from public to private schools.

[20] Johnson (1972, pp. S287–88) attributes to Anne Krueger a similar argument with respect to allocation and the optimal quantity. He says: "Krueger argued, using a model that allowed for the presence of private universities that have to be paid for by parents in addition to the taxes they pay for state universities that they do not patronize with their children because quality is too low, that the income redistribution might go the other way and that there might, in consequence, be either overallocation or underallocation of resources to higher education as a whole." I could not, however, locate Krueger's own statement.

will be improved if every household is allowed to obtain its own desired quantity of schooling rather than an amount that satisfies some average household.

References

Barlow, Robin. "Efficiency Aspects of Local School Finance." *J.P.E.* 78 (September/October 1970): 1028–40.

Barzel, Yoram. "Two Propositions on the Optimum Level of Producing Collective Goods." *Public Choice* 6 (Spring 1969): 31–38.

Buchanan, James M. "Notes for an Economic Theory of Socialism." *Public Choice* 8 (Spring 1970): 29–43.

Gallup Opinion Index. Report no. 47. Princeton, N.J.: Gallup International, May 1969.

Johnson, Harry G. "The Alternatives before Us." *J.P.E.* 80, no. 2, suppl. (May/June 1972): S280–89.

U.S., Department of Health, Education, and Welfare, Office of Education. *Biennial Survey of Education in the United States 1954–1956*. Washington: Government Printing Office, 1960.

Washington State Temporary Special Levy Study Commission. *Research Report*. Vol. 1. March 1971.

5

IS THE ACT OF VOTING RATIONAL?

Yoram Barzel and Eugene Silberberg

I. Introduction

Recent work by several economists has shown that certain phenomena heretofore considered within the realm of political science are amenable to analysis via the use of "economic" models. In particular, the pioneering works of A. Downs [3] and J. Buchanan and G. Tullock [2] showed that testable hypotheses about political behavior could be formulated from the assumption of maximizing behavior on the part of individual voters. The purpose of this paper is to apply this economic reasoning to the problem of voter participation. We wish to demonstrate that varying voter turnout at different elections can be explained in part on the basis of rational, wealth-maximizing behavior on the part of the electorate.

Superficially, it seems odd that individuals bother to vote at all. The literature often expresses the view that in any issue of wide scope, the insignificant weight of his single vote would induce a rational individual to save his time and effort by not voting.[1] The fact that many nevertheless choose to vote is therefore frequently

*Department of Economics, University of Washington. We wish to thank Dick McDonald for his help with the computations.

[1]For example, in Downs [3, p. 267], "In fact, since each citizen's vote value is usually quite small, any [voting] cost at all may threaten the political system with collapse through lack of participation." Also, in a logically similar context, Tullock [7] totally discounts the effect that any one individual might have on the outcome of a revolution in the individual's decision to participate or not.

interpreted as "irrational" or else as consumption activity on the part of an individual who derives utility from being a "responsible citizen" and discharging his civic duties.[2]

To say that a single vote is trivial, however, is to assert that individuals make decisions on the basis of average rather than marginal quantities. The crucial element in a choice-theoretic analysis of voting behavior is not the absolute number of voters, but rather, whether a given voter may prove to provide the swing vote. If the individual expects the issue to be very close to a tie, his vote could matter a great deal; otherwise he will view his (marginal) effect on the outcome as insignificant. The one who does not vote is therefore not necessarily uninterested in the result. He may be greatly interested, but may also feel that since he is unlikely to affect the outcome, the costs associated with voting outweigh the expected benefits.[3]

II. The Theoretical Model

Consider now an individual who anticipates the turnout on a particular issue to be n, where each voter is expected with probability p to vote "yes" on an issue and (1 - p) to vote "no." Assuming independence of voters, he expects the outcome of the vote to be np yeses and n(1 - p) noes with a standard deviation of $\sqrt{np(1-p)}$. If, for example, n = 1000 and p = 0.52, he expects 520 yeses with a standard deviation of about 15. Using the normal approximation to the binomial, he would expect the actual outcome to be yes with a probability of about 0.9. On the other hand, with n = 1000 as before, but with p = 0.6, np = 600 with a standard deviation still of about 15 and the probability of a yes outcome is now better than 0.999999. Obviously, the potential of a single additional vote to change the result differs greatly in the two situations.

More precisely, if an individual voter is to change the result of an election, the original outcome will have had to be either a tie when n is even (the extra vote will break the tie) or a majority of one when n is odd (the extra vote could create a tie if cast against the majority). Given n and p, the question then is about the probability of $\frac{n}{2}$ *yes* votes when n is even and of $\frac{n+1}{2}$ (or $\frac{n-1}{2}$) *yes* votes when n is odd.

This probability, or rather probability density if the normal approximation is used, is given by the density of the unit normal distribution at $\frac{np - n/2}{\sqrt{npq}}$. The higher the density, the larger the chance that the n + 1th voter will affect the outcome.

[2]For example, consider the following statement by Kenneth Arrow:

> To some extent, certainly, the voter is cast in a role in which he feels some obligation to consider the social good, not just his own. It is in fact somewhat hard to explain otherwise why an individual votes at all in a large election, since the probability that his vote will be decisive in so negligible [1].

Also, in Chapter 3 of Downs [3], a model of voting behavior is developed on the basis of expected "utility income" of voting. And on p. 267, Downs states that "rational men in a democracy are motivated to some extent by a sense of social responsibility relatively independent of their own shortrun gains and losses." Downs argues throughout his book that individuals vote in order to preserve the political system (see, e.g., the quote in the previous footnote). This argument fails to come to grips with the obvious "free-rider" problem associated with political choice. In Buchanan and Tullock [2, p. 133], the authors duly note the social pressures to vote out of "citizen's duty."

[3]Since the distribution of non-voters is presumably symmetric with respect to their positions on outcome, the social pressure to participate in elections, if effective, does not generally affect the outcome of the election.

A refutable hypothesis thus implied is that, other things being equal, voter participation in a given election will tend to be smaller the more lopsided the anticipated margin of victory.[4] In elections forecast as very close, we should expect a heavier percentage turnout of voters, since each voter will perceive a greater probability of affecting the outcome. For p which greatly differs from 0.5, the incentive to vote is low for members of both parties; and, when p is close to 0.5, supporters of both parties have a strong incentive to vote.

For instance, until recently the outcome was always extremely lopsided in state elections in the South; the Democratic party won, usually with majorities of 70 percent to 100 percent. We observe that in these elections voter turnout has been very low, usually only 20 percent to 30 percent of the voting-age population.[5] Clearly, such majority percentages discouraged most voters from incurring the cost of participating in elections. The crucial point is that these data are inconsistent with the hypothesis that individuals vote *solely* because of the influence of consumption variables (e.g., "civic duty," etc.). Unless tastes vary across the population (an hypothesis which explains any phenomenon), there is no reason to expect a relationship between the closeness of the election and the degree of voter participation, if the participants are motivated solely by their own consumption expectations.

We now consider a second issue. It seems reasonable to assume that not everyone views the potential outcome of an election in the same manner; i.e., the estimate of the probability p will vary across individuals. The effect of this variance of p in the population on voter turnout, however, itself depends on the (mean) value p. If the average p value is very close to 0.5, then a large variance in the estimated p on the part of voters will probably tend to disminish voter participation.[6] As we move away from p = 0.5, the opposite might be true. If p = 0.6 with little variance of opinion among voters, then a marginal vote will almost surely not count. However, with an extremely volatile voter population (large variance), the probability is heightened that a sample of voters favor election of the presumed minority candidate. Therefore, variance of the estimate of the anticipated outcome may increase voter participation if the election is not considered to be close. Since, then, the placement of the mean determines the relation between the dispersion around the mean and voter participation, we merely recognize that each voter formulates a different notion of the true p. In other words, we view the variance around the mean as a potentially relevant variable, but we do not formulate a testable hypothesis regarding it.[7]

Many other elements, of course, affect the payoff function of voting. First, the outcome of the vote may be viewed as unimportant: many individuals viewed Nixon and Humphrey as equally good (or equally bad). The more significant the outcome, the higher the incentive to vote, and voters may differ in this respect

[4]This hypothesis is mentioned in Tullock [6], where reference is also made to a paper later published by W. H. Riker and P. C. Ordeshook [5]. This latter work contains results consistent with those of this paper. However, their analysis is clouded by their use of questionnaire data rather than actual voting behavior, and the fact that their data pertained to presidential elections which, because of electoral college considerations, makes direct testing of the above hypothesis more difficult.

[5]Until recently, registration was also a relatively low percentage of total voting-age population in the Southern states. This reflects the same issue: i.e., low probability of affecting the outcome. The data are from various U.S. Statistical Abstracts.

[6]In the extreme case where p = 0.5 with no variance, the marginal voter will almost surely vote, since he will very likely change the outcome. A large variance with p = 0.5 will lessen this likelihood of changing the outcome.

[7]The variability in the value of p makes it virtually impossible to obtain an exact expression of the "distance" of the average p from 0.5 in terms of the probability of the actual outcome being 0.5.

within voting units as well as between them. Second, the cost of voting depends on whether one is already registered or not; how far from the polling place one lives; how convenient are the polling hours; and whether one planned to be in the polling place anyhow to vote on some other issue.[8] In the empirical work we attempt to capture the effect of some of these variables.

III. The Empirical Test

The actual form of the estimating equation where the unit of observation is a state is,

$$y = a + b_1x_1 + b_2x_2 + b_3x_3 + b_4x_4 + b_5x_5 + b_6x_6 + u,$$

where:

- y = ratio of voters that actually voted in a given gubernatorial election to to total voting-age population;
- x_1 = ratio of votes for winner to that of total vote (ex post);
- x_2 = total voting-age population of state;
- x_3 = fraction of voting-age population registered to vote;
- x_4 = absolute difference in proportion voting Democrat between current and last election;
- x_5 = 1 if presidential election held that year, 0 otherwise;
- x_6 = 1 if senatorial election held that year, 0 otherwise.

Data for the above variables are obtained entirely from the United States Statistical Abstracts. Gubernatorial elections were chosen because it was felt that the issues raised in this paper were relevant for such elections, and the number of observations is large enough to obtain conclusive results. Also, the issues were not clouded by electoral college considerations which affect presidential elections. We now explain briefly the roles of the variables in the regression equation.

The self-explanatory voter participation variable (y) is what we seek to analyze. Its variation is substantial, ranging from a low of 17 percent (Georgia, 1962) to a high of 76 percent (Utah, 1964). With regard to x_1, the ex-post winning majority is used as a proxy for the anticipated outcome of the election; that is, we assume that deviations of the actual from the expected result are not large.[9] It should be noted that the measurements of x_1 and y are basically independent, and spurious correlation between them is most unlikely. At worst, a positive spurious correlation may occur when one party gets a larger turnout than usual, increasing both its majority and its overall participation. Since our model predicts a negative relation between x_1 and y, any resultant bias in that case would be against our hypothesis.

The total voting-age population (x_2) is used because the closeness of an election depends upon the size of the electorate. For example, with a 52 percent expected majority in, say, New York state, a marginal vote would have almost no chance of changing the outcome. However, the probability of changing the out-

[8]In cases where the outcome of a vote depends on some minimum turnout we may get the perverse result that a person voting against a certain issue may actually make it win, since this could be the crucial vote in terms of required minimum, but it would be outweighted by a majority of more than one among other votes already cast.

[9]A more complete analysis might use the results of pre-election polls as a measure of the anticipated result.

come is much larger, given the same figure, in, say, Nevada, since the variance of the sample mean will be much greater.[10]

The percentage of registered voters (x_3) is a proxy for the intensity of feeling regarding the outcome of the election. If the election is deemed important, a larger fraction of the electorate should be moved to register. The absolute difference in the percentage of Democratic votes between the current and the last election (x_4) is used as a measure of the variance of the estimate of the election outcome. In other words, we assume that voters give little weight to elections earlier than the previous one in formulating their decisions with regard to the present election. Finally, the two dummy variables, x_5 and x_6, are included to measure the effect of the presence of other issues on the ballot.

The data used to test the hypothesis are for four years: 1962, 1964, 1966, and 1968. Since gubernatorial elections are normally held only once every four years, we have fewer than 50 observations per year. Data on registered voters are available for 1968 only, so the effect of this variable is examined only in a subset of the data. Finally, some observations were missing or inappropriate, which further reduced the number of observations.

The regression results for the four years combined are presented in Table 1. The overall regression is highly significant, and about half of the original variance is

Table 1

Variable	*Coefficient*	*t ratio*	
x_1 = winning majority	-.768	-7.24	n = 122
x_2 = voting age population (000)	-.006	-1.41	R^2 = 0.493
x_4 = difference in fraction of democratic vote	-.291	-2.41	$\bar{R}^2$ = 0.472
x_5 = presidential dummy	0.111	5.75	
x_6 = senatorial dummy	0.055	2.62	

accounted for. This is quite substantial, in view of the fact that limitations in data entirely precluded the use of any factors reflecting the importance of the outcome to the individual voter. The difference in fraction of Democratic votes between the current and the previous election, reflecting the uncertainty of voters about the value of p, proved significant. Given the sign of the coefficient, "close" elections dominate the relation.

Our hypothesis predicted a pattern of signs with respect to the other four variables, and all four coefficients obtained the right signs. The coefficient of the size of the state variable (the total voting age population) is significant at the 10 percent but not at the 5 percent level; the other coefficients are very highly significant.

The coefficients of variables for presidential and senatorial dummies indicate that in years and states in which such elections were held, the turnout of voters increased by 11 and 5 percent, respectively. On the other hand, the larger the state, as measured by voting-age population, the smaller the turnout—an increase of one million in voting-age population tends to reduce turnout by 6 percent.[11]

[10]The anticipated number of voters is the ideal variable here, and the voting-age population seems a satisfactory proxy.

[11]The relation here is clearly nonlinear, and the statement in the text applies only around the observed mean of the variable.

The most significant, and the most important, result is the coefficient of the variable for the winning majority. As this majority increases the turnout declines, as predicted by our model. A 1 percent increase in the winning majority leads to about 3/4 of 1 percent decline in turnout. If hypotheses are correct in regarding the act of voting as a civic duty or as a consumption activity, voter turnout should be independent of the majority by which a candidate wins (and, similarly, of the size of the state in which the voter resides). Since that turnout is clearly and strongly affected by the winning majority, we have to reject the above hypotheses, at least as the sole explanation of why people vote, and tentatively accept the notion that their tendency to vote increases as the likelihood becomes greater that their vote may actually decide the final outcome.

Table 2

Variable	Coefficient	t ratio	
x_1 = winning majority	–.547	–1.93	n = 22
x_2 = voting-age population (000)	–.009	–.89	$R^2 = 0.815$
x_3 = fraction of x_2 registered	–.884	5.58	$\bar{R}^2 = 0.757$
x_4 = difference in fraction of democratic vote	–.154	–.70	
x_6 = senatorial dummy	0.004	0.12	

In Table 2 we present the results for 1968 alone, for which voter registration data are available. Again, for all the variables for which our model predicts the sign, the outcome is consistent with the model. The t ratios are lower, as one would expect with fewer observations. The strongest variable here is that of the ratio of registered voters to the population of voting age, but the coefficient of the winning majority variable is also significant.[12] We also ran a regression using as the dependent variable the fraction of registered voters who actually voted. The hypothesis being tested with this regression is that, among those individuals who had already indicated their interest in the voting outcome(s) by taking the trouble to register, the ones who actually voted were motivated by their perceived chance of affecting the outcome. Here again, the signs of the coefficients are consistent with the hypothesis and the most significant coefficient is the winning majority.

IV. Some Conjectures and Conclusions

The hypothesis that political activity is determined partly by the influence each individual perceives himself to have on the outcome of elections has been tested only for one particular subset of all political activity. We feel, however, that the results are encouraging enough to offer some speculations on other aspects of

[12]By 1968 the dominance of Democrats in the "Old South" and the accompanying low participation was less pronounced. Nevertheless, a regression for 1968 deleting the variable for registered voters still explains about 50 percent of the variance, in spite of the absence of the presidential dummy that does not apply to a single year.

political choice. As an initial example, consider the campaign behavior of candidates for office. When faced with a bipartisan audience, we would expect them to stress the superiority of their platform and personality and at best give lip service to the need to vote. On the other hand, when facing a sympathetic audience, candidates can be expected to encourage voter turnout. Given our hypothesis, we predict that in front of the latter audience, candidates will stress the anticipated closeness of the outcome, trying to impress each individual in the audience that *his* vote might be the decisive one.

The same reasoning suggests that the anticipated closeness of the outcome will be a major theme in the solicitation of campaign contributions. Casual empiricism indicates that in order for candidates to receive substantial contributions, their credibility at the polls—e.g., in early presidential primaries—must be established. Also, candidates will not want to impress their supporters as being too far out in front of the other candidates, lest their contributions fall off for similar reasons. The above behavior is consistent with the hypothesis that an individual engages in political activity at least partly out of the belief that he has a significant chance of affecting the outcome.

If individuals believe that their votes have no effect on the outcome, participation rates should be independent of the benefits derived from the election of the candidate most preferred by them. The observed disproportionate participation of high income individuals, who in general tend to be affected more by the outcomes of elections, is further evidence that an individual tends to vote when he views his role as decisive. Thus our model provides an additional, and probably simpler, explanation of the high participation rate by high income people than that of Frey [4].

By the same token, our model should predict the participation rate in revolutions. Specifically, when a regime is near the brink of collapse, not only would revolutionary participation increase, but so also would counter-revolutionary participation, since individuals on *both* sides will view themselves as decisive.[13]

Our model has an interesting implication regarding the cost of operating a party machine whose objective is to win elections. Consider a state for which initially p = 0.50, with a normal voter turnout of one million, giving a standard deviation of the outcome of 500.[14] If the party recruits, say, 500 new voters, the actual winning majority will tend to deviate from 0.5 towards the party running the machine. It would seem that the chance that the party will win is increased from 50 percent to 68 percent. But as a result of the deviation of p from 0.5, voter turnout (from both parties) will fall somewhat and the chance of winning the election becomes higher than 68 percent. Now, if the party machine is maintained for further elections, since turnout is declining the effect of the 500 extra votes will be more decisive than before. This process (assuming the other party remains passive) will converge to the point where only the 500 recruited voters actually vote. The party machine will then tend to reduce the budget for its guaranteed vote, since the outcome of the vote becomes more and more certain with time. This converging process may explain the observed experience in the South (until fairly recently) where Democrats got almost the entire vote, and voter turnout was extremely low. Probably a large fraction of the actual vote is by individuals dependent on political patronage.[15]

[13] See, e.g., Tullock [7], in which this point is ignored.

[14] Standard deviation = $\sqrt{npq} = \sqrt{1{,}000{,}000 \times .5 \times .5} = 500$. This, however, is based on the assumption that p itself is not a random variable. If it is, as is likely the case, the standard error will be more than 500.

[15] Recipients of patronage can be relied upon to side with their patron party; if they vote, their vote then is not too secret. And since the list of actual voters is not secret, it is easy to apply pressure on this group to vote and be confident in the results.

To recapitulate, our basic hypothesis is that wealth-maximizing behavior can explain, in part, why people bother to vote. The individual's incentive to vote increases the larger his estimate of benefits to be derived from his candidate being elected, the smaller his cost of voting, and the larger the chance he perceives of his being the decisive vote. This last item is the crucial element in our analysis. Examining the extent of turnout in gubernatorial elections, we show that in fact people tend to vote when the cost is low (as the number of issues on the ballot increases the cost of voting for each decreases) and that the fraction of individuals actually voting increases, the larger the probability that they will affect the outcome. The strong confirmation of this last hypothesis is also a refutation of the hypothesis that individuals vote solely to meet their civic duty.

REFERENCES

[1] Arrow, Kenneth. "The Organization of Economic Activity: Issues Pertinent to the Choice of Market Versus Nonmarket Allocation." *The Analysis and Evaluation of Public Expenditures: The PPB System,* Part I (Joint Economic Committee, 91st Congress, 1st Session, 1969), p. 61.

[2] Buchanan, James M., and Tullock, Gordon. *The Calculus of Consent,* Ann Arbor, Michigan: Ann Arbor Paperbacks, 1965.

[3] Downs, Anthony. *An Economic Theory of Democracy.* New York: Harper and Row, 1957.

[4] Frey, Bruno S. "Why Do High Income People Participate More in Politics?" *Public Choice,* XI (Fall, 1971), 101-105.

[5] Riker, William H., and Ordeshook, Peter C. "A Theory of the Calculus of Voting." *Am. Polit. Scie. Review,* LXII (March, 1968), 25-42.

[6] Tullock, Gordon. *Toward a Mathematics of Politics.* Ann Arbor: University of Michigan Press, 1967.

[7] Tullock, Gordon. "The Paradox of Revolution." *Public Choice,* XI (Fall, 1971), 89-99.

1

Voting Behavior, Efficiency, and Equity

YORAM BARZEL and ROBERT T. DEACON*

Introduction

The received literature on public expenditure, with the expection of Buchanan, implicitly assumes that goods and services provided collectively are not also simultaneously available through private markets. In real situations, however, private supply is commonly found alongside public provision. This phenomenon poses some interesting and important analytical questions regarding the effect of private supply upon voting behavior, the efficiency of public policy, and equity in the provision of public services.[1]

To address several of these questions, this paper first postulates a model of voting and analyzes the conditions under which voters will choose an efficient rate of public output. Within this context, the equity implications of alternative tax structures are explored. The remainder of the paper incorporates into the analysis the existence of private markets for services that are also collectively supplied. Specifically, it examines the effect of private supply on voting behavior and on the progressivity of public policy.

Voting is introduced into the analysis as the instrument of collective decisions. The collective choice model employed is that of simple majority rule in a case

*University of Washington and the Hoover Institution; University of California, Santa Barbara respectively.

[1] Barzel analyzes the necessary modifications of Barlow's model to account for private supply.

where voters, subject to a structure of individual tax shares fixed prior to the election, simultaneously choose the level of taxes and the associated rate of output for a single, collectively provided service (as is often the situation with local education). It is assumed that the voting franchise is general and that citizens fully informed about the costs and benefits of various public expenditure proposals vote their private preferences. Given an issue on the ballot, a voter weighs its potential added benefit against the extra tax cost and votes accordingly. Finally, it is assumed that the outcome of the election corresponds to the median of the individual optima, i.e., the rate of provision desired by the median voter.[2]

A Pure Public Good

According to the definition we adopt, consumption of a pure public good by one person does not interfere with or subtract from anyone else's consumption of that good. Since the economies of joint consumption are complete, n individuals can each be supplied a unit of such a good at the same cost as for one individual. The level of output of a public good is Pareto optimal if the sum of individuals' marginal valuations equals the marginal cost of the good (provided, of course, that second-order and total conditions are satisfied).[3] Governments presumably are engaged in providing some purely public goods for which these efficiency conditions apply.[4] However, in many instances the joint consumption economies of collectively provided goods are less than complete, and in such cases the above conditions require careful consideration.

To examine the case of a purely public good, consider a society of n citizens in which incomes differ, but individual utility contours are identical. Suppose further that there is one public good and m private goods and that individual demand functions for the public good are all of the form

$$Q_i = k\, Y_i^{\alpha}\, T_i^{-\beta}\, P_1^{\eta_1} \ldots P_m^{\eta_m} \quad (i = 1 \ldots n) \qquad (1)$$

where Q_i is the quantity of the collective good demanded by the ith voter, Y_i is his income, T_i is the tax price (or cost share) paid for provision of a unit of the collective good, $P_1 \ldots P_m$ are the prices of private goods and k, α, β, $\eta_1 \ldots \eta_m$ are parameters (β is preceded by a minus sign to make it positive).[5] In general, it is possible to devise a structure of tax prices which will induce all citizens to demand the same rate of collective supply. This tax structure can be found by

[2]This outcome would be attained if ballot proposals take the form of increments to an existing rate of supply and new proposals are offered until one fails to obtain a simple majority (see Howard Bowen). Alternatively, one could specify that successful politicians offer the voters tax expenditure packages that are identical to the optimum position of the median voter (see Anthony Downs).

[3]Implicit in this statement is the notion of a costless mechanism to provide the necessary information.

[4]Though even here there are problems. See Buchanan and Demsetz.

[5]These are not demand functions in the usual sense, as they do not represent observable market behavior. Rather, they describe behavior that would be observed if the good Q exhibited no joint consumption economies and were offered to individual i at price T.

equating $Q_i = Q_j$, which yields:

$$kY_i^{\alpha} T_i^{-\beta} P_1^{\eta_1} \ldots P_m^{\eta_m} = kY_j^{\alpha} T_j^{-\beta} P_1^{\eta_1} \ldots P_m^{\eta_m} \quad (2)$$

$(i, j = 1 \ldots n)$

Thus, in terms of the demand functions specified, individual tax rates must be a function of income,

$$\frac{T_i}{T_j} = \frac{Y_i^{\alpha/\beta}}{Y_j^{\alpha/\beta}} \quad (i, j = 1 \ldots n), \quad (3)$$

for unanimity to obtain. If the good can be produced at constant marginal cost c, then a Pareto optimal rate of supply can be obtained by charging each citizen a tax price

$$T_i = \frac{c}{\sum_{j=1}^{n} Y_j^{\alpha/\beta}} Y_i^{\alpha/\beta} \quad (i = 1 \ldots n). \quad (4)$$

The outcome of such an arrangement would be the familiar Lindahl solution.[6] Notice that individual tax prices are constant and exponentially related to incomes.

These notions are illustrated by the example in Figure 1 of an electorate composed of three individuals with demands D_A, D_B, D_C where D_T is their vertical summation. If the marginal cost of producing the quantity OR is RT then OR satisfies the marginal condition for an optimum. With a tax system devised to impose a marginal tax rate RA for OR units on the first individual, and similarly RB and RC on the other two individuals, not only will the quantity OR be approved, the vote will be unanimous.

In the Lindahl solution depicted in Figure 1, each individual's marginal valuation, or willingness to pay for a marginal unit, is represented by the height of his demand curve at output OR and is identical to his tax price. Suppose, however, that output rate OR had been provided under a tax scheme which imposed a tax price on individual C equal to RB. If this were the case, then individual C would desire a rate of output larger than OR, *and* his marginal valuation of OR units would no longer equal RC. To see the latter point, notice that a Lindahl tax scheme would require person C to contribute RC · OR in taxes. Under the alternative taxing policy, his tax bill would be only RB · OR, implying a positive income effect upon demand, which will either increase or decrease his willingness to pay, depending upon whether the collective good is normal or inferior, respectively. Likewise, if this policy imposed a tax price of RB on individual A as well, a negative income effect would result, shifting A's marginal valuation schedule.

Notions of equity in the literature of public finance usually apply to tax systems. A tax which takes a larger (smaller) share of income from the rich than from the poor is designated progressive (regressive). When these notions are applied

[6]Pareto optimality requires that the public good be produced in an efficient, cost-minimizing fashion. Further, the Lindahl solution characterized in (4) is, of course, only one of the infite number of possible Pareto optimal arrangements.

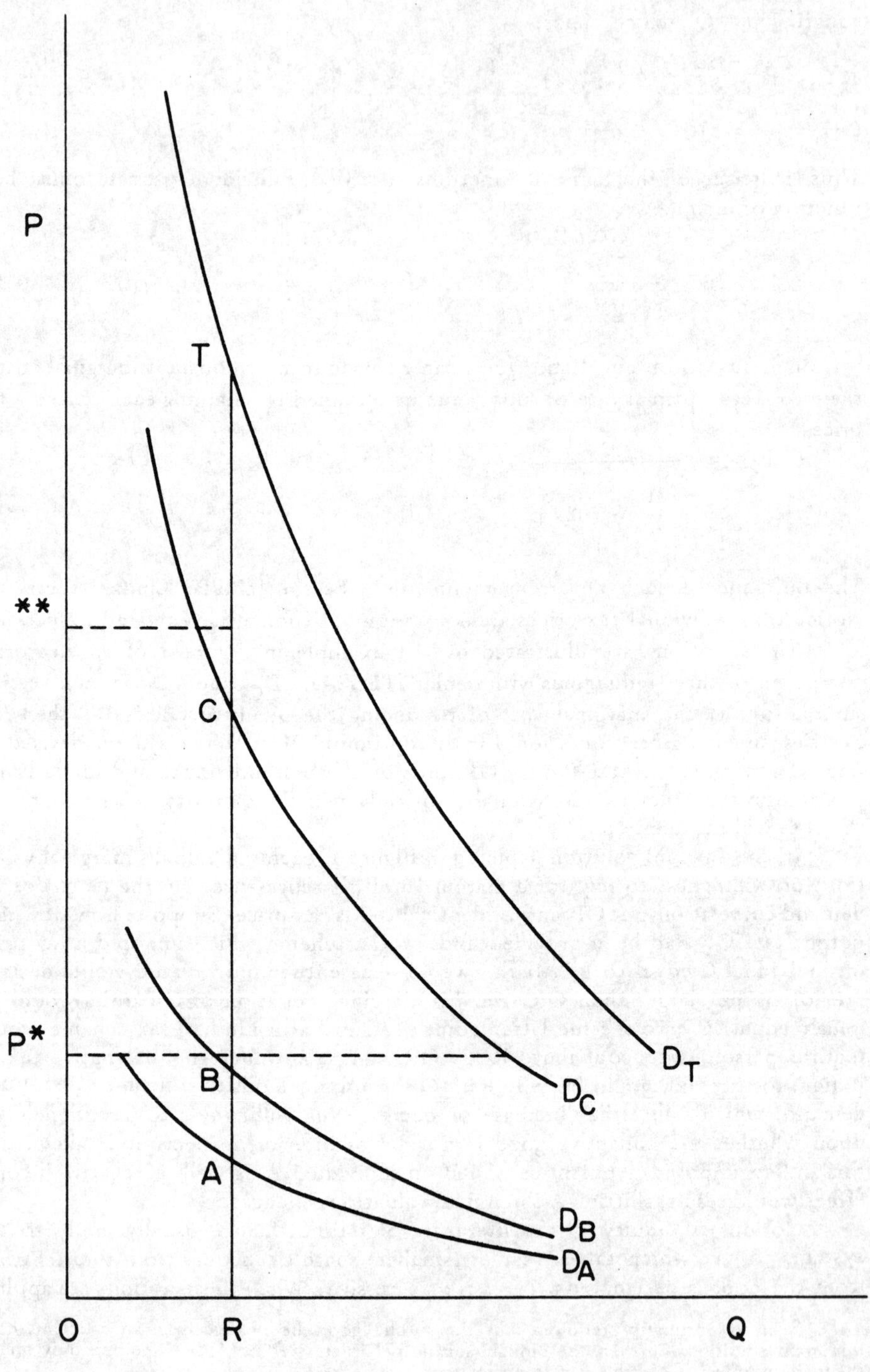

FIGURE I

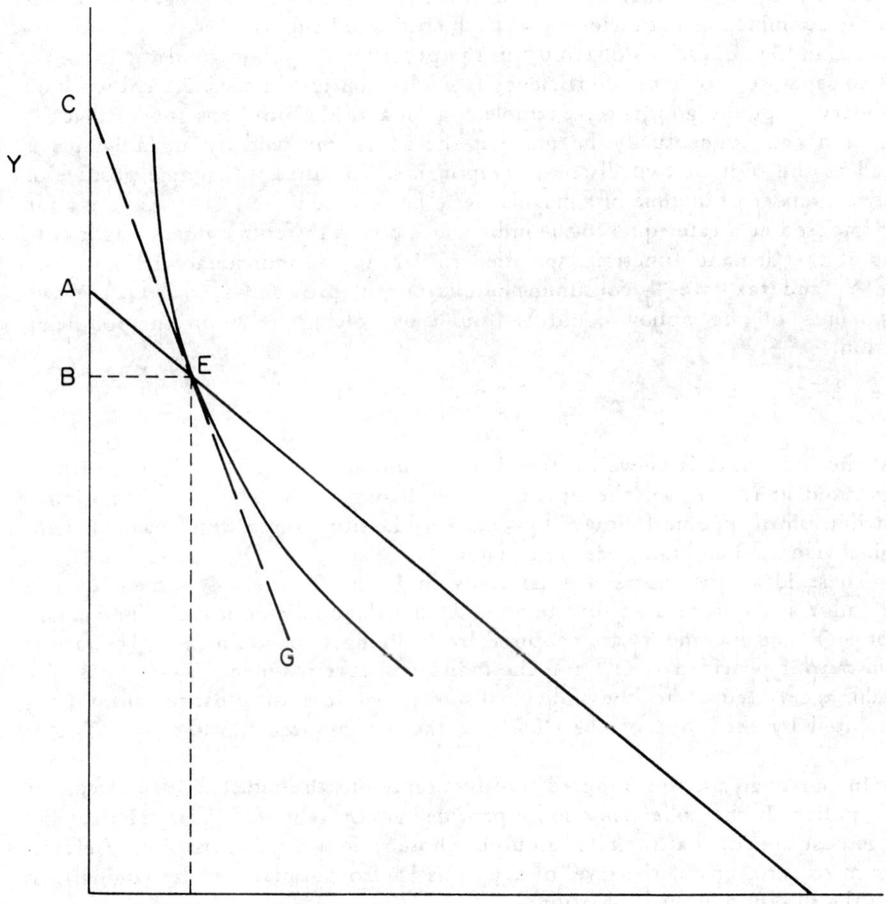

FIGURE 2

to distribution of a good by the government, a question frequently asked is whether the poor get a larger share of it than the rich. If the good is collective, all obtain the same amount, which may appear equitable. However, one should consider not only the physical quantities received by individuals, but also their valuations, which in turn depend upon income. The "progressivity" of any public program depends upon the combined or net incidence of both costs and benefits.

To address questions of equity in the provision of public goods, it is convenient to separate problems of efficiency from distributional issues. Recent work on the theory of public goods (for example, Aaron and McGuire) has shown that the distinction can conceptually be made if the actual tax paid by an individual is treated as the sum of two discrete components. The first is a simple positive or negative transfer of income of a magnitude to be specified later. The second is a tax price imposed at a rate equal to the individual's post-transfer marginal valuation. In terms of the demand functions specified earlier, for an individual with initial income Y_i and tax rate T_i consuming public output provided at rate $\bar{Q}$, the two components of the policy could be found by solving for τ_i in the following equation:

$$\bar{Q} = k[Y_i + (\tau_i - T_i)\bar{Q}]^{\alpha}\tau_i^{-\beta}P_1^{\eta_1} \ldots P_m^{\eta_m}. \qquad (5)$$

Thus, the individual is viewed as receiving an initial transfer $(\tau_i - T_i)\bar{Q}$ and then being taxed at rate τ_i for the provided level of output $\bar{Q}$.[7] The result is an initial redistribution of income followed by a market-like situation in which each citizen's marginal valuation and tax price are equated.

These ideas are expressed graphically in Figure 2, where Q is the collective good and Y is an aggregated private good. Under the public policy, the individual's tax price T_i and income Y_i are captured by the budget constraint, AF. The rate of public output provided is $O\bar{Q}$ and the individual's tax payment $(T_i\bar{Q})$ is AB. The Lindahl tax τ_i (equal to the individual's marginal rate of substitution at E) is represented by the slope of line CEG, and the net imputed transfer $(\tau_i - T_i)\bar{Q}$ is CA.

In our analysis, the imputed transfers represent the redistributive effects of public policy. If the collective good is provided at constant cost (or if marginal and average cost are equal at the rate of output chosen), individual redistributive effects will sum to zero only if the level of supply is Pareto optimal, i.e., if marginal cost equals the sum of marginal valuations.

By examining the implied redistributive effects (as defined above) of a Lindahl solution, one can establish a benchmark against which other policies may be compared. With a Lindahl policy, individual tax prices per unit of public output equal marginal evaluations at the amount provided. If the good is produced under constant costs (as we assume throughout the remainder of the paper), the public budget will be balanced and redistributive effects will be zero, not only in sum, as would be the case with an Pareto optimal policy, but identically for each citizen. Such a policy is, therefore, "neutral" with respect to the initial, pre-policy, income

[7] In the terminology of Aaron and McGuire, $\tau_i\bar{Q}$ is the "income value" of the policy for the ith individual. Notice also that $(\tau_i - T_i)\bar{Q}$ is the implicit income effect mentioned earlier.

distribution. Accordingly, a policy will be termed regressive or progressive, depending upon whether it results in net imputed redistributions to the rich or to the poor, respectively.

In terms of the demand functions specified, suppose that $\alpha = \beta$ so that $\alpha/\beta = 1$. In this case, a policy of providing the good in a way that is neutral with respect to the initial income distribution requires that individual tax rates be proportional to income [see Equation (4)]. If on the other hand, $\alpha/\beta \neq 1$, say $\alpha/\beta > 1$, then from the tax side the arrangement appears progressive, since taxes rise α/β percent for a 1 percent rise in income. However, individual valuations of benefits rise with income in exactly the same manner; while the rich are paying more proportionately, their valuation of benefits is also proportionately larger, and the income distribution is unchanged. Although the tax structure appears progressive, the policy overall is just neutral.[8] By the same token, if $\alpha/\beta < 1$, taxes appear regressive even though the policy as a whole is still neutral. Further, if the good is inferior, $\alpha/\beta < 0$ and a neutral policy would require the rich to pay less in taxes than the poor.[9]

Maintaining the requirements that tax rates be exponentially related to income and that total tax payments cover the total cost of collective supply, consider now the effect of a change in the rate of tax progression. By the first requirement, individual voter optima will be monotonically related to income, and except for the median-income citizen, all voters will prefer quantities different from the one actually chosen. If the degree of tax progression is less than α/β, then provision of the good is regressive; i.e., imputed transfers from poor to rich are involved. Accordingly, the ranking of voters by income and desired levels of output are the same. If, on the other hand, taxes progress at a rate greater than α/β, the rankings are inverted and the policy exerts a net progressive effect upon the income distribution.[10]

Voting Behavior with Private Substitutes

The cost of supplying a unit of a purely public good to one individual is the same as the cost of supplying it to n individuals. But a unit of a purely private good

[8]If one applies the usual notion of progressivity, the tax system will be classified as progressive. Since everyone consumes the same amount of the good, distribution of the good would probably be classified as neutral. Combined, the system may appear progressive, even though the distribution of income is not changed.

[9]It should be noted that, while the above tax will provide a Pareto optimal level of the public good, the tax the individual pays is related to his income and is virtually independent of the quantity of the good he receives. The conventional disincentives associated with taxes operate here as well, and would persist for any measure of income (even one that imputes value to leisure), as long as measured income for tax purposes is not identical with real income as perceived by the individual. For example, if $\alpha/\beta > 1$, then given some mean income to an individual, the larger the variability around that mean, the larger the tax payment. We would expect individuals to reduce their tax payments by selecting among alternative income streams open to them in a way that would reduce variability over time and across individuals (and, conversely, for $\alpha/\beta < 1$). In the remainder of the paper we abstract from this source of misallocation.

[10]The resulting rate of output may or may not be Pareto optimal (it will certainly not coincide with the outcome of the Lindahl policy). If it is not Pareto optimal, then imputed transfers to individuals will not sum to zero. Despite this, one can unambiguously characterize the overall policy as progressive or regressive. Since (with exponential tax rates) individual voter optima are monotonically related to income, and since redistributive effects are always absent for the median-income citizen, it follows that the signs of imputed transfers for all citizens on either side of the median income level are determinate.

can be supplied to each of n individuals only at a cost n times greater, if returns to scale are constant. It is generally considered efficient to provide the former goods collectively and the latter privately. In the case of semi-private goods, the cost of supplying n persons is larger than that of supplying one, but not n times as large. This may give rise to a mixed arrangement—a certain amount of the good to be provided collectively and the balance privately.

Assume that the cost of producing a unit of the good is the same whether it is produced privately or by the government. To clarify the meaning of this assumption, consider the following total cost function:

$$C = cQn^{\gamma}, \tag{6}$$

where C is the total cost of providing each of n consumers with Q units of the good in question. Thus, the marginal cost of providing additional units *to the group is:*

$$C' = cn^{\gamma}. \tag{7}$$

The term c may then be interpreted as the (constant) marginal cost of supplying the good to one individual and, under our assumption, this cost is the same for public and for private producers. For a purely public good, $\gamma = 0$ and the cost of serving additional consumers is zero; if the good is private, $\gamma = 1$. The intermediate range for semi-public goods lies between these extremes.[11]

If the good is semi-public, potential consumers of private supply face a price that exceeds the average tax price faced by all voters. However, since collective provision basically satisfies the median demand (or, more accurately, attains the median of the individual optima), those with relatively intense demand may turn to private supply in spite of its higher cost. In such situations, the availability of private supply may drastically affect voting behavior.

Among goods supplied both privately and collectively, one may distinguish between some cases where private supply supplements public supply, and others where private and public supply are alternatives. This distinction arises because consumption of some goods requires certain inputs on the part of the consumer, particularly time. Further, the quantity and quality of collective supply is uniform for all consumers. For example, when a child attends public school, there is little choice as to the amount of instruction he receives,[12] especially with respect to consumption per unit of time, because he spends so many hours in class each day that substantially greater schooling can be achieved only by using the given time more intensively. Private education, therefore, must largely replace rather than

[11]Essentially the same cost function appears in Borcherding and Deacon. In this context, the degree to which joint consumption economies are present measures the "public" nature of provision. It is likely with some goods that $\gamma = 1$ (so that costs rise in direct proportion to the number of individuals served), but exclusion of non-paying beneficiaries is excessively costly. In such instances, collective agreement is required for efficient provision, even though the goods do not exhibit the "public" characteristics defined above.

[12]Where goods are provided by local governments, the citizen does have some range of choice when determining his place of residence. It seems clear, however, that diversity in individual demands for collective goods exists, even within local jurisdictions.

supplement public education.[13] In the absence of such constraints, or when they are not excessive, private supplements will be preferred to private alternatives.[14]

Consider first the case where private supply supplements a good that was publicly provided under a progressive tax structure (the progression of taxes is at a rate greater than α/β). If the median voter bears no more than the average tax burden, the cost to him of private supply is higher than that of public supply. Demand for the private supplement is also zero among individuals with lower than median income (assuming that the good is not inferior). So the median voter retains his position, and the outcome of the election is not affected by the availability of private supplements. High income individuals continue to vote against increasing public supply, and those whose demand at the private price exceeds the amount publicly provided will supplement their consumption.[15] However, if tax burdens and the final outcome of the vote are unaffected by the availability of private supplements, the net redistributive effects of the public policy are likewise unaffected.

If the tax structure was originally regressive, the analysis is a bit more complex and significant changes in the outcome will occur. Originally, all high income citizens voted to expand public supply, but those facing tax prices above the price of supplements now reverse their voting decision. This shifts the median to a lower income individual and reduces public supply. The new median voter and those with incomes lower than his, clearly gain, as do those high income citizens who reversed their votes. The "old median voter" loses, as do those citizens who occupy neighboring positions in the income distribution. So, the extremes benefit at the expense of the middle class.[16]

The preceding assumed that the median voter paid less than the average tax. Is this likely to be true? Given that income is distributed approximately log-normally, mean income is greater than median income. In any actual tax scheme where tax rates rise with income, it is unlikely that the median voter will pay more than the average tax—although he may indeed do so if significant numbers of low-income voters are exempt from paying taxes. In this case, the tax price of the good to the median voter *may* be greater than its market price; if both the private and the public good are produced under constant cost, he will then choose to

[13] It is true that such activities as religious instruction, music lessons after school, reading in the home, etc., offer some range for supplementing public schooling, but these possibilities are clearly restricted. Introduction of a voucher plan to finance local education would, however, make the use of private *supplements* quite possible (see Footnote 16).

[14] We assume that use of private supply by some consumers bestows no external consumption benefits upon others.

[15] If, for instance, the price in private markets is P* (Figure 1), individual C will purchase some of the good privately. Buchanan has shown that the optimal public supply may be less when private supplements are available than when they are absent. A necessary condition for this is that the demand curves of some individuals extend into the negative quadrant, which may occur if disposal costs are present. (Swimmers may gain utility from the warming up of water in the vicinity of electric generators. But for those who prefer colder water, the service reduces utility since unwanted heat is not costlessly disposable.)

[16] This is essentially the same conclusion reached by Eysenbach (see pp. 869–870) in her analysis of voucher plans for education. Eysenbach's analysis differs somewhat from ours, as she focused specifically upon the provision of education. Since a voucher system affords citizens the opportunity to augment the amount of education provided publicly (equal to the face value of the voucher), it is, therefore, equivalent to introducing the opportunity to use privately supplied supplements.

obtain his entire supply from private sources. This holds even more forcefully if half the voters are paying a higher tax price, in which case a majority will vote down any collective provision of the good.[17] Given its assumed cost advantage, some public output is presumably desirable; thus, this outcome is clearly non-optimal and illustrates an often overlooked way in which taxation can affect the allocation of resources. The analysis of inefficiencies caused by excise and income taxes is, of course, well known (see Footnote 9). However, when a model of individually rational behavior subject to a structure of tax rates is superimposed upon a collective decision-making process such as majority rule, the allocative effects of taxation take on an entirely new dimension.

In the case where private supply is, for some individuals, an alternative to public supply, significant changes in the voting outcome are likely. An individual who opts for a private alternative refrains from using the publicly supplied good, but since he is not excepted from paying taxes, his choice does not immediately affect the tax revenue or the total public expenditure on the good. If the good is semi-public, an unchanged level of tax revenue will permit the reduced number of consumers to enjoy a higher level of consumption. This may be viewed as an equal proportional reduction in the effective tax prices levied on the remaining consumers, which will cause them to demand more of the public supply.[18]

A necessary condition for some citizens to choose private alternatives is that the quantity they would demand at the private price exceeds the level publicly provided. This may occur under either a progressive or a regressive tax system. Consider, first, the case where the original policy is progressive, so that individually desired levels of public output are inversely related to incomes. In terms of Figure 1, Individual C, if faced with a tax price of P** and consuming a public rate of output OR, may opt for the private alternative if it is offered at a price of P*. In such instances, the introduction of private alternatives will lead to an unambiguous rise in the level of public supply.[19] The final voting outcome may be viewed as the result of a sequence of intermediate decisions. When the private alternative becomes available, n_1 (where n_1 is less than a majority) consumers choose to abstain from the public supply (offered at level Q_1), which reduces the tax prices for remaining consumers. In light of lower tax prices, a larger public output, Q_2, is chosen by the electorate. Since this new level is closer to the private optimum of high-income voters, n_2 ($< n_1$) of those who previously opted for private alternatives will now resume consumption of public output, tax prices will rise slightly, and public supply will, consequently, be reduced to Q_3 (where $Q_1 < Q_3 < Q_2$), inducing n_3 ($< n_2$) citizens to switch back to private supply, and so on.

[17]See Eysenbach, p. 868.

[18]A complication arises in that a reduction in the rate of public supply will induce a greater number of high-income citizens to switch to private alternatives. Thus, effective tax prices decline for those continuing to consume collective supply as the rate of public provision is reduced. To the extent that this effect is noticeable, voters may behave like price-setters and base their decisions upon marginal rather than average tax price. Further, since the margin will lie above the average, it is possible that such price-setting behavior could induce voters located near the median to prefer a net reduction in the rate of public supply when private alternatives become available. (Of course, if the reduction in public supply were large enough to induce a majority of voters to switch to private alternatives, public supply would disappear entirely.)

[19]The resulting change in total expenditure will, of course, depend upon the elasticity of demand for the collectively provided good.

The introduction of private alternatives does not alter the progressive nature of the tax scheme for those who continue to use the public supply. However, those high-income citizens who switch to private alternatives are still paying taxes while receiving no public benefits, thus augmenting its progressive impact.

The introduction of private supply alternatives can have a more dramatic effect upon voting outcomes in the case where taxes are regressive in the sense defined earlier. Under such conditions, as long as private supply is prohibited voters with above-median income desire a larger public supply than the median voter does. Suppose that Individual C in Figure 1, a wealthy citizen whose marginal valuation of public supply is RC, faces a tax price P*. At that price, he initially prefers, and votes for, a quantity larger than R. When private supply becomes available, however, he and other high-income individuals may switch from public to private sources if their demand is sufficiently high relative to the private price. Their interest as voters is abruptly reversed; since they contribute to public tax revenue but reap no benefits, they will now vote against any public supply whatever.

This change in allegiance by high-income voters changes the identity, and the income level, of the median citizen. When private supply was prohibited, the median voter was the citizen with median income, and the only information needed to predict the outcome of the vote was to discover his choice of quantity. Now, however, the median voter will be one with lower than median income, and it is much more difficult to identify the crucial voter and the quantity he desires because of the fundamental changes in voting behavior just described.

Under such conditions, is the chosen level of public supply likely to increase or decline? Suppose, as before, that the marginal cost of supplying the good publicly to n individuals is cn^{γ} where c is the (constant) marginal cost of supplying it to one, and $0 < \gamma < 1$, indicating semi-publicness. Then, if 1 percent of the (high-income) public consumers switch to private substitutes, the marginal cost of supplying those remaining will fall by γ percent, reducing their effective tax rates by γ percent. The switch by 1 percent of the voters with high income will shift the median voting position to a person whose income is, say, δ percent below the median-income level. The actual magnitude of δ will, of course, depend upon the parameters and the form of income distribution. Given, however, that the distribution of income is approximately log-normal, one can expect δ to be close to unity.[20] Thus, both the tax price and the income level of the median voter have been reduced. The effect of these two simultaneous changes can be examined by taking a logarithmic differential of the original demand function,

$$d(\log Q) = -\beta\, d(\log T_i) + \alpha\, d(\log Y_i). \tag{8}$$

[20]If income follows a log-normal distribution exactly, it can be shown that a switch in voting allegiance by 1 percent of the high-income citizens will reduce the income level of the median voter by $\sigma\sqrt{2\pi/2}$ percent, where σ^2 is the variance of the log of income. One may approximate σ by noting that the ratio of mean to median income is $e^{(\sigma^2/2)}$. Thus, δ will equal unity if the ratio of mean to median income is approximately 1.38.

The last term captures the effect of having changed the identity of the median voter. Since tax prices have been reduced by γ percent and the income level of the median voter has fallen δ percent, the percentage change in the rate of public supply is:

$$d(\log Q) = \beta\gamma - \alpha\delta = \delta\beta\,(\gamma/\delta - \alpha/\beta), \tag{9}$$

so that the rate of public supplywill fall if $\gamma/\delta < \alpha/\beta$. Assuming that $\delta = 1$, then $\gamma/\delta < 1$ and will approach zero as the supply becomes more nearly public. Recall, also, that the tax structure was assumed to be regressive (i. e., the degree of tax progression is less than α/β), so that, in all likelihood $\alpha/\beta > 1$. In general, then, one would expect the equilibrium rate of public supply to decrease when private alternatives become available.

The change in price and the displacement of the median voter, both effects due to the availability of the private alternative, tend to reduce the level of collective supply chosen. This reduction is accompanied by a decline in the number of individuals consuming the public output. However, even if the tax price to the median voter led to a Pareto optimal level of supply when private substitutes were unavailable, there is no reason to believe that the new arrangement will be optimal. In fact, it is difficult to visualize how one could even set the rules of a system that would result in an optimal level of public supply when private supply is allowed.

The income distribution effects of private supply are fairly obvious in this case. If, before the introduction of private supply, the system was regressive, in the sense that the progression of taxes is by an exponent less than α/β, it cannot now be thought of as globally regressive. Within the group continuing to use public supply the system is still regressive, whereas within the group using private supply the tax is unrelated to benefits and represents strictly a progressive transfer payment. So, only up to a certain income is the tax regressive, and the system as a whole cannot be clearly characterized either way.

Collectively supplied goods have an additional impact on voter behavior and equity, arising from the fact that the consumer frequently has to use some of his own resources to obtain them. Examples of such requirements are the need for television sets to receive television signals, transportation and time costs to use public recreation facilities, automobiles to make use of public highways, and the high school diploma, books, and time to take advantage of college education. For some individuals, such costs may be high enough to cancel out the value of the publicly supplied good, even though it is free.[21] If costs are the same for all individuals (and the good is not inferior), then low-income citizens as a group are most likely to be deterred by them.[22] If the tax system is regressive to begin with, these incidental costs will now lead low-income voters, instead of demanding a relatively small quantity of public supply, to demand none at all. Although the identity of the median voter will not change, the tax price will decrease for those continuing to consume, the rate of collective supply will increase, and (if demand is

[21]The demand for a commodity should be "net" of such costs; their consideration at this point simply indicates that the explicit demand function used earlier in the paper cannot represent the situation described here.

[22]Considerations of this type hold for elementary compulsory education. In that case, the income distribution effects are most curious: not only do poor parents pay taxes which exceed their valuation of the commodity, they are also forced to consume the service even though they may consider its net contribution to their welfare as negative.

price elastic) the tax burden, shared by those who refuse to consume the good, will rise.

So, one may encounter situations where 1) the richest subsidize the rest; 2) the poorest subsidize the rest; or 3) both effects occur simultaneously, as with public higher education where the rich often attend private colleges, the poor do not go to any college, and the middle class benefits at the expense of both extremes ("Director's Law").[23] The tax system may superficially appear to be either progressive or regressive, but under the above conditions it is in fact just muddled.

The muddle gets worse when the assumption that all utility functions are identical is relaxed to allow for diversity of tastes. Individuals may then opt out of public supply not only for its wrong quantity but also for its lack of right features. Probably the most important example is the case of parochial schooling, where the level of expenditures in public school may be "right," yet its character leads some families to prefer private schooling. Given that such tastes are not perfectly correlated with income, neither are the distributional effects of such programs.

To summarize then: with the notable exception of Buchanan, accepted theories of public expenditure and collective choice have implicitly assumed that such goods are available solely through public provision. In actual fact, private supply frequently affords the consumer a feasible supplement or substitute, depending on the type of good, which may alter his consumption of public goods or replace it entirely. In the latter case, it has been shown here that the introduction of private supply may exert a marked effect upon the vote. A combination of tax structure and collective-choice mechanism which yields an efficient level of public output in the absence of private supply will, in all probability, not remain optimal when private supply is permitted; indeed, an efficient combination would be most difficult to specify. The impact of private supply upon the distribution of income may in many cases be significant enough to render the notion of tax progressivity meaningless.

REFERENCES

1. Aaron, Henry, and Martin McGuire. "Public Goods and Income Distribution." *Econometrica,* 38 (November, 1970), 907–20.
2. Barlow, Robin. "Efficiency Aspects of Local School Finance." *Jour. Pol. Econ.,* 78 (September, 1970), 1023–40.
3. Barzel, Yoram. "Private Schools and Public School Finance." *Jour. Pol. Econ.,* 81 (January, 1973), 174–86.
4. Bator, Francis M. *The Question of Government Spending.* New York: Harper and Bros., 1960.
5. Brocherding, Thomas E., and R. T. Deacon. "The Demand for Services of Non-Federal Governments." *Am. Econ. Rev.,* 62 (December, 1972), 891–901.
6. Bowen, Howard R. "The Interpretation of Voting in the Allocation of Economic Resources." *Quart. Jour. Econ.,* 59 (November, 1945), 22–48.

[23]Pechman observed such a case for higher education in California in 1965.

7. Buchanan, James M. "Notes for an Economic Theory of Socialism." *Public Choice*, 8 (Spring, 1970), 29–43.
8. Demsetz, H. "The Exchange and Enforcement of Property Rights." *Jour. Law and Econ.*, 7 (October, 1964), 11–26.
9. Downs, Anthony. *An Economic Theory of Democracy*. New York: Harper and Row, 1957.
10. Eysenbach, Mary L. "Voucher Plans, Voting Models, and the Efficiency of Local School Finance." *Jour. Pol. Econ.*, 82 (September, 1974), 863–71.
11. Pechman, J. A. "The Distributional Effects of Public Higher Education in California." *Jour. Hum. Res.*, 3 (Summer, 1970), 361–70.

PART V

INDUSTRIAL ORGANIZATION

[16]

Excess Capacity in Monopolistic Competition

Yoram Barzel

University of Washington

Will a monopolistic competitor operate at the minimum point of his average cost curve? Demsetz argues that this is possible (1959, 1964). In this paper Demsetz's argument is critically examined and then rejected in favor of a necessarily negative slope at equilibrium and, hence, "excess capacity" in that average cost is higher than marginal cost.

According to Chamberlin (1957, chaps. 5 and 6) the firm under monopolistic competition faces a downward-sloping demand curve. Since the firm is forced to operate at zero profit, the average cost curve is tangent to such a demand curve at the equilibrium point. With falling average cost "excess capacity" is said to exist. Furthermore, since marginal cost is lower than price, a Pareto-optimum condition is thereby violated.[1]

Demsetz (1959, 1964) claims that Chamberlin's analysis is based on a partial relation between quantity and price that fails to recognize that at different levels of output the profit-maximizing firm will attempt to shift the demand curve facing it by changing its expenditures on quality, location, and promotion simultaneously with changes in its expenditures on quantity. Consequently, the demand curve associated with one quantity is obtained for a given level of selling expenditures and in general will differ from that associated with another quantity, since the selling expenditures change with quantity. The market-equilibrium locus of consumers' quantities and prices then is not on a single demand curve, and the negative-slope property of a demand curve does not apply to the market-equilibrium locus. So far so good. Demsetz, however, claims that the market-equilibrium locus is the relevant curve and says that since a zero slope is a likely result, the excess-capacity argument no longer holds. The purpose of this paper is to refute Demsetz's claim.[2]

I wish to thank G. C. Archibald, S. N. S. Cheung, J. E. Floyd, J. A. Hynes, L. G. Telser, J. S. McGee, and E. Silberberg for their comments.

[1] It should be pointed out that while he recognized the problem of nonoptimality, Chamberlin did not wholly subscribe to it (1962, chap. 5).

[2] The market-equilibrium locus for consumers is denoted by Demsetz as MAR (*mutatis mutandis* average revenue). A substantial part of the argument between

We should first note that if one does not view expenditures on quality, location, or promotion as utility-generating expenditures, misallocation occurs by definition. We will follow Demsetz, however, in proposing that such expenditures, including those on promotion, do in fact generate utility. We want to show that when price and quantity are appropriately measured, contrary to Demsetz's argument, average cost necessarily falls at equilibrium. We will proceed by first showing that for quality-improving costs, if the quantity-price locus has a zero slope at equilibrium the slope is negative at equilibrium for quality-adjusted units. The argument will be extended to cover other types of cost, and it will be shown that regardless of the slope of the quantity-price locus at equilibrium, the slope of the properly measured average cost curve has to be negative.

In figure 1 (following in general outline Demsetz's figure 1), the demand curve D_1 and the average cost curve F_1 are derived when quality per unit of output is held constant.[3] These two curves are tangent at X_1—the "Chamberlinian" equilibrium point. At levels of output other than Q_1, the optimum level of expenditures on quality is likely to change, and when expenditures on quality are accounted for and included as part of the total cost we may obtain a (*mutatis mutandis*) cost curve such as C, with X_1 at its minimum point. According to Demsetz, the cost curve C, rather than F_1, is the one relevant to a determination of whether "excess capacity" is present. He argues further that since this curve may have a minimum point at X_1,[4] excess capacity is not a necessary result in monopolistic competition.

But the switch from F_1 to C is not the innocent operation that Demsetz implicitly makes it appear. To draw our demand schedule properly we should deal with homogeneous units. Expenditures on the quality of the product are explicitly designed to change the product; while D_1 is obtained for a homogeneous set of units, C must deal with heterogeneous units as a result of the product improving expenditures. Even though C may have a zero slope at X_1, this can no longer be used to determine any optimal properties for such a point. Into the two-dimensional discussion

---

Archibald (1967) and Demsetz (1967) is an attempt to determine what can be said about the shape of that curve. In this paper it is shown that the presence of excess capacity is independent of the properties of the MAR curve, and that the MAR curve is not only of little use but also is likely to mislead.

[3] Demsetz sets *total* outlays on quality at a constant level for deriving his D_1 and F_1. Constant total outlays imply that per unit outlays vary inversely with the number of units and, consequently, that quality declines when quantity increases. The failure to maintain a set of homogeneous units appears to be the source of Demsetz's error, as will be shown below. Defining D_1 and F_1 conventionally, as we do, still requires a negative tangency for the zero-profit equilibrium.

[4] Where it is tangent to the *mutatis mutandis* demand curve MAR (not shown in fig. 1).

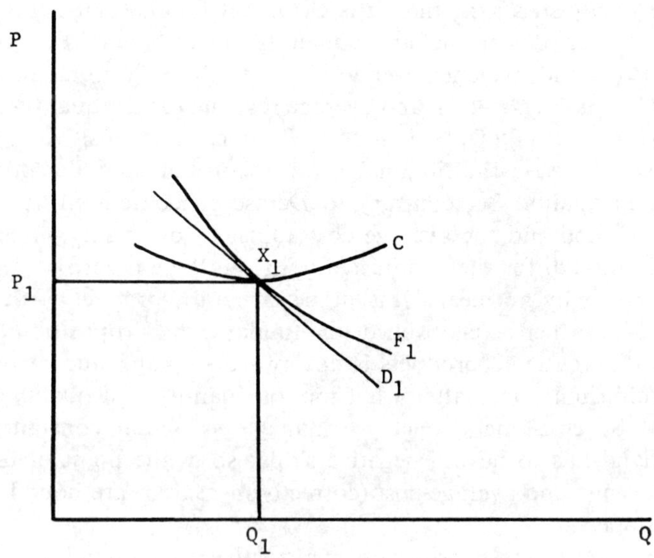

FIG. 1

of quantity and price Demsetz introduces a third dimension more fully than Chamberlin has done, but yet not fully enough. In particular, he does not sufficiently examine the relation between quality change and utility.

To achieve Demsetz's result that C has zero slope at Q_1, quality must rise in the neighborhood of Q_1. If it were to remain constant, D_1 and F_1 would be the relevant curves, and we would be back at the original Chamberlin model. If quality were to deteriorate, production costs would be less than with constant quality and utility would be smaller, too; so the quantity-price path for consumers and that for producers both would have even steeper slopes (in absolute terms) at X_1, which would also disallow Demsetz's results. We may concentrate, then, on the case where, in the neighborhood of the optimal mix, quality per unit is positively related to quantity. Following Demsetz, let us assert that the average cost, C, of producing this optimal quantity-quality mix has a minimum point at X_1. But since the mix itself changes with quantity, the price and the quantity axes fail to deal with homogeneous units. When we move along the quantity axis from Q_1 to $Q_1 + 1$, we move to a set of improved units. If we try to adjust the horizontal scale to bring the old and the new units into a common denominator, the distance between the two quantities is not 1, but $1 + \Delta$ where Δ is the positive correction factor for quality. Similarly, when we consider the price axis and note that due to the zero slope of C at X_1 the equilibrium price is P_1 for both Q_1 and $Q_1 + 1$

along the unadjusted axis, then it is clear that for the unit-adjusted axis the price associated with the larger quantity has to be less. Total revenue at Q_1 is P_1Q_1 and average revenue is $(P_1Q_1)Q_1 = P_1$; total revenue at the new point is $P_1(Q_1 + 1)$, and average revenue for the quality-adjusted units is $[P_1(Q_1 + 1)]/(Q_1 + 1 + \Delta) < P_1$ since Δ is positive. The real price is less, because the nominal price is constant and the product is improved in quality. So, contrary to Demsetz's contention, at equilibrium the demand and the average cost adjusted for quality slope downward, even though for the unadjusted units the slope is zero.

This result is by no means just an arithmetic by-product of the above example. It is rather a reflection of the fundamental proposition that demand for differentiated products is downward sloping,[5] and of the zero-profit equilibrium. No matter what mix of quantity and quality may be demanded by consumers, once we manage to obtain constant-quality units demand has to have a negative slope; so at the point of tangency average revenue and average cost (correctly measured) are bound to have negative slopes.

In one respect Demsetz brings up an attractive way of handling demand-increasing costs by considering such costs as contributing to the value of the good produced and to the utility generated by it, but he does not pursue this approach far enough. Such a relation will be now made explicit. We add to the price and quantity dimensions a third dimension—R/Q—where R reflects attributes of the commodity such as its quality, its closeness to the consumer, and even the image of pretty girls provided by the advertiser.[6] We assume that R can be measured quantitatively along a continuous scale.[7] Improvements in quality may sometimes come in discrete steps rather than along a continuous scale; the analytical difficulties due to such discontinuities, however, are shared by us and by Demsetz alike.

The demand function can be written as $P^* = D(Q, R/Q)$[8] where P^* is not the observed market price (per unit of Q) but the real price of the quantity-quality package as viewed by the consumer. The size of the package will increase with an increase in conventional quantity as well

[5] I doubt that Demsetz will try to preserve his argument by applying it only to Giffen goods; the possibility of such goods will be ignored in the rest of the paper.

[6] Each of these attributes should be separately treated for the argument to be more general. It is clear, however, that the three-dimensional results can be easily extended to more dimensions without altering any of the basic conclusions, and the presentation is simpler if the dimensions are thus restricted.

[7] This is similar to the approach adopted by Robert Dorfman and Peter O. Steiner (1954). Fat content of milk provides a good illustration: the amount of fat is a continuous variable, and its total as well as its amount per quart of milk can readily be changed.

[8] Analytically it is preferable to have P^* as a function of Q and R rather than of Q and R/Q. The substantive results are invariant between the two formulations, and the latter is used in the text since it better corresponds both to usage in the literature and to popular characterization of commodities.

as with an improvement in quality. And the consumer will buy a larger package only if its price per unit is declining. Holding quality constant, we obtain the usual demand curve such that $\partial P^*/\partial Q < 0$. Similarly, holding Q constant we have $\partial P^*/\partial(R/Q) < 0$, indicating that the amount of the quality characteristic demanded is inversely related to price.[9]

Average cost can now be treated symmetrically with demand. We write $AC^* = F(Q, R/Q)$ where the relation between AC^* and the conventional AC parallels that between P^* and P. The equilibrium point of the monopolistically competitive firm earning zero profits has to satisfy two conditions simultaneously. Average cost has to equal average revenue both when quantity changes but quality per unit is held constant, and when quality per unit changes but quantity is held constant.

Diagrammatically, figure 2*a* shows the relation between P and Q for different levels of R/Q; X_1 is the tangency point between $D_1[(R/Q)_1, Q]$ for which R/Q is held constant at $(R/Q)_1$, and the average cost curve $F_1[(R/Q)_1, Q]$ which is also obtained for $(R/Q)_1$. For another value of R/Q—$(R/Q)_2$—the demand curve is $D_2[(R/Q)_2, Q]$. Figure 2*b* portrays the relation between the price per unit of quality and R/Q for different levels of Q. The demand curves $D^1(R/Q, Q_1)$ and $D^2(R/Q, Q_2)$ drawn for constant levels of Q—Q_1 and Q_2, respectively—are implicit in figure 2*a*.[10] Given Q_1, the average cost function for R/Q is $F^1(R/Q, Q_1)$. The zero-profit condition requires a tangency between $F^1(R/Q, Q_1)$ and $D^1(R/Q, Q_1)$ at X_1 which is, of course, the same point as X_1 in figure 2*a*. In both figures the cost curve is tangent to a demand curve and consequently slopes down in both directions.

We can now return to the basic argument. According to Demsetz, given the zero-profit (hence price = average cost) equilibrium point X_1 with coordinates P_1 and Q_1, a point such as X_2 for which $Q_2 > Q_1$ and $P_2 > P_1$ could at the same time be both on the optimal selling path of the firm and on a constant or rising portion of its average cost curve. We will show that this cannot hold without contradicting demand theory and that the appropriately defined average cost function necessarily slopes down in the neighborhood of X_1.

What can be said about the demand curve on which X_2 lies? If we denote this curve as $D_2[(R/Q)_2, Q]$, the condition $(R/Q)_2 > (R/Q)_1$ has to be satisfied. This is so since, if quality is held constant, quantity demanded

[9] This statement should not be confused with the consumer's willingness to pay a higher price per unit of Q when quality improves. The P^* is the price index of quantity and quality combined, and may be obtained as the ratio of total revenue to some weighted average of quantity and quality. An improvement in quality is a move along the demand curve to a larger quantity of the composite good. The numerator of this ratio may increase, but the denominator will increase relatively more.

[10] Vertical sections of fig. 2*a* represent varying values of R/Q, holding Q constant, and corresponding values of total revenues. These are translated in 2*b* into quantity demanded of R/Q for different unit prices of R/Q, holding Q constant.

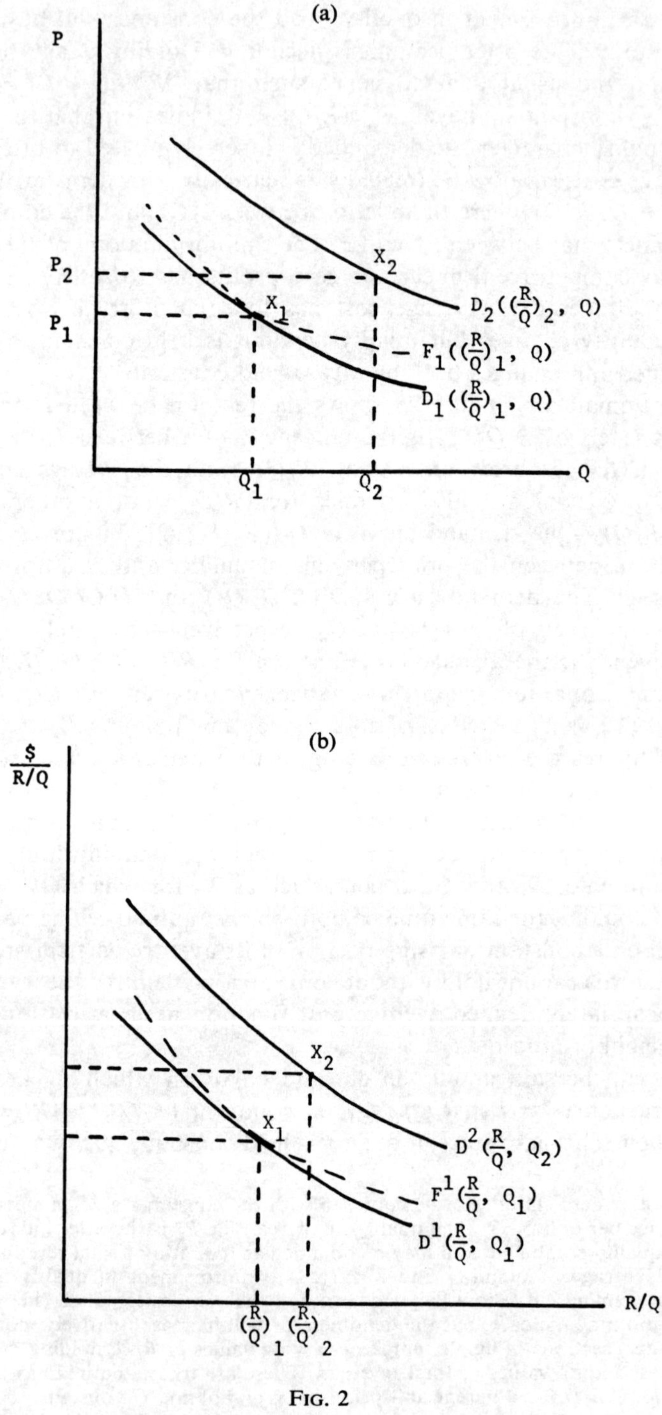
(a)
P
P_2
P_1
X_2
X_1
$D_2((\frac{R}{Q})_2, Q)$
$F_1((\frac{R}{Q})_1, Q)$
$D_1((\frac{R}{Q})_1, Q)$
Q_1
Q_2
Q
(b)
$\frac{\$}{R/Q}$
X_2
X_1
$D^2(\frac{R}{Q}, Q_2)$
$F^1(\frac{R}{Q}, Q_1)$
$D^1(\frac{R}{Q}, Q_1)$
$(\frac{R}{Q})_1$
$(\frac{R}{Q})_2$
R/Q

FIG. 2

will increase only if (nominal) price falls, and only if quality is improved may a larger quantity be demanded without a fall in nominal price. So if X_2 satisfied Demsetz's specification that $Q_2 > Q_1$ and $P_2 > P_1$, it also has to satisfy $(R/Q)_2 > (R/Q)_1$. Given demand theory, the consumers' willingness to move from X_1 to X_2 (which involves an increase in both dimensions of the composite commodity) is indicative that consumers view the real price P_2^* as lower than P_1^*. Otherwise they would not buy more of this composite commodity.[11]

The three-dimensional demand surface (due to the zero-profit condition) is tangent to the three-dimensional cost surface at X_1, and the two have the same slope in any direction. Since $P_2^* < P_1^*$ when the correct set of units is used, it follows that AC_2^*, the correctly measured average cost of producing X_2, is less than AC_1^*, the average cost of producing X_1. So in the neighborhood of X_1 the average cost must fall, and X_1 cannot possibly be the minimum point of the average cost surface. Regardless of the shape of the *mutatis mutandis* curve C, equilibrium necessarily is at the downward-sloping range of the average cost surface, marginal cost is less than average cost and price, and "excess capacity" is still with us. "Excess capacity," of course, implies that marginal cost is less than price. What the above argument brings up most clearly is that marginal cost is less than price not only in the conventional quantity dimension, but also in the quality dimension.[12] To achieve a Pareto optimum, not only output has to be expanded but quality as well (and, for that matter, advertising too!).

This is hardly a surprising result. We deal here basically with two commodities, each subject to the "law of demand." They are produced at a point where the average cost of producing each is declining. It does not seem reasonable to expect a Pareto-optimum solution under such circumstances.

Demsetz's claim that the presence of demand-increasing costs precludes the use of the conventional demand curve in welfare economics falls with the rest of his argument. If such costs are present, one should use demand curves either where quality is held constant or where both price and quantity are adjusted for changes in quality. It is totally inappropriate to disregard changes in quality (and in location and promotion) in defining quantity and price. Similarly, we cannot accept Demsetz's argument (1968) that there are no substantive reasons to distinguish between competition and monopolistic competition, since this contention is based on the argument that no excess capacity exists in the latter.

[11] Analytically, given that $\partial P^*/\partial Q < 0$ and $\partial P^*/[\partial(R/Q)] < 0$, we can unambiguously state that $dP^* = \partial P^*/\partial Q\, dQ + \partial P^*/[\partial(R/Q)]d(R/Q) < 0$, since, when moving from X_1 to X_2, both dQ and $d(R/Q)$ are positive. So P^*_2, the real price of X_2, is less than P^*_1, that of X_1.

[12] I am indebted to D. F. Gordon for bringing this point to my attention. This is not unlike the argument made by Levhari and Srinivasan (1969).

References

Archibald, G. C. "Monopolistic Competition and Returns to Scale." *Econ. J.* 77 (June 1967): 405–12.

Chamberlin, E. H. *Towards a More General Theory of Value*. New York: Oxford Univ. Press, 1957.

———. *The Theory of Monopolistic Competition*. Cambridge, Mass.: Harvard Univ. Press, 1962.

Demsetz, H. "The Nature of Equilibrium in Monopolistic Competition." *J.P.E.* 67 (February 1959): 21–30.

———. "The Welfare and Empirical Implications of Monopolistic Competition." *Econ. J.* 74 (September 1964): 623–41.

———. "Monopolistic Competition: A Reply." Ibid. 77 (June 1967): 412–20.

———. "Do Competition and Monopolistic Competition Differ?" *J.P.E.* 76 (January/February 1968): 146–48.

Dorfman, Robert, and Steiner, Peter O. "Optimal Advertising and Optimal Quality." *A.E.R.* 44 (December 1954): 26–36.

Levhari, David, and Srinivasan, T. N. "Durability of Consumption Goods: Competition versus Monopoly." *A.E.R.* 59 (March 1969): 102–7.

PART VI

DEMAND ANALYSIS

[17]

THE TESTABILITY OF THE LAW OF DEMAND

YORAM BARZEL*
University of Washington

Slutsky, in his magnificient article on demand, has attempted to formulate a law that would always hold true. Against such a formulation, contradictory empirical evidence would then be decisive. Slutsky's own statement is most eloquent: "One cannot call *law* any rule which admits of exceptions—it matters not whether they are few or many. . . ." Thus, the law can be "tested on the basis of scientifically arranged, empirical observations," (Slutsky, p. 45).

The law relates the price of a commodity to the quantity demanded by a person whose income is subject to "compensated variations." The Slutsky equation for an individual's purchase of commodity X is

$$\frac{\partial X^M}{\partial P} = \frac{\partial X^I}{\partial P} - X^M \frac{\partial X^M}{\partial M}, \tag{1}$$

where P is the nominal price of X, and M is money income. The superscript M indicates that money income is held constant, and the superscript I indicates that (apparent) real income is held constant. The law of demand states that $\frac{\partial X^I}{\partial P} < 0$. To test the law, the compensating variations have to be effected. In

I wish to thank M. Hashimoto, L. Kochin, K. Leffler, T. Ozenne, and W. F. Sharpe for their valuable comments.

Slutsky's own formulation the consumer is endowed with *money*, which he allocates among commodities. When a price rises, the value of the money declines, and a positive compensation is needed to restore its real value.

Two major problems impede empirical implementation: how to control for the second right-hand term in the equation; and how to perform the test, given that in reality consumers are endowed with resources, not with "money."

The term $\frac{\partial X^M}{\partial M}$ is the effect of income on consumption when relative prices are constant. To control for it, one needs data capable of yielding a satisfactory estimate of this magnitude. It is contended here that the income measures commonly used in empirical studies are themselves the *result* of price changes and might, therefore, lead to apparent refutation of an otherwise valid law. This issue is discussed in the following section.

We next discuss the transition from a model in which the consumer holds money into one in which he holds resources. Armed with the proper account of these holdings, one can readily identify a class of observations free of any income effect. Since the effect of substitution is already isolated, the law can then be directly tested. The following section enumerates instances where the hypothesis might be tested. Finally, we identify an error in the accepted analysis of portfolio selection.

The analysis here is on the individual level; price changes are treated as exogenous. Thus, only seldom are the results applicable to the market as a whole. On the other hand, a more complete account than is usually the case is taken of the constraints of the individual's resources.

THE DEPENDENCE OF MEASURED INCOME ON PRICE

Consider a simplified version of a common demand-estimation equation:

$$X = b_0 + b_1P + b_2I \tag{2}$$

where X is the quantity of a commodity purchased by a person, P is its relative price, and I is the person's real income.[1] It is said that the law of demand is refuted when $b_1 > 0$.

Data needed to estimate b_1 cannot vary in the nominal price of X alone, since then the income effect of the price change would not be isolated. Variability in I independently of P is essential to the estimation of b_2 to remove the effect of a change in nominal price on income. A more complete specification which separates the two income components is

[1]The simplification consists of the use of a linear form and the omission of customary control variables, neither of which is relevant to our problem. Moreover, since we are concerned with an economic rather than an econometric problem, the error term is suppressed. Similarly, in terms of this paper's objective, there is no loss in considering only a single commodity out of a whole system.

$$X = b_0 + b_1 P + c_1 I_1 + c_2 I_2 \quad (3)$$

where I_1 is income from changes in the nominal price of X, I_2 is other income, and $I_1 + I_2 \equiv I$. An assumption implicit in the received approach, then, is that $c_1 = c_2 = b_2$. Now c_1, the coefficient of I_1, is what we wish to estimate so that the effect of I_1 can be netted out. Only if the effect of other income I_2 on X is the same as that of I_1 (that is, only if $c_1 = c_2$), can the effect on income of a price change be removed. By its definition, I_1 is a "pure" income change, maintaining relative prices constant. For the equality $c_1 = c_2$ to hold, variability in I_2 has to be free of changes in relative prices. It will now be shown that almost all components of income differences, as measured, are brought about by changes in relative prices.

In Slutsky's formulation, the individual can be viewed as receiving a cash endowment at the beginning of each period. However, as commonly used in empirical studies, income is a function of the individual's command over resources. It consists of earnings from assets, wages, and (sometimes) transfer payments. For the present we abstract from the latter. Income, then, depends on the quantities held by a person of each asset including human wealth (from which wages are the earned return) and the prices of those assets. The quantity of one asset held by a person can be increased only when he relinquishes a corresponding amount of another asset. Only a change in asset prices, then, can produce a change in personal income. Now asset prices depend ultimately on commodity prices; thus, personal income also depends, although indirectly, on commodity prices. The use of income in the estimation of demand for X, therefore, is inappropriate. When it is used, the coefficient c_2 would reflect both income and substitution effects, and the requirement that $c_1 = c_2$ would be violated.

The difficulties are compounded when the main, or only, source of income is wages. A wage change is equivalent to a change in the price of a particular commodity—leisure. Like any other price change, it will affect the quantity demanded of X through the (cross-) substitution effect and the income effect.[2] Moreover, as measured, the income effect is overstated. Wage income has to be "earned." At equilibrium in the labor market a person is indifferent about working or not working one more hour. The earnings from the last unit of time, therefore, contain no true income component; the "income" from the marginal hour should be imputed wholly to the substitution effect.[3]

The problematic nature of income, as measured, is not confined to income variability experienced by a single person. Incomes will differ across persons with the levels of their asset holdings or their assets' prices. As with a wage change for a single person, differential wage earnings exert not only an income

[2]There is no a priori reason to expect the order of magnitude of this substitution effect to be smaller than that of the income effect.

[3]For any asset, the quantity held is expected to change with a change in its price. Common methods of income accounting, however, are more likely to handle such a change correctly for nonhuman assets.

effect but also a substitution effect.[4] Thus, in this case c_1 also does not equal c_2, and in general, the estimate of b_1 is likely to be biased.

The difference in income from differential asset holdings across people provides the best opportunity to isolate the income effect; nevertheless difficulties abound here also. Income, as measured, may vary as a result of differences in human capital. Like income from work, human capital has to be earned. Two persons with different stocks of human capital will not necessarily differ in their "true" or "permanent" income—the larger holdings in one asset may well be at the expense of others. Consumption of X by the two may nevertheless differ because of differences in factors such as access to capital markets associated with varying levels of human capital. Obviously, such changes in consumption have little to do with income. We will return to this issue.

Nonhuman asset holdings which vary with the life cycle represent merely a change in the composition of permanent wealth rather than a change in its level. Such differences, then, would not yield the desired information. Additionally, the level of nonhuman assets a person holds will tend to affect both his borrowing rate and the value of his time. Therefore, a difference in income from that source is likely to be accompanied by (induced) differences in relative prices.[5]

Consider now transfers. To the extent that transfers are in the form of subsidies on commodities, as with food stamps or low-cost housing, these clearly are not "pure" income changes, and their lower price will induce substitution towards them. It is necessary to *know* the substitution effect in order to obtain their net effect on income.

Other types of transfers may be more directly related to income. Nevertheless, unless they are unanticipated, they are not pure and have to be "earned."[6] In general, the gain in income is obtained only at a cost, as in the case of the requirement that some transfer recipients must meet certain criteria. To establish their claims, they have to expend resources, particularly in foregone leisure.[7]

The observed or measured change in income resulting from transfers, then, is higher than the real change; therefore, the income effect will be biased toward zero. Not only is the size of the bias unknown; it is likely to differ among individuals and types of transfer. Moreover, income and substitution effects are confounded in cases in which, because *measured* income must be low, some transfers will lead to a reduction in the implicit price of leisure.[8]

[4]Jacob Mincer recognizes that income differences arising from wage differences imply that the price of a consumption good is correspondingly affected. He limits his discussion, however, to the time cost of acquiring commodities.

[5]These differences may be controlled for, in part, by estimating the income effect of assets while holding age and education constant.

[6]Unanticipated transfers, including unexpected losses, are proper measures of income (or wealth). Data on such transfers, however, are hard to come by.

[7]These issues, while in different settings, are discussed in my paper on rationing by waiting.

[8]One other difficulty in obtaining the appropriate income correction is that since only nominal income is subject to income tax, changes in income induced by changes in consumption-basket prices are not taxed, whereas changes in earnings and other income are subject to tax and often at varying rates.

Indeed, it is exceedingly difficult even to conceive of an experiment which might isolate the pure income effect. People will spend resources to increase their chances of receiving the award (or its size), and such efforts annul the "purity" of the income.[9] Stated more generally, what are needed are observations of income changes accompanied neither by price changes nor by expenditure of resources to increase the income. Unacceptable by their very nature are those income changes generated by price changes, including that of leisure. Most other components of measured income are also unacceptable since, as objects of maximization, resources will be spent to acquire the income.

DIRECT OBSERVATION OF THE SUBSTITUTION EFFECT

The difficulty in discovering income changes independent of price changes does not mean that the law of demand cannot be tested. On the contrary, such a test can be readily performed. In a wide variety of circumstances, a change in price simply will not affect income, thus dispensing altogether with the need for a correction.

Given the specification of the Slutsky equation, it is evident that an exogenous fall in price results in a positive income effect. When applied to leisure, however, the Slutsky equation is commonly written rather differently:

$$\frac{\partial X_e^M}{\partial P_e} = \frac{\partial X_e^I}{\partial P_e} + (24 - X_e)\frac{\partial X_e^M}{\partial M}, \qquad (4)$$

where X_e is the per-day amount of leisure and P_e is its price. A fall in price here—that of leisure—results in a negative income effect. The justification given for treating leisure differently than other commodities is that one can expend one's time as one wishes. In other words, people are assumed to be the owners not only of "money," but also of a stock of time whose value rises when its market price increases.

A person may own no asset other than himself, but in general, individuals must own other assets. Indeed, the *entire* stock of X (or of the resources used in producing it) has to be owned by somebody. To correctly analyze the demand for any commodity, such holdings have to be accounted for.[10] The Slutsky equation thus becomes

$$\frac{\partial X^M}{\partial P} = \frac{\partial X^I}{\partial P} + (X^0 - X)\frac{\partial X^M}{\partial M}, \qquad (5)$$

[9]It may appear that income differences generated by lotteries might be useful here. Even those, however, are subject to several, though perhaps unimportant, problems. If lotteries are unfair, or only just fair, only risk-seeking individuals will participate. If their expected value is positive, individuals will be willing to spend resources to participate. Random selection, then, would have to be strictly enforced for the experimental results to be valid.

[10]A. Alchian and W. R. Allen present a clear and satisfactory analysis of this point.

where X^0 is the initial endowment of X.[11] The received way of writing the equation, then, implicitly sets the endowments of commodities other than leisure at zero whereas the endowment of leisure is implicitly set larger than its consumption level. This, however, cannot hold for all individuals. People not only sell labor and buy commodities, they also buy labor and sell commodities. Slutsky's assumption that the individual is endowed with "money" rather than with real commodities (or factors) does not seem useful.[12]

The superior formulation immediately draws attention to the question whether, for any particular commodity, $X_0 - X$ is positive, negative, or zero; whether the individual is a net seller, a net buyer, or is "self-sufficient" with respect to X.[13] When $X_0 = X$, there is no income effect. The price line rotates through the consumption point, and actual income and "compensated income" are the same.

With respect to the bias in the Slutsky compensation, it is well known that for small price changes the bias can be ignored.[14] Note also that if $X_0 = X$ prior to the price change, the substitution effect always dominates in the Slutsky measure, no matter how large the change in price. That is, despite the presence of a nonvanishing income effect due to the Slutsky "overcompensation" (which is identical to the Laspyeres price index bias), the good can never become a Giffen good. The reason is that *only* by substituting toward the commodity with the lowered price can the increase in income be realized. The predictive capability, then is not impeded by overcompensation.

Two major forces may induce individuals to choose to be at the compensated point $X^0 = X$ before the change in market conditions occurs—a desire, first, to economize on transaction costs and, second, to insure against price fluctuations. One who acquires enough of a commodity to cover his consumption needs for several periods is reducing the number (hence, the cost) of transactions and is insulating himself from part of the risk associated with a change in price.[15] He will still be expected to trade when the price changes. He is insured, however, since he will be hurt neither by a price increase nor by a price fall.[16] When these

[11]George Stigler sets out this form, but he does not generalize the role of assets. Ronald Heiner also considers it, but he is mainly concerned with aggregate demand.

[12]Leon Walras, strictly concerned with excess demand, took proper account of initial holdings. Note, however, that since he assumed away inferior goods, the Giffen Paradox had no room in his model. On the other hand, he overlooked the possibility that demand might be positively sloped for a net seller of a commodity.

[13]Stigler's discussion of the Giffen Paradox makes it clear that Giffen was concerned only with *net* buyers of bread. (As Stigler pointed out to me, the price of bread in that period was set abroad, and Englishmen actually were net buyers.) Stigler's own analysis alternates between net buyers and the whole market, as does Marshall's in one of the citations in Stigler. Neither seems aware of the shift in the level of aggregation. See Stigler (1947).

[14]Jacob L. Mosak (with a proof he attributes to A. Wald) shows that the difference between the Slutsky compensation and a constant utility compensation tends to vanish.

[15]There is no presumption that most people most of the time are averse to risk. But since the range in which risk is preferred is "inefficient," people would not be observed, except temporarily, in that range. See Bailey et. al. (1980).

[16]This analysis is incomplete, and it cannot be stated that a risk-averse person would, other things being equal, prefer ownership. A sufficient condition for preferring ownership is the hom-

two forces are powerful enough, the consumer will place himself at the "compensated" position.

Compare the ownership of a condominium with the short-term lease of an apartment. Abstracting from life-cycle changes in demand, from depreciation, and from the differential costs of transacting, the quantity demanded at a given rental rate would then be the same whether it were obtained by short-term lease or by purchase. The two arrangements differ, however, in the predictability of the effect of a price change. The direction of the change in quantity is ambiguous in the first case but not in the second.

When rent increases, if apartment service is an inferior good a tenant may purchase more. On the other hand, if it is a "normal" good, the landlord may purchase more.[17] In either case, no prediction is possible. It is not even certain that the substitution effect will dominate when the effects on the landlord and his tenants are combined, although this seems likely.[18]

The owner of the condominium, however, rents from himself. Thus, he provides himself with an automatic adjustment of the rent component of the cost of living, and when rentals change he actually experiences a Slutsky compensation.[19] Because the income term in his Slutsky equation has vanished, he is unambiguously predicted to demand less housing when rents increase.

We now wish to take into account the costs of transacting for different levels of service and to determine the effects of this factor on predictability. A person's pattern of demand for consumer durables (as for other commodities) changes with age. Moreover, the flow of services generated by a consumer durable will decline as the asset depreciates. Except for a brief moment, then, the quantity of service demanded will not be equal to that provided by a particular durable good. If transacting were costless, people would change their durables constantly; but as it is, the assets held in a particular moment are not, in general, "optimal."

To proceed with the analysis, we use automobiles rather than housing for illustration. Consider the allocation of the budget between automobile services and other goods. In Figure 1, *A* is the flow of automobile service and *B* is other

otheticity of the utility function. Since inferior goods are incompatible with such a function, homotheticity cannot be assumed for the purpose of this paper. In its absence, the effect of price changes on income depends on, among other considerations, the income elasticity of demand for the commodity. The simple notion of risk-aversion seems not to apply here.

[17]This is a partial equilibrium analysis and *cannot* apply to the whole market. Rather, it is confined to those for whom the price change is exogenous and who are not substantially affected by other changes related to the initial change. If the change is due to the award of a major federal project, the only proper subjects of our study would be those whose income and other relevant prices are only negligibly affected.

[18]See Barzel and McDonald (1973) for an elaboration on the notion of cancellation.

[19]Owners of condominiums will benefit from either an increase or a decrease in rents, which they therefore prefer to stable rents! A risk-averse person may wish to remove this source of income variability too, but the required contractual arrangement may become rather complicated. It should not be inferred that instability is to be preferred in general. In the aggregate, variability in prices is the consequence of change in endowment; thus, it is impossible for all individuals simultaneously to stay at their income-compensated points.

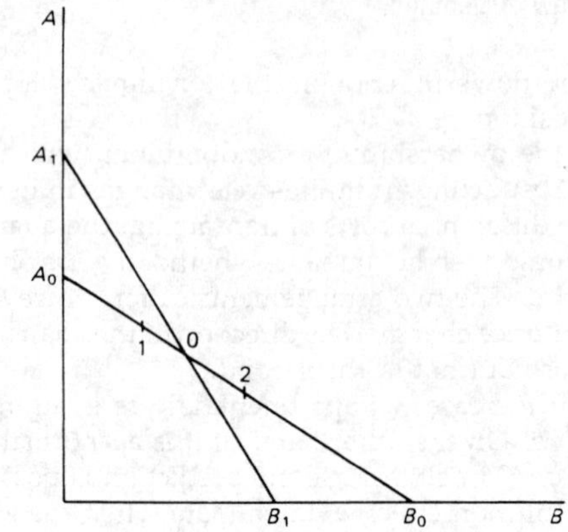

Figure 1 Asset Choice under Costly Transacting

goods. The holdings[20] of an individual with a budget A_0B_0 are initially at point 0. Had a move been costless, it is possible that prior to any change in price he would have chosen to be at 1 or 2 rather than at 0. The individual purchased an automobile which, at the going price, he planned to hold, say, for 5 years. Only in the third year is his holding "optimal," in the sense that when the car was newer he obtained "too many" automobile services; when it is older, he will have too few. Given that point 0 represents his actual holding, if the car is still new, he is obtaining too much service. Point 2 may then be the point of tangency with an indifference curve. On the other hand, if the car is old, Point 1 may be preferred. However, he remains at 0 because to move away would be costly.

What will be his reaction to a fall in the price of *A*? The new price line (A_1B_1), which passes through Point 0 is steeper. Had the initial point of tangency been 0, the conventional incentive would now be to consume more *A*. There is an even stronger incentive to increase *A* if 1 were the tangency point, since "too few" automobile services were consumed to start with. What if 2 were the initial point of tangency? Points superior to those on the segment $0B_1$ were available before but not chosen, so no point on $0B_1$ will be chosen now. No one, then, has the incentive to consume less of *A* than before, while some have an incentive to consume more. Thus, an unambiguous prediction is almost as fully warranted, in spite of the costs of making a change.

[20]The units in Figure 1 are of flows of services. By "holdings" we refer here to those assets which generate the indicated flows in the current period.

THE PREVALENCE OF ISOLATED SUBSTITUTION

It was pointed out in the previous section that, in principle, it should be possible to find situations of price change where an income effect is absent. We now show that such cases are common and that data for testing them should not be difficult to obtain. The ownership of consumer durables is but one instance where changes in some particular prices do not affect income. We now consider some other circumstances where individuals seem to find, or to place, themselves at the Slutsky-compensated position.

Take the case of a worker whose main source of income is wages and whose consumption basket resembles that underlying the consumer price index. If his wage is tied to the index, a change in price is automatically subject to a Slutsky compensation. It is predicted then that he will purchase less of the commodity for which the price has increased. In the early 1970s the price of coffee rose sharply; it is not known whether, in general, the income effect of that increase dominated the substitution effect. But for those working under cost-of-living escalation clauses only the substitution effect was present. For them, the prediction would be clear cut.

Some workers, it seems, are implicitly guaranteed constant real wages (and hours) even when wages in their industry fluctuate. It is predicted that the supply of labor of such workers will never bend backwards. Since the level of their apparent real income is guaranteed a change in the market wage will not affect their wealth, but the prediction holds because they have an incentive to change their behavior on the margin.

For most individuals the life-cycle pattern is to borrow when young and to lend later in life. At the point in the cycle where net borrowing is zero, a change in the rate of interest will have no income effect. Substitution then is the only effect and a clear prediction follows.

Consider now advance purchase of commodities by consumers. The quantities contracted for are presumably at the expected consumption level given the price at the time of the agreement. The effect of a change in price is equivalent to a Slutsky-compensated change; thus, the quantity consumed is expected to move in a direction opposite to the change in price.

The household is often "self-sufficient" in some commodities. A farmer, for example, may keep a few hens so that he usually neither buys nor sells eggs. It is predicted that a fall in the price of eggs will result in some purchase of eggs whereas an increase in price will result in selling. Self-sufficiency precludes any price-induced wealth effect; the only effect is that of substitution.[21]

Some price changes are endogenous to the individual, and of these, that of

[21]Income may, however, increase because of the opportunity to adjust production; thus, some ambiguity is reintroduced.

leisure is the most notable. Education increases the value of time. Since this effect is fully anticipated, it takes place within the framework of a constant permanent income; only the substitution effect remains, and it is predictable that the demand for leisure will fall as education and its associated wage rate increase.[22] A complication appears, however, at this point. Individuals who are identical in every respect will obtain the same education; thus, when two people differ in education they must also differ in some other attribute. In particular, they have to face some nonidentical prices or costs—for instance, their cost of capital or (due to diverse talents) their cost of acquiring education may differ. Spelling out the effects of such differences is beyond the scope of this paper. Nevertheless, prediction is possible since, being fully anticipated, the true income of the individual remains constant while the price of his time changes. A similar statement seems to apply to changes in costs that accompany aging and the associated accumulation of physical assets.

We now turn to a final example of price changes free of income effect. Sometimes a whole structure of prices changes simultaneously: Disneyland may raise the prices of all individual attractions while at the same time lowering the general admission fee. Suppose we can identify patrons for whom the two income effects cancel out at the level of past utilization. It is predicted that at the new price structure, these patrons will visit Disneyland more often and will buy fewer tickets not only per visit, but also per period. Similar predictions apply to a change in the rate structure of public utilities, to a change in medical insurance coverage accompanied by a change in premiums, and so on.

A remark on the income effect is now in order. It should by now be clear that in setting up a demand study it is not appropriate to allow automatically for the income effect of a given change in price. Since this effect may be lacking, its "correction" may introduce bias into an otherwise bias-free relationship.[23]

THE INCOME EFFECT AND PORTFOLIO SELECTION

A central premise in the analysis of portfolio selection is that, other things equal, unexpected fluctuation of income is to be avoided. It is clear from the foregoing discussion as well as from the literature that one can minimize price-induced fluctuations in income by purchasing in advance the commodity bundle he plans to consume.[24] Such a purchase may take the form of direct ownership of the

[22]Lindsay emphasizes that since education has to be "earned," substitution is the dominant factor in the demand for leisure. The point here is that since a person plans his education, he is immediately incorporating in his permanent income whatever wealth effect may result.

[23]Once the constant-real-income price elasticity is obtained, the income elasticity of demand can be estimated by observing the behavior of those for whom real income is affected (in the received way) by price changes. Given the difficulty in discovering pure income changes, however, the knowledge of income elasticity does not seem useful in positive analysis.

[24]See, particularly, an analysis by Jack Hirshleifer (1975).

commodities themselves (or of the assets which generate the consumption services). Alternatively one may hold corporate stocks whose prices vary with those in the consumer's consumption basket.

As already seen in comparing apartment rental to condominium ownership, a consumer is not indifferent to a choice of owning an asset or renting it. In discussing a firm's decision whether to buy or to lease, Merton H. Miller and Charles W. Upton (1976, p. 767) argue that under a lease arrangement the lower risk for a lessee is countered by a greater risk for the lessor. Competition will force the rental terms offered by a lessor to reflect the cost of this uncertainty; thus, the user bears the cost of the risk whether he buys or leases. Risk consideration is accordingly deemed irrelevant to the decision. This, however, ignores the asset holdings of individual lessees and lessors.

It has been pointed out above that price fluctuations generate income fluctuations for those whose endowments differ from their initial consumption—that is, when $X^0 = X$, and P fluctuates. When $X^0 = X$, the fluctuation in P does not introduce (first-order) income fluctuations. Thus, the risk of price fluctuations disappears for a consumer who owns the asset generating his consumption services but is present if he leases. The risk to the lessor does not cancel the risk to the lessee; on the contrary, the two coincide. Given risk-aversion, then, ownership is preferred.[25]

By a proper selection of assets, including corporate stocks, individuals can eliminate some otherwise inevitable price risks. The question whether a "firm" is subject to price risk is not meaningful—its individual stockholders are those to be considered. The purchaser of that firm's stock acquires insurance against price fluctuations of those commodities produced by the firm and correlated with the price of its shares. Such stockholders will not be indifferent as to whether the firm owns or leases.[26] As an example, take the case of mutual funds. Regardless of covariance considerations, some of these will hold in their total assets a fraction of residential properties expected to equal the fraction of total (uninsured) income represented by rents; other mutual funds will hold no residential properties. Apartment dwellers are expected to favor the former funds, home or condominium owners the latter. Such a prediction seems to be neither made nor implied by the received models of portfolio selection.[27] Consider, similarly, differences in the portfolios held by mutual funds as compared with pension funds. The latter are directed toward the needs of older people and are thus predicted to be heavily weighted toward commodities or services which loom large in senior budgets.

[25] This prediction, however, is subject to the same caveat stated in Footnote 16.

[26] If individuals could cheaply change their portfolios, they would simply realign their holdings toward the owner of the asset should the previous owner switch to a lease. Such a change presumably will have little effect on the values of the two stocks. Thus, firms may still be indifferent as to owning or leasing. Thanks are due to Harry DeAngelo for this point.

[27] David Mayers shows that the optimal market portfolio will vary across groups of individuals as they work for different firms and are subject to specific wage fluctuations within those firms. He does not, however, address the issue of avoiding the price risk by advance contracting.

More generally, a person is protected against price fluctuations to the extent that his assets generate services matching his consumption pattern. One such asset is a long-term labor contract protecting against fluctuations in the relative price of leisure. If the contract is also tied to the cost of living, the person is protected against price fluctuations within the index as well. Assets such as consumer durables are often held directly. Protection against fluctuations in other prices can be provided by mutual funds with the appropriate asset composition.

People differ in their choice of directly owned assets or long-term commitments and thus their exposure to price risk is not uniform. It is predicted that mutual and pension funds will refrain from holding assets in which their clients are self-protected and will, instead, seek assets to protect them against remaining risks of price fluctuation.

CONCLUDING REMARKS

Discussion of the pure income effect is prominent in virtually any price theory text. An impression persists that income changes independently of relative price changes and that it need not be "earned." In reality, such instances are rare. Indeed, it is difficult even to conceive of an experiment to generate pure income changes. Since measured income changes are themselves the result of price changes, it is not appropriate to use them for testing the law of demand.

The law, however, *can* be tested readily without income corrections. This becomes evident when the Slutsky equation includes, as it should, the initial endowment of the commodity studied. When the endowment equals consumption, there is no income effect and substitution is the only effect of a change in price. Consumers have certain incentives to assume in advance a "compensated" position so that their real income is not affected by price changes. Identifying such situations, which is not difficult, allows for a direct test of the law.

Those wishing to avoid the risk of price fluctuations will hold assets whose streams of service match their consumption. To the extent that these assets are not held directly, a person's market portfolio is predicted to include such assets (thus, apartment dwellers will hold mutual funds heavy in residential properties whereas home owners will select mutual funds that shun such properties).

References

Alchian, A. A., and **W. R. Allen,** *Exchange and Production.* Belmont, Calif.: Wadsworth, 1977.

Bailey, M. J., M. Olson, and **P. Wonnacott,** "Marginal Utility of Income Does not Increase: Borrowing, Lending and Friedman-Savage Gambles," *American Economic Revue* (June 1980), 372–79.

Barzel, Y., "A Theory of Rationing by Waiting," *Journal of Law Economics* (April 1974), 73–95.

Barzel, Y., and **R. J. McDonald,** "Assets, Subsistence and the Supply Curve of Labor," *American Economic Revue* (September 1973), 621–33.

Heiner, R. A., "A Reformulation of the Law of Demand," *Economic Inquiry,* 2 (December 1974) 577–83.

Hirshleifer, J., "Speculation and Equilibrium: Information, Risk, and Markets," *Quarterly Journal of Economics* 79 (November 1975), 519–42.

Lindsay, C. M., "Measuring Human Capital Returns," *Journal of Political Economy,* 79 (November/December 1971), 1195–1255.

Mayers, D., "Portfolio Theory, Job Choice and the Equilibrium Structure of Expected Wages," *Journal of Financial Economics,* 1 (1974), 23–42.

Miller, M. H., and **C. W. Upton,** "Leasing, Buying, and the Cost of Capital Services," *Journal of Finance,* 31 (June 1976), 768–86.

Mincer, J., "Market Prices, Opportunity Costs, and Income Effects," in *Measurement in Mathematical Economics and Econometrics in Memory of Yehuda Grunfeld.* Berkeley, Calif.: Stanford University Press, 1963.

Mosak, J. L., "On the Interpretation of the Fundamental Equation of Value Theory," in *Studies in Mathematical Economics and Econometrics,* Oscar Lange, et al., eds., Chicago: Chicago University Press, 1943.

Slutsky, E. E., "On the Theory of the Budget of the Consumer," trans., reprinted in *Readings in Price Theory,* Homewood, Ill.: Richard D. Irwin, 1952.

Stigler, G. J., "Notes on the History of the Giffen Paradox, *Journal of Political Economy,* 55 (April 1947), 152–56.

——, *The Theory of Price,* (3rd ed.), pp. 65–68. New York: Macmillan, 1966.

Walras, L., *Elements of Pure Economics,* pp. 116–18. London: Allen and Unwin, 1954.

The Economic Journal, **102** (*July* 1992), 896–905
Printed in Great Britain

THE DEMAND CURVES FOR GIFFEN GOODS ARE DOWNWARD SLOPING*

Yoram Barzel and Wing Suen

The Giffen paradox is one of the most prominent curiosities in economics. Few price theory textbooks fail to mention the possibility that a utility-maximising consumer may consume more of a good at a higher price. Fewer textbooks, however, show awareness as to why the precise nature of the price increase is a crucial element in the Giffen curiosity. This paper will demonstrate that the Giffen curiosity is an artifact of simplification. It only arises when people do not exploit available options and do not plan their consumption in anticipation of (certain or probabilistic) price changes. In a fully specified model, a maximising individual will never buy more of a good when its price increases.

Imagine, for example, that a consumer's demand for fresh vegetables displays the textbook Giffen property. We will show that this same person's demand is downward sloping once the analysis properly accounts for the optimal response to the seasonal price pattern of vegetables. In order to maximise utility, the marginal utility of income between the seasons has to be equalised. This paper demonstrates that the price of a Giffen good is positively related to the marginal utility of income. The consumer will therefore structure his expenditures such that he will spend more in the higher price period and less in the lower price period. Giffen goods being inferior goods, the consumer will consume less vegetables when the price is high and more when the price is low.

In this paper we first demonstrate that where the Giffen good would be present, individuals can gain by buying the appropriate price insurance which will eliminate the Giffen outcome. Even if such insurance markets are not available, individuals can operate on their asset holdings or on their consumption allocation over time. Each alone will also eliminate the Giffen paradox. Thus, if our theory is right, there is a strong presumption that people will find ways to avoid the Giffen good traps.

I. OPTIMAL INSURANCE AGAINST PRICE RISKS

The received mathematical analysis of the Giffen paradox can be stated as follows. If the optimal demand for a good at price p^0 is x^0 and the optimal demand for the good at price $p' > p^0$ is x', and if the price of other goods and money income are the same in the two situations, then the postulate of utility maximisation alone is not sufficient to rule out the possibility that $x' > x^0$. Thus stated, the Giffen paradox is a comparative statics relationship; it shows how the quantity demanded would vary at hypothetically different prices. In the

* We thank Douglas Allen, Steven Cheung and the referees of this JOURNAL for their valuable comments. Christopher Hall helped clarify our exposition. Remaining inadequacies are ours.

analysis the consumer is assumed to respond passively to variations in price in the sense that x^0 is chosen without regard to p', and x' is chosen without regard to p^0. Money income is also assumed to be exogenous. Such an analysis would be appropriate if the price change were completely unanticipated. If consumers can at least assign subjective probabilities to possible price changes, they will make consumption plans that take into account the price risk. In that case optimal consumption at p^0 and at p' cannot be determined independently of one another. Moveover, money income in different states is not longer exogenous to the consumer given the possibility of insurance. An explicit analysis using a framework of expected utility maximisation is necessary.

The theory of consumer behaviour under uncertainty suggests that, under certain conditions (see for example Luce and Raiffa, 1957), consumer preferences can be represented by the utility function:

$$U = \sum_{j-1}^{J} \pi_j u(x_{1j}, \dots, x_{nj}), \tag{1}$$

where π_j is the probability of state j and x_{ij} is the consumption of good i in state j. For a given money income in state j, denoted y_j, the consumer will choose $x_{1j}, \dots, x_{nj}$ to maximise the von Neumann-Morgenstern utility function u subject to the budget constraint $\Sigma_i p_{ij} x_{ij} = y_j$. The solution to this problem yields the indirect utility function $v(p_{1j}, \dots, p_{nj}, y_j)$, and quantity demanded in each state can be obtained by using Roy's identity, $x_{ij} = -v_i(j)/v_y(j)$.

Let state j correspond to the state in which the price of good 1 is equal to p_{1j} (and the prices of other goods are the same across states). Then the utility function (1) can also be written as

$$U = \sum_{j-1}^{J} \pi_j v(p_{1j}, p_2 \dots, p_n, y_j), \tag{2}$$

If the consumer has money income M and if he can purchase actuarially fair income insurance (i.e. state-contingent claims to financial resources), he will choose $y_1, \dots, y_J$ to maximise (2) subject to the constraint:

$$\sum_{j-1}^{J} \pi_j y_j = M. \tag{3}$$

The left side of equation (3) is the cost of an actuarially fair insurance policy that pays an amount y_j in state j. Necessary conditions for the solution to this optimal insurance problem include:

$$\left.\begin{aligned} v_y(j) &= \mu, \quad \text{for all } j; \\ \pi_j v_{yy}(j) + \pi_k v_{yy}(k) &\leqslant 0, \quad \text{for all } j \neq k. \end{aligned}\right\} \tag{4}$$

The first order conditions imply that the marginal utility of income (v_y) is the same across all states. The second order conditions require that the utility function U be quasi-concave in $y_1, \dots, y_J$ at the optimum. They imply that the marginal utility of income is increasing ($v_{yy} > 0$) in at most one state. However, if $p_{1j} = p_{1k}$, then $y_j = y_k$ and v_{yy} must be negative. By continuity v_{yy} is negative if the difference between p_{1j} and p_{1k} is small. Moreover, if the consumer can take fair gambles, he will gamble out of the convex region of the von Neumann-Morgenstern utility function so that the marginal utility of income is always decreasing (Friedman and Savage, 1948).

With optimal insurance against price risks, total spending in the two states must be such that the marginal utilities of income in these two states are equal, i.e.,

$$v_y(p_{1j}, \ldots, y_j) = v_y(p_{1k}, \ldots, y_k). \tag{5}$$

Taking a first order Taylor expansion on (5), and letting $p_{1k} - p_{1j} = dp_1$, $y_k - y_j = dy$, we get

$$dy = \left(\frac{-v_{1y}}{v_{yy}}\right) dp_1. \tag{6}$$

Let $dx_1 = x_{1k} - x_{1j}$ be the difference in the quantity of good 1 purchased in the two states. Using Roy's identity and equations (4) and (6), we have

$$\begin{aligned} dx_1 &= \left[\frac{-v_1(k)}{v_y(k)}\right] - \left[\frac{-v_1(j)}{v_y(j)}\right] \\ &= \frac{[v_1(j) - v_1(k)]}{\mu} \\ &= \frac{(-v_{11}\, dp_1 - v_{1y}\, dy)}{\mu} \\ &= \left[\frac{(v_{1y}^2 - v_{11} v_{yy})}{v v_{yy}}\right] dp_1. \end{aligned} \tag{7}$$

Thus if x_1 is a Giffen good (by this we mean that the demand function for x_1 resulting from the maximisation of the von Neumann-Morgenstern utility function u subject to the constraint $\Sigma_i p_{ij} x_{ij} = y$, has a positive own price derivative), it will have a downward sloping demand curve under our specification if and only if

$$v_{1y}^2 - v_{11} v_{yy} > 0. \tag{8}$$

To prove that condition (8) is true, we need the following lemma.

LEMMA. If good 1 is a Giffen good, then

(*a*) $$-v_y v_{11} + v_1 v_{1y} > 0;$$

(*b*) $$-v_y v_{1y} + v_1 v_{yy} < 0;$$

(*c*) $$-v_y^2 v_{11} - v_1^2 v_{yy} + 2 v_1 v_y v_{1y} < 0.$$

Proof. Roy's identity gives $x_1 = -v_1/v_y$. Since x_1 is a Giffen good, $\partial x_1/\partial p_1 > 0$, which implies part (*a*) of the lemma. Since a Giffen good is also an inferior good, $\partial x_1/\partial y < 0$, which implies part (*b*). Since the substitution effect is negative, $\partial x_1/\partial p_1 + x_1(\partial x_1/\partial y) < 0$, which implies (*c*).

With the above lemma it is not difficult to prove the main proposition of this paper.

PROPOSITION. For any Giffen good x_1 and any two states j and k, holding money income M and the price of other goods $p_2, \ldots, p_n$ constant, $p_{1k} > p_{1j}$ implies $x_{1k} < x_{1j}$.

Proof. Part (*c*) of the lemma can be written as

$$v_y(-v_y v_{11} + v_1 v_{1y}) < v_1(-v_y v_{1y} + v_1 v_{yy}), \tag{9}$$

and part (*b*) can be written as

$$v_1 v_{yy} < v_y v_{1y}. \tag{10}$$

Since the four terms in (9) and (10) are all positive, we can multiply the two inequalities to get

$$v_{yy}(-v_y v_{11} + v_1 v_{1y}) > v_{1y}(-v_y v_{1y} + v_1 v_{yy}), \tag{11}$$

which simplifies to condition (8).

Our proposition demonstrates that, when consumers can insure against price risks, they will purchase a relatively low quantity of a Giffen good when its price is relatively high. *A fortiori*, if Giffen goods have downward sloping demand curves, other goods also have the same property. For completeness, we prove this assertion in an Appendix (available upon request from the authors). Note that our proposition also implies factor supply curves are always upward sloping (see Rosen, 1985).

Let us consider why Giffen goods have downward sloping demand curves in our formulation. What is crucial is that marginal utility of income is high when the price of a Giffen good (or, more generally, the price of an inferior good) is high (see also Marshall, 1895). From part (*b*) of our lemma, we have

$$v_{1y} > \frac{v_1 v_{yy}}{v_y} > 0. \tag{12}$$

Silberberg and Walker (1984) demonstrate that the compensated change in the marginal utility of income in response to a change in price is always of opposite sign to the income effect. The result in (12) is consistent with this. In Fig. 1 we

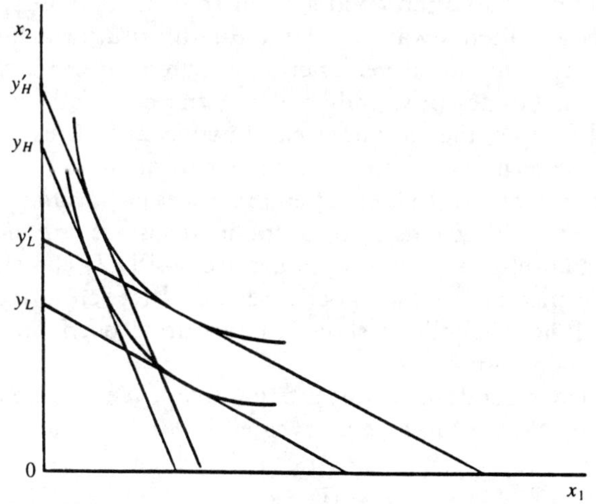

Fig. 1. The marginal cost of utility is low when the price of x_1 is high.

have drawn the indifference map for two goods, x_1 and x_2, where x_1 is a Giffen good. The indifference curves are more tightly packed together in the northwest than in the southeast part of the quadrant. When the price of x_1 is high, the budget line needs to shift only slightly to achieve a higher utility level (from y_H to y'_H). When the price of x_1 is low, the budget line needs to shift a great deal to achieve the same increase in utility (from y_L to y'_L). This means that the marginal cost of utility is low when the price of x_1 is high—in other words, the marginal utility of income is high when the price of the Giffen good is high. Optimal insurance then implies that the consumer will reallocate total spending from situations when p_1 is low to situations when p_1 is high. Formally,

$$\frac{dy}{dp_1} = \frac{-v_{1y}}{v_{yy}} > 0. \tag{13}$$

When p_1 is high, the consumer receives a high income from his insurance policy. Since x_1 is inferior, the high income will cause the consumer to reduce the purchases of x_1. The income effect *reinforces* the substitution effect to produce a downward sloping demand curve.

II. GIFFEN GOODS AS ASSETS

Our result in the previous section depends on the argument that consumers can acquire an optimal portfolio in anticipation of possible price changes. In this section we will show that holding commodity bundles as assets will serve as an imperfect substitute to a perfect insurance market. When a person's portfolio consists of commodities instead of money income, a rise in the price of a good does not necessarily entail a fall in real income. If a person holds an amount of a Giffen good greater than what he consumes, his real income will actually rise when the price of the Giffen good rises. Since the marginal utility of income is positively correlated with the price of Giffen goods, the person's optimal policy is to hold an amount of a Giffen good greater than the amount he consumes. The income effect will then always reinforce the substitution effect to produce a downward sloping demand curve. There are many ways to include a Giffen good in one's assets besides physically holding the commodity. If bread is a Giffen good, for example, the consumer can buy wheat futures or invest in the stock of bakeries. Alternatively, the consumer can arrange to have his wage indexed to the price of bread. In fact, when the prices of consumption goods are variable, consumption decisions and portfolio decisions are not separable. Individuals tend to prefer assets whose values are positively correlated with the price of inferior or income-inelastic goods (see also Breeden (1979) and Besley (1989)). The analysis that follows shows that optimal portfolio decisions will avert the Giffen good trap.

Suppose the price of good 1 in state j is equal to p_{1j}. We assume that the price of good 1 before the state of nature is revealed is equal to the expected price:

$$p_1 = \sum_{j=1}^{J} \pi_j p_{1j}. \tag{14}$$

The consumer first purchases a_i units of good i at price p_i and holds them as assets. After the state of nature is revealed, his final income at state j will be equal to

$$y_j = p_{1j}\, a_1 + \sum_{i-2}^{n} p_i\, a_i, \tag{15}$$

and he can then spend y_j to achieve indirect utility $v(p_{1j}, p_2, \ldots, p_n, y_i)$. At the first stage the consumer will choose an asset holding $a_1, \ldots, a_n$ to maximise expected utility subject to a budget constraint:

$$\text{maximise} \quad \sum_{j-1}^{J} \pi_j\, v(p_{1j}, p_2, \ldots, p_n, y_j)$$

$$\text{subject to} \quad p_1\, a_1 + \sum_{i-2}^{n} p_i\, a_i = M, \tag{16}$$

where p_1 is given by equation (14) and y_j is given by (15).

The first order conditions for the solution to problem (16) can be combined to get

$$\sum_{j-1}^{J} \pi_j\, v_y(j)\, (p_{1j} - p_1) = 0. \tag{17}$$

Equation (17) says that, at the optimum, the covariance between the marginal utility of income and the price of good 1 is zero. Thus, on average, marginal utility of income is equalised across high-price and low-price states. In other words, holding assets or buying futures in the Giffen good serves as a method of partial insurance against price risks. When the price of a Giffen good is high, other things equal, marginal utility of income is also high. Under that situation it is especially advantageous to have a high money income. This is achieved by a long position in the Giffen good because money income will rise automatically when the Giffen good appreciates in value. When a positive amount of the Giffen good is held as asset, the Slutsky equation is written as:

$$\frac{\partial x_1}{\partial p_1} = s_{11} + (a_1 - x_1)\frac{\partial x_1}{\partial y}. \tag{18}$$

Here s_{11} is the pure substitution effect, and it is negative in sign. In the Appendix available from the authors, we show that the optimal asset holding implies $a_1 - x_1 > 0$. Since $\partial x_1/\partial y$ is negative when x_1 is a Giffen good, the expression in (18) is always negative. When the price of a Giffen good rises, people will consume less of it.

III. GIFFEN GOODS IN AN INTERTEMPORAL CONTEXT

When the price of a good is uncertain, consumers will take actions to mitigate the price risks. We have shown that buying insurance or holding Giffen goods as assets will eliminate the possibility of upward sloping demand curves. When the price of a good changes over time and such price variations are anticipated, consumers can also respond to the change in relative prices across time through intertemporal substitution. Assuming lifetime utility is additively separable, we will show in this section that the time series observations of price-quantity pairs will produce downward-sloping demand curves.

We assume preferences are additively separable in time such that the utility function can be written as:

$$U = \sum_{t=1}^{T} u(x_{1t}, \dots, x_{nt}), \tag{19}$$

where x_{it} is the consumption of good i at time t. This is not the most general specification of preferences because it precludes habit formation and life-cycle variations in tastes. We have also ignored discounting for simplicity, but the analysis is unchanged as long as the subjective rate of discount is equal to the rate of interest.

The consumer maximises lifetime utility (19) subject to the lifetime budget constraint:

$$\sum_{t=1}^{T} \sum_{i=1}^{n} p_{it} x_{it} = W, \tag{20}$$

where p_{it} is the price of good i at time t and W is money wealth, and where we again ignore discounting. Suppose x_1 is a Giffen good. (That is, the demand function for x_1 resulting from the maximisation of the per-period utility function subject to a per-period budget constraint has a positive own price derivative.) If the price of x_1 jumps unexpectedly and permanently to a higher level, $p_{11}, \dots, p_{1T}$ will be proportionally higher than they were before. Using Hicks's composite commodity theorem, the demand for x_1 will jump permanently to a higher level since x_1 is a Giffen good. The situation, however, is markedly different when we consider the demand for x_1 if the consumer anticipates the price variations over time. Since the price of x_1 in one period relative to another period changes, and since prices at other periods also affect consumption at the current period, an explicit dynamic analysis is required.

The intertemporal maximisation problem can be solved in two stages because utility is additively separable in time. For a given total expenditure at time t, denoted y_t, the consumer will choose $x_{1t}, \dots, x_{nt}$ to maximise per-period utility u subject to the per-period budget constraint $\Sigma_i p_{it} x_{it} = y_t$. The solution to this problem will yield per-period indirect utility functions $v(p_{1t}, \dots, p_{nt}, y_t)$. Having solved this second stage problem, the consumer will choose $y_1, \dots, y_T$ in order to

$$\left.\begin{aligned} &\text{maximise} \quad \sum_{t=1}^{T} v(p_{1t}, \dots, p_{nt}, y_t), \\ &\text{subject to} \quad \sum_{t=1}^{T} y_t = W. \end{aligned}\right\} \tag{21}$$

The conditions for the solution to this problem include:

$$\left.\begin{aligned} v_y(t) &= \mu, \quad \text{for all } t; \\ v_{yy}(t) + v_{yy}(s) &\leqslant 0, \quad \text{for all } t \neq s. \end{aligned}\right\} \tag{22}$$

Conditions (22) are the same as those in the insurance model. Optimal intertemporal allocation of resources requires that the marginal utility of income be equal across all time periods. Since marginal utility of income is high when the price of a Giffen good is high, the consumer will allocate greater total spending to time periods when the Giffen good is relatively expensive. The higher total spending in turn depresses the consumption of the Giffen good since it is inferior. The formal analysis of the situation is identical to that in Section I. Thus time-series observations of price-consumption pairs will always yield a downward sloping demand curve even for a Giffen good. As in Hall (1978), our proposition describes the consumption pattern that maximising individuals must satisfy; it does not specify a structural demand equation. This specification of the demand curve is closest in spirit to the 'marginal-utility-of-income-constant' demand function of Frisch (1959) and MaCurdy (1981).

In reality, price changes are not perfectly foreseen. Were there an unexpected increase in the price of a Giffen good in the last period, for example, the consumer would not be able to reallocate expenditures already spent towards the last period so that the income effect might give rise to an increase in quantity demanded. However a slight extension of the model along the lines of Section I would cover the case of uncertainty. Suppose consumers are able to purchase actuarially fair insurance. Then maximisation of expected utility implies that the marginal utility of income will be the same across all states of nature. If there is some chance that the price of the Giffen good is high in the last period, consumers will buy insurance to cover this possibility because the marginal utility of income will also be high. When the price increase actually occurs, consumers will receive income from their insurance policies. This additional income from insurance policies will wipe out the effect of the reduction in real income from the price increase. Combining lifetime utility maximisation with expected utility maximisation increases the domain of our proposition.

IV. CONCLUSION

The standard theory of utility maximisation is not strong enough to rule out the logical possibility of an upward sloping demand curve. Yet most economists do not take the alleged exception to the law of demand seriously. Economists' skepticism towards the Giffen paradox can be attributed to several reasons. (1) When the share of expenditure on a good in total spending is small, the magnitude of the income effect is likely to be small (e.g. Hicks, 1946). (2) At the aggregate level, the income effect of a price change is approximately zero (e.g. Friedman, 1949; Heiner, 1974). (3) With an upward sloping demand curve, a decrease in supply would result in a lower price, which is inconsistent with reasonable market dynamics and is counter to the facts (e.g. Dougan, 1982; Dwyer and Lindsay, 1984). (4) Empirical research has not produced a convincing case of an upward sloping demand curve (e.g. Stigler, 1947). We believe the skepticism towards the Giffen good paradox is well-founded. Consuming more of a good when its price is high seems to be a pathological response. In this paper we demonstrate that the Giffen paradox will not arise when consumers plan their consumption in anticipation of price changes. Using a framework of expected utility maximisation or of lifetime utility maximisation, we show that maximising behaviour is inconsistent with upward sloping demand curves. Our paper thus provides a theoretical justification for the empirical regularity known as the law of demand.

University of Washington

University of Hong Kong

Date of receipt of final receipt of final typescript: December 1991

References

Besley, Timothy (1989). 'A definition of luxury and necessity for cardinal utility functions.' ECONOMIC JOURNAL, vol. 99 (September), pp. 844–9.

Breeden, Douglas T. (1979). 'An intertemporal asset pricing model with stochastic consumption and investment opportunities.' *Journal of Financial Economics*, vol. 7 (September), pp. 265–96.

Dougan, William R. (1982). 'Giffen goods and the law of demand.' *Journal of Political Economy*, vol. 90 (August), pp. 809–15.

Dwyer, Gerald P. and Lindsay, Cotton M. (1984). 'Robert Giffen and the Irish potato.' *American Economic Review*, vol. 74 (March), pp. 188–92.

Friedman, Milton (1949). 'The Marshallian demand curve.' *Journal of Political Economy*, vol. 57 (December), pp. 463–95.

—— and Savage, L. J. (1948). 'The utility analysis of choices involving risk.' *Journal of Political Economy*, vol. 56 (August), pp. 277–90.

Frisch, Ragnar (1959). 'A complete scheme for computing all direct and cross demand elasticities in a model with many sectors.' *Econometrica*, vol. 27 (April), pp. 177–96.

Hall, Robert E. (1978). 'Stochastic implications of the life cycle-permanent income hypothesis: theory and evidence.' *Journal of Political Economy*, vol. 86 (December), pp. 971–87.

Heiner, Ron (1974). 'A reformulation of the law of demand.' *Economic Inquiry*, vol. 12 (September), pp. 577–83.

Hicks, J. R. (1946). *Value and Capital*, 2nd ed. Oxford: Oxford University Press.

Luce, R. D. and Raiffa, H. (1957). *Games and Decisions*. New York: Wiley.

MaCurdy, Thomas E. (1981). 'An empirical model of labor supply in a life-cycle setting.' *Journal of Political Economy*, vol. 89 (December), pp. 1059–85.

Marshall, Alfred (1895). *Principles of Economics*, 3rd ed. New York: Macmillan.

Rosen, Sherwin (1985). 'Implicit contracts: a survey.' *Journal of Economic Literature*, vol. 23 (September), pp. 1144–75.

Silberberg, Eugene and Walker, Donald A. (1984). 'A modern analysis of Giffen's paradox.' *International Economic Review*, vol. 25 (October), pp. 687–94.

Stigler, George J. (1947). 'Notes on the history of the Giffen' paradox. *Journal of Political Economy*, vol. 55 (April), pp. 152–6.

Appendix

(A) We want to show that

$$\frac{dx_{1t}}{dp_{1t}} = \frac{(v_{1y}^2 - v_{11}\, v_{yy})}{v_{yy}} < 0,$$

i.e., that condition (8) in the text is true for all goods. The condition is satisfied if $v_{11} \geqslant 0$, so we need only to consider the case when $v_{11} < 0$. Part (*c*) of our lemma in the text is true for all goods because it is derived from the negativity of the substitution effect. Rearranging part (*c*), we get

$$v_{1y} > \frac{(v_y^2\, v_{11} + v_1^2\, v_{yy})}{2v_1\, v_y} > 0,$$

for $v_{11} < 0$.

In the case of an inferior (but not Giffen) good, $\partial x_1/\partial p_1 < 0$ and $\partial x_1/\partial y < 0$. Thus our lemma will be modified to

$$(a') \qquad -v_1 v_{1y} > -v_y v_{11};$$

$$(b) \qquad v_y v_{1y} > v_1 v_{yy}.$$

These four terms are all positive and we can multiply the inequalities to obtain the desired result.

If x_1 is a normal good, the compensated and uncompensated price derivatives are both negative. Our lemma will be written as

$$(a') \qquad -v_1 v_{1y} > -v_y v_{11};$$

$$(c) \qquad -v_y(-v_y v_{11} + v_1 v_{1y}) > -v_1(-v_y v_{1y} + v_1 v_{yy}).$$

Again the four terms are positive and we can multiple the inequalities to get the desired result.

(B) to show that $a_1 - x_1 > 0$, we take a Taylor approximation around p_1 to equation (17) in the text. Let the variance of p_1 be σ^2, we get

$$(v_{1y} + a_1 v_{yy})\,\sigma^2 = 0.$$

The expansion involves no covariance terms since we assume the prices of other goods are fixed. Using the above equation and Roy's identity,

$$a_1 - x_1 = \left(\frac{-v_{1y}}{v_{yy}}\right) - \left(\frac{-v_1}{v_y}\right)$$

$$= \frac{v_1 v_{yy} - v_y v_{1y}}{v_y v_{yy}},$$

which is positive by part (*b*) of our lemma.

PART VII

PROPERTY RIGHTS AND TRANSACTION COSTS

[19]

Reprinted for private circulation from The Journal of Law and Economics, Volume XVII (1), April, 1974, Copyright 1974, The University of Chicago.

A THEORY OF RATIONING BY WAITING*

YORAM BARZEL
University of Washington

When limited quantities of commodities are provided free by the government, it is frequently asserted that not all demand is satisfied. Such commodities are often allocated on a first-come-first-served basis. It will be shown that rationing by waiting, which is the economic counterpart to first-come-first-served, is just another way to "satisfy all demand." The mechanics and the implications of such rationing are the subject matter here.[1]

Compared with the price mechanism, rationing by waiting generally entails a different resource cost—the time spent in the queue.[2] The extent of that cost, sometimes designated "dissipation of rent," will be examined and the conditions specified under which it equals the entire consumer's surplus. The cost arises because no well-defined property rights originally exist to the "free" good. To establish a claim to such rights, one must spend whatever time is necessary to gain priority in the queue.

The provision of goods free of charge is often justified on grounds that the action will benefit the poor. However, it will be shown that even when the poor actually have a lower time cost and therefore a lower cost of waiting, they may not benefit from such action. Indeed, in some empirically relevant cases the rich rather than the poor will stand in line to obtain such goods.

Assuming that every individual is costlessly informed of the waiting time necessary to acquire a subsidized good, what can we say about the length of

* I wish to thank Mary Eysenbach, Chris Hall, Reuben Kessel, John McGee, Mike Rahm, and particularly Steve Cheung for their valuable comments. I was first exposed to the notion of the real costs induced by price control in Harberger's price theory course in Chicago in 1957. Thanks for secretarial help are given to the National Science Foundation Grant to the University of Washington for the investigation of contracts.

[1] The literature on rationing is extensive, but with few exceptions the rationed quantities are assumed to be allocated by mechanisms such as a point system, for which this kind of waiting does not arise. Some queuing problems are discussed by D. Nichols, E. Smolensky, & T. N. Tideman, Discrimination by Waiting Time in Merit Goods, 61 Am. Econ. Rev. 312 (1971) [hereinafter cited as Nichols]. Gary S. Becker discusses briefly the cost associated with queues in A Theory of the Allocation of Time, 75 Econ. J. 493 (1965).

[2] Queues occur also in unregulated markets. While some of the analysis of this paper may apply to such situations, we concentrate here on queuing problems emerging from government actions.

the queue or, more precisely, about the length of waiting time for each individual in line? For this type of market to clear, the *marginal* individual is at a point where *total cost* (time plus money) is equal with his *total* valuation of the good to be obtained. In other words, to the marginal individual the consumer's surplus is zero.

A recent event, verging on a controlled experiment, confirms that allocation by waiting is not just an economist's fancy but is actually a market phenomenon. On June 14, 1972, the United States of America Bank (of Chicago) launched an anniversary sale.[3] The commodity on sale was money, and each of the first 35 persons could "buy" a $100 bill for $80 in cash. Those farther down the queue could each obtain similar but declining bonuses: the next 50 could gain $10 each; 75, $4 each; 100, $2 each, and the following 100, $1 each. Each of the next 100 persons could get a $2 bill for $1.60 and, finally, 800 (subsequently, it seems, expanded to 1800) persons could gain fifty cents each. The expected waiting time in such an unusual event was unpredictable; on the other hand, it was easy to assess the money value of the commodity being distributed.

First in line were four black brothers aged 16, 17, 19, and 24. Since the smallest was 6′2″, their priority right was assured. "I figured," said Carl, the youngest brother, 'that we spent 17 hours to make a $20 profit. That's about $1.20 an hour."

"You can make better than that washing dishes," added another of the brothers. Had they been better informed they could have waited less time. The 35th person to join the line arrived around midnight, had to wait just 9 hours, and was the last to earn $20—$2.22 per hour. To confirm her right, she made a list of all those ahead of her in the line.

"Why am I here?" she asked. "Well, that $20 is the same as a day's pay to me. And I don't even have to declare it on my income tax. It's a gift, isn't it?"

Information is sparse on how the rest of the queue evolved, but by opening time an estimated 500 persons were in line. Between then and the noon deadline, another 1800 or so joined the queue to get fifty cents apiece. What emerges most clearly from this experience is that the identity of those in the queue was not random and that waiting time fell as the bonus declined. The money value of the "free" good was largely matched by waiting time, viewed as a cost by those in the queue.[4]

[3] The information is obtained from the Seattle Times, June 12, 1972, and from four Chicago daily newspapers, the Chicago Sun Times and Chicago Today, June 14, 1972, and the Chicago Tribune and Chicago Daily News, June 15, 1972.

[4] From the viewpoint of the bank, which apparently sought publicity, waiting time was simply a purchased input; indeed, it turned out to be most productive, as attested by the prominent newspapers' writeups.

Time as a Market Clearing Price

The term "rationing" is traditionally identified with disequilibrium, a condition under which individuals are unable to equate costs and values on the margin, as seems apparent when the price imposed is not at the intersection of demand and supply. But since time is costly, waiting provides an additional route whereby individuals can again equate on the margin. Adding the time constraint allows us to apply "equilibrium" analysis to this form of rationing.

In Figure I the horizontal axis measures the quantity of a commodity and the vertical axis its money price. The conventional demand curve of a single individual is represented by $d(t_0)$. (Implicit is the notion that the pecuniary price represents the full cost of purchase where waiting time is zero, that is, $t_0 = 0$.) For each of the other curves, waiting time is assumed to be positive and, at the higher time price, these curves have to lie below $d(t_0)$. At $d(t_2)$ waiting time per unit of the commodity is $t_2 > 0$; at $d(t_3)$ waiting time is $t_3 > t_2$.

When the money price is reduced to zero and per-unit waiting time is t_3, the quantity demanded is k. If k is the per-person quantity being distributed "free" by the government, the individual will be willing to stay in line up to $k \times t_3$ minutes to obtain his share.[5] By letting t vary continuously, every point inside $d(t_0)$ is a point on a demand curve. In this space, for every combination of quantity and money price there is a time price at which the individual will be able to equate on the margin and be in equilibrium. In particular, all points on the horizontal axis to the left of the $d(t_0)$ horizontal intercept, combined with the appropriate amounts of waiting, are equilibrium points. Holding the pecuniary price constant, we can trace the relation between the quantity demanded and the minutes-per-unit waiting price to obtain a demand curve in terms of waiting, as we will do below for the special case where the monetary price is set at zero.

It is important to recognize that when money price is zero, waiting time serves as a total price, and the analogy with pecuniary price is complete: demand with respect to this price will slope downwards. In the absence of discrimination among consumers only one time-price will prevail in the market.[6]

[5] If it is impossible to get fewer than k units at a proportionately lower waiting time, all-or-nothing demand becomes relevant. Such a demand relation is introduced *infra.*

[6] The conclusion that waiting time is constant is derived under the assumption of certainty. P. Naor, The Regulation of Queue Size by Levying Tolls, 37 Econometrica 15 (1969) shows that with a random stream of customers the length of the queue will vary but will never exceed a given level equivalent to our uniform waiting time. He implicitly assumes there is no cost in ascertaining the length of the queue, so that at its maximum level there is no incentive to join. Symmetry would require, then, that when the queue is shorter then maximum, there is an incentive to join thereby lengthening the time in the queue towards the maximum. In any case, when the cost of information is taken into

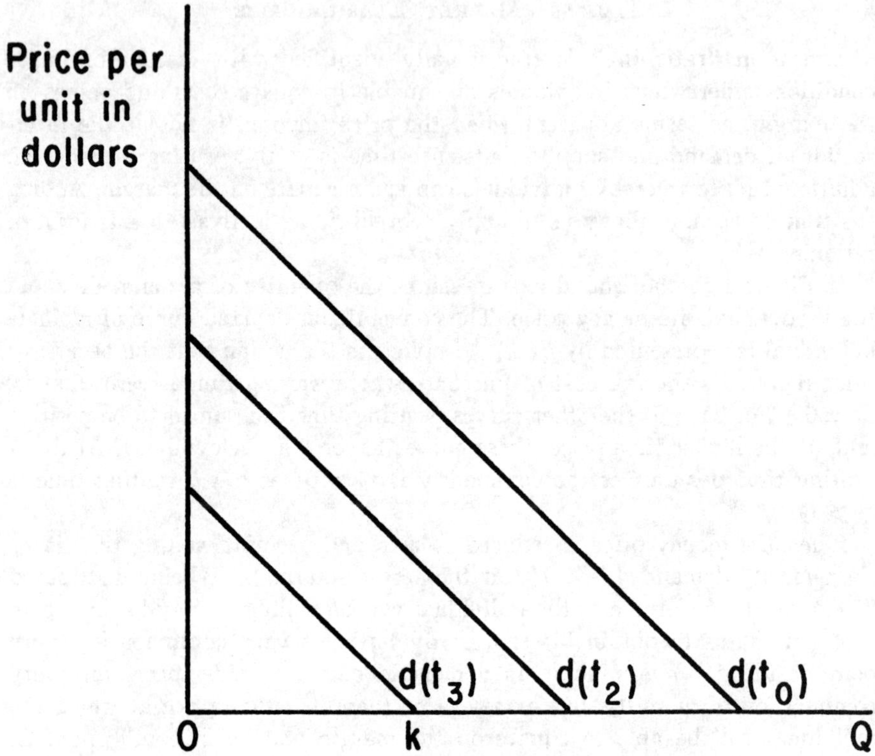

FIGURE I

The marginal valuation here is in terms of waiting time: as the quantity offered increases, the marginal valuation and, consequently, the per-unit waiting time will decline, giving the curve its negative slope.[7]

Unless the individual allotment of the "free" good is restricted, one person may take the entire available supply. Thus the rules for distribution will fix quotas and may also stipulate whether each may join the queue only once

---

account, the decision whether to join will depend on the probability that the queue is shorter than the critical level. The higher this probability the stronger the incentive to explore, which in turn reduces the variability in the length of the queue.

[7] Given that a certain quantity of a commodity is distributed at a zero price, what can be said with respect to changes in the quantity? The cost of increasing the quantity is positive; but as the quantity increases, so does the rent to consumers since waiting time falls. If one is willing to add up dollar valuation of different individuals, a local maximum will occur when the rate of change in the sum of rents to consumers is equal to the rate of change in total cost of production. Second order as well as total conditions have to be also satisfied. In addition, it seems possible that several local maximum points may exist.

per period or as many times as he wishes. The former arrangement prevails with the food stamp program and housing subsidies; the latter implicitly governs the utilization of public parks and roads. Both techniques are considered here.

The time-price an individual is willing to pay per unit of the good falls when the individual allotment increases. And, holding the per-person quantity constant, the number of demanders will increase as the time-price falls. Just as with regular demand, so these two factors account for the negative slope of the aggregate demand curve when waiting time is the price. It might appear paradoxical that time decreases per unit of the good as more is made available for distribution and as the number waiting in line increases. The length of the queue may grow longer when the number of persons being served is larger. But regardless of the efficiency of distribution, for fixed individual allotments per-person waiting has to decline as the number of allotments is increased.

We will now demonstrate that per-person time in the queue is basically independent of the mechanics of distribution, first for a most efficient and speedy organization and then for a relatively slow one. Suppose that for a given amount of a commodity to be distributed free, one batch to a person, the per-person waiting time needed to clear the market is one hour. Now if the entire available amount can be dispensed instantaneously, the *whole* queue will have to form instantaneously one hour before distribution starts so that the time price is the same to all. If the line does not form instantaneously, the early joiner wastes his time, since he could still have obtained the commodity by coming later. He will do his best to join as late as possible, which is when the marginal man is indifferent between being in or out. Waiting cannot, however, be reduced to less than one hour, since positions will then be preempted by extramarginal individuals.

When the number of batches being distributed is increased, the number of individuals in the queue obviously will be larger, but, since the newcomers value a batch of the commodity less than they value one hour of their time, the market-clearing waiting time is shorter—say half an hour. Individuals will now line up only half an hour before distribution starts, or pressure will be exerted to bring it to that level. Thus the queue is longer, but per-person waiting time is less.

If the distribution arrangement is less efficient so that—say—six minutes are required to give out to one person the same amount as before, the first individual will arrive 54 minutes before distribution commences,[8] and from then on others will join the queue at six-minute intervals so that each

[8] This is so because 54 minutes are spent in line before distribution starts and 6 minutes for actually getting the good.

spends one hour waiting. No other spacing would persist, because if waiting takes more than one hour, some individuals will drop out; if less, some extra-marginal individuals will join. After the process is stabilized, the number in the line will be exactly 10, with accretions matching completers, and that level will hold until the last man appears one hour before closing time. For a larger quantity the waiting time required to clear the market is shorter. The total process will be streched over a longer span (or over more distribution centers) so that the additional unit can be distributed; but at any point in time, except at the two ends, fewer individuals will be in the queue.

In the first situation it may seem that if the distribution were started one hour earlier, the line would disappear; but as the new opening time becomes known—instantaneously under the assumptions here—the queue would simply form yet one hour earlier. In the second situation, it may seem that if only the bureaucrats took fewer coffee breaks, less time would be wasted standing in line. But again the queue would eventually adjust to the new conditions and equilibrium waiting time would be restored to one hour.[9] An important corollary is that, given a fixed amount to be distributed free, attempts to improve efficiency will be wasted, since time in the queue will not change. Conversely, the lowest-cost method of distribution, no matter how cumbersome it may appear, is the most efficient in economic terms, since consumers' valuation is independent of such costs.

The speed of the distributing arrangements, however, may affect waiting time in two minor ways. First, under the terms of our numerical illustration, if the available quantity is so large that the equilibrium waiting time is less than six minutes, "technical" conditions then force the waiting price to six minutes. At that time-price some of the available amount will not be demanded and quicker handling is needed to reduce time below six minutes. Second, the distributing organization may be so small that it can handle only part of the available amount. The analysis may now be carried on as before, with the quantity capable of distribution rather than the quantity available constituting the effective constraint.

Even when individuals are allowed to reenter the queue, the available supply may already have been exhausted by the time the first person is

[9] Gary S. Becker, *supra* note 1, at 516, n.3, states, "Time costs . . . often result in external diseconomies: for example, a person joining a queue would impose costs on subsequent joiners." This may appear contrary to our conclusion that the larger the number of batches to be distributed, the larger the number of waiters and the *lower* the waiting per person. Becker's statement, however, seems to apply to the process by which a queue evolves in the absence of adequate information rather than to differences among equilibria of distinct queuing situations for which a *larger* number of persons going through a queue results in a *shorter* per-person waiting time.

ready to step in line again. The quicker the distribution, the greater is the chance this will happen. Here, then, is a case where the distribution arrangement may significantly affect the market-clearing waiting time: speedier distribution shortens the waiting time, since there is less opportunity for multiple approaches.

Several major implications which, at least in principle, are testable emerge from the above discussion. We argue that time-price plays the same role as money price and that for a given stock of a "free" commodity a market-clearing time-price will be reached. Consequently, as the per-person allotment is increased with the number of persons served held constant, we predict that total per-person time in the queue will increase but that this increase will be less than proportionate to quantity, since time per unit is predicted to fall. In addition, holding the per-person allotment constant, per-person time in the queue will decline as the number of allotments is increased. And finally, since we argue that knowledge of the per-person quantity and of the number of persons served is sufficient to determine the market-clearing price, a testable implication is the invariance of waiting time in the queue with respect to the speed of the distribution.

The Resource Cost of the Queue

In the main part of this section it is implicitly assumed that the only cost of getting a commodity to the final consumer is the cost of its production. Let us look briefly at some of the problems associated with this rather basic assumption. In the case of private markets, costs associated with selling are often considerable. On the other hand, for freely disbursed commodities such as roads, elementary public schools, and parks, no resources are used in rationing the available quantity among consumers. The reduction in selling costs as compared with private markets is real enough. We cannot expect, however, that either the quantity supplied or the quality mix will be the same as those supplied by the market.

In any case, it is possible to avoid explicit rationing of roads, schools, and public parks because the rate at which consumers can acquire services is basically restricted to one unit per unit of time. Moreover, it is often prohibitively costly to resell such commodities. In the case of food, on the other hand, the first man in the queue may acquire the entire stock, either for his own consumption or to sell to others. The cost of a rationing organization to prevent this parallels the cost of selling in private markets. Adequate comparison between the two forms of providing commodities would require full assessment of the two types of rationing costs and would be beyond the scope of this paper, therefore we abstract from this problem, as follows.

What is the nature, and measure, of the cost associated with queuing? The mere presence of non-price rationing suggests that the quantity supplied differs from what would be offered in the absence of government intervention. The "misallocation" or "waste" associated with the government action may be measured, say, by the appropriate triangles. Time spent in the waiting line is an additional cost.[10] A pecuniary market price represents a transfer of resources from the buyer to the seller to the extent of the resource cost of producing the good. When a queue is the means of rationing, the time-resource spent to acquire the good is not captured by the producer. If the quantity provided free is equal to what the market would provide, no misallocation triangle appears, but the resource cost of the queue must still be accounted as additional to that of producing the good. Indeed, the two types of cost are basically the same for the marginal unit and are of the same order of magnitude for the entire quantity.

Suppose it were possible costlessly to identify in advance all those planning to be in the queue and to provide them with coupons to claim the good. The saving of time in the lineup would be a net gain, since no other resources were expended. In the absence of such arrangement, since the marginal man in the queue is indifferent between spending his time there or in some alternative use, the extent of the cost for that individual is identical with his total valuation of the "free" good.[11]

Consider a situation in which a large number of individuals have access to a good to be rationed at zero monetary price by means of a queue. In Figure IIa the demand curve d_i of the ith individual is drawn with price in terms of waiting time. Points on this demand curve are implicit in Figure I and can be obtained by matching the quantity and the per unit time price at the intersection of each demand curve with the horizontal axis where pecuniary price is zero. For instance, as evident in Figure I, the time price the individual is willing to pay for k units is t_3 minutes per unit, which gives the point (t_3, k) on d_i in Figure IIa.

[10] At a deeper level, "misallocation," "waste," and time in the queue may be viewed as costs similar in nature to those of selling and transacting. We might hypothesize that these are among the costs which the economy will attempt to minimize. Thus it is conceivable that the existing arrangement is the lowest in cost for achieving certain objectives, and we will touch on this notion later.

[11] In popular discussion of conditions associated with consumption of free goods, the nature of the cost involved is usually (at best) only implicit. However, to cite one exception: "Of course, public [tennis] courts are free or relatively cheap but not always freely available for playing on. In Houston the public courts have become so overtaxed by the tennis boom that players must appear in person a full week before they want to play in order to sign up for their hour on the court. What the poor or parsimonious player may save in money, he can easily spend in time and inconvenience." Sophy Burnham, Tennis: A Whole New Ball Game, Saturday Review, July 29, 1972, at 44, 46.

IIa.

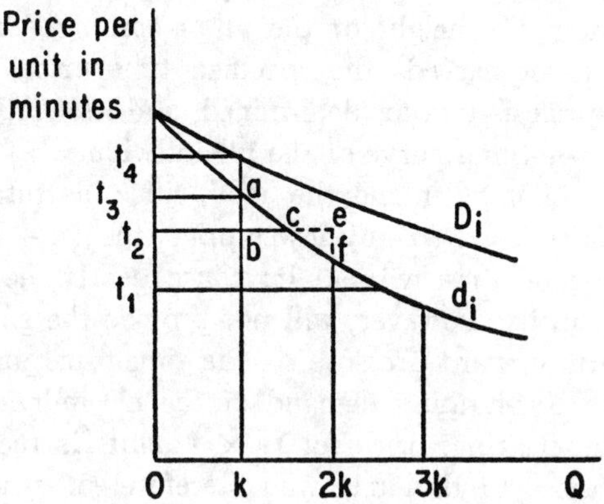

IIb.

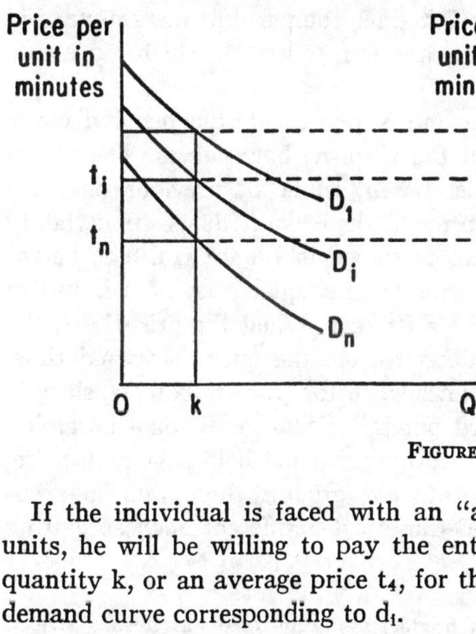

IIc.

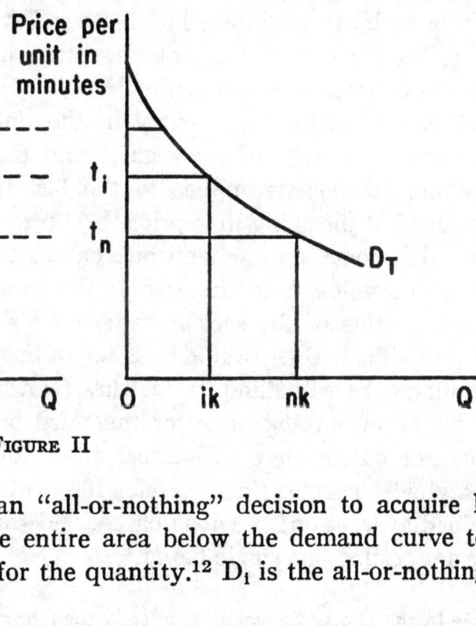

FIGURE II

If the individual is faced with an "all-or-nothing" decision to acquire k units, he will be willing to pay the entire area below the demand curve to quantity k, or an average price t_4, for the quantity.[12] D_i is the all-or-nothing demand curve corresponding to d_i.

In Figure IIb, the all-or-nothing demand curves for several individuals are drawn, ordered (in the relevant range) from highest to lowest. While only a few individuals are represented in the drawing, we assume that the total number is large and that at any quantity the distance between adjacent curves is small enough to be ignored. If the batch size is k, for any time-price

12 We abstract from the difference between income underlying the all-or-nothing decision and that underlying the regular demand curve.

we obtain the number of batches demanded by simply counting the number of individuals for whom the height of the all-or-nothing demand curve at quantity k is equal to or exceeds the specified time price. Given a fixed supply of n batches, price is market determined, and its equilibrium level is the height of the all-or-nothing curve of the nth individual. At that price, the $(n + 1)^{st}$ individual will not demand the good, since his total valuation of the batch is less than his cost. At any lower price, the $(n + 1)^{st}$ individual is better off with the good than without it; consequently, he will be in the line. The available quantity, however, will not provide the good to all those waiting, and this exerts upward pressure on the time-price, bringing it back to the height of the all-or-nothing demand of the nth individual. Thus the equilibrium, or market-clearing, price for $n \times k$ units is the all-or-nothing price for k units for the nth individual, who therefore earns no surplus since his total valuation is precisely exhausted by waiting.

The aggregate demand curve with batch size k and a single access to the queue is drawn in Figure IIc. Notice that since the per unit market-clearing price for n batches is t_n, total waiting time is $n \times k \times t_n$ which represents the total time spent in queuing.[13]

When more than one entry in the line is permitted, the demand curve becomes a mixture of the regular and the all-or-nothing curves. The all-or-nothing component applies to the last batch, while all previous ones are obtained at the going time-price.[14] At price t_2, the ith individuals will certainly join the queue and demand one batch, as shown in Figure IIa. The height of t_2 determines that the area of the triangle abc equals that of cef, and so the valuation of the second batch equals its cost. When the price is t_2, the ith individual, then, would just be willing to join the queue a second time. Similarly, he will stand in line three times when the price falls to t_1, since t_1 is his all-or-nothing price for the third batch.[15] For an individual obtaining just one batch, the conventional all-or-nothing demand holds. At each price, marginal consumers can be classified into two groups: those who have obtained at least one previous batch, and those just indifferent between getting or not getting one single batch.

[13] In the above discussion, n, k (and their product nk) were treated as given. Provided that some quantity is distributed free, one may wish to explore why the particular values of n and k were selected.

[14] Again we abstract from differential income effects.

[15] This analysis differs from the common textbook analysis of demand in that the units of the commodity being distributed are assumed discrete rather than continuous. If the batch size goes to zero, a regular demand curve results. But in the real world the unit by which commodities are sold is seldom fully divisible, consequently the analysis here is more appropriate than that found in most textbooks.

Now n batches will be distributed among fewer than n individuals since at any time-price we would expect, in general, some consumers to obtain more than one. But some will enter the line only once and to the marginal individual in this group, the "free" good provides zero rent just as in the case of single access to the queue. Total time spent in queuing here is $n \times k \times t'_n$ where t'_n is the market-clearing time-price for multiple access (which will be higher, in general, than t_n). We have shown, then, that whether the rule is single access or multiple access, the entire consumer's surplus that the marginal man in the queue derives from the good is exhausted by waiting.

If all individuals under consideration are identical in their utility functions, incomes, and time costs, then the marginal and the average individual are identical. Since the market-clearing waiting time is such that the marginal person in the line receives zero rent (or surplus), so too does the average person. Each is indifferent between having and not having the good, and the entire valuation of the good is lost in waiting.[16]

If those obtaining the good are not identical, the marginal individual is the only one for whom the entire economic rent is lost, and each of the intramarginal ones receives some rent. The rent is equal to the difference in valuation between the maximum amount of time that the particular individual is willing to wait and the actual waiting time. Given a quantity to be distributed free, the aggregate rent is larger the more diverse are those in the queue in terms of their willingness to wait. Homogeneity leads to highly elastic demand for a good whose price is in waiting time, to low returns to those in the queue, and to relatively high cost of waiting in terms of loss of alternative output. Thus the notion that the cost of the free good is low is not generally correct, and we might reject the statement that "to the low wage people, the money cost of the queue is *minimal* and they will receive a *substantial* benefit due to the lower money price."[17]

Turning the problem around, we gain added insight into the political process involved. Queuing uses resources the return from which, on the average, is larger the lower the demand elasticity of the subsidized commodity. If the demand is perfectly elastic, no consumer gains from the subsidy; consequently, little political support can be expected from consumers for the subsidization of such commodities, the less elastic the demand, the larger the gains on intramarginal units and the greater potential political support. We predict, then, that commodities provided free and distributed on a first-come-first-served basis will have, on the average, lower demand elasticities in terms

[16] Instead of "There is no such thing as a free lunch," we have now "If there is a free lunch, it will come to have zero value."

[17] Nichols, *supra* note 1 at 316 (italics added).

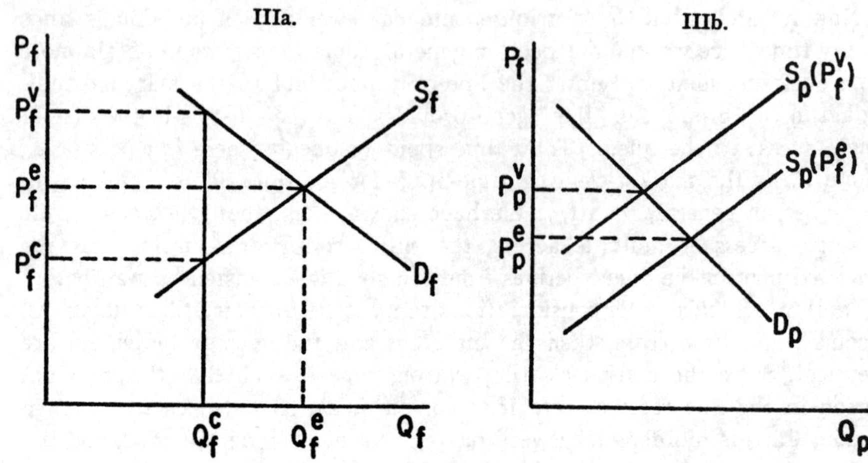

FIGURE III

of waiting time than the average for all commodities and we will show that such commodities are less likely to be obtained by the poor.[18]

Once the consequences of the first-come-first-served rule are recognized, one can readily analyze the effect of a strictly maintained price ceiling[19] on the demand for related goods. In panel IIIa of Figure III, Q_f^e and P_f^e are the initial equilibrium levels of quantity and price of a commodity f. A ceiling price is set at $P_f^c < P_f^e$, at which the quantity supplied is $Q_f^c < Q_f^e$. A queue will form to allocate the limited quantity among demanders, of such length that on the margin the price in money-plus-time must equal the valuation. While the money price is only P_f^c the waiting price is $P_f^v - P_f^c$ which brings the total price to P_f^v, a level *higher* than the initial equilibrium price.[20] At the higher total price the demand for substitutes will shift to the right and that for complements to the left. Since, however, the real price paid by buyers is higher than that received by sellers, the difference being the value of waiting time, we have here a net resource cost resulting in a negative income effect that for superior goods will shift demand to the left, enhancing the price effect on complements but reducing that on substitutes.[21]

18 A similar argument applies on the supply side. The lower the supply elasticity, the larger the gain to suppliers from subsidized purchases.

19 If lax maintenance of the ceiling permits development of a black market, the analysis becomes much more complex, but the basic qualitative results still hold.

20 We abstract from the problem that the demand curve under the new conditions will not be identical with D_f since not all demanders convert time to money price at the same rate.

21 This result differs from that obtained by J. R. Gould & S. G. B. Henry, The Effects

Along the same lines, consider the effect of imposing a ceiling on the price of a factor of production. To the demander of such a factor, the control constitutes an effective increase (the cost of his time) in the price of that factor, which in turn will lead to an increase in the price of the final product. This is shown in panel IIIb of Figure III where, prior to the imposition of the price ceiling, the factor price underlying the supply of the product S_p was P^e_f. Since the price ceiling raised the effective factor price to P^v_f, the supply curve of the product shifted upwards to $S_p(P^v_f)$. The price ceiling in the factor market will, then, increase the price of the product from P^e_p to P^v_p Thus, a refutable implication of our model is that fixing the price of a factor *below* its market price will *increase* the market price of the product. A price ceiling on food will result in an increase in restaurant meal prices; wage control on lumber workers will lead to higher lumber prices; and a "roll-back" of steel prices will bring higher automobile prices.[22]

Property Rights on the Free Good

Many government goods are disbursed at lower than market price, mostly at zero price. Are they all allocated by queues subject to the associated costs? In the market process, goods are provided in exchange for other goods, whereas in the political process goods are transferred from one group to another. In the market, exchange will continue until on the margin the gain equals the cost. In the political arena the situation is more complex. The preceding discussion has evidenced that under certain circumstances individuals will spend resources to affect transfers to themselves to the point where on the margin, as in the market, the gain equals the cost. But is this unique to certain types of political transfers or is this the rule for all such transfers?[23]

---

of Price Control on a Related Market, 34 Economica 42 (1967). When they view the ceiling as the effective price paid by the "satisfied" consumers for whom the price fell while for "unsatisfied" consumers the price is infinite, they fail to recognize that the "unsatisfied" consumers can effectively bid up the price by waiting and thus can restore equilibrium. And, of course, they implicitly assume that the resource cost of waiting time is zero. Note also that, given their model, they make the hardly necessary distinction between gross and net substitutes, not realizing that if consumers gain by paying at the lower rate, producers lose the same amount and the income effects of the two groups combind tend to wash out. (If the slopes of the Engel curves of the two groups are identical, the income effect will cancel exactly).

[22] Note that the results are basically unaffected if the price ceiling P^c_f is replaced by a price floor P^v_f. When analyzing the behavior of sellers the effective price they receive, however, is not the price floor P^v_f but rather the lower P^c_f.

[23] Some transfers take place in the private sector, as with theft, with so-called "externalities," and to some extent within what is conventionally viewed as strictly market exchange.

A position in the queue implies a certain priority right to the good that was originally unassigned. But when property rights to the good, or to the transferred wealth, are once clearly assigned so that current or future action cannot further affect the transfer, there is no motive to spend resources on such action.[24] Thus, point rationing precludes the costs of queuing by turning over property rights to those receiving points. Where such preassignment is not made resources will be spent to obtain the rights to the subsidy (or, by the same token, to avoid paying taxes). On the margin the value of these resources will equal the rate of the subsidy.[25]

Suppose, for illustration, that each of the poorest individuals in the community is to be provided free one unit of a commodity. If eligibility is determined by the level of income reported on a prior tax return which cannot be amended, then the right is clearly defined. But poverty may also be defined in terms of income to be shown on a future tax return. Whether an individual proves to be "poor" will then depend on his own action, and he may devote resources to qualifying himself—particularly by reducing any components which are measured as income for purposes of the subsidy but which do not entirely constitute real income. For instance, when he consumes more leisure and fewer market goods, his measured income declines more than his real income. To the marginal individual, the value of these resources (that is, the fall in real income) is exactly matched by the subsidy.[26]

If a subsidy is anticipated by some firm or individual as yet undesignated, resources may be spent in the present to assure future property rights. In this case, it may appear when the subsidy is eventually given that no resources were spent on acquiring the property rights, but they have simply been paid in advance.

In other cases, the property right can be obtained only when actual distribution takes place, as in queuing and the closely related phenomenon of crowding. In a classc article published half a century ago, Knight demonstrated the costs associated with crowding.[27] Where congestion occurs under conditions of free entry, individuals who have the pertinent information will

24 The property right to this idea is Steven N. S. Cheung's. See, A Theory of Price Control, 17 J. Law & Econ. 53 (1974).

25 P. Naor, *supra* note 6, recognizes the inefficiency associated with the queue and suggests improvement either by charging tolls or by administratively limiting the length of the queue. The latter arrangement, however, implicitly assumes that individuals could not affect the decision whether they would be admitted; if they could do so, the administrative control would not yield the desired result.

26 This last notion is discussed in detail by Gordon Tullock in a seminal article, The Welfare Costs of Tariffs, Monopolies and Theft, 5 Western Econ. J. 224 (1967).

27 F. H. Knight, Some Fallacies in the Interpretation of Social Cost, 38 Q.J. Econ. 582 (1924), reprinted in Readings in Price Theory 217 (Amer. Econ. Ass'n, 1952).

continue to crowd as long as the value of the service exceeds the time-and-money cost of acquiring it. In the case of crowding, the service is usually consumed during the waiting period, instead of later as with queuing.[28] Otherwise there is little difference between them.

Would the previous conclusion be altered if we consider the possibility of bribery? It may appear that bribery will eliminate, or at least reduce, the resource cost of obtaining the right to the subsidy, since waiting in the line will be replaced by a transfer from consumers to officials. Such an arrangement, however, may simply shift the cost from the final consumers to the officials. The value of a disbursing job will be increased by the valuation of the bribes; in the absence of property rights on such jobs, potential workers will then spend resources in queuing or whatever other activity may increase the chance of employment, to the point where the value of these resources equals the valuation of the bribes. The possibility of bribes, then, does not affect the conclusion that the resource cost of acquiring the good will be eliminated only if property rights to the disbursed goods are well defined. Note, however, that the cost of establishing property rights on the intramarginal units will differ in magnitude among different methods of allocation. With one important exception, only queuing as a means of distribution will be considered in the rest of the paper.

Distributive Effects of Free Goods

Assuming temporarily that the free good will not be transferred, would the poor always get it? The lower the cost of time, the lower the cost of waiting—and the time cost of the poor is normally low. However, the question of benefits should not be overlooked. It is obvious that goods for which the income elasticity of demand is high would produce more benefits to the rich than to the poor. It is also clear that if the government-supplied good is available at the same time in the private market, the poor may be expected to pay by waiting while the rich will tend to pay the higher money price.

Consider the formal relation for a special case—where the demand for the good by every individual is of the form $q = \alpha p^{\beta} y^{\gamma}$ where q is quantity, p is price, y is income, price elasticity is β and the income elasticity is γ. Individuals may differ in their incomes, but the quantities they receive are the same, and all pay the same time-price. Suppose also that time-costs (wages) are proportionate to income. Then only if $-\frac{\gamma}{\beta} < 1$ will the queue be com-

[28] Similarly utilities are often required to price their output at a level lower than the unregulated price and simultaneously meet the entire demand. When they fail, instead of queuing or crowding we experience "brownouts" and "blackouts."

posed of the poorest individuals. If $-\frac{\gamma}{\beta} > 1$ the richest individuals will be standing in line to obtain the good.[29] We find, then, that the higher the income elasticity and the lower the price elasticity the less is it likely that the poor will stand in line. This result is entirely general in that it holds, though not as a simple ratio, for other forms of demand.

In light of these findings, it seems evident that government giveaways aimed toward the poor should be commodities with low income elasticities and high price elasticities. This would suggest products for which close substitutes (or the identical goods) are available in private markets. Taking highways as an example: where private toll roads are allowed to operate side by side with free public roads, the latter become more attractive to the poor because their price elasticity is thus raised.

On the other hand, the subsidizing of opera is totally misdirected from the viewpoint of helping the poor. The apparently high income elasticity and low price elasticity of demand for opera results in a redistribution towards the rich since they, rather than the poor, will take advantage of the opportunity. Another example is the municipal golf course where use is normally rationed not by money price but by waiting in lengthy lines, especially on weekends. Most private golf courses are not close substitutes, since they often restrict membership and sometimes are out of municipal limits. Thus, the price elasticity of demand for the municipal course is probably low while the income elasticity is in all likelihood high, and again the rich tend to benefit from this government service. A casual scrutiny of the set of goods freely supplied by the government and rationed by some form of queuing suggests that many of them fail to meet these two elasticity criteria and so are unlikely to end up in the hands of the poor.

It is often claimed that some of the goods provided free by the government

[29] With $q = \alpha p^{\beta} y^{\gamma}$ we can write $p = \alpha^{-1/\beta} q^{1/\beta} y^{-\gamma/\beta}$ where p may be interpreted as the marginal valuation of the qth unit. To avoid infinite total utility, however, assume that the valuation of the entire first unit is, say, at the same rate as the valuation at $q = 1$. Given q, the relative valuation of the marginal unit by two individuals i and j with incomes y_i and y_j is $(y_i/y_j)^{-\gamma/\beta}$. Since this holds for any value of q common to the two individuals, it is also true of the total valuation. Given the assumption that across individuals time-costs, denoted by w are proportionate to income, the relative cost for the two individuals is $w_i/w_j = y_i/y_j$ and will exceed the relative valuation $(y_i/y_j)^{-\gamma/\beta}$ only if $-\gamma/\beta < 1$. For such values of γ/β, then, time-cost rises faster with income than does the valuation of the good. Consequently, if $-\gamma/\beta < 1$, as the number of units to be distributed increases, the order in which individuals will join the queue is from the poorest to the richest. If $-\alpha/\beta > 1$, the order is reversed. Both Becker and Nichols then, err in implying that queuing will necessarily result in a redistribution towards the poor. Finally, if $-\gamma/\beta = 1$, the time-cost rises at the same rate as income. At a low time-cost all individuals are indifferent whether they get the good or not, and for any individual in the queue the waiting cost equals the entire consumer surplus.

are chosen on the ground that their actual consumption, especially by the poor, yields benefits to others. It is also claimed that the presence of such "public benefits" may explain why trading of the goods is frequently banned.[30] Still, abstracting from interdependence we might try to discover what would be the consequences of such trade. The time of the rich, as measured by the market, is usually more valuable than that of the poor. Would it not be more efficient to let the poor wait in line and then sell the good to the rich who value it more highly?[31] In analyzing this problem we assume that nobody wants to consume more than one unit of the commodity, as might be the case for a theater performance. With one important exception, at the (private) margin here, as elsewhere, rent is zero. But we will now show that when trading is allowed a greater rent accrues to *all* the previous intramarginal individuals in the queue and to some extramarginal ones.

To see this, suppose n units of the good are distributed, one unit per person. The analysis depends on whether the number of individuals in the community is less or more than 2n. We will commence with the case where this number is 2n or more. In the absence of trade, and assuming once more that incomes are proportionate to wages and that tastes are identical, the good will be obtained either by the n poorest individuals or by the n richest ones. We will first analyze the effects of permitting trade where under prior restriction the good was obtained by the rich.

Suppose that H_R is the market-clearing price when trade is banned. The nth richest person, who is marginal in the queue, is indifferent between waiting H_R hours in the queue or paying a money price of $W_R H_R$ for the good where W_R is his wage rate. If trade is allowed, "waiting" is purchased in the market, and n units of this service will be demanded by the n richest individuals. As to supply, we assume that each individual is willing to supply any number of hours at his alternative market wage, but that each may acquire only one unit of the good. Obviously, the poorest n individuals will supply the waiting service. Since the money price they will receive for selling the commodity is $W_R H_R$, the number of hours each will have to spend in waiting is $(W_R \cdot H_R)/W_P$ where W_P is the wage rate of the nth poorest individual. If waiting time needed to acquire the good is longer, the units of the good available will exceed the number of waiters, exerting a downward pressure on the time price; the converse will hold if the number of hours is less than $(W_R \cdot H_R)/W_P$. Since neither the marginal man performing the waiting

[30] Nichols, *et al.*, designate these "merit goods," hence the title of their article. That characteristic seems to be the reason Nichols ignores the question of trading in these goods.

[31] If the good is not inferior, the rich always value it more highly.

services nor the marginal man buying the services earns any rent, for this unit, the valuation equals the cost of waiting.

But consider now the intramarginal individuals. Before trading was allowed, the poor ones obviously received no rent since they did not wait in line and did not get any of the commodity. To the extent that the supply price for waiting services of the intramarginal individuals is less than that of the marginal one, they receive some rent. With respect to the rich, all previously had to wait H_R hours, and now they all pay $H_R W_R$ dollars. The intramarginal man whose wage is $W_S > W_R$, previously had to pay $H_R W_S$ as the alternative cost of waiting in line; now he has to pay only $H_R W_R < H_R W_S$, and is better off. Both the rich and the poor, then, gain from the trade.[32]

What occurs in the case where the n poorest individuals would previously have obtained the good? When trade is initiated, since the rich value the good more, they eventually will get it at a price determined as above. All the intramarginal rich will now earn some rent. As to the poor, the same ones will be waiting in the queue, but they now wait longer. Those that previously earned rent will earn proportionately more. Again, both the rich and the poor are better off. Notice that in both cases the move is "Pareto optimal" in that the n-1 richest and the n-1 poorest are better off, while no other individual is worse off despite the fact that total time in the queue is larger.[33]

If the size of the eligible group is less than 2n and n units are being distributed, the set of the n richest partly overlaps that of the n poorest, which means that some of those in line will also consume the commodity. The money and waiting prices now have to satisfy the condition that those in the overlapping group feel sufficient incentive first to acquire the good by waiting in line and then to keep it rather than to sell it. Consequently, the money price of the commodity cannot exceed its valuation by the poorest in the middle group, otherwise he will not choose to retain it. Conversely, waiting time has to be short enough so that the richest in the middle group will choose to wait in line rather than to purchase the good. The simultaneous satisfaction of these two conditions guarantees no fewer than n waiters and no fewer than n consumers. The joint effect of the two conditions is that the poorest and the richest individuals in the middle as well as the rest in that group now earn some rent. All other individuals, as before, earn some positive rent

[32] The above analysis fits rather well some theater experience. Queues sometimes form even though ticket price is not directly controlled, but while an incentive is thus created for additional trading, the law often bans resale at so-called scalping prices.

[33] Note that time in the queue here performs the function of transferring the good to those who value it more.

and so it turns out that loss on the margin is not complete. In this case, then, every individual is better off when trade is permitted.

The importance of this case arises from a fact of political life: Majority voting is often the agent that generates the distribution of the free good. It seems likely, then, that a large fraction of the electorate expects to benefit from many of the approved government programs, so normally the number of units distributed free should be large relative to the population size in the electoral unit. Political considerations also suggest that individuals with low time costs relative to their incomes possess substantial political power. It is unfortunate then (or perhaps one should say "unaccountable") that trading of the good is not more widely permitted.[34]

We have seen that, given the assumption of proportionality between time costs and incomes, all the rich would be better off if permitted to purchase the freely distributed good from the poor who have substituted for them in the service of waiting. It is clear that they would pay a money-price identical with that which would prevail if the same quantity were directly offered under free enterprise. For that given quantity, then, none of the rich would be made better off when the good has been distributed free even when they have contributed nothing in taxes.[35]

This conclusion does not necessarily hold when a greater quantity is distributed free than the market equilibrium one. More importantly, since time-prices are not uniform within levels of income, those with the lower time-price benefit from waiting for the free good rather than paying the money-price in the market. Taking the case of state hunting areas as an example, we would expect that most hunteres on these lands view the time-price they pay in crowding or in actual waiting in line as less costly than the money-price implicit in private hunting preserves. In fact, they will support the provision of public lands only if they consider their saving to be greater than their share of tax payments to maintain the public areas.

It is clear from the analysis of the last few sections that the relation between wages and incomes plays an important role in questions of distribution. Since some people who start life with a substantial amount of non-human wealth have little incentive to improve their own market skills, the wage rate for such individuals when they do join the labor force may be lower than the wage rate of many of those with a lower total income.[36] Obviously, the

[34] If, however, the rationale for providing a free good is to benefit not the poor but rather, say, the producers of that good, it is not difficult to understand the restriction on trading.

[35] Note that the equivalence between waiting and money price does not hold when the poor are those that will be in line to obtain the free good. So, disregarding the question of taxes, the poor are better off with the free good.

[36] Similarly low might be the shadow price of their time when not in the labor market.

subsidizing of this high-asset and low-wage group is a curious way to help the poor, yet when the cost of time is an effective criterion for the subsidy, members of this group would be among those obtaining the free good. Similarly, we have been assuming that preferences are identical. Since in fact they differ widely, the provision of a free good benefits those who happen to have a taste for it at the expense of all others. Within any income group, then, some are aided by the subsidy more than others.[37]

Waiting by Suppliers

Thus far the discussion has dealt only with prices set below the market-clearing level: paying particular attention to zero money-price allowed us to concentrate on the time-price. If the intended subsidy is for suppliers rather than demanders we have to deal with both money-price and time-price simultaneously, since the polar case to a zero demand-price is an infinite supply-price. Otherwise, little is changed in turning to a consideration of subsidies to suppliers. Thus when the government attempts to help the unemployed by fixing wages in some public works above the market-clearing level, we are likely to observe applicants for jobs standing in line; and the properties of the queue will be similar to those analyzed earlier. It is possible to find actual instances where sellers rather than buyers engage in lining up. Still, why is it that queues are predominantly manned by buyers, not sellers? The answer lies in the value of the good to be expected in each case.

Suppose the Chicago bank had offered to recipients amounts 1,000-fold larger than those actually given; that is, the first 35 claimants would have obtained $20,000 apiece, the next 50, $10,000 apiece, and so forth. Even with sufficient lead time it seems unlikely that sheer waiting would have determined the recipients. In the actual situation the gain to the 36th claimant from bumping the 35th would have been only $10. The first 35, however, had an incentive to provide some policing of the queue, and the bank itself had a similar incentive. The result was a sufficient policing to deter bumping—the cost of bumping exceeded $10—and the queue was "orderly." The hypothetical case changes that situation because the prizes now seem so valuable as to preclude counting on the "good behavior" of those farther back in the line or out of it altogether. A device such as writing down the names of persons in

[37] As mentioned earlier, restriction on the trading of "free" commodities is sometimes recommended on the ground that other members of society value the consumption of certain goods by the subsidized individual and that while the recipient might benefit from trading away his subsidized good, others would be made worse off. However, when trading is prohibited, the poor are thereby brought to the point which is optimal, not to them, but to the rest of society—their "benefactors." Thus the attempt at efficiency actually annuls the fundamental reason usually advanced for the distribution of goods free of charge—that is, to help the poor.

order of priority would be totally inadequate. Rights to these amounts might have to be established by such forceful means as physical violence, full-fledged legal services, or what not. In such cases individuals would continue to spend resources to obtain the "free" good, but passive waiting would become subsidiary.

The prevalence of queuing when consumer goods are distributed free may be explained in terms of the low value of the individual allotments. When sellers rather than buyers are being subsidized, the value to each seller is usually high, and so we observe forms of rationing either added to that of waiting or replacing waiting altogether.[38]

Consider the supply of candidates to the restricted number of positions in medical schools. Let us assume that the rate of return in practicing medicine is higher than in alternative occupations. Would a loss of surplus take place here also? And if it would, in what form? It may appear that the selection process used by medical schools will avoid the resource costs associated with queuing. This, however, would be correct only to the extent that the selection is fully predetermined because some individuals hold property rights to the available positions (for example, by virtue of having an M.D. as a father). Many positions, however, are allocated by criteria such as grades and course contents in college. If it could be known in advance who would meet these criteria, the rent associated with acceptance to medical school would once more be appropriated. But since individuals can affect their ranking, they will spend resources to qualify. With perfect knowledge as to conditions in this market, when n positions were available, we would expect that exactly n individuals would attempt to qualify. To the marginal individual the expected return from resources invested to qualify to practice medicine would equal that in his best alternative occupation.[39] So here too, on the margin, the extra value of the good is exactly matched by the resource cost of acquiring it.

Relaxing the assumption of certainty does not change the results substantially although they may change greatly in appearence. Abstracting from the possibility of risk aversion, the marginal individual will be indifferent between medicine and his other alternative opportunities only in the expected sense. If he is "unlucky," his realized rate of return will be lower than normal. If he is "lucky" he will be practicing medicine, and his realized return will

[38] Anne D. Krueger, The Political Economy of the Rent-Seeking Society, 64 Am. Econ. Rev. 291 (1974), considers some ways in which resources are spent to acquire the rights to import quotas.

[39] Better performance in college may lead to a higher return when practicing medicine. This higher return, however, would be incorporated in the student's calculations, and the equality of return on the margin is after this extra return is accounted for.

be above normal. But to the marginal individual among those contemplating going into medicine the rate of return cannot be higher than normal, otherwise "entry" will take place to drive down the return. The empirical observation of a high rate of return to those practicing medicine may be accurate enough; but these studies seldom, if ever, account for the resource cost of unsuccessful candidates to medical school.

In this situation, no literal queue exists but, as with congestion on highways, some waiting takes place side by side with other economic activities. Since admittance to medical schools is not first come first served but rather is based on other criteria, resources are spent which for the marginal individual bring the net present value from practicing medicine down to the level of the next best alternative.

Without elaborating, we again hypothesize (following Cheung) that since economic forces will tend to reduce to a minimum the cost associated with rationing, and since on the margin all the rent is used up, the best choice among a variety of devices for allocating the subsidized good is that which reduces cost with respect to the intramarginal units—that is, the most inelastic arrangement.

Summary

When a good is available in limited quantity and below market price, in the absence of formal rationing individuals will achieve equilibrium by paying the pecuniary price and spending such additional resources on acquiring the good as will bring them to the point at which the marginal individual neither benefits nor loses from obtaining it. Queuing is a customary form of obtaining such goods. The main implications of this hypothesis are that the length of waiting time is basically independent of the speed with which the good is actually handed out and, rather, depends on the size and number of batches to be distributed. The larger each of these is, the shorter the time per unit of the good an individual must wait. An additional implication is that a price ceiling below market price imposed on a factor will result in an increase in the price of the product.

The resource cost of this form of allocation, time spent in the queue, represents a cost of establishing property rights in the good and is over and above the cost required to produce it. To individuals in the queue, the resource cost of producing the good is immaterial. For the marginal individual, his waiting time completely exhausts the benefit of obtaining the "free" good. Intramarginal individuals may benefit; and the less elastic their demand, the larger is their gain.

The attempt to redistribute income through the provision of free goods is costly because the time spent may be substantial compared with the distributive effect achieved. Moreover, not every good provided free necessarily helps the poor; the beneficiaries may often be among the rich. Within any income class the benefits are unevenly distributed: those with lower time cost as well as those with a "taste" for the free good benefit more. Finally, when the poor do obtain the commodity, they, as well as the buyers, could be made better off by being allowed to trade it. The ban on such action cannot benefit them.

[20]

An Alternative Approach to the Analysis of Taxation

Yoram Barzel

University of Washington

Because commodities as transacted are complex, tax statutes could not cover all margins subject to optimization. A tax will induce, then, substitution within the commodity away from the taxed attributes and into the others. The results of a test on cigarettes are consistent with our prediction that the effects of unit and ad valorem taxes will differ both from each other and from those predicted by the conventional model. It is shown that, although the market will adjust in numerous changeable characteristics, the adjustment is constrained by the condition that the sum of the dollar value of the inefficiencies and of the tax paid is minimized.

The Dog and the Accountant

A dog whose fleas had become unbearable sought the advice of an accountant.

"Can I claim these fleas as exemptions?" he asked.

The accountant smiled and shook his head. "Under certain conditions," he explained, "ticks can be claimed as blood relatives. Fleas, on the other hand, are considered luxuries and, far from being deductible, are actually subject to tax."

The following day, the dog had no more fleas; or he didn't declare them, which comes to the same thing.

Moral: There can be no taxation without misrepresentation.

[J. B. Handelsman][1]

Thanks are due to numerous individuals for their comments, particularly to Dan Benjamin, Steve Cheung, Bill Schworm, and Dan Wisecarver. The paper was written, in part, during a visit at the Hoover Institution.

[1] Reprinted by permission; © 1973 by The New Yorker Magazine, Inc.

[*Journal of Political Economy*, 1976, vol. 84, no. 6]

This paper offers an extension of the traditional approach to the analysis of taxation capable of explaining observations attributable to taxation which were not previously explicable. Underlying the change in approach are the premises that *every* commodity is composed of a set of characteristics whose levels are economically determined and that no tax will be so comprehensively specified as to control all the characteristics of a commodity. Market adjustments to a tax will take place not only in the quantity of the good but also in the make-up of its characteristics.

By standard analysis, a tax on the tonnage of ships would simply lead to a substitution resulting in lower tonnage. Such analysis, however, is incapable of explaining why "shipowners had vessels built excessively long, deep and narrow, 'all more or less crank' [i.e., poor in seaworthiness]" (Lane 1964). In the above instance, the tax definition of tonnage (motivated, it seems by considerations of the costs of measurement) was basically proportionate to the length of ships and negatively related to the square of their width. Although deeper and narrower ships took a toll in handling, they did achieve from 1.1 to 1.4 tons of carrying capacity for each "ton" as measured for the purpose of tax.

In this paper it will be shown that, subject to the relevant constraints, the losses to market participants resulting from either unit or ad valorem taxes are treated as a magnitude to be minimized, rendering the adjustments in characteristics predictable.

I. The Setting of the Problem

A consumer's evaluation of a commodity rests on its various characteristics. The commodity "gasoline," for example, is demanded for its potential for generating energy, for its octane rating, and for its additives, as well as for such peripheral services as windshield cleaning. The choice open to consumers of commodities composed of many characteristics has been analyzed by Griliches (1961) in his empirical work on automobile prices and by Lancaster (1966) in his theoretical work on demand. We wish to proceed further by attempting to explain how the market will determine the levels of a commodity's characteristics in response to a tax.

For any given commodity tax, it is crucial to know how the statute defines the unit of the commodity, how that unit is measured, and how the tax is to be enforced. The unit for tax purposes may correspond to the market norm—gallons of gasoline, or packages of 20 cigarettes. Granted that the legal definition of the unit will certainly be more detailed, it is still highly unlikely to cover all revelant characteristics.[2] Furthermore,

[2] The legal definition will almost inevitably become more detailed as inadequacies become evident. For example, the present tax-purpose definition of a cigarette will presumably expand eventually to cover the newly emergent "little cigars." Earlier, a maximum length for cigarettes had to be specified to counter the marketing of extra-long cigarettes, taxed at a constant rate per unit, which could subsequently be cut into standard lengths.

entire characteristics are subject to inclusion or exclusion with varying economic conditions. We seek to discover the nature and extent of these adjustments. As will become evident, the results depend critically on whether the tax is fixed per unit of the commodity or is ad valorem.

With a few explicit exceptions, we assume that prior to the imposition of a tax the market is competitive and free of distortions. A partial equilibrium framework is used throughout the analysis, and we abstract from possible feedbacks due to the effect of the tax on the level of income or on income distribution.

Because existing studies of the effects of commodity taxes employ demand and supply elasticities estimated prior to the tax, their results reflect only the change in volume of the commodity as a whole with no allowance for change in the mix of characteristics or any resultant effect on allocation. In a more careful analysis, this bias would be avoided by the treatment of different varieties as separate commodities, taking into account not only the individual elasticity of each but also their cross-elasticities, as noted by Harberger (1964, pp. 25–70). While this is a step in the right direction, it still does not allow for possible tax-induced changes in the characteristics of each variety. ("Cigarettes," for instance, may shift through a wide spectrum: the quality of tobacco and of its wrapping; the per-package retail services afforded for a given brand; the menthol or other components; and, of course, the length of the cigarettes themselves.) This paper explicitly takes into account this capacity for internal change within each commodity.

II. The Constant per Unit Tax

The traditional theory of taxation under competition is based on the comparison between the systems $D(P) - S(P) = 0$, and $D(P^T) - S(P^T - T) = 0$, where $D(P)$ is the market demand for a commodity, $S(P)$ is its supply, P is the price per unit before the tax, P^T after the tax, and T is the tax per unit. Misallocation occurs because resources shift away from the taxed industry into less highly valued alternatives. For the marginal unit the value of the misallocation is equal to the tax rate. Under common but rather restrictive assumptions, the economic waste as a result of the tax is measured by $\frac{1}{2}[\eta\varepsilon/(\eta + \varepsilon)](T/P)^2$ where η and ε are the respective demand and supply elasticities.

For a commodity composed of several characteristics, equality between the marginal valuation of the commodity as a whole and its marginal cost is a necessary, but not a sufficient, condition for competitive equilibrium. The marginal valuation (MV) of each of the characteristics must equal its marginal cost (MC).[3]

[3] In what follows, we assume that each of the marginal valuations is falling and each of the marginal costs is rising.

Consider a commodity possessing n characteristics. At the pretax equilibrium $MC_i = MV_i$, $i = 1, \ldots, n$. Defining

$$MC = \sum_{i=1}^{n} MC_i \quad \text{and} \quad MV = \sum_{i=1}^{n} MV_i$$

for the commodity as a whole,[4] the equality for each characteristic implies also that MC = MV.[5] After a tax-induced reduction in number of units, but prior to any change in the levels of the characteristics per unit, the following equality will hold:

$$\sum MC_i^T + T = P^T = \sum MV_i^T. \tag{1}$$

The reduction in quantity of the commodity as a whole constitutes a downward move along each of the MC_i schedules and an upward move along each of the MV_i schedules, so that

$$MC_i^T < MC_i = MV_i < MV_i^T \quad \text{for all } i.^6 \tag{2}$$

Suppose now that the tax statute defines the commodity in terms of the pretax equilibrium levels of characteristics, $i = 1, \ldots, k$; but that characteristics $k + 1, \ldots, n$ are not specified in the tax statute. We can decompose (1) into

$$\sum_{i=1}^{k} MC_i^T + \sum_{i=k+1}^{n} MC_i^T + T = P^T = \sum_{i=1}^{k} MV_i^T + \sum_{i=k+1}^{n} MV_i^T. \tag{1'}$$

Given (1′) and the inequalities in (2), prior to any change in the characteristics per unit of the commodity we have

$$\sum_{i=1}^{k} MC_i^T + T > \sum_{i=1}^{k} MV_i^T, \tag{3a}$$

and

$$\sum_{i=k+1}^{n} MC_i^T < \sum_{i=k+1}^{n} MV_i^T. \tag{3b}$$

Here (3a) relates to characteristics specified by the tax statute and (3b) to those which escape the constraint. The tax, strictly speaking, is imposed only on characteristics $1, \ldots, k$. Since the tax-inclusive cost of the first k characteristics exceeds their valuation, while the converse holds for the

[4] To fix units of measurement we set the pretax level of each of the characteristics at one unit per unit of the commodity. Thanks are due John Floyd for correction of a previous error.

[5] An MV_i should be construed as the change in the total value of the commodity induced by a unit change in the ith characteristic and similarly for MC_i.

[6] We abstract from cross-effects among the characteristics in either cost or valuation functions which could conceivably reverse the inequalities.

other $n - k$ group, there is incentive to contract the former relative to the latter. Since the tax statute determines the level of the former per unit of the good, adjustment will have to take place by reducing the number of units produced while increasing the levels of the uncontrolled characteristics per unit of the good. Expansion of the untaxed characteristics constitutes an effective substitution against the tax. Adjustment will continue to the point where the inequality in (3a) and all of the $n - k$ components in the inequality in (3b) turn into equalities.

Since characteristics $1, \ldots, k$ are constrained to a maximum level by the tax statute and since there is basically no incentive to raise them, their level will stay unchanged and we can consider them as one. Characteristics $k + 1, \ldots, n$ are not constrained; but to simplify we shall assume that their relative levels are maintained. Let us call the taxed set of characteristics *A*, the untaxed *B*, and the commodity as a whole *C*.

The tax will cause a decline in the number of units of *A* demanded. The demand for *B* may increase or fall, depending on whether *A* and *B* are substitutes or complements, but that of *B* relative to *A* will have to increase.[7] While each unit of *C* will contain the same *A* as before, the tax will cause it to include more of *B*. In other words, the tax will induce an upgrading in the "quality" of *C* inasmuch as each unit will contain more *B*.[8]

The opportunity to modify the composition of the commodity reduces the tax burden implied in the fixed-quality model, and the equilibrium quantity will increase correspondingly. The "welfare triangle," therefore, is smaller than in the fixed-quality case. The change in resource allocation induced by the tax, however, is no longer confined to a reduction in quantity of the taxed good but now includes the costs of producing an inefficient mix of characteristics within the good.[9]

Thus participants in the market for the commodity suffer three kinds of losses from the tax: the tax payments,[10] the welfare triangle from re-

[7] In a two-commodity world and holding individual incomes constant the demand for *B* per unit of *A* will remain unchanged only if they are perfect complements. Even though basically the tax will not affect aggregate income, it will affect its distribution. The individual income effects will not necessarily cancel out and may produce a perverse outcome. In addition, as noted by Gould and Segall (1969), interaction with other commodities could conceivably upset the results. Finally, the change in the quantities of *A* and *B* implies movements along the (pretax) supply schedules. The two supply elasticities may differ sufficiently to change the expense of *A* relative to *B*. None of these possibilities seems empirically important. In what follows, we abstract from all of them.

[8] The term "quality" is not used in a normative sense. Indeed, if *B* rather than *A* were being used as a unit of measure the "quality" would be reduced by the lesser proportion of *A*. It is used here as a shorthand notation for the quantity of given characteristics per unit of the commodity.

[9] A more complete discussion of these points in relation to a special case is presented in Section V, following.

[10] As already mentioned, we abstract from whatever benefits may arise from the use to which the tax is put.

duced production, and the loss of efficiency in production. Consumers and producers of the taxed commodity will benefit most by minimizing the sum of these losses. Our central proposition is that market forces will actually produce that result.

To demonstrate the proposition: consider the market for our commodity in a (taxless) economy in full competitive equilibrium. From all possible positions open to the economy, equilibrium is at the point at which the sum of consumers' and producers' surplus is maximized. Although most economic models consider one-dimensional goods, the fundamental properties of equilibrium are not affected when commodities have more than one characteristic.

With any change in the price of a factor used in producing the commodity, the economy will move to a new equilibrium. Suppose now a change occurs which has no effect on B but which raises by T the real cost of producing A. From the previous analysis of the effect of the tax (and abstracting from resultant differential changes in the rest of the economy) it is clear that the same equilibrium will be reached at the new factor price as would have occurred under the tax. Given the change in cost, the new equilibrium is again a position of maximum surplus, representing the smallest possible loss as compared to the prior situation. The market will react to the higher factor cost by economizing in its use (1) by contracting the output of the commodity itself and (2) by substituting toward those of its characteristics which use relatively less of the high-priced factor. In short, the market reaction is identical to that in the tax case; in both instances the adjustments constitute a minimization of the sum of the two cost components. Thus the proposition is demonstrated that following the imposition of a tax the market will move to minimize the sum of the tax paid and the welfare loss.

This proposition has been set out in terms of only two characteristics, but its logic is equally applicable irrespective of their number. At competitive equilibrium for any such commodity, economic surplus is maximized. Suppose an increase in the price of a factor used to produce some, but not all, of the characteristics takes place. The levels of each will be so adjusted that all the marginal conditions will be satisfied. The new equilibrium, subject to the higher factor price, will again be a position of maximum surplus, and the move to the second equilibrium will have entailed the smallest possible loss in surplus. Given the complete analogy of impact between a tax and an increase in factor price, the fundamental result enunciated above is entirely general.[11]

[11] Such terms as welfare triangle, misallocation, inefficiency, distortions, and the like carry normative connotations. We have just shown, however, that they possess positive properties as the subject of market minimization. This terminology, ingrained in the literature, is retained here but is used only in its positive sense.

III. The ad Valorem Tax

Suppose an ad valorem tax of rate t is imposed on a commodity having n characteristics. The tax statute here defines the commodity in terms of the *minimum* levels of characteristics $1, \ldots, k$. The after-tax equilibrium prior to any change in characteristics can be written as:

$$(1 + t) \sum \mathrm{MC}_i^t = P^t = \sum \mathrm{MV}_i^t, \tag{4}$$

which is the counterpart of (1) for the constant-unit tax. Expression (4) can be decomposed, as is (1′), into the constrained and unconstrained components:

$$(1 + t) \sum_{i=1}^{k} \mathrm{MC}_i^t + (1 + t) \sum_{i=k+1}^{n} \mathrm{MC}_i^t = P^t = \sum_{i=1}^{k} \mathrm{MV}_i^t + \sum_{i=k+1}^{n} \mathrm{MV}_i^t \tag{4'}$$

Economic choice again determines both what characteristics will constitute a given commodity and their levels. A characteristic will be included in a commodity only if it is cheaper when part of the package than when sold separately. Since characteristics $k + 1, \ldots, n$ are not constrained, reduction of their levels will serve to evade some of the tax. Most important, these characteristics are taxed only so long as they are sold as part of the commodity.[12] Thus, if the pretax advantage of selling the $k + 1$st characteristic as part of the package exceeded that of selling it separately by less than $tx\mathrm{MC}_{k+1}$, it may be removed altogether from the package when the tax is imposed.

To simplify, let us again lump the first k characteristics into A and the remainder into B, and assume that A and B are consumed in fixed proportions. Suppose that, prior to the tax, a package was preferred. This is shown in figure 1, where D is the demand for the package, $S(P)$ is the supply of the package, $S(A)$ is the supply of one component, and $S(A + B)$ is the sum of the supplies of the two components (plus assembly, if necessary).

What would be the effect of an ad valorem tax? If the definition of the commodity for tax purposes is $A + B$, then the conventional analysis

[12] In at least some situations, substantial savings accrue to buying a package rather than its individual components. A study published in *Money Magazine* (1972) shows that while the retail price of a Ford Maverick was then $2,506.55 the retail price for its more than 10,000 parts, unpainted and unassembled, would have totaled $6,435.22. To this could be added the cost to the buyer of time spent in searching and buying.

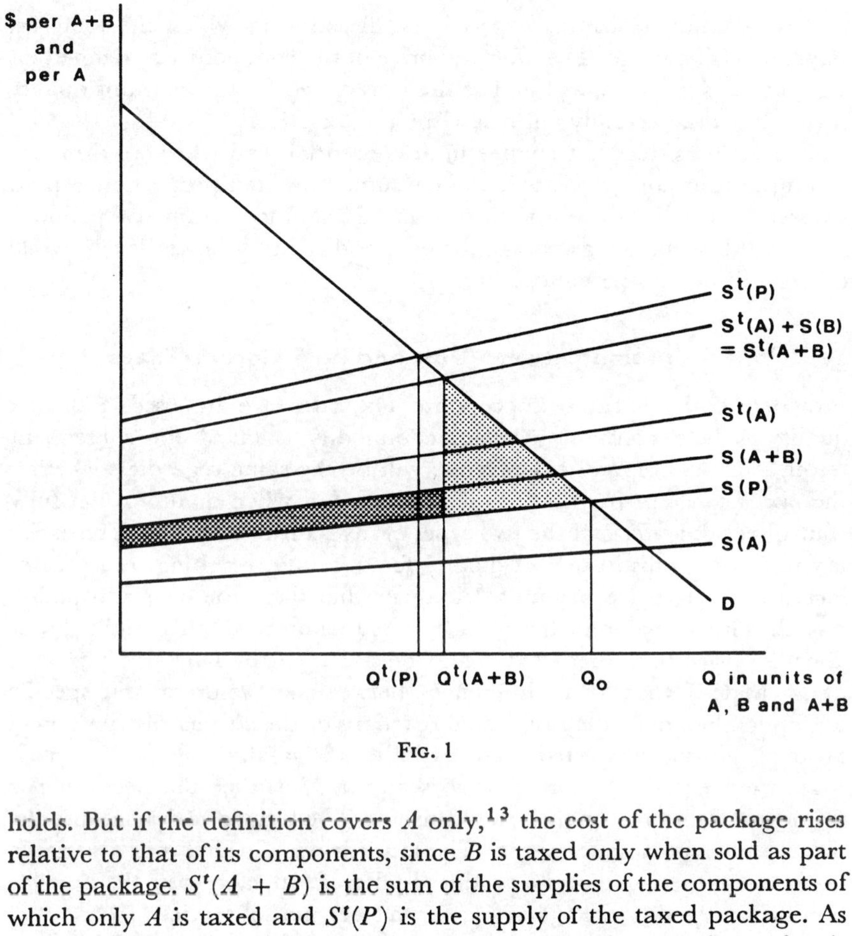

FIG. 1

holds. But if the definition covers A only,[13] the cost of the package rises relative to that of its components, since B is taxed only when sold as part of the package. $S^t(A + B)$ is the sum of the supplies of the components of which only A is taxed and $S^t(P)$ is the supply of the taxed package. As drawn, the former intersects the demand curve at a lower point and so is preferred. The price for $A + B$ paid by the consumer is less if he buys the components separately, so the after-tax quantity falls only to $Q^t(A + B)$ rather than to $Q^t(P)$, which would be the equilibrium quantity were the whole package taxed. As a result, the welfare triangle is also smaller than when quality is unchanged. But the reduced output is now produced at a resource cost according to $S(A + B)$ rather than to the lower $S(P)$, and this inefficiency adds to the welfare cost of the tax. The two components of the total welfare loss form the shaded areas in figure 1.

Tax revenue is now obtained from a larger number of units—$Q^t(A + B)$ rather than $Q^t(P)$; but as the tax base is smaller, the tax per unit is less

[13] Such would be the case where a new air-conditioned car is taxed at the same rate as one lacking that option and where separately purchased air-conditioning units are untaxed. For the tax to apply to all components of a car, the statute would have to cover each of many thousand parts, specifying for each a minimum standard of quality.

and we cannot determine a priori the direction in which the total tax payment will change. The after-tax price of the commodity as defined for tax purposes not only will be less than predicted by the constant-quality model but may actually fall below the pretax price.[14]

The analysis does not change in any essential way when we drop the assumptions of only two attributes consumed in fixed proportion. An ad valorem tax will induce a reduction in all the unconstrained attributes; some will be retained as part of the commodity but at lower levels, while others will be dropped altogether.[15]

IV. The Distinction between Unit and ad Valorem Taxes

Provided both that the appropriate tax rates are imposed and that quality is held constant, when a commodity is taxed the subsequent resource allocation and tax revenue will be the same regardless whether the tax is constant per unit or ad valorem. But when quality is not fully controlled, the effects of the two types of taxes differ radically. The excise tax induces a substitution of quality for quantity, resulting in a greater increase in the price per unit[16] than predicted by the constant-quality model. The ad valorem tax induces a reduction in quality and a lower after-tax price than predicted. Thus the statement by Due (1959, p. 298, italics added) that "this difference [between ad valorem and specific taxes] does not alter the *basic* initial reactions or the *ultimate* distribution of burden" has to be rejected if our hypothesis is valid.

It is evident that when quality is adjusted, neither the per unit nor the ad valorem tax remains truly constant. The former varies because the taxable unit has been changed. The latter is transformed into a variable tax because the value of the product is altered. In each case, the motivation for the quality change is a lower tax per unit of service.

The relation between the two taxes can be traced to an essential feature of commodities transacted in the market. Consider again a commodity possessing n characteristics and assume that the tax statute defines the product in terms of the first k. If deletion of characteristics were costless, the reaction to either a per-unit or an ad valorem tax would be the same. Characteristics $k + 1, \ldots, n$ are untaxed by the excise tax; their removal

[14] The corporate income tax is fundamentally an ad valorem tax. When such a tax is imposed or raised, it can be evaded in part by switching to corporate financing based more on debt and less on equity. The risk borne by equity holders will then increase. The measured rate of return to equity, reflecting this risk, might exceed the change in the tax rate, giving the impression of more than 100 percent shifting.

[15] It may appear that a general sales tax on final consumer commodities (or a uniform income tax) will avoid these problems. However, in addition to the difficulty of taxing home production, there is an incentive for employers to provide their employees with consumption goods such as air conditioning and uniforms—classified under the tax as intermediate and not subject to tax—thereby still partly evading the tax.

[16] The unit referred to is that defined for tax purposes.

from the commodity will exempt them from the ad valorem tax; thus substitution toward these characteristics is implied in either case. We can predict a reduction in the consumption of the first k characteristics, and a relative increase in the consumption of the others.

Suppose now that the ad valorem tax is set at such a rate that the amount realized after the elimination of characteristics will equal that attainable under a unit tax. The two taxes would now have *identical* effects on resource allocation. If we measure the commodity in units as defined by the tax statute, the tax-inclusive price will be lower for the ad valorem tax, but this is simply because the characteristics $k + 1, \ldots, n$ are sold separately.

Of course, it is invalid to assume that the deletion of characteristics will be costless, since they would not originally have been incorporated in the commodity unless this offered advantages. An ad valorem tax will still lead to a reduction of the levels of all the $k + 1, \ldots, n$ characteristics per unit of the good. While some characteristics may be completely eliminated, others will merely be reduced. The two taxes, then, will result in quite dissimilar effects on resource allocation as well as in different observed prices and tax revenues.[17]

V. Tax and Durability

In this and the following section, the analysis will be confined to a commodity with one continuously variable attribute—durability. This simplification not only will clarify some of the foregoing conclusions, but will help in the analysis of additional relevant issues. Thus, for the commodity selected for illustration—light bulbs—we consider only the variable of durability. The bulbs are assumed to be homogeneous in such dimensions as strength and color, and while they last they provide a constant-quality flow of services (the one-horse-shay model).

Consumers, we assume, value the flow of light services but not durability per se. A consumer, then, would be willing to pay the same price for 12 1-month bulbs as for a single 1-year bulb. This valuation scheme becomes plausible if we conceive of the consumer as renting the bulbs, that is, purchasing the light service rather than the product. The cost of changing bulbs is then transferred to the seller and can be incorporated in his cost function.[18] Under these conditions the durability offered in the market will be that for which the price of light services is lowest, satisfying the condition that the cost of an infinitesimal increase in volume of service will be the same whether obtained by an infinitesimal increase in the number of bulbs or in their durability.

[17] It would be interesting to discover under what conditions one type of tax would be selected over the other.

[18] We also assume that for any given volume of service there is always a single durability for which the cost is lower than for any combination of durabilities.

Now consider an excise tax on light bulbs. We assume that the tax statute does not constrain durability. This is not unreasonable, since in our model durability is not an explicit feature of bulbs as only one durability is provided by the market at a point in time. A tax which is constant per bulb raises the marginal cost of bulbs by the amount of the tax but does not affect the marginal cost of durability. The least-cost method of obtaining any given output of light services after the tax is to increase durability to the point where equality on the two margins is restored.

When we compare the constant durability model—fundamentally the accepted model—with the unconstrained durability model, several major differences emerge. With the removal of the constraint, the tax-inclusive cost of service will be lowered and the quantity of services increased. In general, competition drives the price to the lowest level consistent with cost. Here a move to a higher durability reduces the tax-inclusive cost per unit of service and competition will guarantee that more durable bulbs will actually be provided.

Received theory predicts that an excise tax will result in an increase in price not larger than the rate of tax. However, since the increase in durability will itself tend to increase the price of light bulbs, the actual increase in price per light bulb may easily exceed the rate of tax.[19]

Much of the content of the above results can be presented diagrammatically. In figure 2, the units on the horizontal axis represent light services and on the vertical axis, dollars per unit of service. Since the demand for service is independent of durability, a single demand curve suffices. For each durability, however, there is a different cost curve. To simplify graphic exposition, it is now assumed that cost curves for varying durabilities do not intersect. We denote by $S(x)$ the cost curve for durability x. Two such cost curves are drawn in figure 2. Suppose that the lower one, $S(2)$, provides light services at lower resource cost than any other durability, either shorter or longer. Before taxation, then, $Q(2)$ and $P(2)$ are the market quantity and price.

A tax of T per light bulb is now imposed. Each of the $S(x)$ curves will shift upward by amounts inversely proportional to x; the tax per unit of service on a 4-month bulb is half that on a 2-month bulb. The lowest curve will now be one of longer durability; the higher the tax, the greater

[19] Following Harberger (1964), one could alternatively argue that the tax is actually imposed not on a single commodity but rather on a whole array of commodities where each durability constitutes a separate commodity. It is clear that the tax-induced increase in the consumer price for each would not exceed the rate of the tax. But the elasticity of substitution in consumption between alternative durabilities is such that the old durability is entirely replaced. This is formally correct but does not seem useful. In most empirical studies of taxation, the level of aggregation of the taxed commodity is quite high, indicating lack of awareness of the problem of tax-induced substitution within what is classified as a homogeneous commodity.

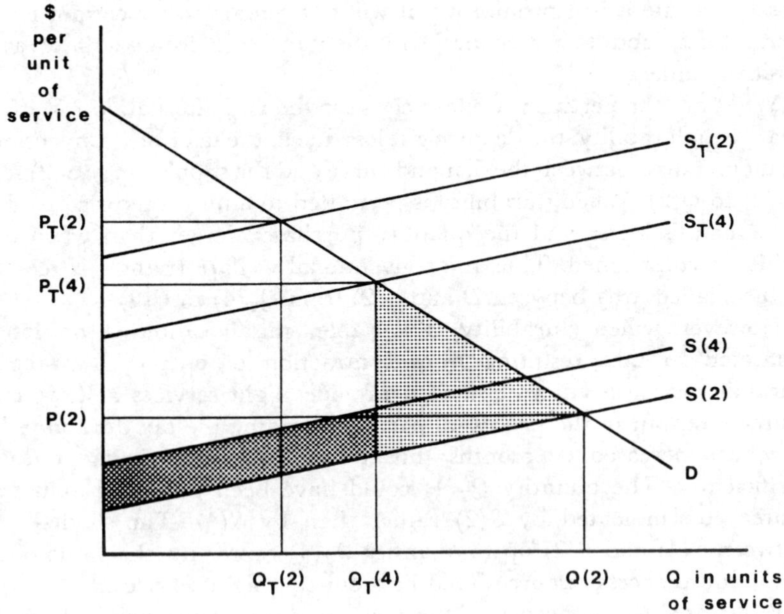

FIG. 2

that durability. We denote by $S_T(x)$ the tax-inclusive cost of light services obtained from bulbs of durability x, and suppose that among all these $S_T(4)$ is lowest.

After the tax, $Q_T(2)$ and $P_T(2)$ are the equilibrium quantity and price if durability is constrained to 2. But if durability is not constrained, the final price per unit of service will be lower and the final quantity of services higher, since $S_T(4)$ lies below $S_T(2)$. Note, however, that the price observed in the market is not per unit of service but per bulb. Thus even though $P_T(4) < P_T(2)$ and $P_T(2) - P(2) <$ tax, the increase in the price per bulb may exceed the tax rate because the after-tax bulb is more durable. Indeed, if the supply curves are perfectly elastic, the increase in the price per bulb will *necessarily* exceed the rate of tax.

Let us now turn to tax receipts. In figure 2 these are represented by the product of the after-tax market quantity and the difference between the after-tax market price and the pretax cost. It is easy to see that tax receipts may go up or down when we compare the constrained with the unconstrained durabilities. For instance, if the tax is originally set to yield maximum tax revenue while constraining durability to its pretax level, when the constraint is relaxed the substitution towards higher durability will necessarily result in a revenue loss.[20] On the other hand, if the im-

[20] Finding the tax rate that yields maximum revenue is equivalent to finding the largest rectangle that can be inscribed between the demand and supply curves to the left of their intersection. Since higher durabilities reduce the area between the two curves, the new largest rectangle has to be smaller than the old one.

posed tax rate is just prohibitive, it will not remain so for certain longer durabilities, and tax revenues will then increase from zero to some positive value.

What are the pertinent welfare costs for the two alternatives? With no change in durability, the deadweight loss due to the tax is the conventional triangular area between the demand curve and the supply curve $S(2)$ from $Q_T(2)$ to $Q(2)$. When durability is permitted to adjust, the price paid by consumers is lower and the quantity purchased larger than when durability is constrained. Thus the conventional welfare triangle is reduced to the shaded area between D and $S(2)$ from $Q_T(4)$ to $Q(2)$.

However, when durability is variable, misallocation is no longer restricted to that resulting from contraction of output. Two-month durability is most efficient since it provides light services at lowest resource cost, but in the process of partially evading the tax durability has now been increased to 4 months; thus the *entire* quantity is being produced inefficiently. The quantity $Q_T(4)$ could have been produced at the resource cost indicated by $S(2)$ rather than by $S(4)$. The shaded area between $S(4)$ and $S(2)$ up to quantity $Q_T(4)$ represents the value of the tax-induced excess resources used in producing light services.

What are the properties of the new equilibrium position? Together, producers and consumers search for that durability for which the effect of the tax is minimized: that is, for the real price that results in the smallest contraction of service output. In other words, market participants search for the durability that leads to the lowest after-tax price per unit of service. The tax paid per light bulb is still T, but now a bulb provides more services, thus the real tax is lower by a corresponding amount.

To depict further the properties of the after-tax equilibrium, figure 3 adds to the demand and supply curves of figure 2 the supply curves of 3-month bulbs, both before and after the tax and a new curve denoted H.[21] Each point on H represents a net-of-tax market equilibrium position if durability is constrained to a particular value. Thus, point 2 is the after-tax equilibrium to suppliers if durability is constrained to 2 months. Similarly for points 3 and 4. Points 2′, 3′, and 4′ are the corresponding points of demand. That is, given the tax and the constrained durabilities, these are the optimal points to consumers. The distance between 2 and 2′, for instance, is the tax per unit of service for a bulb of 2-month durability. The H curve is tangent to $S(2)$ at point 2, since $S(2)$ is the lowest supply curve.

As we move from point 2 through higher durabilities, output is produced at increasing resource cost. In the durability range from 2 to 4 months, however, this increase in cost is more than matched by tax savings. In that range, then, the price paid by consumers is declining, the quantity purchased rises, and the welfare-loss triangle shrinks correspondingly.

[21] The discussion of figure 3, and a following related consideration of subsidies, were stimulated by a conversation with Al Harberger.

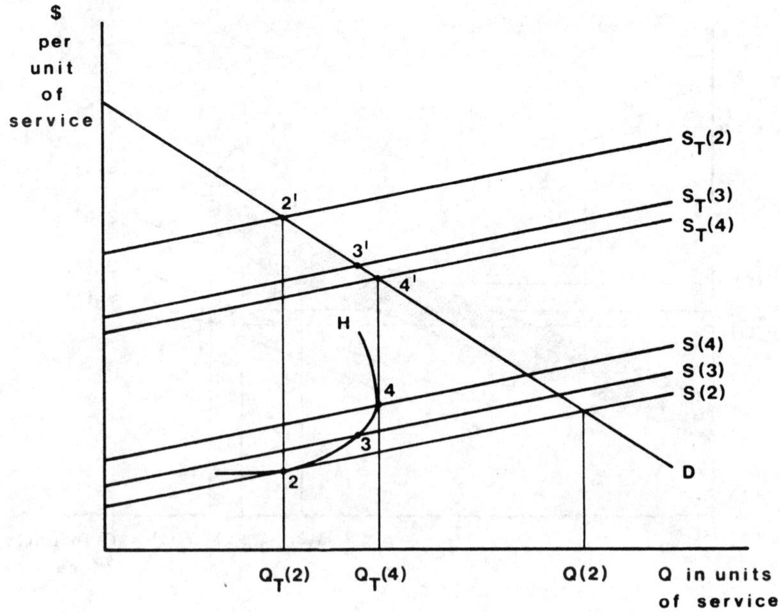

FIG. 3

Beyond point 4 the tax saving of increased durability is less than the extra resource cost. At point 4, where durability is identical to that chosen in the absence of constraint, the *H* curve is vertical and the incremental gain from a further saving in taxes is exactly matched by an increase in cost of production. That point, then, satisfies the first order condition for a minimum. Since point 4 is market determined, the earlier proposition that the market will minimize the dollar value of the sum of welfare losses and tax paid is again demonstrated, though from a different angle.[22]

VI. Subsidies

It may appear that a discussion of subsidies at this point is superfluous: Aren't subsidies the "mirror image" of taxes? Why would not a subsidy simply reverse the signs of the tax case? It is true that a tax is a negative subsidy; the effect of the former is to reduce market quantity and of the latter to increase it. But the effect is not symmetric with respect to resource allocation. *Both* lead to positive welfare triangles and to inefficient moves from the optimal mix of characteristics into mixes which use up more

[22] In the case just discussed, would an ad valorem tax affect durability, or would it be "neutral"? If the tax is on bulbs, but not on their installation, the buyer has a stronger incentive to install his own bulbs. As the cost of installation relative to bulbs is then lower, durability will be shortened.

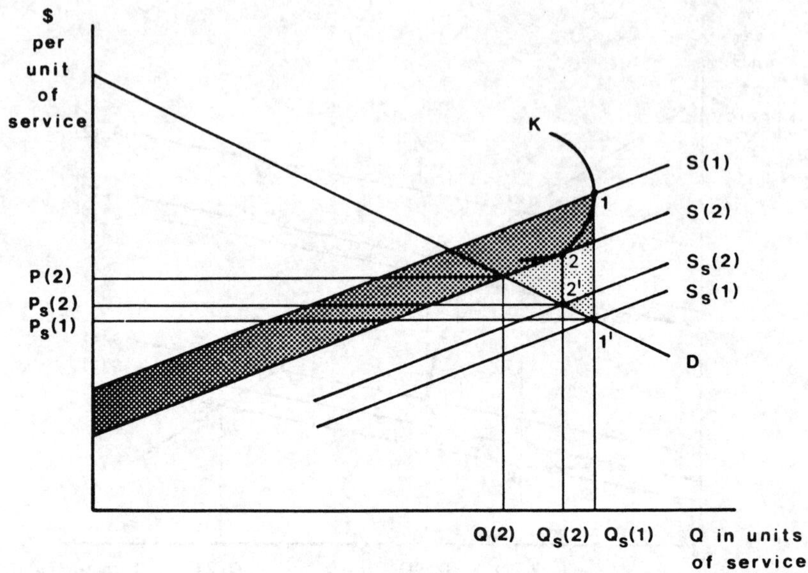

FIG. 4

resources. In the remainder of this section we examine this aspect of the effects of a constant per unit subsidy on a durable commodity.

In addition to directly increasing quantity, a subsidy will lead to an added expansion in quantity because of substitution against durability, since the price per unit of service is thus reduced. In figure 4, $S(2)$ and D are again the same as in figure 2. A subsidy, S, is granted per light bulb of whatever durability. If durability is constrained to remain at 2 months, the price paid by consumers per unit of service will decline to $P_S(2)$ and the quantity will increase to $Q_S(2)$. But for durabilities shorter than 2 months the subsidy per unit of service is higher, thus light service will be cheaper. Suppose that among bulbs of shorter life those of 1-month durability are best; $S(1)$ and $S_S(1)$ as drawn in figure 4 show that when the durability constraint is removed the price per unit of service will fall to $P_S(1)$ while the quantity of service consumed will increase to $Q_S(1)$.

In regard to welfare loss, since the market quantity of services is lower when durability is held constant, the removal of that constraint leads to a *larger* welfare triangle—the shaded triangle in figure 4. In addition, bulbs of 1-month durability provide light service at a higher resource cost than 2-month bulbs, consequently the entire output is produced inefficiently. The total resource cost of this inefficiency is the area between $S(1)$ and $S(2)$ to quantity $Q_S(1)$, which is also shaded in the diagram.

It is evident that if the rate of the subsidy just discussed equals the rate of the tax considered earlier, and given linear demand and cost curves, the adjustment to the subsidy is larger than that to the tax.[23] If the tax and subsidy rates are the same, the changes which will occur in price and quantity under conditions of constrained durability are of the same size (in absolute terms). When durability is allowed to change, a downward move is induced along the demand curve by either the tax or the subsidy. This mitigates the initial effect of the tax but enhances that of the subsidy— which thus has the greater total impact.

More generally, a series of constant tax doses will result in successively smaller adjustments in the price and quantity of service. The intuitive explanation for this is that since each tax increment leads to the production of more durable bulbs for the market, the new levy has a smaller proportionate effect.[24]

The curve K in figure 4 is obtained similarly to H in figure 3. This curve, too, is tangent to S_2 and is vertical at output level $Q_S(1)$. If durability is constrained to 2 months, producers will operate at point 2 after the subsidy is granted. As they are permitted to produce shorter durabilities they will move along the curve K as far as, but not beyond, point 1. At that point the benefit from obtaining a larger subsidy by switching to a still shorter durability is exactly nullified by the increase in cost of the shorter durability. Point 1 produces the largest welfare triangle; as durability was reduced from 2 months to 1, the triangle was increasing continuously; but it then begins to shrink because still shorter durabilities lead to a decline in market quantity. At point 1, which will be chosen by the market in the absence of constraint, the sum of welfare loss and the (negative) tax paid is at a minimum—a small move leaves the area of the triangle unchanged while the change in welfare loss due to inefficient production is exactly matched by the change in subsidy.

Consider now a change away from point 2. Here, an infinitesimal reduction in durability will result in an increased subsidy, but the efficiency in production will not be affected. This, then, will lead to a fall in price paid by consumers, to a corresponding increase in output, and hence to a larger welfare triangle. It is evident, then, as stated earlier, that any move to a shorter durability must result in an unambiguous increase in welfare cost.

When it is possible to tighten the legal definition of the commodity with the objective either of increasing tax revenue or of reducing the dollar value of the misallocation, more information is needed to determine

[23] Of course, a simultaneous tax and subsidy of the same size will identically cancel out. Here the starting point of the subsidy is the end point of the tax. In the textual comparison, the starting point for both is the same.

[24] Note, however, that the observations in empirical work typically correspond to those on light bulbs rather than on light services. It is not entirely clear, then, that the observed price increases will continue declining with successive equal tax doses; a result which anyhow depended on the assumption of linearity.

which way the tightening will work in the case of a tax. With a subsidy, on the other hand, a move to prevent substitution among qualities will always reduce both subsidy payments and misallocation.[25]

VII. A Test of the Hypothesis

Our fundamental hypothesis is that the effect of a tax on the price of a commodity, as measured, will differ from that indicated by conventional analysis. Specifically, we predict that a tax which is constant per unit will increase consumer price, as normally measured, more than is predicted by the received model, whereas an ad valorem tax will raise price less than a comparable per-unit tax.

Consider also the "mark-up" hypothesis which states (inconsistently with demand theory) that when the price to the seller is increased by whatever reason, he will raise the retail price by a larger amount. We argue that the effect produced by an ad valorem tax will differ radically from that of a constant per unit tax. Data on the effects of the two taxes may enable us to test the received model and also to choose between the mark-up hypothesis and ours.

Reported in the following paragraphs are tests of the hypotheses using data on cigarettes.[26] Starting in 1954, the Tobacco Tax Council (1972) has compiled and reported the retail price of cigarettes on a state-by-state and year-by-year basis.[27] The "prices" are actually within-state indices using a set of fixed weights for all states in all years. Weights are given to three types of cigarettes—regular, king, and filter (both 85 mm and 100 mm)—and to three types of sale—single pack over the counter, vending machine, and carton lot.[28]

Cigarettes provide an almost ideal setting for testing our hypotheses. The bulk of cigarettes originate from around North Carolina and are distributed nationally. Apart from the effect of shipping costs (which is possible to control for), the observed price differences at a point in time are presumably due largely to state taxes.

While a federal tax remained constant at 8 cents per package for the entire period, state taxes varied greatly within states and over time. In 1972, the most recent year used, these ranged from 2 cents per package in North Carolina to 21 cents in Connecticut. In the same states the taxes had been, respectively, 0 and 3 cents in 1954.

[25] Incidental to the central theme of this paper is the hypothesis that the quality constraints actually imposed would be more severe for a subsidy than for a tax.

[26] Attempts to test our hypothesis against data on gasoline and liquor are reported in the Appendix.

[27] For most years, the data are given as of November 1. For 1957, 1958, and 1959, the date used is October 1.

[28] Information provided in a letter from the Tobacco Tax Council.

TABLE 1

Cigarette Regression Results*

Variable	Coefficient	Standard Error	*t*-Value
Constant	14.801	0.201	73.564
Tax (in cents per package)	1.065	0.011	101.439
New Hampshire dummy	−0.072	0.014	−5.078
Distance (in 100 miles)	0.011	0.004	3.072
$R^{-2} = .93$			

* A set of year dummies included in the regression showed an upward drift from − 1.9 (cents per package) in 1954 to 0.8 in 1970 declining back to zero (the "base" year) in 1972.

It seems reasonable to expect that the supply elasticity of cigarettes to a single state is very high. Thus if the conventional model is correct, a 1-cent difference in tax per package between two states will result, *ceteris paribus*, in close to a 1-cent difference in price. Using our model, we predict a price increase larger than 1 cent if the tax is constant per unit and a smaller increase if it is ad valorem.

Table 1 presents results from a regression based on 931 observations.[29] The dependent variable is the retail price, deflated by the consumer price index for October of the given year. The coefficient of the tax (also deflated by the consumer price index) indicates that a 1-cent increase in tax raises retail price by 1.065 cents, which is significantly larger than one, as the *t*-ratio for that test exceeds 6.[30] The received notion that the price will increase at most by the amount of the tax can be rejected.[31]

In New Hampshire the tax is ad valorem. The regression coefficient for the dummy variable for that state, measuring the differential from other states with the comparable unit tax, is −0.072 and its standard error is 0.014. The retail price in New Hampshire, then, is significantly less than that predicted for a state with a comparable per package tax,[32] and the hypothesis can be rejected that comparable per unit and ad valorem taxes will have identical effects.[33] Also rejected is the mark-up

[29] These are one observation each for 19 years (1954–72) for the District of Columbia and for each of the 48 continental states. Alaska and Hawaii, for which data are available for only part of the period, were deleted from the sample because of the ambiguity of the distance measure. Note that Hawaii imposes an ad valorem cigarette tax at the wholesale level. Data sources are: for road distances between largest metropolitan areas, Rand McNally *Road Atlas* (1972); for cigarette prices and taxes, Tobacco Tax Council (1972); for consumer price index, U.S. Bureau of Labor Statistics (various years).

[30] We would expect within states a tax-induced shift toward higher-priced cigarettes such as 100 mm and those from vending machines. As a result, the average price per package should have risen. Since weights are fixed in the data, the regression coefficient does not reflect this phenomenon.

[31] The cost of financing the tax in terms of extra interest can account for only a small fraction of the amount by which the coefficient differs from unity.

[32] The size of New Hampshire makes it unlikely that cigarettes would be tailor-made for it. The scope for removing characteristics is quite limited, then.

[33] In scatter diagrams for individual years the slope of the unit tax, fitted by free hand, is consistently higher than one, and New Hampshire has consistently the largest negative deviation.

hypothesis, as it fails to predict differential effects from the two types of tax. Finally, the coefficient of the distance variable, inserted to control for the differential shipping costs from North Carolina, is positive, as expected, and significant.

VIII. Final Comments

If economists are set to offer policy prescriptions, the preceding analysis warns of a serious pitfall. Our model, and our results, cast doubt on the notion held by many economists with respect to second-best solutions—that taxes can be used to correct distortions—as we argue that a tax will have additional "side effects."

For instance, a gasoline tax is often regarded as a means to combat air pollution. Since the tax is actually constant per gallon, market substitution will occur toward high-octane gasoline which has become relatively cheaper. But high octane ratings are produced by lead, now believed to be a major air pollutant, and the tax which results in a higher per-gallon use of lead may actually have increased the absolute level of pollution. The asserted purpose of the tax thus may have backfired.[34]

While taxes do affect resource allocation, the common normative statement that they misallocate resources makes little sense. If that is all they do, why would they ever be imposed? Until we can spell out the objectives of policymakers and the constraints they face we cannot attach meaning to terms such as misallocation or distortion. What we can do, however, is to determine the exact nature of any tax so that we can more accurately predict its effects.

Let us briefly summarize the thrust of the argument. Commodities as transacted in the market are complex, and the margins with respect to which optimization takes place are numerous. Because commodity tax statutes will not generally cover all these margins, any tax will induce multiple changes not only in resource allocation away from the taxed commodity and into others but also in the "quality" of the commodity and how it is transacted, a substitution away from the taxed attributes and into the others.

Adjustment in the face of incomplete specification of commodities implies upgrading of quality in the case of a unit tax and downgrading in that of an ad valorem tax. A test of the effect of taxes on cigarettes refutes the conventional hypothesis that quality will not change with a tax.[35] The results are rather consistent with our model, which claims that the effects of unit and of ad valorem taxes will differ both from each other and from those predicted by the conventional model.

[34] Plott (1966, pp. 84–87) arrives at a similar result for a similar reason.

[35] The results for gasoline and liquor are also consistent with our model.

The two taxes produce different effects because of the different specification of what, exactly, is being taxed. Given the definition (and enforcement) the market will adjust with respect to each of the changeable characteristics. Although these changes are bound to be numerous and will differ depending on the type of tax, their extent is sharply constrained. They will be carried only to the point that minimizes the sum of the dollar value of the resultant inefficiencies and of the tax paid.

Appendix

Tests for Gasoline and Alcohol

Gasoline.—An attempt to test our hypothesis using data on gasoline taxes produced mixed results, vaguely encouraging but quite erratic. The main problems seem to be that (1) at any moment the wholesale price differs widely across markets, and (2) identification is hard to establish.

The data used are reported by the monthly magazine, *National Petroleum News* (1971), where for several years monthly observations are given on the wholesale price, tax, and retail price of regular gasoline in 55 cities.[36]

Regressions were run for 4 months in 1971. The dependent variable was retail price per gallon and the independent variables were wholesale price and tax. With unlagged independent variables the coefficient for tax is 0.78 (0.078 SE) and for wholesale price 1.18 (0.031 SE). The forces that make us expect a "large" coefficient for the tax variable apply to other cost components.[37] The coefficient for the wholesale price variable, at least, is comforting.

The variability in the wholesale price may well be due to differing demands among cities, while our hypothesis is in terms of shifts of cost schedules rather than shifts along them. Thus one cannot accept the above results at face value. When the two independent variables were lagged in an attempt to assure that the direction of causality in the data is from the independent to the dependent variable, the coefficient for the tax became 1.05 (0.23 SE) and that for the wholesale price 0.29 (0.09 SE).

It is clear that a more complete model and possibly better data are required to obtain satisfactory results for gasoline.

Alcohol.—The data used are from a secondary source.[38] A price breakdown is provided of 12 distilled spirits in New York State for 1971. These data enable us to run a regression in which the retail price per case is the dependent variable and tax per case and wholesale price (net of tax) are the independent variables. Since measurement of one of the observations (imported brandy) presented problems, regressions were run with and without it. With the entire 12 observations the tax coefficient was 1.31 (0.40 SE) and that for the wholesale price 1.30 (0.15 SE). With 11 observations the respective coefficients were 1.51 (0.43 SE) and 1.26 (0.14 SE).

36 "Regular" gasoline does not sufficiently define the commodity; octane ratings and other characteristics differ among regions and brands. I was unable to correct for these, however.

37 Therefore, the two coefficients should be approximately equal, but here the difference between them is significant.

38 Daniel Wisecarver (1974) kindly permitted me to use his data from an unpublished paper (tables 1 and 6).

The tax coefficients are larger than one, but not significantly so, and they are of the same order of magnitude as the coefficients for the wholesale price variable. The results, while not overwhelming, tend to confirm the hypothesis.[39]

References

Due, John F. *Government Finance: An Economic Analysis*. Rev. ed. Homewood, Ill.: Irwin, 1959.

Gould, John P., and Segall, Joel. "The Substitution Effects of Transportation Costs." *J.P.E.* 77, no. 1 (January/February 1969): 130–37.

Griliches, Z. "Hedonic Price Indexes for Automobiles: An Econometric Analysis of Quality Change." In *The Price Statistics of the Federal Government*, National Bureau of Economic Research. New York: Nat. Bur. Econ. Res., 1961.

Harberger, A. C. "Taxation, Resource Allocation, and Welfare." In *The Role of Direct and Indirect Taxes in the Federal Revenue System*, National Bureau of Economic Research and Brookings. Princeton, N.J.: Nat. Bur. Econ. Res., 1964.

Lancaster, Kelvin J. "A New Approach to Consumer Theory." *J.P.E.* 74, no. 2 (April 1966): 132–57.

Lane, Frederic C. "Tonnages, Medieval and Modern." *Econ. Hist. Rev.* 17 (December 1964): 213–33.

Money Magazine (November 1972).

National Petroleum News (various issues, 1971).

Niskanen, William A., Jr. "The Demand for Alcoholic Beverages." Ph.D. dissertation, Univ. Chicago, 1963.

Plott, Charles R. "Externalities and Corrective Taxes." *Economica* 33 (February 1966): 84–87.

Rand McNally & Co. *Road Atlas*. 103d ed. San Francisco: Rand McNally, 1972.

Tobacco Tax Council, Inc. *The Tax Burden on Tobacco: Historical Compilation*. Vol. 7. Richmond, Va.: Tobacco Tax Council, 1972.

U.S. Bureau of Labor Statistics. *Consumer Price Indexes*. Washington: Government Printing Office, relevant years.

Wisecarver, Daniel. "The Comparative Resource Allocation Effects of Specific vs. ad Valorem Taxation of Distilled Spirits." Unpublished paper, March 1974.

[39] In a study by Niskanen (1963) one of the findings is that in the taxation of alcoholic beverages consumers bear more than 100 percent of the tax. This offers additional confirmation of the hypothesis.

Reprinted for private circulation from THE JOURNAL OF LAW AND ECONOMICS, Volume XX (1), April, 1977, Copyright 1977, The University of Chicago.

AN ECONOMIC ANALYSIS OF SLAVERY*

YORAM BARZEL
University of Washington

INTRODUCTION

THIS paper seeks to explain certain observations pertaining to slavery. Several of the implications will be tested against data provided in Fogel and Engerman's recent work on the subject,[1] in conjunction with a scattering of information from numerous other sources.

In a nonslave economy, an individual determines the amount of labor he is willing to supply simultaneously with his consumption decisions. In this respect, labor differs from any other factor of production. In a slave economy, however, both the amount of labor to be extracted from a slave and his consumption or "feeding" are determined by the slave owner. Thus, the labor market for slaves differs from that for freemen by the decision-making unit through which options are exercised.

In what follows I postulate that in his labor-supply decision a freeman will take into account nonpecuniary dimensions of his work and of his leisure time. On the other hand, the slaveowner is assumed to act as a wealth maximizer in deciding what amount of labor to demand from his slaves. Thus we abstract from any nonpecuniary aspects in master-slave relationships. At the same time, we recognize that while the slave is subject to the dictates and enforcement of his owner's will, his action also depends on his own preferences for pecuniary as well as nonpecuniary goods.

Under these postulates, how would slaves be treated? How would their performance differ from that of free workers, and from that of such other factors of production as machines?

The following section compares the work effort and consumption levels of slaves with those of freemen, largely under an assumption of zero policing

* My thanks go to Gary Becker, Steve Cheung, Douglass North, William Schworm and John Umbeck for their helpful comments. Credit is due to Lee Edlefson for uncovering a serious error. Lastly, I benefited greatly from numerous discussions with Aaron Director. This paper was written in large part while I was visiting the Hoover Institution.

[1] Some of the hypotheses advanced in this paper are not new. In particular, see Robert William Fogel & Stanley L. Engerman, Time on the Cross (2 vols. 1974) [hereinafter cited as Fogel & Engerman]; Paul A. David & Peter Temin, Slavery: The Progressive Institution?, 34 J. Econ. Hist. 739 (1974).

costs. The effects of positive costs for policing are then considered in the remainder of the paper.

Effort and Consumption

A major tool in our analysis is a modified model for labor-leisure choice. A central proposition of the conventional model for allocating time between work and leisure is that an individual will choose that amount of work which equates his wage rate to his subjective marginal rate of substitution between leisure and goods. This is tangency Point E in Figure I between an indiffer-

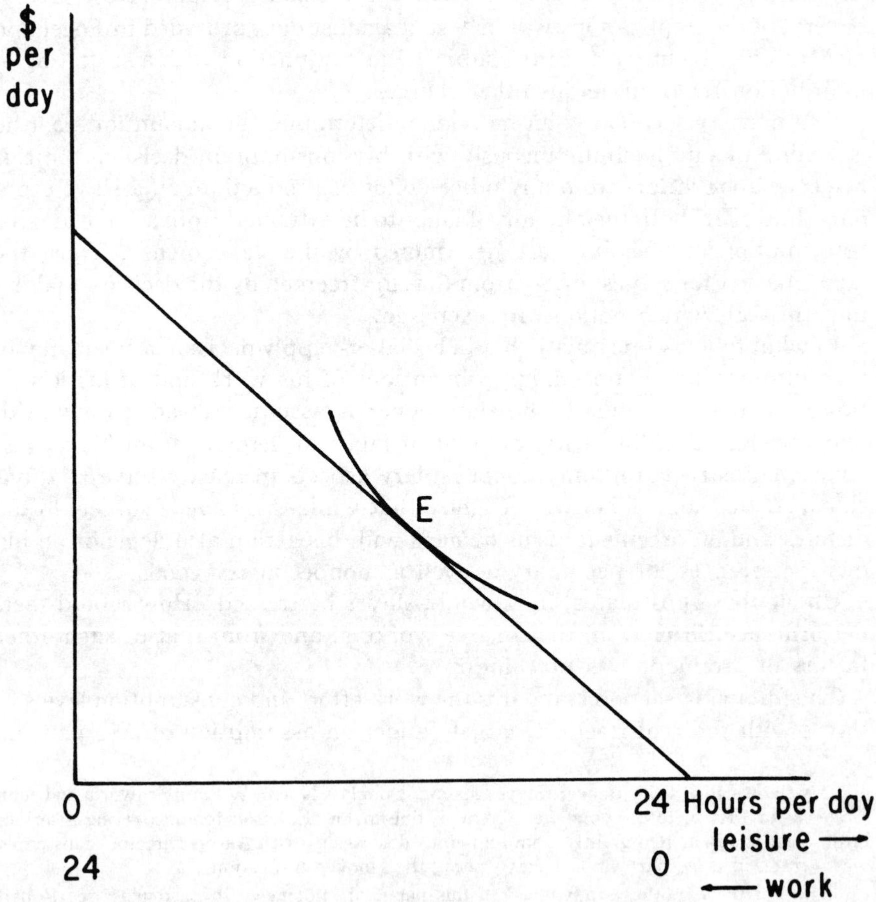

FIGURE I

ence curve and the "wage line" he faces. To serve our purpose, the conventional model has to be further articulated and somewhat modified.

The (competitive) wage rate facing an individual should not be viewed as just a technological datum, but rather as a result of choice. Implicit is the notion that the individual paces himself optimally to satisfy two distinct objectives. One is to properly distribute work effort over his career. The other is to insure that available leisure time, and possibly the working day itself, may be pleasurable. Equalization will take place with respect to each of the margins.

A wealth-maximizing owner, while obviously concerned with proper pacing, does not benefit from his slave's inactive time or leisurely work. He has no incentive to reduce the work-effort requirement to provide leisure or pleasant working conditions. For any given number of working hours, then, a slave will be held to a more intense work pace than a freeman would choose. As a result, the wage line for a slave will *necessarily* lie above that of an equally productive, but free, man. Indeed, except for the optimal distribution of effort over time, a slave's wage line is a technological datum.

For both a freeman and a slave, some consumption is requisite to any given work effort. In conventional analysis this is implicitly incorporated into the utility function, probably because it is both difficult and usually unnecessary to separate "productive consumption" from other consumption. Such separation is desirable, however, in the present analysis; we assume merely that productive consumption increases with the level of effort.

As a final point in modifying the conventional approach, we consider the issue of daily hours. The height of the wage line in a model for labor-leisure choice represents what the employer is willing to pay, which is proportional to the individual's contribution to output. In Figure I, that contribution is highest at twenty-four hours a day. An owner will not force his slave to work that long, however, because, as hours of work increase, fatigue causes the (absolute) slope of the wage line to decline until it eventually reaches zero, which is the point of its maximum level.[2]

In Figure II, GP_S and GP_F relate the value of the gross product associated with different numbers of hours worked by a slave and by a freeman, respectively. The two individuals are assumed to possess identical skills and to be equal in every other relevant aspect. The heights of the curves differ only because the slave is forced to pace himself harder than the other would choose. The line PC_S is the value of productive consumption of a slave who is required to produce on GP_S whereas PC_F is the line for the freeman; the latter is lower because of the lower per-hour work effort. Finally, NP_S and NP_F are

[2] For a more detailed discussion of this point, see Yoram Barzel, The Determination of Daily Hours and Wages, 87 Q.J. Econ. 220 (1973).

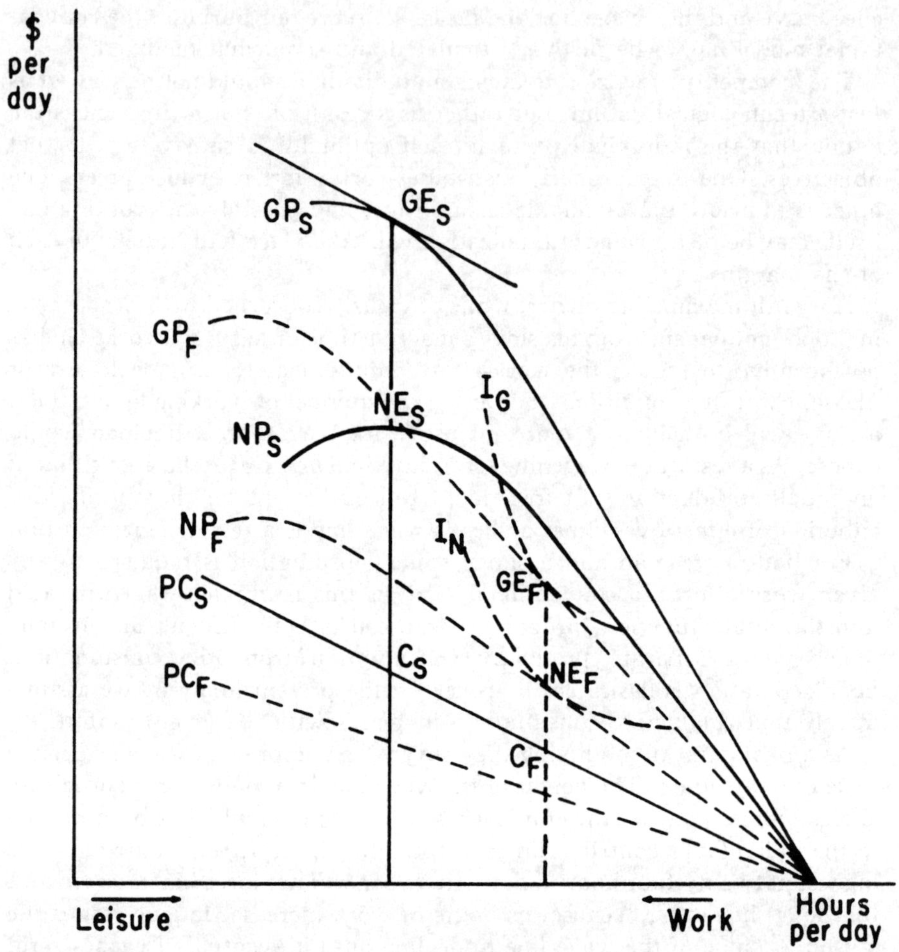

FIGURE II

the respective net product curves—the gross product curves from which productive consumption is netted. NE_S is the equilibrium point for a slave, since there his net output is highest. The consumption associated with this level of effort is C_S; NE_F is the equilibrium point for a freeman.[3]

Let us look at the problem from a different angle. In the analysis underlying Figure II, it is implicitly assumed that the nonhuman wealth of the free individual is zero; he owns no assets, neither is he a debtor. Thus, the curve

[3] I_G and I_N represent a single utility level; productive consumption is netted from the former to obtain the latter.

GP_F represents his entire market-opportunity set, from which he chooses Point GE_F. Consider, however, a net debtor who has to repay an amount $NE_S = GE_S - C_S$—the maximum net output for a slave.[4] To be able to pay that amount *and* to stay alive, the individual has to exert himself to the limit; he has to produce at Point GE_S on GP_S and to consume at C_S. At any other point on GP_S (or any of the others requiring less effort) the value of output would not suffice to meet both loan payment and productive consumption need. It is clear that due to his extreme poverty, his "choice" is limited to a single point. Note that at NE_S, the NP_S curve is horizontal and the net marginal product of his time is zero.

More generally, the move from GP_S to GP_F and the move of the equilibrium points associated with these curves can be viewed as continuous, and dependent on the level of wealth. As wealth declines, the individual chooses to operate on higher curves. Equating on the margin takes place constantly as GP_S is approached. PE_S is the limiting point of the process where the individual operates under conditions of the most extreme poverty.[5]

In the absence of policing costs, it is immaterial whether we designate the individual as a freeman who chooses to be at GE_S and to consume at C_S, or whether we call him a slave whose owner forces him to operate at Point GE_S and supplies him with consumption goods at C_S. If the foregoing is correct, and if policing cost is the only relevant aspect absent in the above analysis, then the determination whether the poorest individual will be a slave or a freeman rests entirely on the costs of policing.

It will later be pointed out, however, that in the presence of policing costs the distinction is substantive. A person who borrows an amount as large as $GE_S - C_S$ could not remain free under the prevailing institutional arrangements. Thus empirically a quantum gap exists between the wealth status of "slaves" and that of "freemen." The term "slave" seems cogent, then, not only to characterize a worker under a particular kind of contract, but also to differentiate him in terms of wealth from even the poorest freeman who will not, in general, be nearly as destitute.

Returning to the comparison between the two classes of workmen, two immediate and major implications appear. (1) The total output and, therefore, the measured "productivity" of a slave will be higher than that of an equally productive free worker. Equilibrium for the former is at GE_S; the latter will choose Point GE_F. (2) The productive consumption of a slave will be correspondingly higher, at C_S, while that of a freeman will be at C_F. It will

[4] To simplify, the analysis is confined to one period.

[5] The same basic notion underlies the derivation of the supply of labor when asset holdings decline to the minimum consistent with survival; this point is made by Yoram Barzel & Richard J. McDonald, Assets, Subsistence, and the Supply Curve of Labor, 63 Am. Econ. Rev. 621 (1973).

be shown below that these two implications still hold when the assumption of zero policing costs is dropped.[6] Therefore, it is not inappropriate to examine the evidence right here.

The findings of Fogel and Engerman strongly confirm these two hypotheses: they found both that slaves were more productive and that they consumed more calories. With respect to productivity, the main finding is that "southern slave farms were 28 per cent more efficient than southern free farms,"[7] where efficiency is measured in terms of *total* factor productivity. The findings on productivity are for whole farms, in which some free labor joined that of slaves. However, where slaves provide a greater proportion of a farm's labor the measured productivity also rises.[8]

Our model predicts a higher output per man, but not necessarily both more effort and more hours: it is only necessary that one of the two be higher. With respect to hours, the evidence is ambiguous. Although Fogel and Engerman did not find longer daily hours for slaves, they did discover more time-input along a whole array of other margins: earlier age for starting

[6] The perspective in interpreting observed behavior, however, will change rather sharply.

[7] 1 Fogel & Engerman 142. The findings on productivity are by no means universally accepted. A number of reasons indicating a bias in the findings are given by (among others) Paul A. David & Peter Temin, *supra* note 1; and by Gavin Wright, Prosperity, Progress and American Slavery, in Reckoning with Slavery 302 (1976). They do not, however, provide a comprehensive recomputation to show that the results would be reversed. Wright also offers a critique of the Fogel and Engerman economies-of-scale argument. I find it even less persuasive than that on productivity.

[8] Indeed, the measured "economies of scale to farm size" may simply be due to the increasing proportion of slaves on the larger plantations. Assume quite arbitrarily that a slave works twice as hard as a freeman. Then the measure of labor input has to be doubled for its slave component. This would affect the productivity measure by a factor of $[(L_s \times 2 + L_f)/(L_s + L_f)]^{0.58}$ where L_s and L_f are the respective shares of slaves and of free labor and 0.58 is labor share in total input (2 Fogel & Engerman 132). In the table below, data on the share of slave labor by farm size is read from 1 *id*. at 195, fig. 44. The third column is the calculated correction of the productivity measure.

Persons per Farm	Per cent Slaves	Productivity Correction Factor
1–10	11%	1.062
11–20	48%	1.255
21–30	73%	1.374
31–40	81%	1.411
41–50	86%	1.433
51–100	91%	1.455
100+	95%	1.473

Since the ratio of slaves to total labor increases with farm size, the correction factor for productivity is correlated with farm size and therefore is not easy to distinguish from Fogel and Engerman's estimate of the scale economy to farm size.

Indirect support for this relation and for the productiveness of slaves is given by the observation that capital/man ratio rises with productivity as would be predicted by a conventional factor proportions analysis. "[O]n large plantations slaves generally worked on better land than free southern farmers and had more equipment." 1 *id*. at 210.

work, higher labor force participation by women, more work by the "disabled," and longer working life.[9]

The intensity of work is just one of the factors affecting the desirability of a job. The conclusion that slaves worked more intensively than freemen leads, by analogy, to the corollary that work assigned to slaves would have offered fewer amenities than the tasks performed by freemen.[10]

Consider now some of the large-scale activities in cotton plantations which required coordinated effort by a large number of workers. Such effort yielded, according to the evidence in Fogel and Engerman, most impressive results. "[T]he slave plantations of the newer southern states exceeded the average efficiency of free northern farms by 53 per cent."[11] The number of slaves in these plantations was large. "[T]he county average in the alluvial regions of short-staple cotton production ranged as high as one hundred twenty-five slaves per holding."[12] In spite of the higher productivity and the implicit higher wages accompanying such intensely coordinated effort, freemen did not choose to work in these plantations. "Economies of scale were achieved only with slave labor. There were no large scale southern farms based on free wage labor."[13] The reason is not hard to find. Olmsted, for instance, notes that the "stupid, plodding, machine-like manner in which they labor, is painful to witness"[14] and elsewhere cites an owner saying, "You never could depend on white men, and you couldn't *drive* them any; they wouldn't stand it."[15] Little wonder that freemen refused to pay the psychic price apparently necessary to maintain the large "efficient" scale. There was no reason, of course, for slave owners to spare their slaves such a regimen.[16]

[9] 1 *id.* at 207-09. More recently, Olson and Fogel have suggested that annual hours for slaves were shorter than for free northern farmers. If this is so, our model implies a more intense effort. Their findings, however, are based on a mixture of observations on slaves and freemen and are not entirely satisfactory. John Olson & Robert William Fogel, Clock Time vs. Real Time: A Comparison of the Length of the Work Years in Northern and Southern Agriculture (1974) (unpublished paper at U. of Rochester).

[10] A related prediction is that a slave with a comparative advantage in performing a job where amenities are important would have been more likely to buy his own freedom than other slaves. As a slave, his consumption of job amenities relative to other goods was high. When freed, however, he would have been willing to work harder to get more market goods. Note that this argument hinges on the initial presence of costs of policing him as a slave. (See discussion on "self-purchase" pp. 18-21 *infra*).

[11] 1 Fogel & Engerman 200.

[12] *Id.* at 200.

[13] *Id.* at 194.

[14] 2 Frederick Law Olmsted, Cotton Kingdom 202 (1861) [hereinafter cited as Olmsted].

[15] 1 *id.* at 83 (italics in original); 1 Fogel & Engerman 205 also cite this and the preceding quotation.

[16] In the U.S. South the comparison was often by color. The fundamental distinction, however, is between freemen and slaves. " 'It is a known fact,' wrote a leading member of the

The attempt by Fogel and Engerman to extol the "superiority of the plantation system of organization," and to conclude that the slaves' labor was of "superior quality" is entirely meaningless. There is no reason to think that white slaves would have performed differently or that freed slaves would have been willing to maintain that effort. The "special quality" of plantation labor was simply "slave quality."[17]

Carrying forward the hypothesis that slaves would have been expected to perform the less desirable tasks, consider now a broader interpretation of the term "amenities" to include the health conditions of different locations. Engerman notes that "the healthier areas apparently attracted more whites relative to blacks [i.e. slaves], leaving the relatively unhealthier areas with almost completely black populations."[18] This is consistent with the prediction that freemen will have more job amenities than slaves can obtain.[19]

Another dimension is the amount of leisure. A major difference between northern and southern agriculture is that little agricultural work can be accomplished during the winter months in the North. Even indoor work was formerly limited by the paucity of artificial light, therefore labor alternated with large amounts of leisure. In the South, however, the winter days were relatively long and the soil was workable. This difference may explain why slavery, at least within agriculture, was confined to hot climates and seldom played a role in the northern United States or in other less temperate regions.[20] More direct evidence relates to the production of sugar, where seasonal variation in labor requirements seemed low: "During slavery [in British Guiana] field and manufacturing operations were carefully timed and co-ordinated with one another and with the weather to permit the produc-

---

plantocracy, 'that without compulsion . . . [manumitted slaves] will not engage in agricultural labor. Wages will not induce them to undertake it . . . A state of slavery alone can ensure such labor from them.' " Jerome S. Handler, The Unappropriated People: Freedmen in the Slave Society of Barbados 117 (1974).

[17] Fogel himself makes the same point. Robert William Fogel, Three Phases of Cliometric Research on Slavery and its Aftermath, 65 Am. Econ. Rev., pt. 2, at 37 (Papers & Proceedings, May 1975).

[18] Stanley L. Engerman, Comments on the Study of Race and Slavery, in Race and Slavery in the Western Hemisphere: Quantitative Studies 200 (Stanley Engerman & Eugene Genovese eds. 1975).

[19] A distinction should be drawn between, on the one hand, the ability to come up with evidence consistent with a hypothesis and, on the other hand, the specification in advance of what evidence will be sought that could refute the hypothesis. The former procedure is inferior since the researcher may, consciously or otherwise, bypass evidence inconsistent with the hypothesis. Some of the evidence presented here is, unfortunately, of the former kind.

[20] The higher level of schooling in the northern farm sector of the United States, as compared with the southern, may also be explained partly by the long, severe winters which reduced the alternative cost of time. That slavery was also unimportant in the northern parts of the Roman Empire is noted by William L. Westermann, The Slave Systems of Greek and Roman Antiquity 131 (1955).

tion of two full crops of sugar every twelve months. Emancipation and the increasingly irregular nature of the labor supply, however, gradually forced planters to abandon this practice in favor of single cropping."[21]

To analyze some aspects of consumption by slaves, we begin with the question of energy. A slaveholder who starved his workers would be comparable to a truck owner who deprived his truck of gasoline. So long as owners required higher effort than they could obtain from freemen, the energy input for slaves had to be correspondingly higher. Fogel and Engerman conclusively demonstrate that slaves' diet contained substantially more calories—in excess of 10 per cent—than freemen's.[22] The fact bears directly on their more intensive effort regardless of whether it constituted "good treatment."

Calories, of course, can be obtained in a variety of ways. Abstracting for a moment from other dietary considerations, to the extent that a freeman will select any food at a price above a basic minimum per calorie, we should observe a difference between his diet and a slave's, since poverty will constrain slaves to the least expensive choice. Fogel and Engerman's data show that such differences did exist. "Much has been made of the fact that corn was the principal grain consumed by slaves, while wheat was the principal grain in the free diet. Yet from a nutritional standpoint, both are excellent foods. . . ."[23]

It would be expected that the diet of slaves would be high in just such nutritional qualities as well as in calories, since food "good for them" by contemporary standards would keep up their productive strength. Like children, they would have been forced to swallow their pills but they would not be given a lollipop as reward.[24] Freemen, on the other hand, would not concern themselves merely with diet optimization. Here, also, the evidence points to a difference in consumption behavior. "[B]oth slaves and freemen ate large quantities of potatoes, slaves consumed virtually nothing but sweet potatoes, although most of the potatoes consumed by freemen were white. The significance of this dichotomy is that sweet potatoes are much better food than white potatoes."[25] So the empirical observation that slaves were fed a "better" diet has little bearing on the question of how well they were treated in general.

[21] Michael Moohr, The Economic Impact of Slave Emancipation in British Guiana, 1832-1852, 25 Econ. Hist. Rev. 588, 599 (2d ser. 1972).

[22] 1 Fogel & Engerman 109-15. It is likely that (within the relevant range) the income elasticity of calories is positive. Given their higher income, freemen are expected to consume more calories. Fogel and Engerman's finding, then, is in spite of this factor.

[23] *Id.* at 113.

[24] The element of compulsion indicated here and in the next paragraph has to do with policing costs to be discussed in the next section.

[25] 1 Fogel & Engerman 113.

There is no need to dwell on the medical treatment and hygienic conditions of slaves; the situation completely parallels that of diet.[26] The distinction between slaves and freemen, however, is most strikingly illustrated by the following: "The *punishment* for slaves who failed to keep themselves personally clean was a *forced* scrubbing by the driver and two other blacks,"[27] and "sometimes the negroes were told at night that any one who came into the field the next morning without being clean would be whipped."[28]

The Policing of Slaves

Slaves, as pointed out earlier, were extremely poor. This was obviously so of forced slaves, most of whose possessions were stolen from them. It was also true of voluntary slaves who were enslaved when unable to repay loans obtained with their own persons as collateral.

As an alternative to slavery one may conceive of conditions where a borrower would have been allowed to remain free, sell his services in the labor market, and use his earnings to provide for his own consumption and for loan payments to his creditor. That this did not occur implies that creditors insisted on (voluntary) slavery because it entailed sufficiently lower policing costs. Since policing costs seem pivotal throughout the institution of slavery, various aspects of such costs are examined below.

In a world in which policing (and transacting) is costless, joint maximization of output will prevail, as demonstrated by Coase.[29] Not only is income maximized, its distribution is also clearly determined by the pattern of ownership. As shown earlier, under such conditions the net income of forced slaves would be zero.

Consider now a world in which policing is costly, and maximization takes place only subject to the additional constraint. Any given method of policing slaves will consume some resources. Moreover, if diminishing returns prevail, the optimal use of resources will necessarily fall short of that required to eliminate all policing problems. Therefore, slaves will not produce to their capacity, and even gross output (prior to subtraction of policing costs) will be less than if policing were costless.

[26] On the ground of striving for productivity, slaves' medical care would be better than freemen's, but for wealth considerations the reverse is true. So we can predict neither a differential in health levels nor in life expectancy for slaves compared with freemen. The evidence presented in Fogel and Engerman shows little difference between the two. The ambivalence of slaves towards their own health is illustrated by the following: "They [slaves] conceal pills . . . and declare that they have swallowed them . . . [as they] were loth to be made quite well enough to have to go to work again." 1 Olmsted 118-19.

[27] 1 Fogel & Engerman 122 (emphasis added).

[28] 1 Olmsted, *supra* note 14, at 200.

[29] R. H. Coase, The Problem of Social Cost, 3 J. Law & Econ. 1 (1960).

But now the income of slaves is no longer zero. First, since policing is optimized, a certain amount of "shirking" and similar behavior will take place. Second, "policing" may take the form of directly remunerating slaves. The value of the *net* output of a slave, however, has to exceed the pay of freemen providing the same kind of services, otherwise the incentive to hold slaves will disappear. Under these conditions, some positive remuneration to a slave is consistent with maximization, even though it would be a contradiction in terms were policing costs zero.

The costs of policing a slave consist of identifying, in terms of Figure II, the curves GP_S and PC_S (and particularly Points GE_S and C_S on them) and then enforcing the appropriate performance. Errors in overestimating productive capability and in underestimating the requisite consumption are costly both to the owner and to the slave. Errors in the opposite direction, however, while costly to the owner, constitute a transfer favorable to the slave.[30] Since it is argued that policing costs are at the heart of the entire institution of slavery, we wish to derive and test implications of their presence. Several specific policing problems are discussed in the following pages.[31]

A. *Policing of Consumption*

One class of observations with regard to slavery is so universal that it is routinely taken for granted with no attempt at explanation: provision for consumption at whatever level was *in kind*. Housing was on plantation grounds, clothing was distributed periodically, medical care as required, and food rations usually weekly. Why did owners not hand out the value of these goods in cash, to be used as the slaves pleased? Payments in kind, particularly when distributed according to a simple formula, are often explained as a way to reduce the cost of transacting. In my view, that was not the fundamental motive for this practice. The explanation rather lies in the distinction between slaves maximizing their own utility and owners maximizing their slaves' (net) productive capacity. Because a slave would be highly unlikely to consider the maximization of his productivity as a prime goal in spending any money he might have, his freedom of choice would almost certainly result in output loss. An owner directly controlling allocation would obviously come closer to maximizing the value of that net output. As Olmsted noted, one owner who pondered whether to rent out some of his hands "did not know whether he ought to let them go, though. They were worked hard, and had too much liberty, and were acquiring bad habits.

[30] This asymmetry, however, would make the term of the contract less favorable to a freeman when offering himself as a slave.

[31] The attention to various policing devices is not according to their importance but rather to my ability to advance explanations.

They earned money by overwork, and spent it for whisky, and got a habit of roaming about and *taking care of themselves*."[32]

Slaves quite often were able to earn extra income by means such as "moonlighting," raising food on their allotted patches, hunting, or stealing. To the extent that this income was used to supplement their food intake, owners had no reason to object; if anything, productiveness would be enhanced. Quite another matter was the acute problem cited by Olmsted; alcohol is notorious for its adverse effect on productivity. Our prediction therefore would be that masters would have spent resources to prevent slaves from obtaining it. Fogel and Engerman do not dwell on alcohol consumption, but the subject is mentioned about a dozen times by Stampp.[33] His discussions center on how owners attempted to deny slaves access to liquor with the single exception of Christmas drinking, which was condoned.

Olmsted time and again refers to the matter. He tells of a planter who "has a store, usually well supplied with articles that they [the slaves] most want, which are purchased in large quantities, and sold to them at wholesale prices; thus giving them a great advantage in dealing with him rather than with the grog-shops."[34] He describes other practices which are clearly inconsistent with minimizing transaction costs, as owners spent resources to prevent slaves from trading. For instance, "the general allowance of food . . . is distributed to them . . . on the better managed plantations, sometimes on Wednesday, to prevent their . . . selling it for whiskey on Sunday."[35] And, "they [slaves] generally save from their ration of meal . . . too often the exchange was for whiskey, which, against his [the owner's] rules, they obtained of some rascally white people in the neighborhood, and kept concealed. They were very fond of whiskey, and sometimes much injured themselves with it."[36] Finally, "the manager endeavours to encourage this practice [of buying flour]; and that they may spend their money for flour instead of liquor, he furnishes it to them at rather less than what it costs him at wholesale . . . each [of the white liquor sellers] have a standing offer of much more than the intrinsic value of their land, from the manager, to induce them to move away."[37]

The hypothesis is here refuted that goods were given to slaves merely to reduce transaction costs. Rather, observed behavior is consistent with the hypothesis that where slaves' desired consumption patterns conflicted with their productivity, masters acted to induce the latter.[38]

[32] 1 Olmsted 60.

[33] Kenneth M. Stampp, The Peculiar Institution (1956).

[34] 1 Olmsted 254-55.

[35] *Id*. at 102.

[36] *Id*. at 103.

[37] 2 *id*. at 196.

[38] It may appear that some constraints on drinking imposed under the British Truck System

B. *Self-Purchase*

The costliness of policing the effort and consumption of slaves has additional important implications. Consider, hypothetically, capital markets in which, first, future labor earnings are not discounted more heavily than earnings of other kinds of capital and, second, where costs of policing work effort are zero. Under these conditions a slave should be able to buy out his "contract," but his subsequent performance would not change one iota.[39] The value of a forced slave to his owner reflects conditions where he is driven to the limit (Point GE_S in Figure II) and every ounce of productiveness is squeezed out of him. The amount he will have to pay his owner to buy his freedom is the present value of his output under these most adverse circumstances. Being a slave, he has no capital and can finance himself only through the loan market; to repay his loan he will have to work precisely as hard as when he was a slave.

When policing costs are positive, slaves will not always be more productive than freemen. Net of these costs, the GP_S curve in Figure II is not necessarily higher than GP_F since the former will in general require more policing. Only in a subset of activities, then, will slaves be more productive. To economize on the costs of policing, owners may sell their contracts to slaves whose comparative advantage is in other activities. Granted that capital market forces pull in the opposite direction—the discount rate facing a slaveholder (based in part on placing a lien on slaves' output) is likely to be lower than that facing a freed slave who has only his own future earnings as collateral for securing a loan. Nevertheless, when occupations or activities are compared, the narrowing of the difference between GP_S and GP_F reduces the profitability of slavery. Thus the observed "greater productivity of slaves" occurs nót because slavery is more productive per se[40] but because slavery endured only where it proved to be more productive.

We are unable to predict what types of slaves would be expected to buy their freedom.[41] Available evidence, however, is consistent with the notion that policing costs were high for slaves who subsequently bought their own contracts. As indicated earlier, in the absence of policing costs a forced slave would need his entire working life to pay for his freedom. In actual cases,

are of similar nature. These are discussed in George W. Hilton, the British Truck System in the Nineteenth Century, 65 J. Pol. Econ. 237 (1957). These, however, were by voluntary arrangement. A possible explanation is that the absenteeism associated with drinking decreased the firm's output by an amount greater than the lost wages of the absentees.

[39] Note that if these conditions were to apply universally, *forced* slavery would never emerge.

[40] This is the position Fogel and Engerman take.

[41] Note, however, that "in the West Indies, . . . slave domestics and tradesmen generally had greater chances for manumission than did field slaves. This was so not only because domestics and artisans had more personal contact with their masters but also because they had relatively greater opportunities to acquire cash resources to effect self-purchase." Jerome S. Handler, *supra* note 16, at 53.

payments sometimes extended over two or more decades, although "[s]ome skilled slaves were able to accumulate enough capital to purchase their freedom within a decade."[42] In such a case, the sum of payments made within a decade provided a higher net present value than the individual's remaining lifetime potential as a slave.

A somewhat different arrangement, pointing however to the effect of the same set of forces, allowed a slave to sell his own labor and to take care of himself while paying his master an annual fee. Full freedom was eschewed by these slaves, perhaps because of the precarious status of free blacks and the loss of the master's protection. The master, on his part, reduced the costs of collecting his fee by retaining formal ownership in his slave. In any case, the observation that "most slaves eagerly accepted that arrangement when it was offered to them"[43] attests the advantage of reduced policing.

In the United States, the number of slaves who actually redeemed themselves does not seem to have been substantial. Although free blacks lived throughout the South, their numbers were small and their freedom was constrained in various ways. The presence of large enclaves of free blacks in the South would have made escape by slaves much easier. (Indeed, as a corollary, the earlier disappearance of white servitude may have been due largely to the difficulty in identifying escaped bond servants.) It is not surprising that the selling or giving of freedom to slaves was frowned on both by public opinion and often by state legislation.[44]

The individual slave owner could have used the lure of manumission to induce higher output. On the other hand he had an incentive to let it be known that under no circumstances would he sell his slaves their contracts, since he thereby forestalled any effort on their part to reduce their own value to him. It was not unheard of for slaves to risk acts of insubordination or malingering in the hope of lowering the costs of buying their freedom.[45]

[42] 1 Fogel & Engerman 151.

[43] Kenneth M. Stampp, *supra* note 32, at 73.

[44] " 'It was admitted to be a rule,' observed a parliamentary commission which investigated Barbado's legal and judicial system in 1823, 'that every Negro is presumed to be a slave unless he can legally prove the contrary.' " Jerome S. Handler, *supra* note 16, at 59. Manumission fees (*id*. at 39-44) might have been imposed for the same reason.

[45] Olmsted tells of an estate executor who had "one very smart man, who, . . . ought to be earning for the estate $150 a year, . . . yet those wages for a year, . . . had amounted to but $18, while he had paid for medical attendance upon him [$] 45. Having failed in every other way to make him earn anything, he proposed to him that he should purchase his freedom and go to Philadelphia where he had a brother. He told him if he would earn a certain sum ($400 I believe), and pay it over to the estate for himself, he would give him his free papers. The man agreed to the arrangement, and by his overwork in a tobacco factory, and some assistance from his free brother, soon paid the sum agreed upon, and was sent to Philadelphia." 1 Olmsted 99.

Self-purchase took place at a small, but steady, rate in Barbados (and elsewhere in the West Indies). One reason for the resistance to self-purchase given by the archdeacon of Barbados was that "the slave will lessen his value by willful misconduct, with a view to obtain his freedom at a low price." Jerome S. Handler, *supra* note 16, at 36; see also his tables at 51-52.

C. *Life Expectancy*

The mortality rate in childbearing was higher for southern white women than for slaves, but the death rate among infants to age one was higher for slaves. This leads Fogel and Engerman to note the "strange paradox of planters who treated pregnant [slave] women and new mothers quite well while abusing their offspring."[46]

But compare the market value of a female slave at the childbearing age to that of an infant: about tenfold.[47] The mother's market value of some $400 to $500 implied that a slave owner would be willing to spend up to that amount to save her life, whereas the high discount rate on human capital and the prohibition of voluntary white slavery might well have precluded a poor, but free, white family from raising such an amount to protect the mother. On the other hand, a slave owner would spend only up to $50 or so to save an infant slave, while the family of a white infant might be able and willing to spend considerably more.

In some respects the slave status offered an advantage. It is possible to show that under certain conditions a free man will, if permitted, sell himself into slavery.[48] For instance, given that same high discount rate to human capital, a change in economic conditions might turn the present value of a "free" child negative, although as a slave he might command a positive price.[49] Under such conditions, the legal prohibition on white slavery put freemen at a disadvantage. One indication may be the higher maternity death rate among whites than among slaves, as just noted. A more dramatic case in point relates to crimes punishable by death. "In cases such as murder, the sentences of slaves who would otherwise have been executed were frequently converted to severe whipping, coupled with exportation to another state or a foreign country" so that "the state could recover a substantial part of the value of a slave that would have been lost through his execution."[50] This avenue was foreclosed to freemen.[51]

[46] 1 Fogel & Engerman at 123.

[47] Values are read from *id*. at 72, 76, Fig. 15, 18.

[48] This apparently was observed at times in the U.S. See Kenneth M. Stampp, *supra* note 32, at 92. It was common practice in the ancient world and until recently in Africa.

[49] "Famine . . . encouraged an intermediary variety of slave. . . . children, sold into slavery by their families in times of need . . . This resort, to the sale of children, may have been widespread in cases of extreme dearth . . . ." And again, "a British official, attempting to check the traffic, intercepted and freed 200 children in less than three months!" Allan G.B. Fisher & Humphrey J. Fisher, Slavery and Muslim Society in Africa 62-63 (1970). (One wonders how the term "freed" may be interpreted).

[50] 1 Fogel & Engerman 144-45. Consider also the following: "In many cases, he [a Portuguese official] asserted, the slave owed his very life to slavery, for some of the slaves brought from the interior were prisoners of war, and would have been executed but for the profitable market ready to receive them." Henry W. Nevinson, A Modern Slavery 54 (1st Schocken ed. 1968) (1st ed. 1906). Notice, however, that the number of prisoners is not independent of slavery.

[51] This was not always so. For a long period, English convicts were sent to the colonies as indentured servants.

D. *The Policing of Performance*

Certain plantation activities involved the simultaneous work of large numbers of slaves, and frequently such work was assigned under a "task system" of uniform daily quotas.[52] That such a policy was followed despite obvious disparities in strength and capability among workers allows the derivation of additional implications regarding both life expectancy and policing costs.

Consider the occasional reference to slaves expiring from exhaustion. Since they were valuable assets, it might appear that only sadism on the part of the owner would allow such an outcome. However, a possible alternative explanation is consistent with a policy of wealth maximization.

Two questions arise. Instead of the task system, why was not each individual assigned a task commensurate with his ability? And, how was the size of any uniform quota determined? An answer to either query would certainly rest largely on the costs of policing. Had it been apparent that the quota would be set to the perceived ability of any particular slave, that individual would have had incentive to understate his capability. But where the quota was set at some "customary" level, no such incentive was present. A standard could, of course, be imposed only on a uniform basis. The less able slave might be driven to exhaustion in a vain attempt to meet the quota, and the signal to abler workers would be clear.

An implication of the model, then, is that occasionally slaves of wealth-maximizing owners would die of exhaustion.[53] One statement supporting the hypothesis is: "Continuously, or at least for long intervals, they [masters] drove their slaves at such a pace that was bound, sooner or later, to injure their health. Such hard driving seldom occurred on the smaller plantations and farms in urban centers; it was decidedly a phenomenon of the large

[52] The decision as to when to monitor output rather than input is of considerable interest. Monitoring inputs requires continuous policing while monitoring output requires policing only after the job is completed but must be supplemented by control of output quality. A hint of how the choice was made is given in the following. "The main object of this operation is to kill all the seeds of weeds, or of rice, on the ground. Ordinarily it is done by tasks—a certain number of small divisions of the field being given to each hand to burn in a day; but owing to a more than usual amount of rain having fallen lately, and some other causes, making the work harder in some places than others, the women were now working by the day, under a direction of a 'driver,' a negro man, who walked about among them, taking care that they left nothing unburned. Mr. X inspected the ground they had gone over, to see whether the driver had done his duty. It had been sufficiently well burned, but not more than a quarter as much ground had been gone over, he said, as was usually burned in task-work—and he thought they had been very lazy, and reprimanded them for it. The driver made some little apology, but the women offered no reply, keeping steadily, and it seemed sullenly, on at their work." 1 Olmsted 243. (*Id.* at 245 brings up the issue of monitoring quality).

[53] Owners had to be careful, however, not to err in imposing too high a quota. A mechanism was provided to correct such an error. "If after a hard day's labor, he [the driver] sees that the gang has been overtasked, owing to a miscalculation of the difficulty of the work, he may excuse the completion of the tasks; but he is not allowed to extend them." *Id.* at 249.

plantation."[54] In quite different circumstances, owners were less subtle. "It was the usual fate of such laggards [in slave caravans] to be killed by their disappointed masters, anxious to discourage any thought of feigning incapacity as a means of escape, just as in the Congo area it was usual to kill slaves who fell ill while carrying ivory."[55]

Some variability may be present among machines also. As the notion of "shirking" does not apply to machines, we would not expect a machine to be driven to destruction. The maximizing behavior of slaves, in the above instance, is the source of their plight.

The hypothesis has a couple of closely related implications. One is that slaves who fulfilled their quota early in the day would not have been required to perform additional tasks. "Short hours" for the abler slaves were, indeed, occasionally observed.[56] Any variation in ability around a required performance level involves a cost (which constitutes a lower bound of the saving in policing costs required to operate individual quotas); the larger this variability, the larger the cost. Another implication, then, is that within a plantation, uniformity of productive ability among the slaves would be highly valued. On this issue several rather scanty pieces of evidence are present in Olmsted. For instance, he observed that "on [large] plantations on the Mississippi, . . . the laborers were, to a large degree, tall, slender, sinewy, young men. . . ."[57] Elsewhere he says, "twenty men, or boys, for none of them looked as if they were full-grown, were ploughing, . . . Their task was nominally an acre and a quarter a day. . . ."[58]

More important was the system of classification of slaves. "The field-hands are all divided into four classes, according to their physical capacities; the children beginning as 'quarter-hands,' advancing to 'half-hands,' and then to 'three-quarter hands'; and, finally, when mature, and able-bodied, healthy and strong, to 'full hands.' "[59]

The monitoring of a slave's effort could relate either to his output or to his effort. In regard to the latter, the apparent contradiction between observations pointing respectively to the "hard work" performed by slaves and to their "laziness" in performing their "duties" may simply reflect the views of outsiders observing different degrees and forms of supervision.[60] In some

[54] Kenneth M. Stampp, *supra* note 32, at 81.

[55] Allan G.B. Fisher & Humphrey J. Fisher, *supra* note at 48, at 78.

[56] 1 Fogel & Engerman 206. Also, "The more industrious and active hands finish them [their tasks] often by two o'clock." 1 Olmsted 248.

[57] *Id.* at 13-14.

[58] *Id.* at 244. See also 2 *id.* at 146.

[59] 1 *id.* at 246. He then describes additional elements in the classification system and, on the following page, several specific tasks.

[60] If output can be monitored, the *threat* of the whip will be an incentive to perform. If only inputs are monitored, when the whip is not immediately present all effort will cease. Note also

cases, slaves were rewarded with positive payments for increased output. In others, the only incentive to work was the whip, and effort predictably tended to fall to zero when the overseer was not at hand.[61]

It is puzzling why Fogel and Engerman so assiduously resist the notion of "laziness" and try to impute to slaves the "Protestant ethic."[62] Granted that owners had reason to encourage such an attitude, the slaves had at least as strong incentive to violate it.[63] Fogel and Engerman's castigation of Stampp for not recognizing the slave's "superior" work attitude seems wholly misplaced. Idleness rather than adherence to the work ethic would have been the rational behavior.[64] Indeed, as suggested earlier, slaves would be kept only where the cost of extra supervision coupled with remaining uncontrolled shirking was less than the productivity due to the policing effort.

VOLUNTARY SLAVERY

The institution of voluntary slavery poses two major problems. Why would a free individual commit himself as a slave? And, given that he does so, in what ways, if at all, will his status differ from that of a forced slave?[65]

Most of what can be said on the first question is embodied in previous sections and requires here only a brief summary. The rate of interest one has to pay for a loan depends on the security that he can offer, including future labor earnings. As the fraction of future earnings to be assigned as lien increases, the lender tends to require a contract securing not only the flow of labor earnings but also the capital asset—the person himself. The reason seems to be that the increasing cost of policing the loan makes possession of the asset preferable to a mere claim on the income flow it generates—itself an

that if equipment failure will increase leisure, an incentive is present to induce it. "Sabotage" was a constant complaint by owners.

[61] "[A]s often as he [the overseer] visited one end of the line of operations, the hands at the other end would discontinue their labor, until he turned to ride towards them again." 1 Olmsted 208.

[62] "The logic of his [Stampp's] position made it difficult to acknowledge that ordinary slaves could be diligent workers, imbued like their masters with a Protestant ethic."

[63] Olmsted records the explicit reaction of one owner as follows: "Slaves never really felt under any moral obligation to obey their masters. Faithful service was preached to them as a Christian duty, and they pretended to acknowledge it, but the fact was that they were obedient just so far as they saw that they must be to avoid punishment. . . ." 2 Olmsted 101. This notion is captured well by Stampp. "Masters measured the success of their methods by the extent to which their interest in a maximum of work of good quality prevailed over the slaves' predilection for a minimum of work of indifferent quality." Kenneth M. Stampp, *supra* note 32, at 54. See also *id*. at 75, 100.

[64] Note that we have no reason to expect idleness to be carried over from slavery to freedom—from conditions where remuneration does not depend on performance to those where it does.

[65] A third question is: Why do all modern societies (and many ancient ones) ban such an arrangement?

object of choice to the borrower. The borrower, presumably, could have avoided the possibility of enslavement by paying a higher interest while offering inferior security. Obviously some, viewing these latter costs as excessive, chose instead to offer themselves as security.

What can be said regarding the condition of voluntary slaves? In Figure II the curve GP_S is drawn for a person who owes an amount $GE_S - C_S = NE_S$ and the curve GP_F for a person who is neither a debtor nor a creditor. A person who is not a net debtor does not have to submit to slavery. A person who owes a small fraction of NE_S perhaps can maintain his freedom, but presumably he will lose the status before the fraction becomes unity. Abstracting from a person's legal status, suppose he owes some fraction of NE_S. At that level of wealth, the corresponding productivity curve is somewhere between GP_F and GP_S and the equilibrium point between GE_F and GE_S. Such a person's net income exceeds his subsistence requirement; he could, for instance, accumulate assets.

If we now consider the entire set of individuals who, having posted themselves as security are unable to pay their debts, it seems clear that we can anticipate a whole spectrum of degrees of default and an equally broad range in the severity of their slave contracts. On average, we would expect their contracts to be more lenient than those of forced slaves who, by the very nature of their position, lose all the income that can be extracted from them.

One would expect, for example, that voluntary slaves should obtain more consumption goods than forced slaves, should be allowed more freedom of action (as their incentive to escape is less), should be able to work in occupations with more amenities, and should more easily be able to buy their freedom.

Westermann's description of slavery in Greece and Rome lends support to the last three expectations. With respect to the first, too little is said to permit inference. A difficulty with Westermann's description is that most of the time he does not differentiate voluntary and forced slavery. Nevertheless, the overall impression is that voluntary slaves were engaged in a wide range of crafts, were allowed considerable freedom of movement, and could manumit themselves readily.[66] Associated particularly with the right of self-purchase was the quasi-legal right to own property that could be used for manumission.[67] Indeed, Westermann observes that "manumissions had constantly occurred upon a wide scale and the barrier between slavery and freedom had

[66] In Athens in the years 349-329 B.C., out of 79 *former* male slaves only 12 were occupied in agriculture; and out of 56 females, none. Most females were in manufacture and most males in manufacture and distributive service. William L. Westermann, *supra* note 20, at 13. See also *id.* at 35, 68-74. With respect to freedom of movement, it may be observed, for instance, that slaves were often used as messengers.

[67] *Id.* at 83; see also 25.

never been a rigid one."[68] In a few cases, a distinction was made between slaves employed on plantations (*latifundia*) and those employed elsewhere. The treatment of the former seems similar to that of slaves in the American South, including the difficulty of manumission and the way slaves were driven.[69]

In a monograph on slavery in Ptolemaic Egypt, Westermann briefly but explicitly discusses "debtor slaves." Their status ranged from the mild form of "debtor bondage" to full-fledged slavery. In general, slavery terminated when the debt was paid. During slavery, various restrictions were placed on the owner, customarily including a ban on sale abroad, presumably to prevent the imposition of forced slavery.[70]

In Africa, where both voluntary and involuntary slavery were common, some evidence points to different treatment of the two groups. In a brief survey of slavery in five African areas late in the nineteenth century and early in the twentieth, the societies are divided between those that practiced voluntary slavery—Ibo, Ila, and ("to a lesser extent") Ashanti—and those that did not—the Kanuri and the Zanzibaris. "The manumission, or freeing of slaves, was an automatic process among the simpler societies such as the Ila, Ibo, and even among the Ashanti." . . . "Only in the more complex states like the Bornu [where, presumably, lived the Kanuri] and Zanzibar was slavery a status inherited over a number of generations." "In Zanzibar the bulk of the slaves worked on the farms and were an economic benefit just as they were in the southern United States."[71]

The comparison between forced and voluntary slaves makes it clear that indentured servitude is simply one step down in the severity of the "slave contract." Indeed, the indenture contract was not designed to recover past loans but rather to assure increased earning potential to the recipient, secured by a few years of slavelike service (and often accompanied by a substantial severance pay). Similarly, "serfdom" can be viewed as a step away from slavery in that the rights of the lord over his serfs were more constrained, as in the matter of what they might own.[72]

[68] *Id.* at 120. Note also that slaves and freedmen had often the same legal status. See *id.* at 119. One cited instance of limited slavery is that of an indentured son who was to work for the creditor until his father's debt was repaid. *Id.* at 137.

[69] Westermann himself makes this comparison. *Id.* at 154. See also his citation of Cato the Elder. *Id.* at 76.

[70] William L. Westermann, Upon Slavery in Ptolemaic Egypt 48 (1929).

[71] Ronald Cohen, quoted from his introduction to a special supplement, Slavery in Africa, in Trans-action, Jan.-Feb., 1967, at 45. At 54 in the same supplement, Victor Uchendu, Slavery in Southeast Nigeria, explicitly states that for debtor slaves, "the period of their servitude depended on the time it took their primary owners to redeem them."

[72] Slavery is also often compared with conscription and with imprisonment. The assumption of owners' wealth maximization, however, does not seem fruitful in those cases. Another

SOME SPECULATION ON NECESSARY CONDITIONS FOR THE EXISTENCE OF SLAVERY[73]

Slave trade usually involved the capture and the enslavement of previously free men. Such capture is an act of stealing. Although theft is a most pervasive phenomenon, organized stealing among states is usually confined to short periods. The normal course is for looting to be quickly converted into some form of tribute—and the explanation for this is straightforward. Like other objects of theft, loot has greater value to the victim than to the thief, otherwise it would already have been sold to him. Once a relationship of conqueror and conquered has been established, it is advantageous for both parties to transform tribute into cash payments to minimize the resource cost of the transfer. The persistence of forced African slavery therefore poses a puzzle.

In the Roman Empire, slaves were acquired only from border and transborder areas; districts ruled by Rome paid tribute and were sheltered from raids. Thus as the size of the empire expanded the number of new slaves declined. In Africa, however, the thefts of humans continued on a large scale and in a highly organized form for several centuries. Why was the process not converted into tribute? And why was Africa the main source of slaves? The answers, it seems, lie in the uniqueness of the human factor, on the one hand, and in the absence of territorial rights in the African interior, on the other.

As just suggested and as Coase[74] demonstrated, the greater value of an item to its owner than to a thief provides an incentive for a bribe. Moreover, in Coase's own illustration where cattle "steal" the farmer's crop, as long as the farmer's net market value is increased by keeping the cattle away, the means for the bribe payments can be readily found.

With the theft of humans the issue is more problematic. In general, a prospective slave possessing only his human capital *cannot* bribe his captor and still keep his freedom. His pecuniary return, as indicated earlier, may well be higher as a slave than as a freeman. Even if he were willing while remaining free to work as hard as a slave, capital market constraints might still prevent a sufficiently alluring bribe to his captor.

Moreover, slave raiders did not keep control of the invaded territory; rather it was under constant threat of raids from others. In other words, prospective slaves were in the "public domain" and were unable to offer

---

distinction is that although the individual's wealth may exceed NE_S, no direct, legal mechanism is provided for manumission.

[73] Several of the points in this section can be found in Stanley L. Engerman, Some Considerations Relating to Property Rights in Man, 33 J. Econ. Hist. 43 (1973).

[74] R. H. Coase, *supra* note 29.

their raiders an acceptable alternative based on their future local earnings. Thus the relative value of the stolen item loses its meaning in this context. By the same token, the action *does* depend on who is liable for the damage. This is not because the Coase Theorem is incorrect; rather, in this case the distributional effects and transaction costs are essential, and the results obtained by abstracting from them are not applicable. If the slave is fully compensated, he will simply repurchase his freedom and stay in his former activity. But if a freeman is permitted to bribe his captor not to enslave him, in general he will be unable to raise the bribe and so will be enslaved.[75] His "behavior" will, of course, be drastically changed. We conclude, then, that a condition for the emergence of slavery is that the captives be unable to "bribe" their captors to maintain their freedom; that their *pecuniary net* present value as freemen must be lower than their price as slaves.

The value of a slave, obviously, would depend on his skills; but because of policing costs, the valuation of skills in freedom may differ greatly from their value under slavery. Free Europeans possessed market skills much more valuable than those of Africans; but apparently due to the differential in cost of policing, an African slave could command a price almost as great as that of the type of white European who might have been captured. On the other hand, in the era of the transatlantic slave trade the pecuniary net present value when free was in all likelihood considerably higher for a European than for an African, both because of the more valuable skills possessed by the former and because the latter faced a greater threat of recapture. A white man was thus in a better position to compensate a captor for his freedom,[76] and European raids resulted in loot and in various kinds of tribute but not in slavery.

Let us return to the issue of theft. Since transaction costs are not zero, theft does occur, and the state undertakes various measures to curtail the loss it generates. When an asset is stolen from a person, the legal machinery of the state is available to help him attempt recovery. But suppose a human being is stolen within the jurisdiction of a state? In any slave society, the legal status of a slave is almost invariably that of an object; he is not recognized by law as a person. Thus if the "stolen" person is deprived of his legal status by enslavement, how is he to go about reclaiming his "asset"?

States that permitted slavery as a general policy often imposed heavy penalties on forcible enslavement inside their borders.[77] The costs arising

[75] The capital market constraint is fundamentally due to positive "transaction costs." If these costs were zero, the Coase Theorem would apply.

[76] An in-between situation occurred when some war prisoners were freed after ransom was paid for them (which often they became obligated to repay) while other prisoners were sold as slaves. William L. Westermann, The Slave System of Greek and Roman Antiquity, *supra* note 20, at 7, 63, 65, 70.

[77] See, for instance, *id*. at 6.

from theft within the state and with measures to reduce it have to be assessed against benefits from "legitimate" slavery. In the U.S. South, the restriction of slavery to blacks served to retain the bulk of benefits, while the cost to whites of forcibly enslaving free blacks could not have been large. Where the distinction between "genuine" freemen and slaves was more costly to make[78] there was greater incentive to abolish slavery altogether; freemen otherwise were in constant hazard of being snatched inside their own areas.

Concluding Remarks

Slavery is a complex institution marked by greatly varied practices across societies in which it was found. To properly derive hypotheses in this area requires thorough knowledge of the institution. Because of the historical diversity of slavery and of the varying constraints across them, inference about any one society drawn from observations about another is risky. It is difficult, then, to find data for testing a hypothesis which are independent of those used in its formulation.[79] Thus the tests provided here have less power than one would hope.

Forced slavery and, to a lesser degree, voluntary slavery can be viewed as an extreme form of poverty. To keep alive, a slave had to work harder than a freeman, and to be able to maintain the more rigorous work pace he had to be fed more as well and to be provided with adequate "maintenance" such as medical care. The observed high levels of nourishment and of health of American slaves, then, does not necessarily mean that they were well treated; rather it is consistent with their required higher performance level which is also observed.

As a maximizer, a slave would be expected to "malinger," and since policing is costly, some malingering should be observed. Indeed, slavery endured only in areas and occupations where their productivity net of policing costs still exceeded that of freemen; otherwise, selling slaves their freedom was more advantageous. Slavery was viable neither in occupations in which supervision is costly, nor in temperate zones where due to climate much "leisure" was consumed in winter. Where slavery was practiced, the importance of policing costs was demonstrated by the deliberate monitoring of consumption to maintain the slaves' productive capabilities. The task system is another instance where some potential output was sacrificed in order to reduce the cost of supervision.

The whole institution of slavery seems to have hinged on the question of policing costs. In their absence, a slave could always have bought his freedom and involuntary slavery would have disappeared. Voluntary slavery was also the consequence of policing costs, evolving when personal debt

[78] In such instances, the costs of preventing the escape of slaves were also higher.

[79] This problem seems common to much economic history.

became large and the costs of collecting it appeared to be reduced by the enslavement of the debtor.

Since, on the whole, voluntary slaves were not as poor as forced slaves, the former were observed to enjoy more freedom and more amenities than the latter. They also redeemed themselves more readily. Finally, where it was difficult to distinguish slaves from freemen, both the cost of preventing escape and the cost of preventing free people from being forcibly turned into slaves were high. Under these conditions, the viability of the whole institution was lessened.

Reprinted for private circulation from THE JOURNAL OF LAW AND ECONOMICS, Volume XX (2), October, 1977, Copyright 1977, The University of Chicago.

SOME FALLACIES IN THE INTERPRETATION OF INFORMATION COSTS*

YORAM BARZEL
University of Washington

It is probable that all efforts to prove a continued bias in the working of competition as such, . . . are doomed to failure.[1]

IN recent years, one of the areas singled out as having the potential for wasteful behavior is that of information. It is claimed that expenditures on certain kinds of information will yield negative social value.

In their maximizing behavior, people seek and use discovered opportunities, whether or not they are "socially desirable." For instance, stealing is practiced. Not surprisingly, great moral pressure and resources are used to restrain thieves. One cannot expect individuals, however, to refrain from all socially undesirable behavior since, even if they wanted to, they cannot always be certain which activities are undesirable.

Two types of wasteful behavior with respect to information have been identified. One is associated with speculative activities,[2] and the other with signaling or sorting.[3] Great ingenuity has gone into the construction of models describing them. Common to both sets of models is the notion that some kinds of knowledge neither affect allocation nor increase social product. Nevertheless, they will be procured by those who benefit from them, though their benefit is entirely at the expense of others. In some fundamental sense, "waste" doubtless does occur in that situation.

Even the most casual observation reveals numerous actual instances

* I wish to thank Armen Alchian, Steven Cheung, Paul Cootner, Sanford Grossman, Christopher Hall, Richard Hartman, Jack Hirshleifer, and Richard Parks for their valuable comments. Thanks are also due to Marion Impola who should be credited with greatly reducing offenses against the English language and for markedly improving clarity of exposition.

[1] F. H. Knight, Some Fallacies in the Interpretation of Social Cost, 38 Q. J. Econ. 582, 605 (1924), reprinted in Readings in Price Theory 160, 178 (Richard D. Irwin ed. 1952).

[2] Eugene F. Fama & Arthur B. Laffer, Information and Capital Markets, 44 J. Bus. 289 (1971); Jack Hirshleifer, The Private and Social Value of Information and the Reward to Inventive Activity, 61 Am. Econ. Rev. 561 (1971).

[3] Kenneth J. Arrow, Higher Education as Filter, 2 J. Pub. Econ. 193 (1973); Michael Spence, Job Market Signaling, 87 Q. J. Econ. 355 (1973); Joseph E. Stiglitz, The Theory of "Screening" Education, and the Distribution of Income, 65 Am. Econ. Rev. 283 (1975). Preceding all these is George A. Akerlof, The Market for "Lemons": Quality Uncertainty and the Market Mechanism, 84 Q. J. Econ. 488 (1970). We will discuss this paper in a later footnote.

where the same information is collected time and again. These authors, then, should be credited for drawing attention to a real enough and seemingly major problem, largely neglected previously. In my view, however, their lines of argument (not necessarily their "internal logic") are seriously flawed.

The fact that many information situations have the potential for waste does not necessarily mean that waste actually occurs. If, in the aggregate, these actions produce a negative product, arrangements that successfully restrain them or reduce their impact will generate a positive return.

An implicit, but crucial, assumption of the models is zero costs of transacting. Transaction costs include those required to formulate and to police contracts. Zero costs of transaction then implies that one can write a contract containing as many stipulations as desired, all fully enforced, without expense. In such a world (abstracting from transport, storage, and so forth) there would be no spread between retail and wholesale prices, or between selling and buying prices; they become identical. Conversely, the use of a single price, common to all these models, implies zero costs of transacting. These authors, however, fail to appreciate the implications of that assumption.

To deal with speculative situations, contracts may be written covering any conceivable occurrence (the state-preference notion) if transacting is costless. Similarly in the case of signaling, one could set up as elaborate an employment contract as desired. It is my contention that with costless contracting, it is possible to find distortion-free transactions which are perfect substitutes for the wasteful informational activities. Being costless and profitable, they will be adopted.

Without attempting to demonstrate the validity of the contention, a brief discussion may indicate its force. Consider a risk-neutral individual owning a member (possibly himself) of a class of assets. Although the item is valued at the same amount by the market and by its owner, its "true" value is subject to variance that can be reduced at a cost. The expected value to the individual of the reduced variance is zero, but costly to achieve. He will not, then, undertake that action.

Maintaining the assumption of risk neutrality, we now permit a different valuation of the asset by the market from that by its owner. It is plausible that when the owner's assessment is higher than the market's, it is to his advantage to spend resources to demonstrate the correctness of his valuation. If his action does not reduce the valuation of other assets, no cost is imposed on others and no problem of waste arises. We assume, however, that apart from the owner's expense the total valuation of all the assets is constant, so a rise in the value of a particular item reduces that of the rest by the same amount. Because the asset owner incurs expense, his net gain is smaller than the losses he imposes on others. This difference constitutes the resource misallocation.

The losers here have both incentive and means to bribe the gainer not to spend resources on the collection of information. But how are the losers to identify potential gainers and, indeed, how will they discover that they are about to become losers? For the market to accept the individual's higher valuation of his asset, there must be present an *independent* market observation where the true value is actually revealed. In the speculative case, this automatically occurs as time unfolds. With signaling, as Spence points out, it "takes time to learn an individual's productive capabilities."[4] Whatever the process, the eventual market valuation can be used to circumvent the informational resource expenditure. As long as the cost of transacting is zero, resources otherwise used to collect information can, though perhaps indirectly, be offered to the owner of the asset to dissuade him from entering into transactions based on costly information. Thus, a costless transfer is effected and the dissipation of resources is bypassed. Specific means toward such dissuasion are discussed below in conjunction with an analysis of the various models offered by the cited authors. It is worth our while, however, to clarify further some underlying issues.

The notion that information is overproduced was preceded in the literature by a diametrically opposing one—that due to the difficulty of capturing its returns, "too little" information is produced. The conflicting views may have been generated by many economists' total reliance on "theory." Conflicting results often simply reflect different assumptions and the failure to spell these out fully. The applicability of the results is a matter of real-world relevance which can be determined on empirical grounds alone. Thus it seems imperative not only to check the consistency of the logic behind the theories but to formulate them in such a way that they can be tested with actual data.

The assumption of zero transaction cost is in violent conflict with reality. When the costliness of transacting is recognized, transacting ceases to be a perfect substitute for information, and duplication in collecting information is then implied. This is so since, given diminishing returns, the informational expense will not be completely eliminated if contracting involves costs. When transacting costs are positive, the "optimal" level of such avoided information activity is not zero but rather that amount for which the cost of eliminating an extra unit of information equals that unit's resource cost. The production of "excess" information, therefore, is consistent with the efficient use of resources.

By incorporating positive costs of transacting in the analysis, this paper

[4] Michael Spence, *supra* note 3.

provides an alternative approach which is capable of empirical test. The models offered by the above-cited authors, at least as they stand, are not amenable to empirical verification; by my interpretation, however, they yield implications rather different from my own. In what follows, I attempt to demonstrate first how, in the absence of transaction costs, the "excess" informational expense will be avoided. Empirical implications based on positive costs of transacting are then proposed and it is shown that some actual experience can be used to choose between the competing models.

It should be recognized that we do not contest here the notion that the availability of some kinds of information will have no effect on resource use or allocation (except for that required to get the information). Though such cases are hard to conceive in reality, the assumption is useful in isolating the effect being studied. When information does lead to a change in behavior, this effect has to be netted from the total effect so that we can impute to distributional forces their proper share. This complicates the analysis and could be a source of confusion. It seems reasonable, then, to first obtain results from studying distributional effects in isolation. Thus, the assumption that some information will have no effect on allocation is retained through much of this paper.

The Speculation Model

In Hirshleifer's exposition of an elementary exchange model,[5] C_0 is the individual endowment of corn today. If state *a* (of weather, say) obtains, C_{1a} is the endowment to be available next period, or C_{1b} if state *b* obtains. It is believed by all that the probability of state *a* is 0.6 and that of *b*, 0.4. These probabilities, along with assumptions about the utility functions and endowments of a set of indentical individuals, yield an expected price of $P_{1a} = 0.3$ for C_{1a}, and $P_{1b} = 0.5$ for C_{1b} given that $P_0 = 1$.

"Now, suppose that a single individual at time 0 secures *private, prior,* and *sure* information that state *a* will obtain at time 1." Knowing that P_{1a} will actually turn out to be 0.5 and P_{1b} zero, he is in a position to gain by reallocating his expected endowment of C_{1b}, which he alone knows to be worthless, to the purchase of more C_0 and C_{1a}. Hirshleifer then continues, "[s]uch information [when becoming public] would be absolutely valueless to

[5] Jack Hirshleifer, *supra* note 2, at 563. Fama and Laffer's model is virtually identical in logic with Hirshleifer's, so discussion of the latter suffices. As Hirshleifer points out, the argument was anticipated by Samuelson fourteen years earlier. Discussing the effect of a speculator just one second quicker than his competitors, he concludes that "[t]here is no necessary correspondence between the income effects realized by any person's actions and the amount of meritorious substitutions that his actions can alone bring into being." Paul A. Samuelson, Intertemporal Price Equilibrium: A Prologue to the Theory of Speculation, 79 Weltwirtschaftliches Archiv 181 (1957), reprinted in The Collected Scientific Papers of Paul A. Samuelson 946-84. (Joseph E. Stiglitz ed. 1966).

the community as a whole. . . . The only thing that could happen, given the new public information, is that prices shift immediately to permit 'sustaining' the endowment vector in the face of changed beliefs entering into the utility function."[6]

At period 1, then, uninformed individuals necessarily realize less than the prior expected value of their endowments. They discover after the fact that they have traded away a valuable asset for a worthless one because better informed traders have taken advantage of their ignorance. Obviously, for such a result to hold, it has to be maintained that no adjustment in behavior takes place in anticipation of the potential loss. Even though the model is confined to two periods, similar informational opportunities presumably existed in the past, and thus individuals are aware of their vulnerability.

Once market participants realize that their expectations are *consistently* disappointed or, better still, once they discover the nature of the informational opportunity,[7] how will they modify their behavior? For the informed individual to gain, he has to bid for the commodity he discovered to be valuable. In a finite world, the price of that commodity will have to increase. But under the idealized conditions of Hirshleifer's model, in the absence of speculation, future prices are believed known with absolute certainty. The slightest price deviation thus reveals that a speculator is in action. Losses will then be averted by suspending trade, and the return from the speculation will be zero. Note that there is no need here to identify the speculator, since his action speaks for itself.[8]

To explore further the notion of the overproduction of information, suppose a crop of a particular wheat farmer is expected by all to be one million bushels and the price six months hence at harvest time, depending on weather conditions elsewhere, to be either 50 cents or $1.50 per bushel with a probability of 0.5 for each. Assume that *currently,* before the harvest, the harvest-time futures contract price of wheat is $1 per bushel. Suppose also that at a resource cost of $100,000, it is possible to predict with certainty which state of the weather will prevail. Assume further that the forecast, however, will be too late to affect the crop, the holding of existing wheat, or any other possible action. Such improved knowledge, by Hirshleifer's reasoning, will yield the forecaster a net gain of $400,000.[9] But the $100,000 worth of resources devoted to gathering information will not have affected any resource allocation, only distribution, hence the misallocation.

[6] Jack Hirshleifer, *supra* note 2, at 564 (italics in original).

[7] The knowledge that an informational opportunity exists is presumably common, thus uninformed individuals should be suspicious.

[8] See Sanford J. Grossman & Joseph E. Stiglitz, Information and Competitive Price Systems, 66 Am. Econ. Rev. 246 (1976), and in particular *id.* at 251 n.9.

[9] We abstract from the application of the forecast elsewhere.

The gain from forecasting is obvious. Under the stated conditions it can be shown that the expected purchase price facing the forecaster is 75 cents while the expected sale price is $1.25. Half the time he will discover he should buy a future contract or future wheat from the farmer at a price of $1.00 and sell, after the harvest, at $1.50. The other half of the time he will find he should sell at the future price of $1.00 and buy a contract or buy wheat to deliver after the harvest at 50 cents. Of course, this means 75 cents is also the expected price the wheat farmer will receive when *confining his dealings to the forecaster*. He gets $1.00 half the time and 50 cents the other half. Similarly, $1.25 is the expected price the ultimate consumer will pay. Since the expected market price is $1.00 per bushel, arrangements that would yield the farmer, on average, more than 75 cents and would cost the ultimate buyers less than $1.25 can be conceived. Such arrangements, obviously, would be preferable to contracting with the informed forecaster.

When the uninformed farmer deals with the informed forecaster, he is taking a basically "unfair" gamble which he can avoid, for instance, by committing himself sufficiently early—before the speculator can effect his forecast—and then standing pat.[10] If he wishes to reduce the risk he is facing, he can enter into a long-term contract with consumers at a sufficient time before the harvest at some prespecified price or price structure, say, $1.00. Since this kind of arrangement will be adopted by all farmers and consumers, there will simply be no later transactions after the forecast, and advance information could not possibly pay off. Alternatively, as in the previous case, the moment the future price deviates from $1.00 (either up or down), everyone is tipped off that a speculator has entered the market and all trade will cease. It seems *always* to be the case that in a world of costless transactions, particularly that described by the state-preference models, nobody will deal with these informed individuals. The only trades that will take place are those valued by "society as a whole."[11]

Consider the above problem in terms of property rights. The situation described by Hirshleifer implies doubt about the future value of what farmers own. The informational expenses can be viewed as a means to establish rights over any later value changes. These value changes seem to be in the public domain, and the expense of information, then, constitutes the dissipation.[12] It was just shown, however, that when transaction costs are zero, the

[10] This may appear to incur the cost of lesser liquidity. But when transaction costs are zero, liquidity has no value.

[11] John M. Marshall, Private Incentives and Public Information, 64 Am. Econ. Rev. 373 (1974), also takes exception to the notion of wasteful collection of information. His criticism, however, is based on an unrelated line of argument. He also accepts part of Hirshleifer's results.

[12] The farmer can be viewed as offering to sell his wheat at 75 cents a bushel. Since its market value is $1.25, this is equivalent to setting a price ceiling at 75 cents whereas valuation is at $1.25. Competition as to who will appropriate the difference will result in resource expense of 50 cents a bushel for the marginal unit.

commodity whose future value initially seemed in doubt is actually "fully" owned by its nominal owner rather than being in part in the public domain. With property rights thus fully defined, the (excessive) informational expense will not take place, and resource allocation is optimal.

Transacting in the markets considered by Hirshleifer was assumed to be costless, and in the preceding few paragraphs the same assumption underlies our discussion. However, these costs are, in fact, substantial. Of special relevance here is that particular prices will vary around their expected values, and that experience has to be acquired before individuals realize that they consistently lose by dealing with the informed individuals at any other than the "expected" price. Learning and other safeguards against being cheated require expenditures.[13]

When transaction costs are positive, arrangements to escape the loss to the forecaster may become so costly as to lose any advantage. Given the whole array of potential forecasts and their alternatives, only a subset of the latter will be adopted, since, in general, some alternatives will prove more costly than the forecasts themselves. Similarly, to the extent that a forecast and the possible ways to bypass it are subject to diminishing returns, the usual marginal conditions apply. As some forecasting is likely to remain cheaper than its alternatives, its use cannot meaningfully be termed inefficient.[14]

The "inefficient" information will be procured only when its elimination would be too costly. Now we have a model which allows for the exercise of choice and under which cost minimization is expected. If it is possible to identify conditions where, for instance, the costs of transaction decline, we could test the prediction that less of such information will then be collected.

The Screening Model

The essence of the "screening" or "sorting" or "signaling" model is similar and is as follows. Individuals differ in their productivity, but perfectly sort-

[13] For instance, one could restrict his dealings to established, reputable traders. For this, however, he would have to pay a premium over dealing with "fly-by-night" traders (and thus a wedge between buying and selling prices is introduced). This premium will not disappear with competition, since acquiring the reputation of a fair dealer also consumes resources. Alternatively, one can switch to an activity with lower expected return, but that is also less susceptible to speculation.

[14] When new knowledge does have potential positive net value, if rights to it are not initially owned, it is said that it will be "overproduced." Even though this is a case where information does affect allocation, the overproduction argument still applies. We predict with respect to this kind of information also that the market will seek arrangements to minimize the inefficiency. When viewed more widely, the entire literature on the overexploitation of resources in the public domain (including my own contributions) is subject to the same criticism that we are making of the information models: it fails to recognize the possibility of the directing of market forces toward minimizing the dissipation. Harold Demsetz, Information and Efficiency: Another Viewpoint, 12 J. Law & Econ. 1 (1969), makes a similar statement under similar circumstances. My own contributions to this literature include The Optimal Timing of Innovations, 50 Rev. Econ. & Stat. 348 (1968) and Investment, Scale, and Growth, 79 J. Pol. Econ. 214 (1971).

ing them in advance is too costly. Therefore, they will be paid for services in the labor market on the basis of average, or expected, productivity. Because education reveals productivity of the individual without, in this situation, affecting it, the better-educated, already more productive individuals will be paid a higher wage than those who do not attend college and thereby implicitly reveal themselves to be less productive. Thus, the resources spent on education have produced merely a signal which only affects the distribution of total output but does not increase it. Therefore, those resources have been misallocated.

We will show that the reasoning by Spence, Arrow, and Stiglitz used to obtain this asserted misallocation is flawed.[15] Rather than starting with labor, we will first illustrate with land. Consider many small, individually owned plots of wheat land of differing productivity. If it was impossible to sort land, all plots would be valued equally at the average productivity of the group. If, however, it is possible to determine the productivity of a given plot by an expensive procedure, the owner of one of the more productive plots will spend some resources to estimate and reveal to others its productivity. Its market value will increase. Now, prior to any determination of the productivity of individual plots, the aggregate productivity of the entire group of plots will obviously be quantitatively equal to the average productivity times the number of plots. Determination of the values of any of the "subplots" will change the value of the remaining area in the opposite direction by the same amount. This operation will yield no increased output in the aggregate, even though it is costly. The *net* aggregate value of the land, therefore, is higher when no resources are spent on signaling.[16] Under the assumption of zero transaction cost, none will be spent on signaling. All land would be assembled to begin with into a single ownership unit and any incentive for determining the value of individual plots will disappear.

Moreover, how does an owner of a plot know that his is more productive? If he knows it on a priori grounds, there is no need for the additional test. If he cannot know it a priori, the expected value of the outcome is zero[17]

[15] In a most elementary model offered by Michael Spence, *supra* note 3, at 357, 361, "there are just two productively distinct groups in a population facing one employer," and the wage "is taken to be [the expected value of] the individual's marginal contribution to the hiring organization." Taken at face value, one employer means no alternative use of time by individuals. As the *only* user of labor, a maximizing employer will pay a wage which will approach zero regardless of the revealed productivity of an employee. Since private return to education here is zero, there will be no demand for it. Therefore, it will not be produced and there is no misallocation. This result, however, depends on the absence of competition, which is not germane to the thesis of this paper.

[16] By assumption, the relation between the intensity of cultivation and production is independent of the quality of land; otherwise, sorting would be of value.

[17] It is assumed that the outcome of the test cannot be concealed. Note that the ability to

and, except for the risk factor, the resources are simply wasted from the individual viewpoint. That same proposition is demonstrated by Arrow with respect to college education. Arrow shows that under such assumptions, *ex ante,* a college entrant does not stand to benefit from the education he receives since "the expected income of college entrants equals that of non-graduates. . . ." It is curious, then, that he proceeds to say that "we have the remarkable possibility that if college is a filter, its abolition may help everyone."[18] Why abolish an institution that could never survive on its own? And how can "social waste" occur if there is no incentive to do privately what is deemed socially undesirable?

Whereas the owner of a plot of land may not know beforehand that his is superior, a person may possess subjective, but valid, evidence that he himself is more productive. The expected value of education to him is positive and it may seem, then, that resources would be spent to effect a redistribution. Arrow argues that this is an additional source of misallocation.

For concreteness, suppose that college education takes four years while the employer needs ten years before he can sort his workers according to their productivity. Consider now the following contract offered by an employer: For the first ten years, every employee will be paid slightly more than the value of the product of an individual in the less productive group. At the end of the period, when the productivity of each is revealed, if it turns out that he is in fact one of the less productive persons, no adjustment is made. But if he is found to be more productive, he will receive a bonus equal to the value of his extra output during the past decade (inclusive of accumulated interest) minus slightly less than the cost of college.[19] This contract is preferred by both groups of workers and by the employer over an alternative in which the more productive individuals would go to college. Furthermore, under competition, the contract terms for both groups of workers will approach the respective values of their product, and the employer's net gain from this superior arrangement will disappear. Education, then, will again simply be bypassed.

Here Spence's and Arrow's models imply that abler workers do not have a well-detected contribution to output in excess of that of the less able workers, and resources are spent (on education) to detect that contribution more clearly. We have shown, however, that under costless transactions, the rights of each group over its output are unambiguous, and thus there is no

---

conceal the outcome is essential in Hirshleifer's model. The ability to conceal is maintained above when Hirshleifer's model is discussed.

[18] Kenneth J. Arrow, *supra* note 3, at 200.

[19] "Performance bonds" would achieve the same result. By their terms, all workers would first be paid at the higher rate and, subsequently, the less productive ones would be required to reimburse the employer.

private return from the added expense. Given the real-world costliness of transacting, not all signaling education will be eliminated since the cost of eliminating some of it would exceed the return. Thus, certain "excessive" education will remain. Here, also, we predict that signaling activity will change directly with the cost of transacting.

Stiglitz[20] introduces a significant modification of the previous model by assuming that any screening by employers is prohibitively expensive. The question then arises: How would the employer know or discover that those screened through education are in fact more productive? It is not at all clear that this is possible. Given such constraints, I am unable to think of a way in which a costless redistribution could take place.[21] However this issue is resolved, it will now be shown that resource use will not take the form indicated by Stiglitz.

If employers were able costlessly to identify the relation between input and output and compensation is by performance, employees would exert themselves to the point where, on the margin, labor generates disutility. But where employers are unable to identify the relation between labor input and output, the individual's pay is set at the average output of all employees. This critical inability implies that the employer has no way to police his employees' contribution to output. How would an employee perform under these circumstances? Since (on the margin) the individual will exert himself only if he is compensated for the (extra) effort, when the number of employees exceeds one, an unpoliced worker gets a "free ride" on his fellows and will always work less than when paid according to his marginal contribution. When the number is large, the output of each will approach zero.

Relaxing the assumption that nothing is known about the relation between input and output, let us assume that the relation is known for the less productive workers, but not for the more productive ones. In other words, it is costless to monitor the lower common denominator for the two types of workers but prohibitively expensive to monitor the differential. As their extra effort cannot be rewarded, the more productive workers have no incentive to work to capacity and will tend to produce as little as the other group. Each will be paid the average of all contributions and each will tend to produce the average contribution. The potential of the abler individual remains untapped, and his mere identification is fruitless. The inability to monitor inputs then implies that the signal generated by college education is of no value to any individual. Unlike the previous models, here output will fall short of its potential in the absence of schooling. In this context, how-

[20] Joseph E. Stiglitz, *supra* note 3, at 284.

[21] Perhaps a solution lies with firm size. Since no screening problems arise with one employee and since, when transaction cost is zero, there is no penalty to smallness of firms, the problem of screening and waste disappears if all firms are reduced to one employee each.

ever, unless schooling happens to resolve the policing problem also, it cannot possibly lead to a higher output and so it will not be undertaken.

In terms of property rights, the individual employee has well-defined rights only insofar as the value of his output equals that of the less productive group. The costliness of policing the extra output deprives the more capable workers of the right over their potentially greater product. A potential income thus tends to be dissipated, and the individual responds by reducing his work, thereby minimizing the dissipation.

Suppose now that the signal produced by education is such that it allows monitoring the output of the more productive group. We should expect, then, a deliberate attempt to produce such a signal. Given that monitoring is costly but not prohibitive, it will take place to the point that maximizes the difference between the addition to the value of the output and the cost of monitoring. If this occurs at sufficiently low cost, the education is worthwhile: the signal increases not only the pay of the more productive individuals, but the total product as well. The higher pay that the productive individuals will receive is now attributable to the higher total *net* income. Still, since monitoring is optimized, not maximized, the output of the more productive workers will fall short of its potential.[22] The cited authors claim that in the absence of signals allocation is optimal and that signals would result in waste. However, in Stiglitz's setting, the absence of signals will lead to dissipation, and signals would tend to restore efficient allocation.

The Conformity of the Hypotheses with Actual Practices

The aforementioned authors all imply that informational opportunities are available to affect income distribution solely, and that resources will be used to take advantage of them. No alternatives are considered to eliminate or minimize such use. Repeating Hirshleifer's words, "[t]he *only* thing that could happen, given the new public information, is that prices shift. . . ."[23] We argue that people will seek alternatives to bypass and reduce such wasteful use of resources.

To choose between the two approaches, it is necessary to identify situations meeting the specified conditions in which these authors assert that excess use of resources will take place and to observe which model is consistent with actual practice. Two major and related difficulties hamper empirical tests. If the earlier models are indeed logically flawed, it is impossible now to derive implications from them. Not only did their authors fail to provide refutable implications (which could be tested regardless of their

[22] If the cost of monitoring the less productive workers is positive, their output will also fall short of its potential.

[23] Jack Hirshleifer, *supra* note 2, at 564-65 (emphasis added).

logical consistency with the model), they also made virtually no effort to spell out factual counterparts to their theoretic concepts. Yet some of the authors formulated policies.

The next few paragraphs show that, according to my reading of these authors' models, it is possible to identify opportunities that will lead to the wasteful use of resources. If it is found that people bypass these opportunities, the validity of the models is denied.[24]

The medical insurance industry[25] is an area where the affinity between the Hirshleifer-type and the Spence-type models may be demonstrated. More importantly, since the information models rest on conditions where behavior does not change, and since I am unable to discover such conditions, the actual change in behavior has to be accounted for to test these models. It will be shown that acceptance of these authors' models, even when false, is favored when one ignores the expected change in behavior induced by group medical insurance. Thus it becomes more difficult to confirm the hypothesis advanced here.

Consider some people whose expected medical expenses are identical. Medical insurance, then, is sold to them at a uniform premium. With the progress of science, it is suddenly discovered that these expenses vary systematically across individuals. In a Spence-type world, we would now expect individuals who know that they are healthier to spend resources to convince insurance companies that they qualify for lower premiums. Let us momentarily maintain that, except for the change in premiums, other behavior would not be affected. The decline in premiums to healthier individuals will be accompanied by increases to all others. A redistribution of income from the sickly to the healthy, then, takes place at a positive resource cost.

In Hirshleifer's world, an insurance organization, taking advantage of the surge in knowledge, would scrutinize individuals' medical records to sort out the healthier ones and would offer them slightly lower premiums to attract them to its program. This would result first in a loss to other insurance companies and eventually in higher premiums to their remaining less healthy clients. Still assuming that the change in the structure of premiums induces no change in behavior, this is also a case of a redistribution that consumes resources.

Spence's and Hirshleifer's models coincide here in that both view such market action as completed. It is evident that they are also very similar logically. Indeed, in the Hirshleifer-type situation, we should expect competition to produce a normal rate of return to all insurance companies so that

[24] An even more ambitious objective (which will be pursued in another paper) would be to show that observed behavior is consistent with the maximization of net values.

[25] The assumption of risk neutrality is relaxed here. This, however, does not introduce any difficulty to the problem at hand.

any gains from the collection of information would accrue to the healthier individuals. The resulting income distribution would be identical with that obtained in Spence's model if the two forms of collecting information cost the same.[26] (Even here, there is choice when these costs differ. If the lower cost arrangement prevails, an element of cost minimization is present.)

What change in behavior will be induced? Once the risk class of an individual is determined, his insurance premium will be set to reflect the (expected) cost he imposes on the insurance program. From the multitude of margins of action available to reduce the premiums, consider preventive measures. The closer the conformity between the individual's "true" risk class and the risk class in which he is placed for insurance purposes, the nearer are his expenses on preventive measures to what is usually deemed the "socially optimal" level. The discovery of how to sort individuals, then, not only provides the opportunity for some to gain at the expense of others, it also results in a higher level of output.

Medical insurance is sometimes offered to whole groups, such as employees of a certain firm, members of a union, or students in a given college. A major feature of group health insurance is that no medical examination is required; individuals qualify simply by belonging to the group. Thus, a major sorting expense is bypassed.[27]

Our fundamental argument is that some sorting is indeed "wasteful," but that people will search for means to minimize this loss. The information models considered here simply ignore that possibility. If such activity can be observed, it refutes those models and tends to support ours. In the case of medical insurance, it was just shown that sorting is likely to contribute to output and, for that reason alone, there is an incentive for sorting. This makes the confirmation of our hypothesis more difficult, because sorting will

[26] The similarity between the two models is also implicit in Akerlof, whose examples (including medical insurance) seem to fit both types of models. He is much more willing than the other authors to use real-world examples; thus he is even less justified in ignoring the multitude of actual market arrangements to avoid information costs.

In terms of his major illustration, that of used cars: concerned with the prospect of getting "stuck with a lemon," he fails to recognize the possibilities of avoiding this by such means as trading among friends; guaranteeing used cars; testing used cars; buying from reputable dealers, and more thorough quality control by automobile producers. All these are costly to arrange, but they avoid the presumably greater cost of dealing with the speculator. Akerlof, however, tends to use absolutist terms such as "it is ***impossible*** for a buyer to tell the difference between a good and a bad car" (emphasis added), and "it is quite possible . . . that no market exists at all." George A. Akerlof, *supra* note 3, at 489-90. Furthermore, as argued earlier, the absence of markets for certain activities may be interpreted as a way of avoiding waste rather than as a sign of some failing of the market.

[27] Sorting costs do not entirely disappear, as the insurance company has to acquire information on the distribution of health within a group to decide on its eligibility for the insurance. The determination of the features of sets of individuals attractive enough for group insurance is a question of considerable interest, but it need not be pursued here.

not be bypassed unless the savings from not sorting are sufficient to negate the positive contribution of sorting to output. Since group medical insurance does indeed bypass a sorting opportunity by not requiring medical examinations,[28] the various sorting models are refuted.[29]

Another class of market activities which also tends to refute the excess-information model can be characterized as the "pig-in-a-poke" phenomenon. Even though economists are aware of such activities, thus far no satisfactory explanation for their existence has been offered. Most dramatic of these is De Beers' sale to dealers of bags of assorted diamonds, each bag fetching a price ranging from fifty thousand to a quarter million dollars. A single prospective buyer is offered, and usually chooses to buy, a bag (sometimes several bags) at the price set by De Beers.[30] Had the contents of a particular bag been available for appraisal by all buyers, each probably would have spent resources to determine the properties of the diamonds. The ultimate resource allocation presumably would hardly be affected. The actual form of sale avoids this extra resource cost.[31] Indeed, the moment the seal on a bag is broken, the bag as a whole loses part of its market value.[32]

It should be recognized, however, that some additional costs have been incurred. For instance, De Beers has had to establish such a reputation that prospective buyers can be confident that the ultimate value of the bag exceeds its price. Thus, an individual buyer does not need to spend resources to investigate a questionable offer. The incentive for De Beers to engage in this peculiar form of trade seems to be that buyers are now in a position to spend

[28] Note that by a line of reasoning similar to that which produced the above models, one may argue that "too little" sorting now takes place.

[29] The rejection is definite, however, only when no forces except the ones considered here could induce group insurance.

[30] "The buyers' list comprises a carefully selected, limited group of over 240 cutters and dealers with whom the company wishes to do business. . . . [S]ales . . . are made periodically (usually once a month) in London. . . . The buyer is given ample time to study his allotted parcel and then can accept or reject it, *in toto*. There is no bargaining over the price, which is paid immediately in cash, or over the composition of the parcel." Michael Szenberg, The Economics of the Israeli Diamond Industry 14 (1973).

[31] Other market transactions of this kind can be mentioned. A former practice (prohibited by court order since 1948) was "block-booking" whereby a theater owner could contract with a movie producer for a whole batch of movies, knowing almost nothing about the prospective content of films, most of which were not even produced at contract time. Currently, the U.S. Post Office and some private moving companies regularly hold auctions for unclaimed trunks and other containers where bidders are not allowed to see the contents. The seller, in turn, usually claims that the trunks have not been opened.

A less dramatic case is the sale of apples or oranges in grocery stores. These fruits are not homogeneous, and stores often offer them both in bulk and in bags, so customers can either spend time choosing the ones they prefer or can buy the whole bag, where the opportunity for sorting is minimized.

[32] This and some of the previous information was provided by a diamond dealer.

on the actual purchase of the diamonds the amount they otherwise might have spent on collecting information.

It is important to clarify what can be claimed regarding the refutation or confirmation of the competing hypotheses in light of the foregoing evidence. Since a fact inconsistent with prediction based on a model tends to refute that model, it is entirely proper to explicitly "fish" for any such instance as a basis for rejection. We have shown that the Hirshleifer-Spence information models are inconsistent with the existence of either group medical insurance or of the De Beers arrangement.

The problem of confirmation is more problematic. As is well known, a test that fails to refute a theory lends it some support. The case is vastly weaker when one can merely point to some facts consistent with a model—even an utterly fallacious theory may agree with some observations. Thus, while it is justifiable to reject the information models on the basis of inconsistent evidence, only minimal support for our alternative has been gained in the process. The successful prediction and observation of an occurrence[33] consistent with our model and inconsistent with the other models is needed for that support.

Concluding Remarks

To this point the word "government" has not been mentioned. Yet it seems plausible that government has a role to play in the market for information. It would be desirable to construct a model that could determine under what conditions government would be more efficient in the gathering of information. I could hypothesize that it will intervene when it is more efficient. A thorough knowledge of transaction costs, particularly those differentiating market from government actions, is essential for such a task. Lacking that knowledge, I am unable to incorporate government in the analysis.[34]

The same knowledge is prerequisite, also, to any prescription for government action. The above discussion points to a previously unrecognized cost of government action. Even within the models under consideration, there is more choice than appears on the surface: alternative screening modes or alternative ways to collect information are surely available, and the one actually selected in a particular situation will presumably be the least costly. Now governmental banning of the activity does not, and probably cannot, imply banning *all* the alternatives. Suppose that in the case of medical

[33] It is preferable that the occurrence is new, or at least previously unknown, so that the integrity of the investigator becomes irrelevant.

[34] Perhaps the advantage of government lies in the relatively low cost of attaining uniformity of behavior when such is desirable.

insurance, insurance companies can sort individuals at a lower cost than individuals can sort themselves, and therefore sorting will be undertaken by insurance companies. Government intervention may take the form of banning this activity. The prohibition, however, is unlikely to cover self-sorting. Overlooking this possibility seems natural since initially individuals were not engaged in sorting. Individuals, then, may now turn to self-sorting in spite of its lesser efficiency. Similarly, if the U.S. were to prohibit college education, individuals could still acquire the education more expensively abroad; contrary to Arrow, it would thus be possible that if college is a filter, its abolition might hurt some and help none.

Let us briefly summarize. Both the speculation and the sorting models contend that individuals pursuing private ends will seek information, the net social value of which is negative; they inflict on others losses which exceed their own net gains.[35] One may reply, in Knight's words: "But under private appropriation and self seeking . . . the course of events is very different. It is in fact the social function of ownership to prevent this excessive investment. . . ."[36]

Any divergence between private and social gains necessarily implies the existence of an unexploited gain from exchange. In both types of the excess-information models, transaction costs are implicitly assumed to be zero. It is shown here that in each of the cases under consideration, if transacting had been costless, the profit potential could be converted into actual profit, thereby restoring the conformity of private and social values.

In a world in which transaction costs are positive, we argue that while some of the above "wasteful" information will be collected, alternative arrangements will be sought so as to maximize net value. The information models seem to deny such alternatives. It is shown that the practice of group medical insurance is consistent with the hypothesis of net value maximization but not with the alternative models, which are consequently rejected.

Although our hypothesis implies that some "wasteful" information will be produced, such production can be regarded as inefficient only in comparison with an ideal world in which government action is costless. When these costs are positive, as seems inevitable, the information produced is part of the maximization of net value. We argue that in each situation people will first assess the resource cost of obtaining a particular piece of information which subsequently will have little effect on resource allocation, and will then compare its assessment with the cost of various alternatives that would

[35] By this reasoning, the resources used to affect *any* redistribution, including those to reduce inequality and to avert theft, are wasted.

[36] F. H. Knight, *supra* note 1, at 163.

preempt the use of information. The lowest cost method will prevail. Consequently, we hypothesize that as the cost of obtaining information rises, and as the cost of alternative arrangements declines, less and less of such information will be produced.

[23]

COMPETITIVE TYING ARRANGEMENTS: THE CASE OF MEDICAL INSURANCE

YORAM BARZEL*

The most compelling argument for tying arrangements presented in the literature is that it serves a monopolist in extracting consumers' surplus.[1] To succeed in the practice the seller must have monopoly power, and the tied commodities must be complementary. In this paper it is argued that tying may also occur under certain competitive conditions, and that the tied commodities will then be substitutes.

By competition we mean least cost production and zero profits, but not product homogeneity and costless information. Given the costliness of transacting, it is seen that the constraints on choice imposed by tying certain services and excluding others are found to be consistent with the attempt to maximize the net value of productive resources.[2] The argument, entirely general, is illustrated and tested by medical insurance. The remainder of this paper assumes that insurance is offered competitively.

Medical insurance is deemed inefficient when it admits persons whose total cost to the program exceeds their total valuation and excludes some whose total valuation exceeds the total cost they would have imposed, and when it permits the marginal valuation of medical services to fall below their incremental cost. If every person seeking insurance were to obtain coverage matching his specific need at a premium equal to the expected cost of serving him, no medical service would be covered unless its valuation exceeded the expected cost of providing it. The problem of "adverse selection" would then fail to manifest itself. Perfect screening of the insured, however, is prohibitively expensive; thus the expected costs of serving different persons paying the same premium is not uniform within each market and within each insurance plan. Furthermore, if every insured person could be induced to consume the amount of medical services he would have consumed when paying the full price, the "moral hazard" problem would not arise. Imposing the appropriate restraints is costly, and some discrepancy will persist.

The extent of the inefficiency varies with the exact specification of the insurance contract. As long as insurers charge premiums commensurate with their expected costs the greater the inefficiency of a contract, the higher the premium. The more efficient the contract, then, the more

*University of Washington. I am indebted to Douglas Conrad and to Masanori Hashimoto for their comments. This study was supported by "seed money" from the Center for Health Services Research of the University of Washington and by a research grant from the Department of Health, Education and Welfare. Barzel (1979) is an earlier version of this paper.

1. Posner (1976), pp. 171-184, particularly footnote 9. This argument is universally attributed to Aaron Director.

2. Had transacting been costless the need for tying, and for our story would disappear; but then resource misallocation due to monopoly would disappear too.

Economic Inquiry
Vol. XIX, October 1981

attractive it is to at least some consumers, and competing insurers will tend to provide it. Thus inefficiency is subject to constrained minimization. Here we focus on coverage as one approach to such minimization, and study the effect of coverage on admission and on utilization.[3]

The majority of medical insurance plans cover a wide array, though never the entirety of medical requirements; certain medical costs are explicitly excluded and others are covered only in part. It is hypothesized in this paper that insurance packages tend to tie together services which are close substitutes while excluding complements. This kind of insurance will be chosen by fewer people who impose costs in excess of their valuation and by more of those whose valuations exceed their costs; moreover, with such packaging the extent of excess use will decline.

The intuitive explanation of why tying substitutes and excluding complements have the desired effects is as follows. When a medical service is covered by medical insurance its marginal price is less than its full market price and its consumption is higher. The quantity consumed of a commodity will increase less when the prices of its substitutes decline along with its own price and when the prices of its complements are not allowed to fall with it. When an insurance plan ties substitute services, their effective marginal prices fall together, thus curtailing excess use. Excess use is similarly curtailed when complements to insured services are excluded from the package.

Adverse selection can occur because not all people who are offered participation in the insurance program have the same demand. It will be shown that the appropriate tying and exclusion of services can induce appropriate self selection. A person for whom an insured service substitutes well for some other service is expected to become a heavy user of the insured service. After buying the insurance the consumption of the substitute service will fall greatly. By tying both services in a single package, the insurance loses its special attraction to the heavy users, and thus tends to weed them out. Excluding complements serves a similar purpose.

In the empirical work pairs of medical services which are better substitutes for some groups of people than to other groups are identified. The hypothesis is then tested that insurance plans will tie together the pair of services more often for those considering the two close substitutes.

I. THEORY

Insurance inevitably causes a discrepancy between what people pay for the service and the resource cost of producing it. The greater the demand

3. The central interest here is the comparison between *alternative* insurance arrangements, not what the motivation for insurance is, which is taken as given. An insurance plan will be in demand only if it responds to whatever consumers seek, and given the cost, an insurance plan preferred by consumers will drive the less popular ones out of the market. Thus, in terms of response to the demand for insurance, our comparisons are between plans that differ in detail only and thus essentially will affect people only on the margin.

elasticity for the service, the greater the associated loss. Constraints on the insured, however, can make the demand less elastic and reduce the loss. It is first shown that adverse selectors' demand for the insured services is more elastic than that of others. It is then demonstrated that when substitute services are tied and when complementary services are excluded adverse selectors tend to abstain from buying the insurance whereas favorable selectors tend to join.

A. *Adverse Selectors' Demand Elasticity.* Consider an insurance plan covering a particular medical service. Suppose that the per unit cost of providing the service (inclusive of insurance cost) is C^* and that the average annual quantity obtained by those insured in the particular plan is Q^*. Given the zero profit condition, the insurance premium then is C^*Q^*. C^* and Q^* are marked in panels 1A and 1B of figure 1.

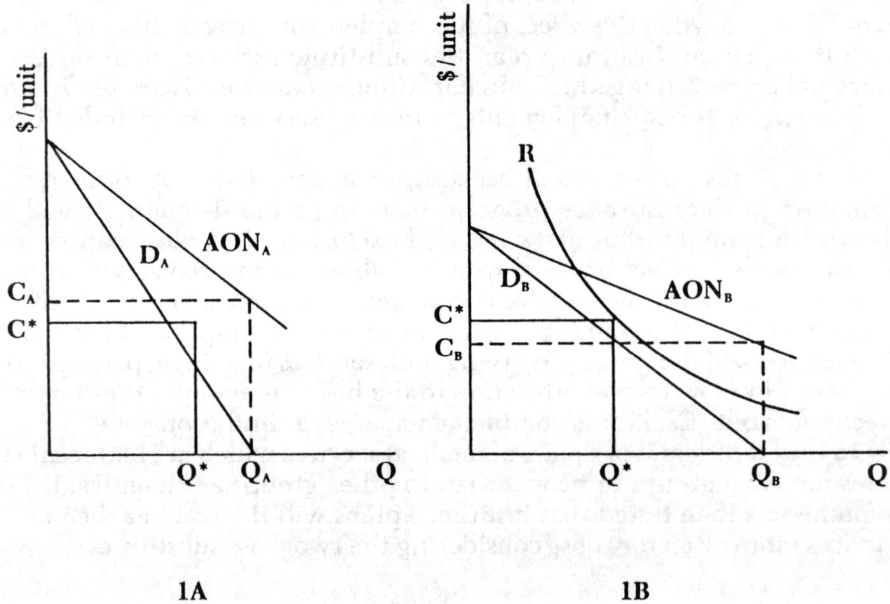

FIGURE 1

In panel A the demand D_A of person A is drawn and in panel B the demand D_B is drawn for person B. These demands are comprised of each person's expected demand for the insured service and the demand for insurance.[4] Moreover, the insured consumer is assured throughout to be

4. The desire to be insured, as mentioned in the last footnote, is taken for granted, but not explored here.

unconstrained in his use of insured services. In other words, he consumes to the point where his marginal valuation is zero. To see more easily whether a person would find the purchase of the insurance worthwhile the "all or nothing" or AON demands are also drawn in. AON_A in panel 1A is the all or nothing demand of person A corresponding to D_A, and AON_B in panel 1B corresponds to D_B. Q_A and Q_B, respectively, are the quantities A and B expect to consume if they buy the insurance as the marginal charge then is zero, and C_A and C_B are their respective per unit or average valuations.

It is evident that to person A the insurance is a good buy. His total valuation is $C_A Q_A$ and since $C_A > C^*$ and $Q_A > Q^*$, $C_A Q_A > C^* Q^*$, so his total valuation exceeds the insurance premium. Person B's average valuation of the quantity he expects to consume is C_B and it is less than C^*; his quantity Q_B, however, is larger than Q^*. Through the point (C^*, Q^*) in figure 1B, a rectangular hyperbola R is drawn for comparison purposes. A person will buy the insurance if at some quantity the average cost, measured by the height of R, is less than his average valuation, measured by the height of his *AON*. As drawn, the height of AON_B exceeds the height of R at Q_B, making insurance a good buy for B as well.

If each person would have been required to pay a premium equal to the cost he imposes on the insurance program, A would have still purchased the insurance as $C_A > C^*$; but since $C_B < C^*$, B would have refused it. We term B an "adverse selector" — a person who will buy the insurance at the going premium, but not when required to pay the expected cost he imposes. By this definition, then, an adverse selector's unit valuation is less than C^*, but more than the height of R at the expected quantity, which implies that expected consumption is more than Q^*.[5]

On *a priori* grounds, it can be shown that within a given insurance plan the demand for insured medical services by adverse selectors — those whose average valuation is less than unit cost, is more elastic than that of others. This elasticity relation is first demonstrated for selected pairs of insured persons, and then is shown to hold for the aggregate of the insured within a plan. In figure 2, Q^* is the average quantity of insured services provided by an insurance plan, C^* is their unit cost, and R is a rectangular hyperbola passing through the point (C^*, Q^*). A person whose all-or-none demand curve is anywhere on or above R will buy the insurance since his total valuation of the insurance exceeds its cost. Compare now two persons; the total valuation by each is equal to the insurance premium so that each of their *AON* demands is just tangent to R. The *AON* demand of one designated AON_N is set tangent to R to the left of Q^*, say at N; the other's — AON_M — tangency point is set to the right of Q^*, say at M. Q_N is the quantity coordinate of N and Q_M that of M. Denote the demand curve of the first

5. This definition of an "adverse selector" seems preferable to the conventional one in which expected consumption is greater than average, but the valuation is not constrained.

person D_N and that of the second D_M.[6] Whereas the total valuations by the two are the same, their total costs are not. The total valuation of the person with demand D_N is greater than the cost he imposes; he is a favorable selector. The other is an adverse selector. Under none-too-restrictive assumptions, D_M can be shown to be more elastic than D_N in the relevant range.

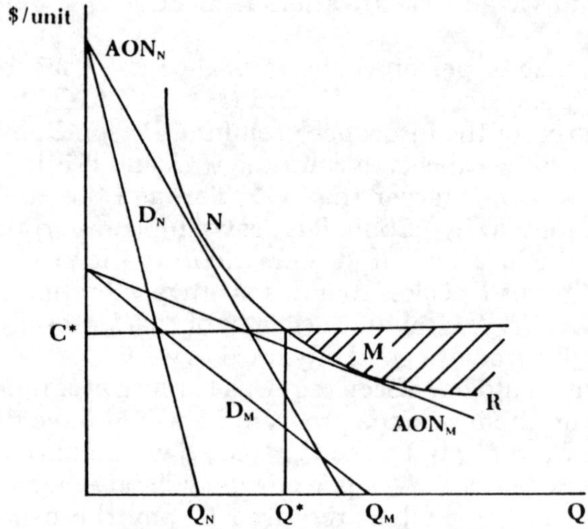

FIGURE 2

Since by assumption both *AON* curves are tangent to the rectangular hyperbola *R*, the area under D_N to quantity Q_N is equal to C^*Q^*, as is the area under D_M to Q_M. If D_M was to lie entirely above D_N, the area under it would necessarily have been larger than that under D_N, an implication which is inconsistent with the equal total valuation assumption. The two demand curves, then, must intersect. Assuming that the demand curves intersect only once, D_M has to intersect the vertical axis below D_N's intersection. Thus the arc elasticity of the entire demand D_M has to exceed that of D_N, as is true for each of the two pairs of segments below and above the intersection. For linear demand curves, D_M's arc elasticity is greater than D_N's between any given pair of prices. In particular, D_M is more elastic than D_N in the price range between C^* and 0, which is the difference between the full unit cost of the service and the zero marginal price under the insurance. Linearity, however, is not a necessary condition here; D_M is still more

6. Since *R* is unit elastic, and since *N* is a point of tangency between an *AON* curve and *R*, the curve marginal to that *AON* curve, i.e., the demand curve D_N has to intersect the horizontal axis exactly under *N*. Thus Q_N lies exactly underneath *N*. Similarly Q_M lies underneath *M*.

elastic if the two demand curves are "well-behaved"; for instance, if they are both concave, or if they are both convex (and intersect only once). Thus assuming that the demand curves for the two persons considered are well behaved, the demand D_M of the adverse selector is more elastic than D_N, that of the favorable selector.

The above analysis was carried for persons whose total valuation of the insurance is just equal to the insurance premium. The same analysis applies when both persons value the insurance by an equal amount above cost. Thus if each values the insurance $1 more than he pays for it, the demand of the heavier user still has to be more elastic.

As a final comparison consider two persons who, at zero marginal price would obtain the same amount of service, say Q_S units such that $Q_S > Q^*$, but whose average valuations differ; one's average valuation is less than its cost and the other is greater than its cost, as can be seen in figure 3. Suppose one person's demand is D_S so his average valuation is $\overline{SQ_S}$ and that of the other, with demand D_T, is $\overline{TQ_S}$. The latter is assumed to value the service more. It is easy to see that since the area under D_T is greater than that under D_S, D_T has to lie largely above D_S.[7] If these demand curves are also "well-behaved" so that D_T lies entirely above D_S are drawn, then D_S is more elastic than D_T at any price range, including that from C^* to zero.

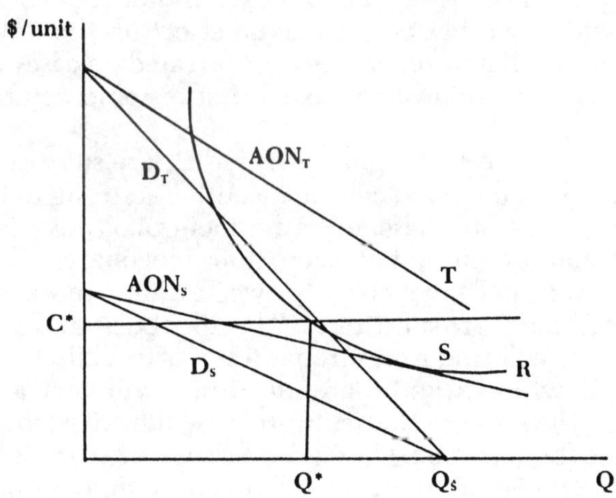

FIGURE 3

In the previous paragraphs it is shown that for certain insured pairs, the demand of adverse selectors is more elastic than that of favorable selectors. If every adverse selector in the program can be matched with one or more favorable selectors, then the demand of adverse selectors as a group is

7. Linearity is a sufficient condition for D_S to lie entirely above D_M.

more elastic than that of favorable selectors.[8] Now all adverse selectors have to cluster at points on their all-or-none curves that lie in the shaded area in figure 2, since only in that area is valuation greater than the premium but less than cost. Within any insurance plan these adverse selectors can be more than matched with favorable selectors whose average valuation exceeds C^* because the distribution of subscribers is subject to the constraint that the average quantity obtained by all subscribers to the plan is Q^* and because all those who obtain less than Q^* units of service as well as some of those who obtain more are favorable selectors. Thus the demand by adverse selectors as a group has to be more elastic than that of the rest of the insured.

B. *Tie-Ins.*[9] Consider two alternate insurance arrangements: in one, two medical services are covered by separate insurance contracts and each eligible applicant can choose whether to buy one, both, or none; in the other a single insurance contract covering both services is offered — the tie-in case, where the choice is between obtaining insurance for both services or for neither.

When the two services are neither substitutes nor complements, a person's decision to buy either is independent of his decision regarding the other. Combining the two services in a single insurance package will force an all-or-nothing choice. Since the demand for each is independent of the price of the other, tying the two has no systematic effect on the adverse-selection problem. Attention, therefore, can be concentrated on cases where the two are related. Substitutes will be discussed first in some detail and complements briefly later.

When the two services, designated A and B, are substitutes and insurance is offered separately for each, the incentive is strong to buy one of the two, but not both. The purchaser of, say, A incurs a positive "admission fee" equal to the annual premium, but a zero marginal charge. However, much of his demand for B can be met cheaply by consuming more of A at no extra charge because A and B are substitutes. The direct demand for B, then, will fall and the person will find its insurance less worthwhile.

The degree to which A and B are substitutes will vary among persons. Those for whom the two are close substitutes will have a stronger incentive to buy insurance for only one. Thus a decision whether to tie the two serves to "separate" the potential applicants.[10] It is now shown that A and B are better substitutes for adverse selectors than they are for others, and that tying the two in a single plan will discourage its purchase by adverse selectors.

8. The possibility that the numbers of the two types are not equal for some of the comparisons and that the unequal weights within the two groups will reverse the relationship between the two elasticities is ignored.

9. Some of the propositions expounded in this section are more formally analyzed in an appendix prepared by Mark Plummer available on request from the author.

10. This separation bears resemblance to that discussed by Rothschild and Stiglitz (1976).

To proceed, denote the own-price elasticity for commodity A as Σ_{AA}, the cross price elasticities as Σ_{AB} and Σ_{AC} where B is a good related to A, and C is the composite of all other goods, and Σ_{AM} is the income elasticity. Consider now the identity $\Sigma_{AA} \equiv -\Sigma_{AB} - \Sigma_{AC} - \Sigma_{AM}$, otherwise known as Hick's "Third Law." Abstracting from the income elasticity,[11] a person's own demand elasticity for a commodity is identical with (the negative of) the sum of all the cross elasticities of that commodity. The identity makes it clear that when one person's own demand elasticity for a given commodity is higher than that of another person's, at least one of his cross elasticities must also be higher. Supposing that B's elasticity with A is known to be higher for one person than for another, then the first person's own price elasticity will also be higher (provided that there is no full compensation through C's cross elasticity with A, which seems unlikely). The differential effect of changing the price of A alone can now be compared with that of changing the price of the substitute in the same direction, as will occur with the insurance tie-in. It is obvious that for both persons the change in quantity will be less in the latter case than when the own price changes alone. More importantly, the relative difference in the quantity of A consumed between the two persons will narrow down with the simultaneous fall in the own and the substitute prices since the cross elasticity is higher for the person with the higher own elasticity.

How would the packaging of A and B in a single plan affect those seeking insurance? The merging will have little effect on a person for whom these are not close substitutes, but for those to whom the two are closer and closer substitutes, the incentive to avoid buying the package becomes increasingly strong. When A was offered alone, it could substitute for B, but this advantage has disappeared — an advantage that to begin with was largest for those deeming the two close substitutes.

Whether a person will buy the package now depends on his assessment of the loss from packaging as compared with his net valuation of the insurance to begin with. The smaller the difference between an individual's initial valuation of the insurance and its premium, the stronger is the incentive not to buy the package. In terms of figure 2, of those who lie in the shaded area, the ones located close to R will be the first to refuse to buy the package. Thus packaging weeds out some of the "worst" adverse selectors.

This weeding process, coupled with the curbing of utilization of A by all others for whom A and B are substitutes lowers the implicit premium for A and thus the premium for the package as a whole. At the lower premium, more eligible persons will now buy the insurance. Among these, however, adverse selectors still have less incentive to join than they would had the

11. At issue here is not a regular price change but rather a change in the method of pricing. The offer of insurance for a service reduces the marginal charge fo that service, but a lump sum payment is required for admission. Real income is higher because of the lower marginal charge, but it is lower because of the admission fee. For a marginal buyer the two cancel each other exactly. For the general case the income term vanishes as a first approximation, particularly since alternative plans are compared.

premium been lowered for *A* alone. Since the incoming group contains a disproportionately large fraction of those with low utilization rate, with their entrance the premium will further decline. Thus through self choice the tying of substitute services lessens the abuse of the insurance plan: adverse selectors do not find the joint insurance as attractive as when the components were insured separately. This method would not eliminate persons who from the beginning were adverse selectors with respect to both *A* and *B* but who nevertheless would have purchased insurance for both. Even so, there is no added loss in packaging the two into a single insurance plan.

Turning to complementary medical services *A* and *B*, the demand for each is increased when the price of the other is lowered. Suppose that *A* and *B* are covered in a joint package. As before, the adverse selectors for the combined services have more elastic demand than that of the favorable selectors. It is intuitively clear that the greater the complementarity, the greater the reduction in adverse selection when one of the services is taken out of the insurance package. This can be seen by reasoning in reverse. If the two persons have the same price elasticities for each of the two services, the person for whom the two are better complements will have the greater demand elasticity for the package. Thus by excluding one or the other of the two complementary goods from the package, the person with greater price elasticity will be more severely denied the opportunity for excess utilization.

The emphasis in the last few sections centered on the effects on participation of tying substitutes and of removing complements from the insurance package. As was mentioned in passing, however, these practices also reduce the excess utilization of the insured services. The simultaneous lowering of the prices of substitute services tends to restrain the consumption of both, and similarly avoiding the simultaneous lowering of the prices of complementary services tends to restrain the consumption of both. Thus these packaging practices achieve the dual result of restraining the moral hazard as well as adverse selection.

In practice it seems easier to implement and police those insurance packages that cover several services rather than those that exclude some services, since the excluded services may be sold separately by other insurers.[12] Nevertheless the complementarity relationship may explain a major insurance practice: namely, coinsurance. In the following discussion some of the general aspects of this practice are considered first and then attention is directed to its relation with complementarity.

When the insured is subjected to a positive coinsurance rate, his expected payment is proportional to the quantity of insured services he expects to consume. The demand for insured services *net* of the coinsurance payments then will fall by his expected payment per unit. The entire previous analysis still applies provided that we replace "net" with regular demand; an ad-

12. It is implied, but not tested, that insurers (perhaps aided by insurance commissioners) will attempt to impose constraints on the provision of supplementary insurance.

verse selector then will tend to have a more elastic net demand than a favorable selector.

The function of the coinsurance rate as a check on the moral hazard is well recognized, and this simultaneously limits adverse selection. A positive coinsurance rate implies a larger expected payment by an adverse selector than by a favorable one. When the coinsurance is introduced, the insurance premium will be lowered by the same amount to both, and the adverse selector's total payment for insured medical services tends to be larger. If both were just indifferent between buying or not buying the insurance when the marginal charge was zero, a positive coinsurance rate will tip the scale so that the adverse selector will tend not to buy the insurance and, given the reduction in premium, toward an affirmative decision by the favorable selector. This, of course, is hardly surprising, since it is a step towards charging each according to the cost he imposes.

Many medical services are provided in discrete units. It seems plausible that the valuation of two halves of such a unit is more than double the valuation of one half of a unit: in other words, that the two parts can be viewed as complementary goods. A coinsurance payment is equivalent to the exclusion of one of the two complementary goods from the package. Thus this aspect of "packaging" medical insurance serves again to alleviate the adverse selection problem.[13] It is predicted that coinsurance payment will be more common (and higher) for indivisible medical services.

II. SETTING THE THEORY FOR EMPIRICAL TESTS

The inference the theoretical model offers is that pairs of medical procedures which are close substitutes to consumers will be tied in medical insurance contracts. However, tie-ins are not free of cost, and it cannot be simply predicted that they will occur for any pair of substitutes. A more discriminating prediction is required. The prediction is, rather, that tie-ins will be more prevalent the higher the gain they generate. Circumstances have to be found, then, where benefits of the tie-ins or their costs vary systematically across insured people. In particular, if classes of insured who differ in their cross elasticity between two medical services can be identified, the prediction is that the tie-ins will be more prevalent for the class with the higher elasticity.[14]

It may seem that differences in elasticities are a matter of "taste," which evades classification. Some differences in elasticities, however, can be readily identified on basically *a priori* grounds. Consider, for illustration only, two possible treatments of tooth infection — extraction and root-canal treatment. It is evident that to some extent the two are substitutes.

13. Whereas deductibles will achieve similar results they are more difficult to analyze, since their effect depends not only on the expected demand but also on its distribution across periods.

14. Substitution in medical services is the subject of a number of studies. As a rule, these seek to determine whether the services are substitutes, not how substitution varies across groups, and thus their results are not useful here.

They are not, however, equally good substitutes to different people. For instance, the closer a person is to requiring dentures, the lesser the incentive to save the tooth. Thus the cross elasticity between the two procedures is higher for a typical person fifty years of age than for one sixty years old. It is predicted, then, that dental insurance for the older group is less likely to cover both procedures than the insurance offered the younger one. More generally, suppose that of two alternative treatments one is a larger investment. Since younger people are expected to benefit from the investment-type treatment for more years than older people,[15] the cross elasticity between the two treatments will change with age.

Age is but one dimension by which the elasticity may vary systematically. Another is the cost of time. Obviously of two alternative procedures, the one requiring lengthier treatment will be less attractive to persons with a high cost of time. Another relevant consideration is the relationship between the "life style" of a person or the kind of job he holds and the effectiveness of alternative procedures. A treatment that is less effective for physically active people than for sedentary ones will attract fewer blue- than white-collar workers.

The concurrent offering of alternate treatments for the same problem implies that each is preferred by some people. If the difference is due to age, then at some particular age a person will be indifferent between the two and exactly then his cross elasticity goes to infinity. The elasticity is declining *both* when age is declining and when it is increasing around the break-even age. Thus tie-ins should be less common as age deviates in either direction away from the break-even point. It does not seem likely that one can tell, on *a priori* grounds, what the break-even age will be for a given service. However, this can be estimated by examining (for uninsured persons) how the utilization of the two treatments varies with age. Alternatively, by comparing groups at either extreme of the age distribution one can be quite certain that the elasticity declines as older people are compared to less elderly people at the high age end, and younger to less young people at the low age end. A similar *a priori* statement can be made with respect to the cost of time where testing can be performed for the two tails of the distribution.

Sometimes the classification is dichotomous as with male/female or sedentary/active. If it is known that of two alternative procedures, one class of people tends to use both procedures whereas the other uses only one, it is clear that substitution is greater for the first. It is predicted then that the two treatments will be tied more frequently for the class using both procedures.

15. See Becker and Stigler (1977).

III. EMPIRICAL EVIDENCE

Two tests of the hypothesis are now presented. They both concern comparisons between younger and older people. In the first test, insurance coverage for hospital stay is predicted to be tied with insurance coverage for nurse visits and for nursing homes more commonly for older than for younger people. In the second test the frequency of co-payments by the insured are predicted to be higher for older people.[16]

Data for the tests are obtained from a compilation of Blue Cross plans as of January 1966,[17] providing information on various plans then offered in each of 76 U.S. areas served by Blue Cross.[18] An attractive feature of these data is that within an area all those insured by Blue Cross are covered by variants of the same basic contract, and the coverage offered to senior citizens and to other classes of insured is typically described as affording benefits "the same as those of the standard certificate *except* . . . ."[19] Thus the comparisons are straightforward since in most major respects other than the criteria relevant here the coverage is uniform within each area, and the *ceteris paribus* condition is reasonably well satisfied.

A. *Nurse Visits and Nursing Homes.* Two services that seem to be good substitutes to hospital stay are staying at nursing homes, and (home) nurse visits. It is predicted that insurance for hospital stay is more often tied in with insurance for stay in nursing homes or with insurance for nurse visits for older persons. More specifically, it is hypothesized that "senior citizens," usually defined as those having reached the eligible age for Medicare, 65, but sometimes those age 60 and over, would tend to be covered for all three services, whereas younger people would tend to be covered only for hospital stay.

The time cost for older people tends to be lower and their ailments of a more chronic nature. Older people, then, would more readily substitute time in the hospital for home visits by a nurse. The more chronic nature of their ailments makes the less intensive medical care available in nursing homes a better substitute for hospital stay. An insurance contract covering only hospital stay will induce substantial substitution away from other treatments by older people but not much by younger ones.

The compilation of the 76 insurance programs just described does not provide information on senior-citizen insurance for 14 of the areas. The data on the remaining 62 areas is presented in table 1, classified by

16. It is often claimed that insurance is offered on basis of "need," or of the magnitude of the expense. Of our two predictions the first conforms to common notions. The second, however, is the reverse of common notions and thus has the power of discriminating between the two hypotheses.

17. *Blue Cross Guide* (1966).

18. Also listed, but not used here, are one plan for Puerto Rico and four for Canadian areas.

19. *Blue Cross Guide* (1966), p. 155. Italics in original.

whether the plan is "standard" (or "basic") from which senior citizens are excluded, or whether it is open for senior citizens. The entries in the table show how many, and what percentage of the different plans include coverage for nursing home stay or for nurse visits (which is additional to coverage for hospital stay). It is strongly confirmed that senior-citizen plans are more likely to tie coverage for each of these two services to that of hospital stay than are standard plans. Even the differential between plans that define a senior-citizen as one above 60 years old and those that define such a person as above 65 years of age produce significant differences (using the χ^2 test at the 10 percent level) between the two groups for both categories, again supporting the hypothesis.

TABLE 1

Nursing Homes and Visiting Nurse Coverage for Standard and Senior Citizen Insurance Plans*

		Standard Plans	Senior Citizen Plans 60+	65+	All
Nursing Homes	Covered	1 (2%)	2 (20%)	22 (42%)	24 (39%)
	Not Cov.	61 (98%)	8 (80%)	30 (58%)	38 (61%)
	TOTAL	62	10	52	62
Visiting Nurse Service	Covered	2 (3%)	3 (30%)	31 (60%)	34 (55%)
	Not Cov.	60 (97%)	7 (70%)	21 (40%)	28 (45%)
	TOTAL	62	10	52	62

*This coverage is additional to that of hospital stay.

B. *Co-Payments.* The function of coinsurance or of co-payment was discussed above. It is expected that the lower is a person's time cost, the larger the share of pecuniary medical costs in total medical costs and thus the greater the demand elasticity with respect to pecuniary price. As we consider insured persons with lower time cost, the more severe are the adverse selection and moral hazard problems, and therefore the stronger are the incentives to have them contribute in the form of co-payments towards the costs they impose.

Among the insurance plans in the above-mentioned compilation are those designated "standard," "left employee," and "senior citizen." The first is the basic plan for those insured in groups through their place of employment. The "left employee" plans are designed for those previously insured through a group who had quit the group. A major reason for the status change is leaving the labor force. The time cost of senior citizens is asserted to be typically lower than that of left employee which, in turn, is lower than that of those covered by a standard plan. It is therefore predicted that the required co-payments will decline as one moves down the line from senior-citizen plans to left employee plans and then to standard plans.

The data for the test are presented in table 2. Some of the plans do not provide information on co-payments. In column 2 the number of plans providing information is given. The number of plans in which co-payments do not differ between the pair of plans compared is entered in column 3. Of the plans where co-payments differ, column 6 presents the percentage of the cases in which the direction of the difference conforms with the hypothesis. The evidence from each of the three comparisons is in conformity with the hypothesis. A χ^2 test against the alternative that the difference is equally likely to go either way confirms the hypothesis at better than 10 percent level in each of the three comparisons.[20]

TABLE 2

Comparing Co-Payments by Senior Citizens
Left Employee Plans and Standard

Comparing	Total number of plans (1)	Number of plans detailing co-payments (2)	Number of plans where co-payments are equal (3)	Number of plans where co-payments differ (4)	Number of plans where the direction of the difference supports the hypothesis (5)	Number of plans where direction co-payments difference supports the hypothesis (5)/(4) × 100% (6)
Left Employee with Standard	76	51	22	29	21	72%
Senior Citizen with Left Employee	76	48	25	23	18	78%
Senior Citizen with Standard	76	51	8	43	34	79%

20. In these tests plans where co-payment are equal are ignored. If, instead, these are equally divided between "support" and "no support" of the hypothesis the first comparison becomes insignificant, but the other two remain significant.

IV. CONCLUDING REMARKS

Medical insurance inevitably drives a wedge between the resource cost of medical services and their valuation, both in total and on the margin. On the assumption that the loss associated with the divergence is subject to minimization, it is shown that by insuring substitute medical services together and by insuring only one of complementary pairs of services, adverse selection and moral hazard losses are reduced.[21] The evidence on nursing homes and on nurse visits, both substitutes for hospital stay for older people but not for younger ones, is consistent with the hypothesis as is the evidence on differential levels of co-payments being higher for older people.

A fixed admission charge and a zero marginal price are not unique to medical insurance. Indeed, such practice is ubiquitous. Restaurants charge for meals, but not for the length of stay; various clubs charge an annual fee and do not restrict usage; and similarly, but less obviously, landlords charge monthly rent, but seldom for the cost of wear and tear imposed by the tenant.[22] In all such cases, losses similar to the insurance's adverse selection and moral hazard can be identified, and the appropriate packaging will predictably reduce the losses. Thus beside medical insurance, much can be gained from an investigation of observed "packaging" behavior in other industries.

REFERENCES

Barzel, Yoram, "Tie-In in Medical Insurance," *Proceedings of the Social Statistics Section, ASA*, 1979: 117-121.

Becker, Gary S. and Stigler, George J., "De Gustibus Nom Est Disputandum," *American Economic Review*, March 1977, Vol. 67, No. 2: 76-90.

Blue Cross Guide, A Summary of Benefits and Regulations of Non-Profit Blue Cross Hospital Service Plans (Blue Cross Association, Chicago), 1966.

Posner, Richard A., *Antitrust Law*, (University of Chicago Press, Chicago), 1976.

Rothschild, Michael and Stiglitz, Joseph E., "Equilibrium in Competitive Insurance Markets: An Essay in the Economics of Imperfect Information," *Quarterly Journal of Economics*, November 1976, Vol. 90: 629-649.

21. It might seem a happy coincidence that both adverse selection and moral hazard are restrained by the same kind of packaging. Moral hazard and adverse selection, however, are two manifestations of the same problem; of getting the marginal unit or the marginal batch of units at a price less than resource cost. The packaging tends to bring the price closer to the resource cost thus restraining any excess use.

22. Even less obvious, but still logically the same kind of practice is the uniform charge in movie theaters, where the seating "quality" (within class) is a free attribute.

MEASUREMENT COST AND THE ORGANIZATION OF MARKETS*

YORAM BARZEL
University of Washington and Hoover Institution

PEOPLE will exchange only if they perceive what they get to be more valuable than what they give. To form such perceptions, the attributes of the traded items have to be measured. Some measurements are easy to obtain; others pose difficulties. For example, determining the weight of an orange may be a low-cost, accurate operation. Yet what is weighed is seldom what is truly valued. The skin of the orange hides its pulp, making a direct measurement of the desired attributes costly. Thus the taste and the amount of juice it contains are always a bit surprising. The grower, more knowledgeable than the consumer, may gain by making the surprise an unpleasant one. The potential errors in weighing the commodity and in assessing its attributes permit manipulations and therefore require safeguards. The costs incurred by the transactors will exceed those under joint maximization.

A sampling of activities that arise solely because these costs are positive may hint at how costly the measurement of commodity attributes is.[1] Had product information been costless, warranties would disappear since attribute levels and defects could be effortlessly identified at the time of exchange; fancy packaging (unless valued for its own sake) as well as the *Consumer Report* and the Good Housekeeping Seal would be super-

* Steven Cheung should be credited with pointing out the importance of the "measurement problem." Thanks are due to Christopher Hall for his penetrating comments. I also received valuable comments from Keith Acheson, Armen Alchian, Steven Cheung, John Hause, Keith Leffler, and John McManus.

[1] A trifling episode dramatically illustrates how costly some measurements might be. In one of Eddie Bauer's sporting goods stores, sneakers were marked down to almost a third of the regular price after a single "defect" was found: their size markings were missing. (Thanks to Dean Worcester for the information.) Presumably, the cost to Eddie Bauer of measuring the sneakers' sizes, and perhaps of convincing consumers that nothing else was faulty, was perceived as more than half the retail price. The inducement required to compensate consumers for undertaking the measurement was obviously smaller than Eddie Bauer's cost, but still very substantial.

[*Journal of Law & Economics*, vol. XXV (April 1982)]

fluous, as would professional certification and recruiting efforts; and beautiful but rotten apples would fetch the appropriate price.

Virtually no commodity offered for sale is free from the cost of measuring its attributes; the problem addressed here is pervasive. "Market signaling" and "adverse selection" are seemingly instances of the general case. In both cases, the costs of measuring the attributes of individuals are high, and the resulting errors permit people to transfer wealth to themselves at a resource cost. Costly measurement is a factor common to these and various other instances where individual and joint maximization do not coincide.

The accuracy of measurement differs fundamentally from other valuable attributes. The presence of random errors introduces the opportunity for costly transfers of wealth. Of concern here are the effects of such behavior and the market arrangements that emerge to reduce the losses from the exploitation of the inaccuracies.[2]

The Nature of Measurement Error

Consider a model adopting all but one of the Walrasian assumptions for a competitive economy; the exception is that product information is costly to obtain. Product information is defined as information on the levels of the attributes per unit of the commodity and on the actual amount contained in the nominal quantity. Measurements of these magnitudes are subject to error. The greater the variability of the measurement around the true value, the lesser the information about the commodity.[3]

Had product information been freely available, equally valued units would sell at the same price and, so long as choosing does not damage the commodity, a seller would not be harmed from allowing buyers to pick and choose. The seller then would have no incentive to constrain choice. It will be seen that when product information is costly, the seller may gain from imposing such a constraint.

The purchase of oranges when the desired good is fresh orange juice can illustrate the measurement problem. Suppose that oranges are identical in the quality of their juice, but the amount each yields varies; that the cost of squeezing oranges at the sellers' premises is prohibitive; that buyers and sellers are able to form estimates of the amount of juice any

[2] John C. McManus, The Costs of Alternative Economic Organizations, 8 Can. J. Econ. 334 (1976), takes a rather similar approach. Steven Cheung, A Theory of Price Control, 17 J. Law & Econ. 53 (1974), it seems, was the first to introduce the notion that markets are organized to minimize dissipation.

[3] Measurement is the quantification of information, and its use will facilitate in making the model operational.

orange contains and that the cost of greater accuracy is increasing. The amount of the attribute desired by consumers (and its price) then is subject to measurement error.[4]

Suppose further that numerous sellers sell the commodity. Each sorts it to as many classes as he wishes and then posts a price, say, in dollars per pound, for each class, permitting consumers to select any item provided they pay the posted price.

A consumer's periodic demand for the desired good is downward sloping, reflecting substitution within the period and the increasing cost of storage. The selection of a seller to buy from entails a fixed cost assumed to be so large that the entire period's quantity is obtained from a single bin of a single seller. After deciding which seller to patronize, a consumer will meet the period demand from that seller's offerings.

Had the units in the bin been identical and the amount of the desired attribute they contain known, the quantity purchased by a consumer would be determined by his demand for the attribute and by the price of the commodity. Had the units been varied, but not enough to justify *any* selection effort by the buyer, the quantity purchased would depend in part on the buyer's aversion to variability. At the going price for the commodity, the *expected* price for the attribute is determined, but the quantity obtained is subject to error. For now this effect of the error is abstracted from.

The quantity purchased in a particular period depends on the cost of selection in the following way. If, for instance, a buyer plans to buy only units estimated to be at the top quarter of the distribution, it is expected that four units will be inspected for each unit selected. The total cost of a purchased unit then is the sum of the posted price and the cost of inspecting four units. If, relative to its posted price, the commodity seems a better buy, so that the buyer plans to buy units from the top one-third of the distribution, then for every unit bought only three units will be inspected.

Thus, the interaction among the buyer's demand for the attribute, the buyer's cost of measuring the commodity, the posted price, and the estimated distribution of the attribute determines the amount purchased. That amount will increase as the demand for the good rises, as the cost of selection falls, as the posted price of the commodity falls, as the average quality increases, and, most important, as the *variability* of the commod-

[4] The assessment of how long a machine will last, the quality of a particular performance of a long-running play, and the cost of preparing a site for construction are a few additional examples of commodities that are difficult to evaluate or to measure, and thus their measurements are subject to error.

ity offered increases. The reason for the last result is that there is no added penalty for inspecting an exceptionally poor item, but there is an added gain to finding an exceptionally good one.

What are the constraints on the seller in posting his price? Buyers, it is assumed, make use of their past experience to predict the relationship between a seller's posted price and the distribution of his commodity. They will stop patronizing a seller who they determine has a high price relative to the distribution offered. This is the route by which competition from other sellers enters the model. Subsequent to a buyer's decision to buy from a particular seller, that seller faces a downward-sloping price function. To survive, however, the relationship between a seller's price and the quality of his offering cannot "exceed" that of other sellers too often.

How finely will a seller sort his commodity? Assuming that the cost of estimation increases with the accuracy of the estimate, suppose first that this cost is the same to the seller and to his buyers and that all buyers are identical in their aversion to variability. When the variability of the commodity offered at a given price is very low, buyers will forgo selecting and will take whatever is handiest. As variability increases, a point will be reached where selection will begin.

Under the assumptions here, sellers will sort the commodity to that break-even point in variability, that is, just finely enough to dissuade buyers from any sorting. When the seller effects such sorting, each item is measured *exactly* once. On the other hand, when buyers effect the measurement, each item will be measured *at least* once; some will be measured twice or more. Thus the net price—that is, price net of the cost of measuring—at which the commodity can be offered is lowest when the seller effects the measurement. Competition will force sellers to effect the measurement.

The conclusion that the seller will be the one to measure does not depend on the level of this cost so long as this cost is the same to buyers and to the seller. Whatever that cost is, the seller will always measure just finely enough to prevent buyers from measuring regardless of how averse to variability they are. The other side of the coin is that even when buyers do not value a better-sorted product, they will gain from measuring by getting the more highly valued units selling at a given price.

Suppose now that the buyers' cost of measuring is higher than the sellers', say, because a tax on measurement by buyers is imposed or because they are constrained in some way. It immediately follows that the sellers' level of sorting will fall to the new level that would just prevent buyers from any sorting. A striking feature of this result is that when the buyers' cost of measuring is increased, the net price they pay for the commodity, or for the desired attribute, will fall.

Buyers perform their measurements in the market in two steps. In the first they estimate the distributions different sellers offer to decide from whom to buy; in the second they determine the properties of individual items. If the increase in buyers' cost applies only to the second step, then the analysis is complete. If, however, it applies to the first step also, a new problem arises.

If buyers' cost of determining what the distribution is is increased, a seller could more easily entice buyers to buy from him even when his merchandise is "overpriced." In that case, buyers must rely more heavily on their past experience or on some other proxy measure and less on assessing what they are offered on a particular shopping trip. The role of a seller's reputation, warranty, and so forth acquires, then, greater prominence. Constraining buyers' choice in that case will generate some gains but will also introduce new problems. Moreover, the imposition of such a constraint is unlikely to eliminate all measurement by buyers since buyers need to convince themselves that they do not receive worthless merchandise.

The earlier assumption that sellers' measurement cost is not higher than that of buyers seems satisfactory for single-attribute commodities. In reality, most commodities have numerous attributes whose levels vary across units. If a commodity is sorted by all its attributes, each unit may occupy a class by itself. If a commodity is not sorted so exhaustively, various buyers will find it worth their while to pick and choose by attributes that they value highly, but not ones by which the seller sorted the commodity. Whereas such sorting will generate a gain, it will be carried "too far" in comparison with the joint-maximization level.[5]

Because of the cost of measurement, the seller cannot capture the entire value of his merchandise had it been costlessly described. This was shown to be the case when the seller sorted to prevent consumers from any choosing. It is also the case when consumers engage in choosing, selecting items valued more than their price. Because of competition among consumers, however, they will be able to obtain the differential in value only by spending resources—those used on measuring the commodity and perhaps on rushing to the top of the line.

In the remainder of the paper, an attempt is made to determine whether particular market practices are designed to cope with the excess-measurement problem, and implications capable of refuting the hypotheses are derived. Some casual empirical observations are made, but no serious tests are conducted. The particular practices considered below are selected on the basis of their apparent "importance" or "interest."

[5] The buyer will sort to the point where an extra dollar's worth of sorting effort yields one dollar in value. Whereas the valued attribute is costly to produce, it is obtained by the buyer at a zero marginal charge from the seller.

An examination of some of the earlier considerations may facilitate in the derivation of hypotheses. A consumer who is convinced that he received a random selection from an optimally measured commodity will not use additional resources for measuring. This requires that trust is established, perhaps by acquiring brand names. The seller still has to select a method of selling to avoid excessive sorting. One such method is to raise the buyer's measurement cost. DeBeers's diamond "sights" seem a case in point. The approved dealers have diamonds chosen for them by DeBeers, and they are not allowed to pick and choose from different offerings.

A buyer's incentive for excessive measurement can also be lowered if he is compensated for items ultimately revealed to be of exceptionally low value, which may explain product warranties. The terms of exchange for warranted products depend on subsequent performance rather than relying entirely on measuring the commodity by the time of exchange. The arrangement, however, lowers the buyer's cost of the careless handling of the product. The severity of this problem depends on the nature of the commodity and on the contractual ability to curb abuse. Share contracts rely even more fully on subsequent performance and obviate the need for certain measurements at the time of exchange. Such contracts are expected, then, when the determination of the value of the exchanged property at the time of exchange is exceptionally costly.

The next four sections discuss product warranties, share contracts, brand names, and the suppression of information. Hypotheses are offered to explain these arrangements, and testable implications are derived. Later sections further expand the model and its applications to such diverse issues as vertical integration and futures markets.

Product Warranties

In every exchange, both the seller and the buyer will require some verification of the measurements of the exchanged goods: the seller to assure himself he is not giving up too much, the buyer to assure himself he is not receiving too little. The process of producing a commodity spans a period of time; the costs of measuring the attributes and of verifying the measurements will vary along the way and will be different for the buyer than for the seller. Which quantitites, then, will be measured, when, and by whom? The remainder of this section concerns measurement by the consumer at the time of consumption.

As a rule, measurement is by the seller, whether in advance or at the time of exchange. Quite often, however, measurement is automatic, or its cost is greatly reduced as the commodity is used. Therefore, substantial savings will result if measuring is left to the buyer to be performed at the time of consumption. A prevalent arrangement for vesting in the consumer the responsibility for certain measurements is that of the guarantee. Presumably, it is too costly for the seller to determine which of his products may have defects. The consumer, on the other hand, can obtain this information cheaply at the time of consumption.[6] In the absence of a guarantee, to avoid getting stuck with a bad item, the consumer will examine several to identify the one with the fewest defects. Given the expected cost of selection by buyers, the seller must price the items he sells below the expected valuation of the best unit; otherwise he will not be able to sell any unit. The differential between the price and the valuation of the units offered for sale is effectively left in the public domain, and buyers will spend resources to acquire it. Selling a commodity with a warranty is essentially a promise to provide one *good* unit at the going price. Thus, the warranty reduces the differential in value received by consumers for given payment and reduces correspondingly the attendant resource expenditure.

The fact that some new cars have numerous defects is not necessarily a sign of poor workmanship. The consumer may simply be more efficient than the seller in providing quality control. When no guarantee is offered, however, a buyer would inspect several cars before choosing one. This excessive examination is avoided when the product is guaranteed. A seller who guarantees his product, then, can raise his price not only by an amount equal to the expected cost of repair, but by a premium representing the cost to the consumer of a prior examination.[7] Guarantees are routine for new cars, but not for used ones. The apparent reason is that a new-car seller can relatively cheaply verify the measurement supplied by the buyer, which is not the case for used cars.[8]

When a warranty is too expensive to supply, two types of arrangements can be used to reduce excess measurement. One is a higher degree of

[6] The same consideration may explain certain return privileges. For such items as paint, tiles, and wool it may be difficult to match the items if a second purchase is needed. Since the consumer can measure his requirements most economically at the time of consumption, he is promised a refund for excess quantities of these goods he may buy originally.

[7] In his seminal "lemon" paper, George Akerlof discusses this role of warranties. See George Akerlof, The Market for "Lemons": Quality Uncertainty and the Market Mechanism, 84 Q. J. Econ. 488 (1970).

[8] The warranty is warranted only if buyers cannot easily exercise it even though they, rather than the seller, are at fault. The ability of one party or the other to abuse his position seems to correspond to Williamson's notion of "information impactedness," where "circumstances relevant to the transaction, or related set of transactions, are known to one or more parties but cannot be costlessly discerned by or displayed for others." See O. E. Williamson, Markets and Hierarchies 31 (1975).

quality control, which one would expect, for instance, with commodities designed for the tourist trade. The section on brand names continues this discussion. The other arrangement is to get the consumer to act as if his choice were random. The sale of used cars, where dealers often obliterate potential distinctions among cars, is, seemingly, a case in point. This issue is further developed in the section on the suppression of information.

Share Contracts

Share contracts are often said to reflect the desire of the risk averse to moderate the effect of risk. Had this been their sole explanation, it would be refuted by the royalty payment to authors. The royalty contract between author and publisher stipulates that the author will receive a given share of the revenue from the sale of the book. Since the success of the book and the total revenue its sale will generate are not known when the contract is drawn, the author's income is uncertain. Had authors been paid a lump sum, their entire risk would have been shifted to publishers. Publishers are often diversified to start with, and thus paying a lump sum would increase the riskiness of their operations only moderately. The desire to reduce risk, then, would have generated the outright purchase of rights to books rather than the common royalty contract.

What else, then, could explain the sharing arrangement? In the royalty contract the share, or share structure, is set in advance, but the absolute amounts the two parties will receive are contingent on consumers' actual demand subsequent to publication. Because of the difficulty in predicting the ultimate success of the venture, the determination of the appropriate lump sum is expensive to reach. If publishers make competitive lump-sum bids, each of them will require some market research. Even the successful bidder's effort is excessive, since subsequently the information will emerge anyhow. Had publishers attempted to lower the cost by spending only a small amount on research, their bids would be subject to large errors, and the winning bidder might turn out to be a big loser.[9] By sharing, the need for market research is reduced and the error is largely limited to the sharing percentage, making the expected value of the royalty contract larger than the lump sum would have been.[10]

Share contracts are subject to incentive problems absent from lump-

[9] Their loss is similar to the loss to speculators in Hirshleifer's model. See Jack Hirshleifer, The Private and Social Value of Information and the Reward to Inventive Activity, 61 Am. Econ. Rev. 561 (1971). In that model, speculation is with respect to price; here, it is with respect to quantity.

[10] Similarly, owners of mineral rights usually do not sell their rights but rather agree to a share of the unknown revenues.

sum contracts and in this regard are more costly. For instance, the publisher will tend to advertise less than when he does not share added revenues with the author. The lesser the information problem, the more attractive the lump-sum arrangement; thus share contracts are expected to be more common with new authors than with established ones,[11] with the first editions than with subsequent ones, and with novels than with "how-to" manuals.

The sharing arrangement, then, makes some search less profitable. Market forces dissuade publishers and authors from acquiring prior information on the value of the traded property.[12] But because such acquisition would have been wasteful, the sharing arrangement is a more efficient solution.[13]

Brand Names

Since consumption yields direct measurement, it is often advantageous to let consumers do the measuring, which may explain warranties and contracts as argued above. Consumers, however, can gain by understanding the value of the good, and it is often difficult to verify their measurements. On the other hand, at the time of transaction, measurement or verification may be rather costly.[14] How can costly measurement be avoided?

Suppose one wants to buy a six-pack of beer. To determine whether the beer is cold enough, he will touch one or two bottles, but not all of them. Similarly, if he looks for a rope of certain strength, he will test just a small segment. In both examples the procedure followed is not as innocuous as it may appear. The beer seller can reduce refrigeration costs if the easiest-to-reach bottles are coolest, and the rope maker can strengthen just the exposed end of the rope. When the buyer does not engage in a

[11] The more books an author publishes, the smaller the proportionate effect of risk from variability in the royalty income from any of the books. The risk-aversion model then implies that sharing, or royalties, will become more common as the number of books an author publishes increases, which is the opposite of this paper's prediction.

[12] See Yoram Barzel, Some Fallacies in the Interpretation of Information Costs, 20 J. Law & Econ. 291 (1977).

[13] Hashimoto hypothesizes that the Japanese wage-bonus payment is a sharing arrangement induced by the cost of evaluating a worker's contribution. He finds that the evidence conforms with this hypothesis. See Masanori Hashimoto, Bonus Payments, on-the-Job Training and Lifetime Employment in Japan, 87 J. Pol. Econ. 1086 (1979).

[14] Various contests and calls for bids are subject to a time limit. Presumably, the caller would wish to have all the materials assembled by a given time. The restriction imposed, however, is on the time marked on the posting, since this seems a much cheaper validation method.

more comprehensive test, he is implicitly trusting the integrity of the seller. But convincing others of one's integrity is a costly activity.

If the buyer is to buy without measuring every item, he has to be persuaded to rely on the seller's assertion of the prior measurement. In some instances, the seller will try to convince the buyer that his purchase will actually be "representative" of the lot; in others that the good is quite uniform and would not vary significantly from sample to sample. Uniformity is the subject of the remainder of this section; suppression of information is the subject of the next section.

A canner known to change the quality of peas (e.g., size, tenderness, sweetness) from one season to another will induce buyers to conduct a fresh, costly test every season. If, on the other hand, the canner is known to maintain tight quality control, much less testing is required. The canner's reputation, or brand name, serves here to guarantee that the product is, and will remain, uniformly good.[15]

The canner incurs costs in establishing reputation,[16] both in controlling quality to assure uniformity and in the maintenance of uniformity when external pressures would call for a change,[17] as any change endangers the canner's reputation, reducing the value of his brand name. Even a higher quality offered at the old price will cause problems by reinducing costly sorting. Thus, it is expected that when the seller's reputation is used to back the product, quality will fluctuate less than when the consumer is to measure it.

Product uniformity lowers the cost of measurement to the consumer. It is probable that to provide continuing uniformity, extensive measurement is required by the seller. However, a seller of established reputation can choose to measure at the cheapest point in the production process rather than at the time of exchange, as would be necessary if the buyer were to insist on verification of the measurement.[18]

[15] In an article on the growing and canning of peas, Susan Sheehan gives a detailed description of the extraordinary effort by Green Giant to guarantee product uniformity at all grades. See Susan Sheehan, Peas, The New Yorker, September 17, 1973, at 103.

[16] If it is easier to convince a consumer of the uniformity of a widely distributed product than of each of several narrowly distributed ones, horizontal integration is advantageous.

[17] This point was contributed by Levis Kochin. The pursuit of constant quality by Mars, a candy maker, is detailed in an article in Business Week (August 14, 1978, at 291). "One source of that mystique is Mars' fanaticism about the quality and freshness of its products. . . ." "While other manufacturers were . . . reducing the quality of their candy because of the price of sugar and cocoa . . . Mars [did not]." "[Mars] was the first candy manufacturer to date its products and to guarantee to take back and credit merchandise still on the shelf in four months."

[18] Brand name also involves "standards." Had the most desired characteristics of peas been easy to measure, the label of each can could have stated their amounts. A shopper then

When a buyer receives a bad unwarranted item, his money is lost. Thus, to gain the buyer's patronage the seller must persuade him that he himself will suffer a substantial loss if his product is found deficient. By backing the quality of the item with a brand name, a bad item sold under that name will tarnish the entire brand. The more likely the consumer is to encounter the brand in the future, the more severe the penalty he can impose on the seller and thus the less he has to worry about being cheated.[19] It is expected that the more difficult it is to measure commodities at time of exchange or to warrant them, the more extensive would be the brand under which they are sold. It is also expected, paradoxically, that a seller committed to compensate the buyer for defective products will sell relatively more defective units than a seller who makes no such commitment.

The Suppression of Information

The provision of uniform commodities would some of the time be too costly. A commodity may be defined as heterogenous if, when allowed, its consumers will spend resources on choosing among equally priced units. Thus, patrons line up for preferred seats in a single-price movie theater; produce and meat in a grocery store are routinely subject to selection; and prospective employers spend resources in recruiting among equally paid, but diverse, workers. As already noted, the competition for the high-valued items is a costly activity; spared of the added cost, a consumer would have offered more for the item.[20]

How much is a buyer who is not permitted to inspect and to choose willing to pay for a commodity? This depends on his guess of the quality of the unit handed to him, which, in turn, depends on how much he trusts the seller. He expects to be given an item from the low-quality end from a mistrusted seller. Suppose, however, that the seller is able to persuade the buyer that he is offering a random or a "representative" selection.

---

could choose his exact preference and uniformity would lose value. A consumer seeking uniformity would simply buy units having the same specifications. Thus the capability to measure implies the existence of "standards." These appear to be a substitute for brand name, and the usage of the two will be negatively correlated. It is expected that the fewer the dimensions of a commodity amenable to standardized measurement, the greater the emphasis on the brand name. Even for commodities that can be cheaply measured, however, brand name helps to assure that the measurements are correct.

[19] Klein and Leffler discuss the nature of brand names and particularly the "last-period" problem. Benjamin Klein & Keith Leffler, The Role of Market Forces in Assuring Contractual Performance, 89 J. Pol. Econ. 615 (1981).

[20] Precisely the same reasoning led to the conclusion that consumers will pay a premium (apart from those for risk reduction and for saving on the expected cost of repair) for commodities sold with warranties.

The buyer will have to submit to the choice effected by the seller, but the resource expense of duplicate sorting is bypassed. Thus, abstracting from risk aversion, he will be willing to bid up to his expected valuation.

Operating within the framework of competitive markets, it is argued that information on the quality of goods that inspection would have generated is deliberately suppressed.[21] On occasion, sellers may even offer buyers "a pig in a poke." There is no difficulty in opening the poke to inspect the pig. When trust can be created cheaply enough, trusting consumers will offer a higher average price for the entire batch when inspection is not allowed, and this arrangement will prevail. In some cases inspection might damage the commodity. In other cases, however, the arrangement is deliberately contrived at a cost of resources.

This may explain why apples are often sold in opaque bags filled in advance by the seller. The consumer spends less time per apple on inspection than when choosing them individually. He obviously will not buy the bag unless he believes that on average he gets a better buy; thus the seller's "fairness" becomes a factor in his decision. It is predicted that sellers catering to transient trade will sell a smaller fraction of their apples by the bag and will sort them into more uniform grouping than will sellers whose credentials are well established.[22]

The advantage of suppressing information may explain some of the practices associated with the selection of physicians by patients. As a rule, a physician has an immense edge over a patient in measuring the service delivered because of the complexity of medical problems and because of the great variability in outcome of a given treatment, even for a single person at different times. Since the patient's cost of measuring the service is much higher than the physician's, resources can be saved if physicians rather than patients engage in measuring. But how can patients be stopped from spending resources trying to identify the best buys? One way is to enhance even further the asymmetry in information between physician and patient.

Sellers of medical services, through the AMA, ADA, etc., spend a large amount of resources to persuade buyers to choose among physicians as if the choice were random.[23] Various measures taken by the AMA lower still further the return to measurement by patients. A high uniformity of skill among physicians is attained through the control of training, of qual-

[21] This parallels the argument that with the royalty-payment scheme, authors and publishers will abstain from collecting duplicate information on the value of a manuscript.

[22] The hypothesis could be tested by comparing the behavior of shopkeepers in resort areas during the tourist season with that during the off-season.

[23] The assumption of competition through free entry does not hold in this case. As will be shown presently, however, in at least one dimension the restriction on entry may prove to be efficient.

ifying examinations, and of admission to medical schools (where, e.g., large fellowships are less readily available than in other graduate programs). Not surprisingly, then, medical school graduates seem more uniform in ability than those in other professions.[24] Moreover, the gap between the training of nurses and physicians is so wide that only seldom would patients compare the services of the two.

Comparison among physicians also is discouraged. Physicians are constrained from criticizing one another, and until recently were not allowed to advertise and were severely restricted with respect to office signs, yellow-page entries, and the like. Additionally, price information is kept in low profile. Thus, a patient can compare physicians only by expedients such as word of mouth.

If the preceding hypothesis is correct, the following observations are implied: (1) The AMA would resist moves to make comparisons easier. (2) The easier it is for patients to measure a medical service, the looser will be its control by the AMA. (3) Income variability among doctors would be less than in other professions that require a comparable amount of training, such as law. Casual observations on the first two implications are in conformity with the hypothesis. The tenacious fight of the AMA against prepaid medical insurance is consistent with the first implication. The question as to whether to join such an insurance group itself requires comparison, and when a compensation schedule is provided, price comparison becomes easier.

With respect to the second implication, consider the distinction between acute and chronic medical problems. A person afflicted with a chronic problem gains experience which in time increases his ability to measure the service he receives. To that extent, he has a comparative advantage over someone with an acute problem. From this it is predicted that the treatment of chronic problems will be less tightly controlled by the AMA. This seems to be borne out by the fact that chiropractors, whose specialty is treating predominantly chronic ailments, are allowed to compete with physicians.

Vertical Integration

When production is specialized, the product will change hands before reaching the ultimate consumer. In this section, some of the problems associated with measuring the product in its intermediate stages are analyzed.[25] Home production is an extreme form of vertical integration.

[24] Medical societies also deny membership, and the right to practice, to physicians who prove "incompetent."

[25] Cohen's discussion of the firm is based, in part, on the difficulties in measurement. L. R. Cohen, The Firm: A Revised Definition, 46 S. Econ. J. 580 (1979).

Since all stages of production are carried out by a single person, the motive for excess measurement is absent but the advantages of specialization are lost. What role does the vertically integrated firm play regarding the problem of measurement?

Consider a production process requiring several workers. A firm employing these workers will incur the costs of contracting with them and policing their activities. These costs would be avoided if the process were divided among firms, each consisting of one worker who would buy the intermediate good from the one preceding him on the production line. He may also buy other needed materials and buy, or rent, the space and equipment he uses. These factors, combined with his own work, would enhance the value of the intermediate good which he subsequently would sell to the next man on the line.[26] If production is so organized, the problem of "shirking" disappears.[27]

At most points, however, the value of the intermediate product may be difficult to assess, and therefore its sale may be accompanied by excess sorting. Thus, costs are incurred also in the exchange among such firms. Sometimes the relationship between input and output is well understood. The change in input may then serve as a satisfactory proxy for the change in output value.[28] As will now be shown, the use of input as a proxy for output does not by itself necessitate exchange within a firm, though it is a condition for this form of organization.

Would separate one-worker firms be formed in a production process spanning the tasks of several workers where output is easily measured at the end points but not at others? If the first step is organized as a separate one-worker firm, its output has to be sold to the firm performing the next task. As asserted, it is more costly to evaluate that output directly than to

[26] During the 1860s, several major industries in Birmingham were composed of numerous one-man firms. See G. C. Allen, The Industrial Development of Birmingham and the Black Country, 1860–1927 (1929; reprinted ed. 1966).

[27] Jensen and Meckling analyze the problem of borrowing and of the associated policing when the amount of capital required for the efficient firm size diverges from what the entrepreneur can supply. For their analysis to hold, firm size has to be independent of what they call "agency cost." This would be the case if optimal firm size were an exogenous "technological" datum. It is suggested here that this size is itself economically determined. See M. C. Jensen & W. H. Meckling, Theory of the Firm: Managerial Behavior, Agency Costs, and Ownership Structure, 3 J. Fin. Econ. 305 (1976).

[28] Alchian and Demsetz state, ". . . Suppose a farmer produces wheat . . . with subtle and difficult quality variations determined by how the farmer grew the wheat. A vertical integration could allow a purchaser to control the farmer's behavior in order to more economically estimate productivity." A. A. Alchian & H. Demsetz, Production, Information Costs, and Economic Organization, 62 Am. Econ. Rev. 785 (1972). This statement comes close to the basic argument here. Alchian and Demsetz, however, do not make the crucial distinction between random and biased errors.

measure the value of the products entering the first step plus its additional inputs. Thus, to determine the value of the product it receives, the second firm will have to monitor the inputs of the first firm. So long as the transition to the third-step output can be measured cheaply, however, there is no clear advantage in integrating the first two steps.[29]

When inputs have to be measured at two successive junctures, a rationale for an integrated firm emerges. If the second firm is also a one-worker enterprise whose output is difficult to measure, the firm performing the third step will have to monitor not only the inputs in the second step but also the value of the product entering the first step and the inputs within the step. Thus, the inputs of the first firm have to be monitored by both the second and the third firm. Although the second firm could provide the third with its own evaluation of the first firm's inputs, it stands to gain from overstating the case. The third firm, then, would need to verify the figures in some way. The problem is obviously compounded as the number of steps increases. If a separate organization performs this function for all steps, the conservation of information is clear: There is no longer a need for each firm to monitor the inputs in all prior steps. It is hypothesized that this is a function of the "firm."[30]

In view of this explanation, the notion of residual payments so commonly associated with the firm obtains an entirely different interpretation. When output is easily measured directly, the contribution of a worker can be assessed by his output, and there is a strong incentive for him to become self-employed. At other times, output can be measured by inputs more cheaply than by measuring it directly. If output is measured by inputs, remuneration of inputs cannot be based on output. Employees of a firm are paid by inputs rather than by output not because of lack of "entrepreneurship," but rather because their input is measured more eco-

[29] Indeed, airlines employ engineers to inspect the airplanes assigned to them while they are being built by Boeing. Similarly, in other equipment contracts and in construction it is not uncommon that the buyer retains the right to inspect the production process.

[30] Coase pointed out two forces favoring organizing production by the firm rather than by the market. One is the cost of "discovering what the relevant prices are"; the other is "the costs of negotiating and concluding a separate contract for each exchange transaction which takes place on a market." R. H. Coase, The Nature of the Firm, reprinted in Readings in Price Theory 336 (1952). Suggested here is another force—the cost of measuring intermediate outputs which, it is argued, favors production within a firm. The motive for vertical integration suggested here resembles that offered by Klein et al. See Benjamin Klein, Robert G. Crawford, & Armen A. Alchian, Vertical Integration, Appropriable Rents, and the Competitive Contracting Process, 21 J. Law & Econ. 297 (1978). Their argument, however, hinges on small numbers; at the extreme, one buyer facing one seller. There is no restriction here on the number of either buyers or sellers. In Williamson's view also, small numbers are a necessary condition, since vertical integration "harmonizes interests" and reduces the hazard of cheating between firms (see Williamson, *supra* note 8, at 82).

nomically than their output; otherwise they would have become self-employed. Having employees bear the risk in output value through direct ownership has no desirable incentive effect and thus is of little purpose. When tasks are performed by employed workers, "shirking" becomes a problem and the entrepreneur is remunerated for his monitoring of inputs, which implies that he has to assume the risk of price and other fluctuations.[31]

Distinct firms will form and trade with each other at junctures where output can be readily measured, but where output is difficult to measure the different steps will be performed within the firm. Between the time that a commodity such as canned salmon leaves the manufacturer and the time it reaches the consumer, its physical properties and its value will have changed only slightly. Other goods such as produce and bread may change a great deal. The ownership of a commodity may not change at all between production and consumption, as is the case with home-grown vegetables, or it may change several times. It is predicted that ownership will change more frequently the less the commodity is subject to change. Thus, canned salmon is expected to change ownership more times than fresh salmon, powdered milk more than fresh milk, cookies more than fresh bread, and so on. A comparison, admittedly casual, of cookies and bread is in conformity with the prediction. Grocers buy the cookies they sell, but only rent shelf space to bakeries for bread sold through them.[32]

Errors of Proxy Measurement

Often, the units by which a commodity is exchanged differ from those for which it is desired. For example, tires are measured by ply, size, and tread, whereas they are valued for strength, road-holding ability, and longevity; oranges are sold by weight, which includes the seldom-wanted skin. In this section, some of the problems that arise from the use of proxies are discussed.

Consider the tastiness of apples. Suppose that taste is extremely costly to measure and that it is correlated with color, which can be measured by the naked eye.[33] Color, then, is used as a measure of taste, and the market price of apples becomes a function of their color—the redder are Red

[31] This argument strongly parallels that of Alchian and Demsetz, *supra* note 28. Their "team production" output can be measured cheaply, but because of scale economies the output of a team member cannot. Team members, then, have to be policed and are remunerated according to their inputs.

[32] Coor's beer, which is more difficult to keep fresh because it has no preservatives, is supposedly monitored by that brewery more vigorously than do other breweries.

[33] John Umbect says (personal communication) that in Tangier, tangerines offered for sale are displayed on a branch with a leaf or two. The apparent reason is that a leaf is a better visual indicator of freshness than is the fruit itself.

Delicious apples, the higher is their price. Thus, an orchardist will optimize with respect to color.

When the proxy measure can be manipulated, here, too, people will redistribute income at the expense of resources. Suppose that a chemical fertilizer can enhance apples without affecting their taste. Abstracting from the asesthetic value of apples, if the consumer cannot discern whether the chemical has been used and obtaining that information is too costly, the orchardist will then apply the chemical.[34]

Since consumers ultimately value apples for their taste and not their color, had it been possible effortlessly to stop the use of the fertilizer, the cost of the extra reddening would have been avoided without incurring any other loss.[35] The use of the proxy seems wasteful—the apples are made "excessively" pretty. The proxy, however, is presumably used because the alternative of not using it is still more costly.

The use of the chemical will affect the relationship between color and value. Assuming diminishing marginal valuation, R_0 in Figure 1 is the original relationship between the two attributes. The application of a given amount of the fertilizer will shift the curve to the right to R_1. Apples of any given color are now valued less. Still, the redder an apple is, the tastier and more valuable it is. The shift in the curve, however, is not likely to be uniform. Rather, the redder the apples are to start with, the smaller is the shift. This is due to two factors, each of which is sufficient for the argument here. First, the originally redder apples are likely to gain less in value from a given increase in color. Second, a given dose of the fertilizer is expected to affect them less noticeably.

Thus R_1 is steeper than R_0. Given the cost and the error of measuring redness, the steeper relationship constitutes a reduction in the informational value of the color of apples. This is a force constraining the application of fertilizer, but it also guarantees that some amount will be used. To see this, assume momentarily that the relationships between redness and value and between redness and the amount of fertilizer are both linear. This means that R_0 and R_1 are parallel straight lines. If the return from the application of one unit of the chemical is positive, then a reapplication will yield the same return. Eventually, however, consumers would cease to employ color as a measure of taste. At this point, the return from its use in *any* amount will drop to zero. But as the use of the fertilizer is discon-

[34] A grower using the fertilizer need not be aware that his behavior is dissipating. He is informed by the market-price structure that consumers value redness, and that is what he is providing.

[35] Spence's "signal" is also a measurable attribute which is correlated with the "true" one and subject to manipulation. See M. Spence, Job Market Signaling, 87 Q. J. Econ. 355 (1973).

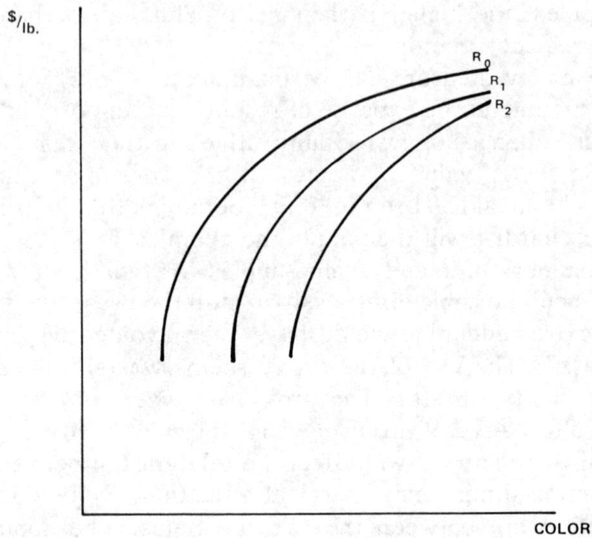

FIGURE 1

tinued, the relationship between color and value will be restored, returning us to the starting point of the cycle.[36]

When returns are diminishing, however, the dilemma disappears. In Figure 1, R_2 represents the effect of a second dose of the fertilizer. The return is lower because the effect on color is less than that of the first dose, and also because an extra unit of color increases revenue less than it did before, as R_2 is steeper than R_1. As more fertilizer is used, a point will be reached at which the return from an extra dose is equal to its cost.

If the simplifying assumptions—that the fertilizer does not affect taste and that color is valued only as a proxy for taste—are relaxed, the analysis grows more complicated but the logic remains the same. To the extent that taste would be improved by the use of the fertilizer, dissipation is decreased. If taste is affected adversely, but the correlation between taste and color remains positive, dissipation will exceed the cost of the fertilizer. If taste is affected more than color, too little of the chemical will be used; indeed, it will not be used at all if it does not alter color even though it improves the taste.

Now, relaxing the second assumption, suppose that the color of apples is valued for its own merit. In this case, the fertilizer will be applied apart from its effect on taste, and it will be used beyond the point that would

[36] Rothschild and Stiglitz present another "no-equilibrium" result. Their setting is competitive insurance markets. See Michael Rothschild & Joseph Stiglitz, Equilibrium in Competitive Insurance Markets, 90 Q. J. Econ. 629 (1976).

have been dictated if color were merely a proxy for taste. The rest of the analysis remains unchanged.

The color of apples can undoubtedly be affected in other ways, such as the choice of harvest time, of storage temperature, and so on. Each of these methods will be used (and the information content of color function "degraded") to a point where the return equals the cost. The general principle is that maximization occurs with respect to whatever measures consumers use to determine market values. Presumably, the measures in actual use combine a high correlation with the desired ones while possessing high resistance to degradation.

Activities directed toward the market measures will, in general, be off the mark in terms of their effect on the "true" measures. Nevertheless, a grower who applies less of the fertilizer will find his revenue declining more than his cost since, given the assumptions here, he is unable to convince consumers that his less colorful apples are as tasty. This is an instance where the "bad" drives the "good" out of the market. Similarly, a consumer cannot gain by buying apples that are not as red as his own preferences dictate, since the price structure of applies of different shades of red is itself determined by consumers' valuation.

It is tempting to think that if a grocer would mark a bin of apples "ugly but tasty," and if the apples indeed proved flavorful, he could overcome the problem of the spurious measure.[37] The difficulty in convincing buyers that what looks unattractive may nevertheless be good is illustrated by the owner who spends resources to "beautify" the house he plans to sell in a way he did not feel was worthwhile when he was living there. Buyers are well aware of this common practice, but its survival demonstrates that the skin-deep treatment does affect their decisions. In the case of apples, the greatest benefits accrue to those growers able to convince consumers that they avoid the fertilizer while in fact using it. It is difficult to allay consumers' suspicions, since for each type of apple the redder it is the better it tastes.

Still, suppose that to a particular grower the cost of convincing consumers that no fertilizer was used is low enough.[38] It is predicted that on average the grower's apples will look less attractive, or rather, less red, than those grown with the fertilizer; that for given redness, the unfer-

[37] Safeway stores seem to harp on this theme when advertising their "Scotch Buy" brand as "It ain't fancy but it sure is good!" This brand, however, is backed by Safeway's own brand name. Two other examples (supplied by Marion Impola) of attempts to dispel mistrust are a seller's sign by his Kiwi fruit, "Ugly, but interesting," and Smucker's ad, "With a name like Smucker's, it's got to be good."

[38] If a growers' association can police its members more cheaply than consumers can police a grower, the association is expected to prohibit the use of the fertilizer. This restrictive practice actually promotes efficiency.

tilized apples will be more expensive; and that the unfertilized apples of a given taste will be cheaper, an implication that is easy to verify subjectively but not objectively.

Given the last implication, the unfertilized apples should drive the other apples out of the market. However, the cost of upholding the no-fertilizer claim will vary among consumers. It is expected, then, that both types of apples will continue to be provided. It seems plausible that the farther consumers are from the grower, the higher the cost of creating "trust." The notion that better Washington apples or California oranges will be shipped to the East Coast then applies to the better-looking, but not to the better-tasting, fruit.

FUTURES MARKETS[39]

The impersonality that characterizes markets in received models does not appear to hold for most actual markets, where the identity or brand name of transactors is essential to functioning. In "futures" markets, however, the trustworthiness of the parties is inconsequential, since apart from the enforcement role of the exchange there is no continuing relationship. The exchange certifies that the traded commodities meet the required specifications and that payment is forthcoming. Thus, the buyer need not worry about receiving defective merchandise and the seller does not have to spend resources to collect his pay. However, far from the accepted view, it appears that such impersonality is attained at high cost.

Suppose that the rate at which a good will deteriorate can be controlled. If the present price decreases as expected deterioration increases, the seller will spend resources to retard that process. Suppose, however, that measurement of the expected deterioration at the time the exchange is agreed upon is so costly that it will not be performed. Now, if the exchange is strictly by specifications, as in the futures trade, the prevention of deterioration will not occur since it will not be remunerated. On the other hand, in the spot market, where sellers operate under a brand name, deterioration will be controlled because a positive return is expected.[40]

This distinction may explain an otherwise puzzling phenomenon: Farm products traded in futures markets tend to be characterized as of "low-quality" or "garbage" grade.[41] How can such a term apply to a commod-

[39] An earlier analysis of these markets by Acheson and McManus is not unlike the one presented here. See K. Acheson & J. McManus, The Costs of Transacting in Futures Markets (August 1979) (unpublished paper, Carleton Univ.).

[40] Lindsay draws a similar distinction between government output that is evaluated strictly by specification, and private output, in which unspecified margins are (somehow) adhered to. See Cotton M. Lindsay, A Theory of Government Enterprise, 84 J. Pol. Econ. 1061 (1976).

[41] The costliness of measuring the protein content of wheat and the resulting allocation of

ity that meets all stipulated specifications? The answer may well be that other *non*stipulated attributes will be underproduced when the commodities are destined for futures markets. The levels of the valuable qualities could have been increased at a lower cost than their valuation except for the cost of measurement—which has prevented such action. For this reason, producers are not expected to plan to produce for the futures markets. Only when the commodity is found unsuitable for regular customers would they divert it toward the futures market.

Since commodities sold in futures markets are also sold in spot markets, two testable implications are suggested. First, the price in the spot market is predicted to be higher than that in the futures market for what appears, in terms of specifications, to be the same commodity. Second, specifications are expected to be more comprehensive in futures markets than in spot markets. Since brand name is already established in the spot market, some direct measurements can be dispensed with.

Uncertainty and Dissipating Behavior

Diminishing marginal utility of income implies that the more income varies around a given mean the less it is valued. The presumption that in reality the marginal utility of income is indeed diminishing is the basis for the accepted explanation of insurance, product warranties, and sharing arrangements that are said to reduce the uncertainty facing the individual. It was suggested, however, that warranties and sharing arrangements may be explained by a quite different force: the cost of getting reliable information about a good. This argument is now more generally related to the problem of uncertainty.

Some uncertainty is truly and entirely random; in most situations, however, opportunities abound for the human hand to affect the odds. A person facing an uncertain situation has reason to fear that if the odds are tampered with, they will not be in his favor. A used-car buyer who suspects that the salesman will attempt to saddle him with a worse-than-average car will take some countermeasures. Both the odds tampering by the seller and the protective steps by the buyer consume resources. The buyer, then, would pay a premium independent of any "risk aversion" to convert the uncertain situation into a certain one.

The risk-aversion model predicts that risk will be shifted toward the party for whom risk is less costly. The prediction here is that whoever is in a position to affect the odds will tend to assume the risk, though the two are not mutually exclusive. The payment of royalties rather than a lump

---

high-protein wheat to regular channels and low-protein wheat through impersonal channels is described by Carl L. Alsberg, Protein Content: A Neglected Factor in Wheat Grades, in 2 Wheat Studies of the Food Research Institute 163–76 (1926).

sum to an author, and particularly to a novice, tends to support the latter hypothesis.

The offering of warranties or of some other means to reduce uncertainty is itself costly. It is predicted that the more easily tampering can be detected and the larger the subsequent loss, the less frequently will a warranty be offered. Indeed, people are expected to expose themselves deliberately to detection to reduce the buyer's fear of being cheated.[42] It is predicted, though most tentatively, that well-established law firms will set fixed fees or fixed hourly charges rather than contingent fees more often than will less prestigious law firms. The highly reputable law firm having more of a reputation to protect is expected to monitor its members to provide clients with satisfactory service. To attract business, law firms of lesser reputation in effect offer insurance when they base their fees contingent on good performance.

Concluding Remarks

The problems and costs of measurement pervade and significantly affect all economic transactions. Errors of measurement are too costly to eliminate entirely. The value of equally priced items will differ, then, and people will spend resources to acquire the difference. Such resource expenditure is wasteful, and it is hypothesized that exchange parties will form such contracts and engage in such activities that reduce this kind of resource use. The customer's random selection from an already optimally sorted commodity will avoid the excessive expense. Thus, for example, it is expected that some readily obtainable information will be suppressed to preempt opportunities for excessive measurement.

Because inputs are sometimes the best available proxies for measuring output, vertical integration in the form of organizing output within firms can conserve some measurement costs. Measurement losses also can be lowered by other expedients such as share contracts and warranties. "Trust," "brand name," "repeat purchases," and the like also lower the need for costly measurements, though they are too costly to produce.

The fragments of evidence presented are only illustrative and should not be construed as a test of the model. Even the hypotheses offered are rather tentative; more thorough knowledge of the details of market organization are needed to make firmer predictions. They help to demonstrate, however, that the concept of "measurement" is operational and that the model based on it is capable of generating testable implications.

[42] The owner of a race track has less incentive to tamper with the results of a horse race when betting is on a parimutuel basis, which may explain the prevalence of that arrangement. In general, it seems that organizers of games of chance are rewarded not on the basis of their risk but of gross income. Sellers of insurance, on the contrary, subject themselves to substantial risk.

Zeitschrift für die gesamte Staatswissenschaft (ZgS) 141 (1985), 4–16
Journal of Institutional and Theoretical Economics

Transaction Costs: Are They Just Costs?*

by

YORAM BARZEL

What are the main effects of the cost of transacting, and what distinguishes them from other costs? In this paper it is argued that when transaction costs are positive, people are able to gain at each other's expense. In order to minimize the associated loss, people will agree to restrain themselves in various ways, and will erect social institutions to impose and enforce the restraints. Such institutions have no significant function when transacting is costless.

The model presented here is compared with a stylized, costless transaction, Walrasian model to bring out some of the unique features of positive costs of transacting. Even though the Walrasian model asssumes that the cost of transacting is zero, some practitioners use it to analyze transaction cost problems. For instance, the Pareto conditions as obtained from a zero transaction cost model are routinely used for the assessment of advertising. It is sufficient to observe that ignorance is a precondition for advertising, whereas the Walrasian model assumes full knowledge of exchanged products[1].

The division of labor is a major contributor to the maximization of the total value of the resources used. A result of specializing is that the producers of a good are distinct from its consumers. Resources are required then not only for producing goods (and for shipping them to consumers), but also for effecting exchange – identifying potential buyers, describing the good to them, setting the terms of trade, and transfering rights.

In much of the theory of perfect competition, particularly as developed by Walras and his followers, it is assumed that homogeneous commodities are traded at a point in space. Moreover, buyers are assumed to be fully informed regarding the attributes of every unit of every good, and know the market clearing prices of various sellers[2]. All units of the same commodity must, then, be traded at a uniform price. As the costs of effecting exchange in this model are assumed to be zero, resources are needed for 'production'

* Thanks to Aaron Director for providing the stimulus for this paper.

[1] An extensive critique of one branch of this literature is carried along these lines in BARZEL [1977].

[2] Some relevant features of the Walrasian system are described in detail by DAHLMAN [1980].

only, and maximization of value implies the minimization of the costs of production[3]. This result is underscored by the 'Coase Theorem', which states that had the cost of transacting been zero, the maximum output would have been produced regardless of initial resource ownership pattern.

In the Walrasian system income (or wealth) is maximized, and its distribution is costlessly determined in the process of determining resource allocation. A common contemporary assertion is that resources which are used solely to redistribute wealth are wasted, or 'dissipated', a statement, however, that is usually made without specifying whether it refers to a zero or to a positive transaction cost world. The mere observation that resources are used to affect redistribution constitutes evidence of waste only in a Walrasian, zero transaction cost, world. Because waste would be instantly eliminated if the cost of transacting were zero, such an observation would refute the Walrasian model[4]. It will be shown below that in the presence of transaction costs, resources must be used in the determination of the distribution of wealth. Thus observing such resource use cannot, by itself, be construed as waste.

In what follows, three of the results derived from the Walrasian model are of particular relevance: (1) Given the initial ownership of resources (as well as tastes and technology) the distribution of wealth is uniquely determined. (2) Whenever any person commits errors in the use of resources or singly changes his behavior, he alone will be affected[5]. And (3) if, for whatever reason, some constraint on resource use is newly imposed by the government, for example, income will necessarily decline. It will be shown below that none of these results hold when the cost of transacting is positive.

1. Transaction Costs and Dissipation

The central proposition here is that exchange costs, which have been ignored in the Walrasian model, differ in essence from the Walrasian costs. Exchange costs acquire their special character from the cost of product information. Certain real world problems that would disappear had this cost been zero are discussed in this section.

The assumption of product homogeneity, or alternatively of costless information of products, is the one allowing the Walrasian model to dispense with exchange costs. To many modern observers this assumption may appear

---

[3] It is not easy to envision how resource ownership is initially determined under these conditions. On the other hand, it seems that once ownership is determined, it is entirely secure and that policing costs are zero.

[4] Christopher Hall suggests that it is always possible to form a rationale for what appears as an inefficiency since it is costless to have as elaborate an arrangement as one wishes. The Walrasian model, then, is empty of empirical content and is impossible to refute. I will leave this issue alone.

[5] We abstract from the effects of such behavior on aggregate demand and supply.

eminently reasonable. Buyers often spend no resources in choosing among equally priced units of a good offered by a seller, thus treating them as homogeneous. The offering of warranties testifies that people do not view the warranted goods as homogeneous[6]. Moreover, it can be shown that where product information is more costly to transmit, producers will spend more resources to enhance the uniformity of their products, or set prices more in accord with quality[7]. If so, the observed homogeneity in the market may be the result of a costly process adopted by the producer rather than one emerging as a free byproduct of mechanization[8]. Indeed, quality control would have been superfluous had product homogeneity, or at least the identification of product quality, been a free outcome of the production process.

In any case, many commodities and services are patently nonhomogeneous. Labor services, whether of unskilled workers or of highly trained engeneers vary widely within groups of equally paid individuals; equally priced hotel rooms vary in attributes such as exposure to noise and distance from the elevator; the tomato bin in the grocery store contains some overripe ones and some which are still green; the list can be extended indefinitely. Homogeneity could be enhanced by explicitly charging for additional attributes or by sorting commodities into more homogeneous groups. Nevertheless, as sold in the market, such commodities distinctly lack in homogeneity.

Why is the assumption of costless product information singled out? It is my contention that costly (intermediate and final) product information is the central problem of transacting, leading to all other transacting problems. To see this, suppose that product information were costless. It seems that a whole array of other costs of transacting would then disappear.

Consider first the use of labor services. It can be readily seen that product homogeneity would render the supervision of labor easy, and perhaps altogether dispense with it. In order to supervise a worker one need only find the quality and value of one of the units, count the number of units he produces, and the value of the product is known. Other inputs can similarly be measured, and thus the value of net product is easy to determine as well. There is no obvious remaining reason for the worker to fail to perform as an independent contractor.

To further demonstrate the validity of the assertion, consider the problem of policing, or of the protection of property rights. Suppose that two individuals claim the same item. How will such a dispute be resolved? In isolation the stronger one will win. Costless product (and factor) information implies

[6] Walter Oi correctly pointed out to me that if differences are truly random, ex ante the units are homogeneous. If, however, resources can be spent to distinguish among units, the argument in the paper holds.

[7] See BARZEL [1982].

[8] The observed heterogeneity in commodities transacted in the market most likely is much less than heterogeneity in all commodities since non-market exchange becomes more attractive as heterogeneity increases.

that in future performances of the two activities the appropriate individuals' attributes are costlessly known, as are those of the contended item. Before the dispute erupts, then, its outcome is fully anticipated by both individuals. The 'designated' loser will do best to concede immediately. Why spend his energy in addition to losing the asset? The certainty of the outcome of the dispute, which is the result of costless product information, eliminates the dispute.

A more complex social setting will require more information to settle the dispute. Ultimately, however, the outcome is still costlessly known beforehand and thus the dispute will again be settled in advance. It is like one chess grandmaster conceding to another in what appears to be the middle of the game. Grandmasters, however, can see a great number of moves in advance, and they concede when they recognize that their situation is hopeless, not when they are actually check-mated. When information on products and on people's abilities is complete, the outcomes of disputes are known and people will not bother to fight[9].

The same reasoning applies to robbery. If I can foil a robber, he will know that beforehand, and will not attempt the theft. If I know that I will fail, I can, at least, spare myself the futile effort of trying to stop him. Similarly, the parties will 'know' how they would have fared in the presence of the police and the courts and thus these controlling bodies are not needed.

Broadly interpreted, costless product information is a far reaching assumption. By maintaining that product information is costless, the Walrasian model is consistent then in also maintaining that property rights are complete and costlessly enforced.

We now examine some of the effects of the costliness of product information. Homogeneity of a good is itself a valuable attribute; people will pay extra to know more accurately what they receive. By the Walrasian model the level of any attribute will be produced to the point where its marginal cost equals its marginal valuation. Had this applied to the attribute 'homogeneity', one would expect commodities to be sorted to the point where the marginal valuation of the added homogeneity would equal its marginal cost[10]. The same principle used by a producer to produce a good will govern the decision to produce homogeneity. The producer of the good will engage those resources with comparative advantage in sorting to produce the desired level of homogeneity.

If the production of the homogeneity attribute is subject to increasing cost and its valuation is declining, its optimal level, as a rule, will fall short of

---

[9] Whenever the parties fully agree on the outcome, whether or not information is free, there will be no dispute. Costless information is a sufficient condition for such agreement.

[10] In the approach pioneered by STIGLER [1961] and adopted by ALCHIAN ([1970], pp. 27–52), information is treated as just another commodity whose (competitive) production meets the condition of equating its marginal cost to its marginal valuation.

perfect homogeneity. As some heterogeneity will then persist, the nonidentical units must somehow be allocated among buyers. If the units of the good sold to any customer are randomly selected from an already optimally sorted population, joint wealth will be maximized since customers will then be provided with the optimal level of homogeneity. It is now shown that in the implementation of such an exchange one encounters difficulties alien to the Walrasian system.

When a buyer receives sub-par units, he can never tell with certainty whether he was unlucky or whether he was cheated. Repeat purchase, a practice which serves no function in the Walrasian model, reduces the severity of the problem but does not eliminate it[11]. Thus the seller can get away with some cheating, and given maximization, cheating will occur. Under competition, price will adjust to the cheating. What is costly, however, is not the cheating per se; rather, resources are devoted to cheating and to its prevention which sharply distinguishes the outcome from that obtained in the Walrasian world.

To better grasp the nature of resource use here, consider another method of selling. When buyers are suspicious of a seller's selection, the seller could realize a higher return by letting buyers inspect the units offered and select the preferred items. For the sake of the argument, suppose that the units offered are already optimally sorted, as would be the case in the Walrasian system where the optimal amount of every attribute is provided. The Walrasian model will prove inapplicable if the optimal level of sorting is not maintained under costly transacting. It is now shown that under the given conditions, consumers will still pick and choose; i.e., they will spend additional resources on sorting[12].

To induce buyers to buy any unit, the price the seller charges must be lower than the expected valuation of some of the units[13]. Indeed, if customers are expected to refrain from choosing, the seller must offer the commodity at the price which will clear the market and which is consistent with its mean and its variability. He must also convince buyers that he is doing just that.

Consumers who spend resources on choosing obtain thereby better sorted, and therefore more valuable units. This alone, though, cannot cover the entire cost of sorting because the items considered are already optimally sorted[14]. When consumers are allowed to pick and choose, they are also able to refuse units they deem worth less than their price. By retaining only units that they

---

[11] Repeat purchase, not a costless procedure, may facilitate exchange by policing the seller (and the buyer too).

[12] See BARZEL [1982] for a more detailed demonstration.

[13] If the price charged is higher than the expected valuation of the most highly valued unit, obviously no sales will occur. Even if the price is equal to the expected valuation of the most valued unit no sales will occur because consumers still have to incur the cost of identifying that unit. Thus, the price must be lower than the expected valuation of the most valued unit.

[14] The seller, presumably, uses the lowest cost method for sorting. The buyer, then, cannot do better than the seller in this regard.

value more than the price charged for them, their sorting expense is made worthwhile[15]. Whereas the joint return from the added sorting must fall short of its cost, a buyer whose sorting cost is the same as the seller's will engage in sorting since he also gains at the seller's expense. Thus, the Pareto conditions used as a starting point cannot be maintained; in the case discussed the amount of sorting exceeds the jointly maximizing level.

In terms of property rights, the seller allows consumers to choose among the heterogeneous units offered because the information required for a better delineation of the product is too costly. That seller, in fact, is placing in the public domain his right over the differential between the more valuable units and the price charged. Buyers will spend resources to capture the differential. The cost of the added sorting, however, is higher than the value, because the gain to buyers who sort consists partly of the capture of the more valuable rights. This demonstrates the dissipating nature of some transaction costs[16]. Whereas the Walrasian system is necessarily free of this action, when the cost of transacting is positive some resources *will* be used in this ostensibly wasteful manner.

In the instance just described, consumers capture rights by rushing to be first to select from a new shipment. Resources are also spent on the repeated inspection of rejected items[17]. Such use of resources may take other forms. When buyers are expected to engage in sorting, a seller's extra dollar spent on sorting beyond the optimal level will increase his income by more than one dollar. The seller's sorting effort increases the (joint) value of the good by almost one dollar; it also prevents (some of) buyers' sorting to capture the seller's wealth. By the added sorting the seller retains the extra valuation which previously was placed in the public domain. Here too the sum of the parties' gains from this extra effort is less than the cost. Nevertheless the seller will sort to the point where an extra dollar spent will yield *him* just one dollar in increased revenues[18].

The seller who has a commodity to sell adopts the method yielding him the highest net gain. The buyer similarly spends his resources as well as he can. The action of capturing rights, however, is subject to competition. The method yielding the largest joint net gain must prevail. Moreover, no third party is involved, and the outcome, therefore, is free from what is sometimes

---

[15] As a corollary, due to Christopher Hall, it can be shown that a maximizing seller who sells heterogeneous items and permits choosing will never plan to sell all the items at the price set initially.

[16] DAHLMAN [1979] shows that other types of costs that are sometimes classified as transaction costs are not dissipating.

[17] Had the information on items inspected but not purchased been marketable the duplication of information would be avoided, but then the rush to head of the line would have intensified.

[18] Another component of dissipation is when buyers spend resources to predict price changes by sellers (this, essentially, is HIRSHLEIFER's [1971] speculation argument).

called externality. Thus 'dissipation' can be said to be present only in comparison with a world that does not exist. Because transacting is costly, resource cost to effect transfers is inevitable. Given the institutional setting, individuals' maximizing behavior, however, generates the smallest possible level of dissipation[19].

It may seem that dissipation would disappear, or at least decline if people would only behave as they should. In some instances the individuals involved may be at least vaguely aware that what they do is not 'right', as when a seller selects for a customer items which are inferior to those displayed. In other situations, however, it is unlikely that market participants are aware that anything is amiss. Why shouldn't a buyer pick and choose to his heart's content when the seller, through the implicit contract, invites him to do so? Obviously, the attempt to behave properly is of little value when people cannot distinguish proper from improper behavior.

Some students of the cost of transacting classify maximizing behavior into 'acceptable' behavior as distinct from 'opportunism' or 'self interest seeking with guile'. WILLIAMSON [1981] goes beyond mere classification; he states that dissipation from 'incomplete contracting' would be avoided 'if economic agents were completely trustworthy'. Whereas, no doubt, some dissipation will be eliminated when agents keep their promises, a major problem remains. For the same reasons that contracts are incomplete, agents cannot possibly know in full detail to what their word applies. They are likely to err, then, when attempting to keep their word, even though sometimes breaking a promise is preferable to keeping it.

People cannot costlessly tell when their behavior is dissipating. If they attempt to do what they perceive as the right things rather than what maximizes their wealth, some of the time they will waste resources. When people can be counted on to take advantage of every opportunity, as is usually assumed, their anticipated behavior itself can affect contract terms. A truck owner employing a driver has the choice of paying by the mile or by the hour. The latter is particularly attractive when the road is in bad repair. A driver employed by the hour is expected to take his time. In this particular case, leisurely driving is desirable because damage to the truck is less. On the other hand, the driver who is anxious to do good work and drives fast does more harm than a self-seeking shirker would.

It is probably true that if each and every person will behave 'as he should', dissipation will be eliminated, and the special features of transacting discussed here will disappear. Such behavior, however, is inconsistent with individual maximization. Moreover, it is not clear what is the operational use of exploring a world in which people behave 'as they should'. The assumption of individual maximization is immensely useful in economic analysis. On the other hand,

---

[19] As far as I know, the notion of the minimization of dissipation was introduced in CHEUNG [1974].

it does not seem possible to operationally identify when maximization is self-seeking and when it is not. This classification, then, adds nothing to the understanding of behavior and in all likelihood serves only to confuse.

2. *Some Effects of Costly Transacting*

As stated earlier, the initial owner will sell his good in the way that he thinks will maximize his wealth. The seller who will provide the jointly maximizing amount of sorting will not adequately protect his wealth from capture by buyers. Thus, the attempt to gain from trade is intermingled with the problem of dividing the gain. The solution to the wealth distribution problem may be complex; nevertheless it is determinate (and unique)[20].

In the Walrasian system a single person's action will not affect the utilities or wealth of others. This is not so when transacting is costly and resources are spent to affect distribution. The more resources a buyer spends on selection, the larger the loss he inflicts on the seller. The seller who charges a uniform price for a set of heterogeneous units of a good will suffer a greater loss from selection by a person whose cost of selection is low than from one whose cost is high. In the Walrasian system, on the other hand, a seller's wealth is independent of the action taken by any single buyer.

In the Walrasian system any advance in productivity increases aggregate output. This is not necessarily true when the cost of transacting is positive. It is not surprising to note that the invention of a superior lock-pick can reduce aggregate wealth. Neither will productivity increases in 'ordinary' and 'legal' activities necessarily increase output. Any change that will permit buyers to extract a larger fraction of the unassigned rights will induce the seller to spend more resources than otherwise to prevent the redistribution, for instance, by reducing the heterogeneity of his product beyond the jointly maximizing level. Thus, when consumers' cost of sorting falls, but remains higher than that of the sorters employed by sellers, sellers are likely to engage in

---

[20] The situation just described has some interesting elements in common with the case of a monopolist selling to the monopsonist. Textbooks based on the Walrasian system have encountered great difficulty in determining output and wealth distribution under these conditions. In more 'modern' texts, joint maximization is a suggested solution. In that case output seems determinate. Wealth distribution, however, is not, and therefore this approach is revealed to offer little more than a comforting terminology while sweeping the real problem under the rug.

As in the case of selling heterogeneous commodities, a portion of the gain from transacting in bilateral monopoly is not assigned and may be competed away. In both cases the parties have the incentive to spend resources to capture a share of the unassigned wealth. It was possible to specify, though just sketchily, what form this resource expense will take in the case of transaction costs. While it seems that the wealth distribution in the bilateral monopoly case can be determined in a parallel fashion, no attempt is made to do this here.

more sorting than before even though that added sorting is not jointly maximizing. The increased productivity of buyers, then, may lower the combined wealth of buyers and sellers[21].

This result is now demonstrated in greater detail. Suppose that the population consists of two homogeneous groups, one being more productive in sorting than the other. When sorting his commodity, a seller will always employ the more highly productive sorters. Suppose that all his buyers belong to the less productive sorting group. As I show elsewhere, the level of sorting effected by the seller will be just low enough to dissuade buyers from sorting on their own (provided that the *jointly* desired sorting level is not higher than that)[22].

Suppose now that the productivity in sorting of the low productivity group increases, but still falls short of that of the better sorters. The seller, then, will choose to effect a higher sorting level; otherwise his customers will capture part of the value of the good that he could have retained. The increased sorting level diverges further from the jointly maximizing level. Thus, the increase in productivity, being useful only to capture wealth, results in a decline in wealth.

When transacting is costly, resources will be devoted to affect the distribution of wealth not only when exchange is directly involved; production itself is affected by the cost of transacting in at least two major ways. First, of two close substitutes, the one whose production cost is lower will not necessarily be the one produced since the cost of transacting it may exceed that of transacting the other by an even larger amount, and the other will then be produced. For instance, it is possible that the varieties of fruits and vegetables offered in the market are not those least costly to produce relative to their valuation. The 'dissipation' associated with transacting for the inherently more homogeneous varieties may be sufficiently lower to give them an edge over other varieties.

Additionally, the technological considerations which are included in the conventional production function notions are not the only ones which determine how resources will be used in production. For example, preference will be given to materials and to products that are difficult to steal and processes which make it easy to monitor workers' performance will be preferred over those which are difficult to monitor.

---

[21] Both in the case of a better consumers' sorting and in that of superior lock-pick some rights are placed in the public domain. In one case it is the rights to the differential in value between equally priced units; in the other it is the value 'expected' to be stolen. In the first, the resource expense of added sorting reduces the loss. In the second, the resource expense on better locks reduces the loss. Property rights are placed in the public domain in one case because of the high cost of policing them; in the other because of the high cost of measuring (or defining) them.

[22] See Barzel [1982]. For simplicity it is also assumed that buyers do not employ their own sorters.

More generally, wealth tends to be dissipated in the process of transacting. Maximization by a seller, then is with regard to that portion of the value of the product he can retain for himself which depends, among other things, on the exact nature of the product. By the time a product is offered for sale, the cost of transacting had already intruded. Thus it is not possible to clearly separate costs directed to 'production' from those directed to 'transaction'. To the individual, they all are costs to be minimized. Nevertheless, a major distinction remains. The Walrasian costs of production cannot be lowered by changes in social institutions whereas the costs associated with those of transacting may be lowered by such institutions. This is the subject of the next section.

3. Constraints on Market Activities

When transaction costs are positive, maximizing individuals spend resources to capture valued attributes from each other. Total income then is less than it would have been under joint maximization. The loss, however, may be lowered by the imposition of constraints – by the deliberate curtailment of the freedom of action. Such constraints cannot serve any useful function under the Walrasian system. In the rest of this section the role of constraints on market activities is discussed and some possible transaction cost explanations for certain privately and publicly imposed constraints on the operations of markets are offered.

Had transacting been costless, curtailing the buyer's right to inspect merchandise and offering him instead a 'pig in a poke' would lower wealth or at best would serve no purpose. When transacting is costly the resources that would have been devoted to inspection might have been dissipated which the constraint may serve to reduce. The same may apply to other constraints, such as imposing a uniform commission rate on residential housing sales, or tying the sale of two or more commodities. Whether it is valid to explain the constraint in this vein can only be determined empirically. The point is that the Walrasian framework is incapable of evaluating such constraints.

Similarly the assessment of government-imposed constraints by the Walrasian standards is improper. For instance, the state-imposed requirement to withdraw dairy products from the market prior to a certain date seems arbitrary and wasteful when judged by the Walrasian criteria. Wouldn't such waste necessarily be avoided by leaving the 'marketing' to competition in the market? Only when transacting is costless can such a statement be made, though in that case the waste can be costlessly avoided. When the cost of transacting is positive some 'waste' is inevitable since it is too costly to equate marginal costs and marginal valuations along all margins. It is conceivable that as a result of the restriction imposed by government, waste is lower than it would have been had government not intervened. The effect of the restriction, then, cannot be construed as true waste on a priori grounds alone.

Suppose, for instance, that an organization such as the AMA is evaluated. If the AMA's objective is to obtain monopoly gains by restricting output, it is bound to fail if it operates inside the Walrasian world. Neither can its objective be the guarantee of quality since in a world of costless product information the effort is superfluous. There is simply no room within the Walrasian model for imposing a minimum level of physicians' training or for restricting the collection of referral fees. Any such constraint will merely lower output. In brief, since in the Walrasian system resource allocation is already efficient, institutions to promote efficiency have no useful role to play and ones that would reduce efficiency could not survive[23].

Whereas social institutions perform no significant function in a Walrasian world, such institutions are capable of lowering costs when transacting is costly, and thus their presence is expected. One of their hypothesized functions is to create conditions such that producers will tend to provide the optimal level of homogeneity on the one hand, and on the other that consumers will act as if that choice were random. An apparently attractive component of such policy is the prohibition of providing items that fall below a certain quality level. This policy will assure consumers that they will not get items whose value is substantially lower than their price, and thus the policy will lower the return from consumers' search among the items offered.

In this light, reconsider the dating of commodities. Sellers often seem reluctant to inform buyers regarding the age or safe life of items they carry, even when the information is not costly to supply[24]. Without the information, consumers are forced to view an item's freshness at random. Consumers, nevertheless will consider buying the goods if they do not think they are consistently receiving relatively stale merchandise. The better the reputation of a seller, then, the less information he is expected to provide on the freshness of commodities offered, and net-of-search cost, the lower the prices of these commodities.

The private action which seems to reduce excess search is sometimes abetted by regulation. States often require the withdrawal of dairy products before a certain expiration date. When this requirement is enforced, consumers will not encounter extremely stale items, and their incentive to identify and capture the fresher units is lessened.

Regulations introduce costs of their own, particularly because of their rigidity. The optimal time for withdrawing a commodity from the market depends on factors such as its price, storage temperature, and buyers' income. Under

---

[23] If I grasp correctly STIGLER's [1961] and ALCHIAN's [1970] approach, there is no room for institutions in their framework either; their information costs are no different from any other cost.

[24] Many commodities are dated in a code; others simply in an unobstrusive way.

the regulation, then, some of the time the commodity will be withdrawn earlier than is 'optimal'. Still, because of the lower consumers' cost of choosing, sellers may be able to charge, on average, a higher price, and consumers' net of search cost price may be lower than when the regulation is not imposed. The expectation of a lower consumer price is the consequence of competition among sellers leading to the transfer of some of the gains to consumers. One implication of this hypothesis is that output is expected to be higher than in the absence of the regulation.

Occupational licensing may serve a similar purpose. Consumers will view licensed professionals as more uniform when some minimum qualifying criteria are imposed[25]. They would then spend less on search and would be willing to spend more on the service itself. Advertising that draws attention to individual differences among professionals is expected to be similarly constrained. The greater the difficulty of measuring professionals' output, the more common and more stringent the licensing and other professional restrictions are expected to be[26].

In closing, consider more generally, though very briefly, the role of social institutions. Virtually no features of Walrasian economics qualifies it as a social science. People interact only in the market, where cheating will not occur since it can be costlessly detected, and the identity of transactors is of no significance. The auctioneer, the only social functionary, plays a strictly mechanical role and provides his service free of charge. Individuals' maximizing behavior leads automatically to Pareto optimum. Moreover, since property rights are well defined and contracts are costless to enforce, even a legal system is not needed. Only in that world is the invisible hand truly supreme.

People trade with each other because they expect to gain, but when transacting is costly, each person spends resources in attempting to capture a greater share of the gain. Traders are not anonymous; their names – their identities – serve to lower the cost of exchange[27]. Thus the social aspect of trade is of fundamental importance. Social institutions are erected to aid in further facilitating the exchange. The study of the cost of transacting then makes economics a useful tool in the study of interactions among people.

---

[25] Professionals could organize in an association which imposes some minimum qualification criteria on its members. Consumers, however, may be more suspicious of the self-policed enforcement of these criteria than when they are policed by government.

[26] Monopoly power is a reason often given to various restrictions. Whereas the reason offered here is the promotion of efficiency, it is to be expected that whoever has the opportunity to exercise monopoly power will do so. It is difficult, then, to determine whether or not monopoly power is the 'primary' factor leading to the regulations.

[27] Both in autarky and in a Walrasian system the notion of socially reprehensible behavior is meaningless. Such behavior may become meaningful only with costly transacting. This might account for the high regard for production activities and the almost universal negative attitude towards trade, speculation, financial activities and the like.

References

ALCHIAN, A.A. [1970] "Information Costs, Pricing, and Resource Unemployment", pp. 27–52, in: E.S. Phelps (ed.), *Employment and Inflation Theory*, New York.

BARZEL, Y. [1977] "Some Fallacies in the Interpretation of Information Costs", *Journal of Law and Economics*, 20, 291–307.

-- [1982] "Measurement Cost and the Organization of Markets", *Journal of Law and Economics*, 25, 27–48.

CHEUNG, S.N.S. [1974] "A Theory of Price Control", *Journal of Law and Economics*, 7, 53–71.

DAHLMAN, C.J. [1979] "The Problem of Externality", *Journal of Law and Economics*, 22, 141–161.

-- [1980], *The Open Field System and Beyond*, Cambridge.

HIRSHLEIFER, J. [1971] "The Private and Social Value of Information and the Reward to Inventive Activity", *American Economics Review*, 61, 561–574.

STIGLER, G.J. [1961] "The Economics of Information", *Journal of Political Economy*, 69, 213–225.

WILLIAMSON, O.E. [1981] "The Modern Corporation: Origins, Evolution, Attributes", *Journal of Economic Literature*, 19, 1537–1568.

Yoram Barzel
University of Washington
Dept. of Economics
Seattle, WA 98195
U.S.A.

[26]

THE ENTREPRENEUR'S REWARD FOR SELF-POLICING

YORAM BARZEL*

The collaboration among people is often subject to shirking; the net gain from the collaboration depends on the contract governing it. I argue that the entrepreneur assumes the role of the residual claimant because his actions are more costly to monitor than those of the factors with which he collaborates. By offering fixed pay contracts to others and himself becoming residual claimant, the entrepreneur curtails his incentive to gain at the expense of his partners, and the net gain from the collaboration is then maximized. Costly monitoring applies to both labor and capital, and thus the entrepreneur may supply both labor services and capital. The entrepreneur's capital serves to guarantee the pay of the other factors.

I. INTRODUCTION

When people collaborate, the contribution of each to the combined output depends on how each is remunerated and on how each is supervised. Those properties of the remuneration and supervision scheme that generate the largest net joint value will be explored here. When the outcome of common effort can vary, "moral hazard" opportunities can arise. These are opportunities of getting goods, at the margin, at less than their resource cost. The hypothesis of this paper is that in order to reduce the moral hazard loss, the person whose contribution to common effort is the most difficult to measure will assume the position of entrepreneur, employing and supervising the other persons. By becoming a residual claimant who bears most of the risk of variable outcome, his incentive to gain at the expense of his partners is curtailed. In order to persuade others to work for him he will commit capital of his own to the venture and form contracts such that the value of his capital will fall if he does not keep his promise to pay them. Capital here serves as a bond, which explains why capital hires labor. Of the contributors to the common effort, those whose pay is fixed will agree to be constrained by their employer so that their newly created moral hazard opportunities can be controlled.

I will make no attempt to cover the entire range of operations or all the sources of variability of large, complex organizations. Rather, I will analyze circumstances requiring a narrow range of contracts; in particular, my entrepreneur always participates in direct production and spends only part of his

* I wish to thank Donald Gordon and Christopher Hall for their most valuable comments. I benefited also from the comments of Thomas Borcherding, James Buchanan, Patricia Danzon, Robert Higgs, Keith Leffler, Frederic Warren-Boulton and Ben Yu. An earlier version of this paper entitled "The Entrepreneur as a Bearer of Risk" was written during a visit at the Hoover Institution.

Economic Inquiry
Vol. XXV, January 1987, 103–116

time in supervision. This paper, then, attempts to offer a theory that applies only to a subset of all firms.

The model developed in the following section shows that the owner of the production factor most costly to monitor will assume the role of the entrepreneur who is the residual claimant; circumstances are pointed out under which the model can be tested. The relationship between risk and transaction cost is then elaborated upon, and the analysis of the role played by the entrepreneur's own capital closes the discussion.

II. MORAL HAZARD, MEASURABILITY AND THE ASSIGNMENT OF RISK

Suppose that one person's comparative advantage is in making a specialty product whereas another's is in pursuing such activities as buying raw materials, arranging for space, getting credit, and selling. The two people can collaborate under various contractual arrangements. They can operate, for example, as two independent "firms," as sharing partners, or as employer and employee. In the last case, whoever is the employer can employ the other by the piece, by the hour, or in some other way.

Suppose the operations of the first person are routine. Measuring his productive effort then is relatively easy; for instance, a small sample of the person's effort or output yields a great deal of information on his performance. The operations of the second person are more difficult to evaluate. The outcome of this person's endeavors depends on such factors as whether or not bargain prices for purchased inputs are available, how much the actual quality of the delivered inputs differs from their expected quality, and which deals can be made concerning the sale of the output. Because of the variability in these factors, it is costly to separate, in any particular instance, the effect of luck from that of the level of effort.

If the two persons trade with each other by operating as independent firms, the business expert, when not monitored, may be able to charge input prices that are too high and to pay prices that are too low when buying output. Competition will eliminate any excess profits from such trades, but elimination of the undesirable, resource-consuming practices will be costly. If sharing is adopted as the method of reward for the cooperators, then again the business expert, whose action is difficult to monitor, will be able to gain from what is viewed here as 'shirking'; he may reduce his effort level and disguise the reduction as bad luck.

Consider the case in which the business expert is the entrepreneur, employing the other person by the hour. Since the productive effort of the properly supervised employee is easy to evaluate and is a good measure of his output, he will receive pay corresponding closely to his contribution to output. The entrepreneur's income, which is the residual, depends both on chance and on his own effort. Since his ability to affect his expected income is a function of his contribution only, his incentive for shirking disappears and it does not matter that the chance component is difficult to isolate.

The price of the service or commodity the transactors produce also must be set. The determination of prices, particularly on a continuing basis, is costly and subject to error. By paying an employee a constant wage rather than the value of his marginal product, the entrepreneur assumes the effect of price-variability of output and becomes the residual claimant in this regard, too.

When the entrepreneur bears the risk of the business he is running, he also bears the full consequence of any reduction in his own effort. Bearing the risk here is an act that promotes efficiency, though not necessarily an act of insurance. Collaboration in the form of employer-employee is not always the least costly arrangement, and no attempt is made here to determine when this form is least costly; I simply concentrate mostly on cases where it is. I hypothesize that the remuneration of the entrepreneur takes the form of a residual because his contribution to output and to its value are difficult to measure.[1] More generally, I hypothesize that among factors contributing to the value of common effort, the greater the difficulty in measuring one factor's contribution vis-á-vis that of others, the more likely is the owner of that factor to assume the position of the residual claimant.[2]

Turning specifically to the employer-employee collaboration, I wish to determine who assumes which role. Both the variability in the physical units and that in their values contribute to the variability in the value of the collaborative outcome. Economists encounter difficulties in detecting variability in physical units; changes in unit value are easier to observe, and are used here to derive a major implication: Changes in relative wages are expected to lead to changes in organization. When two workers, A and B, intend to collaborate, as the market wage of A relative to that of B rises, A tends to assume the employer's role and B the role of employee. A decline in the relative wage of A has the opposite effect. This hypothesis clearly depends on transaction costs, but the test of the hypothesis does not require observations of these costs. The data required to test the prediction are the market wages of two classes of workers and information about whether each individual worker is employer or employee; these are readily observable data.

The prediction that an increase in a worker's market wage will tend to make him the employer is derived from a two person, employer-employee model, the central feature of which is the cost of supervision. Simplifying assumptions serve to isolate the process of determining which of the two will be employer and which employee. The assumptions are as follows.

I. Individuals' working time is the only input, and the total hours of each worker are fixed.[3]

1. Akerlof [1970, 496] comes close to defining the entrepreneur as a guarantor of quality when quality is subject to manipulation. He says, ". . . the important skill of the merchant is identifying the quality of merchandise . . . and guarantee[ing] the quality . . . . And this is one [added] reason why the merchants may logically become the first entrepreneurs."

2. Grossman and Hart [1986] consider a problem that shares some important features with mine and demonstrate a result similar to the one that underlies my hypothesis.

3. The central question here is how role switching by itself affects total output. The assumption

II. The entrepreneur's time is divided between direct production and supervision, and his direct contribution to output is proportionate to the amount of time he spends on his productive task (which equals his total time on the job less that spent on supervising).[4]

III. The employed worker's physical output increases with the amount of time his employer spends on supervising him, but at a declining rate.[5] The declining rate follows from the assumption of variability: no task is truly routine; some aspects of performance therefore are easier to monitor than others.

IV. The per hour output of a person working as his own boss exceeds his output as a supervised employee; in other words, some shirking is inevitable when persons are employees rather than their own bosses.

V. The value of total output is the simple sum of the values of the contributions of the two collaborators.[6]

VI. Finally, the value of the output of each worker is equal to his contribution to output times his exogenously determined wage rate. This is the conventional relationship between physical output and its value.

In order to determine the employer-employee relationship that maximizes the joint wealth of the collaboration, the maximum outputs of the two possible situations must be compared. At either maximum-output point the increase in the value of the employee's output induced by added supervision must equal the loss in the value of output induced by diverting the entrepreneur's time from production to supervision. A diagrammatic description of the model is contained in the next three paragraphs and in Figures 1 and 2.

Figure 1 serves to determine the supervision level that maximizes the output-value for a particular employer-employee relationship. The horizontal axis in Figure 1 measures the daily hours spent on supervision by the employer, and the vertical axis measures the value of daily output. Supposing that A is the employer and B the employee, $O^s(A)$, is A's direct output, which falls linearly with the hours he spends on supervising B; $O_s(B)$ is B's output as a function of that supervision. S denotes supervision when used as a superscript, supervised when used as a subscript. At low supervision levels, the cost of supervision, which equals the rate of fall in $O^s(A)$, is less than the increase in output it induces; but eventually, due to diminishing returns to supervision, $O_s(B)$ rises more slowly than $O^s(A)$ falls. H_0 is the point where $O_s(B)$ rises at

of fixed hours merely isolates this effect. Relaxing this simplifying assumption, as well as the assumption that time is the only input, does not affect the main conclusion.

4. My characterization of the entrepreneur is similar to Oi's [1983]. Oi concentrates, however, not on who will be entrepreneur, but on the quality of the other inputs the entrepreneur will employ.

5. The worker's valuation of less strenuous effort is incorporated into the value of output. The entrepreneur's desired pace of work underlies his $O^s(A)$ in Figure 1 below.

6. This assumption means that differences in input ratios associated with the change in the employment relationship are abstracted from. It is suggested below that some activities may be switched from one worker to the other, making it easier to obtain the desired input mix.

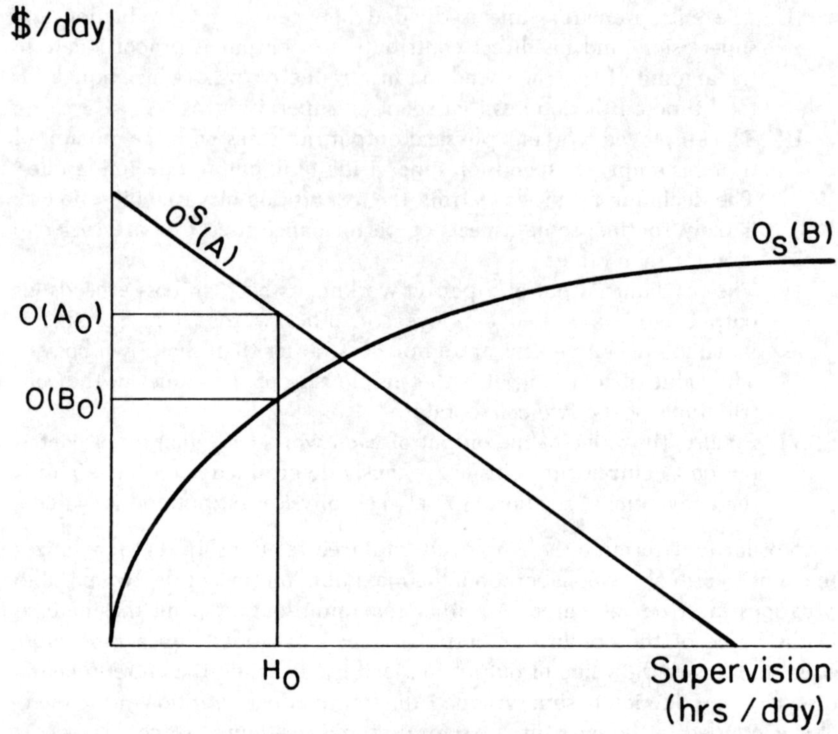

FIGURE 1

the same rate that $O^s(A)$ falls; therefore, at H_0 the sum of $O^s(A)$ and $O_s(B)$ is highest. The value of total output, then, is maximized when the employer devotes H_0 hours to supervision. At the maximum point *A* spends H_0 hours on supervision and produces $O(A_0)$ output with the rest of his time; *B* produces $O(B_0)$ output.

Figure 2, an elaboration of Figure 1, allows for the possibility that *B* will be employer and *A* employee. For ease of comparison, the value of *B*'s direct output when operating as employer, $O^s(B)$, is first set to be the same as $O^s(A)$. Suppose also that *A*, as a supervised employee, is less productive than *B*, so that $O_s(A)$ lies below $O_s(B)$ as drawn.[7] With *B* being the employer and *A* the employee, H_1 is the maximizing supervision level. As drawn, however, total output is higher if *A* is the employer and *B* the employee.

An exogenous increase in *B*'s wage will shift both his $O_s(B)$ and his $O^s(B)$ proportionately upwards. The maximizing levels of supervision will change; the direction of the change, however, depends on whether *B* supervises or is

7. A person's productivity as an employee depends on the ease of monitoring his task and on the complementarity between the other's task and monitoring.

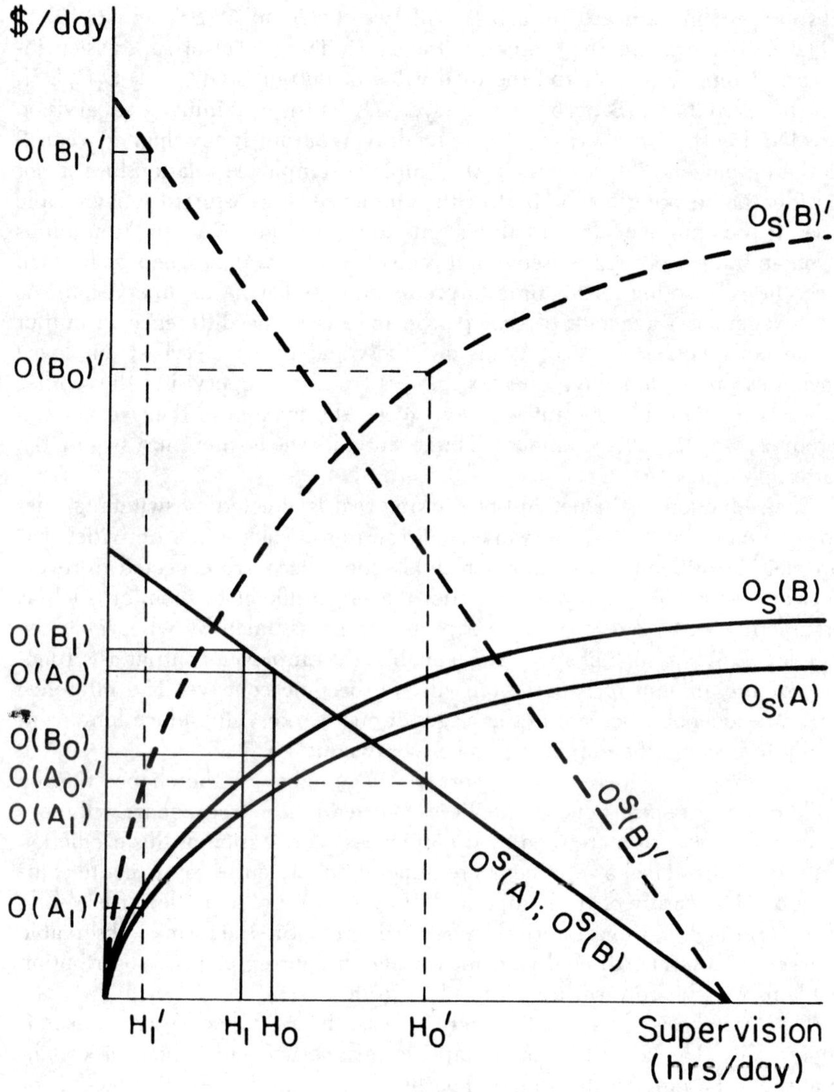

FIGURE 2

being supervised. If *A* is the supervisor, the value of his supervision and with it its maximizing level will increase. If *B* is the supervisor, the cost of supervision will increase, and the maximizing level of supervising *A* will fall.

It will now be shown that as the exogenously determined wage of *B* relative to that of *A* rises, the two eventually switch roles, *B* becoming the employer and *A* the employee. Consider an exogenous doubling of *B*'s wage. Both of

B's curves shift upward by a factor of two; $O^s(B)$ to $O^s(B)'$, and $O_s(B)$ to $O_s(B)'$. If A remains the employer, the maximizing level of supervision increases from H_0 to H_0', and the total value of output is $O(A_0)' + O(B_0)'$. If, on the other hand, B becomes employer, H_1' is the maximizing supervision level and output is $O(A_1)' + O(B_1)'$. As drawn, output is now higher when B is the employer. The reversal in the employer-employee relationships is not accidental. Shirking on the part of the employee is, as asserted, unavoidable even if the employer devotes all his time to supervision. A person's output as even an intensively supervised employee would be less than when, as his own boss, he is devoting all his time to production (and none to supervision). As the exogenous wage rate of that person increases, the difference in output value between his working as his own boss and as a supervised employee increases proportionately, whereas the loss from not supervising the worker whose wage is held constant will not exceed the maximum that worker can produce, which is a fixed amount. Thus eventually the former must swamp the latter.

The reduction in the net cost of shirking that is effected by switching roles may be enhanced if the two workers also swap some activities. Activities that are neither difficult to monitor nor highly specialized are expected to revert to whoever is the employee. Activities that are difficult to monitor, such as transacting with "outsiders," are expected to be assumed by whoever is the employer. When such changes are available, the employer's output as a function of the amount of supervision will also become concave. The inference that an exogenous increase in the wages of one worker will induce him eventually to become the employer, however, remains.

If an exogenous increase in a worker's wage enhances the chance that he will become an entrepreneur, then it is expected that entrepreneurs will more often than not earn more than their employees. Verification of this prediction is problematic. The entrepreneur's remuneration, of course, is subject to competition. The nature of the competition for the entrepreneurs' rewards cannot be determined, however, since these rewards are not in the form of observable market prices. The difficulty in measuring the entrepreneur's contribution explains why his reward takes a residual form.

The hypothesis that an exogenous increase in a worker's wage makes it more likely that he will become employer of another with whom he collaborates can be empirically tested. The hypothesis can be tested directly, for example, in relation to ditch digging, an activity often performed by two workers where one operates a bulldozer and one drives a truck. When the collaboration of bulldozer operator and truck driver takes the form of an employer-employee relationship, the prediction is that as the exogenously determined wage of truck drivers increases relative to that of bulldozer operators, the proportion of truck drivers who are employers also increases.

Additional tests of the hypothesis may be performed provided the model is somewhat generalized. In the model, the pay of an employed worker and of an entrepreneur may be thought of as being obtained from a formula consisting of the combination of a fixed wage and of a residual, with, in this case, the appropriate zero-one weights. In the more general case, non-zero weights apply so that part of a worker's pay is a wage and part is a share of the residual. The greater is the weight of the residual in total expected pay, the closer is the position the worker assumes to that of entrepreneur. This extension of the model yields the prediction that as a worker's productive capacity, and with it market wage, increase, the weight of the residual component in total pay becomes higher.

This prediction may be tested by observing the form of pay in some partnerships and in some professional sports. In such partnerships as those of lawyers or of physicians, the partners' pay formula often consists of a salary plus a measure of each partner's contribution to the partnership income. The prediction is that as partners' total income increases, whether because their exogenous market wage rises, or because they gain experience, the fraction contributed by the fixed salary will decline. A closely related prediction applies to professional team athletes. The higher are athletes' incomes, the greater the share of remuneration based on variables such as gate receipts or attendance is expected to be.

Another implication arises in regard to the division formula of court-awarded rewards between client and lawyer. Clients' role differ greatly depending on the nature of their claims. For instance, a driver claiming collision damages incurred when he drove his car is likely to play a greater role in the ensuing litigation than is one claiming damages to his unoccupied automobile that was hit by another car. The greater the personal role of the plaintiff, the more his reward is expected to be in the form of a residual and that of his attorney is in the form of a fixed fee; conversely, the smaller the role of the plaintiff, the more likely is the lawyer fee to take the form of a share in the total.[8]

III. RISK AND THE COST OF TRANSACTION APPROACH TO CONTRACTS

The term "moral hazard" originated as an insurance term and continues to be used as such, but it clearly has a broader range of application. Units of a commodity that vary in value will be sold at a uniform price if the gain of selling them at different prices is less than the cost. Non-identical workers exerting non-identical efforts, for instance, are sometimes equally paid. Whenever such smoothing out is practiced, people are not marginally penalized for certain types of careless or poor behavior and can be expected to exploit the smoothing out for their own gains; thus, workers "shirk," and patrons of a single price movie theater wait in line to gain the better seats. These practices are logically equivalent to moral hazard in insurance. This view of the moral hazard problem renews the role of risk in explaining economic organization

8. In Canada and the U.K., where contingent fees are prohibited, clients are the court-awards residual claimants in all cases. When seeking court awards, clients are expected to get more involved in the litigation than are their American counterparts.

and provides a link between the risk explanation and the transaction cost approach to contracts.[9]

The unification of risk and transaction cost leaves behind one casualty, namely, risk aversion as a necessary condition for explaining the employer-employee relationship. Risk aversion is often considered the reason for fixed wage contracts. The person who is less risk averse is thought to assume the bulk of the risk of the joint action by employing others for a fixed wage and by absorbing some of the effect of wage fluctuations. I offer an alternative explanation: The person with the greater ability to affect outcome variability will employ the other for a fixed wage. How can the two explanations be distinguished from each other?

Compare the layoff rate of employees whose wages (and hours) are fixed with the unemployment rate of the self-employed. When the price of a product falls because of a fall in demand, an employer who continues to use labor at the original fixed wage will experience a fall in profits. A common reaction of employers is to lay workers off. Expectation of a layoff, however, produces greater income variability and lower income than expectation of a wage reduction produces, and a risk averse person prefers lower-wage employment to unemployment. A risk averse person values the constancy of income; a fixed wage contract that permits layoffs, however, does not produce constant income. The employer also experiences lower income and greater variability with layoffs than with wage reductions. If risk aversion were the sole reason for the form of wage payment, a contract providing for wage reductions with a fall in demand would be preferred to a fixed wage contract accompanied by layoffs. Thus, no difference in the rate of employment between individuals who are self-employed and those who are employed by others would be expected.

The transaction cost hypothesis implies that the fixed wage is designed to prevent the employer from "unjustifiably" reducing wages. The employer, presumably, is more knowledgeable than the employee regarding conditions in the industry. When wages are allowed to adjust constantly to market conditions, the employer is in a position of lowering wages even when true conditions do not merit the action. If, however, he is committed either to keeping his workers employed at the agreed upon wage, or, as elaborated below, to laying them off along with his own resources, he will lay them off only when conditions turn unusually bad.[10] Were the person self-employed, he would have the choice of responding to a fall in demand either by not

9. For a demonstration of some of the organizational implications of moral hazard, see my 1982 paper.

10. The moral hazard explanation of layoffs is given by Hashimoto [1979] and by Hall and Lilien [1979]. In his long term contract with employees, the employer must also agree (perhaps implicitly) not to hire other workers at the lower "spot" wage rates prevailing when layoffs are called for. When demand conditions facing a whole industry deteriorate, many firms may lay off workers and not lower wages even though the laid off workers might be willing to work at lower wages.

working or by working at a lower rate of remuneration and presumably he would choose to work in times when employed workers are laid off.

A comparable fall in the prices of products produced by employees and by self-employed workers is expected to lead to a higher rate of unemployment for the former than for the latter when moral hazard rather than risk aversion is the reason for the fixed wage contract. If such a differential is observed, the risk aversion theory tends to be rejected, whereas the moral hazard one is supported. Thus, a test is available to distinguish between the two explanations of the fixed wage contract.

Some barbershops are operated and owned by one barber; other shops are owned by one barber who employs several others. By my model, a fall in demand for haircuts will lead to a layoff rate among the employed barbers that is higher than the rate of closures of shops owned by self-employed ones. In a similar situation, a fall in the demand for taxicabs is expected to induce a greater layoff rate for employed drivers and the cabs they operate than for owner-operators and their cabs.

IV. THE ROLE OF THE ENTREPRENEUR'S OWN CAPITAL

An explanation is now offered for the observation that the entrepreneur usually supplies capital of his own to the enterprise, first in relation to other sources of finance, and second in relation to the employment of labor. Consider a businessman who discovers that the landed price of an imported good is expected to be lower than the local price. Price fluctuations, changes in shipping costs, and spoilage all introduce variability to the expected return. The businessman can raise capital to finance the project by selling bonds or by floating stock. Suppose that it is known to all that the variability of the venture depends entirely on forces beyond the businessman's control. In that case, the businessman's net pecuniary income from these alternative forms of finance will vary only to the extent that he earns more or less of a premium for bearing risk. Indeed, the businessman could easily become the capitalists' employee without affecting the basic results.

In terms of what Lucas [1981] describes as the "*relationship* between decision maker and observer," the businessman here is the decicion maker, and the lenders are the observers.[11] These observers have no difficulty in detecting what the decision maker is doing; thus, they recognize the risk they assume when they participate in the venture. Subsequent to the discovery of the opportunity, the role of the decision maker in this extremely simplistic situation is trivial. His actions are routine and he introduces no uncertainty to the picture. The risk such a businessman faces, then, can be readily transacted in the market.

In contrast, consider the same person's search for the profitable venture. That search requires the businessman's time, which he may finance himself,

11. Lucas [1981, 236, italics in the original]. See also page 223. I am indebted to Lucas for illuminating this point in a private correspondence.

or for which he may seek outside financing. The expected return and the variability of the return of this investment depend on the businessman's diligence. How can the project be financed if it is costly to monitor both the businessman's effort and his ability to effect a tradeoff of a lower expected overall return for exceptionally high returns at lower probabilities? The cost of monitoring the businessman's effort may be so high that other people may refrain from buying shares in the project. They may be willing, however, to lend him money at a fixed rate which, as compensation for their expectation of default, sufficiently exceeds the market rate of interest. If the risk of default were constant, the businessman would bear the entire expected effect of the project's outcome variability. By the previous assumptions, however, the businessman's ability to affect the probability distribution of outcomes is costly to detect and the default probability cannot be considered constant. Under the stated conditions, as long as the businessman does not finance the whole project, no contract realizing the entire joint gain can be obtained.[12]

Lenders who forward loans to a businessman at a fixed rate fully share losses since the value of the loan can fall to zero, but they do not share gains, since the loan value does not rise with the project's success. The businessman, therefore, can be expected to search for riskier projects at the expense of a lower expected joint rate of return. The expected joint return from the project will be highest, then, with self-financing, and will decline as the share of external financing increases. Lenders may impose constraints on borrowers and warrants may be used. These methods, however, are costly, and even when they are used the joint return will decline with the share of self financing. Since, on average, outside creditors earn the market rate of return, a fall in the return from such projects must ultimately be borne by the businessman.[13]

The change in the businessman's behavior in response to the extent and method of external financing implies that the expected return to the project is itself not a parameter but rather an endogenous variable. The return, then, is subject to "uncertainty." In this situation, it is costly for the observers to isolate the effect of a change in the decision-maker's behavior from the effect of the random factor. This costliness in turn makes it difficult for the decision-maker to induce others to collaborate with him, as the mere act of collaboration implies a fall in the venture's expected return. The smaller is the businessman's contribution to financing, the lower the expected return to the project.

In this stylized operation, the businessman's effort in search of profitable

12. Jensen and Meckling discuss essentially the same problem and arrive at similar conclusions.

13. The notion is common that in corporations, ownership and control are separate and managers are able to gain at owners' expense. The apparent managers' gain, however, must be consistent with owners, in the aggregate, earning the market rate of interest. Managers' apparent ability to gain at owners' expense, then, actually must reduce the demand for managers services and, if supply of managers' services is not perfectly elastic, managers' income is expected to be lower than it would be were such opportunities absent.

opportunities is difficult to observe and thus financing it is problematic. On the other hand, at the stage when the discovered opportunity is acted upon, the businessman's effort is easy to monitor and is thus easy to finance. Self-financing, then, may give way to market financing at a juncture where measuring the product becomes easier.

Self-financing performs one more function which may explain why usually capital hires labor. A person who employs a factor on a continuing basis at a fixed pay schedule must be able to convince the factor's owner that payment will be forthcoming. The value of the contribution of an employee working for fixed pay or of a fixed rate lessor of capital equipment varies over time. Therefore, about half the time their contributions will exceed their pay, and half the time the reverse will be true. Owners of such factors may fear, then, that pay will be forthcoming only so long as business conditions are good and the value of their contributions exceeds their rate of pay, since whenever their pay rates exceed the value of their contributions, their employer gains if he replaces them with inputs obtained in the "spot" market. Employed factors will feel more secure if their contracts are structured so that an employer who fails to pay for the use of others' assets stands to lose, which will happen, for instance, if a commensurate amount of the employer's own capital is idled when he lays off other factors. The person assuming the bulk of the risk, then, is also expected to bring in his own capital, committing to idle it when his hired factors are let go. He thus secures his committment to his employed resources for the new risk he may impose on them.[14] This may explain why in recessions both labor and capital are held idle.

When the businessman takes responsibility for his own action through self-financing, the net return from the project will be higher than when others provide part of the financing. A businessman whose personal wealth is inadequate for financing a particular prospective venture may be unable to develop it, whereas another who can finance his own effort may earn a handsome return from developing the same venture.

V. CONCLUSIONS

In this paper I argue that the entrepreneur assumes the role of residual claimant because his actions are more costly to monitor than those of the factors he collaborates with. There is little conflict between this view and the more common image of entrepreneurs as enterprising capitalists. The present approach is consistent with the views of both Knight [1921][15] and Coase [1937][16] on the firm as well as with a branch of the transaction cost literature, the

14. The explanation offered in the text, anticipated by FitzRoy and Mueller [1984], may be an answer to the puzzle posed by Putterman [1984].

15. In my companion paper in this issue I attempt to show that Knight developed (but then abandoned) such a theory.

16. If one follows Coase [1937] in defining the firm in terms of "master and servant," then this hypothesis constitutes a component of the theory of the firm.

principal contributors to which are McManus [1975] and Jensen and Meckling [1976]. The entrepreneur's newer role as monitor proposed by Alchian and Demsetz [1972] is viewed here as derived rather than as primary. Neither is the entrepreneur, as proposed in the principal-agent literature, necessarily less risk averse than are those with whom he collaborates. Instead, by becoming entrepreneur the more difficult task of having others monitor him is avoided. Moreover, as was seen above, my entrepreneur can be identified empirically. Skills in monitoring and taste for risk are, on the other hand, not readily observable.

Quite often the entrepreneur is characterized as a capitalist or as the discoverer of non-routine trading opportunities. Kirzner [1973], for instance, views the entrepreneur as the person who effects the economy's move towards equilibrium by discovering, and profiting from, opportunities for arbitrage across markets. He argues that the entrepreneur needs no productive resources for his operation, but must only be alert to exploit price differentials. Buchanan [1980] takes a broader view, emphasizing the more dynamic Schumpeterian role of the entrepreneur who uses capital to take advantage of profit opportunities across time periods. These views and mine are in harmony as far as such activities are most difficult to monitor; however, these authors abstract from and, in Kirzer's case, even deny the entrepreneur's organizational role hypothesized in this essay.

I have considered situations where discovered profit opportunities require collaboration among factor owners. I have argued that the (would-be) entrepreneur supplies the factor performing the least routine role since his effort is more costly to measure and to monitor than that of others. In order to reduce the opportunity for moral hazard the entrepreneur becomes the residual claimant and employs the other factors at some fixed terms. Moreover, because new opportunities for morally hazardous behavior are created by the fixed pay contracts, the entrepreneur's own capital serves as his bond; consequently, he is expected to be a capitalist, too.

The basic argument of this paper can be recast in terms of information costs.[17] The variability among units of a commodity or a service being exchanged at a fixed price reflects the costliness of acquiring relevant information. The exchange party whose cost of acquiring the information is lower than the other's also has greater control over variability. Information here is asymmetrical, and it may appear that the uninformed party can be exploited. The incentive for exploitation vanishes, however, if the informed party assumes the effect of variability by becoming employer-entrepreneur. The uninformed exchange parties, through their fixed pay contracts, are guaranteed by the informed ones that they will not be taken advantage of, so they have no incentive to collect the information. At the same time, the entrepreneur's

17. Hayek [1937] opened the discussion on what is the minimum information necessary to make the right decision.

wealth is maximized when he collects that information which is jointly maximizing.[18]

REFERENCES

Akerlof, George A. "The Market for 'Lemons': Quality Uncertainty and the Market Mechanism." *Quarterly Journal of Economics*, December 1970, 488–500.

Alchian, Armen A. and Harold Demsetz. "Production, Information Costs, and Economic Organization." *American Economic Review*, December 1972, 777–95.

Barzel, Yoram. "Measurement Cost and the Organization of Markets." *Journal of Law and Economics*, April 1982, 27–48.

———. "Knight's 'Moral Hazard' Theory of Organization." *Economic Inquiry*, January 1986, 117–20.

Buchanan, James M. "Resource Allocation and Entrepreneurship." *Statsvetenskaplig Tidkrift (The Swedish Journal of Political Science)* 5, 1980, 285–92.

Cheung, Steven N. S. "The Contractual Nature of the Firm." *Journal of Law and Economics*, April 1983, 1–22.

Coase, Ronald H. "The Nature of the Firm." *Economica*, November 1937, 386–405.

FitzRoy, Felix R. and Dennis C. Mueller. "Cooperation and Conflict in Contractual Organization." *Quarterly Review of Economics and Business*, Winter 1984, 24–49.

Grossman, Sanford J. and Oliver Hart. "The Costs and Benefits of Ownership: A Theory of Vertical Integration." *Journal of Political Economy*, August 1986, 691–719.

Hall, Robert E. and P. M. Lilien. "Efficient Wage Bargains Under Uncertain Supply and Demand." *American Economic Review*, December 1979, 868–79.

Hashimoto, Masanori. "Bonus Payments, On-The-Job Training and Lifetime Employment in Japan." *Journal of Political Economy*, October 1979, 1086–104.

Hayek, Friedrich A. "Economics and Knowledge." *Economica* (New Ser.), February 1937, 33–54, reprinted in Friedrich A. Hayek. *Individualism and Economic Order*. Chicago: University of Chicago Press, 1948, 33–56.

Jensen, Michael C. and William H. Meckling. "Theory of the Firm: Managerial Behavior, Agency Costs and Ownership Structure." *Journal of Financial Economics*, October 1976, 305–60.

Kirzner, Israel. *Competition and Entrepreneurship*. Chicago: University of Chicago Press, 1973.

Knight, Frank H. *Risk, Uncertainty and Profit*. Boston: Houghton-Mifflin, 1921.

Lucas, Robert E., Jr. *Studies in Business-Cycle Theory*. Cambridge: MIT Press, 1981.

McManus, John C. "The Costs of Alternative Economic Organizations." *Canadian Journal of Economics*, August 1975, 334–50.

Oi, Walter Y. "Heterogeneous Firms and the Organization of Production." *Economic Inquiry*, April 1983, 147–71.

Putterman, Louis. "On Some Recent Explanations of Why Capital Hires Labor." *Economic Inquiry*, April 1984, 171–87.

18. The argument can also be rephrased in terms of property rights. My basic proposition implies that only if the party able to affect variability in a transaction also assumes its effect are property rights well defined, and then no resources will be spent to capture wealth. These are also the circumstances under which resources are used most productively. The cost of transacting matters here, and thus the Coase Theorem is not applicable. When variability is allocated efficiently, however, property rights are well defined, and, as implied by Coase, output is then at its maximum.

[27]

KNIGHT'S "MORAL HAZARD" THEORY OF ORGANIZATION

YORAM BARZEL*

In this paper I suggest that besides Knight's well recognized "uncertainty" explanation of the firm, he had another one. "Moral hazard" is the central feature in the second, largely overlooked theory. I argue, and attempt to document, that this theory is not a chance excursion but is rather quite well developed by Knight.

Knight, in "Risk, Uncertainty and Profit" [1921], apparently was the first economist making a major, concerted effort to explain the existence of firms. His well recognized explanation is based on "uncertainty" that cannot be transacted in the market, and thus must be borne by the entrepreneur. Alchian and Demsetz [1972], for instance, in analyzing theories preceding their own, consider, besides Coase's, only Knight's theory. They attribute to Knight and to his followers the identification of "the bearing of risks of wealth changes with the director or central employer" (page 784). I will attempt to show that Knight had not one but two theories of the firm. "Moral hazard" is the central feature in the second, largely overlooked theory. This theory is quite well developed by Knight and is not a chance excursion.

Knight's recognized theory of the firm and of the role of the entrepreneur as a bearer of uncertainty is contained in Chapters 9 and 10 of his book. While laying down the foundation for the following two chapters, Knight, in Chapter 8, analyzes in considerable detail another risk-related problem, that of moral hazard. Knight does not define moral hazard; however, he indicates that it will occur ". . . [in] situations where, on account of the impossibility of objective definition and external control of the individual ventures or uncertainties 'moral hazard' prevents insurance by an external agency" (page 256). My own view, which I think is consistent with Knight's, is that behavior is morally hazardous when people are able to obtain services, at the margin, at less than their resource cost.

The term moral hazard originated and continues to be used as an institutional insurance term, but Knight quite clearly recognized its broader range of application. In proceeding from the analysis of risk in Chapter 8 to the celebrated discussion of the entrepreneur and the firm in the following two chapters, however, the problem of moral hazard is abandoned without explanation. Few students of Knight's analysis of the firm seem to appreciate his grasp of the role of moral hazard,[1] even though it is explicitly and elaborately explored, and contains, for instance, some of the ingredients of the view of

* University of Washington, Seattle. Thanks to Donald F. Gordon, Paul Heyne and Dean Lueck for their valuable comments.

1. Alchian and Demsetz [1972] are among those who attribute to Knight only a risk theory which they contrast with their own view of shirking. McManus [1975], the main exception, is well aware of Knight's understanding of moral hazard. He interprets Knight to imply that the

Economic Inquiry
Vol. XXV, January 1987, 117–120

the firm offered by Jensen and Meckling [1976]. Given Knight's own disregard of the moral hazard problem in Chapters 9 and 10, it is easy to understand the lack of appreciation for his earlier discussion. The reason for his abandonment of the concept is more difficult to comprehend.

Knight's view of uncertainty has been a subject of lengthy debate which is not yet fully resolved. I do not intend to take part in that debate except to offer a reason why Knight's notion of uncertainty is so difficult to pin down. Because of moral hazard, some risks, such as developing a new line of business, are prohibitively costly to insure. When such risks are assumed by the entrepreneur, the incentive for morally hazardous behavior disappears.[2] I suspect that initially Knight intended to call such uninsurable risk "uncertainty." When Knight abandoned the moral hazard explanation of the firm, rather than also abandoning the term uncertainty, he attempted to develop a new role for it. This may account for the difficulties the concept has encountered.

In Chapters 9 and 10 Knight considers in detail the problem of acquiring knowledge of the probabilities of various outcomes. In Chapter 8, while analyzing the difficulties of assessing such probabilities, the examples he offers contain a feature foreign to those of the subsequent discussion. In these examples the probabilities are not fixed; instead, they depend on the behavior of the people involved.[3] Knight shifts from merely assigning probabilities to the question of whether they are parametric by tying the problem of moral hazard to the role of the entrepreneur. On page 249 in Chapter 8, Knight explicitly introduces the term and the problem of moral hazard. He stated,

> The fact which limits the application of the insurance principle to business risks generally is not therefore their inherent uniqueness alone, . . . the classification or grouping can only to a limited extent be carried out by any agency outside the person himself who makes the decisions, because of the peculiarly obstinate connection of a *moral hazard* with this sort of risks. The decisive factors in the case are so largely on the inside of the person making the decisions that the "instances" are not amenable to objective description and external control. (p. 251; italics in the original)[4]

A bit later he reiterates that "a 'moral hazard' prevents insurance by an external agency . . ." (p. 256). He proceeds to relate further the role of the entrepreneur to the moral hazard problem.

entrepreneurial solution is "due to the prohibitively high cost of enforcing constraints that would induce one individual, the manager, to maximize the wealth of another, the risk taker" (p. 348). Spiller [1976] and Mayshar [1982] also appreciate Knight's insight of moral hazard.

2. See Barzel, this issue, for an elaboration of this interpretation of the role of the entrepreneur.

3. Knight's characterization of some activities went through a corresponding change. In Chapter 8 Knight emphasizes the difficulty in controlling moral hazard because economic activities are inherently unique. In Chapter 10, on the other hand, Knight asserts that most business decisions are not unique. He goes as far as to state that the employed manager's "decision-making or exercise of judgment is automatically reduced to a routine function" (p. 297).

4. Knight concluded that because of moral hazard incentives, certain instances are amenable neither to external control nor to objective description. This may be the origin of his uncertainty. The difficulty of external control follows from the presence of moral hazard. It is not clear that the difficulty of objective description can be attributed to moral hazard.

> The superiority of the higher form of organization . . . consists . . . in the more effective unification of interest which reduces the moral hazard connected with the assumption by one person of the consequences of another person's decisions. (pp. 252–53)

Knight's view of the causal relationship between moral hazard and economic organization can be readily documented.

> Not less important is the incentive to substitute more effective and intimate forms of association for insurance, so as to eliminate or reduce the moral hazard . . . . Since it is capital which is especially at risk . . . the form of organization centers around the provisions relating to capital. (p. 252)[5]

He elaborates, stating that

> . . . it is the inefficiency of organization, the failure to secure unity of interest, and the consequent large risk due to moral hazard when a partnership grows to considerable size, which in turn limit its extension to still larger magnitudes and bring about the substitution of the corporate form of organization. (p. 253)

Knight vividly portrays the loss associated with morally hazardous behavior when he states that

> . . . the protection of its [the corporation's] various types of members and adherents against each other's predatory propensities, are quite . . . vital . . . . (p. 254)

Any remaining doubt about Knight's view of the relationship between moral hazard and economic organization should be dispelled by his statement that

> . . . nothing but a revolutionary transformation in human nature can apparently solve this [the effective unification of interests] problem finally, and such a change would, of course, obliterate all moral hazard at once, without organization. (pp. 253–54)

Knight's discussion of the effects of moral hazard on organization is fresh and persuasive. It demonstrates an understanding of the principal-agent relationship at least as clear as that found in the recent literature that bears this name. Yet a major puzzle remains: if Knight understood the moral hazard problem so well, why did he revert to what is now widely viewed as a much less satisfactory theory of the firm? I have no satisfactory solution of this puzzle.[6]

5. The special role of capital, as FitzRoy and Mueller [1984] note, is also abandoned in the discussion of the firm in Chapter 9 (see Footnote 1, p. 274).

6. One possible solution to this puzzle is that Knight's moral hazard theory of organization was his only theory and that he retained that theory in Chapters 9 and 10. In other words, moral hazard rather than the difficulty of estimating probabilities is the cause for his "uncertainty." Indeed, the uncertainty referred to in these chapters is largely with regard to the entrepreneur's (or others') character; not to natural conditions. This view is also consistent with Knight's repeated mention of the inseparability of responsibility and control. On the other hand, the theme of "consolidation" which pervades these chapters supports the view that these chapters' theory is that of risk bearing. The view that the moral hazard theory is Knight's only one obviously differs from the usual interpretation of Knight's theory of the firm.

REFERENCES

Alchian, Armen A. and Harold Demsetz. "Production, Information Costs, and Economic Organization." *American Economic Review*, December 1972. 777–95.

Barzel, Yoram. "The Entrepreneur's Reward for Self-Policing." *Economic Inquiry*, January 1987, 103–16.

FitzRoy, Felix R. and Dennis C. Mueller. "Cooperation and Conflict in Contractual Organization." *Quarterly Review of Economics and Business*, Winter 1984, 24–49.

Jensen, Michael and William Meckling. "Theory of the Firm: Managerial Behavior, Agency Costs and Ownership Structure." *Journal of Financial Economics*, October 1976, 305–60.

Knight, Frank H. *Risk, Uncertainty and Profit*. Boston: Houghton-Mifflin, 1921.

Mayshar, Joram. "Risk and Uncertainty in Capital Markets: Knight Revisited." Photocopy, 1982.

McManus, John C. "The Costs of Alternative Economic Organizations." *Canadian Journal of Economics*, August 1975, 334–50.

Spiller, Pablo T. "A Note on Asymmetrical Information and Knight's Nature of the Firm." Falk Institute, July 1976.

THE ALLOCATION OF RESOURCES BY VOTING*

YORAM BARZEL AND TIM R. SASS

A general theory of voting, which explains under what conditiions voting will be chosen as a means for allocating resources and how the constitution that governs the voting will be structured is presented. It is hypothesized that developers of voting organizations will structure their organizations in order to maximize the value of shares sold by minimizing the expected costs of wealth transfer and decision making in the voting organization. Implications regarding the allocation of votes and assessments within the organization, the domain of voting decisions, and the optimal voting rule are tested with data on the constitutional structure of condominium homeowner associations.

Voting is used by many organizations, both public and private, to allocate scarce resources. Economic analysis of the structure of such voting organizations has developed in two essentially independent bodies of literature. The "public choice" literature, based largely on the seminal work of Buchanan and Tullock [1962], focuses on the structure of political voting organizations. Assuming individual maximization, Buchanan and Tullock analyze the choice between voluntary action in the market and political action. Their theory of constitutional structure focuses on the choice of the optimal voting rule as a function of the characteristics of the decision-making group, and of the type of decision to be made. In the twenty-five years since the initial work of Buchanan and Tullock was published, only relatively minor critiques and extensions of their theory have been advanced in the public choice literature.[1]

In contrast, the corporate voting literature, initiated early by Manne [1964], has recently blossomed with the work of Easterbrook and Fischel [1983], Nitzan and Procaccia [1986], and particularly Grossman and Hart [1988] and Harris and Raviv [1988]. This work has focused primarily on two issues: the assignment of votes in relation to income claims within a corporation, and the selection of

*We wish to thank Robert Ellickson and Barry Weingast for their valuable comments. We also received helpful comments from Doug Allen, Linda DeAngelo, Frank Easterbrook, Micha Gisser, Tom Goodwin, John Hause, Michael Pogodzinski, Raymond Sauer, Pablo Spiller, and an anonymous referee. Thanks also go to Keith Burris for excellent research assistance, and the Research Allocation Committee of the University of New Mexico for providing financial support.

1. For example, see Kiesling [1968], Ostrom [1968], and Kafoglis and Cebula [1981].

The Quarterly Journal of Economics, August 1990

the voting percentage required to transfer control of a corporation. The most recent work in this area, that of Grossman and Hart and of Harris and Raviv, has concentrated on the effect of private benefits accruing to management from corporate control on the optimal choice of these two variables.

A general theory of voting should explain under what conditions voting will be chosen as a means for allocating resources, and how the constitution that governs the voting, including the allocation of votes and assessments within the organization, will be structured. The existing public choice literature, while applicable to a wide range of voting organizations with varying collective choice problems, has concentrated largely on the voting rule, thereby neglecting to effectively address of the many other aspects of a voting institution. In contrast, the relatively new corporate voting literature does consider both the voting rule and the assignment of votes, but it does so only in the narrow context of corporate control decisions. In this paper we explain the choice of the various components of a voting organization's constitution in a general context that is applicable to both political and business voting.

In addition to developing a general economic theory of constitutional choice, we provide a number of tests of our theory. No such empirical analysis of the initial choice of rules under which voting is to take place has been previously conducted.[2] Two factors seem responsible for this lack of empirical work on constitutional choice: first, the difficulty in untangling the initial maximization process in political constitutions; and second, the relative homogeneity of vote assignments within the types of voting organizations previously studied.

Although all voting institutions are erected by the same maximizing individuals who operate in markets, and are therefore endogenous, untangling the endogeneity of voting mechanisms in large political units is problematic. Tracing the political entity's historical origins back to the introduction of its constitution—often an impossible task—is required. The study of this seemingly intractable political problem, however, becomes relatively simple

2. Political scientists have conducted some empirical studies of the adoption of "reform" elements in the charters of municipal governments. These elements include electing council members at large, holding nonpartisan elections, and employing city managers rather than elected mayors. However, such studies use indices of the reform elements as the dependent variable in their analyses, rather than specific individual provisions. See Farnham and Bryant [1985] and Maser [1985].

when one observes a business venture that incorporates voting as part of its decision-making mechanism. The criteria for maximization are much easier to delineate in such a private voting organization. Given wealth maximization by its developer, he will select the stipulations of the organizations's constitution that are expected to maximize the net present value of the venture to its prospective buyers.[3]

A second factor contributing to the dearth of empirical analysis is the fact that both purely political bodies and corporations, taken separately, have relatively little diversity in the assignment of voting rights. In political organizations, the one-man-one-vote rule is used almost exclusively, while one-share-one-vote dominates in the corporate voting context.[4] This makes analysis of the choice of voting rights within either type of organization difficult. Fortunately, this problem can also be overcome by studying private, noncorporate organizations that use the voting mechanism for decision-making purposes.

In order to avoid the problems mentioned above, we have chosen to focus our analysis on owners' associations of newly developed condominiums. Such private "governments" are particularly well suited to the study of voting organizations for a number of reasons. First, the constitution of the association is written by the condominium's developer, making the maximand clear. Second, as the association emerges immediately in its "fully grown" state, its evolution is easy to trace. Third, the assignment of voting rights among condominium owner associations is relatively diverse. Fourth, in contrast to purely political voting where benefits are largely nonpecuniary, and corporate voting where benefits are almost exclusively pecuniary, benefits in condominium associations include both pecuniary and nonpecuniary elements, thereby allowing an analysis of the form of benefits on institutional structure. Fifth, and perhaps most important, the study of such associations is

3. The idea that the constitution is part of the maximization process is not new. Grossman and Hart [1980, p. 48], for instance, say "... at the time the [corporation's] charter is written, initial shareholders try to devise self-enforcing mechanisms to ensure good management."

4. Out of the thousands of corporations with publicly traded stock in 1980, DeAngelo and DeAngelo [1985] could identify only 78 corporations that assigned votes on other than a one-share-one-vote basis. See also Lease, McConnell, and Mikkelson [1983], who measure the relative values of voting rights in such dual class stock corporations, and Partch [1987] and Jarrell and Poulsen [1988] who estimate the effect on the market value of stock when a second class of stock with differing voting rights is issued.

empirically tractable since their "constitutions" and relevant physical properties are a matter of public record.

In Section I we begin by analyzing the choice between market organization and the use of voting. It is shown that the use of voting to allocate resources can avert certain moral hazard opportunities associated with market transactions. Voting entails two kinds of costs: those of decision making and those associated with wealth transfer. These voting costs are the subject of Section II. In Section III we analyze the ways in which the developer of a voting organization can structure its constitution in order to minimize the voting costs related to wealth transfers, and thereby maximize his gains. Finally, in Section IV many of the predictions formulated in previous sections, as well as some implications of the Buchanan-Tullock model, are tested using data on condominium homeowner associations.

I. A Rationale for Voting Organizations

In many organizations that allocate resources by voting, voters are both the owners of resources used by the organization and the consumers of its services. By internalizing exchange, such voting organizations avoid certain transaction costs that would be incurred with market exchange. There is a trade-off, however, since operating a voting mechanism also consumes resources.

To illustrate the cost of market exchange, consider a project requiring a large, centrally used amount of capital. When the requisite capital exceeds an individual's personal wealth, he may go to the market and borrow others' capital, paying fixed interest on the loan and becoming the sole residual claimant. It is well-known that forming and policing loan contracts is costly. By undertaking investment projects that are subject to a lower expected return and higher variability than those of other available projects, the borrower can gain at his lenders' expense. The precautions lenders will take in order to reduce their expected losses are also costly. On the margin, lenders will spend one dollar in resources to avert the transfer of one dollar of their wealth to borrowers. Borrowing, a market exchange, therefore involves policing and other transaction costs.[5]

5. The costs of using the market include the costs of writing and enforcing contracts involving contingent claims. While such contracts may prevent some wealth transfers, they must be written ex ante, when it is costly to determine all

Alternatively, the suppliers of capital can invest in equity. As long as all equity holders have the same rights and are subjected to the same costs, there will not be a divergence in incentives, as there is with debt financing. Since the suppliers of capital also decide how it will be employed, no exploitation within the group will take place. However, equity holders require a decision-making mechanism for the collective use of their capital, which allows each of them to remain an owner. Voting, appropriately designed, is a method by which to achieve simultaneously joint ownership and decision making. The use of voting thereby replaces price (interest rate here) as the mechanism for allocating resources.

We can view the choice of voting to allocate resources in another way. Implementing detailed pricing and policing is costly. Market exchange will thus leave some valued commodity attributes in the public domain. Whereas resources spent to effect and to avert transfers are "dissipated," the dissipation can be reduced by "harmonizing" the interests of the two parties.[6]

The problems that voting organizations may eliminate are general; they are present in any exchange. In order to make the model operational, conditions under which voting organizations rather than markets will be used must be specified, either by delineating the characteristics of exchanges that are relatively more prone than others to costly attempts to capture wealth, or by determining circumstances under which the voting organization's costs decline while the gains they generate remain constant. As economists, we lack the expertise to delineate characteristics of commodities that are relatively costly to exchange in the market. We are better equipped to identify factors that affect the costs of voting.

II. The Costs of Voting

Maximization of the net gains from a voting organization implies structuring the organization in order to minimize the two types of costs associated with voting. The first type includes the resources expended in attempts to use the voting process to transfer

possible contingencies. Easterbrook and Fischel [1983] also view voting as an alternative to costly contingent contracts. They say, "voting exists in corporations because someone must have the residual power to act (or delegate) when contracts are not complete" [Easterbrook and Fischel, 1983, p. 403].

6. The dissipation considered here is of the same logical nature as the dissipation from excess measuring. See Barzel [1982].

wealth among members in the organization. In their discussion of this wealth-transfer problem, Buchanan and Tullock focus on the losses that an *individual* expects to incur as a result of others' actions in the voting process, in particular being subjected to voting decisions that go against his interest when in the minority. Many of these costs tend to cancel out across individuals, however; a loss suffered by someone in the minority may be offset by a gain to a member of the majority.[7] If losses due to potential wealth transfers were only of this distributional nature, they would not affect the decision making of a developer seeking to maximize the *total* net value of the voting organization.

Of greater concern to a maximizing developer is the value of resources that voters expect to expend in attempts to effect and avoid wealth transfers among themselves. In order either to transfer one dollar of wealth to themselves or to avoid the transfer of one dollar of their wealth to others, voters will be willing to spend up to one dollar worth of resources. Since voters will pay a developer more when they expect to devote fewer resources to wealth capture and prevention, a developer will attempt to reduce the potential for redistribution through voting.

The second type of voting cost, called "decision-making costs" by Buchanan and Tullock, entails both the effort devoted to reaching decisions by voting, as well as the costs of strategic bargaining by voting members.[8] Strategic bargaining costs are the losses imposed by individual members who prevent agreement by holding out for a disproportionate share of the gains.

Yet another component of decision-making costs (unaccounted for by Buchanan and Tullock) is the cost of acquiring information required to make voting decisions. An individual will collect only that information which he values more than his cost of acquiring it. The information any single voter requires to guide his voting decision is similar to that needed by all other voters; individual voters will not collect information that can be obtained more cheaply by copying fellow voters.[9] This consideration applies to all

7. The losses from wealth transfers, termed "external costs" by Buchanan and Tullock, also include deadweight costs due to inefficient levels of public activities selected by the majority as well as pure transfers. In addition, risk-averse individuals may prefer not to be subject to the uncertainty of possible transfers. We do not attempt to capture either of these effects in our analysis.

8. These two components of decision-making costs, not explicitly delineated by Buchanan and Tullock, are emphasized by Kiesling [1968].

9. This point is made in the corporate voting context by Manne [1964].

voters, and thus some useful information may not be collected at all, while the effort to acquire other information may be duplicated.

Voting organizations are expected to seek methods that minimize the voter information problem. For instance, publicly held corporations furnish their stockholders with information by providing financial and auditor's reports, and data pertaining to directors. Corporations also reduce the information problem by hiring managers who are, in part, information specialists. Such information specialists, by the nature of their function, possess more information than their employers, however, and may attempt to exploit their advantage. Therefore, voters must still collect some information on their own in order to be able to assess the performance of specialists, and decide how to vote.

Voters who do acquire information make more informed choices, the gains from which are shared by all group members. In a shareholder firm, stockholders should therefore be rewarded not only for furnishing capital, but also for contributing to decision making. The incentive to collect information and vote increases with the size of the individual's stock ownership, since the costs are independent of that ownership and the return is proportional to a person's share holdings. It is expected, then, that large holders will both collect more information and be compensated for their extra contribution.[10]

III. The Structure and Constitution of Voting Organizations

Three factors determine a buyer's valuation of an ownership share in a jointly held asset controlled by voting: the value of the asset at the time of purchase (how attractive is the condominium's swimming pool?), his perception of the subsequent time path of changes in the asset's value (will the pool be well maintained?), and

10. Consistent with these expectations, Brickley, Lease, and Smith [1988] find that the percentage of stock voted in antitakeover votes is positively related to the proportion of stock held by nonmanagement owners of large blocks of stock. Nitzan and Procaccia [1986] reason that the one-share-one-vote rule provides such large shareholders a proper incentive to acquire information about voting issues. Also, see Easterbrook and Fischel [1983] who recognize that the right to vote is associated with stock return.

The refund policies of some cooperatives also seem to reward voters' effort. They provide their services to nonmembers and to members on equal terms, yet members (voters) receive "refunds" while nonmembers get smaller refunds or none at all [Bogen, 1968, 12.11], thereby enhancing members' incentives to contribute to the cooperative management.

his expected voting costs associated with the asset (how costly will a dispute over guests' pool use be?). Buyers' valuations of the assets offered by a developer therefore depend, in part, on their expectation of how deciding majorities of members will vote in future periods, and on their own expected expenses in attempts to affect those voting decisions.

If voters' costs and gains were identical, a decision favored by one would be favored by all: votes would be unanimous, and exploitative opportunities absent.[11] In such cases buyers would offer higher amounts than they would offer in instances where votes are contested and wealth transfers occur. Such increases in valuation can be extracted from buyers by developers in the form of higher prices. Developers, then, will gain by structuring their offerings so that buyers' interests are in harmony. We first consider the requisite conditions for harmonizing buyers' interests,[12] and then analyze the methods by which developers can achieve such harmony.

A. Harmonizing Voters' Interests and the Form of Organizational Benefits

If individuals' shares yield uniform net gains, their interests would be in harmony. Uniform net gains and the corresponding harmony of interests are obviously achieved when similar individuals are provided with identical facilities and are assessed equally. However, harmony can also be achieved under less stringent conditions; it suffices that voters agree on issues that come up for vote, even if they disagree on other matters. Harmony is relatively easy to attain in projects that provide only pecuniary benefits, but harder to achieve when projects also provide their owners direct consumption.

Assets are valued for both directly contributing to consumption and for the pecuniary gains they may generate. The larger the proportion of the pecuniary gains in the total valuation of an asset, the easier it is to reach agreement concerning the asset's performance, since then valuation depends on objective criteria. When all returns from an asset are pecuniary and known with certainty, shares that yield uniform net gains can be readily formed, and

11. Decision-making costs, in particular the costs associated with strategic bargaining, would still be present, however.

12. It may appear that the simplest method of attaining harmony of interests is by letting buyers select themselves. Self-selection will obviously attract individuals who value the asset highly. Among these, however, are adverse selectors—individuals who value the asset highly because they can gain at others' expense.

owners are likely to agree on their valuation of the asset. Developers of public shareholder firms are able to achieve such agreement among shareholders most successfully.

Corporate shares possess the following harmony-inducing features: (1) rewards to shareholders are uniform across shares, since shares are valued for their claims to dividends and changes in their market price, rather than for any direct contribution to utility; (2) the buyers of corporate shares are allocated votes in proportion to their share holdings;[13] and (3) assessments are zero. Therefore, any project demonstrably enhancing the value of the corporation will receive unanimous support.[14] The developers of corporations are able to structure their assets and the rights of prospective owners such that there are almost no opportunities for majorities to capture wealth from minorities.[15] In fact, in most stockholder votes the margin of victory is overwhelming.[16] Correspondingly, prospective owners' valuations of the shares offered by a developer of a stock corporation are not diluted by expectations of future resource expenditures to effect wealth transfers among themselves.

Buyers into projects that generate consumption services are also the final consumers of the services and thus obtain utility directly from their purchases.[17] The provision of commodities that contribute to individuals' utilities is difficult to harmonize, as such commodities are in general harder to evaluate and more costly to trade than projects contributing to pecuniary wealth. It is therefore more difficult for developers of projects producing consumption

13. Both Harris and Raviv [1988] and Grossman and Hart [1988] demonstrate that when private benefits from corporate control, such as perquisites, are small, the selection of uniform income claims and voting rights (i.e., one share, one vote) and a majority voting rule maximizes the total value of the firm's securities. Further, Grossman and Hart show that only when there exist significant private benefits from corporate control for both present management and potential management are deviations from one-share-one-vote optimal. This is consistent with our theory in that votes not based on income claims are desirable only when benefits are not strictly proportional to income claims.

14. DeAngelo [1981] demonstrates conditions for unanimity. Three types of decisions came to mind regarding which unanimity may not be achieved in reality: the distribution of dividends, dealings of the corporation with other firms owned by subsets of the stockholders, and decisions regarding management when managers are shareholders.

15. The primary exception is where majority control of a corporation can allow management to extract private benefits at the expense of other shareholders. See Grossman and Hart [1988, pp. 191–95].

16. Shareholders' ignorance or indifference is likely to reduce the participation rate, but seems to be unrelated to the degree of unanimity.

17. Partnerships such as lawyers or physicians are intermediate organizations in that although they produce services for the general public, the effect of working conditions on partners' utility seems to be of particular importance. Fama and Jensen [1983a, 1983b] analyze the structure of such professional partnerships.

services than for developers of stock firms to secure harmony of interest.

Such is the case in political voting where benefits received by voters in a political jurisdiction are primarily nonpecuniary, coming in the form of goods and services provided by government. Because such benefits are mostly nonpecuniary, harmonizing voter interests would be difficult even if that were the policy objective.[18] With heterogeneous preferences, voters' interests may diverge, creating opportunities for majorities to capture wealth from minorities through majority voting.

The more diverse the interests of voters, the greater the potential for contested voting decisions, and for the corresponding costs of potential wealth transfers. For this reason, we expect that in order to protect prospective buyers from wealth capture, developers of utility-generating projects will choose more elaborate constitutional provisions than those made by developers of cash-generating projects. For example, the interests of owners who purchase condominium units as investments generating tax advantages rather than as residences are for the most part confined to the market value of their units. The constitutions of such condominiums are therefore expected to be less restrictive, including fewer precautions against transfers, than the constitutions of owner-resident condominiums.[19] Our theory similarly predicts that the constitutions of commercial condominiums will be less restrictive than those of residential condominiums, since the gains to unit owners in commercial condominiums are primarily pecuniary. In particular, our theory predicts that the voting rule selected by developers of commercial condominiums will be less inclusive, i.e., farther from unanimity, than that chosen by developers of residential condominiums. This implication will be tested in Section IV below.

Maximizing the present value of shares in a voting organization requires that harmony be maintained over time. The ability to maintain harmony will vary, as before, between assets generating pecuniary gains and those providing primary consumption gains. For example, the public stock corporation's objective of wealth maximization remains unaltered with the passage of time. Even if it

18. In the same spirit Manne [1964, p. 1441] states that "a crucial difference between political and corporate elections [is that] with very rare exceptions, there are no conflicts in the corporate interests of voting shareholders."

19. The more closely owners represent their tenants' interests, the higher the rent they can collect. However, since owners are not expected to be perfectly well informed of their tenants' preferences, the prediction in the text is still valid.

is expected that opinions on future issues will be divided, the low-cost transferability of shares makes it likely that current owners will be in agreement on the issues at hand at any given time.[20] Harmony is more difficult to sustain in voting organizations providing nonpecuniary benefits. Take the example of homeowners' associations. Neither homes nor owners age at a uniform rate. A change in ownership can avert exploitation based on differences in personal characteristics; the tendency of families with children to push for the construction of a playground to be funded in part by assessments on childless homeowners is constrained by the latter's ability to sell their units to families with children. While ownership turnover is expected to enhance agreement, the complexity of a dwelling makes it costly to sell; disagreement among owners will therefore continue. Anticipating significant future conflicts, the initial valuation of the units by prospective buyers will be correspondingly lower. In order to raise units' values, we expect the developer to enhance the role of supermajorities and other restraints on wealth capture that might occur as the organization ages. We also predict that a low-cost mechanism to dissolve the organization, or to withdraw from it, will be included in the organization's constitution.[21]

B. Developers' Maximizing Actions

A developer has three major organizational tools with which to harmonize interests and thereby maximize the net present value of his project. The first is the choice of ownership rights that buyers receive with the asset. In particular, the assignment of assessments and voting rights will have a direct impact on the harmony of interests, and hence on the costs of voting. The second is the developer's control of the features of the transferred asset; he can decide ahead of time which features will be outside the domain of subsequent voting and which will be left to the discretion of the voting organization. The third is the rules under which decisions are made. Voting rules that are more inclusive (i.e., nearer unanimity) lower the potential for wealth transfers at the expense of higher decision-making costs.

In addition to its obvious effect on buyers' valuation of units,

20. This point was first made by Manne [1964]. The option of sale decreases the role of voting in the decision-making process. See Easterbrook and Fischel [1983].

21. Fama and Jensen [1983a, 1983b] emphasize the use of redeemable claims in financial mutuals, where shareholders can withdraw their assets on demand, as an important mechanism for controlling agency problems in these institutions.

the assignment of assessments will also affect the degree to which buyers will agree on voting issues. The more voters agree, the fewer resources that will be expended in attempts to effect and prevent wealth transfers. A necessary condition for achieving unanimity among voters is that a project generating net positive value to one generates positive value to all.[22] When the total net gain from a project is positive, there exists at least one set of assessments that yields a net positive value to each participant. However, implementing an assessment scheme possessing such properties encounters some problems. First, if potential projects differ in the distribution of benefits they generate for owners, each project would require its own assessment formulae in order to achieve unanimity on all voting issues. Construction and implementation of such multiple assessment formulae would likely be quite expensive. Second, and more fundamental, is the fact that the assessments for all potential projects must be decided on prior to participants' purchase of shares; otherwise, the setting of assessments itself will require a unanimous vote, which seems very costly to implement. On the other hand, a single assessment formula that applies to all prospective projects is unlikely to generate unanimous votes in all cases. If a single formula is nevertheless selected, the closer it comes to generating unanimity, on average, the lower resource expenditures to capture wealth are predicted to be.

We now turn specifically to the development of a condominium.[23] In order to maximize the value of individual units, the condominium developer can choose the assessment method to be employed, the vote allocation scheme and various other features of his project.

The distribution of benefits among units in a condominium is likely to be a function of both the number and characteristics of residents, as well as the heterogeneity in the attributes and value of individual units. For example, a common facility such as a swimming pool may generate benefits nearly proportional to the number of (swimming) residents in a unit. In contrast, the benefits of a central heating system are likely to be proportional to the area of a unit. Maintaining architectural standards and keeping common

22. The total net gain a project generates can be divided in a number of ways, and thus the condition in the text is not sufficient for unanimity. The discussion of the necessary condition suffices here, however.

23. Ellickson [1982] provides a detailed discussion of voting in condominiums and homeowners' associations.

areas attractive may generate benefits roughly in proportion to a unit's value.

An assessment that is uniform across condominium units is easily implemented and will serve well if most future projects in a condominium tend to generate the same benefits to all unit owners. The more uniform the units themselves, the more likely that this condition will be satisfied. It seems plausible that benefits from some future projects will generally be a function of both area and value. If this is the case, the more varied are the units' areas within a condominium, the less the likelihood that uniform assessments will lead to near unanimous votes, and the greater the likelihood that assessments that are proportional to unit size will enhance unanimity. Similarly, the more units vary in value per square foot, the greater the likelihood that the assessment formula will be based on value in order to serve well, and the more we can expect to see assessments by value. Thus, we test below the hypothesis that the greater the variance in value per square foot of units within a condominium, the greater the likelihood of assessments being apportioned by value; the more units vary by size, the greater the probability that assessments will be allocated by area.

The vote allocation selected by the developer will affect both the wealth transfer costs and decision-making costs associated with voting. Holding constant the costs of carrying out the voting process, when benefits are positive and assessments are strictly proportional to benefits, the method of allocating votes is immaterial.[24] Since under these conditions it is impossible for some group members to gain at the expense of others, resource allocation within the voting organization is independent of the allocation of votes.[25] As we pointed out above, however, deviations from proportionality between assessments and benefits are expected. Decision-making by majority vote allows majorities to form in order to exploit the deviation from proportionality between assessments and benefits, and to gain at the expense of minorities. The ability to form such majorities depends in part on the vote allocation method. Allocating votes by value of investment will not always best prevent majorities from capturing minorities' wealth. For example, if votes were proportional to the value of units but assessments were

24. We abstract from a possible divergence between average and marginal conditions, which, however, does not affect subsequent results.

25. Under the stated conditions, property rights are perfectly defined, and as implied by the Coase Theorem, no resources are spent to capture wealth.

uniform, owners of more valuable units could exploit the voting process to reap gains at the expense of owners of smaller units. The greater the discrepancy between individuals' economic interests (i.e., the assessments and benefits) and the corresponding amount of votes, the greater the opportunity for wealth capture. We predict that votes will tend to be allocated proportionally to the gains or to the assessments. In a stock corporation this condition is clearly satisfied since assessments are zero, and votes are proportional to shares. In the case of a condominium, where gains are costly to gauge, votes are expected to be proportional to assessments.

The vote allocation method will also affect the costs of decision-making within a voting organization, one of which is simply counting votes. In the case of condominiums, uniform allocation of votes allows tallying of votes by a simple show of hands at a meeting. In contrast, votes based on unit values or areas may require tallying of fractional voting shares, as well as producing and policing signed ballots. The greater the number of voting members, the higher these costs will be. Therefore, a bias in favor of uniform allocation of votes is expected. Further, this tendency toward uniform voting is likely to be stronger the greater the number of units in the condominium. Below, in Section IV we test the proposition that deviations in the allocation of votes from the method chosen for assessments are toward uniform voting, and this tendency toward uniform voting is more pronounced the greater the number of units in the condominium.

Another method by which a developer can affect the costs of a voting organization is through control of issues that will be subject to vote. Potentially disputed projects that are undertaken prior to the sale of the assets to individual buyers are simply not subjected to vote. It is therefore expected that developers will undertake ahead-of-time projects whose total net value is positive, but regarding which, opinions are likely to be divided. The clearest example is condominiums with uniform units, where deviations in net benefits among owners should be minimal. In such condominiums it is predicted that amenities are less likely to be installed by the developer. This implication is tested below in Section IV.

One obvious disadvantage of developer-constructed amenities is that they require early commitment, even when waiting may be advantageous. When project benefits are confined to easy-to-identify subsets of buyers, this problem can be avoided by forming "local" governments within the organization. By creating such subunits with their own assessments and voting allocations, one will avoid the potential capture as well as the difficulty of assuring that the majority of all buyers vote for such projects.[26]

The final method by which a developer can seek to minimize costly wealth transfers is through the choice of the voting rule. Buchanan and Tullock [1962] argue that the choice of the optimal voting rule depends on the trade-off between "external costs" (mostly individuals' losses from transfers) and decision-making costs. As the voting rule becomes more inclusive (nearer unanimity), external costs decline, since the size of the minority with potential to be exploited by the majority declines. In the extreme case of unanimity, no voter can impose costs on others without their consent, and external costs would be zero.[27] There would then be no resources devoted to avoiding wealth transfers. Decision-making costs, however, increase with the percentage of votes required to take action for two reasons. First, the greater the percentage for a given size group, the greater the absolute number of voters who must reach agreement. The larger the absolute size of the requisite coalition, the more costly that coalition is to achieve. And second, strategic bargaining costs due to the "holdout" problem also increase with the inclusiveness of the decision rule. Under unanimity, any single voter can determine the outcome, thereby intensifying the problem of strategic bargaining.

Based on this reasoning, Buchanan and Tullock claim that the smaller the size of the decision-making unit, the more inclusive the voting rule will be. Holding constant the voting rule and the method of assigning votes, the larger the group size, the greater the absolute number of people required for agreement, and the higher the decision-making costs. In addition, Buchanan and Tullock argue that external costs are relatively constant across groups of different sizes. Consequently, the sum of external costs and decision-making costs is an increasing function of group size, and the larger the group, the less inclusive is the optimal voting rule.

Kiesling [1968] challenges the Buchanan-Tullock prediction, arguing that as group size increases, strategic bargaining costs fall,

26. Occasionally, a condominium will adopt a general assessment scheme for most issues, and a special assessment formula for a particular service. For example, at least one Parisian developer adopted a clever assessment formula to cover the cost of running an elevator. In this four-story condominium, ground floor units are not assessed at all; first floor units are assessed half of what second floor units are assessed; and one third that of third floor units.

27. The benefits of a unanimity rule are discussed extensively in Buchanan and Tullock [1962, Ch. 7].

since the absolute number of voters required to block the majority and "hold out" for a more favorable outcome increases with the size of the group. He concludes that overall decision-making costs as a function of group size are therefore ambiguous.

Consistent with our theory, Buchanan and Tullock also argue that the more heterogeneous are the voters in a group, the more inclusive the voting rule will be. They reason that while decision-making costs will be high for heterogeneous groups, the potential for exploitation of the minority by the majority will also be higher the more divergent the interests of group members, leading to the choice of a more inclusive voting rule.

To summarize, developers of voting organizations will select the allocation of assessments and votes to members of the organization in a way that minimizes the sum of the costs associated with wealth transfer and decision-making. Issues for which these costs are "too high" will be excluded by the developer from the domain of voting. Further, for those issues that are subject to vote, the choice of the voting rule will depend on the heterogeneity of interests within the voting group.

IV. Empirical Tests: The Constitutions of Condominium Owner Associations

The "declaration" is the constitution of a condominium homeowner's associaton. The declaration is written by the developer of the condominium and must be filed with the clerk of the county in which the condominium is located. Subject to certain restrictions in state condominium acts,[28] the developer is free to choose the declaration's provisions. Thus, the declaration should reflect his attempts to lower the costs of the voting organization in order to maximize the value of the condominium units he is selling. By law, the declaration must describe the physical features of the individual units and common amenities, and specify the allocation of votes and assessments among condominium unit owners. Consequently, many of the implications of our theory of constitutional choice can be tested by analyzing the declarations of condominiums.

Our data include declarations from condominiums in the counties of Bernalillo, Sante Fe, and Lincoln in New Mexico. Albuquerque, the largest city in New Mexico, is located in Berna-

28. For a review of state condominium statutes, see Ellickson [1982] and references therein.

lillo County. The third largest city, Santa Fe, is located in Santa Fe County, where due to high land values, the number of condominiums is greater than in any other county in the state. The resort town of Ruidoso is in Lincoln County where there are also a large number of condominiums. The total sample from these three counties includes the declarations of 120 condominiums. Of these, 101 are residential, seven are offices, four are commercial, five are mixed use, and the remaining three could not be identified.[29] Information contained in this sample of declarations is used to test predictions made in the previous sections.

Consider first the effect of the diversity in attribute levels on the choice of the assessment formula among individual units within a condominium. The theory predicts that the assessment allocation chosen will be the one most nearly proportional to the benefits received. Virtually all condominiums in the sample assign assessments according to one of three formulas: (1) uniform assessments across units, (2) assessments based on the relative area of units, or (3) assessments based on the relative value of units.[30] If benefits are related to both area and value, then our model predicts that the greater the variance in unit areas or unit values, the less likely it is that uniform assessments will be assigned. Similarly, the greater the variance in value per square foot, the more likely assessments are to be based on unit values rather than on unit areas.

In order to test these hypotheses, a multiple logit regression was performed to estimate the effects of differences in the variabil-

29. For Bernalillo County, the sample represents all 40 condominium declarations filed since the initial New Mexico condominium legislation of 1963 through November 1984. For Santa Fe County, records were searched for the period April 1974 through April 1984. This period encompasses the vast majority of declaration filings. A total of 108 declarations were filed during the period. However, for those declarations filed in July 1980 or later, condominiums lacking area or value data are not included in the sample. This excluded 42 condominiums, leaving a sample of 66. The average size of condominiums in Sante Fe County was 9.2 units per condominium compared with 75.2 for Bernalillo County. In Lincoln County only those declarations containing both area and value data were included in the sample. Thus, the sample from Lincoln County includes only 14 out of the 37 condominium declarations which had been filed through August 1985. The average size of condominiums in Lincoln County was 22.1 units. Total sample size is 120 (40 + 66 + 16).

30. Condominium developers were legally constrained to adopt one of these three allocation formulas from 1975 through 1981. During that period New Mexico law required that voting "be based upon: the square or cubic footage in the unit as a percentage of the square or cubic footage in all of the units; the value, as that term is defined in the declaration, of the unit as a percentage of the value of all of the units; or the unit itself as a percentage of all of the units in the property" [New Mexico Statutes Annotated 1978, § 47-7-12]. Before and after this period any allocation scheme could be used.

TABLE I
ASSESSMENT ALLOCATION REGRESSION

Dependent variable	Constant	Standard deviation in area of units	Standard deviation in value per square foot of units
		Unweighted sample	
1. log (P_A/P_U)	−2.934***	0.004	2.023***
	(−3.86)	(1.12)	(2.65)
2. log (P_V/P_U)	−1.867**	0.001	2.066***
	(−2.88)	(0.37)	(2.72)
3. log (P_A/P_V)	−1.067*	0.003	−0.043
	(−1.81)	(1.62)	(−0.28)
		Weighted sample	
1. log (P_A/P_U)	−2.045**	0.005	1.711***
	(−2.06)	(0.92)	(3.04)
2. log (P_V/P_U)	−2.023*	0.002	1.753***
	(−1.71)	(0.39)	(2.86)
3. log (P_A/P_V)	−0.022	0.003	−0.041
	(−0.04)	(1.15)	(−0.24)

Total number of observations = 52
Chi-squared statistic $= -2 \times (L_0 - L_{max})$ = 34.04*** (unweighted sample)
= 31.39*** (weighted sample)

Note. U = uniform, A = area-based, and V = value-based assessments. Asymptotic t-ratios are in parentheses.
*Significant at the 0.10 level; **significant at the 0.05 level; ***significant at 0.01 level in a two-tailed test.

ity of unit areas and unit values among condominiums on the relative probabilities of selecting uniform, area-based, and value-based assessment schemes. The original sample, consisting of 52 condominiums for which data on both unit values and unit areas were available, was weighted to account for sample selection bias resulting from an oversampling of condominiums with value-based assessment schemes.[31] Results for both the original and the weighted sample are reported in Table I.

The dependent variables in the three equations of the multiple logit model are log (P_A/P_U), the log of the probability of selecting

31. As one might expect, condominiums with uniform or area-based assessments were much less likely to report unit values in their declarations than were condominiums with value-based assessment schemes. Therefore, condominiums with value-based assessments were overrepresented in the original sample and condominiums with area-based or uniform assessment formulas were underrepresented. To correct for this, the sample was weighted so that the proportions of condominiums with uniform, area-based, and value-based assessments were the same as in the population. Details of the weighting procedure are specified in Greene [1985, pp. 148–152], and Manski and McFadden [1981].

area-based assessments relative to the probability of selecting uniform assessments; log (P_V/P_U), the log of the probability of choosing value-based assessments relative to the probability of selecting uniform assessments; and log (P_A/P_V), the log of the probability of selecting an area-based assessment formula relative to the probability of choosing an assessment scheme based on unit values. The coefficients of the independent variables in the third equation are not independently estimated. Rather, since log $(P_A/P_V) = \log (P_A/P_U) - \log(P_V/P_U)$, they are simply the difference between the coefficients in the first and second equations.[32]

The coefficient on the area variability variable is positive in the first and third equations, as expected, indicating that increases in the variance in unit areas tend to increase the probability that an area-based assessment scheme will be chosen relative to the likelihood that uniform assessments or value-based assessments will be selected. However, the area variability coefficient is insignificant in the first equation and only significant at about the 10 percent level in the unweighted third equation.[33]

The coefficient on the value variance variable is positive and highly significant in the second equation, as expected, indicating the probability of choosing value-based assessments relative to the probability of selecting uniform assessments increases with increases in the standard deviation in unit values. The value variance coefficient is negative in the third equation, as predicted, indicating that increases in the variability of unit values within a condominium tend to decrease the likelihood that area-based assessments will be chosen relative to the probability that value-based assessments are selected. This effect is not significantly different from zero, however.

The negative and significant coefficients on the constant term in the first and second equations indicate that holding constant the variance in unit attributes, uniform assessments tend to be preferred relative to area-based or value-based assessments.

Our theory also predicts that votes will be assigned in order to conform to owners' gains and costs from new projects. In particular,

32. For a discussion of the precise formulation of the multiple logit model, see Pindyck and Rubinfeld [1981].

33. The lack of significance of the coefficient on the area variability variable may be due to collinearity between the area and value variability measures. A simple binary logit regression of log (P_A/P_U) on the standard deviation in unit areas and a constant yielded a positive and significant coefficient on the area variability measure $(t = 2.45)$.

the method chosen to allocate votes within condominiums is expected to be the same as that chosen for assessments. Other than the potential for dissipation, however, the choice of voting assignments is also influenced by the cost of utilizing the voting mechanism. It is expected that, ceteris paribus, a one-vote-per-unit rule would be preferred, since counting hands is easier than adding up fractional votes. Further, the reduction in decision-making costs resulting from use of uniform voting would be greater with a greater number of voters. Therefore, the larger the size of the voting group, the more likely uniform voting should be.

These predictions are supported by the data. Table II shows that the vast majority of condominiums in the sample employ the same rule for assessments and voting. Further, *all* of the deviations between the voting method and the method of assessment are toward one vote per unit. Table III reports the results of a binary logit regression where the dependent variable equals one if the assignment of votes was uniform and the assignment of assessments nonuniform, zero otherwise. As predicted, the probability of choosing a uniform voting scheme, despite nonuniform assessments, increased with the number of units in the condominium.

The developer may also choose which features to provide in advance, thereby removing them from the domain of voting decisions. Our theory predicts that the greater the potential voting costs associated with decisions about a project, the more likely it is that the project will be undertaken ahead of time. The potential wealth transfer costs of voting will be greater the greater the variation in net benefits among members. Assuming that benefits are related to

TABLE II
ASSIGNMENT OF VOTING RIGHTS BY METHOD OF ASSESSMENT

Method of assessment	Assignment of voting rights			
	By unit	By area	By value	Total
By unit	35	0	0	35
	(100.0)	(0.0)	(0.0)	(100.0)
By area	9	41	0	50
	(18.0)	(82.0)	(0.0)	(100.0)
By value	1	0	26	27
	(3.7)	(0.0)	(96.3)	(100.0)
All methods	45	41	26	112
	(40.2)	(36.6)	(23.2)	(100.0)

Note. Row percentages are in parentheses.

TABLE III
UNIFORM VOTING REGRESSION

Independent variable	Predicted sign	Coefficient (t-ratio)
Constant		−2.867*** (−6.49)
Number of units	+	0.011*** (2.66)
Number of observations = 111		
Chi-squared statistic = $2 \times (L_0 - L_{max}) = 6.69$***		

Note. ***Significant at the 0.01 level in a two-tailed test.

the physical features of units, then in condominiums with units of equal size and value, variation in net benefits will be nearly absent, and we therefore expect that amenities are less likely to be installed by the developer.

The number of developer-installed common amenities will also depend on the demand for such features. To the extent that amenities like swimming pools and lounges are quasi-public goods, net benefits per unit and total demand should increase with the number of units in the condominium. In addition, recreational amenities may be more highly valued in resort areas than in year-round residences. The demand for amenities may also be related to the incomes of unit owners. As incomes rise, it seems that demand for features like hot tubs or lounge areas is likely to increase. However, higher income owners may prefer to consume some of these features individually rather than in common (e.g., a bathtub with a jacuzzi rather than a common hot tub or a large living room rather than a lounge). Therefore, while it is expected that the number of developer-installed amenities is likely to be higher in larger condominiums and resort condominiums, the effect of income on the number of amenities is uncertain.

To test these predictions, we performed a least squares regression in which the dependent variable equaled the total number of amenities (swimming pools, hot tubs, tennis courts, recreation rooms, and meeting rooms) erected by the developer.[34] Only residential condominiums were included in the regression since our theory does not suggest difficulties in adding amenities to nonresi-

34. These five categories of amenities are the only common amenities that exist in any of the condominiums in the sample.

TABLE IV
AMENITIES REGRESSION
(RESIDENTIAL CONDOMINIUMS ONLY)

Independent variable	Predicted sign	Coefficient (t-ratio)
Constant		1.069 (0.45)
Condominiums with uniform units	–	−0.413** (−2.05)
Log of number of units	+	0.353*** (3.82)
Log of average unit value	?	−0.150 (−0.66)
Resort condominiums	+	0.053 (0.24)
Number of observations = 47		R^2 = 0.36

Note. **Significant at the 0.05 level; ***significant at the 0.01 level in a two-tailed test.

dential condominiums. The first independent variable takes on a value of one if units in the condominium have equal areas and values, zero otherwise. The second and third explanatory variables are the natural logs of the number of units and the average real value of units, respectively. The latter is a proxy for the income of condominium owners. The last independent variable is a dummy variable indicating condominiums located in the resort area of Ruidoso. In the amenities regression, summarized in Table IV, the coefficients of all of the variables have the expected signs. The coefficients on both the uniformity and size variables are highly significant.[35]

Finally, supermajority rules are asserted to prevent the majority from exploiting the minority. There are several distinct forces that may influence such voting rules. The first relates to capital improvements such as building a swimming pool or remodeling the exterior of buildings. As discussed above, if there is great potential for conflict, these projects may be undertaken in advance by the developer. Once the facilities are in place, the probability of

35. The variable measuring average unit values could be correlated with the error term since unit values are in part determined by the number of common amenities. To account for this possibility, a two-stage least squares regression with unit area in the instrument list was run. The results were virtually identical to the ordinary least squares estimates reported in Table IV.

additional improvements would be reduced.[36] Consequently, it is expected that the voting rule for improvements would be less inclusive for condominiums with facilities already in existence. In addition, in small developments the per unit cost of major improvements is high, making the initiation of such issues unlikely. If this were the only effect of the number of units, we would expect the inclusiveness of the voting rule to increase with the number of units in the condominium. However, Buchanan and Tullock predict that due to the higher decision-making costs encountered by large groups, the inclusiveness of the voting rule will be inversely related to group size. Therefore, the net effect of the number of units on the optimal voting rule is indeterminate. Buchanan and Tullock also predict that the more homogeneous the voting group, the less restrictive the voting rule. Last, our theory predicts that commercial and office condominiums are more apt to have less restrictive rules than those that exist in residential condominiums, since benefits in the former are primarily pecuniary.

Table V shows the results of a least squares regression where the dependent variable is the minimum percentage vote required to pass capital improvement expenditures voted on by unit owners.[37] Condominiums with less than ten units were excluded, since differences in voting percentages have little meaning for very small groups. The coefficient on the first independent variable, the number of units within the condominium, is positive and significantly different from zero. This result indicates that the effect of increases in the number of units on the likelihood of capital improvement issues dominates the effect such increases in the number of voters has on decision-making costs. The second independent variable is a dummy variable with a value of one if the condominium is located in the resort area of Ruidoso, and zero if located elsewhere. Decision-making costs tend to be high in condominiums located in such resort areas, since many owners are not full-time residents. Further, it is common for resort condominium owners to rent out their units when they are not in residence,

36. A referee points out that the initial placement of common amenities by a developer could be an indicator of unit owners' having a relatively high demand for these goods. If this is the case, then the probability of future debate over installation of amenities could be positively correlated with the existence of developer-installed amenities.

37. In some condominiums the board of directors can make capital improvement decisions independently of unit owners, though such decisions can be challenged by unit owners. The voting rules for representative bodies are beyond the scope of this paper. However, see Sass [1988].

TABLE V
VOTING RULE REGRESSION
(CONDOMINIUMS WITH TEN OR MORE UNITS)

Independent variable	Predicted sign	Coefficient (t-ratio)
Constant		50.529***
		(10.5)
Log of number of units	?	2.433*
		(1.84)
Resort condominium	–	–5.617*
		(–1.87)
Nonresidential condominium	–	–6.160
		(–1.33)
Mixed use condominium	+	7.764
		(1.37)
Number of swimming pools and hot tubs	–	–6.692**
		(–2.29)
Number of recreation or activities buildings	–	7.792**
		(2.04)
Number of meeting rooms and lounges	–	–4.612
		(–1.15)
Number of tennis facilities	–	–8.178
		(–1.40)
Number of observations = 60		$R^2 = 0.28$

Note. *Significant at the 0.10 level; **significant at the 0.5 level; ***significant at the 0.01 level in a two-tailed test.

thereby creating pecuniary as well as nonpecuniary benefits. For both of these reasons, it is expected that resorts in Ruidoso would tend to have less inclusive voting rules; indeed the coefficient on resort condominiums is negative and significant. Since commercial and office condominiums provide mainly pecuniary benefits to their unit owners, they are expected to have less inclusive voting rules than do residential condominiums which provide substantial nonpecuniary benefits. The dummy variable indicating commercial and office condominiums, is negative, as expected. However, this effect was not significant. The fourth variable is a dummy indicating mixed use condominiums that contain both residential and commercial or office units. Due to the heterogeneity of ownership, such condominiums are expected to have more restrictive voting rules. The coefficient on the mixed use variable is positive, but insignificant. The next four independent variables measure the influence of various amenities on the optimal voting rule. We predict that construction of additional amenities is less likely to be a voting issue if some amenities are already in place, thereby making possible the use of a less inclusive voting rule. The coefficients of all four variables are expected to be negative. The results of this test are inconclusive. The coefficient for the number of recreation or activities buildings installed is positive.[38] Of the other three, only the coefficient on the number of swimming pools and hot tubs is significantly different from zero.

V. Summary

The use of voting to determine the allocation of resources is an alternative to use of the price mechanism. Market exchange separates ownership from use, whereas voting organizations are often owned by the same people who consume the services produced by the organization.

The study of allocation by political voting organizations is problematic because the interests of political voters are difficult to untangle. However, it is relatively easy to analyze the behavior of developers who set up the physical operations and structure the constitutions of private voting groups, and then sell voting shares in these organizations. In particular, the more appealing the constitutions of such developers' organizations to prospective buyers, the higher will be developers' gains, since the net revenues elicited from buyers are then also higher.

When resources are allocated by voting, costs associated with majorities' opportunities for capturing wealth (and minorities' preventative efforts) and difficulties of making decisions arise. Developers will attempt to convince potential buyers that these costs are likely to be low.

It is argued that developers will gain (1) by closely matching projects' assessments to projects' benefits; (2) by closely matching projects' net benefits to the allocation of votes among members; (3) by providing ahead of time (or excluding from the organization's jurisdiction) projects that, if proposed later on, are likely to be divisive; and (4) by requiring more inclusive voting rules (larger

38. The positive and significant coefficient on the recreation building variable may be due to the potential capital improvement expenditures of equipping such structures. While swimming pools and tennis courts are essentially complete once installed, potentially divisive decisions regarding purchases of recreational equipment must be made if a recreation building is erected.

majorities) for future projects whose total net value is large, but that make easy targets for the capture of wealth.

The predictions of the theory are tested for one type of voting organization: condominium owners' associations. The decision to study condominiums is the result of the availability of data on their physical features and constitutions and of the wide range of voting and assessment rules they employ. Consistent with the theory, it is first found that the greater the variance in value per square foot among condominium units, the more likely will be the selection of area-based assessments. Likewise, the probability of selecting value-based assessments tends to increase with the variance in unit value per square foot. Second, votes tend to be allocated in the same manner as assessments; when they do deviate, it is always toward the lower cost system of uniform voting. The probability of selecting uniform voting, despite nonuniform assessments, increases with the number of units in the condominium. Third, the greater the potential for divisiveness of a project, the higher the likelihood of developers undertaking them in advance. The construction of common amenities in a condominium is an example of such a project. We found that when condominium units are uniform and thus the divergence in owner's net benefits are low, fewer amenities were put in place by the developer. Finally, we found the inclusiveness of the voting rule selected tends to increase with increases in the heterogeneity of the voting group and the degree to which benefits are nonpecuniary. While not all of these results are significant, all but one of the effects we were able to test for are in the predicted directions, and taken as a whole, they strongly support our theory. Thus, our embryonic theory of constitution, based on maximizing projects' values to their owners, and derived from profit maximization by project developers, gains considerable support from the empirical results.

University of Washington
Florida State University

References

Barzel, Yoram, "Measurement Cost and the Organization of Markets," *Journal of Law and Economics,* XXV (April 1982), 27–48.

Bogen, Jules I., *Financial Handbook,* fourth edition (New York, NY: Ronald Press, 1968).

Brickley, James A., Ronald C. Lease, and Clifford W. Smith, Jr., "Ownership Structure and Voting on Antitakeover Amendments," *Journal of Financial Economics,* XX (January/March 1988), 267–91.

Buchanan, James M., and Gordon Tullock, *The Calculus of Consent* (Ann Arbor, MI: University of Michigan Press, 1962).

DeAngelo, Harry, "Competition and Unanimity," *American Economic Review*, LXXI (March 1981), 18–27.

———, and Linda DeAngelo, "Managerial Ownership of Voting Rights: A Case Study of Public Corporations with Dual Classes of Common Stock," *Journal of Financial Economics*, XIV (March 1985), 33–69.

Easterbrook, Frank H., and Daniel R. Fischel, "Voting in Corporate Law," *Journal of Law and Economics*, XXVI (June 1983), 395–427.

Ellickson, Robert C., "Cities and Homeowners Associations," *University of Pennsylvania Law Review*, CXXX (June 1982), 1519–80.

Fama, Eugene F., and Michael C. Jensen, "Separation of Ownership and Control," *Journal of Law and Economics*, XXVI (June 1983a), 301–25.

———, and ———, "Agency Problems and Residual Claims," *Journal of Law and Economics*, XXVI (June 1983b), 327–49.

Farnham, Paul G., and Stephen N. Bryant, "Form of Local Government: Structural Policies of Citizen Choice," *Social Science Quarterly*, LXVI (June 1985), 386–400.

Greene, William H., "LIMDEP[tm] User's Manual," xeroxed material, 1985.

Grossman, Sanford J., and Oliver D. Hart, "Takeover Bids, the Free-Rider Problem, and the Theory of the Corporation," *Bell Journal of Economics*, XI (Spring 1980), 42–64.

———, and ———, "One Share-One Vote and the Market for Corporate Control," *Journal of Financial Economics*, XX (January/March 1988), 175–202.

Harris, Milton, and Artur Raviv, "Corporate Governance: Voting Rights and Majority Rules," *Journal of Financial Economics*, XX (January/March 1988), 203–35.

Jarrell, Gregg A., and Annette B. Poulsen, "Dual-Class Recapitalizations as Antitakeover Mechanisms: The Recent Evidence," *Journal of Financial Economics*, XX (January/March 1988), 129–52.

Kafoglis, Milton Z., and Richard J. Cebula, "The Buchanan-Tullock Model: Some Extensions," *Public Choice*, XXXVI (1981), 179–86.

Kiesling, Herbert J., "Potential Costs of Alternative Decision-Making Rules," *Public Choice*, IV (Spring 1968), 49–58.

Lease, Ronald C., John J. McConnell, and Wayne H. Mikkelson, "The Market Value of Control in Publicly-Traded Corporations," *Journal of Financial Economics*, XI (April 1983), 439–71.

Manne, Henry G., "Some Theoretical Aspects of Share Voting," *Columbia Law Review*, LXIV (1964), 1427–45.

Manski, Charles F., and Daniel McFadden, eds., *Structural Analysis of Discrete Choice Data with Econometric Applications* (Cambridge, MA: MIT Press, 1981).

Maser, Steven M., "Demographic Factors Affecting Constitutional Decisions: The Case of Municipal Charters," *Public Choice*, XXXVIII (1985), 121–62.

Nitzan, Shmuel, and Uriel Procaccia, "Optimal Voting Procedures for Profit Maximizing Firms," *Public Choice*, LI (1986), 191–208.

Ostrom, Elinor, "Some Postulated Effects of Learning on Constitutional Behavior," *Public Choice*, V (Fall 1968), 87–104.

Partch, M. Megan, "The Creation of a Class of Limited Voting Common Stock and Shareholder Wealth," *Journal of Financial Economics*, XVIII (June 1987), 313–39.

Pindyck, Robert, and Daniel Rubinfeld, *Econometric Models and Economic Forecasts* (New York, NY: McGraw-Hill, 1981).

Sass, Tim R., "Constitutional Choice in Representative Democracies," unpublished manuscript, San Jose State University, June 1988.

This article uses a rational choice model of the origins of democracy to analyze the political history of medieval England from the Norman conquest to the Hundred Years War. Why did a country just taken over by a ruler more autocratic than his predecessors develop a political system increasingly dominated by the rule of law and protodemocratic institutions? The authors argue that protodemocratic institutions such as the Magna Carta, Parliament, and an independent judiciary evolved as unintended consequences of the self-interested wealth-maximizing behavior of rulers and some of their subjects. The evolution of contractual relations between rulers and nobles, towns, and Jewish financiers is shown to be consistent with the theory. The article concludes with a discussion of why the rule of law was more secure and protodemocratic institutions were stronger and more enduring in England than in Continental monarchies.

The Origins of Democracy in England

EDGAR KISER
YORAM BARZEL
University of Washington

The Norman conquest of England, the signing of the Magna Carta, and the development of the English parliament are widely recognized as among the most significant events in the political history of the West. The early unity and centralization of the English state was directly promoted by the conquest. The Magna Carta shaped the contours of political debate and action in England for centuries and served as a model for the constitutions of other countries. The English parliament was the strongest and most enduring of medieval legislative assemblies and had a lasting influence on state policy. To better understand the development of the rule of law and democracy in the West, it is necessary to go back to its medieval origins (Downing 1989). The protodemocratic institutions (i.e., those providing voting and other rights

Authors' Note: *An earlier version of this article was presented at the conference on "Revenue Extraction and the Institutionalization of the State" held in Seattle, WA in April 1991. We would like to thank participants in that conference and Terry Boswell, Paul Burstein, Herbert Costner, Jack Goldstone, Julie Elston, Margaret Levi, Diane Lye, Kevin Neuhouser, Douglass North, Robert Stacey, Gordon Tullock, and four anonymous reviewers for helpful comments.*

RATIONALITY AND SOCIETY, Vol. 3 No. 4, October 1991 396-422

for some subset of subjects) that arose across medieval Western Europe were never totally eliminated in the Absolutist Era. In fact, differences in the policies of European absolutist states can be partly explained by variations in the extent to which preceding protodemocratic institutions survived (Kiser 1987). Here, however, we are interested in the origins of these institutions, not their subsequent development.

Why and how did a country just taken over by a ruler with "unparalleled power" (Teunis 1978, 141) develop a political system increasingly dominated by the rule of law and protodemocratic institutions? More specifically, what explains the proliferation of constitutional contracts, the emergence of an independent judiciary, the independent power of towns, and a strong legislative assembly?

These central questions about the politics of medieval England have not received much attention from social scientists. Historians have produced an abundance of studies of particular aspects of these issues, but a theoretical model capable of incorporating and synthesizing our knowledge of the historical development of protodemocracy and the rule of law in medieval England has yet to be developed. Many scholars have offered inductive generalizations consisting of lists of structural factors correlated with political transformations in this period (Weber [1922] 1968; Hintze 1975; Bendix 1978; Poggi 1978; Downing 1989). However, their ability to understand the politics of medieval England has been limited by their (usually implicit) assumption that the only thing that rulers and other actors are maximizing is power and that the interests of rulers and subjects generally conflict (Weber [1923] 1968, 1013, 1087; Bendix 1964, 42-47; 1978, 189; Hintze 1975, 309, 313; Gintis and Bowles 1984, 21, 24; Poggi 1978, 36-37, 47; Downing 1989, 225; Tilly 1989). To take just one example, Blockmans (1978) argues that "representation appears whenever a government finds itself forced by the concentration of power in the hands of its subjects to share power with them through institutionalized consultation" (p. 192). Although many have noted that cooperation between rulers and some subjects occurs (Tilly 1990; Hall and Ikenberry 1989, 40), it has been seen as the exception to normally oppositional relations. Some scholars argue that rulers cooperated only with the "dominant class" of nobles (Anderson 1974; Gintis and Bowles 1984). Others note limited cooperation with towns (Poggi 1978; Bendix 1978). Yet another suggests that cooperation will occur only when subsistence is threatened (Lenski 1966). These analyses have not recognized that the wealth-generating potential of cooperation between rulers and some subjects provides the foundation for a general explanation of the evolution of medieval political institutions.

As a result of the limitations inherent in their theoretical approach, the development of protodemocracy in England remains "puzzling" to most scholars (e.g., Tilly 1989, 564). One indication of the lack of consensus on this topic is the diversity of the lists of causes of protodemocracy in three prominent analyses (cf. Hintze 1975; Lenski 1966, 60; Downing 1989). Moreover, because the explanations they have provided often cannot adequately account for important empirical facts, they are sometimes compelled to deny well-known aspects of the history of the period. For example, neither Poggi (1978) nor Anderson (1974) can adequately explain relations between rulers and towns. Poggi (1978, 36-37) argues that rulers opposed the autonomy of medieval towns, and Anderson (1974, 161, 195) denies that they had any autonomy. Since these arguments are unable to account for the development of medieval political institutions, it is necessary to construct a different theoretical framework.

We suggest that the rule of law and protodemocracy evolved as an unintended consequence of the self-interested wealth-maximizing behavior of rulers and their subjects. This article uses a rational choice theoretical model of the origins of democracy (Barzel 1991a) and insights from other rational choice work on politics (North 1982; Bates and Lien 1985; Kiser 1987; Levi 1988)[1] to analyze the transformation of the English state between the Norman conquest and the Hundred Years War. Part 1 provides a brief summary of the theory. We then apply the theory to three aspects of English history: the Norman conquest and its immediate aftermath (Part 2); the formation and transformation of contracts between rulers and subjects after the conquest (Part 3); and the evolution of an independent judicial system (Part 4). As will be seen, the major historical trends in this period of the evolution of democracy conform well to the theory.

1. TOWARD A THEORY OF THE EVOLUTION OF DEMOCRACY

Barzel (1991a) has developed a general theoretical model of the process by which an autocratic state[2] will evolve into a democracy.[3] The model is of a country that is taken over by a wealth-maximizing absolute ruler who then utilizes his or her resources so as to yield the highest net present value income stream, subject to personal safety.

Hypothetically, rulers could create and enforce laws arbitrarily and periodically confiscate the resources of their subjects. This strategy, however, is not wealth maximizing. Rational rulers are expected to confiscate as much as they can *immediately* and to refrain from confiscation thereafter. Niccolò Machiavelli ([1531] 1977) understood this strategy well: "When a prince takes a new state, he should calculate the sum of all the injuries he will have to do, and do them all at once, so as not to have to do new ones every day; simply by not repeating them, he will thus be able to reassure people, and win them over to his side with benefits" (p. 28). The extent of the initial confiscation will be determined by the relative power of rulers and subjects. After the initial confiscation, as time passes, rulers will selectively form a sequence of contracts with subsets of their subjects. Each successful contract enriches the parties to it and increases their confidence in contracting, thus encouraging the broadening of the process.

The ruler enters such contracts to increase his wealth. Subjects, however, will not contract with him unless they also gain and their gains are guaranteed. Thus subjects will be granted valued rights and privileges, primarily the rights to own property and to trade. Rulers granting these rights are no altruists; they simply want to increase their own wealth. Subjects who are allowed to keep some of the gains from their production and trade will produce and trade more; they are willing to pay for the opportunity to become richer. This allows the ruler to receive a higher net income, often in the form of higher tax revenue, that subjects willingly grant. Some of these are granted collectively by vote.

Absolute rulers cannot rely on third-party enforcement. Subjects, then, cannot trust absolute rulers to abide by their contracts (Hicks 1966). To gain subjects' trust, rulers must make their commitments credible (Williamson 1985; North and Weingast 1989). Commitments are credible if the loss from breaking them exceeds the gain. Rulers can make their contractual commitments credible by creating an independent mechanism of contract enforcement and can enhance their credibility by insuring the continuity of the relationship.

Consider, first, the creation of enforcement mechanisms. A ruler who intends to make deals with subjects must set rules governing the relationship and methods of enforcing them. When disputes regarding the deals occur, policemen and judges must be called on to settle them. Policemen and judges who are strictly the ruler's subjects will settle all disputes in the ruler's favor, and subjects, then, will be reluctant to deal with the ruler. Rulers can persuade subjects to deal with them only if they can create a judicial system that will obey the law rather than always rule in rulers' favor. Therefore, rulers with attractive prospects to increase their wealth by transacting with their subjects will create an *independent* judiciary to which they *cede some power*. Rulers *gain* by becoming *less* absolute.

The creation of institutions granting subjects the right to make state policy by voting is another aspect of contract enforcement. Suppose that rulers perceive worthwhile large-scale projects in which they would like to invest and that would benefit from subjects taking part in their management and in financing them. Had subjects' financing taken the form of a loan, lenders would fear capture, perhaps in the form of unduly risky projects, and require safeguards against such capture. One method of solving this problem is using equity finance and giving control to investors by writing contracts stipulating that major business decisions will be made by a majority of the investors' votes. Such a method for wealth-maximizing business decision making enhances the rule of law and has many of the rudiments of a democratic institution. Rulers do not abdicate to a full-fledged democracy—they merely provide guarantees to business partners. As the number of profitable investment opportunities increases, the need for capital and for managing partners becomes greater. In the process of undertaking these projects, the ruler (and his subjects) gain by expanding the scope of these institutions and by strengthening the safeguards against confiscation.

Continuity also increases the credibility of commitments. Rulers who renege on promises cannot expect subjects to place much credence in their future promises. If the ruler reneges, then some of the gains expected in future deals will be lost. A ruler will keep a promise if the associated current gain from reneging is less than the present value of the loss on future deals. The greater the expectation of continuity in the relationship between the ruler and subjects, the greater the loss from reneging, and therefore the more trustworthy the ruler becomes. In hereditary systems of government, the continuity of relationships depends on the presence of an heir and the age of the ruler. Rulers who have an heir can make credible commitments into the future, even beyond their expected lifetime. Such rulers, then, are wealthier than heirless rulers. Indeed, an heirless ruler is subject to the "last period problem" (Klein and Leffler 1981), and would be expected to break contacts more often. The closer the kinship ties between the heir and the ruler, the greater the level of continuity and the more credible the ruler's commitments. Thus sons should have the greatest effects on credibility. The problem is less severe for an heirless young adult ruler than for an heirless old ruler, but regardless of age, an absolute ruler is expected to attempt to insure succession.[4]

Cooperation will be sought by both powerful and weak rulers. The terms of the contract, however, will vary in accordance with the relative power of the two parties. Contracts are used for exchanges between the parties and must also provide for enforcement. In this case, restrictions on rulers are necessary to insure compliance with the contract, and these come in the form of privileges granted to subjects. Without imposing such restrictions on themselves, even the most powerful rulers could not find the partners necessary to increase their wealth through contracting. Restrictions by themselves obviously decrease the ruler's power. The added wealth they help produce however may well compensate for the loss. Therefore, powerful rulers will grant privileges to their subjects, simply as a means to increasing their wealth. Indeed, powerful rulers will contract more with their subjects and in the process will grant *more* privileges than weak ones will because they are more secure, fearing less that subjects will overthrow them, and are in a better position to increase their wealth.

Not all relations between rulers and subjects will be cooperative and harmonious; sometimes, rulers will violate contracts, confiscate property, or abuse the judicial system. The theory seems capable of predicting when such events will occur. While contracts are in effect, many random, unforeseen events are bound to occur. Some of these will affect the relative power of the contracting parties. Others will increase the importance of factors that at contract time were not worthwhile stipulating about and consequently are now a cause of dispute. Changes that affect the relative power of the parties are, for instance, that the ruler may win or lose a war, gain a sole heir, or lose one he had. Technological advances may increase the wealth of subjects or create new weapons that alter the balance of power. These changes in conditions may alter the equilibrium contract stipulations. Another kind of change may be in the price of a factor that originally was low enough for one of the parties to supply it without explicitly agreeing to do so. A large increase in the price of such a factor may result in a dispute as to who should provide it.

As the existing contract diverges more and more from the equilibrium one, the cost of breaking the contract will not be deemed large enough, and contract violations and disputes will multiply. The eventual outcome, whether it is reached by negotiation, through the courts, or even by revolution, will be a new contract that better reflects current conditions. As conditions begin to change again, this process will repeat itself. The fewer and milder the changes in conditions, the better the performance of contracts and the greater the advance in the rule of law.

England provides a dramatic example of the evolution toward democracy. Several features of English history make it a suitable case to illustrate our argument. The Norman conquest in 1066 can be taken as a clear starting point of a *relatively absolute* rule. Norman rulers were never complete autocrats, but their power was more absolute than that of the Anglo-Saxons who ruled before them. After the conquest, the external shocks to the system are minimal. England's geographic isolation makes it *relatively free* from serious outside threats for the next few centuries,[5] and there were few natural disasters that would drastically transform relations between rulers and subjects. We end our discussion at the middle of the 14th century, just when two major "shocks" are about to occur – the plague and the Hundred Years War. The combination of conquest followed by continuity in England provides a unique opportunity to examine ongoing relations between rulers and their subjects over a long period of time.

SUMMARY OF PROPOSITIONS

1. Rulers will confiscate as much as they can immediately after taking power. The amount they can confiscate is determined by their power relative to their subjects.
2. Rulers lacking close heirs will be more likely to violate contracts and confiscate from subjects than will rulers with close heirs.
3. External "shocks" change the distribution of resources between rulers and subjects in unexpected ways. The greater the number and severity of external shocks, the greater the number of contract violations and the slower the development of the rule of law.
4. In the absence of frequent external shocks, the number of contracts between rulers and subjects will increase over time, and the contracts will become more detailed and include better enforcement mechanisms.
5. Rulers will often allow, and even fund, defensive fortifications by subjects (such as town walls and noble castles) in order to increase their costs of confiscation and thus make their commitments to subjects more credible.
6. Rulers will give subjects voting rights in order to allow them to protect their investments in joint projects.
7. Powerful rulers will contract more with subjects and grant subjects more rights and privileges than will weak rulers.
8. The form of contracts between rulers and subjects will be a function of the nature of their joint projects. The more wealth that subjects provide, the greater the privileges and voting rights they will be granted.
9. Although scholars have focused on two significant events in medieval English history – the Magna Carta and the origin of Parliament – both of these are parts of larger processes. The Magna Carta is just one of many contracts between rulers and subjects, and Parliament is only one of the institutions created to enhance contractual relations between them.

2. THE NORMAN CONQUEST: CONFISCATION AND THE RULE OF LAW

A major part of our argument is that a new absolute ruler will confiscate right away and then revert to the rule of law, which, in the absence of major shocks, will progress steadily. The conquest of England by William the Conqueror employed a mixture of force and legality. William began by confiscating all property – he claimed that he owned all the land in England

and that all subjects were his tenants. The king himself retained about 20% of all land, significantly more than the former English king (Brown 1969), distributed 50% to the Norman nobles who made his military victory possible (in exchange for their continuing military service),[6] and increased the holdings of the church, a supporter of his conquest, to about 25% (Warren, 1987, 55). As part of the confiscation, the new ruler used every possible precedent of taxation. He also carried out a detailed survey of all taxable property (the *Domesday Book*) in 1086. This survey permitted a quite accurate evaluation of these properties, and thus provided secure property rights for subjects as well as a firmer basis for taxation (Holt 1987).

The Norman conquest took place during a period of contested succession in England. William the Conqueror was one of many who claimed the right to rule, and his may have even been the most legitimate claim (Brown 1969, 109). He had the blessing of the Pope and the support of major elements of the English church (Brown 1969, 148). The legitimacy of his claim to the throne supported William's argument that his use of force during and immediately after the conquest was legal. He argued that all of the people who opposed him, and according to him, all English nobles had, were guilty of treason. The penalty for treason was forfeiture of all of their land to the Crown (Taylor 1889, 235). These acts of confiscation were soon followed by the laying of a legal foundation to his rule. William had himself elected king by the council of nobles, signed a coronation charter promising to respect traditional laws and privileges, and ensured succession to his sons.

The rule of law was not entirely absent even during the conquest. William preserved most of the customary laws of England, the existing central administrative structure, and local political institutions (Richardson and Sayles 1966, 28). However, the lack of institutionalized mechanisms to control the actions of the ruler made it very difficult for him to guarantee his promises to even his most powerful subjects (e.g., nobles had few castles to raise the costs of confiscation). Without such guarantees, the council could not be used to make binding contracts, and its meetings tended to be mere formalities. The immediate aftermath of the conquest thus marks a high point of royal autocracy in medieval England.

3. CONTRACTS, DISPUTES, AND DEMOCRACY

The two centuries following the conquest are characterized by a decline in the autocratic and arbitrary nature of rule. English kings entered into separate contracts with nobles, towns, Jewish financiers, and merchants, granting each of these groups, and individuals within them, certain and very different rights and privileges.[7] These contracts, which form the earliest foundation of the rule of law and protodemocracy, have been difficult for many historians to explain. Treharne (1969) argues that "it was inconceivable that any king other than a minor or an imbecile would willingly agree, without a struggle, to surrender any significant part of his traditional powers" (p. 60). As a specific example, Hollister (1980) notes the difficulty many historians have had trying to explain an early charter voluntarily granted to London: "The terms of the charter seem uncharacteristically generous for a powerful and notoriously stingy king who apparently had nothing to fear from Londoners, and therefore no reason to placate them" (p. 290). Yet many of these contracts were not forced on rulers. What these historians overlook is the reciprocal nature of these relationships; they implicitly assume that English kings were maximizing power and would maintain their autocratic rule at all costs. Our model, based on the assumption that kings were maximizing wealth, can offer an explanation of the evolution of such contracts. We argue that cooperation governed by contracts increases wealth. Therefore, it is capable of benefiting the ruler, but it must benefit subjects as well.

It would be presumptuous to claim that the data we use here provide a test of our model; they definitely do much less. The following discussion of contracts with nobles merely shows that the historical evidence does not contradict our model. The sections on towns, Jewish financiers, and Parliament attempt a somewhat more demanding examination of how well the data fit the model.

CONTRACTS BETWEEN KINGS AND NOBLES: FROM CORONATION CHARTERS TO MAGNA CARTA

This section explores contracts between rulers and nobles, focusing on coronation charters and the Magna Carta. Our model suggests that, over time, these contracts should become more detailed and the mechanisms of contract enforcement should improve. Violations of existing contracts should not occur unless the continuity of the relationship is threatened (e.g., when rulers lack sons or close heirs), or "shocks" to the system alter the relative power of the parties.

The first contracts made by rulers were with the Norman nobility. Nobles were the wealthiest subjects and also the most powerful since they had their own armies. Thus contracts with them would be easiest to guarantee. However, contracts with even this powerful group were difficult to enforce in the first century following the Norman conquest.

The most important change in the relationship between the ruler and nobles brought about by the conquest was the introduction of feudalism. The feudal relation was one in which the ruler who owned all land conditionally granted some land to the highest nobles, who in turn conditionally granted some of their land to nobles below them. The condition in each case was that military service and other feudal obligations were to be provided in exchange for the land. A hierarchy of reciprocal contractual obligation was created, with rights to use land being passed down the structure and military and other obligations passed up.

The "coronation charters" were contracts regulating the rights and obligations between the new ruler and the nobility. The feudal contract was reconfirmed in the charters sealed by each king at the beginning of his reign. There were two main ingredients to the contract enforcement mechanism. First, confiscation by the ruler was costly because the nobles had military power, giving them the ability to revolt. It was made more costly by the construction of castles protecting most noble property. There were few castles prior to the conquest, but, *with the ruler's permission*, many were built in the immediate decades following it (Brown 1969). Second, the nobles had seats on the king's council, giving them an institutionalized position from which to influence state policy. In this early period, members of the council were often unable to exercise much control over policy. However, as the rule of law evolved, council power increased.

The selection of a new ruler was often contested. Thus nobles were in a good position to extract concessions from potential rulers in exchange for their support. The coronation charter signed at the election of William Rufus (William's son) to the throne in 1087 provides a good example. This charter was clearly a contract: The king ceded guaranteed property rights and regulated taxation in return for the support of the English nobles and most Norman nobles. As a rule, monarchs cooperate with subjects on projects and agree to share the benefits. They provide guarantees so that subjects will agree to participate. Here, the "project" is the appointment of the ruler, so the ruler must cede some wealth in exchange for support. William Rufus used this support to defeat his brother Robert and his uncle Odo, allied with a few Norman nobles, in their attempt to take the crown.

However, once he became king, William Rufus did not keep all of the promises made in his charter. He did improve royal justice to some extent, and he protected Jewish financiers (Mason 1977). In spite of this, his rule is known for its "irresponsible despotism," including the regular extraction of many forms of tribute and the use of local courts for extortion (Schwartz 1967; Barlow 1983). William Rufus's partial violation of the contract can be explained by the inadequacies of the contracts themselves, which prior to the Magna Carta were short, imprecise documents (Warren 1973), and the inadequacy of the institutions necessary to enforce them. An independent judiciary and a legislature with control over taxes had not yet developed. Moreover, the king had no son to serve as an heir. Revolt did not prove to be an effective enforcement mechanism. The revolts of 1075 and 1095 did not receive widespread support; many participants lost their property, and some lost their lives.

At the death of William Rufus, there were two main claimants to the throne: William Rufus's brothers, Robert and Henry. Robert again had some of the Norman nobles on his side and again tried to take the crown by force. Henry, on the other hand, offered a coronation charter, called the "Charter of Liberties," to the English nobles in 1100; it was enough to win their support, the election, and his dispute with Robert. For the second time in a row, the promise of the rule of law had won over the use of force alone, and for the second time in a row, the promises made in the King's charter were not entirely kept. As was usual in this period, there were some contract violations by the king. Barlow (1955) notes that "despite Henry's charter, reliefs remained arbitrary, amercements were heavy, heiresses were sold, the wardships of minors stayed with the king, and the English barons were mulcted and controlled" (p. 183). But even more than William Rufus, Henry I abided by many of the terms of the coronation charter. Teunis (1978) suggests "that Henry more or less stuck to his promise, so far as the barons were concerned, was an equally wise course of action [since] he stood to gain more than not" (p. 138).

The charter signed by Henry II in 1154 was "meager," and the two following kings, Richard and John, signed no charters at all. Perhaps these charters atrophied because they could not be adequately enforced. There is no point in requiring rulers to make promises they cannot be made to keep. It is important to note that the absence of a clear enforceable contract was costly to both parties. Some mutually advantageous projects for which rulers would raise the revenue necessary to pursue policies they favored and the nobles would share in the gains as well as limit what they saw as the arbitrary exercise of power by rulers were not implemented because a mechanism to enforce the rulers' side of the bargain was lacking.

The Magna Carta of 1215 can be understood as an attempt to overcome the imperfections in previous contracts and address problems arising from changes that altered the prior relationship between the contracting parties. One of the most important changes was inflation (Harvey 1973). Because taxes were generally paid in money, not in kind, inflation decreased Richard's and John's revenue in real terms and reduced their ability to employ soldiers and purchase weapons. Noble landlords were less hurt by inflation, as many of them could shift from leasing their land to managing it themselves (an option not valued by rulers due to poor administrative capacity; Harvey 1973). The result of this development was a shift in relative wealth away from the rulers and toward the nobility. A series of bad harvests (Mann 1986, 426) further increased the fiscal problems of both rulers.

The conjunction of declining state revenue and almost constant warfare produced an increase in tax requests and petty expropriations (including justice fees and exploitation of wardships and church vacancies) by Richard and John (Taylor 1889). The lack of sons to serve as heirs to the throne during much of this period may have contributed to the increase in "arbitrary" rule. Richard lacked sons during his entire reign (1189-1199), and John had none for the first several years (1199-1207) of his reign.

The outcomes of war also shifted the balance of power between rulers and the nobility. Richard used up the large surplus left by Henry II and all of the money he had extracted by increasing all forms of taxes, but because his wars were successful, his policies enjoyed broad support (Gillingham 1978). John's power significantly declined when his military ventures failed and he lost his lucrative French possessions. This change weakened the crown, thus allowing the nobles to push for a new contract.

The Magna Carta was described by the nobles who drafted it as a return to the contract specified in the coronation charter of Henry I (Holt 1965). However, it differed from all earlier contracts between rulers and nobles in two important ways. First, it was by far the longest and most detailed charter written since the conquest and included technical language that served to reduce ambiguity. Second, it was the first charter to specify a mechanism of contract enforcement, including both monitoring the actions of rulers and describing sanctions that would follow contract violation (Clause 61). Although the enforcement mechanism was crude, amounting to little more than organized confiscation of the king's assets in the event of violation of the contract, it represents an important step in the evolution of contracts.[8]

The Magna Carta primarily delineates property rights, especially concerning relations between rulers and nobles (tenants in chief). It contains many complaints about the arbitrary nature of royal justice, and "one note runs through it: the re-establishment of the rule of law" (Richardson and Sayles 1966, 152). The authors of the contract seem to have been well aware that property rights can only be maintained by a fair and independent judicial system, and the contract addresses that concern. The other main focus of the contract is royal taxation. Two taxes used to finance wars, the *aid* and the *scutage*, are singled out for specific criticism, and constraints are set on the ruler's power to impose these taxes. The Magna Carta sets the stage for the development of protodemocracy by stipulating no taxation without consent. The need for protodemocratic institutions (like the need for the rule of law) however, is at best a second-order concern and not the main focus of the Magna Carta. These stipulations are there because they are necessary to enforce economic contracts (mainly regarding taxation for war) between rulers and nobles.[9]

CONTRACTS BETWEEN RULERS AND TOWNS

Historians have failed to perceive the gains to the towns and the ruler from dealing with each other and thus have had a hard time explaining town charters. They have assumed that relations between rulers and towns were always oppositional and thus that only weak rulers would grant privileges to towns (Blockmans 1989, 739). One case, the "Charter of Liberties" granted to London in 1133, was thought to be a forgery (Brooke, Keir, and Reynolds 1973) because it was literally too good to be true. Historians simply could not understand why a strong king would grant so many freedoms to a relatively weak town. It has now been demonstrated that the charter is real (Hollister 1980).

Social scientists also have had some difficulty explaining rulers' relations with towns. Adam Smith ([1776] 1976, 423-25) argued that rulers aided towns *only* because they needed allies in their ongoing conflicts with nobles (see also Poggi 1978; Downing 1989). However, this argument assumes that rulers had cooperative relations with some groups (towns) but did not cooperate with others (nobles). We argue that rulers had incentives to cooperate with both groups.

The economic activities that characterize towns are highly specialized, and people will not specialize unless their investment can be protected from confiscation. The ruler stands to gain from such specializing and will attempt to accommodate it. We expect an increase in the number of contracts over time and the development of mechanisms to prevent confiscation by rulers. Furthermore, the nature of contracts with particular towns should vary with the wealth-creating potential of the town and the nature of its comparative advantage.

The experience of towns in medieval England fits the model well. In the first few decades after the Norman conquest, English towns retained little autonomy and few privileges. They were monitored closely by the crown (Young 1961, 10-11), and William confiscated from them frequently (Bourne 1866, 9). However, rulers could benefit from the expert knowledge of foreign trade, coinage, building and repairing ships, and naval strategy found only in towns (Young 1961). They could secure these highly skilled services *only* by the cooperation of properly motivated individuals, that is, independent specialists rather than serfs. They had reason, then, to create contractual relations that would effectively further the rule of law.

Henry I granted the first charters – to Lincoln and London – in 1130 and 1131. Between 1130 and 1307, the rights and privileges given to the towns increased substantially (Young 1961, 156). These grants were not unilateral; they brought in fees and taxes. More towns were included, and liberties given to each increased with successive charters. These charters included the right to control justice, to elect town officials such as mayors and bailiffs (an early form of local democracy), to collect their own taxes and thus enhance local civic projects, and to regulate their own commerce (Young 1961, 29). Many of the charters prohibited royal officials from interfering in any of the businesses of the town (Young 1961, 88). Moreover, John, Henry III, and Edward I even financed the building and repair of town walls (Young 1961, 103). Among other things, such walls contributed to the credibility of the ruler's commitments, as they increased his cost of confiscation. Town charters generated income for the towns as well as for the ruler. From about 1150 on, the towns began to grow rapidly (Barlow 1955, 121). The privileges they obtained helped insure their continuing prosperity.

The charters granted to the towns were not all the same – some provided many more privileges than others. The pattern of difference between town charters is consistent with our model. The more wealth generated by trading with a town, the greater the necessary contractual guarantees. Contracts with London, the wealthiest of English cities, contained the most privileges (Stubbs 1921, 46). The "cinque ports" were also given more rights than other towns (Young 1961, 87-88).

The relations between kings and towns were not always cooperative and harmonious. Kings had the power to revoke the charters they had granted, which they occasionally did. The pattern of the revocations has also puzzled some historians. Reynolds (1972) suggests that "it is paradoxical that it should have been the mighty Henry I who made concessions and the weak Stephen who revoked them" (p. 342). This is not as paradoxical as it appears. A ruler who followed the rule of law could be relied on and therefore could gain from trade and become richer (and more powerful). The security of a weakened ruler is threatened. Such a ruler will tend to discount heavily the gains that might be forthcoming in the future and value rather highly immediate gains (Levi 1988). Therefore, confiscation is more likely from a weak than from a powerful ruler.

CONTRACTS BETWEEN RULERS AND JEWISH FINANCIERS

One of the first groups with whom kings made contracts was Jewish lenders. Jews arrived in England under William the Conqueror. Although religious tolerance was not a strong point of medieval England, a maximizing ruler is expected be more tolerant to Jews the more profitable they are to him. Since Jews provided a steady source of royal loans and tax revenue from their income from lending to subjects, both William and William Rufus treated them well (Stokes 1921, 3). All early English rulers protected the Jews from exploitation by others (among other things, they could not be serfs of anyone else), if only to insure the profitability of their relationship. Henry I gave a charter of privileges to Jews in England, allowing them to charge interest on loans (Bourne 1866, 10). Henry II also frequently taxed Jewish income, but they still prospered under his rule (Stokes 1921, 4). By the second half of the 12th century, taxes on Jews provided about 14% of crown revenue (Roth 1964, 16). Henry III required all Jewish loans to be registered with the state, making them both more secure for lenders and easier for rulers to tax (Roth 1964, 28-29; Barzel 1991b). Jewish financiers charged interest rates on their loans that ranged from 21% to 43% per annum (Roth 1964, 106), which enabled them to prosper while paying taxes to the king.

Beginning around 1239, the nature of the relationship between rulers and Jews changed drastically. Prior to that time, taxation of the Jews had been steady but not confiscatory (Stacey 1987, 143-45). Between 1239 and 1250, Jews were taxed at more than double previous rates, and even the wealthiest Jews were financially ruined (Stacey 1987). Finally, the impoverished Jews were expelled from England in 1290. Opposition to Jews in England by both the nobility and the clergy had been present throughout the 13th century (Deighton 1953, 169; Elman 1937). At the parliament of 1290, Edward I was willing to expel the Jews in exchange for one grant of taxation (Elman 1937).

How can we explain this pattern of contracting and confiscation? Why did rulers initially grant such important wealth-generating privileges to a group with so little power? Why did they later terminate contractual relations with Jewish financiers and expel them from the country?[10]

The specialty of Jews – finance – made them very difficult to supervise directly, a situation in which there are clear benefits to the ruler to contracting and honoring contracts. Moreover, Jews primarily loaned money to subjects (Roth 1964) and rulers taxed their profits, making confiscation a less profitable option for rulers (Barzel 1991b). The situation changed early in the 13th century when an alternative source of loans became available: Italian lenders, who started their financial dealings in England then (Roth 1964, 69) and became prominent lenders by the middle of that century. Since the Italians had a different relationship with the ruler than that of the Jews, they had some reason to believe they would not suffer the same fate (Elman 1937, 151-52). Their loans were not registered, so presumably they were not taxed, and they were guaranteed by the new customs taxes. Jewish lenders could not compete with the Italian lenders unless they too were exempted from taxes. Under these conditions, however, Jews were not useful to the king any more. Expropriation then became the ruler's maximizing course. The emergence of an alternative source of loans, then, made it profitable for rulers to confiscate from Jews (Veitch 1986; Barzel, 1991b), which they began to do in 1239.

THE ROAD TO DEMOCRACY: THE EVOLUTION OF PARLIAMENT

Parliament was not the first institutional mechanism of protodemocratic participation in England. Many varied groupings of individuals with some specific voting rights preceded it. English kings were never totally absolute; they could never make policy and tax decisions without consulting the opinions of some of their subjects. As a rule, kings consulted with particular subjects whose cooperation was necessary for certain projects. The main large-scale project in this period was war (Mann 1986; Tilly 1990; Rasler and Thompson 1990).[11] Bisson (1966) showed that rulers often would summon to the council only the nobles whose cooperation for a particular war was required. When rulers wanted to pursue other projects, they chose to meet with different subsets of their subjects. For certain purposes, they called meetings of selected towns (such as the five major ports); for others, they brought together primary owners of forest lands or Jewish financiers (White 1914). These early assemblies were not democratic bodies representing the public, nor were they the most powerful individuals in the realm. They were groups of potential partners in specific joint ventures who were given some rudimentary voting rights in order to insure their cooperation. It is out of these sorts of meetings that the parliament of medieval England evolved.

Of course, these ad hoc assemblies and the parliament that developed after them were not what we would now call "democratic," as only a small fraction of subjects had voting rights. However, the same could be said of the political institutions of 19th-century England. The important points are that they were more democratic than the institutions that preceded them, and they were the seeds of the increasingly democratic institutions that followed them.

Scholars who have analyzed the evolution of parliamentary institutions have come to very diverse conclusions concerning the main causes of the process. For example, Hintze (1975) and Tilly (1989) argue that military competition between states was a primary cause of the rise of representative institutions like parliament. This argument leads Hintze to suggest that parliament developed during the Hundred Years War. Unfortunately, this is several decades after its actual origins. Lenski (1966) and Poggi (1978) argue exactly the opposite: that military competition between states led to the decline of representative institutions and the rise of absolutism in Europe; however, neither of the authors provide sufficient microlevel causal mechanisms for their arguments.

We view the development of the English parliament as a mechanism to enforce contractual relations between rulers and their subjects. The judicial functions of parliament also increased the independence of the judiciary and thus enhanced the rule of law, but that is not the focus of this section.

Most royal revenue after the conquest came from crown lands, land taxes, and the provision of justice (Harriss 1975, 5; Green 1981). Levels of taxation in this period were maintained by custom, and raising any additional revenue required the consent of the nobles in the Council (Mitchell 1951, 156). Although their institutional position was not strong, the fact that many of these nobles had castles and could muster armies and revolt must have set an upper bound on the amount that rulers extracted from them.

In the early period, because the rule of law was in its infancy, opportunities for the rulers to trade their decision-making autonomy for more wealth were only modest. As late as 1190, rulers used revenues from crown lands and feudal prerogatives to cover 75% to 80% of their expenses (Mann 1986, 418). This high level of independent revenue went hand in hand with high autonomy (Kiser 1986-87, 1987). However, their independence also meant that their resources were limited and they could only pursue projects such as limited wars for which they had enough capital and did not require subjects' active cooperation.

Beginning about the middle of the 13th century, kings began to *ask* for aids and other taxes much more frequently (Mitchell 1951, 151). This form of raising funds is viewed by historians as expropriatory, and the fact that kings had to ask remains a mystery. We hold a different view: that rulers *proposed* joint projects and requested nobles' participation. When the nobles in the council were asked to contribute (i.e., to be taxed), as is common with business propositions, sometimes they agreed and sometimes they refused the requests.[12] Refusal was not uncommon; for example, there were nine such refusals of royal requests between 1237 and 1272 (Mitchell 1951, 194). Agreements reached were binding on all voters. Because war affected all of them, it was desirable that all would take part in its financing. This is why a national rather than a local assembly dealt with war finance.

In our view, these refusals were due not to the fact of taxation but to the nature of the projects on which the tax money was to be spent and the nobles' share in the rewards. The nobility did not always accept the ruler's implicit calculation that they themselves would gain from all such wars. They were willing to pay for "national wars" but not for the "king's wars" (Harriss 1975, 34-38). They presumably expected to gain (or avert loss) from national wars but not from the king's wars and therefore would agree to taxation for the former but not the latter.

Moreover, the nobility sought some say about the conduct of war (and other projects), not just a share in financial costs and benefits. The necessary relationship between the payment of taxes and some control over state policy by the nobility was made clear in the Provisions of Oxford issued in 1258. The Provisions of Oxford introduced a significant improvement in contract enforcement mechanisms, replacing the ad hoc committee of nobles suggested in the Magna Carta with a regular national assembly: parliament (Harriss 1981, 29-30). Rulers were not forced to accept parliament; they gained from the opportunity to guarantee their contracts. Indeed, Strayer (1970) notes that "rulers at first seem to have been rather more enthusiastic about representative assemblies than were their subjects" (p. 66). To gain the cooperation of owners of resources necessary to pursue new wars (and other investment opportunities), kings were willing to give up some of their power to manage such projects.

From the protoparliament of 1253 to the "model parliament" of 1295 and beyond, the powers of this new institution continued to grow. Parliament was the locus of the revolt against taxes for offensive wars in 1297, which resulted in a reconfirmation of the Magna Carta and a strengthening of the link between grants of taxes and the redress of grievances (Harriss 1975). In the 40 years following that agreement, Parliament met 44 times (Harriss 1975, 75). Its demands, the quid pro quo for granting taxes, often became law. By 1311, its consent was required to initiate war, and by 1362, it gained the right to grant customs duties in addition to its control over other taxes (Prestwich 1980). That the mechanisms of contract enforcement had improved substantially since the conquest is attested by Parliament deposing a king – Edward II – for violating his coronation oath (Harriss 1981, 31).

Perhaps the best evidence of the success of cooperation made possible by the development of Parliament comes from the financing of the Hundred Years War. The relatively advanced development of parliamentary representation in England meant that in case of agreement it became much easier for rulers to raise the resources necessary to fight. As a result, in spite of their much lower population and wealth, England was the aggressor throughout, and both English kings and many of their subjects were able to profit at the expense of France, their less politically developed adversary (Prestwich 1980, 202).[13]

4. THE RULE OF LAW: THE DEVELOPMENT OF AN INDEPENDENT JUDICIARY

The rule of law is obviously a necessary condition for maintaining contractual relations. The purpose of this section is not to test our model, since the available data are much too meager, but rather to point out that alongside the evolution of contracts discussed earlier, an accommodating legal framework was also being developed by rulers of England. This legal framework not only delineated relations between subjects but, most important for our model, limited the ability of rulers to act arbitrarily. Downing (1989) sees the rule of law as an "obstacle" that rulers tried to avoid and argues that the only benefit that rulers derived from the rule of law was an increase in "legitimacy." We argue instead that rulers facilitated the development of the rule of law because it allowed them to increase their wealth by providing necessary guarantees for contracts.

The development of the English judicial system seems to be characterized by a slow and partial evolution from royal arbitrariness to the rule of law. William insisted on maintaining preconquest laws and generally tried to maintain law and order to facilitate trade (Brown 1969).[14] The independence of the judiciary began to increase in the reign of Henry I, known by contemporaries as the "Lion of Justice." According to Richardson and Sayles (1966), the judicial system of Henry I was more systematic than any in Europe. He created a system of royal itinerant justices that replaced local justices and brought "peace and security" to England. The authors summarized the change brought by Henry I as follows: "Presumably the king's justices sometimes tilted the scales of justice to the king's advantage, but that they heightened the standards of justice everywhere is a truth that cannot be questioned" (p. 39).

In the period of civil war during Stephen's reign (1135-1154), justice declined, but afterwards, the independence of the judiciary began to increase again. Henry II established a "reign of law" by unifying the common law across the country, eliminating many local variations (Cronne 1970). He also increased the number of royal courts, instituted fixed procedures to make justice faster and more uniform, and established controls over which cases went to court (Warren 1973). It is significant that Henry II, the "strongest of all medieval English kings," was also the monarch who did the most to strengthen the rule of law (Treharne 1969, 48).

There seems to have been a decrease in the independence of the judiciary and an increase in the arbitrariness of justice during the reigns of Richard and John (Holt 1965; Turner 1868; Green 1986).[15] The Magna Carta stressed the importance of a return to the rule of law, and subsequent improvements in justice indicate that these deviations from the rule of law were temporary setbacks within a general progression (Warren 1987; Turner 1985).

CONCLUSION: WAS ENGLAND UNIQUE?

Barzel's (1991a) model of the evolution toward democratic government has been used to explain features of medieval English political history. The model, although not seriously tested, is reasonably consistent with the observed relations between rulers and several diverse groups, indicating that it may be fruitfully applied to other cases. This section compares the early evolution of English politics to other European medieval states and suggests a reason for the uniqueness of England. Although a detailed comparative analysis is beyond the scope of this article, we can suggest some of the main issues that such an analysis must address.

The theoretical model used in our study is entirely general, even though its application here is limited to England. We assume that all rulers and subjects will attempt to increase their wealth through cooperation governed by contracts and that all will try to create institutions to guarantee compliance with contracts. England was not the only medieval state to develop toward protodemocracy between 1100 and 1300. Contracts were made between rulers and various subjects in all medieval states, and institutions were developed to enforce them. Yet in England, contracting was more extensive, the rule of law was becoming more secure, and protodemocratic institutions became stronger and more enduring. As a result, early modern England never became as "absolutist" as France or Spain, and the English economy was less fettered by the arbitrary actions of autocratic rulers.

Contracts between rulers and various subjects proliferated in medieval states, and mechanisms to enforce them also were widespread. Although the extent of the rule of law varied, royal judicial institutions developed across Europe (Strayer 1970). Pirenne (1956) argues that the judicial reforms of St. Louis (1226-1270) in France were very similar to those of Henry II and Henry III in England. Reynolds (1984) notes that the French Charters granted in 1314 and 1315 had a lot in common with the Magna Carta. Towns received privileges in most of medieval Western Europe (Pirenne 1956; Weber [1922] 1968). National legislative assemblies (usually, like the English Parliament, with judicial functions as well) arose all over Western Europe, and many had some control over taxation (Myers 1975). The English Parliament was not even the first of these – the Cortes in León in 1188 has that honor.

Although rulers and subjects in any state could increase their wealth by cooperating using enforceable contracts, variations in the structural conditions within which they attempted to create contracts produced important differences in the number and type of contracts and the mechanisms of enforcing them. In the case of protodemocratic legislative institutions, the English Parliament and the Cortes of Aragon were always significantly stronger than the Estates General in France (Marongiu [1949] 1968) and the Cortes in Castile (Myers 1975). In France, provincial Estates became the main locations of contract negotiations between rulers and subjects as the power of the Estates General waned. Charters were granted in France in 1314 and 1315 to 10 different regions (Bloch 1961, 425-26), and regional variations in law were maintained as well. This is in sharp contrast to the national legal systems that developed in medieval England. Although some French towns were granted charters (Blockmans 1989, 743), English towns had much more autonomy than French towns in this period (Downing 1989, 223).[16] Towns in Aragon also had unusually high autonomy and privileges (Albaladejo 1989, 723).

The experience of the Norman conquest of southern Italy and Sicily further demonstrates the uniqueness of England. Although, as in England, the political system was created by conquest and run by rulers from Normandy, contractual relations in southern Italy and Sicily were few (those with the Church were an exception) and fewer institutions to guarantee contracts were developed (Douglas 1969). This suggests that the development of protodemocratic institutions in England was not caused by any particular characteristics of the Normans.

How can we explain the uniqueness of England? Our model suggests that the number of contracts formed will be a function of the costs, including those of enforcement, and benefits of contracting. The benefits of cooperation through contracting for war, construction of infrastructure, and other investments presumably existed for all rulers and subjects. There are no doubt variations in the benefits of cooperation across cases, but our theory does not yield any precise predictions about them. In any case, we believe England's uniqueness is the result of lower costs of contracting.

Several factors made the costs of creating enforceable contracts lower in England than elsewhere. First, England was relatively protected from outside "shocks," particularly from foreign invasion (Bulpitt 1983).[17] Because such shocks will tend to disrupt or invalidate existing contracts, and because, by their very nature, they cannot be controlled by the contracting parties, the more shocks the parties expect, the fewer contracts will be made. Second, England was both small and homogeneous enough to allow national-level institutions to develop. England had only about a third as much land and a fifth of the population of France in the early Middle Ages (Bulpitt 1983). Rasler and Thompson (1990) suggest that France was too large and heterogeneous for any ruler to effectively govern in this period. Protodemocracy developed much more fully in small countries like England and Aragon than in larger ones like France and Castile. Third, although in part a consequence of the first two factors, England had much greater internal stability than most other states in this period. For example, from the 12th through the 14th centuries, England had only 56 internal revolts, compared to 88 in Castile and 94 in France (Rasler and Thompson 1990, 40). This greater internal stability indicates that English kings were more secure and stronger than their Continental counterparts, facilitating more contracting in England. The main intended result of the enhanced contracting was speedy economic development. An important unintended result of contracting was a more rapid evolution of protodemocracy and the rule of law in England.

NOTES

1. Several recent rational choice models of politics have analyzed relations between rulers and subjects as evolving contractual bargains and have discussed some of the determinants of the type of bargains reached (North 1982; Bates and Lein 1985; Levi 1988; North and Weingast 1989; Root 1989). This body of work has also explored the creation of credible commitments through the evolution of institutional mechanisms of contract enforcement. The theoretical model used in this article (Barzel 1991a) differs from previous work in two main ways. First, instead of slicing into ongoing relations between rulers and subjects, the model begins with the creation of an autocratic state. Second, the model is more general than those proposed in previous work. For example, Levi (1988) and Bates and Lien (1985) focus only on taxation (in the latter, the discussion concerns only the distinction between mobile and immobile assets), Root (1989) is concerned only with loans, and North and Weingast (1989) combine the two. Barzel's (1991a) model attempts to explain these as well as many other relations.

2. No pure autocracy has ever existed, and medieval England is no exception. The assumption of autocracy is used to give the model a precise starting point, but none of the arguments we present require that the state is, in fact, totally autocratic.

3. Unless otherwise noted, all arguments in this section are from Barzel (1991a).

4. Although we have focused only on the issue of how heirs produce continuity in relationships between rulers and subjects, they have other effects as well. First, hereditary systems of government are prone to royal minorities (periods in which a minor must inherit the crown). Although it is impossible to predict when these will occur, we can be certain that they will, and that when they do, the balance of power between rulers and dominant classes will be temporarily tipped toward the latter (Kiser 1986-87, 1987 analyzes the effects of royal minorities on politics in early modern Europe). On this issue, two questions are of central importance: How did the ruler's associates attempt to protect their interests during the minority? How were regents prevented from exercising full power? Second, our stress on the advantage of having heirs should not obscure the fact that heirs sometimes try to take power before the current ruler dies. Moreover, in an era of high mortality, more than one heir is often necessary, but this leads to conflicts between potential heirs. Unfortunately, there has been no systematic study of the role of heirs in the relationship between rulers and subjects.

5. Norman England was only relatively free from external threats. For the early part of the period we cover, the French possessions had to be defended, and Scotland was also periodically threatening.

6. William split the land he gave to each of the Norman nobles into several small manors scattered throughout the country. It is plausible that security was the rationale for the splitting. Since dispersed manors are more costly to manage than unitary ones, this entailed a trade-off of wealth for security. The wisdom of this decision is indicated by the fact that three of the four largest land areas (earldoms) that William did give intact to Norman nobles were the site of revolts during the next 50 years (Stenton 1908).

7. Rulers also entered into contracts with the church. Since complications raised by three-party interactions involving rulers, popes, and the English clergy would require a detailed analysis beyond the scope of this paper, we will not provide a systematic discussion of relations between rulers and the church. However, some aspects of this relation suggest that our model may also be useful for analyzing this phenomenon. The cooperation between rulers and the church in England began with the conquest, when the pope supported William's claim to the English crown. Most of the contracts between rulers and the English church concerned property rights. In return for the land that rulers granted to them, the church initially provided military service to the crown and later was given the right to provide the monetary equivalent. The contracts stipulate that when church land was left vacant (e.g., following the death of a bishop), it, and all the income from it, temporarily reverted to the crown. The rulers were obligated also to appoint a successor as soon as possible. Two opportunities for exploitation, however, arose from this situation: Rulers could maintain the vacancy and keep the income from the land themselves, or they could sell profitable offices in the church. Clauses prohibiting these practices appear often in contracts with the church, but violations of the contract seem to have been frequent (Barlow 1983; Warren 1973). It seems that the main reason why contracts with the church were violated so often is that they lacked adequate enforcement mechanisms. King John's dispute with the pope over the election of the archbishop of Canterbury illustrates the problem well (see Warren 1961). Attempting to curb John's power in the matter, the pope used the two main enforcement mechanisms at his disposal: He called a general strike of the English clergy (putting all of the souls in England in jeopardy), and he excommunicated John. The pope, however, overplayed his hand. John's response was to confiscate church property. In retrospect, it transpired that the contract with the church was self-enforcing, as John was unable to gain from the confiscation: His inability to manage the property efficiently led to its return.

8. Perhaps because the enforcement mechanism was so crude, these sanctions were dropped in subsequent versions of the Magna Carta.

9. An ongoing debate concerns the interests of the nobles who drafted the Magna Carta (see Treharne 1969, 63-65). We obviously do not subscribe to the view that they were early constitutionalists furthering the national interest.

10. Neither the initial confiscatory taxation of Jews in 1239 nor the termination of their relations with rulers in 1290 occurred during periods in which rulers lacked heirs.

11. We agree with Tilly (1990) and Rasler and Thompson (1990) that war facilitated "state making." We attempt to elaborate their arguments by specifying microlevel causal mechanisms and by disaggregating the concept of state making into the development of specific proto-democratic institutions.

12. The conquest of England had no doubt demonstrated that some wars could be very profitable for all parties on the winning side. Of course, not all wars are intended to produce gains; some are necessary just to avoid great losses. Nobles in the council had to decide whether particular proposed wars could be justified on either of these grounds.

13. In addition to those already discussed, rulers contracted with several other groups. As the specialization and differentiation of the economy increased, the number of groups with whom rulers could profit by contracting with increased. Edward I (1272-1307) created a contract—the Charta Mercantoria—with foreign merchants trading in England. This contract gave many privileges to foreign merchants, in exchange for an increase in the rate of customs duties they paid (Bourne 1866, 24). In the 14th century, Edward III signed charters granting privileges to many guilds (including the Fishmongers Company in 1363 and Drapers in 1364; Bourne 1866, 34). The privileges granted included internal democracy and control of justice in guild matters, along with monopolistic positions in the economy (Bourne 1866, 37). It is not clear whether or not these were the first such contracts. Carus-Wilson (1954) indicates that money was taken from guilds as early as the reign of Henry I but does not specify what was given in return. Trading companies were also beginning to emerge in the 14th century. The earliest of these, the Merchants of the Staple, was recognized by the crown in 1313 and became a chartered company later (Bourne 1866, 39).

14. In spite of this, the English judiciary after the conquest was not very independent. Interference by the king in local courts became more systematic and more frequent after the conquest, and the will of the king "generally . . . prevailed" (Taylor 1889, 241), especially in the reign of the heirless William Rufus (Barlow 1983).

15. It seems that the same factors that caused an increase in the violation of contracts by Richard and John also caused this regression in the rule of law discussed earlier.

16. Medieval Japan provides another interesting contrast, as both the rule of law and the autonomy of towns developed without any accompanying representative institutions (Hall 1906). A comparative study that includes the Japanese case may thus be able to separate the factors responsible for the development of legal institutions from those that promote protodemocratic representative assemblies.

17. The fact that Swiss mountain cantons had the most democratic form of government in medieval Europe (Blockmans 1978) also supports the notion that isolation may facilitate the development of democracy.

REFERENCES

Albaladejo, Pablo. 1989. Cities and the state in Spain. *Theory and Society* 18:721-31.

Alexander, J. 1985. A historiographical survey: Norman and Plantagenet kings since World War II. *Journal of British Studies* 24:94-109.

Anderson, P. 1974. *Passages from antiquity to feudalism*. London: New Left Books.

Barlow, F. 1955. *The feudal kingdom of England, 1042-1216*. London: Longman.

———. 1983. *William Rufus*. London: Methuen.

Barzel, Y. 1991a. Property rights and the evolution of the state. Manuscript, University of Washington.

———. 1991b. Confiscation by the ruler: The rise and fall of Jewish lending in the Middle Ages. Manuscript, University of Washington.

Bates, R., and D. Lien. 1985. A note on taxation, development, and representative government. *Politics and Society* 14:53-70.

Bendix, R. 1964. *Nation-building and citizenship*. New York: Wiley.

———. 1978. *Kings or people*. Berkeley: University of California Press.

Bisson, T. 1966. The military origins of medieval representation. *American Historical Review* 71:1199-1218.

Bloch, M. 1961. *Feudal society*. Chicago: University of Chicago Press.

Blockmans, Wim. 1978. A typology of representative institutions in late medieval Europe. *Journal of Medieval History* 4:189-215.

———. 1989. Voracious states and obstructing cities: An aspect of state formation in preindustrial Europe. *Theory and Society* 18:733-55.

Bourne, H. R. 1866. *English merchants*. Vol. 1. London: Clowes & Sons.

Brooke, C. N., G. Keir, and S. Reynolds. 1973. Henry I's charter for the city of London. *Journal of the Society of Archivists* 4:558-78.

Brown, R. A. 1969. *The Normans and the Norman conquest*. London: Constable.

Bulpitt, Jim. 1983. *Territory and power in the United Kingdom*. Manchester: Manchester University Press.

Carus-Wilson, E. M. 1954. *Medieval merchant ventures*. London: Methuen.

Cronne, H. A. 1970. *The reign of Stephen, 1135-54*. London: Weidenfeld & Nicolson.

Deighton, H. 1953. Clerical taxation by consent. *English Historical Review* 22:161-92.

Douglas, D. 1969. *The Norman achievement, 1050-1100*. Berkeley: University of California Press.

Downing, B. 1989. Medieval origins of constitutional government in the West. *Theory and Society* 18:213-47.

Elman, P. 1937. The economic clauses of the expulsion of the Jews in 1290. *English Historical Review* 7:145-54.

Gillingham, J. 1978. *Richard the Lionheart*. New York: Wiley.

Gintis, H., and S. Bowles. 1984. State and class in European feudalism. In *Statemaking and social movements*, edited by C. Bright and S. Harding, 19-54. Ann Arbor: University of Michigan Press.

Green, J. 1981. The last century of Danegeld. *English Historical Review* 50:241-58.

———. 1986. *The government of England under Henry I*. Cambridge: Cambridge University Press.

Hall, J. C. 1906. The Hojo code of judicature. *Transactions of the Asiatic Society of Japan* 36:1-44.

Hall, John A., and John Ikenberry. 1989. *The state*. Minneapolis: University of Minnesota Press.

Harriss, G. 1975. *King, parliament, and public finance in medieval England to 1369*. Oxford: Clarendon.

Harriss, G. L. 1981. The formation of Parliament, 1272-1377. In *The English Parliament in the Middle Ages*, edited by R. Davies and J. Denton, 29-60. Manchester: Manchester University Press.

Harvey, P. 1973. The English inflation of 1180-1220. *Past and Present* 61:3-30.

Hicks, J. 1966. *A theory of economic history*. Oxford: Oxford University Press.

Hintze, O. 1975. *The historical essays of Otto Hintze*. Oxford: Oxford University Press.

Hollister, C. 1980. London's first charter of liberties: Is it genuine? *Journal of Medieval History* 6:289-306.

Holt, J. C. 1965. *Magna Carta*. Cambridge: Cambridge University Press.

———. 1987. 1086. In *Domesday studies*, edited by J. C. Holt, 41-64. Suffolk: Boydell.

Kiser, E. 1986-87. The formation of state policy in Western European absolutisms: A comparison of England and France. *Politics and Society* 15:259-96.

———. 1987. Kings and classes: Crown autonomy, state policies, and economic development in Western European absolutisms. Ph.D. diss., University of Arizona.

Klein, B., and K. Leffler. 1981. The role of market forces in assuring contractual performance. *Journal of Political Economy* 81:615-41.

Lenski, G. 1966. *Power and privilege.* New York: McGraw-Hill.

Levi, M. 1988. *Of rule and revenue.* Berkeley: University of California Press.

Machiavelli, N. [1531] 1977. *The prince.* Reprint. New York: Norton.

Mann, M. 1986. *The sources of social power.* Cambridge: Cambridge University Press.

Marongiu, A. [1949] 1968. *Medieval parliaments: A comparative study.* Reprint. London: Eyre & Spottiswoode.

Mason, Emma. 1977. William Rufus: Myth and reality. *Journal of Medieval History* 3:1-20.

Mitchell, S. K. 1951. *Taxation in medieval England.* New Haven, CT: Yale University Press.

Myers, A. 1975. *Parliaments and Estates in Europe to 1789.* London: Thames & Hudson.

North, D. 1982. *Structure and change in economic history.* New York: Norton.

North, D., and B. Weingast. 1989. Constitutions and commitment: The evolution of institutions governing public choice in seventeenth-century England. *Journal of Economic History* 4:803-32.

Pirenne, H. 1956. *A history of Europe.* Vol. 2. New York: Doubleday.

Poggi, G. 1978. *The development of the modern state.* Stanford, CA: Stanford University Press.

Prestwich, M. 1980. *The three Edwards.* New York: St. Martin's.

Rasler, Karen, and William Thompson. 1990. *War and state-making.* Boston: Unwin-Hyman.

Reynolds, S. 1972. The rulers of London in the twelfth century. *History* 57:337-57.

———. 1984. *Kingdoms and communities in Western Europe, 900-1300.* Oxford: Clarendon.

Richardson, H. G., and G. O. Sayles. 1966. *Law and legislation.* Edinburgh: Edinburgh University Press.

Roth, C. 1964. *A history of the Jews in England.* Oxford: Clarendon.

Root, H. 1989. Tying the king's hands: Credible commitments and royal fiscal policy during the Old Regime. *Rationality and Society* 1:240-59.

Schwartz, B. 1967. *The roots of freedom.* New York: Hill & Wang.

Smith, A. [1776] 1976. *The wealth of nations.* Chicago: University of Chicago Press.

Stacey, R. 1987. *Politics, policy, and finance under Henry III, 1216-1245.* Oxford: Clarendon.

Stenton, F. 1908. *William the Conqueror and the rule of the Normans.* New York: Barnes & Noble.

Stokes, H. 1921. *A short history of the Jews in England.* London: Central Board of Missions.

Strayer, J. 1970. *On the medieval origins of the modern state.* Princeton, NJ: Princeton University Press.

Stubbs, W. 1921. *Select charters.* Oxford: Clarendon.

Taylor, J. 1889. *The origin and growth of the English Constitution.* New York: Houghton Mifflin.

Teunis, Henry. 1978. The Coronation Charter of 1100: A postponement of decision. What did not happen in Henry I's reign. *Journal of Medieval History* 4:135-44.

Tilly, C. 1989. Cities and states in Europe, 1000-1800. *Theory and Society* 18:563-84.

———. 1990. *Coercion, capital, and European states.* Oxford: Blackwell.

Treharne, R. F. 1969. The constitutional problem in thirteenth century England. In *Essays in medieval history,* edited by T. A. Sandquist and M. R. Powicke, 46-78. Toronto: University of Toronto Press.

Turner, R. 1968. *The king and his courts.* Ithaca, NY: Cornell University Press.

———. 1985. *The English judiciary in the age of Glanville and Bracton, c. 1176-1239.* Cambridge: Cambridge University Press.

Veitch, J. 1986. Repudiations and confiscations by the medieval state. *Journal of Economic History* 1:31-36.

Warren, W. L. 1961. *King John.* London: Methuen.

———. 1973. *Henry II.* London: Methuen.

———. 1987. *The governance of Norman and Angevin England, 1086-1272*. Stanford, CA: Stanford University Press.

Weber, M. [1922] 1968. *Economy and society*. Reprint. Berkeley: University of California Press.

White, A. 1914. Some early instances of concentration of representatives in England. *American Historical Review* 19:735-50.

Williamson, O. 1985. *The economic institutions of capitalism*. New York: Free Press.

Young, C. R. 1961. *The English borough and royal administration*. Durham, NC: Duke University Press.

Scand. J. of Economics 94 (1), 19–31, 1992

Ronald Coase on the Nature of Social Cost as a Key to the Problem of the Firm

Yoram Barzel and *Levis A. Kochin**

University of Washington, Seattle, WA, USA

Abstract

Thirty years ago "The Problem of Social Cost" [1960][1] was published. It transformed the field of Industrial Organization and greatly expanded its scope. We briefly survey the state of the field before 1960, and then show some of the ways by which Coase's paper changed economic thinking.

Early Developments

In one way or another, transaction costs have always played a role in economics: Economists have long been aware that in a specialized economy the transformation of factors of production into utility involves more than manufacturing and transportation. They have been aware that exchanges are subject to "friction", that the "cost of doing business" is positive, and that buy-sell differentials exist. For a long time, transaction cost problems had not been a subject of analysis. In Walras' model, these costs are implicitly assumed to be zero; in other models these costs are implicitly assumed to be infinite. In *Risk, Uncertainty and Profit* (1921), Knight implicitly introduced significant transaction cost considerations to the analysis of the firm. His uncertainty — the driving force in his theory of the firm — is best understood as being like risk except that it is too costly to transact in the market; see Barzel (1987). The transaction cost basis of the distinction between risk and uncertainty is not explicit in Knight's analysis and the controversies surrounding Knight's uncertainty did not attempt an analysis of the cost of transacting, nor even of the costs that are specifically related to uncertainty.

---

*This manuscript benefited from comments at seminars at Washington University and the UCLA Industrial Organization Workshop; particularly valuable were comments by Benjamin Klein and Harold Demsetz.

[1]Dates in brackets refer to publications by Ronald Coase (see Bibliography) and dates in parentheses to the references listed at the end of this article.

In "The Nature of the Firm" [1937c], Coase argues that the costs of transacting, particularly those of determining prices, are the direct explanation of the firm. This first major attempt to connect these costs of transaction with economic organization for many years fared no better than Knight's; both were widely read and little used. Indeed, it is argued below that Coase's view of the firm is inconsistent with the prevailing cost curves view. "The Nature of the Firm" was reasonably well known in the 1950s and might have been required reading in some programs, but the cost curves view was the only one to appear in economic journals or in textbooks.

The 1950s saw various developments in the areas of transaction costs and property rights. One is due to Alchian (1958). Alchian's concern is with the absence of property rights in government or in non-profit institutions. He argues that the pricing of services supplied by such institutions will inevitably fail to meet the criterion of equating marginal cost to marginal variation. As people attempt to capture the wealth government fails to protect, valuable resources are dissipated. A connection between property rights and resource allocation was thus brought to center stage. In the process of analyzing a property rights problem, a tool for analyzing resource allocation in non-market settings has emerged.

Another development that emerged during the decade of the 1950s was Simon's (1955) concept of satisficing. Simon's fundamental departure from previous practice is in the explicit recognition that the obtaining and processing of information is costly. People do not know precisely what the maximizing solutions to their problems are. Maximization by individuals and by firms ceases to be automatic; rather, "frictions" are superimposed on the analysis. The main message Simon's approach yielded was a negative one: the world does not function as cleanly as the dominant economic model suggested.[2] No clear-cut positive lesson from this alternative view has evolved, however.

Still another 1950s development was made by Aaron Director.[3] Director's exposure to litigation problems seems to have led him to realize the inadequacy of the then contemporary analyses of various aspects of monopoly. The accepted analysis assigned to monopoly great brute power. The discussion of the new questions being raised by the circle of economists and lawyers around Director tended to cast doubt on how great monopoly power is. At the same time, these questions also suggested additional, more subtle dimensions of monopoly power; a case in point is

[2] Harvey Liebenstein's (1966) notion of x-efficiency is in the same mold.

[3] Director's contribution to the profession is probably the most spectacular manifestation of an oral tradition: his considerable influence on the literature is essentially through others' writings.

the pricing practice of punch-cards by IBM, interpreted as a tool for extracting greater monopoly rent in the use of its machines. Aaron Director's questioning led to the realization that certain seemingly monopolistic practices may actually have entirely different objectives. For example, retail price maintenance may prevent consumers from free riding on sellers' information; cf. Telser (1960).

Information problems that are at the heart of the costliness of transacting received direct attention from Hayek in 1937 and from Stigler in 1961. Hayek emphasized the need for information in making allocation decisions and pointed out a mechanism by which individuals are rewarded for contributing to the socially desirable information. While fairly widely recognized, this idea was not integrated in economic literature. The heart of Stigler's contribution is in simply making the commodity "information" a subject of economic analysis, using conventional methods to analyze this unconventional commodity.

Missing from each of these individual ideas and, even more so, from this body of work as a whole is a coherent unifying framework. Whereas each idea hung unconnected until the end of the fifties, the last quarter century seems to have experienced the coalescing of these lines of thought.

The Publication of "The Problem of Social Cost"

We believe that a compelling case can be made showing that Coase's "Problem of Social Cost" [1960] provided the force that unified the diverse ideas.[4] So powerful and pervasive is this force that in its sweep "The Nature of the Firm" for the first time is being integrated with economic thinking. The novel approach in analyzing economic problems has induced major changes in diverse areas and also in the methods employed to tackle problems.

"The Problem of Social Cost" is renowned for what came to be known as the "Coase Theorem". We wish, however, to first consider another feature of that paper — the explicit distinction between an ideal world in which transacting is costless and a world (our own) in which transacting is costly. Whereas much of the analysis in economics is carried under the implicit assumption that transacting is costless, quite often the assumption

[4] Coase's seminal insight on social cost appeared first in one of his articles about broadcasting, "The Federal Communications Commission" [1959]. The notion that the damaged party is as responsible for the damage as is the damaging party, is already fully stated in that article. Coase was concerned there with the allocation of radio frequencies in the face of interference. It is clear that Station B must be in operation if it is to be damaged by Station A, and that Station A's interference with Station B's implies interference in the opposite direction too. Recognizing the symmetry of the parties' positions is easier in this setting than in other settings; recognizing its generality, however, requires a great leap.

of positive, and occasionally infinite, costs of transacting is slipped in, resulting in inconsistencies and confusions. The conventional analysis of monoppoly is one of the instances in which assumptions are switched in mid-course. Virtually no monopoly model requires monopolists to expend resources to determine where their demand curves lie, thus implicitly assuming that this information can be obtained at no cost. This, however, is inconsistent with the notion of prohibitively costly transacting underlying the rather common statement that all output is sold at a single price because price discrimination by monopolists is "too expensive". Another example of inconsistency in assumptions is in the discussion of advertising. Advertising is predicated on consumers' ignorance of commodities' properties. The analysis of advertising, however, is often carried within models that otherwise assume that information is free.

Coase's explicit separation of the zero and positive transaction cost models made economists aware of the need to spell out the transaction cost assumptions under which analysis is conducted. The inappropriateness of using results from one model as a basis of drawing conclusions on the other became clear. Coase himself severely criticized Pigou for making policy recommendations based on the untenable, implicit assumption that certain costs of transactings are zero when the government rather than private individuals takes some action. In the "grass is greener" argument Demsetz (1969) follows through in uncovering and demonstrating other cases in which the "actual" situation where transacting is costly, is compared with the "ideal" situation where transacting is costless.

More significantly, given that transacting is costly, whether it is carried out in the market or by government, Coase pointed out the need to compare outcomes of actions carried out under differing institutional settings. Economists have been paying greater and greater attention to the differences in behavior brought about by organizations that differ in their incentive structures. An important by-product of this approach is the realization that the role of government is a proper subject for the development of positive theories by economists.

The Coase Theorem

We now turn to the Coase Theorem. The theorem states that when property rights are perfectly well defined, production will be efficient, or Pareto optimal regardness of the assignment of property rights.[5] How does

[5] The theorem clearly implies that so long as liability is clearly assigned, if A's damage to B increases by $1, his payment to B must increase by $1. This is obviously so when A is liable. When B is liable; i.e., when A owns the right to damage B, when again A damage to B increases by $1, B's damage restraint payment to A will decline by $1. Thus, the cost to A of damaging B does not change whichever way liability is allocated.

this theorem square with the Walrasian model? A major assumption underlying the frictionless competitive system is that property rights are perfectly well defined; one of its major results is that the economy is always Pareto efficient. The two approaches, then, share at least one fundamental assumption and one major result.

The Coase Theorem, however, holds under more general conditions than those underlying the Walrasian model; it is not derived from any assumption about competition. It must hold, therefore, regardless of the number of players.[6] It was known before the statement of the Coase Theorem in 1960 that a perfectly discriminating monopolist uses resources efficiently. Under the zero transaction costs assumption, which was routinely made before 1960, a person with monopoly power would always discriminate perfectly in order to maximize his income. Thus, when property rights are well defined, the distortions associated with monopoly must be absent. This is not a well known result, and it is not clear to us whether or not Coase himself, who did not address monopoly problems in "The Problem of Social Cost", was aware of it.

The work of economists concerned with industrial organization went through a profound shift in emphasis subsequent to the publication of "The Problem of Social Cost", a shift most likely attributable to a change in direction induced by that paper. Before 1960, the questions that occupied these economists were mostly concerned with the nature and extent of monopoly power, whether by a single buyer or seller, or by oligopolies, cartels and the like and of the methods of containing this power. This was true, for example, for Bain; it was also true for Stigler. These questions make less frequent appearances in today's journals. Awareness of the Coase Theorem is conducive to the reinterpretation of monopolists' behavior.

Action by a monopolist does not necessarily increase the level of distortion. On the contrary, the presumption is that the incentive is greater to take action that will lower the level of distortions; total wealth is then larger and the monopolist, therefore, has more from which to gain. This newer view has brought in its wake another change which is as profound as the previous one. Under ideal conditions monopoly does not result in any distortions. Under actual conditions monopolists may be able to retain a share of the gain from the lowering of distortions and may indeed minimize them. The notion that government should intervene to stop or to reduce distortion is not terribly persuasive if it is not clear that distortions are present in the first place.

One occasionally encounters the notion that the Coase Theorem is self

[6] The assumption of competition is not superfluous, however; it simultaneously aids in determining a solution to the problems of allocation and distribution.

evident. Nevertheless, one of its major insights is overlooked even by individuals that surely are well acquainted with it. In Tullock's and in Posner's discussions of the cost of monopoly the argument being advanced is that the associated distortions exceed the "welfare triangle" and are of the order of monopoly profits since people will spend resources to secure the monopoly position. This is inconsistent with the Coase Theorem if rights are well defined. But these authors fail to qualify their argument to only those instances where such rights were in public domain.

The new approach very quickly absorbed the above mentioned Director-induced work on monopoly and on general business practices. In retrospect it seems likely that Director's approach was leaning towards the conclusions implied by Coase's analysis, and when the latter became available, the merger between the two approaches proceeded quite quickly.

The Theory of the Firm

The role of Coase's "The Nature of the Firm" in the development of the theory of the firm poses a major intellectual puzzle. The traditional view, still dominant in textbooks, is based on two major assertions: I. that factor prices and technology determine the optimal size of the production unit, and II. that the production unit as determined in I is the firm. Under competition a firm's size is simply the size of the production unit that minimizes average cost. These results are derived under the assumptions that all relevant information is costless to obtain and that each factor operates at its socially optimal pace, without supervision.[7] Questions such as whether workers should be employed by the hour or by the piece, how prices are set, or whether capital should be owned or rented are set aside by the first assumption. The second avoids the question of why the productive resources used in a production unit have to be employed within an organization possessing the legal status of a firm. The answers to these questions are by no means obvious.

The question arises whether actual observations are consistent with the theory. The answer is negative; this theory of the firm is severely strained by facts. In order to accommodate the observed coexistence of a wide range of firm sizes within industries, the points of the minimum average cost of different firms must be stretched from a single value — as implied by typical textbook analysis and drawings — to a huge range. The corresponding production function must be rather peculiar. It is not helpful that the traditional theory clearly implies that firms will consist of single plants, since many firms actually have more than one plant. An even greater strain on the theory is posed by vertically integrated firms. The theory seems to

[7] Williamson (1985) has an extensive discussion of this issue.

deal with single production processes; corresponding observations thus should consist of single layers of the vertical production process, particularly when the production facilities are separate. For instance, the assemblers of automobiles — assembly being one of the horizontal layers in producing automobiles — indeed buy parts such as tires and batteries to be used in the assembly. Many other parts however, are made by firms engaged in assembly.[8] These observations strain the theory. Fatal to the traditional theory of the firm are the observed instances of what are clearly optimal size plants, which, however, operate not as a single firm but as many unrelated firms. For instance, the workers in plants called "office buildings" are often employed by numerous firms.[9]

It is often, and seemingly correctly, said that falsifying evidence will not, by itself, induce practitioners to abandon a theory; needed is an alternative theory. In the case of the theory of the firm, such an alternative has been available since 1937 in "The Nature of the Firm". At least until the early 1960s, however, this alternative was not treated as a serious contender. One reason Coase's theory of the firm was ignored is that until 1960, economists who wished to study the problem had to rely entirely on the 1937 piece, since Coase himself did not elaborate on "The Nature of the Firm". Such elaboration evidently was necessary; the discussion of transaction costs in that paper is brief and cryptic, and it does not seem that economists were ready to tackle this elusive problem.

In "The Problem of Social Cost" it is shown that when the cost of transacting is positive, rights are not perfectly well defined, and the Coase Theorem makes it clear that costly transacting must lower the attainable output. Thus "The Problem of Social Cost", in pointing out a relationship between the output that can be obtained from a given set of inputs and the form of organization governing these inputs, provides an elaboration useful in the study of the firm. In the last two decades many economists attempted to tie the problems of production when transacting is costly to the problem of organization.

Alchian and Demsetz' 1972 paper is the best known post Social Cost attempt to formulate a theory of the firm. Even though they offer an alternative to Coase's theory of the firm, their firm, nevertheless, is fundamentally a transaction cost phenomenon — it arises in response to the costs associated with measuring and policing various inputs and outputs. Alchian and Demsetz recognize that different regions in the cost function may be associated with different transaction costs, particularly, with the

[8] The degree of integration cannot be explained by technology alone; in Japan the fraction of purchased parts is much larger than in the United States.

[9] Intermediate cases where films own partial interests in suppliers or customers are also not unusual. Many of Toyota's independent suppliers are in part owned by Toyota.

cost of measuring the contribution to output by each production unit; still, the latter rather than the former constitutes the basic force underlying the firm. Subsequent contributions to the theory of the firm, by Williamson (1975), Jensen and Meckling (1976), Klein, Crawford and Alchian (1978), Cheung (1983), and Grossman and Hart (1986), all rely entirely on the cost of transacting. These efforts are applications of Coase's theory of social cost more than they are elaborations of Coase's theory of the firm.

Voluntary Non-Price Constraints on Behavior

The study of actual contracts has generated one major beneficial side effect: it has revealed a basic feature that distinguishes transaction cost economics from frictionless economics. Contracts have revealed that in the former, people may agree to restrict their behavior, whereas such restrictions cannot play a significant role when frictions are absent. Thus, for example, in a frictionless world, every worker could be self employed even if he were specialized in some intermediate production process. When the cost of information is positive, workers may agree to forgo the direct sale of their products and the associated freedom to conduct their activities as they please and instead sell labor service.

Each party to a contract will agree to a provision which changes an existing contract only if he thinks that the provision increases to him the net value of the contract either directly or through a commensurate compensation in some other dimension of the contract. If a provision raises the total value of the contract but at the expense of only one party, another contract that will be preferred by both parties can be devised. When a contract restricts the parties' behavior, each of the contractors, then, must view the net effect of the restrictions on his wealth as positive. The study of contracts tends to reveal such observations and challenges economists to explain why particular restrictions are put in contract; that contrasts with previous economists' almost exclusive concern with explaining prices and quantities.[10]

One of the earliest, and still one of the most prominent studies of contracts in the wake of Coase is Cheung's (1969) work on share contracts. Share contracts were criticized by many economists for rewarding dissipation. Cheung points out that with the appropriate contract restric-

[10] Kessel (1958) suggests that membership in social groups — a non-price method of allocation — is a useful tool for enforcing price discrimination practices. It seems that the economics profession in general, and Kessel in particular, were not ready to generalize on the use of such non-price methods. Kessel could have, but did not point out that social discrimination may serve a productive purpose in maintaining social cohesion which reduces transaction costs.

tions, the dissipation can be eliminated. Cheung's is one of the first studies to subject a transaction cost hypothesis to empirical test.[11]

The study of contracts inevitably reveals the nature of various costs of transacting — for instance, the costs of finding exchange partners and the costs of contract stipulations. More importantly, the study reveals what lawyers have been well aware of — that transactions have numerous attributes and that it is too expensive to cover every conceivable eventuality in even the simplest transaction. This contrasts sharply with economists' prevailing view of commodities as simple, easy to transact, entities. Only when the usefulness of the assumption that commodities are homogeneous was questioned did it become possible to inquire how people deal with nonhomogeneity. Akerlof pursued this issue first with his "lemons" (1970) analysis as many others proceeded to do.[12]

Property Rights and Economic Organization

The study of the formation and delimitation of property rights is another way of exploring economic problems. In the literature following Pigou on questions such as pollution, the concepts most persistently used are externalities and differences between private and social costs. These concepts do not correspond directly to observable magnitudes; a whole series of links must be established before they can become operational. It is not surprising therefore that this framework was slow in producing refutable propositions.

Stating his theorem in terms of property rights and exploring a series of legal examples, Coase brought to the fore questions of what people actually own and how they go about modifying their property rights, which gave rise to the study of property rights and of their transfer by contract. Since ownership is a feature of actual behavior, it must have an observable counterpart and thus it may be readily made operational. When people deal with each other, each stands to gain from, and is willing to spend resources in order to capture, a larger portion of the available pie; each can also gain by being rewarded for preventing its shrinkage. The former entails a divergence between private and social costs; the latter implies the minimization of the divergence between the two interests. People will cede each other's rights in pursuit of the above objectives. The study of property rights then is useful in discovering both dissipating actions and actions reducing the dissipation.

---

[11] Demsetz' (1968) test of a transaction cost hypothesis is another early example.

[12] These include Arrow (1973), Spence (1973), Stiglitz (1975), Holmstrom (1979), Klein and Leffler (1981) and Barzel (1982). Unlike Coase, however, these economists all suggest the possibility of associated dissipation.

More importantly, the emphasis on property rights, or contracts, and their relationship to harmful or beneficial effects people may have on each other brings one directly back to the question of organization and the economics of the firm. It was suggested above that the firm is a transaction cost phenomenon. Firms, as observed in reality, do not only vary in sizes; their organizational diversity is immense. They include partnerships, coops, franchises, companies with publicly traded equity; they also include a variety of non-profit firms ranging from families to golf clubs to universities governments.

Of the array of studies that have built on the organizational implications of "The Problem of Social Cost", only a few major ones are singled out in any detail. Demsetz' (1967) study of the formation of property rights is one of the earliest. In it, he simply and convincingly shows that as the value of a resource increases, rights to properties that initially were in the public domain get delineated. In his example, this permitted the economical exploitation, or husbanding, of fur resources.

The studies by Williamson (1975) and by Klein, Crawford and Alchian (1978) may appear as attempts to build on "The Nature of the Firm", but as already stated, they descend more directly from "The Problem of Social Cost". These authors are not content to confine their investigation to firms' size; they rather inquire why firms acquire certain structures. In particular, they attempt to explain why firms are more or less vertically integrated. The main explanatory force they offer is the prevention of *ex-post* opportunism in the appropriation of quasi-rent. Transacting parties encounter difficulties in the delineation of rights to this quasi-rent; this rent may be competed away unless protective measures are undertaken. They suggest that the vertical integration of the involved transactors can protect against the dissipation.

Cheung's (1979) study of rent control in Hong Kong may appear first to be a refutation of the Coase Theorem. He shows that a change in the assignment of rights had a monumental effect on the rate of investment on new construction. The apparent inconsistency is resolved when the positive cost of transacting is taken into account. In 1968, the courts in Hong Kong changed the prevailing interpretation of the rent control law. As a consequence of that change, the cost of transacting between landlords and tenants residing in rent controlled apartments declined drastically. This change in the cost of transacting led to a change in the pattern of ownership, permitting the buying out of the tenants residing in uneconomical structures; these structures could then be demolished to provide space for new construction. Thus, it is shown how under conditions of costly transacting changes in the delineation of rights can indeed affect allocation.

Coase's work stimulated the development of a positive economic theory of the evolution of legal institutions. This literature's most important voluminous contributor is Richard Posner. One component of Posner's theory that directly derives from "The Problem of Social Cost" is that common law judges tend to assign rights in such a fashion as to minimize the costs of subsequent reassignments.

> "Coase observed…that the English courts, in interpreting the common law doctrine of nuisance (the doctrine governing pollution and related types of interference with the enjoyment of property), had decided cases in a way that seemed to accord with the economics of the problem. In fact they had exhibited a surer, if wholly instinctive, grasp of those economics than the economists had!" Posner (1981, p. 4).[13]

The transactions cost paradigm has also induced the development of a new theoretical basis for accounting. Accountants have realized that the main purpose of their procedures is to service the demands of principals for an accounting of the acts of their agents. The new theory of accounting seeks to explain the standard accounting techniques as instruments for the pursuit of these aims. The theory of agency which has been developed from transactions cost economics is recognized as the center of any serious study of accounting.[14]

Concluding Remarks

For quite some time economists have been aware of the effects of the costs of transacting and particularly of the costs of information on the functioning of the economic system. Knight, Hayek and Coase recognized the importance of these costs in economic organization before World War II. Only after the publication of "The Problem of Social Cost" in 1960, however, did economists start to realize how to make the analysis of transaction costs operational. As the understanding of these notions advance, empirical work both in entirely new applications such as contracts and in more traditional ones such as comparing piece rates to hourly rates is becoming more common.

The new tools are nowadays most commonly applied to contract problems. They are also extended, however, to such diverse areas as accounting, the functioning of the government, and the evolution of law. In the process, the scope of human relationships covered by economics is greatly expanded from the almost exclusive concern with market activities to a much wider array not governed by prices to include the internal functioning of organizations, the legal system and government regulation.

---

[13] See also Posner (1977).

[14] See Leftwich (1980) and DeAngelo (1981).

References

Akerlof, G. A.: The market for "lemons": Quality and uncertainty and the market mechanism. *Quarterly Journal of Economics 84*, 488, 1970.

Alchian, A. A.: Private property and the relative cost of tenure. In P. D. Bradley (ed.), *The Public Stake in Union Power*, Charlottesville, 1958. Reprinted in Armen A. Alchian *Economic Forces at Work*, Indianpolis, 1977.

Alchian, A. A. & Demsetz, H.: Production, information costs, and economic organization *American Economic Review*, December 1972.

Arrow, K. J.: Higher education as filter. *Journal of Public Economics*, 193, 1973.

Barzel, Y.: Measurement cost and organization of markets. *Journal of Law and Economics*, April 1982.

Barzel, Y.: Knight's moral hazard theory of organization. *Economic Inquiry*, January 1987.

Cheung, S. N. S.: *The Theory of Share Tenancy*, University of Chicago Press, 1969.

Cheung, S. N. S.: Rent control and housing reconstruction: The postwar experience of prewar premises in Hong Kong. *Journal of Law and Economics*, April 1979.

Cheung, S. N. S.: The contractual nature of the firm. *Journal of Law and Economics*, 1–22, April 1983.

DeAngelo, L. E.: Auditor size and audit quality. *Journal of Accounting and Economics*, No. 3, 1981.

Demsetz, H.: Toward a theory of property rights. *American Economic Review*, May 1967.

Demsetz, H.: The cost of transacting. *Quarterly Journal of Economics*, February 1968.

Demsetz, H.: Information and efficiency: Another viewpoint. *Journal of Law and Economics*, April 1969.

Grossman, S. J. & Hart, O. D.: The costs and benefits of ownership: A theory of vertical and lateral integration. *Journal of Political Economy*, August 1986.

Hayek, F. A.: Economics and knowledge. *Economica IV* (New Series, 1937); reprinted in Friedrich A. Hayek, *Individualism and Economic Order*, Chicago, 1948.

Holmstrom, B.: Moral hazard and observability. *Bell Journal of Economics*, Spring 1979.

Jensen, M. C. & Meckling, W.: Theory of the firm: Managerial behavior, agency costs, and capital structure. *Journal of Financial Economics*, October 1976.

Knight, F. H.: *Risk, Uncertainty and Profit*. Boston, 1921.

Kessel, R. A.: Price discrimination in medicine. *Journal of Law and Economics*, October 1978.

Klein, B. & Leffler, K. B.: The role of market forces in assuring contractual performance. *Journal of Political Economics*, August 1981.

Klein, B., Crawford, R. C. & Alchian, A. A.: Vertical integration, appropriable rents, and the competitive contracting process. *Journal of Law and Economics*, October 1978.

Leftwich, R.: Market failure fallicies and accounting information. *Journal of Accounting and Economics*, No. 3, 1980.

Leibenstein, H.: Allocative efficiency vs. "X-Efficiency". *American Economic Review*, June 1966.

Posner, R. A.: *Economic Analysis of Law*. 2nd ed., Boston 1977.

Posner, R. A.: *The Economics of Justice*. Cambridge, 1981.

Simon, H. A.: A behavioral model of rational choice. *Quarterly Journal of Economics*, February 1955; reprinted in *Models of Man*, New York, 1957.

Spence, M.: Job market signaling, *Quarterly Journal of Economics 87* 335, 1973.

Stigler, G. J.: The economics of information. *Journal of Political Economics*, 1961.

Stiglitz, J. E.: The theory of screening education, and the distribution of income. *American Economic Review 65*, 283, 1975.

Telser, L. G.: Why should manufacturers want fair trade? *Journal of Law and Economics*, October 1960.

Williamson, O. E.: *Markets and Hierarchies: Analysis and Antitrust Implications*. New York, 1975.

Williamson, O. E.: *The Economic Institutions of Capitalism*. Free Press, 1985.

Scand. J. of Economics 94(1), 33–36, 1992

Bibliography of Ronald H. Coase's Publications, 1935–1991*

Books and Pamphlets

Published Balance Sheets as an Aid to Economic Investigation – Some Difficulties (with R. S. Edwards and R. F. Fowler), Accounting Research Association (June, 1938).

The Iron and Steel Industry 1926–1935: An Investigation Based on the Accounts of Public Companies, Special Memorandum No. 49 of the London and Cambridge Economic Service (with R. S. Edwards and R. F. Fowler) (1939).

British Broadcasting: A Study in Monopoly (London School of Economics and Longmans Green in Great Britiain and Harvard University Press in the United States, 1950).

Educational TV: Who Should Pay? (with Edward W. Barrett), Rational Debate Seminars, American Enterprise Institute (1968). Also in *Educational Broadcasting Review* (April 1968) and *Television Quarterly* (Winter 1968).

The Firm, The Market and the Law (University of Chicago Press, 1988).

Articles

The Problem of Duopoly Reconsidered, *2 Rev. Econ. Stud.* 137 (1935).

Bacon Production and the Pig-Cycle in Great Britain, (with R. F. Fowler), *2 Economica* (n.s.) 142 (1935).

The Pig-Cycle: A Rejoinder, (with R. F. Fowler), *2 Economica* (n.s.) 423 (1935).

The Pig-Cycle in Great Britain: An Explanation, (with R. F. Fowler), *4 Economica 55*, (1937a).

Some Notes on Monopoly Price, *5 Rev. Econ. Stud. 17* (1937b).

The Nature of the Firm, *4 Economica* (n.s.) 386 (1937c). Also in American Economic Association, *Readings in Price Theory*, selected by a Committee of the American Economic Association (1952) and elsewhere.

Business Organization and the Accountant (a series of 12 articles in *The Accountant*, October–December 1938). Also in *Studies in Costing* (David Solomons ed. 1952); and in a shortened form under the title "The Nature of Costs" in *Studies in Cost Analysis* (David Solomons ed. 1968) and elsewhere.

Rowland Hill and the Penny Post, *6 Economica* (n.s.) 423 (1939).

The Analysis of Producers' Expectations, (with R. F. Fowler), *7 Economica* (n.s.) 280 (1940).

Price and Output Policy of State Enterprise: A Comment, *55 Econ. J.* 112 (1945).

B.B.C. Enquiry? *176 Spectator* 446 (1946).

---

*This bibliography was kindly provided by Professor Richard A. Epstein of the University of Chicago Law School.

The Marginal Cost Controversy, *13 Economica* (n.s.) 169 (1946).
Monopoly Pricing with Interrelated Costs and Demands, *13 Economica* (n.s.) 278 (1946).
The Marginal Cost Controversy: Some Further Comments, *14 Economica* (n.s.) 150 (1947).
The Economics of Uniform Pricing Systems, *15 Manchester Sch. Economics and Social Stud.* 139 (1947).
The Origin of the Monopoly of Broadcasting in Great Britain, *14 Economica* (n.s.) 189 (1948). Also in *Reader in Public Opinion and Communication* (1950).
Wire Broadcasting in Great Britain, *15 Economica* (n.s.) 194 (1948).
The Nationalization of Electricity Supply in Great Britain, *26 Land Econ.* 1 (1950).
British Television Policy: Questions of Control and Finance, *The [London] Times*, September 9, 1950.
The B.B.C. Monopoly, *Time and Tide*, October 7, 1950.
Report on the B.B.C., *Time and Tide*, January 20, 1951.
The Beveridge Report and Private Enterprise in Broadcasting, *The Owl* (1951).
The Development of the British Television Service, *30 Land Econ.* 207 (1954).
The Postal Monopoly in Great Britain: An Historical Survey, in *Economic Essays in Commemoration of the Dundee School of Economics, 1931–55* (J. K. Eastham ed. 1955).
The Federal Communications Commission, *2 J. Law & Econ.* 1 (1959).
The Problem of Social Cost, *3 J. Law & Econ.* 1 (1960). Also in *Readings in Microeconomics* (William Breit & Harold M. Hochman eds. 1968) and elsewhere.
Why Not Use the Pricing System in the Broadcast Industry? *The Freeman*, July 1961a.
The British Post Office and the Messenger Companies, *4 J. Law & Econ.* 12 (1961b).
The Outreach of Government: At What Point Peril? *Analysis*, October 1962.
The Interdepartment Radio Advisory Committee, *5 J. Law & Econ.* 17 (1962).
Evaluation of Public Policy Relating to Radio and Television Broadcasting: Social and Economic Issues, *41 Land Econ.* 161 (1965).
The Economics of Broadcasting and Government Policy, *56 Am. Econ. Rev.*, Papers & Proc. 440 (1966). Also in *The Crisis of the Regulatory Commissions* (P. W. McAvoy ed. 1970).
The Theory of Public Utility Pricing, in *The Economics of Regulation of Public Utilities* (1966).
Consumer's Surplus, in *International Encyclopedia of the Social Sciences* (1968).
Social Cost and Public Policy, in *Exploring the Frontiers of Administration* (George A. Edwards ed. 1970).
The Theory of Public Utility Pricing and its Application, *1 Bell J. Econ.* 113 (1970).
The Auction System and North Sea Gas: A Comment, *13 J. Law & Econ.* 45 (1970).
Industrial Organization: A Proposal for Research, in *Policy Issues and Research Opportunities in Industrial Organization* (Victor R. Fuchs ed. 1972a).

Durability and Monopoly, *15 J. Law & Econ.* 143 (1972b).

The Appointment of Pigou as Marshall's Successor, *15 J. Law & Econ.* 473 (1972c).

The Market for Goods and the Market for Ideas, *64 Am. Econ. Rev.*, Papers & Proc. 384 (1974a). Also in *Price Theory* 559 (Harry Townsend ed. 2nd edition 1980).

Economists and Public Policy, in *Large Corporations in a Changing Society.* (J. Fred Weston ed. 1974b).

The Lighthouse in Economics, *17 J. Law & Econ.* 357 (1974c). Also in *The Theory of Market Failure* 255 (Tyler Cowen ed. 1988).

The Choice of the Institutional Framework: A Comment, *17 J. Law & Econ.* 493 (1974d).

Marshall on Method, *18 J. Law & Econ.* 25 (1975).

Adams Smith's View of Man, *19 J. Law & Econ.* 529 (1976).

The Wealth of Nations. An Address by Professor R. H. Coase. Los Angeles, Foundation for Research in Economics and Education, 1976. Also *15 Econ. Inquiry* 309 (1977).

Advertising and Free Speech, *6 J. Legal Stud.* 1 (1977). Also in *Advertising and Free Speech* (Allen Hyman & M. Bruce Johnson eds. 1977).

Economics and Contiguous Disciplines, in *The Organization and Retrieval of Economic Knowledge* (Mark Perlman ed. 1977). Also in *J. Legal Stud.* 201 (1978).

Introduction, in Armen Alchian, *Economic Forces at Work* (1977).

Economics and Biology: A Comment, *68 Am. Econ. Rev.* 244 (1978).

Payola in Radio and Television Broadcasting, *22 J. Law & Econ.* 269 (1979).

Should the Federal Communications Commission Be Abolished? (with Nicholas Johnson) in *Regulation, Economics and the Law* 41 (Bernard H. Siegan ed. 1979).

The Coase Theorem and the Empty Core: A Comment, *24 J. Law & Econ.* 183 (1981).

Duncan Black: A Biographical Sketch, in *Toward a Science of Politics* 1 (G. Tullock ed. 1981).

Economics at LSE in the 1930's: A Personal View, *10 Atlantic Econ. J.* 31 (1982).

How Should Economists Choose? G. Warren Nutter Lecture in Political Economy (The American Enterprise Institute, 1982).

George J. Stigler: An Appreciation, *6 Regulation* 21 (Nov/Dec 1982).

The New Institutional Economics, *140 Zeitschrift für die Gesamte Staatswissenschaft* 229 (1984).

Alfred Marshall's mother and father, *16 History of Political Economy* 519 (1984).

Professor Sir Arnold Plant: His Ideas and Influence, in *The Unfinished Agenda, Essays in Honour of Arthur Seldon*, 79 (The Institute of Economic Affairs, 1986).

Arnold Plant, in John Eatwell, Murray Milgate, and Peter Newman, eds.: *The New Palgrave, A Dictionary of Economics*, Vol. 3, 891 (The Macmillan Press, 1987).

R. H. Coase Lectures: "The Nature of The Firm, 1. Origin, 2. Meaning, 3. Influence", *4 J. Law, Econ. & Organization* 3–47 (1988).

Blackmail, *74 Va. L. Rev.* 655 (1988). Also as Occasional Paper No. 24, The Law School, University of Chicago, 1988.

How Should Economists Choose?, in Thomas Jefferson Center Foundation, ed.: *Ideas, Their Origins and Their Consequences: Lectures to Commemorate the Life and Work of G. Warren Nutter* 63 (American Enterprise Institute for Public Policy Research, 1988).

Contracts and the Activities of Firms, *J. Law &Econ.* (Supplement, Oct. 1991).

Criticism and Discussion

Discussion of "The Trend of Public Employment in Great Britain and the United States" by Moses Abramovitz & Vera Eliasberg, *43 Am. Econ. Rev.*, Papers & Proc. 234 (1953).

Comments on "Full Costs, Cost Changes and Prices", and "Characteristics and Types of Price Discrimination", in Universities-National Bureau Committee for Economic Research, *Business Concentration and Price Policy* (1955).

Discussion of "Direct Regulation and Market Performance in the American Economy", by Richard E. Caves, and "The Effectiveness of Economic Regulation: A Legal View", by Roger C. Cramton, *54 Am. Econ. Rev.*, Papers & Proc. 194 (1964). Also reprinted in revised form in *The Crisis of the Regulatory Commissions* (P. W. McAvoy ed. 1970).

Discussion of "Achieving Efficient Regulation of a Fishery", in *Economics of Fisheries Management: A Symposium* (A. D. Scott ed. 1970). Vancouver, University of British Columbia.

Comment on "The Muted Voice of the Consumer in Regulatory Agencies", by Colston E. Warne, in *A Critique of Administrative Regulation of Public Utilities* (W. J. Samuels & H. M. Trebing eds. 1972d).

Comments on Steven N. S. Cheung: On the New Institutional Economics, In Lars Werin and Hans Wijkander eds.: *Contract Economics* (Blackwell, forthcoming).

CONFISCATION BY THE RULER: THE RISE AND FALL OF JEWISH LENDING IN THE MIDDLE AGES*

YORAM BARZEL
University of Washington

I. The Problem

THE power to confiscate is a mixed blessing. A ruler who is truly absolute can confiscate from his subjects at will. In practice, however, no ruler is as "absolute" as the term implies. For example, a ruler may have to forgo investment projects that would otherwise increase his wealth because his subjects, fearing confiscation, are reluctant to deal with him and because he is not absolute enough to costlessly force subjects to do so. This problem is especially acute when the ruler stands to gain by borrowing from his subjects. As Bulow and Rogoff show, a debtor who cannot be penalized for repudiating his debt will repudiate.[1] Obviously, the same applies to an absolute ruler. As Veitch points out, however, he will not necessarily repudiate at his first opportunity.[2] As long as he expects his future borrowing to exceed his interest payments, he gains by waiting. What Veitch fails to realize is that no lender can operate indefinitely on such a basis and, consequently, that the ruler will repudiate when the present value of his debt is maximized. Since repudiation is inevitable, it might seem that an absolute ruler would be unable to find willing lenders.

Loans are often repudiated for the more prosaic reason that borrowers lack adequate resources at repayment time. Lenders may try to avert this outcome by lending only to borrowers who demonstrate that they will be

* I wish to thank Douglas Allen, Bruce Johnsen, Levis Kochin, and Robert Stacey for their comments.

[1] Jeremy Bulow & Kenneth Rogoff, A Constant Reconstructing Model of Sovereign Debt, 97 J. Pol. Econ. 155 (1989).

[2] John M. Veitch, Repudiations and Confiscations by the Medieval State, 46 J. Econ. Hist. 31 (1986).

[*Journal of Law & Economics*, vol. XXXV (April 1992)]

able to repay. Such a demonstration might require the borrower or his guarantor to reveal his or her business plans to the lender. Yet borrowers may be reluctant to supply the information because it gives lenders the opportunity to exploit the information to their own advantage by, for example, duplicating the proposed investment.

Though troublesome, these obstacles to lending under an absolute ruler are not insurmountable. One likely solution (perhaps the only solution) to the repudiation problem is to provide the ruler with a source of income that is tied to lending such that it will terminate if he repudiates. Consider the prospect of lending and borrowing among subjects. If this activity is allowed to flourish, it could become a source of substantial tax revenue to the ruler. Lending activities could flourish if lenders are assured that their loan obligations will not be confiscated and if borrowers are assured that lenders and their associates will not compete with their borrowers' businesses. A ruler who firmly agrees not to become a lender himself and, in addition, prevents lenders from competing with their borrowers loses much of the incentive to confiscate loan repayments because of the loss of the tax revenue it entails. The fear of lenders that the ruler will confiscate their claims on subjects' debts is reduced further if they extend loans to the ruler as well. It is evident, then, that absolute rulers can create conditions to avert lenders' fears of confiscation, just as they can create conditions to avert other forms of confiscation.[3] This article develops these propositions and tests their implications against the history of Jewish lending in medieval England.[4]

II. A Rationale for Jewish Lending

During the Middle Ages, the Catholic church adopted the scholastic principle with roots in the Old Testament that everything that accrued to the capital constitutes usury, and, therefore, the church prohibited charging interest on loans. The state's attitude toward usury is more difficult to uncover. The literature I studied shows that some medieval French rulers enforced the church's restrictions whereas others were quite lenient toward Christian lenders. The literature says little regarding the

[3] Yoram Barzel, Property Rights and the Evolution of the State (unpublished manuscript, Univ. Washington, Dep't Economics, March 1992).

[4] Douglass C. North & Barry R. Weingast, Constitutions and Commitment: The Evolution of Institutions Governing Public Choice in Seventeenth-Century England, 49 J. Econ. Hist. 803 (1989). North and Weingast are also concerned with the ruler's confiscatory power. They show how a constitutional solution to the problem eliminated the ruler's power to confiscate. Whereas the ruler was able to borrow before his power was constrained, North and Weingast demonstrate the drastic fall in the cost of borrowing that ensued in the imposition of the constitutional constraint.

English kings' policy on this issue, except for noting that one or two Flemish lenders were in operation (and thus tolerated) in England during part of the twelfth century. Italian lenders were prominent in England during much of the thirteenth century. I found no clue as to why these and not other Christian lenders were permitted to operate. Some Englishmen, of course, lent money to others, but interest was seldom charged openly. There were ways to evade the constraint on interest payments by, for example, overstating the size of the principal or repaying cash loans in underpriced commodities. Such evasions, however, had the drawback of making it difficult to renew loans. In any case, it is clear that in England individuals felt constrained and that, by and large, the church's prohibition on its Christian subjects was enforced by the state. Thus, Richardson states that "what the king's ministers could not do [after confiscation] was to retain the bond and require the payment of interest arising."[5] The enforcements, however, were applicable only within faith. The Mosaic code barred Jews from charging interest within faith, but, like the church, it did not apply across faiths. Jews, then, could freely lend to (and sometimes borrow from) Christians.

In the Middle Ages, the repayment of loans made by Jews was exceedingly vulnerable to confiscation by the ruler. Indeed, confiscation of Jewish property was a recurring event in the Middle Ages. Nevertheless, for much of that time Jews were an important source of loans. I will now examine those factors that enabled Jews to keep their capital in states where the ruler had confiscatory power, and I will discuss the conditions that caused the protection to fail periodically.

The activities of Jews in England were severely circumscribed; they were permitted to engage in financial transactions with Christians but were barred from virtually any other business relationship with them. It is generally taken for granted that capital markets always generate net benefits to their participants, that the church-imposed restrictions on charging interest hindered the realization of such gains from trade, and that the existence of a non-Christian group that could engage in lending raised income by simply evading the restriction imposed by the church. Could it be, however, that lending entails some major, albeit hidden, costs and that Jewish lending was largely free from that hidden cost? As argued above, borrowers may fear that the information they reveal to lenders in order to secure the loans could be used to take over their businesses or to compete with them. In medieval England, Jews, who were the primary lenders to the Christian population, were barred from

[5] H. G. Richardson, The English Jewry and Angevin Kings 75 (1960).

most other occupations where they could have interacted with Christians. They were also restricted in the location of their residences, which increased the costs of their illegal business activity. Borrowers, then, could more readily reveal to their Jewish lenders the necessary information, which may explain the occupational restrictions imposed on Jews. Since the demand for loans is higher if aspiring borrowers do not fear competition from potential lenders, the occupational and residential restrictions imposed on Jews largely eliminated the fear of such competition.[6] The simultaneous restrictions on within-faith lending and on across-faith business dealings other than lending are consistent with the notion that their purpose was to increase the ruler's tax revenue from lending and to lower his gain from confiscation.[7] Indeed, Jews who converted to Christianity lost the right to charge interest and in so doing lost their usefulness to the king; the king confiscated the property of converts.

But how did the ruler allay the fear of confiscation? The ruler would have gained from confiscation had he been the sole borrower.[8] Jewish lenders, however, provided a service valued by the rulers' subjects as well. My argument is that the ruler would not necessarily gain from confiscating Jewish claims if some or all of the borrowing from Jews were done by his Christian subjects and if that service could be taxed. Confiscating the promissory notes Christian borrowers gave to their Jewish lenders would have entailed a cost to the ruler. Any Christian ruler who were to confiscate the promissory notes, called "bonds" in this literature, would personally have become the owner of the agreed repayments. (Christians, apparently on a modest scale, lent money to Jewish lenders by buying their bonds. Such lending has to be netted out to obtain the total amount the ruler could confiscate from Jews.) As a result of the confiscation, borrowers simply acquired a new claimant on their payments. The ruler, however, then had to liquidate the loans or at least refuse to make new ones; otherwise, he would have violated the lending prohibition.[9] The ruler, of course, could use the confiscated funds di-

[6] I am indebted to Ron Barzel for this idea.

[7] The hypothesis above implies that consumption loans should be allowed more readily than business loans. Long ago, however, Jews expressly removed the within-faith restriction from business loans.

[8] J. R. Hicks, A Theory of Economic History (1969). Implicitly considering borrowing only by the ruler, Hicks concludes that confiscation is inevitable.

[9] A ruler who abided by the church's position on charging interest either was not absolute or, alternatively, viewed the constraint on himself as well as on others as advantageous or at least as a worthwhile concession to the church. The discussion in the text suggests that the constraint benefited the ruler.

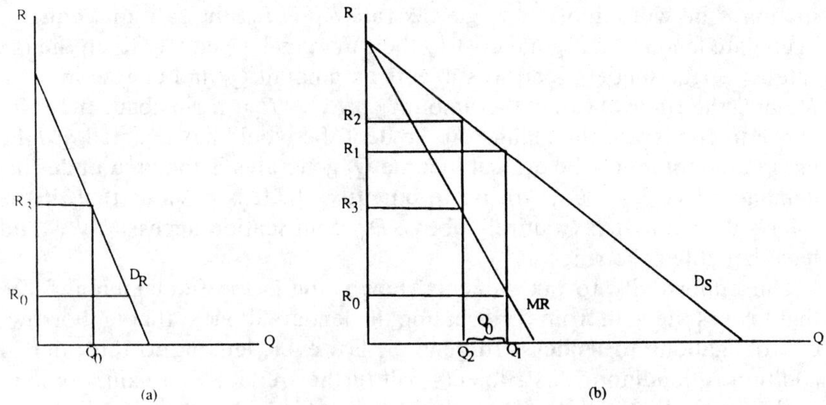

FIGURE 1

rectly, thereby earning whatever rate of return the extra funds yielded when used on his own projects. Instead of confiscating lenders' claims, however, he had the option of allowing subjects to borrow, albeit at a high rate, for their own investment projects and of taxing the lenders. By taxing Jewish lenders, the ruler in effect was able to collect high, "usurious" interest while deflecting the populace's animosity from himself to the Jews. Taxes that are not fees for services are a form of confiscation. The taxes on lending confiscated part of the associated income flow; repudiation confiscated the capital stock. My argument is that under the appropriate conditions the present value of the former could exceed the value of the latter. A rate of taxation at least as high as the rate of return that the ruler would have earned on the confiscated capital obviously would have yielded no less than confiscation. By imposing such a tax, the ruler's promise not to confiscate became self-enforcing; he gained from keeping his word. Under these conditions, lenders would not have been squandering their money when they lent it.

Figure 1 illustrates the argument on the ruler's cost of and gain from confiscation and elaborates on it. In each of its two panels, Q is the amount lent, R is the interest rate, and R_0 is the average and marginal cost of capital to Jewish lenders. In panel *a*, D_R is the ruler's demand for capital. In panel *b*, D_S is subjects' demand for capital net of collection and default costs, and *MR* is the corresponding marginal revenue. A rising cost of capital will be considered below. The ruler's objective is to extract the largest amount of tax revenue. Abstracting from price discrimination,[10] he will impose a single tax rate $R_1 - R_0$; the rate that equates aggregate lenders' marginal cost to their marginal revenue. Given the tax rate $R_1 - R_0$, lenders lend to subjects an amount Q_1 and charge interest R_1, and the ruler extracts the amount $Q_1(R_1 - R_0)$. If, instead, the ruler chose to confiscate the claims on the debt, he would have gained Q_1, the entire amount lent. The annual income Q_1 generates is the area under his demand curve D_R (panel *a*), up to quantity Q_1. It is obvious that, if the ruler's demand D_R lay entirely above D_S, confiscation necessarily would have benefited the ruler.

The opportunity to tax subjects' borrowing is the fundamental force that lowers the gain from confiscating the lenders' bonds, that is, borrowers' obligations to lenders. In general, however, lending to the ruler in addition to lending to his subjects will further reduce that gain. As long as the vertical intercept of the ruler's demand is higher than R_1, diverting a nonzero number of loans from subjects to ruler would generate to the ruler a higher income than he could earn from taxation, correspondingly reducing the incentive for confiscation. The maximizing amount of borrowing by the ruler should satisfy the condition that the return on the last unit he borrows should equal the loss in tax revenue due to the transfer of lending from subjects to ruler. In order for the ruler to maximize his wealth, he should borrow an amount such that the marginal revenue from lending to subjects equals the height of his demand curve at the quantity released by subjects. In the figure, this condition is satisfied when, out of their total lending funds of Q_1, Jews lend the amount Q_2 to subjects and lend the remaining amount Q_0 to the ruler. At Q_2, average revenue is R_2, and this is the rate they should charge subjects. The marginal revenue is R_3, which is the rate lenders should charge the ruler. The ruler's net gains from taxing Jewish lenders, then, is higher when he also borrows. He would then gain less from confiscation since he is already extracting some of the rent that the confiscated funds can otherwise generate.

For clarity of exposition, the focus of the analysis here is the rate, but it can be carried in lump-sum terms. Instead of charging a unit tax $R_2 - R_0$, the ruler could have imposed a lump-sum tax amounting to $Q_2(R_2 - R_0)$, which would have changed the form of the tax but not its total amount. Taxes were usually lump sum.

Two more elements must be introduced into the model—one is the fact

[10] Jews needed the ruler's permission to become lenders. The ruler could have franchised all lending to a single lender. He must have believed, however, that he was better off by allowing competition among lenders, as numerous Jewish lenders apparently competed with each other in England in 1066–1290, the period of this study.

that conditions are not static, and the other is the emergence of alternative lenders. The ruler's demand for capital was likely to fluctuate over time. This is of particular importance. He may have altered the tax rate as his demand changed or, given the cost of change, stayed with whatever tax rate he imposed. In either case, an upward shift in his demand D_R made confiscation more profitable to him. When his demand increased enough, he would confiscate. Regarding alternative lenders, their emergence implies that the demand facing Jewish lenders became more elastic. More elastic demand means a diminished capacity for taxation making confiscation more attractive.

III. Refutable Implications

I hypothesized above that during the Middle Ages confiscation was costly to the ruler because by confiscating he must have forgone the opportunity to tax the net income Jews would earn by lending to his subjects. The ruler's loss from confiscation was larger the lower R_0, the lower D_R, and the more restricted the subjects' access to alternative sources of funds. If this is true, then the following should be observed.

First, Jewish lenders were heavily taxed by the ruler. Assuming that when Jews arrived in England they possessed (or had access to) only a small amount of capital for lending, growth of the Jewish capital stock should be observed since the ruler would have gained from taxes low enough to permit accumulation. The ruler protected his tax base as an asset that was one source of his income. Second, the bulk of Jewish lending was to subjects rather than to the ruler. Third, the rate of interest charged by Jews was higher than they were where usury laws were not as stringently enforced and lending not so easily taxed. Fourth, Jewish claims on subjects' debts were confiscated when competing but untaxed sources of lending became available. Fifth, Jews were not allowed to engage in the same business activities as were their borrowers; and, like Jews, other prominent lenders were easy to distinguish from their borrowers. And sixth, the amount taxed and the likelihood of confiscation of Jewish claims on debts increased as the ruler's demand for loans increased relative to that of his subjects.

IV. The Evidence from Medieval England

I will use the history of Jews in medieval England to test the hypothesis. It seems that no Jews lived in England in the years preceding the Norman Conquest. Jews came to England in the wake of the Conquest as feudal subjects of the monarch.[11] Jews were allowed to engage in lending and were barred from virtually any other occupation outside the Jewish community. Until Henry III ascended the throne in 1216, Jews in England thrived under the king's protection. In the midst of his long reign (1216–72) Henry III departed from his predecessors' practice and imposed a series of confiscatory taxes on the Jewish community. He also provided Jews with much less protection against harassment than did his predecessors. Edward I, his successor, continued these policies. In 1290, apparently yielding to prevailing anti-Semitic sentiments, he expelled the impoverished and decimated Jewish community from England.[12] The relevant period for the tests, then, is from 1066 or soon afterward to 1290.

I will now discuss how the propositions introduced above fare against the facts. First, prior to the confiscation that Henry III initiated, the Jewish community was heavily taxed, as is implied by the hypothesis. Roth states that "[i]t has been estimated that an average of £3000—that is, something like one-seventh of total revenue—was derived at this period [the second part of twelfth century] from the Jews every year."[13] He indicates that this tax was separate from many special impositions that Jews were required to pay. At the same time, the Jewish community was allowed to prosper within these constraints, which is consistent with the implication that the Jewish capital stock would grow. Until the rule of Henry III, the English monarchs vigorously protected the Jewish community and assisted in enforcing repayment of their loans. A major ingredient in the loan-security mechanism was the registry of loans, a procedure introduced in the 1190s. Loans that were registered with the authorities were easier to enforce; such loans were also easier to tax. Registry was compulsory.[14]

The second implication is that Jews are expected to have lent mostly to subjects rather than to the monarch. Roth's discussion makes it clear that Jews extended loans to numerous individuals and that their operations covered the entire country. Although he does not dwell on the

[11] Frederick Pollock & Frederick William Maitland, 1 The History of English Law before the Time of Edward I, at 468 (2d ed. 1898).

[12] Cecil Roth, A History of the Jews in England (1987). Roth is the main source for the historical background.

[13] *Id.* at 16. In a personal communication, Robert C. Stacey maintained that the one-seventh figure underestimates the king's total revenue, particularly if account is taken of the king's revenues from his holdings in France.

[14] *Id.* at 28–29. Six or seven cities were designated as registration centers. "All deeds and contracts had to be drawn up in duplicate, in the presence of [two reputable Jews, two Christians, and two clerks], the counterparts being deposited in a chest (archa, huche) provided with three locks and seals" (*id.*).

extent of lending to the monarch, his account suggests that such lending was on a modest scale. When discussing certain large lenders, he states that the transactions of three or four prominent Jewish businessmen from London were mainly with the nobility and that another large lender was "making advances to the crown also, though of relatively small amounts."[15] The facts, then, are consistent with the hypothesis that the bulk of Jewish lending was to subjects rather than to the ruler.

Third, regarding interest rates, Roth's data indicate that the rates charged by Jewish lenders in England exceeded the prevailing rates in areas where usury laws were not enforced vigorously. Interest rates were usually stated in pence per pound per week. With 240 pence to the pound, a pence per pound per week (not compounded) amounts to 21 2/3 percent per year. Jews were prohibited from compounding the interest. Roth states that Jewish lenders charged from 21 2/3 to 43 1/3 percent per annum and exceptionally would charge 60 percent or even 87 percent,[16] whereas "in southern Europe . . . the standard rate was far less—23 percent to 37 percent in Italy, 20 percent in Spain."[17] Richardson, whose work is subsequent to Roth's, provides no information on non-English borrowing. For England he states that "2 pence per pound [per week, an annual rate of 43 1/3] seems to be the usual rate of interest."[18]

The fourth hypothesis implies that confiscation will occur when alternative sources of loans emerge. Consider first the alternative sources of loans. Italians, who were becoming the most active financiers in Europe, eventually became the chief substitute source of loans. Roth states that Italian lenders began their financial dealings in England in 1223.[19] By the middle of the thirteenth century they were already very prominent. Additional bits of data on the Italian presence in England are provided by Shatzmiller and by Kaeuper. Shatzmiller notes that prior to 1244 the priory of Canterbury dealt with Jews, but in the subsequent fifty years it dealt with Lombards.[20] Kaeuper states that "[t]he Italians . . . had lent money on occasion to Richard (1189–1199) and John (1199–1216) . . . but it was during the reign of Henry III [1216–1272] that they began to flourish."[21] He also states that the Riccardi of Lucca, who were bankers

[15] *Id.* at 7 and 16.

[16] *Id.* at 106.

[17] *Id.* at 107, n.1.

[18] Richardson, *supra* note 5, at 70.

[19] Roth, *supra* note 12, at 69.

[20] Joseph Shatzmiller, Shylock Reconsidered (1990).

[21] Richard W. Kaeuper, Bankers to the Crown: The Riccardi of Lucca and Edward I, at 76 (1973).

to Edward I in the period 1272–94, were also "money-lenders to great and lesser men alike on a considerable scale."[22] In one fundamental respect, Italian lenders were treated differently from Jewish lenders—there was no compulsory registry of their loans. So, Italian lending presumably was not taxed. It is evident that Italian lenders did not consider themselves vulnerable to the forces that led to the confiscation of Jewish property. The reason, however, eludes me.

The emergence of Italian (Christian) lenders more or less coincided with the onset of the imposition of confiscatory taxes on the Jews. Stacey provides a more detailed account than does Roth of the timing of the confiscation, placing the onset of confiscatory taxes in 1239 or 1240. He states that, "[b]efore 1239, Jewish taxation had made a modest but fairly steady contribution to the king's finances."[23] "This pattern . . . changed dramatically when [in 1239] Henry demanded from the Jews the third part of all their chattels."[24] He concludes that "there can be no doubt at all that Jewish fortunes in England changed dramatically and permanently between 1240 and 1260, and that this change was in large part a consequence of the new approach to Jewish taxation initiated by King Henry III and his council between 1239 and 1242."[25] The protracted process of confiscation may be explained by the fact that the ruler could extract more from Jewish lenders by letting them continue to apply their specialized skills while alternative sources of loans were being developed.

I cannot test the fifth implication—that Jewish lenders would be barred from their borrowers' trades—because I formed the hypothesis only after having learned about the Jews' occupational restrictions. That Jews were restricted in residential location and required to wear distinctive clothing or marks is, however, consistent with the hypothesis. The implication that other lenders would be distinct from borrowers is borne out by the evidence. As just discussed, Italian lenders replaced Jewish ones. Moreover, Richardson states that around 1160 there were, besides Jewish lenders, only two other prominent lenders.[26] Both of these lenders were Flemish.

The last implication is that confiscation will occur when the ruler's rate of return from using the capital increases. This implication appears to correspond with the popular notion that the ruler's increased "need" for capital, particularly to finance wars, tends to lead to confiscation. It is

[22] *Id.* at 31.

[23] Robert C. Stacey, Politics, Policy, and Finance under Henry III, 1216–1245 (1987).

[24] *Id.* at 144.

[25] *Id.* at 155.

[26] Richardson, *supra* note 5, at 53.

not, however, a simple matter to identify what the discount rate facing the ruler was. Moreover, the common assertion that such a rate must be high at a time of war is not generally true.[27]

The question that must be answered first is whether the change in the discount rate associated with a war is due to a shift in demand conditions or in supply conditions. Consider a ruler who has standing plans to attack another ruler and is just waiting for the right circumstances. He might go to war, for example, if his adversary has weakened. When this happens, the ruler's demand for funds increases, and on the margin his discount rate is higher. Or the ruler might go to war if there is a rightward shift in the supply of funds he faces, that is, if he faces a more abundant supply of funds.[28] When such a shift occurs, the ruler's discount rate is lower on the margin (as well as on average). Thus, the discount rate of a ruler who is observed to go to war can be lower than it was before the war; it is not necessarily higher. Regarding the discount rate of the ruler's adversary, when the adversary himself is weakened, his demand for funds also increases, and his discount rate is higher. In the case where one side faces a shift in the supply of funds, it is not clear what rate of discount is faced by the other side because, while a ruler may be forced to go to war, the supply of funds facing him may have also shifted out. For medieval England, at least, it is too difficult to sort out these forces and determine what the ruler's rate of return was or how and why it fluctuated. Thus, I am unable to test this implication.

The model predicts not only conditions for (full) confiscation but also conditions for change in the tax rate (or tax amount). The taxes imposed on Jews were indeed changed every so often, and in 1210 an especially heavy tax was imposed. Once again, however, it is too difficult to isolate the factors that could lead to a clean test of the rate of return hypothesis.

A few words are in order regarding the test of the hypothesis under

[27] Historians and political scientists, in their discussions of financing wars, tend to consider the cost of warfare as an exogenous force. Increases in unit costs—of weapons, for example—are often asserted to require a correspondingly higher expenditure to fight a war. This view is fundamentally flawed. Restricting the discussion to fighting for financial gain alone, the cost of weapons has little to do with the cost of war. The expected gain (or the expected loss) is the fundamental determinant of how much to spend on fighting. By and large, an increase in the costs of producing given weapons will, as a first approximation, affect both sides equally. Its main effect is simply reduced purchases, leaving a country's total fighting budget unchanged. The increase in the total cost of warfare is the result of the expected gain and not the cause of the search for war financing.

[28] North & Weingast, *supra* note 4, at 830. They provide a dramatic illustration of how the reduced cost of finance enhanced military activity. They say, "the funds made available by the growth in debt [at lower interest rates] from 1688 to 1697 were surely a necessary condition for England's success in this war with France as well as the next one (1703–1714), from which England emerged the major power of the world" (*id.*).

conditions of the Jewish experience in medieval France. The history of Jews in France has many parallels with that of Jews in England, and French Jews were expelled from (Capetian) France in 1306, just sixteen years after the expulsion from England. The French case is "richer" than the English one. Confiscation and expulsion had several phases and applied differently in different areas.[29] In England, the Jewish policy was much more narrowly a royal policy. In order to test the model for the French experience, many more data are needed than in the English case. As sparse as the English data are, there are even less French data. Therefore, the model is not tested for the French case. It is interesting to note, however, that during the late twelfth and the thirteenth centuries, the Templars, a Christian order active in the Crusades, became major lenders in France.[30] The Templars' property was confiscated by the French king at about the same time he confiscated the Jewish property. These acts of confiscation occurred after Italian lenders acquired a major role in French finances.[31]

V. Summary and Conclusions

An absolute ruler's ability to confiscate hinders his opportunities to strike deals with his subjects. Loans to the ruler are especially vulnerable to confiscation. In medieval England, Jews who were major lenders were entirely at the king's mercy. This article argues that the Jews' exclusive right to charge interest and their exclusion from other business activities enabled the formation of a self-enforced commitment on the part of the ruler not to confiscate. This article then derives several implications. The available evidence is entirely inadequate for testing one of the implications—that on the rate of return. The evidence used to test the other five implications is rather spotty and probably subject to substantial error. Still, in every case the data are consistent with the hypothesis. Taken as a whole, the results provide strong support for the basic hypothesis.

The results tend to confirm the hypothesis that Jewish property was protected from confiscation by the ruler only as long as Jewish lenders were able to produce a higher tax income to the ruler than the ruler could have had by confiscating their property and managing the funds himself.

[29] William C. Jordan, The French Monarchy and the Jews: From Philip Augustus to the Last Capetians (1989).

[30] E. B. Fryde, Public Credit, with Special Reference to North-western Europe, in 3 The Cambridge Economic History of Europe 447 (M. M. Postan & H. J. Habakkuk eds. 1963).

[31] *Id.* at 451.

In turn, the high level of tax revenue depended on Jewish lenders' ability to charge high interest on loans to the ruler's subjects. Once outside (and untaxed) competitors emerged, confiscation of Jewish loans became the maximizing course for the ruler to take, and that is the course he adopted.

Bibliography

Barzel, Yoram. "Property Rights and the Evolution of the State." Unpublished manuscript. Seattle: University of Washington, Department of Economics, 1992.

Bulow, Jeremy, and Rogoff, Kenneth. "A Constant Reconstructing Model of Sovereign Debt." *Journal of Political Economy* 97 (1989): 155–78.

Fryde, E. B. "Public Credit, with Special Reference to North-western Europe." In *The Cambridge Economic History of Europe*, 2d ed., edited by M. M. Postan and H. J. Habakkuk, 3:447–570. Cambridge: University of Cambridge Press, 1963.

Hicks, John Richard. *A Theory of Economic History*. Oxford: Clarendon Press, 1969.

Jordan, William C. *The French Monarchy and the Jews: From Philip Augustus to the Last Capetians*. Philadelphia: University of Pennsylvania Press, 1989.

Kaeuper, Richard W. *Bankers to the Crown: The Riccardi of Lucca and Edward I*. Princeton, N.J.: Princeton University Press, 1973.

North, Douglass C., and Weingast, Barry R. "Constitutions and Commitment: The Evolution of Institutions Governing Public Choice in Seventeenth-Century England." *Journal of Economic History* 49 (1989): 803–32.

Pollock, Frederick, and Maitland, Frederick William. *The History of English Law before the Time of Edward I*, 2d ed. Vol. 1. Cambridge: Cambridge University Press, 1898.

Richardson, H. G. *The English Jewry and Angevin Kings*. London: Methuen Press, 1960.

Roth, Cecil. *A History of the Jews in England*. Oxford: Clarendon Press, 1987.

Shatzmiller, Joseph. *Shylock Reconsidered: Jews, Moneylending, and Medieval Society*. Berkeley and Los Angeles: University of California Press, 1990.

Stacey, Robert C. *Politics, Policy, and Finance under Henry III, 1216–1245*. Oxford: Oxford University Press, 1987.

Veitch, John M. "Repudiations and Confiscations by the Medieval State." *Journal of Economic History* 46 (1986): 31–36.

Name index

Economists of the Twentieth Century

Monetarism and Macroeconomic Policy
Thomas Mayer

Studies in Fiscal Federalism
Wallace E. Oates

The World Economy in Perspective
Essays in International Trade and European Integration
Herbert Giersch

Towards a New Economics
Critical Essays on Ecology, Distribution and Other Themes
Kenneth E. Boulding

Studies in Positive and Normative Economics
Martin J. Bailey

The Collected Essays of Richard E. Quandt (2 volumes)
Richard E. Quandt

International Trade Theory and Policy
Selected Essays of W. Max Corden
W. Max Corden

Organization and Technology in Capitalist Development
William Lazonick

Studies in Human Capital
Collected Essays of Jacob Mincer, Volume 1
Jacob Mincer

Studies in Labor Supply
Collected Essays of Jacob Mincer, Volume 2
Jacob Mincer

Macroeconomics and Economic Policy
The Selected Essays of Assar Lindbeck, Volume I
Assar Lindbeck

The Welfare State
The Selected Essays of Assar Lindbeck, Volume II
Assar Lindbeck

Classical Economics, Public Expenditure and Growth
Walter Eltis

Money, Interest Rates and Inflation
Frederic S. Mishkin

The Public Choice Approach to Politics
Dennis C. Mueller

The Liberal Economic Order
Volume I Essays on International Economics
Volume II Money, Cycles and Related Themes
Gottfried Haberler
Edited by Anthony Y.C. Koo

Economic Growth and Business Cycles
Prices and the Process of Cyclical Development
Paolo Sylos Labini

International Adjustment, Money and Trade
Theory and Measurement for Economic Policy, Volume I
Herbert G. Grubel

International Capital and Service Flows
Theory and Measurement for Economic Policy, Volume II
Herbert G. Grubel

Unintended Effects of Government Policies
Theory and Measurement for Economic Policy, Volume III
Herbert G. Grubel

The Economics of Competitive Enterprise
Selected Essays of P.W.S. Andrews
Edited by Frederic S. Lee and Peter E. Earl

The Repressed Economy
Causes, Consequences, Reform
Deepak Lal

Economic Theory and Market Socialism
Selected Essays of Oskar Lange
Edited by Tadeusz Kowalik

Trade, Development and Political Economy
Selected Essays of Ronald Findlay
Ronald Findlay

General Equilibrium Theory
The Collected Essays of Takashi Negishi, Volume I
Takashi Negishi

The History of Economics
The Collected Essays of Takashi Negishi, Volume II
Takashi Negishi

Studies in Econometric Theory
The Collected Essays of Takeshi Amemiya
Takeshi Amemiya

Exchange Rates and the Monetary System
Selected Essays of Peter B. Kenen
Peter B. Kenen

Econometric Methods and Applications (2 volumes)
G.S. Maddala

National Accounting and Economic Theory
The Collected Papers of Dan Usher, Volume I
Dan Usher

Welfare Economics and Public Finance
The Collected Papers of Dan Usher, Volume II
Dan Usher

Economic Theory and Capitalist Society
The Selected Essays of Shigeto Tsuru, Volume I
Shigeto Tsuru

Methodology, Money and the Firm
The Collected Essays of D.P. O'Brien (2 volumes)
D.P. O'Brien

Economic Theory and Financial Policy
The Selected Essays of Jacques J. Polak (2 volumes)
Jacques J. Polak

Sturdy Econometrics
Edward E. Leamer

The Emergence of Economic Ideas
Essays in the History of Economics
Nathan Rosenberg

Productivity Change, Public Goods and Transaction Costs
Essays at the Boundaries of Microeconomics
Yoram Barzel

Reflections on Economic Development
The Selected Essays of Michael P. Todaro
Michael P. Todaro

Macroeconomics and Monetary Theory
The Collected Essays of Meghnad Desai, Volume I
Meghnad Desai

Poverty, Famine and Economic Development
The Collected Essays of Meghnad Desai, Volume II
Meghnad Desai

Economic Theory and Reality
Selected Essays on their Disparity and Reconciliation
Tibor Scitovsky